Contemporary Cuba

The Post-Castro Era

THIRD EDITION

EDITED BY HOPE BASTIAN, PHILIP BRENNER,
JOHN M. KIRK, AND WILLIAM M. LEOGRANDE

ROWMAN & LITTLEFIELD
Lanham • Boulder • New York • London

Published by Rowman & Littlefield
An imprint of The Rowman & Littlefield Publishing Group, Inc.
4501 Forbes Boulevard, Suite 200, Lanham, Maryland 20706
www.rowman.com

86-90 Paul Street, London EC2A 4NE

British Library Cataloguing in Publication Information available

Library of Congress Cataloging-in-Publication Data

Names: Bastian, Hope, editor. | Brenner, Philip, editor. | Kirk, John M., 1951– editor. |
    LeoGrande, William M., editor.
Title: Contemporary Cuba : the post-Castro era / edited by Hope Bastian,
    Philip Brenner, John M. Kirk and William M. LeoGrande.
Other titles: Contemporary Cuba reader.
Description: Third edition. | Lanham : Rowman & Littlefield, 2023. |
    Includes bibliographical references and index.
Identifiers: LCCN 2023019454 (print) | LCCN 2023019455 (ebook) |
    ISBN 9781538177136 (hardcover) | ISBN 9781538177143 (paperback) |
    ISBN 9781538177150 (epub)
Subjects: LCSH: Cuba—Politics and government—21st century. | Cuba—
    Economic conditions—21st century. | Cuba—Foreign relations—21st century.
Classification: LCC F1788 .C67 2023 (print) | LCC F1788 (ebook) |
    DDC 972.9107—dc23/eng/20230425
LC record available at https://lccn.loc.gov/2023019454
LC ebook record available at https://lccn.loc.gov/2023019455

Contemporary Cuba

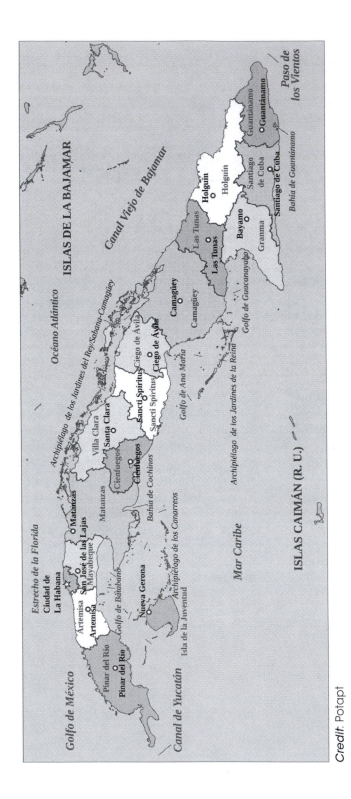

Contents

PART II: ECONOMY   **121**

PART III: INTERNATIONAL RELATIONS   **197**

PART IV: SOCIETY   271

Introduction

HISTORY AS PROLOGUE? CUBA UNTIL 2018

Philip Brenner

When the National Assembly elected Miguel Díaz-Canel Bermúdez as Cuba's president on April 19, 2018, few expected him to chart a course that departed dramatically from the one President Raúl Castro had established during the previous ten years. The Cuban leadership and much of the population seemed to share a consensus that the country should continue its revolutionary commitment to the promotion of economic development with equity, its centuries-old quest to keep Cuba independent from the dominance of a single foreign power, and its sixty-year embrace of the ideals of South-South solidarity. Notably, the 2021 Cuban Communist Party Congress, at which Díaz-Canel replaced Castro as first secretary, proclaimed *Somos Continuidad* (We are Continuity) as its theme. Yet given the economic, demographic, and international political challenges that Cuba faced, 2018 more appropriately might have been recognized as the end of one era and perhaps the start of a new one.

President Díaz-Canel had big shoes and expectations to fill. Fidel Castro and then his brother had led the country for nearly sixty years. Fidel had been the indispensable person without whom the Cuban Revolution would have taken a different course. Yet he was not a stereotypical Latin American caudillo. To be sure, he did shape the country's economy, politics, foreign policy, culture, and social organization from 1959 to 2006, when illness forced him to name his brother as provisional head of state and commander in chief of the Revolutionary Armed Forces.[1] Still, the Cuban Revolution had an organic quality and was not merely a reflection of Fidel's personality and personal predilections. It grew from below and was shaped by the interaction between leader and followers. Sociologist Nelson Valdés explains that this interaction is what made Fidel a truly *charismatic* leader. "His charismatic authority would not have been possible without the revolutionary practices which the Cuban populace embraced."[2]

Maintaining governmental legitimacy without Fidel was the primary task that confronted Raúl in 2006. Of course, as one of the Cuban Revolution's leaders, he could rely on traditional authority. At first, he also surrounded himself with leaders whose right to rule derived from their own participation in the Revolution. Still, Raúl was seventy-six years old, and his colleagues—the "historical" generation that overthrew Fulgencio Batista in 1959—were of the same vintage. He recognized that he had to prepare the country for an era when the legitimacy of the Cuban Revolution and the state would rest on legal-institutional authority.[3] At the same time, he hoped to develop a new economic model appropriate for the twenty-first century that would enable Cuba to maintain its commitment to providing basic needs equally for all Cubans and to sustain the country's high standing in Latin America and the Third World.

This book focuses on the way Cuba has attempted to carry out this agenda since 2018 and the changes that have occurred in the last decade. Still, it is important to recognize the continuity in Cuba's history that still influences its trajectory. This introductory chapter offers an overview of that history.

Colonialism and Neocolonialism

EUROPEAN "DISCOVERY"

Christopher Columbus "discovered" Cuba on his first voyage across the Atlantic in 1492, claiming it on behalf of the Spanish Crown. Prior to Columbus's discovery, native tribes of Cuba—largely Arawak and Ciboney—had lived in peace for centuries, in harmony with their neighbors and nature. The Spaniards outlawed the tribes' religious practices, stole their collective property, and made them slaves for the benefit of the Crown. In contrast to the Indigenous population of mainland Spanish America, the native peoples of Cuba virtually disappeared within a generation of Spain's arrival, wiped out by overwork, disease, and mass suicides.[4] A notable exception were the Taino Arawaks, who waged a fierce struggle against the Spanish. Their example of resistance is still celebrated in Cuba, and Taino tribal leader Hatuey is a national hero.

For much of its time as a colony, Cuba languished as a backwater in the Spanish Empire. It possessed few minerals of real worth; its value lay in its strategic location. The Spanish Crown maintained a monopoly on all of Cuba's trade, stifled attempts to develop Indigenous industry, and imposed high taxes on all imports and exports. As in other colonies, political control in Cuba remained with governors and administrators from the mother country, and Spanish soldiers enforced colonial rule. The Crown rewarded Spanish settlers who came to live in the "most lovely land that eyes have ever seen," as Columbus described Cuba, with immense tracts of land. In the mid-eighteenth century in response to European popular demand, they began to transform their agricultural production from basic food staples to sugar. Sugar was cultivated most efficiently on large plantations, and its harvesting was a labor-intensive process. With profits waiting to be earned and a shortage of workers on the island, Spain legalized slavery, and an active trade in African slaves began in 1763. Slave traders brought approximately 750,000 Africans to Cuba in the next one hundred years. In 1862, Cubans of African descent accounted for more than half of the 1.4 million people on the island, and Cuba produced more sugar than any other country in the world.[5] Slavery did not end in Cuba until 1886.

The Spanish colonial government encouraged the racial divide that slavery produced, doling out almost all prestigious positions in the military and government to whites born in Spain, known as the *peninsulares*—those born on the peninsula of Spain. Children born in the "colonies" to Spanish parents—the *criollos*, or "creoles"—

were branded with an original sin of inferiority despite being "white." The result was a racist society in which one's status, privileges, and rights were based on the color of one's skin and the location of one's birth. Spanish Catholic bishops accommodated and reinforced this standard by allowing only white Spanish priests—many of whom were "parachuted" in for limited-term appointments—to officiate in Cuban churches.

Between 1810 and 1821, people throughout South America successfully struggled to end colonialism, developing national boundaries more or less along the lines of the current configuration of Latin America. But not in Cuba, which became the refuge for the Spanish soldiers defeated in the wars of independence. They tended to reinforce the authoritarianism, rigidity, racism, and great disparities in wealth among Cubans and between regions within Cuba. This resulting tension came to a head in 1868, when Cubans began a ten-year war for independence that would unfold over the following ninety years.

A TEN-YEAR WAR LEADS TO INDEPENDENCE

Agitation for independence had been building for nearly two decades when plantation owner Carlos Manuel de Céspedes proclaimed Cuba's freedom from Spain on October 10, 1868. Joined by other planters, he freed his slaves and declared the *Grito de Yara* (Cry of Yara)—a call for revolution. Starting with fewer than 200 volunteers, the rebel army (called the *mambises*) grew to 12,000 within a few months, gathering small farmers, laborers, and freed slaves. This was a conservative revolution in most aspects other than ending slavery because the planters resented the increases in Spanish taxes and sought political power for themselves. While the rebels defeated superior Spanish forces in several battles, captured cities such as Bayamo, and established a new government and a democratic constitution, both sides were exhausted after ten years of fighting, which left 50,000 soldiers and civilians dead. The conflict ended in February 1878 when Spain agreed to free some slaves, promised future reforms, and gave Cubans a bit of autonomy while maintaining its colonial status. Unwilling to accept continued foreign rule, rebel officers led by Antonio Maceo penned "The Protest of Baraguá," a pledge to continue the independence war. Cuban leaders today still refer to Baraguá as a symbol of defiance against external dominance.[6]

Maceo abandoned the fight after a few months and did not return to Cuba until March 1895, one month after the renewed independence war began. In 1892, José Martí gathered the opposition under the banner of the Cuban Revolutionary Party as he coordinated preparations for the coming struggle. The son of poor Spanish immigrants, Martí began his first attacks on Spanish colonial rule in *La Patria Libre* (Free Fatherland), a newspaper he started in 1869 at the age of sixteen. Jailed for his political activities, he was then exiled to Spain in 1871. In 1881, he moved to New York, where he worked as a journalist, covering US politics for several Latin American newspapers, and became famous throughout the Spanish-speaking world for his poetry.

Cuba experienced a severe depression in 1895, in part caused by a US tariff on sugar imposed the year before. This contributed to the widespread support the rebels received. They started their campaign in the east (Oriente Province), and by the end of the year, the struggle for independence had engulfed the entire island. Martí was killed in combat on May 19, 1895, only six weeks after returning to Cuba with General Máximo Gómez. Yet his concept of *Cuba Libre* continued to inspire the new mambises. It also set the stage for an inevitable clash with the United States. As historian Louis Pérez Jr. explains, "*Cuba Libre* had come to signify more than separation from Spain. . . . The *independentista* formula was simple: Cuba for Cubans—the one eventuality which nearly one hundred years of North American policy had been dedicated to preventing."[7]

Meanwhile, Spain fought back against the revolutionaries with ferocious brutality, razing villages and driving Cubans out of their homes. The 200,000-soldier Spanish garrison at first seemed sufficient to counter the *independentistas*. But by 1898, the army's morale was low, and Spanish repression had stimulated support for the revolutionaries. Both Madrid and Washington assessed that the rebels would likely win the war by year's end.

When the USS *Maine* exploded in February 1898, the rebels were preparing their final offensives. American intervention two months later effectively stole the fruits of the Cubans' thirty years of fighting. Four months after the United States declared war, it signed a bilateral peace treaty with Spain without any Cuban participation. The name commonly applied to the conflict in the United States—Spanish American War—betrays an ignorance about the limited importance of the US contribution in securing victory. It also obscures the US suppression of Cuban hopes for full independence. In Cuba, the conflict is known as the Cuban War of Independence.[8]

American business barons encouraged US intervention, fearing that a rebel victory would mean a Cuba run by Cubans, which might undermine their holdings and privileged trade deals. Even before the war, the United States had supplanted Spain as Cuba's main trading partner.[9] It was in response to concerns about property owned by Americans—and perhaps about the lives of US citizens—that President William McKinley dispatched the USS *Maine* to Cuba in January 1898. Yet there also were US political leaders who convinced themselves that intervention would be a humane and selfless action because an independent Cuba could not govern itself.[10]

DE FACTO COLONIALISM: CUBA'S SPECIAL RELATIONSHIP WITH THE UNITED STATES

Although Cuba was nominally independent from 1903 to 1959, it was a de facto colony of the United States. The United States withdrew its occupation forces from Cuba in 1902 on the condition that the new constitution would include the Platt Amendment, a provision that permitted US unilateral intervention on the island. During the period when the Platt Amendment was in force, from 1903 to 1934, the United States occupied Cuba with troops on three different occasions. At the same time, US corporations and investment banks gained control of Cuba's basic infrastructure. Formal independence did not bring about meaningful sovereignty; Cuba was once again controlled by a foreign country.

The US occupation began on January 1, 1899. Leonard Wood, the second US governor-general, revealed in a letter to President McKinley the patronizing attitude the new rulers had toward their subjects. He wrote that "we are dealing with a race that has steadily been going down for a hundred years and into which we have to infuse new life, new principles and new methods of doing things."[11] In developing the Platt Amendment as a mechanism for control, Senator Orville Platt and Secretary of War Elihu Root manifested President McKinley's vision that Cuba and the United States should have a "special relationship" with "ties of singular intimacy."

In practice, the special relationship stifled Cuban development. Spurred by concessions that the occupation government granted to US investors, the North American hold over Cuban sugar plantations quickly led to US domination of Cuba's nonsugar industries. Sugar operations were quite large, and the *centrales* became thoroughly integrated small cities that linked key sectors of the Cuban economy, most of which were controlled by US firms. Consider that in the mid-1920s, because of ties between sugar mills and railroads, US companies owned 22 percent of Cuba's land area.[12] US-Cuban trade agreements opened Cuba to inexpensive manufactured goods, suppressing the creation of an Indigenous manufacturing sector. The US sugar quota, which specified how much sugar Cuba could sell at a subsidized price, became the most important determinant of year-to-year survival for Cuba's sugar workers and for Cuba's economic planning. A "wrong" decision by a Cuban official, which might upset one US senator, could lead to a filibuster against Cuba's quota. And so, for example, although Cuba was on a course by 1950 to grow enough rice to avoid spending scarce funds to import the grain, US rice producers lobbied to cut off Cuba's sugar import quota, which essentially closed Cuba's rice production.[13] One-third of US rice exports were sold to Cuba in the 1950s.

By the mid-1950s, 90 percent of Cuba's telephone and electrical services, 50 percent of public service railways, 40 percent of raw sugar production, and 23 percent of nonsugar industries were US-owned. The United States was Cuba's largest export market and the main source for its imports: 59 percent of the value of Cuban exports—including 80 percent of its exported sugar—went to the United States.[14]

As US businesses rapidly took root in Cuba, the Cuban upper class came to identify with US cultural values. During the first half of the twentieth century, the Americanization of the creole middle class led to a dominant culture imbued with a North American perspective. Soon anything American was deemed better than anything Cuban, from the arts to the design of buildings to business strategies, and baseball became the national pastime.

During the period of the special relationship, a limited form of democracy did emerge on the island, but it was one that Cubans associated with corruption and foreign domination. In 1933, President Franklin Delano Roosevelt (FDR) feared that the unpopularity of Cuba's president, the dictatorial Gerardo Machado, might lead to instability and a radical government. He dispatched a personal emissary, Ambassador Sumner Welles, who persuaded Machado to resign, and arranged for his replacement by a reformer who would comply with US requests.

Within weeks, a popular uprising—sparked by a sergeants' revolt with Fulgencio Batista in the lead—ousted the US-approved president and established a provisional government. The new government proclaimed that it would bring about national "economic reconstruction" as it began "the march toward the creation of a new Cuba founded . . . upon the most modern concept of democracy."[15] FDR made clear his disapproval of the new government by refusing to grant it diplomatic recognition. Welles then worked behind the scenes to entice key backers, particularly Batista and the military, to defect from the revolutionary coalition, which lasted only four months before being overthrown by the army. Batista continued to be a dependable US surrogate for the next quarter of a century. Cubans learned that FDR's "Good Neighbor Policy" meant only that the United States would not intervene *militarily*. The US success in suppressing Cuban nationalism, though, led nationalist populism to become the dominant theme of Cuban politics in the following twenty-five years.

When Batista overthrew the constitutional government in 1952, ending Cuba's experience with "democracy," there was little public outcry. Nelson Valdés observes that many in the Cuban elite had abandoned the concept of a distinctive Cuban national identity. In addition, the mass of Cubans associated democratic elections with the theft of Cuban nationalism, either by the Mafia or the US government. The revolutionary movement that triumphed in 1959 in part derived its legitimacy from its devotion to Cuban nationalism. This placed the new regime on an inevitable collision course with the United States.

The 1959 Revolution

The active opposition to Batista's dictatorship was organized by several groups and was spread across the island, especially in the cities. Each group of revolutionaries had distinctive goals, but together they shared a desire to rid Cuba of corruption, to modernize the country, and to raise living standards for most of the population. It was not until mid-1958 that the combined revolutionary organizations came together as a unified force. The 26th of July Movement had become the largest and most dynamic group, gaining increased support as it won military victories in the summer of 1958. The group took its name from the date in 1953 on which Fidel Castro and some 160 others stormed the Moncada garrison in Santiago in a failed attempt to spark a general uprising. As founder of the rebel army and head of the 26th of July Movement, Castro quickly became the natural leader of the revolutionary government when Batista fled the country on December 31, 1958. In its first post-Batista edition, the popular weekly magazine *Bohemia* described him as a "national hero."[16]

Superficially, Castro would not have seemed likely to promote revolutionary change. An upwardly mobile lawyer, he was a graduate of the Colegio de Belén, a high school that educated many of the children from Cuba's upper classes. His father was a plantation owner, though not a rich one. His first wife, Mirta Díaz-Balart, was the daughter of Rafael José Díaz-Balart, a wealthy and prominent conservative lawyer who was transportation minister in Batista's cabinet from 1952 to 1954. Yet Castro also had been a leader of the activist student movement at the University of Havana, a member of the leftist Ortodoxo Party, and an ardent supporter of the party's charismatic leader, Eduardo Chibás. With this profile, it is no wonder that US intelligence analysts were uncertain at first whether Castro would try to radically transform the system or institute only modest reforms that would not fundamentally alter the country's subservient relationship with the United States.

Uncertainty vanished quickly, as the new government initiated major changes in 1959 and 1960. The May 1959 Agrarian Reform Law reduced the maximum landholding size to 1,000 acres, and the excess property was largely distributed to landless farmworkers. Forty percent of Cuba's rural property was nationalized. The Urban Reform Law cut rents substantially. Cubans with more than two pieces of property were obliged to hand over the excess to the government, which then reclassified them as social property, transforming houses, for example, into day care centers.

The reforms entailed a massive redistribution from rich to poor as the wealthiest 10 percent of the population lost much of its property, privileges, and political power. They were forced to pay new luxury taxes; their private schools and clubs were closed; private beaches were opened to the public; and private clinics were forced to treat indigent patients. At the same time, poorer Cubans, especially urban Cubans of African descent and most Cubans in rural areas, received immediate benefits because historically they had suffered the greatest unemployment and had received the fewest public services. More than 40 percent of the Cuban workforce in 1958 was either underemployed or unemployed. Sugarcane workers made up approximately 25 percent of the national labor force and averaged less than four months of work a year.

In addition to tangible relief, the revolutionary government set in motion processes that would create new opportunities for the previously dispossessed. It passed laws banning discrimination based on race or gender, it began to train doctors so that good health care would be universal, and it set out to strengthen the education system. The 1961 literacy campaign engaged many young, educated Cubans in the revolutionary process, sparking their idealism and opening their eyes to the vast inequalities in the country. University classes were suspended as students and professors went throughout the country over a nine-month period to teach adults how to read. They succeeded in reducing illiteracy from 23.6 percent of the population to 3.9 percent.

Blacks and mulattoes constitute a much higher proportion of the population in Cuba than in the United States. The 1953 census recorded 26.9 percent of Cuba as Black or mulatto; in the 1981 census, it was 34 percent.[17] Racial discrimination before 1959 may have been less a result of interpersonal prejudice than in the United States, but it was entrenched in the way Cuban institutions functioned. Schools for darker-skinned Cubans were vastly inferior to those for whites. They also had the worst living conditions and held the lowest-paid jobs. There was some social mobility for non-white Cubans: Fulgencio Batista, a light-skinned mulatto, became president in 1940. But the white, upper-class Havana Yacht Club even denied membership to him while he was in office from 1940 to 1944. Still, as Lourdes Casal, a seminal scholar on racism in Cuba, points out, several factors softened the expression of racism. "The most important leaders of the Cuban independence struggle such as José Martí (white) and Antonio Maceo (black)," she wrote, placed great emphasis on "racial unity and integration."[18]

POLARIZATION EMERGES

As the pace of change accelerated, an ideological gulf emerged between moderate and radical reformers. Without the common enemy, their differences came to the forefront. Some moderates joined the campaign because they were appalled by Batista's violent repression and disregard for human rights; others had focused on his regime's corruption and willingness to give the Mafia effective carte blanche over part of Cuba's tourist industry. Some believed that the enormous gap between the country's rich and poor could be closed significantly through liberal democratic reforms. To these moderate Cubans, Castro was "betraying" the goals that led them to join the Revolution. On the other hand, some so-called moderates invoked "democracy" merely to protect their property and privilege. Saul Landau comments that they "had little interest in ending the state of dependency with the United States, and absolutely no inclination to channel their wealth to the services of the majority. This was the essence of the class war that confronted Castro and the revolutionaries by spring 1959."[19]

The class war was only the first of three simultaneous conflicts that the revolutionary leadership faced. The second involved assaults by US corporations with extensive investments in Cuba in alliance with Cuban property owners. These were the very bonds the radical nationalists aimed to cut in the hope that decisions about Cuba's economy could be made in Havana and not New York or Washington. Castro made some attempt to blunt the negative US reaction he expected. On a goodwill trip to the United States in April 1959, he offered to repay owners of confiscated lands a price that was greater than their assessed values in tax records, and he promised Cuba would deliver eight million tons of sugar to the United States at below-market price. But many of his speeches in 1959 and 1960 were rife with derisive and insulting remarks that were seemingly intended to taunt the United States.

The third conflict was cultural. It involved overcoming sixty years of neocolonial acculturation to US values that implicitly denigrated Cuban identity and Cubans themselves. This struggle was the most difficult because it occurred at an ideological, unconscious level, where the enemy was ingrained in each person's conception of the Cuban character. Most often the clash manifested itself as a contest over the meaning of civilization. Defenders of the old order argued that the extent to which Cuba had become civilized could be ascertained by the availability of modern technology and even "luxuries" that would enable a person to live comfortably. In contrast, Castro argued, the level of civilization should be evaluated by the percentage of people who were illiterate and unemployed and by the number of children with parasites. In effect, Louis Pérez explains, the revolutionaries sought "to rearrange in usable form the standards by which to measure civilization and in the process summon a vision of an alternative moral order."[20]

The revolutionary leadership reasoned that victories in these three conflicts would require Cubans to sustain great leaps of faith that could be undermined if there were disunity and dissent. The determination to create and maintain unity led the government to close newspapers, nationalize television and radio stations, and cancel promised elections. Efforts to develop a disciplined party apparatus led to the arrest of some who had fought against Batista but did not want to accept Castro's leadership. These measures left an indelible imprint on the Cuban Revolution. Justified at first by the necessity to galvanize the mass of Cubans and enable them to develop a revolutionary consciousness, repression became routinized by the alleged demands of national security. Over time, as national security came to eclipse other priorities, some threats became exaggerated, and petty officials were given license to engage in acts of cruelty.

To be sure, the Cuban Revolution had serious enemies. Counterrevolutionaries, centered in the Escambray Mountains and located throughout the country, fought tenaciously from 1960 to 1966. In that period, more than 2,000 insurgents and 500 Cuban soldiers were killed in battle.[21] The United States began to support the counterrevolutionaries in late 1959 and attempted to overthrow the regime by mounting the failed April 1961 Bay of Pigs invasion. The Central Intelligence Agency (CIA) then waged a multifaceted "low-intensity" war against Cuba, code-named Operation Mongoose, which included plans for an invasion by the US Marines.[22]

The height of repression came after the Bay of Pigs invasion. The Cuban government rounded up and arrested "tens of thousands of people." While most were released quickly, Castro acknowledged in 1965 that 20,000 political prisoners continued to be incarcerated.[23] Later in that year, the military began to "draft" thousands of people whom the government designated as "socially deviant": homosexuals, vagrants, and Jehovah's Witnesses and other religious missionaries. They were placed in prisonlike camps named "Military Units to Aid Production" (UMAP)—ostensibly to be reeducated—and ordered to do nonremunerated labor. The UMAP program lasted for two years. Castro disbanded it in 1967 after the Cuban National Union of Writers and Artists protested the incarceration of many writers and university professors.

Still, the early years of the Revolution produced an enormous outpouring of vibrant cultural expression. For example, the official newspaper of the 26th of July Movement, *Revolución*, included a literary supplement every Monday, *Lunes de Revolución*, which quickly gained international acclaim from the world's leading avantgarde authors. *Lunes* focused on all the arts. In addition to the magazine, *Lunes* created a record company, started a publishing house that emphasized works by new Cuban writers who broke with traditional themes, and produced a weekly television program that featured modern plays, jazz, and experimental films.[24] In effect, *Lunes* became the forum for debates about Cuban culture.

The explosion of creativity inevitably ran the risk of challenging the government's plan for unity. In June 1961, Castro made clear that the limits of tolerance had been reached. In a three-day meeting with "intellectuals," he laid down a new dictum. The Revolution, he said, must give an opportunity to all writers and artists, even to those who were not "genuine revolutionaries," to express themselves freely and to use their "creative spirit." But this freedom would be available only if their creative work was consistent with the Revolution. Castro tersely summarized the rule by declaring, "Within the revolution, everything; against the revolution, nothing."[25] The trouble was that he did not provide clear parameters as to what lay "within" and what strayed outside the borders of permissible dissent. Without guidelines, enforcement became arbitrary. Writers and artists feared that the pronouncement was intended to stifle and not to endorse freedom of expression, and their interpretation was reinforced in November, when Castro shut down *Lunes de Revolución*.

As the Cuban revolutionaries implemented their plans, disaffected Cubans voted with their feet and left Cuba. The first wave of émigrés (1959–1962) consisted largely of landowners, wealthy business people, former Batista government officials, managers, small proprietors, and professionals such as doctors, engineers, and skilled technicians. Many went to the United States, where those with professional training were especially welcomed as part of a US strategy to undermine the Cuban Revolution by depleting the island of people who had technical expertise. By November 1965, when Castro opened the door to unrestricted emigration, 211,000 Cubans had departed. In the next six years, an additional 277,000 emigrated from Cuba.[26]

DEBATE OVER THE "NEW" CUBAN MAN (MATERIAL VERSUS MORAL INCENTIVES)

At its core, the Cuban Revolution included a socialist humanist vision that contributed to its international appeal. The vision was based on an Enlightenment belief that human beings are "perfectible" and that their institutions make them imperfect. Simply stated, socialist humanists contend that people become alienated from their full potential when a society's institutions—and its consequent relationships—lead them to pursue self-gratification and individual survival. They assert that humans are capable of transcending individualism and selfishness and of acting with a social conscience for the benefit of the whole society.

Scholars have tended to identify Ernesto "Che" Guevara as the main proponent of the socialist humanist vision among the founding leaders of the Revolution. Indeed, Guevara did call for the development of new Cuban citizens—the term he used was "new man"—who would eschew "the satisfaction of their personal ambitions" and "become more aware every day of the need to incorporate themselves into society."[27] The transition, Guevara asserted, involved reeducation that should take place not only in schools, because Cubans needed to learn the meaning and practice of the new morality gradually through their daily activities and relationships. In Guevara's view, the new morality also could emerge only if the government relied on "moral incentives" to motivate people rather than "material incentives," which tend to reinforce individualism.

In practice, the use of moral incentives is usually accompanied by inefficiency. Appeals to a common purpose are less likely to engender consistent hard work than differentiated rewards to individuals. Yet the resulting decrease in the production of necessities would likely undermine popular support for the Revolution itself. The dilemma—posed by the debate over the reliance on material or moral incentives—is one that continues to frame Cuban development decisions even today. Notably, Fidel Castro continued to be a forceful advocate for a new Cuban morality even after Guevara left Cuba in 1965. Invoking Guevara's name, he often railed against evidence of greed and selfishness. Indeed, at key junctures, he implemented significant changes in Cuba's economy to restore what he viewed as a balance between material and moral incentives. In March 1968, following a January purge of "old" Communist Party members who favored material incentives, he nationalized 55,000 small businesses and called for a "revolutionary offensive" to "complete the job of making our people fully revolutionary." Cubans had to learn to develop their revolutionary consciousness from "each event . . . each new experience."[28]

The experiment with moral incentives in the late 1960s contributed to serious economic problems and the failure of Castro's heralded plan to produce ten million tons of sugar in 1970. For the next decade and a half, under pressure from the Soviet Union, Cuba returned to a reliance on material incentives. In 1986, however, Castro once again reacted against what he regarded as the evils of the market. He shut down private farmers' markets and denounced the distributors of agricultural produce who earned sums far greater than those of ordinary workers. At the same time, he criticized managers of state enterprises for applying capitalist principles—favoring the production of higher-priced goods that earned more money for their firms over the production of goods needed for social projects—and "people who confuse income earned through work with what can be got through speculation." These practices had to be "rectified," Castro asserted, by returning to the fundamental principles of the Cuban Revolution. "There are some," he said, "who think that socialism can be brought about without political work. . . . I believe that the problems must be resolved morally, honorably and with principles."[29]

To some extent, Cuba was able to reconcile the first goal—providing universal and quality health care and education, food for everyone, and universal access to necessities, such as electricity and clean water—with the second goal—developing a new Cuban morality as a result of an economic growth spurt in the early 1970s. By the end of the decade, the revolutionary government had eradicated epidemic diseases and lowered the rate of infant mortality to the level in the United States. Rural poverty essentially had been eliminated, in part because of a conscious effort to locate new production facilities in previously downtrodden areas and to increase wages of agrarian workers and provide them with housing, roads, schools, health clinics, and electricity.[30] At the same time, in what was ultimately a failed project, the government attempted to instill a new morality by creating free boarding schools in the countryside. Students at these schools spent part of each day cultivating and harvesting crops. The intention was twofold: to break down urban prejudices about *campesinos* by integrating children from city and rural locales, and to induce a sense of responsibility for the common good by engaging in nonremunerated "social labor."[31]

Two factors mainly accounted for the economic gains in the 1970s. First, the world price for sugar jumped to historic levels—$0.70 per pound briefly in 1974—enabling Cuba to earn hard currency from surplus sugar and to buy modern technology from European firms. Second, in 1972 Cuba joined the Council for Mutual Economic Assistance (CMEA), the socialist trading bloc headed by the Soviet Union. Cuba was designated as a commodity producer for the CMEA countries, providing sugar, citrus, nickel, and cobalt to its new partners. In turn, it was able to import petroleum, machinery, and manufactured goods from them at subsidized prices; defer loan repayments; and obtain new loans with low rates. Although the products from the Soviet Union and Eastern European countries tended to be of low quality, they provided Cuban leaders with the means to begin an effort at diversifying the economy.

In both the 1968 and the 1986 cases, Castro's rejection of Soviet demands reflected his determination to maintain as much independence for Cuba as possible. But just as Cuba's special relationship with the United States from 1903 to 1959 limited Cuba's options, its relationship with the Soviet Union from 1960 to 1991 created conditions that influenced the course of the Cuban Revolution.

Foreign Relations from 1959 to 1991

TESTING THE LIMITS OF SOVIET TOLERANCE

Despite his reputation for rashness and braggadocio, Soviet premier Nikita Khrushchev was quite wary about disturbing the United States in the Western Hemisphere. In the 1950s, the Soviet Communist Party had ordered its affiliated parties in Latin America to distance themselves from any attempts to forcibly overthrow or destabilize their governments. Most Cuban communists, who were organized as the Popular Socialist Party (PSP), also followed this Moscow line and had little if any contact with the revolutionaries during the struggle against Batista. The Soviets thus did not know much about Fidel Castro and the 26th of July Movement, and they were not anxious to support rebels who neither would take orders from Moscow nor were likely to survive US hostility. It took until February 1960 for a Soviet trade delegation to arrive in Havana, though it was a prominent one, headed by Deputy Premier Anastas Mikoyan. Shortly afterward, the two countries reestablished diplomatic relations, which had been broken in 1952.

In the spring of 1960, the Soviets began to supply Cuba with a few light arms, artillery and mortars, tanks, antiaircraft rockets, and technical assistance. But only after the 1961 Bay of Pigs invasion, when it was clear that the revolutionary government had popular support and staying power, did the Soviets promise to send more sophisticated weapons.[32] Of greater importance, when President Dwight Eisenhower barred any further US importation of Cuban sugar in July 1960, the Soviet Union purchased the sugar that Cuba had expected to export to the United States. This began a trading relationship in which Cuba remained dependent largely on its production of sugar. By the 1980s, sugar export earnings from sales to the Soviet Union and Eastern European countries accounted for a larger percentage of total exports than sugar exports to the United States in the 1950s.[33] In addition, Soviet sales of petroleum to Cuba at below-market prices were a form of foreign assistance on which Cuba came to depend.

Yet Cuba's relations with the Soviet Union were never as congenial as US officials and the Western media portrayed them. Tension between the two countries was so great in 1968 that Raúl Castro publicly charged a high official of the Cuban Communist Party, Aníbal Escalante, with treason for conspiring with Soviet officials to replace Fidel Castro as first secretary of the party.

The bitterness that Cuba's leaders felt toward the Soviet Union can be traced to October 28, 1962, the day on which the Cuban missile crisis is commonly said to have ended with an understanding between the US and Soviet heads of state. (The so-called Kennedy-Khrushchev agreement stipulated that the Soviets would withdraw all offensive weapons from Cuba, and the United States would pledge not to invade or support an invasion of Cuba.) The Cubans interpreted the agreement as a Soviet capitulation to US threats and judged that the Soviet Union would be unwilling in the future to put itself at risk to protect Cuba. "We realized how alone we would be in the event of a war," Castro remarked in a speech to the first full meeting of the Communist Party's Central Committee in January 1968. From the Cuban perspective, the Soviet Union had made Cuba even more vulnerable than before the missile crisis. Not only had the Soviets signaled to the United States that its guarantee of protecting Cuba was hollow, but Khrushchev also was asking Cuba to return weapons to the Soviets that the Cubans believed were necessary for their defense. Castro's palpable contempt was evident in 1968 as he characterized the Soviet leaders as "feeble-minded bureaucrats."[34]

After the missile crisis, the two countries locked horns on several issues. Speaking on behalf of the Cuban government at a 1965 conference in Algeria, Che Guevara castigated the Soviets for their regressive ideological views and for their immorality in not adequately supporting liberation movements.[35] In January 1966, Cuba frontally challenged the Soviet Union's claim to be the natural leader of the Third World when it brought together 500 delegates from Africa, Asia, and Latin America at the first Tricontinental Conference with the goal of promoting and supporting armed liberation struggles on the three continents. Soviet leaders had repeatedly admonished Castro to back away from supporting armed struggle. Notably, Castro did not invite any communist parties to be represented at the conference. Then in October 1967, Guevara was killed fighting against the Bolivian government. It was a terrible blow to Castro, who blamed his comrade's death on the Bolivian Communist Party and, by implication, on its Soviet masters.[36]

CUBA JOINS THE SOCIALIST CAMP

Cuba and the Soviet Union had come close to a breaking point. Castro knew he had no other options but to reduce the tension and cease his open challenges to Soviet leadership. This was underscored by a Soviet decision to provide Cuba with less oil in 1968 than it was expecting to receive. On January 2, 1968, Castro reported that troublesome news to the Cuban people. But he held out the hope that the hardships would be temporary, lasting for at most three years. By achieving the goal of a ten-million-ton sugar harvest in 1970, he asserted, Cuba would earn enough hard currency to be self-reliant. It would no longer need to make undignified, "incessant requests" for advance shipments of oil. The ten-million-ton harvest thus embodied a political goal as well as an economic one. Cuba could truly be independent if the plan were successful.[37]

Consequently, virtually the entire economy was subordinated to the task of meeting this unprecedented target. Ultimately, some 8.5 million tons were gathered. Although that set a record, it represented a pyrrhic victory. Other sectors of the economy suffered major losses because so many resources and so many workers had been diverted to the sugar harvest. The failure of the ten-million-ton campaign led directly to Cuba's decision to become a junior partner in the CMEA.

As Cuba tied its economic planning more closely to the Soviet bloc, it also began to link its armed forces and intelligence services to corresponding Soviet agencies. Despite such integration, though, Cuba took its own counsel on foreign policy. Most scholars have concluded that Cuba was neither a puppet of nor a stalking horse for the Soviet Union. While Cuba's choices often coincided with Soviet interests, there were several notable disagreements in the 1970s. In early November 1975, Cuba sent the first contingent of what would be a deployment of 5,000 soldiers to Angola to support the Popular Movement for the Liberation of Angola (MPLA), one of the three parties already engaged in a civil war to determine who would rule the country after independence. Castro did not inform Soviet leaders about the Cuban troop movement, fearing that they were likely to oppose it. Indeed, the Soviets were not pleased because their priority was advancing détente with the United States. Soviet-Cuban engagement in the Angolan civil war was likely to upend delicate negotiations with the United States, which was backing the forces opposed to the MPLA. Nevertheless, Moscow agreed to provide Cuban troops with the military equipment they needed to turn back a South African invasion of Angola.[38]

In contrast, Third World countries, especially those in Africa, lavished praise on the Cubans. Cuba's support for the MPLA and its willingness to fight against the apartheid regime in South Africa was a key reason that the Non-Aligned Movement (NAM) selected Havana to be the location for its 1979 summit. The host country also served as chair of the NAM until the next summit, and Castro saw this as an opportunity to forge unity among poorer countries of the world. He planned to encourage oil-rich countries in the "South" to use their resources for South-South cooperative programs, which he viewed as an essential step to reduce their dependency on the advanced industrial nations.

CUBA'S INTERNATIONALISM

The divergent Soviet and Cuban perspectives—one from the vantage point of a small nation and the other from the vantage point of a superpower—were painfully evident to Castro in December 1979 when the Soviet Union invaded Afghanistan. The invasion vitiated Cuba's ability to serve as an effective NAM leader because Afghanistan was a NAM member and nonintervention was a core NAM principle. Castro had not even been informed in advance about the intervention. But he felt constrained to support the Soviet action by not condemning it, which was a position exactly opposite the one that NAM countries expected their chair to take. The asymmetry between Cuba and the Soviet Union, which had contributed to their friction in the 1960s, continued to generate tension for the next twelve years until the Soviet Union collapsed.[39]

This was most evident around Cuban support for liberation struggles in Central America and southern Africa during the 1980s. For example, Castro did not attend the 1985 funeral of Soviet president Konstantin Chernenko to show his displeasure with the low level of support the Soviet Union was providing the Sandinista government in Nicaragua.[40]

Cuba's commitments to the MPLA's victory in Angola, to the success of the Southwest Africa People's Organization in its struggle for Namibia's independence, and to the consolidation of Sandinista rule in Nicaragua were not based on expedient short-term calculations or spontaneous bursts of revolutionary zeal.[41] They developed slowly, starting in the 1960s, and were deeply rooted in the Cuban revolutionaries' belief that internationalism served Cuba's immediate and long-term interests.

Internationalism also brought ordinary Cubans into contact with the deep poverty many Third World people suffer, and new generations of Cubans who had no memory of the 1950s could gain an appreciation for the achievements of the Revolution. By the mid-1980s, approximately 15,000 Cubans—one out of every 625—were working in civilian foreign aid missions in more than thirty countries. At the same time, 24,000 students from eighty-two countries were enrolled in Cuban high schools and universities.[42] In 1999 Cuba opened the Latin American School of Medicine, a tuition-free institution in Havana created to train students from underserved populations in Africa, Asia, and the Western Hemisphere, including the United States.[43]

CHALLENGING THE UNITED STATES

It may be impossible now to disentangle the different ideological underpinnings of US policy toward the Cuban Revolution in the early years. One strand hearkened to the US patronizing attitude General Wood had evidenced in 1899. At a February 1959 meeting of the National Security Council, CIA director Allen Dulles counseled that "the new Cuban officials had to be treated more or less like children."[44] Similarly, Secretary of State Christian Herter described Fidel Castro as "immature and irrational."[45]

Alternately, conventional wisdom has held that Cold War ideology shaped US policy. Washington was in the grip of a mindset that framed foreign policy decisions in terms of a bipolar, zero-sum view of the world: a country was either for the United States or for its enemy, the Soviet Union. There was no room for an independent country of the sort Cuba hoped to be. Even though Cuba did not establish diplomatic relations with the Soviet Union during the first year after the Revolution, US policymakers worried about the direction of the revolutionary government, in part because of its charismatic chief, Fidel Castro. After an April 1959 meeting with Castro, Vice President Richard Nixon reported in a confidential memo that the Cuban leader "has those indefinable qualities which make him a leader of men. Whatever we may think of him he is going to be a great factor in the development of Cuba and very possibly in Latin American affairs generally."[46]

By the end of the year, the CIA was developing schemes to assassinate Castro and overthrow the Cuban government.[47] In a November 1959 memo to President Dwight Eisenhower, Secretary of State Herter provided the justification for the subversive plans. Cuba threatened the United States, he observed, because Castro "has veered towards a 'neutralist' anti-American foreign policy for Cuba which, if emulated by other Latin American countries, would have serious adverse effects on Free World support of our leadership."[48] In effect, Cuba's stance challenged the legitimacy of what Abraham Lowenthal called the US hegemonic presumption in the Western Hemisphere.[49] Castro made his opposition to US "leadership" explicit in September 1960, openly proclaiming Cuba's duty to make revolution in the hemisphere.[50]

Whether the initial US concern was over the apparent threat to US hemispheric hegemony or the so-called Soviet threat, Cold War assumptions had gained full rein over US policy by mid-1960. At that point, despite the fact that Cuba was not yet ruled by a Communist Party, there was no longer any debate among US policymakers about whether Cuba was in the Soviet camp.

Castro first declared the character of the Cuban Revolution to be "socialist" only on the eve of the April 17, 1961, Bay of Pigs invasion. Within months of the failed US-sponsored attack, President John Kennedy authorized the CIA to undertake a more ambitious effort to overthrow the revolutionary regime. Code-named Operation Mongoose, the project had four components: (1) terrorism—CIA agents and assets based in Florida would conduct raids in Cuba to sabotage factory equipment, burn sugarcane fields, contaminate processed sugar, and provide weapons to counter-revolutionaries who would undertake their own "military" actions; (2) political isola-tion—the United States was able to pressure enough Organization of American States (OAS) members in January 1962 to gain the necessary votes to suspend Cuba from the organization; (3) economic strangulation—in February 1962, Kennedy instituted a full embargo on all transactions between Cuba and the United States, including food and medicine; (4) military intimidation—the US Navy conducted several unusually large exercises in the Caribbean in 1962, including one that involved the practice inva-sion of an island named "Ortsac," that is, "Castro" spelled backward. There was also an associated project that ran concurrently with Mongoose to assassinate Castro and the other Cuban leaders.[51]

Castro interpreted all this activity as prelude to a US invasion. He sought Soviet assistance to defend Cuba, and Khrushchev offered ballistic missiles. The October 1962 missile crisis confirmed the Kennedy administration's worst fears about how the Soviet-Cuban connection could undermine US security. Subsequently, Cuba's supposed threat to the United States, because of its close ties to the other superpower, remained a core assumption of US policy until the Soviet Union imploded in 1991.[52]

For Cuban officials, the possibility of a US attack was ever present after the Bay of Pigs invasion. Even today several US laws stipulate that Cuba is an "enemy" of the United States. A small country like Cuba, adjacent to the world's most powerful nation, does not have the luxury to view such designations casually, as if they had no meaning.

Still, there were three brief periods during the Cold War when the glimmerings of a US-Cuban modus vivendi surfaced.[53] In 1963, Kennedy used unofficial emissaries to probe the possibility of restoring relations between the two countries. But these efforts ended shortly after Lyndon B. Johnson became president. In 1974, Secretary of State Henry Kissinger initiated secret negotiations between US and Cuban officials aimed at normalizing relations. The next year, as a signal of good faith, the United States voted with a majority of members in the OAS to lift the 1964 hemisphere-wide embargo against Cuba. President Gerald Ford then relaxed the US embargo to permit subsid-iaries of US corporations in third countries to trade with Cuba.[54] Cuba's response to the conciliatory US moves, Kissinger believed, was decidedly hostile. He viewed its support for the MPLA in Angola later that year as an assault on US-Soviet détente. In December 1975, President Gerald Ford announced that Cuba's Angola operation "destroys any opportunity for improvement of relations with the United States."[55]

The third opening occurred during the first two years of the Carter administration.[56] Shortly after his inauguration, President Jimmy Carter announced that he would not renew the ban on travel to Cuba by US citizens and that US citizens would be permitted to spend money in Cuba related to their travel. He also approved negotiations with Cuba over maritime boundaries and fishing rights, and an agreement was finalized in April 1977. In September, the two countries opened diplomatic missions in each other's capitals.

However, by 1978, the Cold War had intruded once again as Cuba deployed more than 20,000 troops to Ethiopia to support its conflict with Somalia. US concerns were further fueled by events in Zaire and an alleged Soviet military buildup in Cuba. Even though the Carter administration had misinterpreted these situations, in October 1979 Carter issued PD-52, a presidential directive that ordered key national security agencies to devise ways "to contain Cuba as a source of violent revolutionary change."

Thus, when President Ronald Reagan took office, the US hostility toward Cuba that already was in place provided firm ground from which to launch a more threatening policy. Secretary of State Alexander Haig asserted in February 1981 that the United States must "deal with the immediate source of the problem [in El Salvador]—and that is Cuba."[57] Cuba responded by creating a 1.5-million-person "Territorial Troop Militia" to defend the island with a Swiss-like strategy of a "people in arms."[58]

After the collapse of the Soviet Union, Cuba's apparent threat to US national security largely disappeared. In President George H. W. Bush's view, the change meant that Cuba was no longer a significant foreign policy issue. Instead, domestic political considerations drove US policy, which effectively placed the Cuban American National Foundation (CANF) in the driver's seat.

Founded in 1981 with the assistance and encouragement of Reagan administration officials, the CANF relied on campaign contributions shrewdly spent by its political action committee and the power of a few well-placed senators and representatives who valued CANF's support to influence Congress.[59] By 1990, CANF had effectively gained control of US policy and was determined to restructure it to push the revolutionary regime into the abyss toward which it seemed to be tipping.

Reinventing the Cuban Revolution

In the span of thirty years after the overthrow of the Batista dictatorship, Cuba had developed to the point where infectious diseases had been eradicated and the infant mortality rate was comparable to that of advanced industrial nations. The country had more doctors per capita than any other country in the world and provided free universal health care throughout the island. Universities had been established in every province, education through graduate school was free, and educational opportunities had helped to reduce racial and gender disparities.

Although Cuba was still a poor country by standard measures of gross domestic product (GDP), it was an egalitarian society, and most people could reasonably hope that their children's lives would be better than their own. The great majority of Cubans also had gained an intangible but discernible sense of dignity, in part because of

Cuba's prowess in international sports competitions; the worldwide recognition of Cuban artists, writers, dancers, and filmmakers; and the respect that other Third World countries accorded to this small nation that had repeatedly and successfully defied the hovering giant ninety miles away.

However, the collapse of the Soviet Union in 1991 made clear the continuing weakness of Cuba's monocultural export economy. Cuba's adaptation to its new circumstances altered the very nature of the Cuban Revolution and significantly impacted the economic and political organization of the country, Cuba's culture and daily life, and its foreign relations. In effect, Cuba had to abandon the former revolutionary order and invent a new one.

ECONOMICS AND POLITICS DURING THE SPECIAL PERIOD

Imagine your reaction if you had to substitute sugar water for food every third day for a year and as a result you became blind because of a vitamin deficiency (as happened temporarily to 50,000 Cubans) and lost twenty to twenty-five pounds (the average for Cubans in 1993–1994).[60] Suppose that you could not drive your car and buses ran infrequently because of gasoline shortages, and blackouts meant that food you expected to preserve in your refrigerator was rotting because oil imports dropped by 70 percent over a four-year period, as they did in Cuba from 1989 to 1993. Picture yourself undergoing an operation at a formerly reliable hospital where now several doctors and nurses were absent because of transportation problems and there were hardly any anesthetics, medicines, or bandages. In 1990, few Cubans believed that they would ever live this kind of life, even when President Fidel Castro announced that the country was entering a "Special Period in a Time of Peace."

The collapse of the CMEA, the Eastern bloc's trading system through which Cuba had conducted 85 percent of its international commerce, forced it to find new trading partners who demanded that Cuba pay market prices in an internationally convertible (i.e., "hard") currency for the goods it imported. As its international trade plummeted between 1990 and 1993, Cuba's GDP declined by 30 percent.[61] A further blow came in 1993, when the United States began to implement the Cuban Democracy Act, which banned sales to Cuba by subsidiaries of US corporations abroad, thereby increasing the cost of food and medicine that Cuba imported.[62]

In response, Cuban leaders focused on "a relatively narrow agenda" of immediate solutions.[63] In practical terms, the new reality meant that Cuba had to abandon its economic model of import-substitution industrialization and to insert itself into the international capitalist economy. It had to find new ways quickly to earn hard currency. The export of sugar and nickel had been Cuba's main source of convertible funds, but production in both industries was inefficient and depended on imported oil that Cuba could no longer afford. Backed into a corner, Cuba's leaders opted for three strategies they had eschewed previously.

First, they sought to attract large amounts foreign investment capital. This required removing bureaucratic obstacles, creating new Cuban companies to interact with foreigners, and approving new laws that would enable foreign enterprises to own more than 49 percent of a joint venture with a Cuban entity. The new quasi-private enterprises became staffed largely by former members of the Cuban armed forces (Fuerzas Armadas Revolucionarias [FAR]).[64] In 1995, the government permitted 100 percent foreign ownership in a few specified industries. There were 392 foreign joint ventures in Cuba by 2001.[65]

Hotels became the largest kind of foreign investment, coinciding with Cuba's second strategy for acquiring hard currency, building up its tourist industry. But the decision was not taken lightly. As Marguerite Jiménez explains, "Fidel Castro's reluctance to promote tourism was rooted in memories of pre-1959 Cuba, as an all-inclusive hedonist playground for affluent North American tourists, accompanied by prostitution, corruption, and gambling casinos run by organized crime syndicates."[66] By 2005, more than two million visitors were arriving on the island annually, and tourism replaced sugar as the country's most important source of hard currency.

The government turned to its third strategy in 1993, legalizing the use of US dollars on the island and opening dollar stores (*Tiendas de Recuperación de Divisas*) at which Cubans could purchase imported goods. The goal was to discourage the illegal black market, to capture dollars that could be used to import necessities, and to encourage Cubans abroad to send even more money to their families. The policy succeeded; over the next decade, remittances sent by relatives rose to more than $1 billion annually. At the same time, however, the purchasing power of the Cuban peso receded, exacerbating inequality among Cubans by creating a two-class system of consumption: one for those with access to dollars (e.g., from remittances or tips in the tourist sector) and one for those without.

Cuban officials also sought to reduce the need for hard currency by reorganizing the system of food production. Large state farms required imported equipment, fertilizer, and petroleum. They were replaced by small producer cooperatives called Basic Units of Cooperative Production (*Unidades Básicas de Producción* [UBPC]), in which individual families had land use rights. The government also reintroduced free farmers' markets, in which both private farmers and UBPCs could sell produce to the public at market prices. These reforms only marginally increased food production; at the turn of the century, Cuba still had to import 70 percent of its food.

Perhaps the most difficult decision concerned sugar. Cuban identity had been entwined with sugar for nearly two centuries, and Cuba had long been the world's leading producer of the sweetener. But the production of sugar became unsustainable by the end of the twentieth century.[67] At times, Cuba spent more to harvest and process the cane than it earned in hard currency. For several years, the government subsidized sugar production for political and not economic reasons to avoid dislocations in rural areas where sugar constituted the only source of employment. The day of reckoning arrived in May 2002 when the government announced that half the island's mills would be closed.

RAFTER EXODUS

In 1994, the economic calamity clearly had become a political one as emigration pressures mounted. The number of people trying to leave the island illegally every month rose from dozens to hundreds and then thousands. The deep impact of the economy's decline was evident in the desperation of those who used makeshift rafts—inner tubes, wood slats, anything that would float—to traverse the Florida Straits, one of the world's most dangerous waterways. By some estimates, three-fourths of those who attempted the trip did not survive.[68]

In 1984, as a result of the 1980 Mariel exodus, the United States and Cuba signed an immigration accord under which the United States would grant "up to" 20,000 immigrant visas annually to Cubans. However, just as economic conditions got worse, the United States issued fewer and fewer visas—only 2,003 in 1993 despite more than ten times that number of applicants—which left illegal departure as the only way out.[69] Fidel Castro charged that the United States was encouraging the exodus by granting asylum to rafters, and early in August he announced that Cuba would not constrain anyone from trying to leave Cuba.[70] Thousands began flocking to the shore.

Significantly, most of these emigrants were Cubans who had grown up during the Revolution. They were younger than the wave in the 1960s. Two-thirds of those whose occupations could be identified had been in low-skilled jobs.[71] While it was evident that their principal motive for leaving Cuba was economic, there also was some evidence that they had become alienated from the Revolution. The exodus ended with a US-Cuban accord under which the United States would grant at least 20,000 visas annually to Cubans and would house rafters whom it picked up on the high seas at the Guantánamo naval base. In 1995, the agreement was amended: the United States allowed the 23,000 Guantánamo detainees to apply for visas and committed itself to return to Cuba any illegal émigrés found on the high seas. This became known as the "wet foot, dry foot" policy; Cubans picked up at sea were returned to Cuba, but those who made it to the United States or a US territory such as Puerto Rico were allowed to stay.

CIVIL SOCIETY

As the government's ability to provide employment and a social safety net for everyone diminished, it became more tolerant of religious institutions and allowed nongovernmental organizations to form. While some of the organizations continued to have links to the state and, thus, might not be indicative of a truly emergent civil society, there is little doubt that conditions during the Special Period fostered new networks and groups that provided some opening for the expression of independent views. The Catholic Church, in particular, developed magazines and newsletters that circulated widely.

The Catholic Church had opposed the Revolution in the 1960s. Until the Special Period, active participation as a congregant was an obstacle for anyone who wanted to move ahead professionally or politically. But as the Church accommodated itself to the Revolution, the state softened its stance against religion. In 1994, the Vatican named Havana archbishop Jaime Ortega y Alamino as a cardinal. While he affirmed the Catholic Church's support for the Revolution's social justice accomplishments, he also stipulated that "the Church had an obligation to help the Cuban people transcend the revolution's limitations . . . through a mobilized civil society," as historian Margaret Crahan observed.[72] In 1998, Pope John Paul II made the first papal visit ever to the island. Tumultuous crowds welcomed him, and throughout the country, Cubans placed signs in their windows proclaiming, "No tengo miedo" (I have no fear). During the five-day trip across Cuba, the pope called both for more freedom of speech and religious education and for an end to the US embargo.

One of the most prominent examples of civic engagement emerged from the work of a lay Catholic activist, Oswaldo Payá Sardiñas. In the late 1990s, he organized the Varela Project, which had the goal of collecting a sufficient number of signatures on a petition to trigger a national referendum to promote freedom of speech and assembly, the right to own a business, and the end of one-party rule. Although the 11,000 signatures he submitted to the National Assembly in 2002 exceeded constitutional requirements, the petition was denied, and the Varela Project lost much of its force.

The project lacked both the resources and critical mass to sustain a serious challenge to the government. Similarly, none of the small groups of "dissidents" who had been supported or promoted by US governmental and nongovernmental organizations were able to build an effective network of opposition during the Special Period. While this was partly a consequence of state repression,[73] they also were discredited by working too closely with the US government. In addition, Cubans found nontraditional ways to express their views through media such as film, the plastic arts, and music.

CULTURE AND SOCIETY DURING THE SPECIAL PERIOD

Shortages during the Special Period initially took a heavy toll on all forms of Cuban culture. Money for films was scarce, as was paper for newspapers and books. Baseball games were played only during the daytime to avoid using stadium lights. To survive, Cuban writers and artists turned abroad to publish their works, host dance performances, curate art exhibits, and coproduce films. For example, the Academy Award–nominated 1993 film by Tomás Gutiérrez Alea and Juan Carlos Tabío, *Fresa y chocolate* (*Strawberry and Chocolate*), was produced as a Cuban-Spanish-Mexican venture. The film is also an example of how the new forms of financing for the arts broadened the possibilities for expression. *Fresa y chocolate* probes several previously taboo subjects: homosexuality, ideological rigidity, and even patriotism.

Similarly, as the Havana Art Biennial grew in popularity and drew international crowds, artists pushed the boundaries of what had been acceptable.[74] Musicians also found ever-greater freedom to criticize not only shortages but also the shortcomings of the Revolution. Carlos Varela, a popular folksinger, carried on the *nueva trova* tradition made famous by Silvio Rodríguez and Pablo Milanés. But Varela's songs went right to the edge, in effect calling for major reforms. Consider "William Tell," which recounts the famous story from the perspective of the archer's son. Tired of holding the apple on his head, the boy runs away. William Tell cannot understand why his son would abandon him, so the singer explains: "William Tell, your son has grown up / And now he wants to shoot the arrow himself."[75]

For musicians, the cost of equipment that could replicate the kind of rap music they wanted to play was prohibitive. "Rap was originally an import," sociologist Sujatha

Fernandes explains, but "Cuban rap soon took on a life of its own." She notes that Cuban rappers by the mid-1990s recreated "the rhythmic pulse of hip-hop with instruments like the melodic Batá drums, typically used in ceremonies of the Afro-Cuban Santería religion."[76] As Cuban hip-hop evolved independently of US influence, its lyrics and themes became a distinctive contrast to the American genre that promoted sexual exploitation and consumption. Cuban artists focused on the problems of inequality, prostitution, police harassment, and the difficulty of doing everyday tasks such as buying food and cooking, as well as the way that governmental decisions during the Special Period undermined earlier achievements of the Revolution, such as racial equality.[77]

Historian Alejandro de la Fuente reported that "by the early 1980s Cuban society had made remarkable progress in the reduction of racial inequality in a number of crucial areas, including education, indicators of health care, and the occupational structure. Racial inequality persisted in some areas, but the trend was unequivocally towards equality."[78] But the Special Period undermined these advances, many of which depended on government spending that declined after 1990. While several market reforms engendered inequalities across the races, some had their greatest negative impact on Blacks, who had less access to hard currency from remittances because whites constituted the largest portion of exiles abroad.[79] Moreover, discrimination against darker-skinned Cubans in the tourist sector limited their access to the second source of hard currency. The consequence was that while "all Cubans were equal before the law," those able to *resolver* (find a solution) more successfully during the Special Period tended to be lighter-skinned Cubans.[80]

Not surprisingly, Cubans' health and the quality of their education suffered during the first years of the Special Period. As noted earlier, this was due largely to an inadequate diet and the increased cost of food and medicine because of the US embargo. Basic teaching materials were no longer available, though the greatest impact on education came from two different effects of the Special Period. First, teachers' salaries were so low that many left the profession, and there were few replacements. Second, young people began to devalue education because it no longer was "the main route to a higher standard of living, nor an essential mechanism for achieving social status."[81] A taxi driver could earn in three days what a teacher earned in a month.

Despite the economic conditions, the Cuban government continued to allocate scarce funds to health care, education, social security, and assistance to the poor at a relatively constant percentage of GDP—and at times at a higher percentage. By the end of the decade, teachers gained a 30 percent increase in their wages. Cuban inventiveness led to new forms of volunteerism in staffing day care centers, much as Cuba had relied on volunteers to work in the 1961 literacy campaign. Indeed, Cubans looked to the new millennium with a renewed confidence, in part because changing international circumstances gave it several new allies.

FOREIGN POLICY DURING THE SPECIAL PERIOD

In 1991, Cuban leaders perceived that their country was utterly "alone" in the world, much as Castro did at the end of the missile crisis when it seemed that the Soviet

Union had abandoned Cuba and that the United States remained an even greater threat.[82] But instead of seeking allies by supporting revolutionary movements as Cuba did in the 1960s, it engaged intensely with like-minded countries in multilateral institutions and developed new defensive economic ties with emerging powers. Consider that starting in 1992, the UN General Assembly has voted every year since to condemn the US embargo. While initially more countries abstained than approved the measure, in subsequent years the number of "yeas" grew so that by 2013, 188 countries voted affirmatively. (In 2022, the vote was 185–2–2, with only Israel voting with the United States against the resolution; Ukraine and Brazil abstained because the former was receiving billions of dollars from the United States for its war with Russia, and the latter was still headed by Jair Bolsonaro.)

Cuba had built a deep well of appreciation in the Third World because of its assistance programs and sustained military commitment in Angola against the apartheid South African regime. This was highlighted by Nelson Mandela during a 1991 trip to Cuba, the year after he was released from prison. In a speech on July 26, with Fidel Castro at his side, Mandela declared, "The Cuban people hold a special place in the hearts of the people of Africa. The Cuban internationalists have made a contribution to African independence, freedom, and justice, unparalleled for its principled and selfless character."[83]

By 2003, it was clear that Cuba would concentrate its foreign policy more intently toward the Third World—toward countries with which it could relate based on mutual respect and not asymmetric requirements—rather than Europe or Russia. Consider that Castro blasted the EU's conditioning of loans and aid to improvements in Cuba's human rights. The Cuban leader asserted that the EU's demands were a form of neocolonial intervention and bluntly asserted that "Cuba does not need the aid of the European Union to survive."[84]

China was a different matter. Cuban leaders tended to view China—despite its size, wealth, military power, and potential for domination—differently than countries that previously had dominated Cuba. Until the late 1980s, China had little capacity to provide much support to Cuba, and it had little incentive to do so given Cuba's relationship with the Soviet Union. But as the Soviet Union dissolved, China began a historic spurt in the growth of its economy. In the 1990s, China also started to invest in Latin America as it searched for raw materials to fuel its fast-growing industries. Initially, Cuba was not high on China's target list, though it did ship 500,000 bicycles to Cuba in 1992 and 1993. But in 2001 China began to allocate large sums to Cuba for petroleum exploration and the renovation of nickel production facilities.

Cuba's renewed turn to Latin America was facilitated by the 1998 election of Hugo Chávez as Venezuela's president. Chávez looked to Fidel Castro as his spiritual mentor and turned to the Cuba leader for advice. Together, they began to implement an ambitious project, as Castro described it in October 2000, "to unite the Latin American and Caribbean nations and to struggle for a world economic order that brings more justice to all peoples."[85] That month, Venezuela began to sell oil to some South American countries and Cuba not only at a price that was one-third less than the world market price but that also could be purchased with a loan payable after fifteen years at a 2 percent interest rate.

In 2001, Cuba imported more oil from Venezuela than it had imported from the Soviet Union in 1990. As payment, Cuba sent teachers and doctors to Venezuela. The teachers contributed to the eradication of illiteracy in Venezuela, and the doctors helped that country establish a medical program for the poor, Barrio Adentro (Inside the Neighborhood). In 2006 more than 20,000 Cuban medical personnel were serving in Venezuela, and in 2013 there were 30,000. Venezuela also had become Cuba's major trading partner, accounting for nearly 22 percent of Cuba's imports and exports.[86]

Late in 2004, Cuba and Venezuela launched a new organization intended to achieve their common hemispheric goals: the Bolivarian Alternative for the Peoples of Our America (ALBA in the Spanish acronym).[87] Backed by Venezuela's oil wealth, it aimed to integrate Latin American and Caribbean countries economically, in competition with the US-proposed Free Trade Area of the Americas. ALBA also created a development bank and served as a coordinating mechanism for development projects.

ENGAGEMENT AND DISENGAGEMENT WITH THE UNITED STATES

Cuba's tactical response to the sanctions of the 1992 Cuban Democracy Act was to go beyond trade by attracting new foreign investors. As the plan began to work, hard-liners in US Congress sought to scare off investors with legislation that would enable former Cuban property owners, such as Bacardi, to sue the investors in a US court and obtain compensation by seizing their US-based properties. Officially titled the Cuban Liberty and Democratic Solidarity (LIBERTAD) Act, the bill became popularly known as Helms-Burton after its two principal sponsors, Senator Jesse Helms (R-NC) and Representative Dan Burton (R-IN).

Cubans viewed the act as a challenge to their country's national sovereignty, much like the Platt Amendment. They argued that it arrogated to the United States the right to determine whether there has been an appropriate transition to democracy; that is, whether the Cubans have established a government that the United States can trust to rule the island.[88] In any case, the law had only a limited effect, as US allies demanded that President Bill Clinton waive a key provision that could have been costly to several European corporations.

Moreover, despite the restrictions that Helms-Burton seemed to pose on a president's authority, President Clinton permitted an increase in cultural exchanges (including two baseball games between the Baltimore Orioles and Cuba's national team) and eased travel regulations. This stimulated the creation of several "people-to-people" educational programs by universities and organizations such as the National Geographic Society.

Meanwhile, the weakening of the anti-Castro lobby and the growing interest by US agricultural exporters in selling products to Cuba led to the 2000 Trade Sanctions Reform and Export Enhancement Act (TSRA), which authorized the direct commercial export of food and agricultural products from the United States to Cuban government-operated entities on a cash basis. Despite its financing hurdles, the TSRA provided the mechanism to open trade significantly. In 2008 US sales of agricultural goods reached a high point of $711.5 million, though they declined to half that annual level by the end of 2013.[89]

Still, the anti-Castro lobby had enough clout to influence President George W. Bush to issue a series of executive orders in May 2004 intended to hasten "Cuba's transition from Stalinist rule."[90] The new measures included a reduction in trips to the island by Cuban Americans from once a year to once in three years and a requirement that university programs in Cuba be a minimum of ten weeks. The number of programs dropped within months from more than 300 to 6.

The Revolution under Raúl Castro

On July 31, 2006, a gravely ill Fidel Castro handed the conductor's baton to his younger brother Raúl Castro. At that point, the Cuban government had weathered most of the Special Period hardships that would have destabilized most other countries, and Cubans had demonstrated a remarkable resilience and ability to adapt. But no one could be certain how much longer they would be patient without political and economic reforms that were necessary for the Cuban Revolution to be sustainable. Recognizing that his authority was tenuous, Raúl proceeded cautiously. He quoted Fidel in every speech, wrapping himself in his brother's aura, and made no dramatic moves during his first eighteen months in office. Yet he also began to prepare the country for what he hoped would be a reinvented Cuban Revolution.

ECONOMICS AND POLITICS

An October 2006 investigative report on corruption in *Juventud Rebelde*, the official newspaper of the Communist Party's youth wing, was an early signal of changes to come. Headlined "The Big Old Swindle," the series could not have appeared without Raúl's approval. It officially acknowledged what most people already knew: state-owned stores routinely sold products that weighed less than the amount customers had paid for; food at state restaurants had less meat or cheese than regulations required.[91] Two months later the acting president encouraged university students to engage in the kind of open debate about Cuba's future that his older brother had eschewed.[92]

The following July he offered a frank and critical assessment of Cuba's economic circumstances, pointedly saying that the US embargo was only one of several factors Cuba had to consider to improve its economic performance. The main issue, he declared, was that "no one, no individual or country, can afford to spend more than what they have." He then warned that "structural and conceptual changes will have to be introduced."[93] Members of the Communist Party and Young Communists studied the speech in detail over the next months, not as commandments to be repeated by rote, but as pronouncements to be debated and interpreted. Journalist Marc Frank obtained the guide prepared for discussion leaders and reports that it admonished them to foster a "profound debate."[94]

As discussions moved beyond the Communist Party into work centers, community meetings, and even some publications, a new set of issues replaced the recommended topics. Cubans vented their anger over the dual currency system and their declining ability to purchase necessities with the state salaries they earned. Many complained about bureaucratic red tape that made bribes an increasingly necessary cost in order to obtain a state service or license or to avoid trouble from inspectors or the police.[95]

There were still many achievements for which Cubans could be proud. The UN's 2009 *Human Development Report* ranked at Cuba 51 out of 194 countries, just behind Argentina (49) and Uruguay (50), and ahead of Mexico (53), Costa Rica (54), and Brazil (75).[96] However, the Special Period clearly had taken an enormous toll. Increasing inequality, decreasing universal access to health care and a good education, a growing culture of individualism, and a declining sense of communal solidarity had eroded distinctive aspects of the Cuban Revolution. The wellspring of hope that nurtured Cubans' belief in the future, which had given them the energy and strength to defy the odds in building a new society, seemed depleted.

A PREFERENCE FOR ORGANIZATIONAL ORDER

The 1976 Constitution (and subsequent amended versions through 2002) proclaimed that the Cuban Communist Party (PCC) was "the highest leading force [*la fuerza dirigente superior*] of the society and State." Yet by 2008, the PCC was languishing. Led mainly by white men in their seventies and eighties, and increasingly disconnected from the travails most Cubans felt, it had not held a party congress since 1997, though one was supposed to be organized every five years. In part, its decline resulted from Fidel's efforts to energize Cubans through participation in mass organizations disconnected from the PCC, such as the revitalized Federation of University Students, which he hoped would instill revolutionary fervor among younger Cubans.[97]

Most of these ad hoc efforts ended after the National Assembly formally elected Raúl as the new president in February 2008. In his inauguration speech, he emphasized the importance of institutionalization and reestablishing the role that the constitution had given to the PCC.[98] In contrast to his brother, Raúl had a decided preference for organizational order. He honored well-defined lines of authority and sought to establish accountability for achievements and errors.

The new president waited one year to institute any major reform. Then with one stroke in March 2009, he dismissed three senior party leaders and eight ministers, including Carlos Lage Dávila, the vice president in charge of the Cuban economy, and Foreign Minister Felipe Pérez Roque. At the same time, he combined four existing ministries into two (the Ministry of Foreign Trade and Investment and the Ministry of Food), and he promoted some younger PCC officials whom he viewed as exemplary managers. Most notable was Miguel Díaz-Canel Bermúdez, the Holguín Province party chief, who became minister of higher education and later the first vice president. The National Assembly elected him as Cuba's president in 2018.

Díaz-Canel had a reputation for being an efficient manager. Born in 1960, he studied to be an electrical engineer, spent three years in the army, and then rose in the

Communist Party hierarchy. As PCC first secretary in the provinces of Villa Clara and Holguín, he was also known for fighting corruption.

ECONOMIC REFORMS

The changes in Cuba's political structure after 2006 were accompanied by only minor economic reforms at first. Economist Jorge Mario Sánchez aptly observed that the economic measures "pointed in the right direction but were insufficient to deal with the roots of dysfunctionality."[99] Cuba still had not found a way to generate enough hard currency to develop a sustainable and equitable economy. While its gross domestic product had reached $100 billion, hard currency earnings amounted to only 4 percent of the total. The country continued to spend too much on importing food that it could have grown domestically.[100]

Then in April 2010, Raúl set off an economic shock. Charging that "the budgeted and entrepreneurial sectors have hundreds of thousands of workers in excess," he announced a plan to reduce the size of the state's workforce by one million employees—a cut of nearly 20 percent.[101] Several problems had combined to lead to this one solution. The government was strapped for cash to pay workers. Some laid-off state workers, officials reasoned, might accept the government's offer of up to forty hectares (about one hundred acres) of free land on which they could increase domestic food production. Raúl also believed that government workers treated their jobs as sinecures—guaranteed regardless of what they did—which encouraged sloth that resulted in low productivity.

Popular reaction to the speech was decidedly negative, and resistance to the plan emerged from within the government as well. In August 2010, the president revised his numbers. He said that the reduction would be more moderate—the state would drop only 500,000 from its payroll, with much of the decrease occurring through retirement and attrition. Nevertheless, he was adamant that change had to come, and he pressed senior officials to quicken the pace of change, a process he labeled as "updating the Cuban economy."

"UPDATING" THE ECONOMY BEGINS

In November 2010, "updating" was formalized as a major new program of economic revitalization named "Guidelines for the Economic and Social Policies of the Party and the Revolution."[102] Known as the *Lineamientos*, or Guidelines, it outlined 291 proposals for reform, which became 313 after a nationwide series of meetings.[103] The Sixth Party Congress approved the plan in April 2011.

Included in the 313 *Lineamientos* was a process for expanding the number of permissible private (referred to as "non-state") sector enterprises. It created a commission that initially listed 181 types of private occupations that could be performed legally. The list included mostly service jobs, such as barber or beautician, electrician, bricklayer, plumber, photographer, waiter, truck driver, flower seller, entertainer, sports instructor, and so on.[104]

Cuban economist Juan Triana explained that the *Lineamientos* provided a fundamentally new orientation for the society. The "consensus that without development it will be very hard to sustain Cuban socialism," he wrote, "is a departure from the past in which socialism was the guarantor of achieving development."[105] Notably, Cuba's leaders acknowledged that development might need to prioritize efficiency and growth, which would require a greater reliance on markets in determining wages and even what enterprises produced.[106]

The Seventh Party Congress revised the *Lineamientos* in 2016 and approved two additional documents as a basis for further reform: "Conceptualization of Cuba's Economic and Social Model" and the National Development Plan to 2030. While maintaining aspirations of equity and full employment, the new plans made clear that the non-state sector (private and cooperative enterprises) would be a permanent feature of Cuba's economy. The 2019 constitution affirmed this by recognizing private ownership of productive as well as personal property (Article 22) and guaranteeing that foreign investment is an "important element for the economic development of the country" (Article 28).[107] The Guidelines, the Conceptualization of the Model, and the 2019 constitution roughly indicate the nature and extent of privatization that Cuba's leaders envision for the country: between 40 and 50 percent of Cuba's workers would be employed in non-state sector jobs; strategic sectors (the "axes of development") and major resources—nickel mines, oil fields, energy production—would continue to be state-owned; the state would maintain near exclusive monopoly to provide education, day care, and health care.

In 2011, at about the same time that the PCC approved the original *Lineamientos*, the government eased several regulations related to small businesses. Bed-and-breakfast accommodations in the 1990s and early 2000s had been confined to rooms within a dwelling occupied by the vendor. A modified rule allowed an entrepreneur to rent out a whole apartment or house—which became the most popular option for Airbnb participants when the company entered Cuba in 2015. Late in 2011, the government also decreed that individuals could buy and sell houses and automobiles directly to one another for first time in fifty years.

Slightly more than 75 percent of Cuba's population lived in urban areas in 2009. While the plan to increase food production by enticing city dwellers to rural areas with the offer of free land began that year, there were few takers. Aside from the expectation that the work would be difficult, the incentives were low and the hurdles were high. A family's rights over improvements to the land—such as a barn—remained unclear. Moreover, as political geographer Garrett Graddy-Lovelace reports, there was a "thirty percent rate of food loss from field to store" in 2015 because farmers often lacked "bags, bushels, crates, and boxes to transport harvested crops."[108]

In 2012 and 2013, the government partially responded to the problems by easing and clarifying some regulations, especially for cooperatives. The area of land a cooperative could lease was increased to sixty-seven hectares (about 165 acres), and leases could extend to twenty-five years instead of ten. Cooperatives also were permitted to sell directly to hotels and other tourism entities instead of going through a state entity. Both cooperatives and individual farmers were allowed to retain the right to the structures they had built on the land.[109] But these reforms generated little movement back to rural areas, and food production continued to lag.

RUNNING IN PLACE

Even though small businesses were flourishing when the PCC held its Seventh Congress in 2016, many Cubans complained that all of their bustling still left them only running in place and that Raúl was implementing changes too slowly. Indeed, he acknowledged in mid-2016 that the Cuban economy was suffering severe problems and warned that it would be "imperative to reduce expenses of all kinds that are not indispensable."[110] Similarly, the PCC Congress reported that only 21 percent of the reforms intended to "update" the Cuban economic model had been fulfilled completely.[111]

Two significant problems stood in the path of updating the economy. First, opponents of reform were scattered throughout the government and PCC, especially at key decision points. Some were self-serving survivalists who had found ways to adapt to hardship through informal networks and illegal practices that economic reforms would have disturbed. Others sincerely worried that foreign investments could make Cuba vulnerable to the demands of another country and vitiate Cuba's sovereignty, or that Cuba's unfettered integration into the global economy would lead Cubans to replace values of social responsibility and communal cooperation with extreme individualism and consumerism.

The situation of nonagricultural cooperatives illustrates how opponents of change could slow down the process. A local municipal agency could approve a license for an individual private business (*cuentapropista*). Yet only the national Council of Ministers could authorize the operation of a nonagricultural cooperative. As a result, there were only 450 of these cooperatives functioning in mid-2018, most of which were spun off from state enterprises located in Havana. At the same time, few licenses had been issued for private professional activities—legal representation, architecture, business consulting, accounting—even though post-2011 regulations permitted such professionals to form cooperatives.

The second obstacle was US sanctions. These imposed enormous costs (by some estimates $150 billion over the previous fifty years), discouraged foreign investment on the island, made interaction banking difficult, and essentially placed Cuba's potentially largest and most lucrative market off-limits.

In 2016, the economy experienced two consecutive quarters of negative growth (i.e., a recession). The next year GDP growth was an anemic 1.2 percent and only 1.8 percent in 2018. As Ricardo Torres observed, this is "well below the needs of a country the size and level of development of Cuba" and is incompatible "with a sustained improvement in the living conditions of a majority of Cubans."[112]

FOREIGN RELATIONS UNDER RAÚL CASTRO

No one expected Raúl to shift Cuba's foreign policy from the internationalist path it had taken under Fidel. After all, the new leader had been vice president and minister of the armed forces for more than forty years and was a partner with his brother in establishing the path. Still, there were changes occasioned by new opportunities and challenges in the international landscape.

In 2006, Cuba was at a high point in its relations with countries in Latin America, Africa, and Asia, and at a nadir in its relations with the United States and Europe. In December 2006, Cuba hosted the NAM summit for the second time and became chair for the next three years. (Only Yugoslavia, another founding member of the NAM, had been honored to host the summit twice.) By the end of its three-year term as NAM chair, all of the countries in the Western Hemisphere except the United States had established diplomatic relations with Cuba. In November 2008, Cuba also became a full member of the Rio Group, an informal association of twenty-three Western Hemispheric countries that formalized itself in 2011 as the Community of Latin American and Caribbean States (CELAC in the Spanish acronym) and aspired to challenge the OAS as the main forum for handling hemispheric issues.

In 2006, China provided nearly $400 million in long-terms loans and credits to upgrade Cuba's telecommunication infrastructure and to enable Cuba to purchase Chinese televisions, washing machines, and air conditioners.[113] The next year China became Cuba's second-largest trading partner, after Venezuela, with $2.3 billion in bilateral trade that year. When Chinese president Hu Jintao visited Cuba the following year, he approved a $6 billion investment for the expansion of a Cienfuegos oil refinery and the construction of a liquefied natural gas plant and provided the second phase of a $350 million loan designated for the renovation of Cuban hospitals.[114] On the heels of President Hu's visit, Russian president Dmitry Medvedev came to Cuba to sign trade agreements involving nickel, oil, automobiles, and wheat.

Still, Latin America was the region that offered the greatest promise for Cuba. The leftward shift in Latin America in the first decade of the twenty-first century brought to power several leaders who had long admired Cuba. This was one reason they selected Cuba to host the second CELAC summit, which convened in January 2014 in Havana. In addition, every Latin American country had experienced meaningful economic growth between 1990 and 2010. Brazil's GDP grew by more than 40 percent, and it moved from eleventh to seventh place in the world's ranking. Cuba reached out to Brazil partly as a way of diversifying its trading partners, and it established a joint venture with Odebrecht, the Brazilian engineering conglomerate, to reconstruct the Port of Mariel at a cost of $1 billion. The port opened in January 2014 with a terminal that has an annual capacity of one million containers and the ability to service super cargo ships traversing the recently widened Panama Canal.

In conjunction with ALBA, Cuba provided medical aid, including a program to restore eyesight to more than two million people, in several Latin American and Caribbean countries beginning in 2005.[115] John Kirk explains that Cuba's "tradition of medical internationalism dates back to 1960." As of 2011, the international medical program was sending about 41,000 health workers to sixty-eight nations.[116] While the commitment to medical internationalism continued apace under Raúl, despite setbacks in the domestic economy, it also became an important way for Cuba to earn hard currency—as Cuba charged fees to countries that could afford them—and increase the wages of Cuban doctors. The services they provided in Brazil, Bolivia, Venezuela, and Ecuador brought medical care to rural communities and urban pockets of poverty that had never seen a doctor. In turn, it strengthened popular support for the leaders in those countries, which reinforced their inclination to support Cuba.

Also meeting in Havana at the time of the 2014 CELAC summit were peace negotiators from the Colombian government and the Revolutionary Armed Forces of Colombia (FARC), the main insurgent group in the country. The peace negotiations began in mid-November 2012 in Norway and quickly moved to Havana, where Cuban diplomats played a critical role in helping to bring about an agreement four years later.

SLOW OPENING WITH THE UNITED STATES

Colombia had been the third-largest recipient of US economic and military aid in the world—an average of more than $700 million per year for over two decades. Thus, Colombian president Juan Manuel Santos's stark ultimatum at the end of the 2012 Summit of the Americas shocked US officials. Speaking on behalf of the other heads of state, he declared they would not attend the summit planned for 2015 unless Cuba was permitted to participate.[117] Back in Washington, President Barack Obama fired his national security adviser for Latin America, and shortly after his November reelection, decided to pursue normal diplomatic relations with Cuba. In April 2013, he assigned two top aides to begin negotiations toward that goal.[118]

Cuba had bought a record $711 million worth of food, agricultural equipment, and medicine from the United States in 2008. Despite the embargo, the hovering giant had become the island's fifth-largest trading partner.[119] Some Cuban officials hoped that the purchases would encourage major US companies to lobby for a changed US policy, but the Obama administration's policy during his first term disappointed them.

During the 2008 presidential campaign, Senator Obama said he would be willing to meet with President Castro. His margin of victory in Florida—204,600 votes—included approximately 35 percent of Cuban American ballots, which indicated that a significant group of moderates favored improved relations between the two countries.[120] He also had political cover created by a flurry of proposals for better relations from several ad hoc groups made up of former US government officials and members of Congress, leading scholars, and prominent public intellectuals, several of whom had previously supported harsh measures against Cuba. This context provided enough political space for President Obama to fulfill a campaign promise by removing restrictions on remittances sent by Cuban Americans. He also reversed President George W. Bush's restrictive travel policy for Cuban Americans. In 2011, President Obama increased the level of remittances all US citizens could send to Cuba and eased restrictions on educational travel, most significantly by restoring the people-to-people travel license under which most non-Cuban Americans visited the island until President Bush abolished it. Moreover, the administration restarted semiannual migration talks with Cuba and increased diplomatic contacts at a slightly higher level than before.

From the Cuban perspective, the administration's actions were too modest, because they did little to reduce major US economic sanctions and the Obama administration had made no move to remove Cuba from the US State Department's list of state sponsors of terrorism. Meanwhile, Washington continued several programs that

Cuba perceived as harmful or threatening. One project, the Cuban Medical Professional Parole (CMPP) program created in 2006, was designed to encourage Cuban doctors serving abroad to give up their citizenship and emigrate to the United States. By the end of 2015, the United States had approved more than 7,000 applications by Cuban medical personnel.[121]

The US Agency for International Development (USAID) was the lead agency in spending funds on covert programs that Cuba considered subversive. In 2009, it spent $45 million on these projects.[122] The one that created the greatest obstacle for improved relations involved Alan P. Gross, a subcontractor for Development Alternatives International. The Cuban government arrested Gross in December 2009 and asserted his mission was to create a covert system of communications for the purpose of subversion. The US State Department claimed he was in Cuba merely to provide the small Jewish community with telecommunications equipment that would enable its members to access the internet without Cuban government interference or surveillance. The Jewish community had not requested such assistance.

In fact, what Gross provided was sophisticated satellite communications transmitters that included a subscriber identity module (SIM) card usually available only to the US military or intelligence community. The SIM card could prevent the detection of signals from the transmitters for a radius of 250 miles.[123] The communications setup Gross established would allow a Cuban enemy to communicate with its operatives inside Cuba or allow subversive groups to communicate across the island by tapping into the equipment that Gross had given to Cuba.

Following Gross's arrest, the State Department ended the renewed migration talks and refused to consider offers by Cuban representatives to discuss a variety of bilateral issues. (However, US and Cuban officials continued monthly meetings at the Guantánamo Naval Base fence line and maintained cooperation over drug enforcement.[124]) Judging that the Obama administration was unlikely to make any major move to improve relations, the Cuban government cut back its purchases of US exports to $533 million in 2009.

Several events and circumstances in 2013 offered renewed expectations for improved relations. A new Cuban law enabled most citizens to obtain passports, to leave the country for up to two years without an exit permit, and to return without forfeiting their property. The United States previously had highlighted Cuba's travel restrictions in attacking its human rights record.[125] In November 2013, President Obama hinted at big changes. He remarked at a fund-raiser that "the notion that the same policies that we put in place in 1961 would somehow still be as effective as they are today . . . doesn't make sense."[126]

OBAMA OPENS THE DOOR AND TRUMP CLOSES IT

On December 17, 2014, Presidents Castro and Obama revealed what had been in the works for the previous eighteen months, announcing that their countries would resume diplomatic relations. President Castro also announced Cuba had released Gross, the USAID subcontractor, on humanitarian grounds, had commuted the sentence for a

CIA agent arrested in the 1990s, and would also release fifty-three political prisoners. President Obama did the same for the three remaining members of the Cuban Five still in prison and returned them to Cuba. The Cuban Five were intelligence agents who were monitoring the activities of US-based terrorist groups engaged in disrupting Cuban tourism by planting bombs in hotels. A US federal court found them guilty of conspiracy to commit espionage. President Obama also indicated he would consider removing Cuba from the US list of state sponsors of terrorism.

As the two governments sought to make the movement toward normal relations "irreversible" in 2015 and 2016, they engaged in a flurry of activity and produced almost two dozen agreements. Negotiations ranged across a variety of issues, including environmental cooperation, law enforcement, combating trafficking in persons, property claims, and human rights. Regularly scheduled airline service, direct postal services, advanced telecommunications connections, and new avenues for commerce were made possible when the United States relaxed some sanctions and the State Department removed Cuba from its list of state sponsors of terrorism. One notable agreement led to new Treasury Department rules that allow US citizens to engage in joint medical research projects with Cuban nationals and permit the importation of Cuban-origin pharmaceuticals. This enabled the Roswell Park Cancer Institute in Buffalo, New York, to begin clinical trials on CIMAvax, a Cuban drug that may pave the way to developing a lung cancer vaccine. In March 2016, President Obama even traveled to Havana with his family, along with a large contingent of US senators and representatives and business executives.

Republican presidential candidate Donald Trump correctly asserted that as president he would have the authority to reverse nearly all of President Obama's initiatives because they had been achieved through executive orders and not legislation. Yet by mid-2017 he reversed only one of the sanctions President Obama had relaxed, requiring that US citizens travel to Cuba for educational purposes only with a licensed travel provider. He also added a new sanction that banned any commerce with a Cuban entity owned or controlled by the military, which placed many hotels, restaurants, and stores off-limits to Americans.

Far more significant was the State Department's decision to label a series of illnesses experienced by twenty-four US embassy personnel as "sonic attacks," for which it asserted Cuba should bear responsibility. The illnesses, which in the most severe cases mimicked the kind of concussion that occurs from a physical blow to the head, occurred over a period of several months in late 2016 and 2017. Yet a May 2019 *New York Times* article reported "the claims of an attack by an invisible weapon remain not only unproved but also highly contested by prominent physicists and engineers in the United States and abroad."[127] In January 2022, a CIA study concluded that "it is unlikely that a foreign actor, including Russia, is conducting a sustained, worldwide campaign harming U.S. personnel."[128]

Despite the uncertainty about the cause of the problems, and with no evidence that Cuba had caused or had taken insufficient action to prevent the harm, the Trump administration evacuated most of the embassy staff from the country and designated Cuba as an unaccompanied post. It then demanded that Cuba reduce the size of its embassy staff in Washington and issued a travel warning about Cuba. Consequently, several US organizations canceled planned educational trips to the island, and Cubans seeking a US visa had to travel to a third country to obtain one.

In November 2018, US national security advisor John Bolton launched an additional series of attacks on Cuba that brought relations to their most contentious point since the end of the Cold War. He announced there would be additional sanctions and characterized Cuba as one of three countries in a "troika of tyranny" (the other two being Venezuela and Nicaragua).

SOFT POWER

"Soft power" is a term that connotes the ability of a country to influence others by example rather than by coercion. Cuba had accumulated its soft power through several mechanisms by the time Raúl became president. In addition to international medical and cooperative aid programs, these included appealing to other Third World countries as an underdog who resists US oppression; supporting solidarity groups throughout the world; focusing on Cuba's own war against terrorism and its suffering from terrorism; and exporting Cuban films, music, and ballet. All have contributed to a positive image that enables Cuba "to be seen as a trusted and valued partner in many international arenas and institutions," despite its lack of Western liberal democracy, as historians Julia Sweig and Michael Bustamante observed.[129]

Cuba's soft power explains its success at the 2012 Summit of the Americas, despite being absent from the meeting. Its soft power in effect countered the hard power—military strength and financial levers—Washington traditionally used to dominate the hemisphere, when the United States backed down and agreed to allow Cuba to participate in future summits. Political scientist Tom Long describes such a case as "collective foreign policy," where a small country can influence a larger one because of its "ability to win international allies and to work with other small and medium states."[130]

In addition to medical internationalism, Cuba made itself a center for regional culture events with arts, jazz, and film festivals that attract tens of thousands of attendees. Latin Americans accord the annual writing prizes from Casa de las Americas the level of prestige that the Pulitzer Prize has in the United States. Cuban music, films, and art—and, of course, Che Guevara T-shirts—are popular throughout the world.

Culture and Social Relations

NEW SPACES FOR EXPRESSION

In 2012, Cuba's Ministry of Culture and the National Book Institute awarded the National Literature Prize to Leonardo Padura for *The Man Who Loved Dogs*. The decision to give Padura the country's most prestigious award for writing was, in effect, an open acceptance of dissent. All of Padura's detective novels had a political edge, exposing some form of corruption beneath the official facade of normalcy. *The Man Who Loved Dogs* is an epic work that weaves three stories into one. Each challenges an aspect of Cuba's politics, alleged ideological rigidity, or seemingly blind adherence to Soviet dogmas.

The shift toward greater freedom of expression began before Raúl became president. *Temas* magazine, for example, celebrated its twenty-fifth anniversary in 2019. By publishing articles on topics rarely covered in the official media, and with views well outside the mainstream, the magazine helped to expand the borders of what was acceptable. Its July/September 2012 issue, for example, examined the subject of "social development," which included an article about the lack of social mobility and the transmission of poverty from one generation to the next. *Temas*'s editor, Rafael Hernández, argues that increased access to digital media also accelerated the transformation of Cuba's civil culture, including mass cultural consumption and production.[131] By 2014, there had been a revival of periodicals and public spaces for debate on topics as diverse as the nature of socialist democracy, human rights, citizen participation, violence, local initiatives, urban and community problems, religious faiths, and gender.[132]

Yet Cuba lagged behind many other countries in providing access to the internet. By the end of 2013 less than 5 percent of the population had full access.[133] In part, this was due to the US embargo, which prevented Cuba from using the services of US companies that dominated global connectivity or accessing the undersea fiber optic cables that literally surround the island. It was due, also, to technical problems in building a fiber-optic cable connecting Cuba to Venezuela, which began operation only in January 2013. Within four years, though, the percentage of Cubans using the internet had risen to 57 percent.[134] Moreover, in December 2018 the Cuban government made internet access even more readily available by enabling Cubans to purchase 3G cellphone service. In addition to cyber platforms, digital information was widely disseminated across the island through the *paquete semanal* (weekly package), a non-state digital data distribution system. The *paquete* gathered thousands of hours of material from sources worldwide, mostly in violation of international copyright.[135]

Until the Special Period, the Cuban Institute of Cinematographic Art and Industry (ICAIC) was the only distributor of Cuban films and provided most of the support for production. However, as filmmaking with limited resources grew ever more difficult, the government permitted filmmakers to search for funding outside of the country. Coproduction gave them the opportunity to explore subjects previously taboo in Cuba.[136] This was ever more apparent in the 2010 to 2013 period, with films such as *Revolución* (2010) on underground culture, *Habanastation* (2011) on inequality, and *Melaza* (2012) on the necessity to engage in petty corruption in order to survive. In 2011, Cuba released its first "zombie" movie, *Juan de los Muertos*, a comedy in which the government attempts to cover up the existence of the living dead by alleging they were dissidents trying to overthrow the Revolution.

Given their experience with increased openness, artists were especially troubled late in 2018 when the government issued Decree 349, which would have allowed inspectors to close down any public performance or display if the artists were not members of a registered Cuban organization. Critics viewed the decree as a vehicle for censorship and, for a time, succeeded in limiting its force. Notably, in March 2019 the government approved the "new cinema law" (Decreto Ley 373), which provides legal protections for independent filmmakers and seemingly led to the creation of several production companies.[137]

INEQUALITY, RACISM, AND LGBTQ RIGHTS

The Cuban government does not gather data on income distribution. Yet, increasing inequality is evident from the clothing Cubans wear, their choices in transportation and communication, the quality of their housing, and their differential abilities to enjoy restaurants and recreation. Anthropologist Hope Bastian reports that inequality has not only created gaps in consumption but also altered social relations because local community ties have begun to disintegrate, generating new patterns of social stratification, and it has changed Cubans' values with a greater emphasis on materialism and individualism.[138]

Significantly, economic inequality emerged "along clearly visible racial lines," sociologist Katrin Hansing has observed.[139] A greater proportion of darker-skinned than lighter-skinned Cubans were living in substandard housing, which made them unsuitable for rent to tourists, depriving them of one source of hard currency. Darker-skinned Cubans also lacked access to capital from remittances and suffered discrimination due to racist norms in hiring for the tourism industry. As a result, antiracism organizations reemerged across the island after 2006, focusing on fields from legal rights to youth, culture, communications, and barrio-based community organizing.[140]

Journalist Jon Lee Anderson argues that considerable credit should be given to Alfredo Guevara, the founder of ICAIC, for helping to "usher in an era of gradual sexual glasnost" in producing *Fresa y chocolate* (*Strawberry and Chocolate*) in 1993.[141] Directed by Tomás Gutiérrez Alea and Juan Carlos Tabío, the film examines the developing friendship between a gay artist and a committed young communist whose aim initially is to spy on the so-called deviant. *Fresa y chocolate* not only portrays a gay Cuban sympathetically; it also clearly criticizes the ways the government penalized homosexuality in the 1960s and the lame excuses the PCC offered to justify discrimination and repression against homosexuals.

The film's appearance marked a turning point for LGBTQ Cubans. Less fearful about acknowledging their orientations, they began to gather openly in clubs, perform as transvestites, and speak out. While subsequent films reinforced their courage, unquestionably the most significant support came from Mariela Castro Espín, the director of the National Center of Sex Education (CENESEX) and daughter of Raúl Castro and the late Vilma Espín. Established in 1989 with the aim of promoting sexual education, Mariela Castro refocused CENESEX in 2004 to concentrate on LGBTQ issues. Her crusade for LGBTQ rights engendered a national conversation, educated Cubans, and empowered the LGBTQ community.[142] In 2009, she took to the streets to lead a parade on the International Day against Homophobia and prominently led the Conga against Homophobia and Transphobia in subsequent years (it was canceled from 2019 to 2022, and resumed in 2023). Fidel Castro acknowledged in 2010 the injustice of sending thousands of gay men and others deemed unfit for military service to the UMAP labor camps in the mid-1960s, and a 2013 law banned workplace discrimination based on sexual orientation.[143]

A New Era?

When one era ends, a new one does not necessarily replace it. The change in Cuba's leadership in 2018 certainly signified the close of the Castro era. Yet the nature of the next era is still uncertain. In his first speech as the new president, Díaz-Canel emphasized that he would maintain current policies and goals rather than pursue change. He asserted, "I assume this responsibility with the conviction that all we revolutionaries, from any trench, will be faithful to Fidel and Raúl." He added that Raúl, who was reelected in 2016 to a five-year term as first secretary of the PCC, "will take the lead on decisions of greatest importance for the present and future of the county."[144] Six weeks later the National Assembly named Raúl to head a commission to draft a new Cuban constitution.

Yet the new Cuban leader was handed a portfolio of challenges—creating a sustainable developmental model that would maintain Cuba's egalitarian and communitarian values, establishing a single currency and encouraging foreign investment, strengthening partnerships with other countries while avoiding dependence on a single partner, stemming the discontent and emigration of Cuba's youth—which could be met only by change in the existing rules and institutions. Notably, three of the six vice presidents named to the Council of State in 2018 were new, and they ranged in age from forty-eight to fifty-two years. More than half of the members of the newly elected National Assembly that anointed Díaz-Canel as president were first-time deputies. Also, for the first time, its membership closely reflected the gender (53 percent women) and racial (41 percent Black and mulatto) percentages of the country.

In short, Cuba attempted to close out the Castro era by making some headway in implementing the changes Raúl Castro had sought. But it fell short of fully addressing the problems Cubans and the Cuban leadership alike had identified, and it did not provide a clear trajectory for Cuba's new leaders to follow. What follows in the chapters of this book is an attempt to describe and assess how Cuba has responded to these challenges since 2018.

Notes

1. Fidel Castro continued to serve formally as first secretary of the Communist Party of Cuba until 2011.

2. Nelson P. Valdés, "The Revolutionary and Political Content of Fidel Castro's Charismatic Authority," in *A Contemporary Cuba Reader: Reinventing the Revolution*, ed. Philip Brenner, Marguerite Rose Jiménez, John M. Kirk, and William M. LeoGrande (Lanham, MD: Rowman & Littlefield, 2007), 27.

3. Raúl Castro Ruz, "Speech Delivered at the Close of the Inaugural Session of the Seventh Legislature of the National Assembly of People's Power," Havana, February 24, 2008, accessed at www.cuba.cu/gobierno/rauldiscursos/2008/esp/r240208e.html; also see Carlos Alzugaray Treto, "Continuity and Change in Cuba at 50: The Revolution at a Crossroads," in *A Contemporary Cuba Reader: The Revolution under Raúl Castro*, ed. Philip Brenner, Marguerite Rose Jiménez, John M. Kirk, and William M. LeoGrande (Lanham, MD: Rowman & Littlefield, 2014), 40–42.

4. There were an estimated 112,000 Indians on the island in 1492 and fewer than 3,000 by the mid-1550s. See Eduardo Torres-Cuevas and Oscar Loyala Vega, *Historia de Cuba 1492–1898*, 3rd ed. (Havana: Editorial Pueblo y Educación, 2006), 25, 50–58; Irving Rouse, *The Tainos: Rise and Decline of the People Who Greeted Columbus* (New Haven, CT: Yale University Press, 1992), 157.

5. Louis A. Pérez Jr., *Rice in the Time of Sugar* (Chapel Hill: University of North Carolina Press, 2019), 29.

6. For example, see "Discursos pronunciados en el Acto Solemne, el 20 de junio del 2002 Intervención de Ricardo Alarcón de Quesada, Presidente de la Asamblea Nacional del Poder Popular," June 20, 2002, accessed at http://www.cuba.cu/gobierno/documentos/2002/esp/a200602e.html.

7. Louis A. Pérez Jr., *Cuba and the United States: Ties of Singular Intimacy* (Athens: University of Georgia Press, 1990), 80–81.

8. Louis A. Pérez Jr., *Cuba: Between Reform and Revolution*, 4th ed. (New York: Oxford University Press, 2011), 137–38.

9. Jules Robert Benjamin, *The United States and Cuba: Hegemony and Dependent Development, 1880–1934* (Pittsburgh, PA: University of Pittsburgh Press, 1977), 4–5; Pérez Jr., *Cuba and the United States*, 61.

10. Lars Schoultz, *That Infernal Little Republic: The United States and the Cuban Revolution* (Chapel Hill: University of North Carolina Press, 2009), 22.

11. Lars Schoultz, *Beneath the United States: A History of U.S. Policy toward Latin America* (Cambridge, MA: Harvard University Press, 1998), 145.

12. Leland Hamilton Jenks, *Our Cuban Colony: A Study in Sugar* (New York: Vanguard Press, 1928), 286.

13. Pérez Jr., *Rice in the Time of Sugar*, chapter 5.

14. Leland Johnson, "U.S. Business Interests in Cuba and the Rise of Castro," *World Politics* 17, no. 3 (1965): 443, 453; Robin Blackburn, "Prologue to the Cuban Revolution," *New Left Review*, no. 21 (October 1963): 59–60.

15. As quoted in Luis E. Aguilar, *Cuba 1933: Prologue to Revolution* (New York: Norton, 1972), 163–64.

16. Julia E. Sweig, *Inside the Cuban Revolution* (Cambridge, MA: Harvard University Press, 2002), 165–82.

17. Lourdes Casal, "Race Relations in Contemporary Cuba," in *The Cuba Reader: The Making of a Revolutionary Society*, ed. Philip Brenner, William M. LeoGrande, Donna Rich, and Daniel Siegel (New York: Grove Press, 1989), 475; Alejandro de la Fuente, "Recreating Racism: Race and Discrimination in Cuba's Special Period," *Socialism and Democracy* 15, no. 1 (Spring 2001).

18. Casal, "Race Relations in Contemporary Cuba," 477.

19. Saul Landau, "Asking the Right Questions about Cuba," in Brenner et al., *The Cuba Reader*, xxiii.

20. Louis A. Pérez Jr., *On Becoming Cuban* (Chapel Hill: UNC Press, 1999), 42.

21. James G. Blight and Peter Kornbluh, eds., *The Politics of Illusion: The Bay of Pigs Invasion Reexamined* (Boulder, CO: Lynne Rienner, 1998), 10–13; Jorge I. Domínguez, *Cuba: Order and Revolution* (Cambridge, MA: Harvard University Press, 1978), 345–46.

22. Brig. Gen. Lansdale, "Review of Operation Mongoose," memorandum for the Special Group (Augmented), July 25, 1962, Office of the Secretary of Defense, declassified January 5, 1989, in *The Cuban Missile Crisis 1962: A National Security Archive Documents Reader*, ed. Laurence Chang and Peter Kornbluh (New York: New Press, 1992), 47.

23. Domínguez, *Cuba*, 253.

24. William Luis, "Exhuming *Lunes de Revolución*," *CR: The New Centennial Review* 2, no. 2 (Summer 2002): 254–57.

25. "Discurso Pronunciado por el Comandante Fidel Castro Ruz, Primer Ministro del Gobierno Revolucionario y Secretario del PURSC, Como Conclusion de las Reuniones con los Intelectuales Cubanos, Efectuadas en la Biblioteca Nacional el 16, 23 y 30 de Junio de 1961," accessed at http://www.cuba.cu/gobierno/discursos/1961/esp/f300661e.html.

26. Susan Eva Eckstein, *The Immigrant Divide: How Cuban Americans Changed the US and Their Homeland* (New York: Routledge, 2009), 10–12; Felix Roberto Masud-Piloto, *From Welcomed Exiles to Illegal Immigrants: Cuban Migration to the U.S., 1959–1995* (Lanham, MD: Rowman & Littlefield, 1996), 58–59.

27. Ernesto Che Guevara, "Man and Socialism in Cuba," in *Man and Socialism in Cuba: The Great Debate*, ed. Bertram Silverman (New York: Atheneum, 1971), 343–44.

28. Fidel Castro, "Speech Delivered on March 13, 1968, at Ceremonies Marking the 11th Anniversary of the Attack on the Presidential Palace, at the University of Havana," in *Fidel Castro Speaks*, ed. Martin Kenner and James Petras (New York: Grove Press, 1969), 271, 283.

29. Fidel Castro, "Speech Delivered on the 25th Anniversary of the Bay of Pigs Victory, April 19, 1986," in *Cuban Revolution Reader: A Documentary History*, ed. Julio García Luis (Melbourne: Ocean Press, 2001), 243–45.

30. Susan Eva Eckstein, *Back from the Future: Cuba under Castro* (Princeton, NJ: Princeton University Press, 1994), 129–37, 151–54.

31. Marvin Leiner, "Cuba's Schools: Twenty-Five Years Later," in *Cuba: Twenty-Five Years of Revolution, 1959–1984*, ed. Sandor Halebsky and John M. Kirk (New York: Praeger, 1985), 28–29, 32–36.

32. Carlos Lechuga, *In the Eye of the Storm: Castro, Khrushchev, Kennedy and the Missile Crisis*, trans. Mary Todd (Melbourne: Ocean Press, 1995), 18; Aleksandr Fursenko and Timothy Naftali, *One Hell of a Gamble: Khrushchev, Castro, and Kennedy, 1958–1964* (New York: Norton, 1997), 146.

33. Marifeli Pérez-Stable, *The Cuban Revolution: Origins, Course, and Legacy*, 2nd ed. (New York: Oxford University Press, 1999), 88.

34. James G. Blight and Philip Brenner, *Sad and Luminous Days: Cuba's Struggle with the Superpowers after the Missile Crisis* (Lanham, MD: Rowman & Littlefield, 2007), 36, 60.

35. Ernesto (Che) Guevara, "Speech in Algiers to the Second Seminar of the Organization of Afro-Asian Solidarity, February 25, 1965," in *Che Guevara Speaks*, ed. George Lavan (New York: Pathfinder Press, 1967), 107–8.

36. Fidel Castro, "A Necessary Introduction," in *El Diario del Che en Bolivia* (Havana: Editora Política, 1987), xvii–xviii.

37. "Discurso Pronunciado por el Comandante Fidel Castro Ruz, al Conmemorarse el IX Aniversario del Triunfo de la Revolución, en la Plaza de la Revolución, el 2 de Enero de 1968," accessed at http://www.cuba.cu/gobierno/discursos/1968/esp/f020168e.html.

38. Piero Gleijeses, *Conflicting Missions: Havana, Washington, and Africa, 1959–1976* (Chapel Hill: University of North Carolina Press, 2002), 260, 305–7.

39. Mervyn J. Bain, "Cuba-Soviet Relations in the Gorbachev Era," *Journal of Latin American Studies* 37 (2005): 773–76.

40. William M. LeoGrande, "Cuba," in *Confronting Revolution: Security through Diplomacy in Central America*, ed. Morris Blachman, William M. LeoGrande, and Kenneth Sharpe (New York: Pantheon, 1986), 253.

41. William M. LeoGrande, *Our Own Backyard: The United States in Central America, 1977–1992* (Chapel Hill: University of North Carolina Press, 1998), 15, 24–25. Eckstein, *Back from the Future*, 186–88.

42. H. Michael Erisman, *Cuba's Foreign Relations in a Post-Soviet World* (Gainesville: University Press of Florida, 2000), 98–99; Donna Rich, "Cuban Internationalism: A Humanitarian Foreign Policy," in Brenner, et al., *The Cuba Reader*.

43. John M. Kirk, *Healthcare without Borders: Understanding Cuban Medical Internationalism* (Gainesville: University Press of Florida, 2015), chapter 2.

44. As quoted in Schoultz, *That Infernal Little Republic*, 90.

45. Quoted in Louis A. Pérez Jr., *Cuba in the American Imagination: Metaphor and the Imperial Ethos* (Chapel Hill: University of North Carolina Press, 2008), 241.

46. Richard M. Nixon, "Rough Draft of Summary of Conversation between the Vice-President and Fidel Castro," April 25, 1959, reprinted in Jeffrey J. Safford, "The Nixon-Castro Meeting of 19 April 1059," *Diplomatic History* 4, no. 4 (Fall 1980): 431.

47. Peter Kornbluh, "Introduction: History Held Hostage," in *Bay of Pigs Declassified*, ed. Peter Kornbluh (New York: New Press, 1998), 9.

48. "Memorandum from the Secretary of State to the President: Current Basic United States Policy toward Cuba," in US Department of State, *Foreign Relations of the United States, 1958–1960*, vol. 6, *Cuba* (Washington, DC: Government Printing Office, 1991), doc. no. 387, 657.

49. Abraham F. Lowenthal, "The United States and Latin America: Ending the Hegemonic Presumption," *Foreign Affairs* 55, no. 1 (October 1976).

50. "First Declaration of Havana," September 2, 1960, in *Cuban Revolution Reader: A Documentary History of 40 Key Moments of the Cuban Revolution*, ed. Julio García Luis (Melbourne: Ocean Press, 2001), 45–51.

51. US Central Intelligence Agency, Inspector General, "Report on Plots to Assassinate Fidel Castro," May 23, 1967, National Archives and Records Administration, JFK Assassination System, Record Series: JFK, record no. 104-10213-10101, agency file no. 80TO1357A (released June 23, 1998).

52. McGeorge Bundy, "Memorandum for the Record," November 12, 1963, in US Department of State, *Foreign Relations of the United States, 1961–1963*, vol. 11, *Cuban Missile Crisis and Aftermath* (Washington, DC: Government Printing Office, 1997), doc. no. 377, 889; Gregory F. Treverton, "Cuba in U.S. Security Perspective," in *U.S.-Cuban Relations in the 1990s*, ed. Jorge I. Domínguez and Rafael Hernández (Boulder, CO: Westview Press, 1989), 71.

53. William M. LeoGrande and Peter Kornbluh, *Back Channel to Cuba: The Hidden History of Negotiations between Washington and Havana* (Chapel Hill: University of North Carolina Press, 2015), chapters 2, 4, and 5.

54. LeoGrande and Kornbluh, *Back Channel to Cuba*, 139–42.

55. Henry Kissinger, *Years of Renewal* (New York: Simon & Schuster, 1999), 785–87; "Ford Says Angola Acts Hurt Detente, Cuba Tie," *New York Times*, December 21, 1975, 3.

56. Austin Scott, "Carter Outlines Basis for Better Ties with Cuba," *Washington Post*, February 17, 1977.

57. Richard Halloran, "From Washington and El Salvador, Differing Views on Fighting Rebels," *New York Times*, February 21, 1981.

58. Philip Brenner, "Change and Continuity in Cuban Foreign Policy," in Brenner et al., *The Cuba Reader*, 263–65.

59. Patrick J. Haney and Walt Vanderbush, *The Cuban Embargo: The Domestic Politics of an American Foreign Policy* (Pittsburgh, PA: University of Pittsburgh Press, 2005), 32–36.

60. Diane Kuntz, "The Politics of Suffering: The Impact of the U.S. Embargo on the Health of the Cuban People" (report to the American Public Health Association of a fact-finding trip to Cuba, June 6–11, 1993), *Journal of Public Health Policy* 15, no. 1 (Spring 1994);

Katherine Tucker and Thomas R. Hedges, "Food Shortages and an Epidemic of Optic and Peripheral Neuropathy in Cuba," *Nutrition Reviews* 51, no. 12 (1993): 349–57. By 1993, the average daily caloric intake in Cuba had fallen below the World Health Organization standard. Diet insufficiency led to outbreaks of disorders that had long vanished from Cuba, such as neuropathy (damage to nerves that can produce sharp pains in the fingers and feet), loss of a sense of touch, an inability to control muscle movement, and even temporary blindness.

61. Jorge I. Domínguez, "Cuba's Economic Transition: Successes, Deficiencies, and Challenges," in *The Cuban Economy at the Start of the Twenty-First Century*, ed. Jorge I. Domínguez, Omar Everleny Pérez Villanueva, and Lorena Barberia (Cambridge, MA: Harvard University Press, 2004), 19.

62. The 1992 Cuban Democracy Act bars subsidiaries of US corporations in third countries from selling goods to Cuba. Food and medicine made up more than 90 percent of Cuba's imports from these subsidiaries in 1991. Donna Rich Kaplowitz and Michael Kaplowitz, *New Opportunities for U.S.-Cuban Trade* (Washington, DC: Paul H. Nitze School of Advanced International Studies, Johns Hopkins University, 1992), 57–64.

63. Pedro Monreal, "Development as an Unfinished Affair: Cuba after the 'Great Adjustment' of the 1990s," in *A Contemporary Cuba Reader* (2007), 117–18.

64. Hal Klepak, "The Revolutionary Armed Forces: Loyalty and Efficiency in the Face of Old and New Challenges," in *A Contemporary Cuba Reader* (2014). The military's involvement in the economy served two purposes. First, it provided jobs to the FAR, which suffered a reduction in its size from 300,000 to 100,000 members during the Special Period. Without work, the newly unemployed soldiers and officers might have been a source of instability. Second, the discipline instilled in the FAR reduced the possibility for corruption by those working in the new companies.

65. William M. LeoGrande, "The United States and Cuba: Strained Engagement," in *Cuba, the United States, and the Post-Cold War World: The International Dimension of the Washington-Havana Relationship*, ed. Morris Morley and Chris McGillion (Gainesville: University Press of Florida, 2005), 18.

66. Marguerite Rose Jiménez, "The Politics of Leisure," in *A Contemporary Cuba Reader* (2014).

67. Philip Peters, "Cutting Losses: Cuba Downsizes Its Sugar Industry" (Arlington, VA: Lexington Institute, December 2003), 3. In 1989, the price of sugar on the world market was $0.13 per pound and barely $0.06 per pound in 2002, while Cuba's rank in world production dropped from third to tenth.

68. Holly Ackerman, "The 'Balsero' Phenomenon, 1991–1994," *Cuban Studies* 26 (1996): 173.

69. Schoultz, *That Infernal Little Republic*, 466–67; "137 Cubans Land in Florida; Largest Boatload since 1980," *New York Times*, July 2, 1994, 6.

70. Under the 1966 Cuban Adjustment Act, a Cuban who remained on US territory for one year and one day could become a US permanent legal resident, receiving enhanced benefits not available to refugees from any other country. Until 1994, the United States also had the practice of nearly automatically allowing Cubans who arrived on US territory to claim asylum and to stay in the United States while their claims were investigated, a process that invariably took more than one year. In addition, Radio Martí regularly broadcast detailed weather conditions for the Florida Straits as a guide for rafters.

71. US Immigration and Naturalization Service, *Statistical Yearbook of the Immigration and Naturalization Service, 1996* (Washington, DC: Government Printing Office, October 1997), table 21, accessed at http://www.dhs.gov/archives. See also Susan Eckstein and Lorena Barberia, "Cuban Americans and Their Transnational Ties," in *A Contemporary Cuba Reader* (2007), 269.

72. Margaret E. Crahan, "Civil Society and Religion in Cuba: Past, Present, and Future," in *A Contemporary Cuba Reader* (2007), 331–32.

73. In 2003, seventy-five so-called dissidents were arrested, tried, and sentenced (some to long prison terms) for accepting US assistance in violation of Cuban law. However, more than one dozen turned out to be double agents working for state security agencies.

74. Sandra Levinson, "Nationhood and Identity in Contemporary Cuban Art," in *A Contemporary Cuba Reader* (2014).

75. Carlos Varela, "Two Songs," in *A Contemporary Cuba Reader* (2014), 327. Also see María Caridad Cumaná, Karen Dubinsky, and Xenia Reloba de la Cruz, *My Havana: The Musical City of Carlos Varela*, trans. Ana Elena Arazoza (Toronto: University of Toronto Press, 2014).

76. Sujatha Fernandes, "Straight Outta Havana," *New York Times*, August 6, 2011.

77. Margot Olavarria, "Rap and Revolution: Hip-Hop Comes to Cuba," in *A Contemporary Cuba Reader* (2007), 367.

78. de la Fuente, "Recreating Racism," 68.

79. According to a study by the Pew Hispanic Center, about 86 percent of Cubans in the United States self-identified as "white" in 2004. "Cubans in the United States," Pew Hispanic Center Fact Sheet no. 23, August 25, 2006, accessed at https://www.pewresearch.org/wp-content/uploads/sites/5/2011/10/23.pdf.

80. Esteban Morales, "Notes on the Race Question in Cuba Today," in *A Contemporary Cuba Reader* (2014).

81. María Isabel Domínguez, "Cuban Youth: Aspirations, Social Perceptions, and Identity," in *A Contemporary Cuba Reader* (2007), 294.

82. Fidel Castro Ruz, "Discurso en el acto central conmemorativo del XXX aniversario de la victoria de Playa Girón, efectuado en el teatro 'Carlos Marx,' el 19 de abril de 1991," accessed at http://www.cuba.cu/gobierno/discursos/1991/esp/f190491e.html. See also Fidel Castro Ruz, "Discurso en el acto estudiantil con motivo del xxxiv aniversario del asalto al Palacio Presidencial y a Radio Reloj, efectuado en el antiguo Palacio Presidencial, el 13 de marzo de 1991," accessed at http://www.cuba.cu/gobierno/discursos/1991/esp/f130391e.html; Blight and Brenner, *Sad and Luminous Days*, 60.

83. Nelson Mandela, "Speech at the Rally in Cuba," July 26, 1991, in Nelson Mandela and Fidel Castro, *How Far We Slaves Have Come!* (Atlanta: Pathfinder Press, 1991); Richard Boudreaux, "Mandela Lauds Castro as Visit to Cuba Ends," *Los Angeles Times*, July 28, 1991.

84. Fidel Castro, "Speech at the Ceremony Commemorating the 50th Anniversary of the Attack on the Moncada and Carlos Manuel de Cespedes Garrisons," Santiago de Cuba, July 26, 2003, accessed at http://www.cuba.cu/gobierno/discursos/2003/ing/f260703i.html.

85. Fidel Castro Ruz, "Key Address to a Solemn Session of the National Assembly," Caraças, Venezuela, October 27, 2000, accessed at http://www.cuba.cu/gobierno/discursos/2000/ing/f271000i.html.

86. H. Michael Erisman and John M. Kirk, "Cuban Medical Internationalism and 'Soft Power,'" in this volume; Cory Fischer-Hoffman and Greg Rosenthal, "Cuba and Venezuela: A Bolivarian Partnership," *Monthly Review*, January 13, 2006, accessed at http://mrzine.monthlyreview.org/2006/fhr130106.html; *Anuario Estadístico de Cuba 2011*.

87. In 2009, the name was changed to the Bolivarian Alliance for the Peoples of Our America.

88. Philip Brenner and Soraya M. Castro Mariño, "David and Gulliver: Fifty Years of Competing Metaphors in the Cuban-U.S. Relationship," *Diplomacy and Statecraft*, no. 20 (2009): 247.

89. US Census Bureau, Foreign Trade Statistics, "Trade in Goods with Cuba," accessed December 31, 2022, at http://www.census.gov/foreign-trade/balance/c2390.html.

90. US Commission for Assistance to a Free Cuba, *Report to the President, May 2004* (Washington, DC: US Department of State, 2004), xi, accessed at https://2001-2009.state.gov/p/wha/rt/cuba/index.htm.

91. Yailin Orta Rivera y Norge Martínez Montero, "La vieja gran estafa," *Juventud Rebelde,* October 1, 2006, accessed at www.juventudrebelde.cu/cuba/2006-10-01/la-vieja-gran-estafa.

92. Anita Snow, "Cuba's Raul Castro Signals More Openness to Debate of Divergent Ideas than Brother Fidel," Associated Press International, December 21, 2006.

93. Raúl Castro, "Speech at the Celebration of the Attack on Moncada," Camaguey, July 26, 2007, accessed at www.granma.cu/granmad/secciones/raul26/02.html.

94. Marc Frank, *Cuban Revelations: Between the Scenes in Havana* (Gainesville: University Press of Florida, 2013), 73–74.

95. Frank, *Cuban Revelations,* 74.

96. United Nations Development Program, *Human Development Report 2009* (New York: UNDP, 2009), 167–68.

97. Denise Blum, "Cuban Educational Reform during the 'Special Period': Dust, Ashes and Diamonds," in *A Contemporary Cuba Reader* (2014), 424–27.

98. Raúl Castro Ruz, "Speech before the National Assembly," February 24, 2008, accessed at http://www.cuba.cu/gobierno/rauldiscursos/2008/esp/r240208e.html.

99. Jorge Mario Sánchez Egozcue, "Challenges of Economic Restructuring in Cuba," *A Contemporary Cuba Reader* (2014), 129.

100. Ricardo Torres Pérez, "Concluding Reflections of the Current Reform Process in Cuba," in *No More Free Lunch: Reflections on the Cuban Economic Reform Process and Challenges for Transformation,* ed. Claus Brundenius and Ricardo Torres Pérez (Heidelberg: Springer, 2014), 225; Armando Nova González, "Cuban Agriculture and the Current Process of Economic Transformation," in *A Contemporary Cuba Reader* (2014), 153–54.

101. Raúl Castro Ruz, "Speech at the Ninth Congress of the Young Communist League," April 4, 2010, accessed at www.cuba.cu/gobierno/rauldiscursos/2010/ing/r030410i.html.

102. Sixth Congress of the Communist Party of Cuba, *Resolution on the Guidelines for the Economic and Social Policies of the Party and the Revolution,* April 18, 2011, accessed at www.cuba.cu/gobierno/documentos/2011/ing/l160711i.html.

103. Philip Brenner and Peter Eisner, *Cuba Libre: A 500-Year Quest for Independence* (Lanham, MD: Rowman & Littlefield, 2018), 310.

104. Richard E. Feinberg, *Open for Business: Building the New Cuban Economy* (Washington, DC: Brookings Institution Press, 2016), 140.

105. Juan Triana Cordoví, "Moving from Reacting to an External Shock toward Shaping a New Conception of Cuban Socialism," in Brundenius and Torres Pérez, *No More Free Lunch,* 234.

106. Antonio F. Romero Gómez, "Economic Transformations and Institutional Changes in Cuba," in *Cuba's Economic Change in Comparative Perspective,* ed. Richard E. Feinberg and Ted Piccone (Washington, DC: Brookings, 2014), 33–34; Feinberg, *Open for Business,* 28–29.

107. "La Constitución de la República de Cuba" (2019), accessed at http://www.cubadebate.cu/noticias/2019/04/09/descargue-la-constitucion-de-la-republica-de-cuba-pdf.

108. Garrett Graddy-Lovelace, "United States–Cuba Agricultural Relations and Agrarian Questions," *Journal of Agrarian Change* 18, no. 1 (January 2018): 47.

109. Romero Gómez, "Economic Transformations and Institutional Changes in Cuba," 34–35.

110. Raúl Castro Ruz, "The Revolutionary Cuban People Will Again Rise to the Occasion: Speech to the Closing Session of the National Assembly," July 18, 2016, accessed at https://en.granma.cu/cuba/2016-07-13/the-revolutionary-cuban-people-will-again-rise-to-the-occasion.

111. Communist Party of Cuba, "Seventh Congress of the Communist Party of Cuba, Resolution on the Results of Implementing the Lineamientos," April 18, 2016, accessed at http://www.cubadebate.cu/especiales/2016/04/18/resolucion-sobre-resultados-de-la-implementacion-de-los-lineamientos-de-la-politica-economica-y-social-del-partido-y-la-revolucion-aprobados-en-el-vi-congreso-y-su-actualizacion-el-periodo-2016-2021.

112. Ricardo Torres, "Cuba's Economy: Reforms and Delays from 2014–2018," in *Cuba at the Crossroads*, ed. Philip Brenner, John M. Kirk, and William M. LeoGrande (Lanham, MD: Rowman & Littlefield, 2020), 47.

113. Adrian H. Hearn, "China, Global Governance, and the Future of Cuba," in *A Contemporary Cuba Reader* (2014), 231–39.

114. "China Signs Trade Deals with Cuba," *BBC News*, November 19, 2008, accessed at http://news.bbc.co.uk/2/hi/americas/7733811.stm.

115. John M. Kirk, "Cuban Medical Internationalism under Raúl Castro," in *A Contemporary Cuba Reader* (2014), 258.

116. Kirk, "Cuban Medical Internationalism under Raúl Castro," 251.

117. Brian Ellsworth, "Despite Obama Charm, Americas Summit Boosts U.S. Isolation," Reuters, April 16, 2012, accessed at http://www.reuters.com/article/us-americas-summit-obama-idUSBRE83F0UD20120416.

118. LeoGrande and Kornbluh, *Back Channel to Cuba*, epilogue.

119. US Department of Commerce, Census Bureau, "Foreign Trade: Trade in Goods with Cuba," accessed December 31, 2022, at https://www.census.gov/foreign-trade/balance/c2390.html.

120. Philip Brenner and Soraya M. Castro Mariño, "Untying the Knot: The Possibility of a Respectful Dialogue between Cuba and the United States," in *A Contemporary Cuba Reader* (2014), 278.

121. Victoria Burnett and Frances Robles, "Cuba-U.S. Ties Being Strained as Doctors Flee," *New York Times*, December 20, 2015, 1.

122. Fulton Armstrong, "Time to Clean Up U.S. Regime-Change Programs in Cuba," *Miami Herald*, December 26, 2011.

123. Desmond Butler, "USAID Contractor Work in Cuba Detailed," Associated Press, February 12, 2012.

124. LeoGrande and Kornbluh, *Back Channel to Cuba*, 387–94.

125. US Department of State, "Country Reports on Human Rights Practices for 2012, Cuba," April 19, 2013, accessed at https://2009-2017.state.gov/j/drl/rls/hrrpt/2012humanrightsreport/index.htm#wrapper.

126. Barack Obama, "Remarks by the President at a DSCC Fundraising Reception," November 8, 2013, accessed at http://www.whitehouse.gov/the-press-office/2013/11/08/remarks-president-dscc-fundraising-reception-0.

127. Dan Hurley, "Was It an Invisible Attack on U.S. Diplomats, or Something Stranger?" *New York Times Magazine*, May 19, 2019.

128. Shane Harris and Missy Ryan, "CIA Finds No 'Worldwide Campaign' by Any Foreign Power behind Mysterious 'Havana Syndrome,'" *Washington Post*, January 20, 2022, accessed at https://www.washingtonpost.com/national-security/cia-havana-syndrome-investigation-russia/2022/01/20/2f86d89e-795c-11ec-bf97-6eac6f77fba2_story.html.

129. Michael J. Bustamante and Julia E. Sweig, "Cuban Public Diplomacy," in *A Contemporary Cuba Reader* (2014), 269.

130. Tom Long, "Small States, Great Power? Gaining Influence through Intrinsic, Derivative, and Collective Power," *International Studies Review* 19, no. 2 (2017): 198–200.

131. Rafael Hernández, "Intellectuals, Civil Society, and Political Power," *Social Research: An International Quarterly* 84, no. 2 (Summer 2017): 415.

132. Teresa García Castro and Philip Brenner, "Cuba 2017: The End of an Era," *Revista de Ciencia Política* 38, no. 2 (2018): 269–70, accessed at http://ojs.uc.cl/index.php/rcp/issue/view/298.

133. Nancy Scola, "Only 5 Percent of Cubans Can Get on the Same Internet Americans Do. That Could Soon Change," *Washington Post*, December 17, 2014, accessed at https://goo.gl/x1Pxye.

134. International Telecommunications Union 2019, "Percentage of Individuals Using the Internet," accessed July 25, 2019, at https://www.itu.int/en/ITU-D/Statistics/Documents/statistics/2019/Individuals_Internet_2000-2018_Jun2019.xls.

135. Antonio García Martínez, "Inside Cuba's DIY Internet Revolution," *WIRED*, August 2017, accessed at https://www.wired.com/2017/07/inside-cubas-diy-internet-revolution. Also see El Paquete Semanal, https://elpaquetesemanal.org, accessed December 31, 2022.

136. Ann Marie Stock, "Zooming In: Making and Marketing Films in Twenty-First-Century Cuba," in *A Contemporary Cuba Reader* (2014), 351–53.

137. Lauren Marrero Tamayo, "Nueva Ley de Cine y productoras independientes en Cuba," *Vistar*, March 11, 2022, accessed at https://vistarmagazine.com/nueva-ley-de-cine-y-productoras-independientes-en-cuba.

138. Hope Bastian, *Adjusting to the Adjustment: Inequalities and Mobility in Everyday Life in Havana* (Lanham, MD: Lexington Books, 2018).

139. Katrin Hansing, "Race and Inequality in the New Cuba: Reasons, Dynamics, and Manifestations," *Social Research: An International Quarterly* 84, no. 2 (Summer 2017): 331.

140. Sujartha Fernandes, "Afro-Cuban Activists Fight Racism between Two Fires," *The Nation*, May 24, 2016, accessed at https://www.thenation.com/article/archive/afro-cuban-activists-fight-racism-between-two-fires.

141. Jon Lee Anderson, "Cuba's Film Godfather," *The New Yorker*, April 24, 2013.

142. Emily J. Kirk, "Setting the Agenda for Cuban Sexuality: The Role of Cuba's Cenesex," *Canadian Journal of Latin American and Caribbean Studies* 36, no. 72 (2011): 146–63.

143. Hope Bastian, "After Marriage Equality, Cuba's LGBTQ Activists Still Have Work to Do," *World Politics Review*, November 29, 2022, accessed at https://www.worldpoliticsreview.com/cuba-family-code-lgbt-gay-marriage.

144. Miguel Díaz-Canel Bermúdez, "Speech to the National Assembly," April 19, 2018, accessed at http://www.granma.cu/elecciones-en-cuba-2017-2018/2018-04-20/asumo-la-responsabilidad-con-la-conviccion-de-que-todos-los-revolucionarios-seremos-fieles-al-ejemplar-legado-de-fidel-y-raul-video-20-04-2018-04-04-02.

The Past Is No Longer a Source of Inspiration

A CONVERSATION WITH LOUIS A. PÉREZ JR.

Louis A. Pérez Jr. has been described as the "dean" of US historians studying Cuba. This conversation with the editors occurred on January 17, 2023, shortly after Pérez and they returned from research trips to Cuba.

Editors: You remarked recently that you have the impression young people in Cuba don't have a sense of history. Please describe that impression.

Louis A. Pérez Jr. (LP): It would perhaps be useful to examine the latter years of the twentieth century, with attention to the 1990s and the collapse of the Soviet Union. When Cuba became untethered from the socialist bloc and subsequently subjected to the 1992 Torricelli act [Cuban Liberty and Democracy Act] and the 1996 Helms-Burton law [Cuban Liberty and Democratic Solidarity (LIBERTAD) Act], and the attending scarcities and shortages, the island plunged into an apocalyptic crisis. Cuba was governed by political leaders who proclaimed themselves to be the defenders of a historic struggle—a struggle with origins in 1868 and rendered as *cien años de lucha*—and having been consummated in 1959. They inscribed themselves into the history from which they claimed to have emerged, to right the wrongs visited upon Cuba in the nineteenth century by Spanish colonialism and in the twentieth by US imperialism. It was a very effective discursive device through which Cubans prevailed in the 1990s during the Special Period.

In many ways the strategy was brilliant, for many Cubans have venerated their past. And with justification: heroic figures and acts of heroism, struggles that entailed sacrifice all through the nineteenth and into the first half of the twentieth century. As something of a survival strategy, the invocation of the past implied the need for Cubans—the generation of the 1990s—to keep faith with their past, to honor the sacrifices made by previous generations, to which Cubans during the 1990s could do no less.

This implied a moral obligation to discharge a debt incurred by virtue of a patriotic covenant, Cubans as heirs to a legacy of the sacrifice and struggle of their parents and grandparents. Billboards across the island all through the 1990s exhorted the need to keep faith with the past as a matter of duty.

This was history writ large. Cuba in the 1990s was rendered in terms of an *eterno Baraguá*, referring to 1878 when Antonio Maceo gathered his officers and soldiers at Mangos de Baraguá to repudiate the peace settlement with Spain ending the Ten Years War and vowing to continue to fight until Cuba had obtained its independence.

The image of Cuba during the 1990s in a condition of an "eternal Baraguá" established the parameters of a collective sense of resolve and resilience. Fidel's 26th of July speech in 1991 was filled with allusions to the past, that is, Cubans imbued with a sense of historical purpose. The young men and women of the 1990s came of age at a time suffused with historical allegory. After the 1990s, as the urgency of the crisis diminished, historical discourse as a politics continued. Increasingly history was appropriated as political discourse, that is, as a source of subsidy for the political project.

History thus insinuated itself into the political culture on a scale perhaps never before experienced. Historical discourse that appeared in popular periodicals and daily newspapers on national commemorative occasions and holidays was placed at the service of political purposes to "explain" the logic of the political problematic.

Editors: Are you saying since the 1990s young people do not perceive history as an integral part of their lives but as something that was foisted on them as propaganda?

LP: I would not use the word *foisted*. This implies a concerted action, that is, of malice aforethought. Rather, it was a process that assumed something of a life of its own, in part because there was no alternative process through which to render comprehensible the unexpected outcomes of foreign policies and domestic programs. It evolved into an excellent discursive device through which to sustain the summons to national solidarity. And not without consequences. I recall a colleague recounting with dismay visiting an elementary school in the 1990s, on the occasion of José Martí's birthday, when students were asked by the teacher "Who was José Martí?"—and the students responded that José Martí was "the intellectual author of Moncada." Consider the implications of that response: Martí's principal virtue was deemed to be the inspiration for Moncada. Does the appropriation of historical icons recruited into political service of a government suffering from diminishing popularity—that is, Antonio Maceo, Máximo Gómez, Mariana Grajales, Antonio Guiteras, among others—men and women long invoked for righteous purposes, act to diminish the "value" of historical actors and their historical acts?

Editors: Is it your sense that young people are taught history in a way that doesn't allow them to connect with the real past?

LP: I have not had the opportunity to be present in a classroom listening to the teaching of history. But a review of the teaching manuals and textbooks for historical pedagogy reveals the teaching plans for history hewing closely to political purport. If the political system experiences a loss of credibility, so too will supporting moral infrastructure that sustained its logic.

Editors: Are you saying that under these circumstances, history no longer becomes an inspiration?

LP: This is not the end of history in the [Francis] Fukuyama sense. But it may be worse: history relegated as irrelevant, without purpose and function. I have not examined closely the narratives and the pronouncements of July 2021 [during the demonstrations]. At first blush, however, there seem to be few allusions to the past—to history—as a means through which to "legitimize" protests. From the 1830s and 1840s through the 1990s, mobilization for political purpose in Cuba has been inscribed in some measure in the pursuit of redemption of a historical ideal. In other words, to make history by invoking history. The change of motif from *patria o muerte* to *patria y vida* is not without significance. Cuban history is rich with accounts of a people who contemplated self-immolation on the altar of the *patria* with equanimity as a matter of moral imperative. The lyrics of the Cuban national anthem promises everlasting life to those who die for the *patria*. No more *patria o muerte*?

Editors: So if history is not the source of inspiration, what is?

LP: Immediate and urgent needs. A demand for relief, respite, and remedy. All perfectly understandable. Conditions in Cuba in the early 2020s are in every sense as deplorable and as urgent as they were during the 1990s. Perhaps worse. Certainly, psychically worse. Many Cubans confronted the multiple crises of the 1990s as circumstances that were perceived to have come from without, that cascaded upon Cuba as a result of tectonic global shifts. Cubans took it upon themselves to meet the challenge. Tens of thousands of men and women emigrated, of course. But many more remained and took it upon themselves to meet the challenge. Cuban ingenuity was celebrated: Cuban resourcefulness, Cuban recycling and home gardens, Cubans on bicycles. Yes, this was crisis as a chronic condition. Yes, there were shortages. Yes, there were scarcities and blackouts. All rendered as one more challenge to the Cuban Revolution. Fidel Castro was alive. The United States added to Cuban woes with Torricelli and Helms-Burton. Another source of a rallying cry.

The crisis of the 2020s appears different. It is not perceived to be entirely external. This is a crisis that is generally looked upon as coming from within. There is skepticism about the political leadership. There is no rallying cry for heroism. Mostly resignation, a malaise. The situation is materially as grave as the Special Period. But even more profoundly at a moral and a psychological level.

Editors: And without any sense of the past, that Cubans today are part of a continuum of history, they've lost a sense of future, they don't have a sense that there is any continuity?

LP: Yes. A rupture appears to have occurred. An examination of the proposition of the future in Cuba—the "future" as an idea, an idea with a history—often offers insight into a prevailing national mood. The sources are rich and include short stories, novels, plays, poems, lyrics, and political discourses, expressions through which Cubans contemplate the future. A historian can chronicle the history of the idea of the future as early as the nineteenth century as a means through which to take measure of the character of daily life. The times when the future looked bright, the times the future looked dark, when the possibility of the future existed and when it did not. And those times when Cubans understood the need to seek a future elsewhere.

One of the striking facets of the early years of the Cuban Revolution was the degree to which Cubans mobilized for the future. Men and women summoned the idea of the future with the confidence of having redeemed the past. They had fulfilled the historic goals of national sovereignty and self-determination: Cuba as an independent nation, Cuba for Cubans. An ideal with origins early in the nineteenth century, thwarted again and again: thwarted in 1878, thwarted in 1898, thwarted in 1933.

But in 1959, Cubans had finally made good on the ideal of the sovereign nation. That was the dominant—and recurring—narrative. Sovereignty as a means, where the nation was now free to attend to the needs and the interests of its people as a matter of priority of public policy. A sense of January 1, 1959, being different. The speeches of the leadership during the early years were exhilarating. Some of the most poignant passages in Oscar Lewis's three-volume oral histories [*Four Men, Four Women, and Neighbors*] include first-person accounts of rising expectations, Cubans exuding optimism for a bright future if not always for themselves, certainly for their children. They saw with clarity a future worth struggling for because the promise of the sovereign nation, of Cuba for Cubans, had been fulfilled. The early speeches of the leadership were driven by the promise of better material conditions for the Cuban working class, predicted to reach the level of the European working class. The middle class would attain the standard of living of the American middle class. That was the promise. Yes, there would be struggle. Yes, there would be sacrifice. Yes, there would be difficult times ahead. But the better future was at hand.

Alas . . . . Sixty years later the future had arrived bearing empty promises, and worse still: there was no more future. Or perhaps more correctly: there was no more future in Cuba.

Editors: Are you saying that freedom is no longer something Cubans feel they need to struggle for; now they need to struggle for survival?

LP: A qualified yes. Cubans desire a reasonably tranquil life, where they can be reasonably certain of a steady diet, adequate health care, access to the amenities of life. To believe their children might have the opportunity for a better life. The driving force that has summoned Cubans to heroic action for almost 200 years—national sovereignty and self-determination—having been fulfilled, thereupon to discover that it did not deliver what it had promised.

Editors: Let's go back to your point about the 1990s. In the 1990s, Cubans could still believe they were fighting for freedom from external forces, because the source of the problem seemed to be external. But now the source of the problem is internal. So fighting for the idea of freedom from external control no longer holds weight?

LP: The principal driving force of Cuban history, self-determination and national sovereignty—independence not as an end but as a means—having been attained. If fulfillment of self-determination and national sovereignty failed to deliver all that it promised, is then the paradigm self-determination and national sovereignty discredited? To what degree has the proposition of *patria* as a plausible source of collective cohesion been bruised? To ask this another way: has the salient purpose of a history deployed as a means of national independence suffered the disappointment of a future only fulfilled with empty promises?

Part I

POLITICS

William M. LeoGrande

As Cuba emerged from the global pandemic caused by the severe acute respiratory syndrome coronavirus 2 (SARS-CoV-2), its political leadership faced three interconnected challenges: (1) completing the transformation of the economy to a new model of "prosperous and sustainable" socialism; (2) establishing the legitimacy of a new generation of leaders; and (3) adapting Cuba's one-party system to political demands from an increasingly heterogeneous and vibrant civil society. It was, by far, the most daunting complex of problems faced by Cuban leaders since the Special Period in the 1990s.

Prosperous and Sustainable Socialism

When Raúl Castro succeeded his brother Fidel as president in 2008, the Cuban economy was plagued by serious and persistent structural problems. Most state salaries were inadequate to cover basic needs, productivity in state enterprises was poor, and foreign reserves were chronically low. Agricultural production was so bad that Cuba had to import more than 60 percent of its food at a cost of $2 billion annually.[1] A dual currency and exchange rate system that originated in the 1990s produced severe distortions in the labor market and external sector, discouraging exports. Opinion polls consistently identified the economy as the greatest source of popular discontent.[2]

Raúl Castro was unsparing in his criticism of the hypercentralized economic system imported from the Soviet Union in the 1970s. "No country or person can spend more than they have," he reminded his comrades. "Two plus two is four. Never five, much less six or seven—as we have sometimes pretended."[3] His drumbeat of criticism foreshadowed an ambitious and transformative economic reform. In 2011, Castro launched the "updating" (*actualización*) of the economy to replace Cuba's Soviet-era top-down economic model with a Cuban version of market socialism. The Sixth Congress of the Communist Party endorsed the "Guidelines for the Economic and Social

Policies of the Party and the Revolution," a document of 313 economic objectives comprising the blueprint for a new economic policy to unleash market forces, require state enterprises to make a profit, allow the development of the private and cooperative sectors to generate jobs and tax revenue, and attract foreign direct investment (FDI) to stimulate economic growth. The state's role would be restricted to strategic sectors. Decision-making would be decentralized to give managers greater authority, wage incentives would reward productivity, and market mechanisms would balance supply and demand. At the same time, the social programs emblematic of the Revolution— free health care and education—would continue and, Raúl Castro promised repeatedly, no one would be left behind.[4]

The pace of change was intentionally deliberate—"without haste, but without pause," in Castro's oft-repeated phrase. But slow progress implementing the guidelines signaled that some of Cuba's leaders had doubts. At the Seventh Communist Party Congress in 2016, Castro reported that only 21 percent of the guidelines adopted in 2011 had been fully implemented, a pace that Castro blamed on "the burden of an outdated mentality."[5] The reform program was not embraced enthusiastically by state and party bureaucracies socialized in a centrally planned system where ministries in Havana made all the important—and sometimes unimportant—economic decisions. Resistance came from people who feared that concessions to the market were a slippery slope leading to capitalist restoration or even regime collapse, as happened in Eastern Europe and the Soviet Union. They could invoke Fidel Castro's warning that trying to construct socialism with capitalist methods was "one of the great historical errors."[6]

Ideological suspicion also hampered Cuba's search for FDI. In 2014, Cuba adopted a new FDI law with competitive tax rates and concessions, hoping to attract $2 billion in FDI annually. By the end of 2016, however, only $1.3 billion had been approved in total. The biggest problem was interminable bureaucratic delays in the approval of proposed projects. "It is necessary to overcome, once and for all, the obsolete mentality of prejudices toward foreign investment," Castro insisted. "We must rid ourselves of unfounded fears of foreign capital."[7] Ideological concerns were reinforced by self-interest. If economic management was decentralized and nonstrategic economic activity devolved to the private sector, the role of the central government bureaucracy would be much diminished, along with the number of bureaucrats and perquisites available to those who remained.

The Seventh Party Congress in 2016 approved a new document, the "Conceptualization of the Cuban Economic and Social Model of Socialist Development," a theoretical blueprint of what "prosperous and sustainable" socialism would look like once the economic transformation was complete.[8] The document reflected tensions within the political elite about how to retain the socialist character of the system while giving markets and private property a greater role. Discussion began five years before the Party Congress, and the document went through eight drafts.[9]

While the reform process had limited success stimulating growth, it produced a noticeable rise in inequality, price increases that outpaced wage growth, and rumblings of political discontent. The increase in inequality, caused by both the wider scope given to markets and the population's differential access to convertible foreign currency, posed an ideological challenge to a regime that built its foundational legitimacy on reducing the deep inequities in prerevolutionary Cuba.[10]

The Succession Challenge

The Seventh Party Congress convened under a huge banner featuring a photograph of a young, smiling Fidel Castro and the slogan "The Communist Party of Cuba is, now and forever, the party of the Cuban nation." A fragile Fidel briefly appeared in person wearing an Adidas jogging suit rather than his emblematic olive-green uniform. Alluding to his own mortality, he told the delegates that this would probably be his final appearance at such a gathering.[11] He died seven months later on November 25, 2016. Castro's death prompted an outpouring of emotion among Cuban citizens. Thousands lined up well before dawn and stood for hours to pay their respects. Thousands more lined the streets to salute Castro's ashes as a caravan carried his remains the length of the island from Havana to Santiago, retracing the triumphal march he made in January 1959 after the fall of Fulgencio Batista's regime.

Despite the discontent many Cubans felt over their government's anemic economic performance, the Cuban state still retained significant legitimacy, especially among those old enough to remember prerevolutionary Cuba. As Raúl Castro remarked, the founding generation enjoyed some "power of moral authority" based on their historic role.[12] But the founding generation, *los históricos*, was on its way out. Raúl stepped down as president at the end of his second term in April 2018 and retired from his post as first secretary of the Communist Party in 2021. Miguel Díaz-Canel, who was born after the triumph of the Revolution, took over both posts.

For any state born in revolution, the first transfer of power to a new generation is fraught with the question of how the new rulers establish their legitimacy. More so in Cuba, where for decades Fidel Castro's charisma was a pillar of regime support. Raúl Castro tried to strengthen governing institutions to smooth the transition, and he elevated young new leaders to responsible positions while the older generation was still in place to assure stability and continuity. Nevertheless, Cuba's new leaders needed to establish their right to rule by superior performance—first and foremost by completing the restructuring of the economy Raúl began and delivering on the promise of economic growth and a living wage.

Generational change was high on the agenda at the Party Congress in 2016, as it had been at the previous congress in 2011, when Raúl Castro emphasized the need to build a contingent of experienced young men and women for the inevitable succession. To ease out the old guard, he introduced term limits for top government and party positions—no more than two five-year terms—and pledged to abide by the limits himself. At the Seventh Congress, Castro reiterated the importance of rejuvenating the party. An aged leadership was "never positive," he said, reminding listeners that three leaders of the Soviet Communist Party died within months of one another a few years before its collapse.[13] The new Central Committee elected at the congress included a large new cohort of fifty-five members younger than age sixty, while retaining a core of experienced elders. The new committee also reflected a commitment to make the party's leadership look more like Cuban society by expanding the membership from historically underrepresented groups. Forty-four percent of the new Central Committee were women, up from 42 percent in 2011 and just 13 percent in 1997; and 36 percent were Afro-Cuban, up from 31 percent in 2011 and just 10 percent in 1997.[14]

In April 2018, Cuba's National Assembly elected Díaz-Canel president. He began his inaugural speech with a paean to Raúl Castro's leadership. He promised to continue Raúl's policies, adopting the social media slogan "We are Continuity" (#SomosContinuidad) to allay concerns about the presidential succession. He also pledged that Raúl would continue to "lead the most important decisions"—a new president hoping to share his predecessor's mantle of legitimacy. Díaz-Canel stressed the theme of unity within the party and with the broader public while promising a more collective and participatory leadership style—a necessary virtue for a president who lacked the inherent authority of being a Castro.[15] He repeatedly asserted the need for greater popular participation in government and a government more responsive to the popular will. He spent the first few months of his presidency traveling around the country on a get-acquainted tour, meeting with local and provincial officials.

Díaz-Canel's rise exemplified Raúl Castro's commitment to strengthening institutions and promoting people based on experience and merit, as opposed to Fidel's penchant for elevating promising but inexperienced young people to top positions for which they were often unprepared—people Raúl derisively called "test-tube leaders." Díaz-Canel was a seasoned, pragmatic politician who rose through the ranks of the Communist Party, serving as first secretary (the party's equivalent of state governor) in his home province of Villa Clara for a decade and as first secretary in Holguín for six years. He joined the Communist Party's Central Committee in 1991 and the Political Bureau in 2003. At forty-three, he was the youngest person ever named to the party's highest body. In 2012 he was named one of several vice presidents and in 2013 first vice president and likely successor to the presidency. In the provinces, Díaz-Canel earned a reputation as an honest, efficient manager. Although his speeches tended to be flat and uninspiring, in small groups he was said to be relaxed, humorous, and willing to listen. When Cuba was plagued by fuel shortages during the economic crisis of the 1990s, he abandoned his official car and security detail to ride to work on a bicycle, endearing him to his provincial constituents.[16]

The Castro era in Cuba came to an end at the Eighth Communist Party Congress in April 2021, when Raúl stepped down as first secretary. Three of the Political Bureau's four other veterans of the of the struggle against Batista also retired: José Machado Ventura, architect of the party apparatus; Comandante Ramiro Valdés, former interior minister; and General Leopoldo Cintra Frías, minister of the Revolutionary Armed Forces. Initially, Raúl kept a relatively low profile after stepping down, appearing in public only occasionally to reaffirm his support for Díaz-Canel at moments of political tension, such as during the nationwide demonstrations in July 2021. Nevertheless, Castro's authority and prestige in both the party and the armed forces meant that, like Deng Xiaoping in China, he remained influential even in retirement. In 2022, as Díaz-Canel faced new political challenges due to a weak economy and a breakdown in the electrical grid, Castro began attending meetings of both the National Assembly and the Central Committee of the Communist Party, although he was a leader of neither. Machado Ventura and Valdés also reappeared at the party meetings.

The Achilles' heel of the new leadership's legitimacy continued to be the dismal performance of the economy. No issue was more important to the Cuban public, and no other issue evoked such popular skepticism about the government's competence. In every independent opinion poll taken in Cuba since 2005, the economy was named the most important issue facing the nation. Discontent was especially high among Cubans younger than age sixty, who were too young to remember prerevolutionary Cuba or the euphoria of the Revolution's early years. They came of age during the hardship years of the 1980s and 1990s, and for them socialism meant privation.[17]

The New Constitution

Just three months after Díaz-Canel assumed the presidency he unveiled a new Council of Ministers and the draft of a new constitution—a flurry of activity that gave the new administration a patina of activism. In February 2019, after four months of grassroots consultations in which 8.9 million Cubans debated the draft in their workplaces, neighborhoods, and schools, the constitution was approved by referendum.[18] The avowed reason for revamping it was to bring it into accord with the economic reform program. The previous 1976 constitution, adopted at the height of Cuba's adherence to a Soviet model of central planning, was incompatible with key elements of the reforms. Nevertheless, two central tenets of the old charter remain unchanged. The new constitution reiterated the Communist Party's leading role as the sole political representative of the Cuban nation and reaffirmed the commitment to a socialist system in which state property predominates and Cubans are guaranteed free, universal social services.

The most important constitutional changes for the economy were the legalization of private enterprise and employment, guarantees for FDI, and a prohibition on expropriating private property except for public purposes and only with compensation.[19] Although private business had been allowed since 1992 as "self-employment" (*cuentapropismo*), the private sector was on shaky legal ground. Cuba's old constitution did not explicitly recognize private economic property other than land owned by small farmers, and it prohibited private businesses from hiring wage labor. Over the years, the fortunes of Cuba's small businesses waxed and waned with shifting political winds, creating tremendous uncertainty and driving many enterprises out of business or underground.[20] Having a firm legal foundation was a major step forward.

The constitution also mandated significant changes in the structure of government, the most important of which was the creation of the new post of prime minister to oversee day-to-day operations of the state bureaucracy. Even Fidel Castro, despite his meticulous attention to detail and long working hours, had trouble keeping tabs on the work of some two dozen ministries. Close supervision was important because getting the reluctant bureaucracy to implement the economic reforms was a constant problem.

The constitution enhanced the authority of local government, giving local officials greater authority to deal with problems as they saw fit rather than awaiting orders from Havana. Provincial governments began imposing a 1 percent tax on all commercial activity and distributed the proceeds to municipal governments to fund social programs and local initiatives.[21] The new constitution also strengthened the legal rights of citizens, especially the due process rights of those charged with crimes, although critics argued that the government frequently failed to abide by those guarantees.[22]

A Heterogeneous and Vibrant Civil Society

Cuba has long been notorious for having the worst digital connectivity in the Americas. In recent years, however, Cuban leaders have acknowledged that being connected to the internet is a necessary condition for building a twenty-first-century economy.[23] So, despite their fears that digital communications could be exploited by their enemies (foremost among them the United States, which has tried to use the internet to undermine the regime), Cuba's leaders expanded access significantly. Between 2009 and 2022, the government opened more than 800 public Wi-Fi hot spots and cybercafés. Home internet access became available in 2017, and by January 2022, 68 percent of the Cuban population had internet access, 39 percent of them from personal cellphones, which were illegal until 2008.[24]

While the government jealously maintained a near monopoly on print and broadcast media (with a few exceptions linked to the Catholic Church), it allowed, albeit grudgingly, greater diversity in the digital public sphere. The absence of legal prohibitions on most expression in cyberspace gave rise to a freewheeling digital arena in which Cuban bloggers and independent journalists offered reporting, commentary, criticism, and debate. The emergent digital platforms ran the gamut from openly dissident (Yoani Sanchez's *14ymedio*), to critically independent (Elaine Díaz's *Periodismo de Barrio*, focused on local news), to political and economic commentary (*El Toque* and *La Joven Cuba*), and entirely apolitical (Pedro Enrique Rodríguez's sports magazine, *Play-Off*). Other digital media based outside Cuba (such as *CubaNet* and *Diario de Cuba*) and funded by the US government or the National Endowment for Democracy adopted an openly provocative, antigovernment stance.

At first, the government tolerated online criticism, but as internet access became more widespread, independent journalists were harassed by the authorities when their coverage became too critical. Sites the state disapproved of were periodically blocked. The government has also pushed back against online critics by expanding its own online presence and supporting *oficialista* blogs like *La Pupila Insomne*. President Díaz-Canel mandated that most senior officials create Twitter accounts to promote government policies.

The expansion of internet access, especially the advent of 3G connectivity, and the blossoming of social media posed a significant challenge to the government's control of information flows. Social media platforms enabled Cubans with common interests to find each other, spurring the growth of social networks that constitute an independent civil society beyond state control, virtual social networks that could be mobilized via social media.[25] Several independent groups have sprung up, organized initially on social media but then meeting in person to pursue common projects—social, artistic, and political. Before the coronavirus disease 2019 (COVID-19) pandemic, people who were not explicitly dissidents but were interested in specific issues used social media to organize to protest state policies.[26] Dissident groups, both in Cuba and Miami, have also taken advantage of social media to build linkages across the Florida Strait, encouraging antigovernment demonstrations.

Cubans developed a variety of strategies to express their disagreement with government policies. Evangelical Christians expressed vocal opposition to the same-sex marriage provision in the draft constitution during the officially sponsored consultation process; artists organized performance art to protest censorship; taxi drivers organized a work stoppage over government price controls; entrepreneurs petitioned the government to repeal restrictive regulatory changes; and animal rights and LGBTQ activists organized street demonstrations to press for protective legislation.

The government's response to these newly mobilized special interest groups was more tolerant than its response to the traditional dissident groups. Protests on specific issues were generally allowed to proceed, and the government frequently made policy concessions. Demonstrations by dissidents, by contrast, were typically broken up by arbitrary short-term detentions. Nevertheless, the government was wary of these new civil society voices. Although it has avoided public confrontations, organizers were frequently harassed by police in the aftermath of protests.

The Artists' Revolt

The arts have been a site of contention between Cuban intellectuals and state authorities since the earliest years of the Revolution. One of the first clashes was triggered in 1961 when censors banned the film *P.M.* on the grounds that its portrayal of Havana night life and Afro-Cubans was insufficiently revolutionary, and then closed the magazine *Lunes de Revolución* for having endorsed the film. In his famous 1961 speech, "Words to the Intellectuals," Fidel Castro defined the limits of cultural discourse: "Within the revolution, everything; against the revolution, nothing."[27] Ever since, Cuban intellectuals and the state have struggled over defining that murky boundary. The determination of intellectuals, artists in particular, to push the boundaries outward has resulted in periods of surprising artistic freedom, punctuated by episodes of intolerance.

The contradiction is neatly illustrated by the Padilla Affair. In 1968, poet Heberto Padilla's collection of critical poems, *Fuera del juego*, won the Julián del Casal national prize, touching off a political backlash that landed him in prison in 1971. That same year, the influential, unconventional social science journal *Pensamiento Crítico* was closed, marking the onset of *el quinquenio gris* (the Five Gray Years) during which artistic and intellectual discourse was tightly controlled by the state's cultural bureaucrats.[28]

In the decades since, Cuban artists, especially in film and plastic arts, have been able to carve out significant space for critical expression. Films have dealt with the sensitive issue of race (*Cecilia*, 1982), homosexuality and the state's denial of LGBTQ rights (*Fresa y chocolate*, 1994), bureaucracy and the hardships of the Special Period (*Guantanamera*, 1995), and the government's ineptitude and deception (*Juan de los Muertos*, 2011). Explicit political criticism is on display in any number of installations at Havana's National Museum of Fine Arts. Cuban hip-hop groups pull few punches calling out racial profiling and discrimination. Novelist Leonardo Padura was awarded the National Prize for Literature in 2012, despite the critical undertone of his novels. Cuba's most popular sitcom, *Vivir del Cuento*, poked fun at the government weekly.

Cuban artists and intellectuals are fiercely protective of the space they clawed back from the cultural bureaucrats, as the government learned the hard way in 2007, when Cuban television featured interviews with three cultural officials who were notorious for enforcing ideological orthodoxy during the Gray Years. Fearing that the reappearance of these apparatchiks foreshadowed a new crackdown, Cuban intellectuals launched an "email war" of protest so intense that Minister of Culture Abel Prieto met with them privately to reassure them and publicly reaffirmed that the leadership still regarded the Gray Years "with great disapproval."[29] Nevertheless, the ministry's penchant for control was such that it still took filmmakers six years to convince the government to allow independent films made outside the auspices of the Cuban Film Institute (ICAIC).[30]

The next skirmish in the battle over the arts was touched off by the promulgation in April 2018 of Decree Law 349, a new law requiring artists, musicians, and performers to register with the state and pay a 24 percent commission on their earnings from private engagements. It also prohibited work with pornographic or racist content, or work promoting violence, and it provided for a corps of inspectors to assure compliance. The arts community mobilized via social media, using hashtags #NoAlDecreto349 and #artelibre, among others. More than one hundred artists signed a letter to President Díaz-Canel calling for the repeal of Decree Law 349.[31] Dissident artists mounted a series of symbolic protests—performance art on the steps of the Capitol, a "concert without permission," and a sit-in at the Ministry of Culture—none of which got off the ground because police quickly detained the dozen or so participants. While the government took a hard line against the dissident artists, it took a more conciliatory approach to the broader arts community. In meetings with arts representatives, officials in the Ministry of Culture claimed that Decree Law 349 had been misinterpreted and promised to modify it to address the artists' concerns.[32]

The San Isidro Movement and 27N

Led by performance artist Luis Manuel Otero Alcántara, the San Isidro Movement (Movimiento San Isidro [MSI]) was founded by a small group of dissident artists during the 2018 protests against Decree Law 349. In November 2020, the arrest of MSI hunger strikers touched off a spontaneous demonstration at the Ministry of Culture by some 300 artists representing a breadth of ideological views.[33] At first, the government tried to engage with the protestors. Vice-Minister of Culture Fernando

Rojas, along with leaders of Cuba's major cultural institutions, met with a delegation of thirty-two demonstrators to hear their demands. Officials agreed to establish an ongoing dialogue with the artists, who referred to themselves on social media as the 27N movement (short for November 27, the day of the demonstration).

Things quickly went awry. Shortly after the protest, state media launched a campaign vilifying the San Isidro artists as mercenaries paid and directed by the United States, and President Díaz-Canel denounced MSI as "an imperialist reality show."[34] The Ministry of Culture refused to meet with artists receiving US "democracy promotion" funding, some of whom had participated in the 27N protest.[35] A meeting meant to reestablish a dialogue turned into a shoving match between artists and Ministry of Culture officials, including the minister himself, ending with the demonstrators being arrested and detained for several hours by police.[36]

The 27N demonstration was unusual for its spontaneity—it was not organized in advance but developed as word spread on social media of the arrest of the MSI hunger strikers. It also involved a broad cross section of the artistic community rallying to defend a dissident group, fueled in part by pent-up grievances over Decree Law 349. In addition, while most of the 27N artists were not themselves dissidents, their demands for freedom of artistic expression and an end to police harassment were more threatening to the state than the demands made by other interest groups that had mounted public demonstrations.

In mid-February 2021, a collection of well-known hip-hop and reggaeton artists living in Miami and two rap artists from MSI released a high-quality music video, "Patria y Vida" (Homeland and Life) that spread rapidly on social media. It was praised by US officials and one of the musicians was invited to meet with President Biden.[37] The title was a counterpoint to Fidel Castro's defiant signature phrase, "Patria o Muerte" (Homeland or Death). The song's lyrics disparaged the revolutionary project and government, building gradually to a climax, declaring, "It's over." The government responded the next day with a blistering attack on the song, accusing the musicians and others of receiving US funding to subvert the Revolution.[38] In November 2021, "Patria y Vida" was named Latin Grammy Song of the Year.

The COVID Crisis

The Cuban economy sustained two major shocks in 2020 that were still reverberating in 2023: the ratcheting up of US economic sanctions and the COVID-19 pandemic. Together, they threw Cuba into a recession deeper than anything since the economic crisis of the 1990s Special Period and posed a serious political challenge to the government.

In 2019–2020, the Trump administration pursued a policy of "maximum pressure" to cut off all sources of foreign exchange. It activated Title III of the 1996 Cuban Liberty and Democratic Solidarity Act to deter foreign investors. It ended most travel to Cuba by non-Cuban Americans and drastically curtailed air service. It tried to interdict Venezuelan oil shipments and pressured Latin American countries to end their medical service contracts with Cuba. In its final months, the administration effectively blocked most remittances and put Cuba back on the list of state sponsors of international terrorism. Cash remittances fell from an estimated $3.7 billion in 2019 to $2.4 billion in 2020 and $1.9 billion in 2021.[39]

The COVID-19 pandemic had an even greater impact. With a preventive health-care system and strict quarantine, Cuba was more successful than most countries at containing the pandemic, but the economic impact was devastating. On March 24, 2020, the government closed the island to all nonresidents, shuttering the tourist sector. The number of foreign visitors fell by 75 percent in 2020, and 92 percent in 2021 compared to pre-pandemic levels.[40] The combined impact of US sanctions, reduced remittances, and the decline in tourism led to a 45 percent reduction in Cuba's total foreign exchange earnings in 2020, necessitating a 27 percent drop in imports in 2020 and a 40 percent drop in 2021.[41] The result was a serious and persistent shortage of food, medicine, and fuel.

The economic recession appeared to break a logjam of disagreement among Cuba's senior leaders, accelerating the pace of economic reform. In May 2020, Raúl Castro told the party's Political Bureau that pushing ahead with the long-delayed reforms was "the main strategic problem we have, to which we must dedicate all our efforts. We must continue working on these issues, get on this train and not get off anymore."[42] In announcing a package of new economic measures in July 2020, Díaz-Canel acknowledged that "reforms entail risks," but "the worst risk would be in not changing and losing popular support."[43] Between July 2020 and December 2022, the government relaxed restrictions on the emergent private sector, greatly expanding the number of allowable private occupations; gave state enterprises greater autonomy; relaxed restrictions on foreign direct investment; opened stores selling goods only in convertible foreign currency; and abolished the dual currency and unified exchange rates (although the latter was partially reversed by late 2022).

The most controversial reform was opening stores selling food and hygiene supplies for freely convertible currency (*moneda libremente convertible* [MLC]), creating a visible social divide between Cubans with access to foreign exchange (mainly US dollars) and those without, a division that some dubbed "economic apartheid."[44] The fact that MLC stores stocked basic products unavailable in other stores angered Cubans without the wherewithal to enter them. Social media bristled with complaints about the MLC stores, which even spilled over into the official media.

In Havana's Pueblo Nuevo barrio, a party member and delegate to the local Popular Power assembly expressed his constituents' dismay: "There is not a single block in this popular council where the *cederistas* [members of the Committees for the Defense of the Revolution] are not indignant. . . . Opening these stores exclusively to buy in dollars is a tremendous mistake by the Party, and it is not only my opinion, but that of other fellow cadres in the territory."[45] The government tried to explain that the MLC stores were for the benefit of all because they enabled the government to capture foreign exchange and use it to import food and medicine to stock non-MLC stores, but the explanation rang hollow in light of the perennially empty shelves in non-MLC stores.[46] To add insult to injury, profiteers bought up goods in bulk from the MLC stores and sold them for Cuban pesos at extortionate prices on the black market.[47]

There is a racial dimension to Cuban inequality. Cubans of African descent are far less likely to have relatives abroad to send them remittances, less likely to work in the tourist sector where they have access to tips, less likely to live in an attractive neighborhood where tourists will rent a room, and less likely to have the capital to open a private business. Consequently, 95 percent of Afro-Cubans have incomes below the equivalent of US$3,000 annually, compared to 58 percent of white Cubans.[48]

Inflation Out of Control

On January 1, 2021, the Cuban government finally implemented the long-awaited unification of the currency and exchange rates (*Tarea Ordenamiento*). The convertible peso (CUC), which had exchanged 1:1 for the US dollar (USD), was eliminated and the national peso (CUP) exchange rate with the USD was fixed at 24:1, which was about what it had been in the retail sector prior to the unification. In transactions between state enterprises and the Central Bank, the prevailing exchange rate between CUP and CUC had been 1:1. Now forced to pay 24 CUP per USD instead of 1 CUP, importers had to raise retail prices drastically. To offset the impact of rising prices, the government increased state sector salaries and pensions by 500 percent.[49] The surge in prices caused widespread anxiety and protests, leading the government to roll back some increases, but most Cubans still reported that their salaries were not adequate to meet basic needs.[50]

As many economists predicted, the unification unleashed far more severe inflation than authorities anticipated. Inefficient state enterprises adapted to the new exchange rates by jacking up prices rather than raising productivity. Meanwhile, the state ran huge budget deficits in 2020 and 2021 as it tried to cushion the impact of the pandemic despite the loss of tourism revenue. In August 2022, the government was forced to devalue the peso again, to 120 CUP to the dollar in the retail sector, but the black-market exchange rate continued to rise, reaching 175 by the end of the year.

Among the most serious aspects of the economic crisis was the shortage of food and medicine. In a country that imports most of its food, food security is always precarious. The drastic decline in the government's foreign exchange earnings meant less imported food, and the closure of the country to foreign travel during the pandemic cut off the supply of foodstuffs brought into the country by Cuban American visitors and Cubans able to travel abroad. The monthly cost of a basic basket of staple foods increased 1,000 percent from 18 CUP to 180 CUP after the currency unification—a rate twice the 500 percent increase in state salaries.[51] The government had to acknowledge that this increase put the basic food basket beyond the reach of many pensioners and promised to remedy that by either raising pensions or increasing the number of people receiving welfare payments.[52] The shortage of medical supplies became critical when the Delta variant of COVID broke out into community spread during the early months of 2021. The lack of personal protective equipment, ventilators, oxygen, and syringes to administer Cuba's homegrown vaccines took a heavy toll, especially in Matanzas Province.

July 11, 2021

On Sunday, July 11, 2021, Cuba was rocked by nationwide demonstrations against the government joined by thousands of people—an unprecedented public display of opposition. The protests began in San Antonio del los Baños on the outskirts of Havana. Organized online by a Facebook hometown group that included Cuban American former residents, the initial crowd of several dozen people grew spontaneously into several thousand as they marched through the streets chanting antigovernment slogans. Participants streamed the march live on social media, sparking similar demonstrations in dozens of towns and cities across the island. Most marches drew no more than a few hundred people, but in San Antonio and downtown Havana thousands participated. As videos of the protests went viral, the government shut down access to some popular social media channels, but news of the day's events continued to circulate regardless.

In most places, people paraded peacefully through the streets chanting "Freedom!" "Down with Communism," "Down with the dictatorship," and "Patria y Vida," the name of the hip-hop music video by popular Afro-Cuban artists abroad. Having never seen anything like this before, the police were befuddled at first. They simply stood by, watching, or walked along with the crowd keeping a wary eye on things. Some of the demonstrations turned violent when groups of young men attacked police, throwing rocks at them and overturning police cars. Rioters looted several dozen stores across the island, most of them in Havana and the province of Matanzas. The protests were driven, first and foremost, by economic desperation over the shortages of food and medicine, a dramatic rise in COVID-19 cases, frequent electricity blackouts, and the runaway inflation unleashed by the currency reform. One of the chants on July 11 was "We want more help!"[53]

Authorities were taken by surprise at the breadth of the discontent, but by afternoon, they had regrouped, dispatching riot police to contain and disperse the crowds. Díaz-Canel went on national television to denounce the demonstrators as counterrevolutionaries and to accuse the United States of launching a "soft coup." He issued a call for "combat," urging loyalists into the streets to defend the Revolution, leading to violent clashes in some places.[54] Regular police and the "Black Beret" riot police deployed in force, backed by "rapid reaction" battalions of plainclothesmen armed with clubs. More than 1,400 people were arrested, several hundred of whom were subsequently convicted of serious crimes of violence or sedition and sentenced to long prison terms.

By Wednesday, July 14, Díaz-Canel had adopted a more conciliatory tone, acknowledging that many of the demonstrators had legitimate grievances and that the state had failed to meet people's needs, especially in marginal communities. He appealed for national unity in the face of economic difficulties and US hostility and announced new programs to improve conditions in poor neighborhoods.[55]

The Protest of 15N

A few months later, dissidents tried to channel the discontent that burst out on July 11 into more-focused political protests. In September, Archipiélago, a Facebook group of artists and intellectuals led by playwright Yunior García Aguilera, partnered with the Council for the Democratic Transition of Cuba, a coalition of dissident groups led by Daniel Ferrer's Patriotic Union of Cuba (UNPACU), to petition authorities in several cities for permission to hold a "Civic March for Change" in November. The aim, according to the petition, was "to demand that all the rights of all Cubans be respected, for the release of political prisoners, and for the solution of our differences through peaceful and democratic means."[56] The petitioners cited Article 54 of the 2019 constitution, which guarantees the right of assembly, demonstration, and association "for legal and peaceful purposes."

The government denied permission for the marches on the grounds that they were aimed at regime change and therefore violated Article 4 of the constitution, which declares Cuba's socialist system "irrevocable."[57] García called the denial of permission a crime and declared the government a "dictatorship." The marches, he said, would proceed regardless.[58] The government launched a series of ad hominem attacks against García and the other organizers, branding them as US agents, harassing them, cutting off their internet and phone service, and staging "acts of repudiation" by regime supporters outside their homes. Sensing that turnout for the marches might be small, Archipiélago rechristened the "Civic March for Change" as a "Civic Day for Change." As an alternative to marching, they urged people to bang empty pots or applaud at the scheduled march time of 3:00 p.m.

On November 15 (15N), march organizers across the island were either detained by police or held under house arrest to prevent them from participating. No one appeared at the appointed hour to march, and no one banged pots or applauded. The complete failure of the planned protest was surprising, given how much attention it received in Cuba's independent, social, and even state media. The failure had multiple causes. First and foremost, the government did its best to minimize participation by declaring the marches illegal and warning that revolutionaries would not allow dissidents to control the streets. Authorities implicitly threatened dire consequences for participants—a threat reinforced by the stiff sentences imposed on those arrested for participating in the July 11 (11J) protests. On 15N, the police presence was heavy and visible in the cities where marches were planned.

Second, Archipiélago's appeal did not resonate with the broader public. The organizers hoped to enlist the anger and frustration expressed on 11J behind a program of political reform. But the spontaneous outburst on 11J did not express a coherent political program, nor did it imply a common set of concerns or demands, notwithstanding antigovernment chanting by some protestors. Archipiélago's message of political reform, delivered by young artists and intellectuals, did not speak to the issue that was the top priority for most Cubans—the state of the economy and their standard of living.

Third, the failure of 15N illustrated the limitations of organizing via social media. Archipiélago was not an organization. It was a Facebook group with a small team of coordinators who spoke on its behalf—and not always with one voice. Because it had no on-the-ground capacity to organize people for political action, it had to rely on people being so discontented that they would respond to a call to march without organizational preparation.

Two days after 15N, Yunior García left Cuba for self-imposed exile in Spain without informing the rest of the Archipiélago coordinating committee. Some movement supporters publicly criticized him for deserting the field of battle after having called others into the streets. The failure of 15N and internal recriminations took a toll on Archipiélago, prompting prominent members of the coordinating committee to resign, most of whom subsequently went into exile. By 2023, the group had effectively ceased to exist as a focal point of opposition.

Emerging from COVID

As 2022 drew to a close, there were signs that the Cuban economy was gradually recovering. The number of foreign visitors in 2022 was up four-fold over 2021, although the total was still just 38 percent of tourist arrivals during 2019.[59] At that rate, full recovery of the tourist sector to pre-pandemic levels would take at least until 2024. Remittances increased as family visits resumed and Cuban Americans could bring cash and goods directly, and found new ways to help family on the island—"topping off" cellphone accounts and ordering groceries through online delivery services.

In November 2022, the US Treasury Department granted a Miami-based travel agency, VaCuba, a license to wire remittances to a nonmilitary Cuban financial institution, Orbit S.A., and in January 2023, Western Union announced it would resume wiring remittances to Cuba. Nevertheless, the rapid rise in inflation and continuing shortages of basic goods, including food and medicine, meant that the crisis was far from over for Cuban consumers. Despite Díaz-Canel's best efforts to reassure people that "we will win,"[60] he failed to paint a convincing picture of a path out of the country's misery. Even among loyalists, there was creeping doubt that the authorities had a workable plan to move the country forward.[61]

One of the most aggravating problems for the public, and one of the most politically dangerous for the government, was rolling electricity blackouts that began in April 2022 and lasted well into the fall. Cuba's dilapidated electrical grid, plagued by constant breakdowns, was unable to meet peak summer demand. In July 2022, the system was operating at less than half of installed capacity.[62] In August, lightning struck the country's largest oil storage facility in Matanzas, igniting a fire that burned for five days, destroying half the facility's capacity and upward of a million barrels of oil, aggravating the shortage of fuel for Cuba's thermoelectric plants.[63]

Power outages lasted up to twelve hours in some areas, leaving people without fans in the sweltering heat of Cuba's summer and causing the spoilage of food that people stood in line for hours to buy. Notably it was a lack of electricity after Hurricane Irma that brought protesters into the streets of Havana's Diez de Octubre neighborhood in 2017.[64] In the summer of 2022, the blackouts touched off similar neighborhood protests in several dozen towns,[65] but none expanded beyond a few hundred people or catalyzed demonstrations elsewhere, as happened in July 2021 (which also began as a protest over blackouts). President Díaz-Canel complained to the National Assembly that the demonstrations, though understandable, were playing into the hands of counterrevolutionaries. "This does not resolve the situation," he lamented.[66]

On September 27, 2022, Hurricane Ian ravaged the western provinces of Cuba, knocking out power to the entire island. In the hardest hit areas, people lost water and telephone service as well. Several dozen protests over the slow pace of restoring power and water broke out in the areas affected, especially in Havana, including the relatively well-off neighborhood of Vedado. In some cases, women banging empty pots blocked streets, demanding action and chanting "Give us light!"[67] The opposition in exile did its best to encourage the demonstrations via social media with the hashtag #CubaPaLaCalle (Cuba to the Streets), and there were reports of people abroad paying Cuban youths for isolated acts of violence and sabotage.[68]

The government's response to the demonstrations was restrained in most places. Police stood aside while government and party officials came out to speak with the crowds to try to get them to disperse. In an interview with state media, Luis Antonio Torres Iríbar, first secretary of the Communist Party in Havana, affirmed the people's right to protest government shortcomings. Altercations broke out in some places when police tried to reopen blocked streets or when pro-government counter-demonstrators clashed with the protestors. On October 2, Díaz-Canel tried to draw a distinction between demonstrators with legitimate concerns expressed "from a civic, decent position" and those taking a more aggressive stance, "challenging and offending" authorities. "We cannot allow that," he warned.[69] As power was gradually restored, the demonstrations subsided.

Cuban officials recognized they had a political problem. Even as they blamed discontent on US subversion and "mercenaries," they worked to rebuild a measure of grassroots support.[70] The programs to improve infrastructure and services in vulnerable communities were the most tangible example. Shortly after 11J, the government launched a nationwide program to plow resources into 302 "vulnerable communities," 65 of them in Havana, including a number that spawned large protests on July 11, 2021.[71]

As COVID restrictions were relaxed, senior officials, Díaz-Canel foremost among them, hit the streets, trying to be more visible to the citizenry. Díaz-Canel traveled the country to preside over every provincial Communist Party *balance* (review) meeting and some municipal meetings, exhorting party members to be more politically active, more exemplary, and innovative in problem solving.[72] A common theme was the need to engage young people, involving them in all levels of work. Roberto Morales Ojeda, organizational secretary of the Communist Party, reported that fewer members of the Union of Young Communists, the party's main recruitment channel, were interested in joining the party—one more sign of the generational divide in Cuban politics.[73] In February 2022, the government launched a "Comprehensive Policy for the Care of Youth and Children," acknowledging the problems of alienation and youth migration. Unless these problems were attended to, Díaz-Canel warned, they could "break the continuity of the revolution."[74]

While the government tried to redress the economic problems at the heart of popular discontent, it toughened its stance toward all manifestations of opposition, introducing new laws with broad scope to criminalize dissident expression. In June 2022, MSI leaders Luis Otero Alcántara and Maykel Castillo were sentenced to nine and five years in prison, respectively, leaving MSI adrift. In August, Patriotic Union leader José Daniel Ferrer was returned to prison from house arrest for participating in the July 11 demonstrations.[75]

After the July 11 demonstrations, during which automated accounts based outside of Cuba flooded social media with photos and video of the protests, the government issued Decree Law 35, a new law on cybersecurity. It imposed criminal penalties for hacking, the dissemination of disinformation, and accessing the internet by satellite without a permit. It also gave authorities enormous latitude to criminalize online commentary "inciting mobilizations or other acts that alter public order," "subverting the constitutional order," or "defamation with an impact on the country's prestige."[76]

The new Penal Code approved in 2022 included several provisions so broad they could be invoked to charge people for nonviolent criticism or protest. Article 120 criminalized the "arbitrary exercise of any right or freedom recognized in the Constitution" that "endangers the constitutional order and the normal operation of the state." Article 143 took aim at the funding of nongovernmental organizations and independent media by making criminally liable anyone who "supports, encourages, finances, provides, receives or has in his control funds, material, or financial resources, in order to support activities against the state and its constitutional order." Specifically mentioned were those acting "on behalf of non-governmental organizations, international institutions, associations, or any natural or juridical person of the country or of a foreign state."[77]

Elections

When the government dropped the same-sex marriage provision from the draft constitution in 2018, it pledged to return to the issue in a new Families Code. The result was another spirited national debate over the draft law in 2022. Once again, the churches, led by evangelical Protestants and Catholic bishops, campaigned vigorously against the law, sending believers door to door urging people to vote no in a referendum on it.[78] The government pushed hard for the law's approval with billboards and saturation media coverage. Two days before the referendum, Díaz-Canel appeared on television calling for people to vote yes "for unity, for the Revolution, for socialism, and . . . for Cuba!" But he spoke respectfully of those opposed to the new law, calling them "people of doctrine and faith who rightly defend their conception."[79]

On September 25, Cubans approved the new Families Code by a substantial margin, 66.9 percent voting yes, 33.2 percent no. Nevertheless, the vote was unusual. Turnout was just 74.1 percent, well below the norm, and the margin of victory was also significantly less than in past referenda and legislative elections, in which "yes" votes typically surpassed 90 percent. Some dissidents urged people to vote no or abstain as a "punishment vote" (*voto castigo*) against the government, but others supported the code as a net gain for human rights. The opposition framed the low turnout as a victory, evidence of the public's disaffection rather than disinterest.

This was the first election in which opponents of the government's position were allowed to campaign more or less openly (in person and not just online) without being vilified as counterrevolutionaries. The government was well aware, based on the popular reaction during the constitutional consultations and its own polling, that a substantial segment of the population was opposed to same-sex marriage, including some government supporters. This made it difficult—and risky—to frame the issue as a vote "for the Revolution," as Díaz-Canel tried to do in his closing appeal. The churches, on the other hand, were able to frame the issue as one of religious and moral values rooted in an individual's personal convictions—a cultural frame rather than a political one.

Two months later, Cubans went to the polls again to elect more than 12,400 delegates to municipal legislative assemblies. Hoping to capitalize on public discontent, a number of dissident groups banded together in a coalition, "D Frente," to propose candidates, who are nominated in open neighborhood meetings. In the 2017 election cycle, more than one hundred dissidents stood as candidates, but the Communist Party mobilized to oppose them and none were nominated. In 2022, several dissident candidates were reportedly prevented from nominating themselves. Only one managed to win nomination, but dropped out of the race, reportedly under pressure.[80] The opposition then shifted to a social media campaign urging people not to vote, to spoil their ballots, or to leave them blank.[81]

Turnout was historically low at 68.6 percent, down from 89 percent in 2017. Average turnout, from the first election in 1976 to 2017, was 96 percent, but it had been gradually declining since 2012. The opposition declared the drop-off in turnout a victory, but the increase in the number of blank and spoiled ballots, which were a clearer indicator of active defiance, rose less dramatically from 8.2 percent in 2017 to 10.9 percent in 2022. At the very least, the 20.4 point drop in turnout represented increasing disenchantment with the political process and doubts that voting was likely to make any difference.[82]

Migration

Every major surge in emigration from Cuba since the mid-1960s has coincided with an economic downturn: Camarioca (1965), Mariel (1980), and the *balsero* (rafters) crisis (1994). The economic crisis of 2020–2022 was no different. In 2022, US Customs and Border Protection encountered more than 300,000 irregular Cuban migrants seeking entry to the United States—more than a five-fold increase over the previous year.[83] Tens of thousands more were emigrating to other countries, Spain in particular, where Cubans with a Spanish grandparent were eligible for a Spanish passport.

For younger people, the motivation was not just the immediate economic hardship but doubts about their life opportunities in Cuba. Growing numbers concluded that their prospects were better abroad.[84] With economic reforms moving slowly and yielding no improvement in the standard of living, and with the channels for expressing dissent narrowing, more and more Cubans concluded there was, in Albert O. Hirschman's terms, no space for "voice" and chose "exit" instead.[85] The departure of young people represented an enormous loss of human capital for a country that invests 15 percent of its state budget on education.[86] It also aggravated the demographic crisis facing Cuba as the average age of the population rises. Finally, as dissidents chose exile, sometimes forced, they reinvigorated antigovernment sentiment abroad, delaying US-Cuban rapprochement and potentially complicating Cuba's relations with Spain and the European Union.

Cuba's Political Struggle to *Resolver*

To *resolver*: in Cuba, it means to find a way through adversity, to figure out a solution. Miguel Díaz-Canel's first term as president was one of the most precarious political moments experienced by the revolutionary government since 1959. A new generation of leaders, lacking the prestige of the regime's founders, had to face the worst economic crisis to hit the island since the Special Period of the 1990s. One disaster after another plagued them: intensified US sanctions, the COVID pandemic, hyperinflation, the fire at the Matanzas oil depot, Hurricane Ian, a collapsing electrical grid, and persistent shortages of food, fuel, and medicine.

Popular discontent ran high, and for the first time since 1994 produced a series of popular demonstrations beginning with the nationwide protests on July 11, 2021, and continuing with local protests through most of 2022. With no organized opposition capable of channeling popular discontent into a coherent political alternative, the public protests never threatened regime survival, but they signaled a new, more complex political landscape that Cuba's leaders had to navigate. The market-oriented economic reforms begun in 2011 produced both winners and losers, widening inequality and creating a more heterogeneous civil society. New interest groups emerged, facilitated by social media, making demands of government and posing new challenges.

Díaz-Canel's political strategy appeared to be two-pronged. On the one hand, he exhorted supporters and the general public to maintain unity in the face of hardship. He worked hard to revitalize the Communist Party's grassroots apparatus as a means of rebuilding popular support by making the party and government more responsive to local needs. When new interest groups emerged demanding policy changes that did not challenge the legitimacy of the socialist system, Díaz-Canel's government engaged with them and offered concessions. When protests broke out in some of Cuba's poorest neighborhoods, the government launched a program to improve infrastructure and services in vulnerable communities.

At the same time, however, the government's tolerance for dissidents who challenged the fundamentals of the one-party socialist system declined in tandem with the economy. The government was determined not to allow opposition forces any opportunity to build a broad movement. Dissident leaders either landed in jail or were forced into exile. The hardening of the government's posture extended to critical voices on social media as well. Independent media outlets that had been previously tolerated came under withering public attack and private pressure by state security.

As Díaz-Canel's first term in office came to a close, his government had survived the global pandemic but still faced daunting economic challenges undermining popular faith in the regime's competence, even among loyalists—a crisis of faith visible in protests, declining participation at the polls, and the surge in migration. Even though dissidents were unable to capitalize on this latent discontent and mold it into a popular movement, politics was becoming visibly more polarized, stoked by social media influencers at home and abroad. For Cuba's leaders, the challenge was whether they could kick the bureaucracy into gear and make real progress toward meeting people's basic needs before the public's desperation and alienation reached a tipping point.

Notes

Portions of this chapter are adapted from "Politics: The Challenges Facing Cuba's New Leaders," in *Cuba at the Crossroads*, ed. Philip Brenner, John Kirk, and William M. LeoGrande (Lanham, MD: Rowman & Littlefield, 2020).

1. "El ministro de Economía afirma que 2008 será un año de 'crecimiento,' pese a los huracanes," *Cuba Encuentro*, November 2, 2008, accessed at https://www.cubaencuentro.com/cuba/noticias/el-ministro-de-economia-afirma-que-2008-sera-un-ano-de-crecimiento-pese-a-los-huracanes-128912; Associated Press, "Cuba Rations Staple Foods and Soap in Face of Economic Crisis," *New York Times*, May 11, 2019, accessed at https://www.nytimes.com/2019/05/11/world/americas/cuba-rationing-sanctions.html.

2. William M. LeoGrande, "Updating Cuban Socialism: The Politics of Economic Renovation," *Social Research* 84, no. 2 (Summer 2017): 353–82.

3. Peter Orsi, "Raul Castro Proposes Term Limits in Cuba," *NBC News*, April 16, 2011, accessed at https://www.nbcnews.com/id/wbna42620105.

4. Communist Party of Cuba, *Resolution on the Guidelines for the Economic and Social Policies of the Party and the Revolution*, April 18, 2011, accessed at http://www.cuba.cu/gobierno/documentos/2011/ing/l160711i.html.

5. Raúl Castro, "The Development of the National Economy, along with the Struggle for Peace, and Our Ideological Resolve, Constitute the Party's Principal Missions," *Granma*, April 18, 2016, accessed at https://en.granma.cu/cuba/2016-04-18/the-development-of-the-national-economy-along-with-the-struggle-for-peace-and-our-ideological-resolve-constitute-the-partys-principal-missions.

6. Fidel Castro, "Speech Delivered at the Commemoration of the 60th Anniversary of His Admission to University of Havana, in the Aula Magna of the University of Havana, on November 17, 2005," accessed at http://www.cuba.cu/gobierno/discursos/2005/ing/f171105i.html.

7. Raúl Castro, "Fidel, Undefeated, Has Left Us, but His Spirit of Struggle Will Permanently Remain in the Conscience of All Revolutionaries," *Granma*, December 28, 2016, accessed at http://en.granma.cu/cuba/2016-12-28/fidel-undefeated-has-left-us-but-his-spirit-of-struggle-will-permanently-remain-in-the-conscience-of-all-revolutionaries.

8. Partido Comunista de Cuba, *Conceptualización del Modelo Económico y Social Cubano de Desarrollo Socialista*, June 18, 2016, accessed at http://www.granma.cu/file/pdf/gaceta/Conceptualizaci%C3%B3n%20del%20modelo%20economico%20social%20Version%20Final.pdf.

9. "Party Congress Less than a Month Away," *Granma*, March 28, 2016, accessed at http://en.granma.cu/cuba/2016-03-28/party-congress-less-than-a-month-away.

10. Randal C. Archibold, "Inequality Becomes More Visible in Cuba as the Economy Shifts," *New York Times*, January 19, 2018, accessed at https://www.nytimes.com/2015/02/25/world/americas/as-cuba-shifts-toward-capitalism-inequality-grows-more-visible.html. For in-depth research by Cuban sociologists, see Mayra Espina Prieto, *Políticas de atención a la pobreza y la desigualdad: examinando el rol del estado en la experiencia cubana* (Buenos Aires: CLACSO,

2008) and Maria del Carmen Zabala Argüelles, "Poverty and Vulnerability in Cuba Today," *Socialism and Democracy* 24, no. 1 (2010): 109–26, 181.

11. Fidel Castro, "The Cuban People Will Overcome," *Granma*, April 20, 2016, accessed at http://en.granma.cu/cuba/2016-04-20/fidel-castro-the-cuban-people-will-overcome.

12. Raúl Castro, "Speech During the Closing Ceremony of the Sixth Session of the Seventh Legislature of the National People's Power Assembly," December 18, 2010, accessed at http://www.cuba.cu/gobierno/rauldiscursos/2010/ing/r181210i.html.

13. Raúl Castro, "Development of the National Economy."

14. "New Central Committee Elected," *Granma*, April 21, 2016, accessed at http://en.granma.cu/cuba/2016-04-21/new-central-committee-elected.

15. Miguel Díaz-Canel, "I Assume This Responsibility with the Conviction That All Revolutionaries Will Be Loyal to the Exemplary Legacy of Fidel and Raúl," *Granma*, April 19, 2018, accessed at http://en.granma.cu/cuba/2018-04-24/i-assume-this-responsibility-with-the-conviction-that-all-revolutionaries-will-be-loyal-to-the-exemplary-legacy-of-fidel-and-raul.

16. Azam Ahmed and Frances Robles, "Who Is Miguel Díaz-Canel, Cuba's New President?" *New York Times*, April 19, 2018, accessed at https://www.nytimes.com/2018/04/19/world/americas/miguel-diaz-canel-bermudez-cuba.html.

17. LeoGrande, "Updating Cuban Socialism."

18. Andrea Rodríguez, "Cuban Constitutional Reform Spawns Unusual Public Debate," AP News, October 11, 2018, accessed at https://apnews.com/article/caribbean-ap-top-news-elections-international-news-cuba-9f2a3d8f9f7c495fb1234c62898f35f4.

19. Anthony Faiola and Rachelle Krygier, "Cuba Moves Toward Officially Recognizing Private Property, Foreign Investment," *Washington Post*, July 21, 2018, accessed at https://www.washingtonpost.com/world/the_americas/cuba-moves-toward-striking-changes-to-officially-recognize-private-property-foreign-investment/2018/07/21/cd5c230a-8c69-11e8-9d59-dccc2c0cabcf_story.html?noredirect=on&utm_term=.706bbb52764d.

20. Archibald R. M. Ritter and Ted A. Henken, *Entrepreneurial Cuba: The Changing Policy Landscape* (Boulder, CO: Lynne Rienner, 2014).

21. Miguel Febles Hernández, "A One Percent Worth Millions," *Granma*, November 8, 2018, accessed at http://en.granma.cu/cuba/2018-11-08/a-one-percent-worth-millions.

22. Marc Frank, "Cuba Approves Laws Granting Greater Rights as Criticism of Protesters' Arrests Heats Up," Reuters, October 28, 2021, accessed at https://www.reuters.com/world/americas/cuba-approves-laws-granting-greater-rights-criticism-protesters-arrests-heats-up-2021-10-28.

23. "Internet es vital para el desarrollo de Cuba," *Juventud Rebelde*, February 6, 2009, accessed at http://www.juventudrebelde.cu/cuba/2009-02-06/internet-es-vital-para-el-desarrollo-de-cuba.

24. ONEI (Oficina Nacional de Estadística e Información de Cuba), *Anuario Estadístico de Cuba, 2021*, Tecnología de la información y las comunicaciones, Table 17.4 (Havana: ONEI, 2022). Accessed at http://www.onei.gob.cu/sites/default/files/17_tic_aec_c_0.pdf.

25. Ted A. Henken, "Cuba's Digital Millennials: Independent Digital Media and Civil Society on the Island of the Disconnected," *Social Research* 84, no. 2 (Summer 2017): 429–56.

26. Glenda Boza Ibarra, "6 Movilizaciones Ciudadanas Impulsadas por los Datos Móviles," *El Toque*, December 9, 2019, accessed at https://eltoque.com/6-movilizaciones-ciudadanas-impulsadas-por-los-datos-moviles.

27. Fidel Castro, "Discurso . . . como conclusion de las reuniones con los intelectuales Cubanos," June 30, 1961, accessed at http://www.cuba.cu/gobierno/discursos/1961/esp/f300661e.html.

28. Kepa Artaraz, "El Ejercicio de Pensar: The Rise and Fall of Pensamiento Crítico," *Bulletin of Latin American Research* 24, no. 3 (July 2005): 348–66.

29. Arturo García Hernàndez, "La política cultural de Cuba, sin dogmas ni sectarismos," *La Jornada* (Mexico), February 26, 2007, accessed at https://www.jornada.com.mx/2007/02/26/index.php?section=cultura&article=a10e1cul.

30. Sarah Marsh, "Cuba Legalizes Independent Movie-Making," Reuters, June 27, 2019, accessed at https://www.reuters.com/article/us-cuba-cinema/cuba-legalizes-independent-movie-making-idUSKCN1TS336.

31. "Cuban Artists Lead Protest against Decree 349," Artists at Risk, accessed January 4, 2020, at https://artistsatriskconnection.org/story/cuban-artists-lead-protest-against-decree-349.

32. Sarah Marsh and Nelson Acosta, "Cuba Defends Controversial Arts Decree but Seeks Consensus on Norms," Reuters, December 8, 2018, accessed at https://www.reuters.com/article/us-cuba-art/cuba-defends-controversial-arts-decree-but-seeks-consensus-on-norms-idUSKBN1O705C.

33. "Ustedes deben ser los que hablen con nosotros, no la Seguridad del Estado," 14yMedio, December 3, 2020, accessed at https://www.14ymedio.com/cuba/Ustedes-deben-hablen-Seguridad_0_2996700306.html.

34. Carmen Sesin and Orlando Matos, "After Historic Meeting, Cuba Slams Protesters, Dashes Hopes for Dialogue," *NBC News*, November 30, 2020, accessed at https://www.nbcnews.com/news/latino/after-historic-meeting-cuba-slams-protesters-dashes-hopes-dialogue-n1249437.

35. Marc Frank, "Cuban Authorities Backtrack on Talks with Protesters," *Financial Times*, December 5, 2020, accessed at https://www.ft.com/content/247afcaa-15e6-4ce1-b401-acc30b849365.

36. Nora Gámez Torres, "Cuban Artists behind Rare Protest Met with Shoves, Insults after New Try at Dialogue," *Miami Herald*, January 28, 2021, accessed at https://www.miamiherald.com/news/nation-world/world/americas/article248828484.html.

37. Aamer Madhani and E. Eduardo Castillo, "U.S. Sets New Cuba Sanctions as Biden Meets with Cuban American Leaders," *Los Angeles Times*, July 30, 2021, accessed at https://www.latimes.com/world-nation/story/2021-07-30/u-s-sets-new-cuba-sanctions-as-biden-meets-with-cuban-american-leaders.

38. Sarah Marsh and Rodrigo Gutiérrez, "Cuban Anti-Communist Anthem Featuring Gente de Zona Goes Viral, Sparks State Fury," Reuters, February 20, 2021, accessed at https://www.reuters.com/article/us-cuba-politics/cuban-anti-communist-anthem-featuring-gente-de-zona-goes-viral-sparks-state-fury-idUSKBN2AK0MA.

39. "COVID-19 puede hacer declinar las remesas a Cuba entre un 30 y 40% en el 2020," Havana Consulting Group, March 20, 2020, accessed at. http://www.thehavanaconsultinggroup.com/en-us/Articles/Article/74.

40. ONEI, *Anuario Estadístico de Cuba, 2021*, Turismo, Table 15.4, accessed at http://www.onei.gob.cu/sites/default/files/15_turismo_.pdf.

41. ONEI, *Anuario Estadístico de Cuba, 2021*, Sector External, Table 8.6, accessed at http://www.onei.gob.cu/sites/default/files/08_sector_externo_2021-_1.pdf; Marc Frank, "Cuba Sees Slow Economic Recovery at 4% in 2022," Reuters, December 12, 2021, accessed at https://www.reuters.com/business/cuba-sees-slow-economic-recovery-4-2022-official-2021-12-12.

42. "Montarnos en este tren y no bajarnos más" *Progreso Semanal*, May 20, 2020, accessed at https://primerocuba.blogspot.com/2020/06/montarnos-en-este-tren-y-no-bajarnos.html.

43. Miguel Díaz-Canel, "¡Fuerza Cuba, que seguiremos viviendo, impulsando la economía y venciendo!," *Granma*, July 17, 2020, accessed at http://www.granma.cu/cuba-covid-19/2020-07-17/version-integra-de-las-palabras-pronunciadas-por-el-presidente-de-la-republica-de-cuba-miguel-diaz-canel.

44. Ed Augustin, "Dollar Back in Cuba as Pandemic and US Sanctions Hammer Economy," *The Guardian*, August 18, 2020, accessed at https://www.theguardian.com/world/2020/aug/18/cuba-dollar-stores-coronavirus.

45. "'Es una traición bien pensada': las nuevas tiendas en divisas vistas desde barrios pobres cubanos," *Diario de Cuba*, July 22, 2020, accessed at https://diariodecuba.com/cuba/1595443194_23914.html.

46. Yisell Rodríguez Milán, "Unificación monetaria: El peso del peso cubano," *Granma*, October 22, 2020, accessed at http://www.granma.cu/pensar-en-qr/2020-10-22/el-peso-del-peso-cubano-22-10-2020-19-10-27.

47. "Diez meses de prisión para un revendedor de Sancti Spíritus," 14yMedio, September 19, 2020, accessed at https://www.14ymedio.com/cuba/meses-prision-revendedor-Sancti-Spiritus_0_2951704804.html.

48. The difference in remittances is especially stark. Only 28 percent of Afro-Cubans receive remittances, compared to 56 percent of all Cubans. Katrin Hansing and Bert Hoffmann, "Cuba's New Social Structure: Assessing the Re-stratification of Cuban Society 60 Years after Revolution," GIGA Working Papers 315, German Institute for Global and Area Studies (2019), accessed at https://www.giga-hamburg.de/en/publications/giga-working-papers/cuba-s-social-structure-assessing-re-stratification-cuban-society-60-revolution.

49. AFP, "Cuba to Increase Minimum Salary Fivefold," France24, December 11, 2020, accessed at https://www.france24.com/en/live-news/20201211-cuba-to-increase-minimum-salary-fivefold.

50. "Los lectores de 'Cubadebate' se rebelan contra la manipulación de la encuesta," 14yMedio, March 5, 2021, accessed at https://www.14ymedio.com/cuba/Cubadebate-manipulacion-encuesta-Tarea-Ordenamiento_0_3051894786.html.

51. *OnCuba* staff, "The Reorganization's Prices (II): With and without Ration Card," February 5, 2021, accessed at https://oncubanews.com/en/cuba/the-reorganizations-prices-ii-with-and-without-ration-card.

52. Mailenys Oliva Ferrales et al., "Tarea Ordenamiento: Nuevas decisiones a partir de la voluntad del pueblo," *Granma*, February 11, 2021, accessed at http://www.granma.cu/tarea-ordenamiento/2021-02-11/tarea-ordenamiento-nuevas-decisiones-a-partir-de-la-voluntad-del-pueblo.

53. William M. LeoGrande, "Explaining the Political and Social Unrest in Cuba," Political Violence at a Glance, July 20, 2021, accessed at https://politicalviolenceataglance.org/2021/07/20/explaining-the-political-and-social-unrest-in-cuba.

54. Gladys Leidys Ramos López, "A la Revolución la defendemos ante todo," *Granma*, July 12, 2021, accessed at https://www.granma.cu/pensar-en-qr/2021-07-12/a-la-revolucion-la-defendemos-ante-todo-12-07-2021-01-07-22.

55. Yaditza del Sol González, "Díaz-Canel: Hacemos un llamado a que el odio no se apropie del alma cubana, que es de bondad," *Granma*, July 14, 2021, accessed at https://www.granma.cu/cuba/2021-07-14/en-vivo-presidente-de-cuba-comparece-en-la-mesa-redonda-videos.

56. "Grupo Archipiélago convoca a una marcha pacífica en La Habana," *Periódico Cubano*, September 22, 2021, accessed at https://www.periodicocubano.com/grupo-archipielago-convoca-a-una-marcha-pacifica-en-la-habana-para-el-20-de-noviembre

57. "Régimen de Cuba responde a Marcha Cívica del 15N," *Diario las Américas*, October 12, 2021, accessed at https://www.diariolasamericas.com/america-latina/regimen-cuba-responde-marcha-civica-del-15n-n4234065.

58. "'Más claro ni el agua, Cuba es una dictadura' dice Yunior García sobre respuesta oficial a Marcha Cívica por el Cambio," Radio Televisión Martí, October 12, 2021, accessed at https://www.radiotelevisionmarti.com/a/el-r%C3%A9gimen-califica-de-ileg%C3%ADtima-la-marcha-c%C3%ADvica-del-15n-por-un-cambio-en-cuba-/305516.html.

59. ONEI, "Turismo. Arribo de viajeros y visitantes internacionales," December 2022, accessed at https://www.onei.gob.cu/sites/default/files/arribo_de_viajeros._visitantes_internacionales_diciembre_2022.pdf.

60. Leticia Martínez Hernández, "Díaz-Canel: Aun en la peor de las situaciones, vamos a vencer," *Granma*, June 14, 2022, accessed at https://www.granma.cu/cuba/2022-06-14/diaz -canel-aun-en-la-peor-de-las-situaciones-vamos-a-vencer-14-06-2022-14-06-22.

61. See for example Silvio Rodríguez's comments in response to Fidel Vascós González, "Propuesta para combatir la inflación desde la oferta," *Segunda Cita*, April 11, 2022, accessed at https://segundacita.blogspot.com/2022/04/propuesta-para-combatir-la-inflacion.html.

62. Randy Alonso Falcón et al., "Ministro de Energía: Situación del sistema eléctrico nacional es compleja, pero tiene solución," Cubadebate, July 18, 2022, accessed at http://www .cubadebate.cu/noticias/2022/07/18/sistema-energetico-de-cuba-actualizacion-y-perspectivas -video.

63. Marianna Parraga, "Devastating Fire May Force Cuba to Resort to Floating Oil Storage," Reuters, August 9, 2022, accessed at https://www.reuters.com/world/americas/devastating -fire-may-force-cuba-resort-floating-oil-storage-2022-08-08.

64. Luz Escobar, "Hundreds of Havanans Protest in Neighborhood Five Days without Electricity or Water," *Havana Times*, September 14, 2017, accessed at http://translatingcuba.com/ hundreds-of-havanans-protest-in-neighborhood-five-days-without-electricity-or-water.

65. "Protestas en Cuba," interactive map, accessed August 30, 2022, at https://maphub.net /proyectoinventario/protestas-verano-2022-en-cuba.

66. "Díaz-Canel pide a los cubanos no protestar por apagones porque no soluciona el problema," CiberCuba, July 23, 2022, accessed at https://www.cibercuba.com/noticias/2022-07-23 -u1-e199482-s27061-diaz-canel-pide-cubanos-protesten-apagones.

67. Camila Acosta and Maria Abi-Habib, "Protests Erupt in Cuba Over Government Response to Hurricane Ian," *New York Times*, September 30, 2022, accessed at https://www .nytimes.com/2022/09/30/world/americas/cuba-hurricane-ian-protests.html.

68. "¿Cómo opera el neoterrorismo promovido por youtubers desde EE. UU.?" *Granma*, August 18, 2022, accessed at https://www.granma.cu/cuba/2022-08-18/como-opera-el -neoterrorismo-promovido-por-youtubers-desde-ee-uu-18-08-2022-00-08-44.

69. Miguel Díaz-Canel, "Díaz-Canel: Todos tenemos la responsabilidad de superar esos daños," *Granma*, October 2, 2022, accessed at https://www.granma.cu/discursos-de-diaz-canel /2022-10-03/diaz-canel-todos-tenemos-la-responsabilidad-de-superar-esos-danos-03-10-2022 -20-10-00.

70. Bertha Mojena Milian, "La esencia del Partido es el trabajo con la gente," *Granma*, February 23, 2022, accessed at https://www.granma.cu/pensar-en-qr/2022-02-23/la-esencia -del-partido-es-el-trabajo-con-la-gente-23-02-2022-22-02-09.

71. Luis Brizuela, "The Cuban Government Tries to Address Social Gaps," *Havana Times*, October 7, 2021, accessed at https://havanatimes.org/features/the-cuban-government-tries-to -address-social-gaps.

72. See for example Ronald Suárez Rivas, "Hay que analizar la realidad desde todos los puntos de vista," *Granma*, March 11, 2022, accessed at https://www.granma.cu/file/pdf/2022 /03/12/G_2022031203.pdf.

73. "Pocos militantes de la Unión de Jóvenes Comunistas desean ingresar al Partido y al régimen le preocupa," *Diario de Cuba*, March 6, 2022, accessed at https://diariodecuba.com/ cuba/1646571171_37896.html.

74. Leticia Martínez Hernández, "Díaz-Canel: La Política para la atención a jóvenes y niños es uno de los proyectos más importantes en los que vamos a trabajar," *Granma*, February 22, 2022, accessed at https://www.granma.cu/cuba/2022-02-22/diaz-canel-la-politica-para -la-atencion-a-jovenes-y-ninos-es-uno-de-los-proyectos-mas-importantes-en-los-que-vamos-a -trabajar.

75. "'Dejen de presionarme con tomar un avión o irme al exilio,' Yoani Sánchez denuncia coacción de Seguridad del Estado," Radio Television Martí, November 5, 2021, accessed at

https://www.radiotelevisionmarti.com/a/yoani-s%C3%A1nchez-presionada-por-la-seguridad-del-estado-para-que-abandone-cuba/306842.html.

76. Ministerio de Justicia de Cuba, Decreto-Ley 35/2021, "De las Telecomunicaciones, las Tecnologías de la Información y la Comunicación y el Uso del Espectro Radioeléctrico" (GOC-2021-759-O92), *Gaceta Oficial de la República de Cuba*, No. 92, August 17, 2021, accessed at https://www.gacetaoficial.gob.cu/sites/default/files/goc-2021-o92.pdf.

77. Ministerio de Justicia de Cuba, Ley 151/2022, "Código Penal" (GOC-2022-861-O93), *Gaceta Oficial de la República de Cuba*, No. 93, September 1, 2022, accessed at https://www.gacetaoficial.gob.cu/sites/default/files/goc-2022-o93_0.pdf.

78. Cristiana Mesquita, "Cuba Holds Unusual Vote on Law Allowing Same-Sex Marriage," Associated Press, September 26, 2022, accessed at https://apnews.com/article/religion-cuba-caribbean-gay-rights-69dbfba5ead550e919294ceca401d82a.

79. Miguel Díaz-Canel Bermúdez, "Es un Código de amor y de afectos que protege a todas y a todos," Cubadebate, September 23, 2022, accessed at http://www.cubadebate.cu/opinion/2022/09/23/es-un-codigo-de-amor-y-de-afectos-que-protege-a-todas-y-a-todos.

80. AFP, "Cuba Holds Local Elections as Opposition Deplores Pressure," France24, November 27, 2022, accessed at https://www.france24.com/en/live-news/20221127-cuba-holds-local-elections-as-opposition-deplores-pressure.

81. Dave Sherwood and Nelson Acosta, "Cuba's Opposition Calls on Voters to Abstain from Sunday's Local Elections," Reuters, November 23, 2022, accessed at https://www.reuters.com/world/americas/cubas-opposition-calls-voters-abstain-sundays-local-elections-2022-11-23.

82. Dave Sherwood, "Cuba Municipal Elections See Lowest Turnout in 40 Years," Reuters, November 28, 2022, accessed at https://www.reuters.com/world/americas/cuba-municipal-elections-see-lowest-turnout-40-years-2022-11-28.

83. US Customs and Border Protection, "Nationwide Encounters," accessed at https://www.cbp.gov/newsroom/stats/nationwide-encounters.

84. "Cuba and Its Youth: The Generational Challenge," *OnCuba News*, March 20, 2022, accessed at https://oncubanews.com/en/cuba/cuba-and-its-youth-the-generational-challenge.

85. Albert O. Hirschman, *Exit, Voice, and Loyalty* (Cambridge, MA: Harvard University Press, 1972).

86. Olivia Marín Álvarez, "Presupuesto estatal para 2021: ¿cómo se usa el dinero en Cuba?" *Periodismo de Barrio*, January 26, 2021, accessed at https://periodismodebarrio.org/2021/01/presupuesto-estatal-para-2021-como-se-usa-el-dinero-en-cuba.

CHAPTER 1

The New State Structure in Cuba
FROM CENTRAL POWER TO MUNICIPAL POWER

Julio Antonio Fernández Estrada

The new constitution of the Republic of Cuba, approved in 2019, modified the political system in its institutional dimension but left its core hard and untouched: the direction of the state and society is in the hands of the Communist Party of Cuba (PCC), now consecrated as unique, Fidelista, and democratic.

The 1976 constitution was in force until this last law of laws was approved, but it went through two modifications that changed the structure of political power. In 1992, constitutional reform introduced important changes in the economic foundations of the state by allowing a new form of property derived from foreign investment. It also incorporated "Martiano" as a moniker for the ideological base of the PCC, in search of a political opening that relaxed and expanded the consensus in favor of political power in the face of the crisis caused by the fall of the Socialist bloc and the start of the so-called Special Period.

Other changes related to power in the constitutional reform of 1992 were the consecration of the secular state; religious freedom; the incorporation of the state of emergency as an exceptional situation; the replacement of the old local executive bodies by the Administration Councils, with functions of government at the municipal and provincial level; and the birth of Popular Councils, which are considered the highest authority in their demarcations and serve as a kind of intermediate link in the chain of power between the municipal delegates and the people.

An electoral law was derived from the 1992 reform, that same year, that allowed for direct, popular voting in the election of provincial delegates and deputies to the National Assembly of People's Power. As of 1976, direct elections were only held at the municipal level, and provincial deputies and delegates came from the suffrage of the Municipal Assemblies of People's Power.

The democratization that was experienced with the constitutional reform of 1992 was trapped in the preservation of the Candidacy Commissions that still survive, although their function has been modified. From 1992 to 2019, these commissions oversaw the creation of the lists of candidates for provinces and the nation at a municipal level. As of 2019, these commissions began to create lists for the candidacies of deputies to the National Assembly because the old Provincial Assemblies of People's Power were dissolved and, in their place, governors, proposed by the president of the republic, were elected by the Municipal Assemblies to preside over provincial governments.

Still in 2002, the 1976 constitution was modified to include a third paragraph within Article 3, which already protected popular sovereignty and the people's right of resistance against attempts to overthrow the Magna Carta. From that moment on, an intangibility clause was incorporated that prevents Cuba from abandoning its socialist path both economically and politically.

Local Power in the 2019 Constitution

The Cuban state changed drastically in 2019. The political system continues to be dominated by the PCC and the Union of Young Communists (UJC), along with other social and mass organizations, but the state has changed its local and national structure.

At the municipal level, the Municipal Assemblies of People's Power and the Popular Councils remain, though mayors have now been included. They are appointed by the Municipal Assemblies at the proposal of the presidents of those bodies; they direct the Councils of Administration, the level of government closest to the people. The management positions within the Municipal Assemblies, such as the presidency and the secretariat, are internally elected by this body without popular participation.

The provincial government is now in the hands of a governor and a Provincial Council. The governor presides over the provincial administration, and the position lasts five years. The Provincial Council is chaired by the governor and is also made up of the vice governors, the presidents and vice presidents of the Municipal Assemblies, and the mayors.

One of the most interesting changes brought by the 2019 constitution has been the Fifth Section of Title II, Chapter VIII, called Guarantees to the Rights of Petition and Local Popular Participation, which allows, in Article 200 of the law of Cuban laws, that the Municipal Assemblies of People's Power convene popular consultations and respond to proposals by the population, as well as their complaints and requests. It also guarantees that citizens in the municipality can propose topics for discussion, ensures that adequate information is updated, and analyzes its own agreements for rights violations.

It must be noted that in the new constitution, Article 168 of Title VII: Territorial Organization of the State already considered municipalities autonomous and clarifies that they have their own judicial body and income, in addition to the allocations they receive from the government of the republic. For its part, the province is only considered an intermediate level between the central and municipal structures, according to Article 167 of the constitution.

The New Territorial Development Policy

In 2020, the Council of Ministers approved a new Territorial Development Policy, which should serve as a framework for the laws and public policies that are approved at the municipal level from now on. The policy of territorial development opens a path to an old desire of the Cuban population, of academic institutions, and of Cuban civil society—that of local development and municipal autonomy.

Municipal autonomy was presented as a state resolution in the 2019 constitution, and local development is outlined in the party guidelines approved during its Sixth and Seventh Congresses. This policy now emphasizes the endogenous possibilities of the territories and considers strategic the production of food and the exploitation of potentiality for each territory. A territorial development policy is proposed in the context of economic crisis in which it is essential to move little by little from an importation economy to one of exportation. The possibility of creating local development projects of municipal, provincial, and national interest is made more flexible.

It is a policy that involves communities, popular power, and above all citizens in the approval of participatory budgets and local development projects with various modes of financing. In this policy, the union of various state and non-state subjects is promoted as a strategy to carry out these projects. The policy encourages the employment of young people and women in these projects. It revolves around sustainability and respect for the environment, in addition to the legality of any local development project.

The policy opens the door for local development projects to use, after fulfilling their tax responsibilities, up to 50 percent of what is earned to develop the work of the same project. It is also a policy that allows productive, sociocultural, and environmental local development projects. It encourages the use of the most advanced scientific knowledge that each territory may have and involves institutions for territorial training. It does not seek to stop the objective of local development with bureaucratization, but rather encourages it with more expeditious and informal mechanisms. It is a policy that is clearly related to the economic measures announced on July 16, 2020.

This document is evidence that those who have worked the most to achieve awareness of the need for local development over the last twenty years have been listened to, including and above all, institutions and research anchored in the same territories.

The approved policy opens the doors to the use of economic salary incentives for local development projects that until now were only allowed for prioritized sectors of the economy. It seeks to develop territories that have long been entrenched in social and economic situations that do not allow for the well-being of the population. Social welfare is precisely one of the fundamental objectives of this policy.

A training strategy for natural and legal persons is outlined by institutions involved in the design of this policy to prepare leaders and individuals interested in new local development projects. It is considered a priority to give all legal security to the new local development projects created, to the point of recognizing the projects as having legitimate, legal backing.

The policy analyzed stands out with its flexible, tolerant, and updated language from the perspective of what has been achieved by Cuban civil society and what is established by the social sciences that work on issues related to territorial development. It is committed to democratization—for popular participation, for considering the results of the assemblies of accountability, for economic flexibility—which is open to the participation of new subjects. It leaves open an interesting possibility: that the relationships between subjects involved in a project are established through association contracts.

In conclusion, it is a policy that, depending on its implementation within laws at a municipal level and others, can be an avenue that encourages new forms of work, community development, and even democracy at the municipal level.

The Law of Functionality and Organization of Municipal Assemblies and Popular Councils

The Law of Functionality and Organization of Municipal Assemblies and Popular Councils was also approved in 2020. It deals with municipalities in general, as well as municipal autonomy; the definition, integration, and constitution of Municipal Assemblies; and the dismissal of principals within the assemblies from their functions. The law also deals with the sessions of the assemblies and the request for information from the president, as well as reports, voting, agreements, and ordinances. It deals with delegates, work commissions, and the rendering of accounts. It guarantees the rights of petition and citizen participation, popular consultation, attention to proposals, attention to complaints, and requests from the population. It also deals with the right of citizens to propose analyzing issues to the Municipal Assembly, for the population to be informed about decisions of general interest, for disclosure of analyses of official agreements at the request of the population, and the revocation of decision-making bodies subordinate to the local assembly.

The labor relations between assemblies and councils of the administration are regulated with the provincial governments and the superior organs of the state. In relation to the Popular Councils, Title II of the law defines what a Popular Council is, its organization, its powers, popular participation, control over production and service entities, and the cessation of functions in office.

It is fundamental in this provision, Article 10, which regulates that the attributions and functions that the constitution and the laws confer on the municipal organs of the People's Power cannot be interfered with or assumed by the provincial government.

The Central Power since 2019

The 2019 constitution created a new state in Cuba with a series of organs that did not previously exist or did not have constitutional importance. The presidency and vice presidency of the republic, the prime minister, and the national electoral council were introduced into the state structure. The general comptroller of the republic was introduced into the Magna Carta after years of the position already working within the state.

The presidency of the republic is a unipersonal body in Cuba that will be elected every five years and is extendable for a second term of equal time. The most important change in what it means for political power is the president's character as head of state and his or her indirect election by the deputies to the National Assembly of People's Power. From 1976 to 2019, the head of state was the president of the Council of State and Ministers, who headed the collegiate bodies of which he was a member.

Perhaps the most radical change that has been ushered by the new Cuban constitution has been the separation of state functions from those of the government and party, which were homogeneous until 2019. On the other hand, the division of powers is still outside of constitutional order in Cuba, and this allows the courts of justice to be considered independent, but the constitution itself provides that they can receive directives from the state.

The principles of organization and operation of the state continue to be those of a socialist democracy, but there has been a decline in the number of positions and bodies that are appointed or constituted through indirect elections. The prime minister now directs the Council of Ministers, where the government of the republic still resides, but this figure becomes in fact and in law the head of government. He is appointed by the national assembly on the proposal of the president of the republic.

Final Thoughts

Political power in Cuba is torn between its legal form and its material manifestations, as in any other place in the world. The 2019 constitution establishes the socialist state of law but does not conceptualize it. It also declares the principle of constitutional supremacy, but the legislative schedule approved shortly after the great text came into force has already been replaced by another, which has postponed, for example, the law that should create a judicial procedure for the defense of human rights.

The Cuban constitution now mentions human rights for the first time since 1959, but it limits the right to create a political organization other than those that already exist in the country, and it does not foresee a specialized institution for the defense of individual and collective rights, nor a mechanism independent of constitutional control.

Popular sovereignty is at stake in the face of a bureaucracy little trained in dialogue, deliberation, or citizen control. Municipal autonomy seems to be the remaining path toward the construction of democracy in Cuba, and there are indications of movement within the state toward this sphere of political life in Cuba.

It is impossible to speak of power and its structure in Cuba without considering its indissoluble relationship with the vicissitudes in the relationship between the governments of the United States and that of the largest island in the Caribbean. Likewise, it is important to evaluate the new economic and political subjects that operate below the public political mesh and that tend to be decisive everywhere.

The first few months of 2021 showed that the island was not as sleepy as it was thought to be and that the new generations have less admiration and are less trusting toward politics, which gives them the possibility to demand and resist, in addition to not having lived the years of splendor of the epic and mystical socialist revolution.

The 2019 constitution is paradoxical in much of its content, and there are nuances of the power that wrote it. In it there is popular sovereignty, human rights, a single party, preponderance of the state enterprise, private property, consideration of foreign investment, and the irreversible nature of socialism.

All that amalgamation of values that sometimes conflict is a sample of the struggle for political power in a Cuba less monolithic than what is believed beyond the sea that surrounds us.

Note

This essay is adapted with permission from the *Cuba Study Group* blog, May 17, 2021.

CHAPTER 2

"Martiano," "Fidelista," and Reformed?

THE COMMUNIST PARTY AFTER THE GENERATIONAL CHANGE

Arturo Lopez-Levy

During the decade between 2011 and 2021, Cuba's one-party political system went through a set of important changes. The center of those changes was the intergenerational transition of leadership. This change represented the end of the Fidel-in-command model. This model was softened by the intragenerational transition from Fidel Castro to his brother Raúl at the end of the first decade of the twenty-first century. The Fidel-in-command model rested on the charisma and historical authority of Fidel Castro combined with the institutionalization of Leninism around the rule of the Communist Party as the dominant organization. By the 1990s, Cuba was—in the typology of nondemocratic regimes proposed by Linz and Stepan (1996)—a post-totalitarian regime in mobilization, pluralism, and ideology, but until his retirement in 2006, the system's legitimacy rested significantly on Fidel Castro's charisma.

This hybrid system implied two tracks of promotion of cadres (LeoGrande 2015). Fidel Castro used a system of promotion by "helicopter" to choose his staff. Fidel would select young celebrities and leaders from sports, science, the Union of Young Communists (Union de Jóvenes Comunistas [UJC]), or the University Students' Federation (Federación Estudiantil Universitaria [FEU]) and add them to his staff. These people mainly trained and learned on the spot while supporting Fidel's campaigns and development projects and disrupting the group thinking in the party-state apparatus. They were chosen mainly because of a combination of their competence, leadership skills, or celebrity status, together with direct capacity "to interpret Fidel's ideas." From this staff position working on the commander in chief's priorities, the best among this group would jump to important executive positions in the party-state machinery. Carlos Lage and Felipe Pérez Roque were archetypical cases of these type of cadres.

Although Raúl Castro used similar prerogatives to create his own most direct support staff, he also was a resolved defender of party policies for choosing and promoting cadres. After the First Congress of the Communist Party of Cuba (PCC) and the ascent of José Machado Ventura as leader of the Organization Department, the party-state consolidated a well-structured Leninist system of step-by-step promotion and socialization in which leaders were formally vetted, supervised, and trained in teamwork and loyalty to the party. The promotion of these leaders follows a well-institutionalized path in the party, armed forces, and government hierarchies. All the generals and provincial party czars followed this path.

The intragenerational transition from Fidel to Raúl Castro ended this duality in cadres' promotion. In the case of the intergenerational transition to Díaz-Canel's presidency, the Central Committee's Organization Department and the Secretariat, a party executive institution restored at the Sixth Congress of the PCC, played the decisive role. This was not the ascension of one leader but the rise to power of a group of leaders with affinities and ways of thinking beyond an age cohort who were born around the same time. Rafael Hernández (2018) demonstrated how, by the moment when Díaz-Canel and his generation took control of the Political Bureau, most of the (real) transition, understood as the renewal of municipal and provincial elites in the PCC and the central organs of government, had already taken place.

In this chapter, I look closely at the specific leadership transition (succession) that took place between the Seventh and the Eighth PCC Congresses (2016–2021) and how the PCC functioned as an actor of reform as well as a target of it. The party-state is a terrain in which Cuban elites' different visions about reforms and the institutionalization of political succession are negotiated. The consensus inside the party defines the policy frontiers (Golob 2003)[1] within which the decisions about further changes are settled. The renewing of elites brought together a transition to a market-oriented mixed economy and a less top-down command relationship between the party-state and civil society. To make viable the economic reform, the PCC adopted a time framework for political and constitutional reforms without abandoning the Leninist vanguard-party paradigm. But this policy agenda requires ideological adjustments that reflect and imply an expansion of the policy frontiers.

Without Fidel's charismatic leadership and Raúl's historical flair of the Revolution's foundational generation, the Díaz-Canel government is trying to catch up with changes postponed by the longest delayed intergenerational transition of all post-revolutionary regimes in history. The arrival of the first post-insurrection generation to the helm of the Cuban party-state came accompanied by a profound economic crisis, and a search for new zones of legitimacy associated with a transition to a mixed economy, the reinforcement of well-rooted nationalism versus the US imperial policies (Domínguez and Yaffe 2017), and some liberalization of state-civil society relations.

The Communist Party of Cuba: Subject and Object of the Reforms

Cuba is ruled by the PCC, not by a family. Fidel Castro's premiership and later presidency was by no means a sultanistic type of regime. His charismatic leadership placed him among the most influential leaders in the Cold War world and definitively in Cuba (Kapcia and Finn 2021). Inside the party-state complex, he was a "minimal winning coalition," using the definition of Linz and Stepan. But he built a Leninist system, not one in which there was "no elaborate or guiding ideology . . . outside of political despotism" (Linz and Stepan 1996).

From the origins of the Revolution, Communist ideology has significantly intertwined with nationalist views (Valdez Paz 2020). The balance of these compatible but different ideologies is changing with the arrival of generations with a less adverse attitude toward market mechanisms, the participation of the Cuban diaspora in the life of the country, and private property. Policies are adopted within new policy frontiers marked by a new constitution approved in 2019. The shift toward a more nationalist orientation in ideology, not abandoning but in balance with the Leninist internationalist approach, is a long trend in policy-making, narratives, and elites' education programs (Berman 2008) for at least the last two decades.

The PCC plays multiple roles within Cuba's political system. In one of the clearest signs of continuity, Article 5 of Cuba's 2019 constitution established: "The Communist Party of Cuba, unique, Martiano, Fidelista, and Marxist-Leninist, the organized vanguard of the Cuban nation, sustained in its democratic character as well as its permanent linkage to the people, is the superior driving force of the society and the State" (Republic of Cuba 2019).

The first role of the party was originally as "unique" and "vanguard" of the "working class," but after the constitutional changes adopted in 1992, it became "vanguard of the Cuban nation." However, the new 2019 constitution includes some notable changes with impacts in the way the role of the PCC was historically understood:

1. There is a change in the sources of the official ideology. José Martí's ideas ("Martiano") that used to be in second place after Marxist-Leninism in the 1976 constitution, moved to first place in 1992 and is now accompanied by Fidel Castro's thoughts ("Fidelista"). Ironically, just when the leaders of PCC reinforce Leninist organizational principles, the text pushed further back the role of Marxist-Leninism as an ideological source.

2. Article 22 in Chapter II identified multiple forms of property, adding private property. Symbolically, and practically, two important policy frontiers have been pushed outward, expanding the political space for dismantling old policies of economic command and control that were up to now indispensable for the vertical structure of party domination of state and civil society.

3. The constitution codified terms and age limits for the mandates of the highest levels in the party-state apparatus, such as the presidency, a position historically held by the first secretary of the PCC. Thus, the "minimal winning coalition" form expressed in the Fidel-in-command model is made less likely by using institutional mechanism of collective controls and separation of functions (the new constitution creates the figure of prime minister in charge of managing the day-by-day government issues).

References to "the party" usually refer to most leaders of the country, including the Political Bureau, the Central Committee, the party bureaucracy, and a set of agitprop cadres that are central to the organization. The supreme authority within the PCC is the Political Bureau, presided over by Miguel Díaz-Canel, in which most substantive questions about the country and party dominance of Cuban society are decided. According to its statutes, the PCC should have a congress every five years in which the mandate of the Central Committee and the Political Bureau is renewed, a schedule it has kept since 2011.

In charge of the PCC's inner governance and guidance of the militants' political action within society is the Secretariat. The Secretariat was historically the staff leadership at the service of the Political Bureau, organizing the work of the cadres and functionaries of the Central Committee headquarters. The Secretariat is the ultimate place of the institutional power of the party bureaucracy. Its members supervise the work of departments of the Central Committee, making the policy decisions of the Political Bureau operational. The Secretariat also oversees the development of the party's national apparatus, selecting and developing leadership cadres.

The most important party reform legacy left by the period between the Seventh and the Eighth Congresses is the consolidation of the Secretariat. The trajectory of the Secretariat shows the different level of institutionalization of Leninist rule in parallel to the charismatic power of the first secretary.[2] This organ disappeared after the Fourth Congress in 1991, as part of the centralization of power in Fidel's hands and a remarkable reduction of the size of the party bureaucracy in the Central Committee and the provincial levels. One of Raúl's early decisions in 2011 as part of the Sixth Congress program of institutionalizing one-party rule was the restoration of the Secretariat. Press reports highlight a renovated, broad, and activist role for the Secretariat members in areas as diverse as the economy, ideology, attention to social organizations under the PCC aegis, and the party's mobilization in response to the COVID-19 pandemic.

The composition of the Secretariat also reflects the balance of power and priorities of the PCC. After the Sixth Congress of the PCC, Raúl, who was elected first secretary, assigned to Machado Ventura, the identified leader of the most conservative faction within the *historicos*, oversight of the work of the Secretariat. Although the ultimate decision-making power is in the Political Bureau, the institutional power and the basis for implementing agendas are in the party apparatus and its network of central, provincial, and municipal cadres that penetrate and oversee state structures. Prominent in the Secretariat is the secretary or member of the Political Bureau who monitors the Organization Department. This position was managed first by Machado Ventura, and after the Sixth and Seventh Congresses by Abelardo Alvarez-Gil, who had worked under Machado Ventura's leadership since 1969. The position is currently held by Roberto Morales Ojeda, who, along with Díaz-Canel, represents the rise of cadres from the provincial party ranks.

The Organization Department as a Gatekeeper of Leadership Prospects

References to the party have other connotations beyond the top elites and decision-makers. There is also the PCC as a party-state complex pursuing the proclaimed goals of the country and sustaining its political legitimacy. Most high positions in the government are held by members of the party. They act as implementers of policies discussed under the inspiration or supervision of strategies dictated by the party congress's or Political Bureau's decisions. Crucially, there are the base-level party members and the UJC—a subordinate body in charge of implementing the party policy toward youths and children.

At the base, party members are average people who join the party out of conviction or convenience. They are consulted and oriented but do not play any major role in decisions. It would be an exaggeration to classify these people as elites if one understands by this concept the groups whose policy preferences tend to prevail. But these intermediate cadres and rank-and-file members are the ultimate pillars on which the one-party system has rested. At the grassroots levels of the party and the organizations under its aegis—according to even PCC documents—there are trends to formalism, disconnection between the official discourse and the members' practice, and other forms of moral corruption. In a rational model of party-state decision-making, such trends should keep party leaders awake at night because they steadily undermine the government's edifice of legitimate authority one piece at a time.

The outcome and turnout of recent referendums about the 2019 constitution, the 2022 Families Code, and the 2022 municipal assembly elections sent clear messages that although the PCC won in an uneven field skewed in its favor, it has lost significant political ground. The economic crisis and the dynamics of corruption, rent-seeking, and rising inequality accompanying partial reform equilibrium (Lopez-Levy 2016) are daily eating away former zones of legitimacy of the system.

The ties that connect these three roles of the PCC are the local party cadres in the provinces and municipalities. The gatekeeper for the promotion of these cadres and monitor of the policies and incentives for them is the Organization Department of the Central Committee. Together with the strengthening of the Secretariat, the second most important feature of the role of the PCC in Cuba's political system between the Seventh and Eighth Congresses is the consolidation of its institutional rule around policies agreed to and implemented with the Organization Department as the spinal cord of its inner governance.

Raúl Castro's ascent to the leadership of the PCC empowered two important groups inside Cuba's one-party system: the military high command and the PCC apparatus, fundamentally the provincial party czars and the Organization Department of the Central Committee. The institutionalization of a Leninist party structure strengthened these two groups, already in an advantageous position due to the end of the executive groups that worked as a support staff for Fidel Castro and derived all power from the proximity to him (the Battle of Ideas group, the Coordination and Support group, and a set of cadres such as Carlos Lage, Felipe Pérez Roque, Otto Rivero, and Carlos Valenciaga, who emerged from working directly for Fidel Castro).

For most leaders of the party, the Organization Department is the main entrance of approval to the ladder of Cuban politics. The work of the department does not invalidate the role of informal politics, such as personal, work, regional, and family ties, but these elements of networks do not operate arbitrarily but within institutional boundaries better defined since 2011. This institutionalization increases the cohesiveness of the party elites because it conceives the top leadership succession as connected to systemic elites' renewal. Díaz-Canel is regarded as "the first among equals" in a coalition government that included other leaders of his generation such as the prime minister Manuel Marrero and the recently deceased General Luis Alberto Rodríguez López-Calleja. Such characteristics help consensus building and systemic coherence on recruitment and retirement of cadres but, at the same time, reinforce common trajectories and the selection biases that lead to "group think."

The PCC has a widespread system of party schools in which cadres receive professional and political training. At the top of the PCC education system is the national party school Antonio "Ñico" López. There, party cadres study and discuss doctrinaire issues such Marxism-Leninism, Cuban history, PCC documents, and Fidel Castro's thought. But the party school programs also include courses on economics, world politics, and even religion. At the school, professors and classmates evaluate the cadres' performance and skills. These evaluations go to the files at the Organization Department, which routinely evaluates the performance of members of each graduation.

The Organization Department manages the files of all cadres from the municipal committees of the party to the Central Committee. But this department is not only the equivalent of the human resources section of the party, because it also monitors the promotion of thousands of state cadres in Cuba's economic, cultural, and social life. For instance, all ministers and vice ministers, directors of major government companies and radio and TV stations, provincial governors, and municipal administrators are vetted by the department. The dossiers managed by the PCC Organization Department are primordial information shaping the path for most leaders. There, the party not only records one's age, race, education, and jobs but also collects all the annual evaluations of every cadre including any criticism or positions he or she has defended. The Organization Department provides guidelines to provincial and municipal party organization offices.

One of the most difficult challenges for the Organization Department created by decisions of the Sixth, Seventh, and Eighth Congresses is the management of the age and term limits. The fact that the *historicos* generation is on its way out does not mean that other leaders will not try to remain at the top of decisions after their terms have expired. Raúl's solution of creating advisory bodies as soft-landing retirement positions was supposed to be temporary. The arrival of new cohorts with their own agendas might create some conflicts down the road.

There is also a system of political orientation and party organization (Dirección Política) within the Revolutionary Armed Forces (FAR) and the Ministry of Interior (MININT) subordinated to the military high command but connected to the PCC Central Committee through a military affairs department. More than in any other communist country, the FAR play a key role in Cuba's governance. Fidel and Raúl Castro founded the armed institution with the high command of cadres who mainly came from the guerrillas and the underground resistance of the July 26 Movement.

"It makes no sense to ask," Perlmutter and LeoGrande (1982) wrote of those foundational institutional years of the Cuban Revolution, "whether the dual elite functions as the agent of the party within the army or the agent of the army within the party. It is both." As part of this tradition, the Political Bureau has reserved a quota of members for the military or people who had been associated with it in their leadership trajectory. But the professionalization of the functions of the party and the military has affected this dynamic, now shaped by the intragenerational transition. In the past, the military quota inside the Political Bureau and the Central Committee was assigned to commanders based on their roles and legacies from the insurrection. In the Eighth Party Congress, the slots were assigned based not on a historic nostalgia but on institutional ranks and functional positions: the minister, General Álvaro López-Miera; Rodríguez López-Calleja, due to his new generation and position directing the military's business conglomerate; the first vice minister; and some regional commanders.

If acting cohesively, the FAR-MININT complex today constitutes a veto player for any major decisions. Its role is extended from national security to the most sophisticated and internationally linked parts of the Cuban economy. In terms of civil-military relations, General Rodríguez López-Calleja's death represents a challenge for Díaz-Canel, the first civilian leader of the post-1959 process. Both leaders worked in coalition and Rodríguez's unique standing (primus inter pares of his generation) in the high military ranks guaranteed a unified support. Today, Díaz-Canel is in no condition to push the military back to the barracks even if he wanted to. He relies more on Raúl Castro's support, and within a likely horizon without Raúl, civil leaders must respect military zones of autonomous decisions.

"Martiano," "Fidelista," and Reformed: Updating the Party and Its Ideology

The PCC remains inextricably linked to Fidel Castro's legacy in Cuban history. The party arose from the revolutionary insurrection against Batista, and a coalition of revolutionary forces that opted for a communist orientation as the optimal form of Cuban nationalist resistance against US opposition between 1959 and 1961. These guerrilla origins of the PCC were combined eventually with Leninist principles of organization, cadre education, and control of the state. Levitsky and Way (2022) demonstrated how the dynamics of revolution and prolonged counterrevolutionary conflict—arguably present until today in the form of the "blockade" or "economic war"—played a decisive role in fostering "elite cohesiveness" and a durable, strong, one-party state. The structure of the party and the role of a strong military faction within its upper echelons is in large measure a product of the guerrilla path to power that preceded its creation.

From his early years of conflict and consolidation of power, Castro extracted three important lessons, a legacy he left for future generations of leaders of the PCC: First, although he understood that the United States is a complex society with many views about Cuba, Cuban patriots could not rely on any US moral restraint for the protection of their sovereignty. The United States should not be trusted. Second, the barrage and radicalism of external and internal counterrevolutionary forces has been of such caliber that triumphant revolutionaries rallied around a one-party system in which the FAR and the PCC must remain totally loyal to each other. Third, even in case of improvement of relations, Cuban patriots should remain skeptical about the political evolution of the United States and its attitude toward Cuba (Castro 2016).

This nationalist idea of preserving sovereignty and independence is central to the moral purpose of the Cuban postrevolutionary party-state. If there is an external factor that contributed to rally most of the party around Miguel Díaz-Canel's leadership, it is the continuing policy of regime change applied by the United States against Cuba. The Seventh Congress took place in April 2016, in the middle of the two-year interregnum of President Barack Obama's normalization policy, after his historic visit to Havana.

Although far from lifting the sanctions of the embargo/blockade, Obama's actions motivated a debate inside Cuban society about the proper domestic political organization to cope with a horizon of some détente with the United States. Hardliners in the ideological apparatus of the PCC tried to present Obama as the same wolf but in different clothes, but they could not disqualify demands for deep reforms in the middle of a détente. By the time of the debate over the new constitution (2018), President Donald Trump had returned to a policy of regime change, so Cuban reformers had lost the opportunity to set the agenda by invoking chances of US-Cuba rapprochement. The political reform process was postponed or canceled by the rise of Trump and the continuation of his policies by the Biden administration, even in the middle of the COVID-19 pandemic.

Democratization—to the extent it is mentioned—is conceived as a tool to expand zones of legitimacy for nationalism and the Leninist system (Chase and Lopez-Levy 2018). Multiparty elections in the presence of US war against the Cuban economy remain anathema to all segments of the PCC. The reform process launched at the Seventh Congress had nothing to do with any reappraisal by the leadership of the virtues of liberal democracy. Support for a transition to a mixed economy reflected a search for legitimacy based on economic performance in response to Cuba's desperate economic circumstances.

But the reforms toward a market-oriented economy, respect for religious liberties, the adoption of a "socialist rule of law," and private property redefine the ideological boundaries in which policies are adopted. Even when the changes are managed by a conservative Political Bureau, they are not implemented in a vacuum or laboratory but in permanent interaction with other domestic and foreign actors. Implementation is not a passive process by the officials down the hierarchy in charge of making the new economy and society a reality. Although the organization of the system is still Leninist, and the leadership has proclaimed continuity within this paradigm, such an outcome is not assured. Change sometimes takes on a dynamic all its own.

The economic crisis is the most urgent challenge to the PCC. The command economic model is exhausted, unable to guarantee minimal levels of energy and food security. However, the most difficult challenge for the party consists of the political consequences of implementing the already approved economic reforms of the last three PCC congresses. If the economic reform is carried out as designed, the PCC will have to rule a more unequal, open, and market-driven society than anything that has existed in Cuba since 1960.

The implementation of these within-regime reforms most likely will lead not to a steady state of political stability but to pressures for advancing to a more open system. It is difficult to believe that empowered new actors with middle-class status, strongly connected to a diaspora ninety miles north in the United States, with bourgeois values and economic autonomy, would remain quiet, renouncing further demands for political change. Leninist experiences with market economies and liberalized societies in East Asia have demonstrated that such a mission is not impossible. Such a challenge in the middle of a Western culture demands a vision of dynamic, not static, stability well beyond the partial reform logic and excessive gradualism showed by the PCC in Cuba's recent past.

Notes

1. For the concept of policy frontiers, I use here the definition by Stephanie Golob (2003) in her study about the origins of NAFTA. According to Golob: "Policy frontiers develop as certain elements of the 'national interest'—sovereignty, security, and identity—become equated with the legitimation of state elites. When these leaders defend the policy frontier (ostensibly to defend the nation), they are also defending their own political power. These barriers are constructed in a path-dependent fashion, through a critical juncture that first establishes the frontier, and then are maintained over time by institutional and ideological mechanisms of reproduction. For the frontier to be transcended, a critical juncture combining an exogenous shock with an internal legitimacy crisis must undermine, and then reconfigure, both mechanisms of reproduction."

2. In "After Fidel," William LeoGrande (2015) provides a short discussion of the history of the PCC and its evolution under Raúl Castro's rule before the Seventh Congress.

References

Berman, Salomon. 2008. "Rowing against the Stream: Elite Regeneration and the Question of Regime Continuation in Cuba." PhD diss., Georgetown University, Washington, DC.

Castro, Fidel. 2016. "El Hermano Obama." *Granma*, March 28. Accessed at https://www.granma.cu/reflexiones-fidel/2016-03-28/el-hermano-obama-28-03-2016-01-03-16.

Chase, Michelle, and Arturo Lopez-Levy. 2018. "Democratizing Cuba?" NACLA, November 14. Accessed at https://nacla.org/news/2018/11/14/democratizing-cuba.

Domínguez, Ernesto, and Helen Yaffe. 2017. "The Deep Historical Roots of Cuban Anti-imperialism." *Third World Quarterly* 38, no. 11: 2517–35.

Golob, Stephanie. 2003. "Beyond the Policy Frontier: Canada, Mexico, and the Ideological Origins of NAFTA." *World Politics* 55, no. 3: 361–98.

Hernández, Rafael. 2018. "Por fin, la (real) transicion politica cubana." *Foreign Affairs Latinoamerica* 18, no. 4: 53–62.

Kapcia, Antoni, and Daniel Finn. 2021. "Revolutionary Cuba and the Legacy of Fidel Castro." *Jacobin*, September 26. Accessed at https://jacobin.com/2021/09/cuban-revolution-castro-fidel-raul-socialism-soviet-ties-embargo-diaz-canel-protests-pandemic.

LeoGrande, William. 2015. "After Fidel: The Communist Party of Cuba on the Brink of Generational Change." In *The Revolution under Raúl Castro*, ed. Philip Brenner, Marguerite Rose Jimenez, John Kirk, and William LeoGrande, 59–72. Lanham, MD: Rowman & Littlefield.

Levitsky, Steven, and Lucan Way. 2022. *Revolution and Dictatorship: The Violent Origins of Durable Authoritarianism*. Princeton, NJ: Princeton University Press.

Linz, Juan, and Alfred Stepan. 1996. *Problems of Democratic Transition and Consolidation.* Baltimore, MD: Johns Hopkins University Press.

Lopez-Levy, Arturo. 2016. "Cuba After Fidel: Economic Reform, Political Liberalization and Foreign Policy Adaptation (2006–2014)." PhD diss., Josef Korbel School of International Studies, University of Denver.

Perlmutter, Amos, and William LeoGrande. 1982. "The Party in Uniform: Towards a Theory of Civil-Military Relations in Communist Political Systems." *American Political Science Review* 76, no. 4: 778–89.

Republic of Cuba. 2019. "Constitution of Republic of Cuba." Accessed November 24, 2022, at https://www.constituteproject.org/constitution/Cuba_2019.pdf?lang=en.

Valdez Paz, Juan. 2020. *La evolucion del poder en la Revolucion Cubana.* Mexico: Rosa Luxemburg Stiftung. Accessed at https://www.rosalux.org.mx/sites/default/files/evolucion-poder-rev-cubana-2_0.pdf.

CHAPTER 3

Civil Society, Nation, and Conflict in Cuba

Julio César Guanche

Translated by Ann Halbert Brooks

On July 11, 2021, the largest protests in Cuba since 1959 took place. These protests, known as the 11J protests in Cuban discourse, further illuminated a landscape of serious social conflict. In this analysis of the protests and that landscape, I question the relevance of the term *civil society* in the Cuban context. In particular, this chapter addresses the social foundations of the conflict from which the 11J protests arose, the sectors of the Cuban political system that engaged with that conflict, and the characteristics of those sectors that the 11J protests made more visible. Finally, I analyze the contemporary challenges faced by the Cuban justice system regarding civil society and social protest.

Civil Society: Which Version, Which Focus?

My first question is whether the concept of civil society is the best one to explain the social conflict in Cuba today. I propose that the most apt term is not civil society but rather *el pueblo*, the Cuban people. The idea of el pueblo incorporates the idea of social difference and the layers of domination that arise from these differences. Through this analytical lens, we can analyze nuances such as the segregation of citizens from noncitizens, or first-class citizens from second-class citizens. In contrast, the concept of civil society assumes a universal community of citizens equal to one another, not embedded in an existing network of social asymmetries.

Furthermore, the concept of civil society does not include the whole of society or the population; it is a group of affiliated citizens. Citizenship, however, is almost always a rare commodity. That is, one cannot automatically assume access to citizenship. Instead, the term *civil society* alludes to organized movements, whether based around intellectual, market-focused, entrepreneurial, media, private, or social interests. The idea of civil society is less useful when studying social inequality and asymmetries among social actors in political life. One example of citizenship being a rare commodity was the official rhetoric that the 11J protestors were "vandals" and "delinquents," terms that divided Cuban citizens from one another based on the protestors' demands for representation, self-determination, and inclusion.

A class-based analysis also reveals that the current landscape of social conflict in Cuba cannot be fully explained with the concept of civil society. However, it can be better analyzed with the more radical concept of *el pueblo*, and particularly the idea that el pueblo can be an "oppressed subject." Protestors on 11J and, more recently, in a 2022 protest in the town of Nuevitas, have organically adopted the term *pueblo*, as in the slogan "The people, united, shall never be defeated" ("El pueblo unido jamás será vencido"). According to the philosopher Wilder Pérez Varona (2021), "That possibility is nothing other than its right to exist and to act as a people—their sovereign right without mediation, a right to exercise self-determination that cannot be delegated. It is the right to engage in untimely plans, strategies, and programs that are alien to their reality. It also includes the right to make mistakes. It is a supreme right that cannot be transferred or possessed in usufruct by another."

El pueblo is not an inevitable fact of society, but rather an act of institutionalization, of political creation. Classical Marxist perspectives continue to explain why Cuban protests have employed this discourse of el pueblo. Gramsci, for example, described the people—"the plebeian" in his writing—as "the social bloc comprised of the oppressed," and in opposition to the "historic bloc" in power (Dussel 2006, 94). From this perspective, the only source of political power is the national political community of plebeians: the people. More recent Marxist perspectives in Cuba have also refined this theory of el pueblo. For example, Roberto Zurbano (2015) has used the concept of "internal colonialism" to explain the relationship between socialism and racism and to illuminate the racialization of poverty in the interior of the nation and the necessity of promoting antiracist political agency by the people.

The Social Origins of the 11J Protests

Questioning the relevance of the concept of civil society to explain the context of the conflict is also based on the need to understand that the class-based essence of this situation goes beyond any explanation of the concept of civil society. A key component of the current situation is precarity (i.e., being in precarious living conditions), "the central sociological reality of post-Soviet Cuba" (Santiago Muiño 2021). The concept of precarity in Cuba is expressed in the use of the term *the struggle—la lucha*—a reference to the difficulty and complexity of daily activities. This struggle is not explicitly political, but rather an anthropological fact and set of conditions in which an immense mass of people without an official salary, or with insufficient income, must "invent" or "struggle" to acquire basic necessities by seeking outside income. Both those with salaried employment and those without are involved in this "struggle," as both groups experience degrees of precarity as they seek informal income to live on a day-to-day basis.

Instead of analyzing this day-to-day struggle as an anthropological example of survival strategies, the Cuban government sees it as evidence of the need for programs that "struggle against crime." In poor neighborhoods, the struggle against crime comes into conflict with strategies for survival, stigmatizing individuals who are, arguably, workers living in precarious conditions but labeling them as delinquents. It is not uncommon to hear the political opposition voiced on 11J in these neighborhoods, particularly against the police patrols launched as part of the "struggle against crime." Precarity in these communities has been reproduced in large part due to the shrinking of the Cuban state since the 1990s in terms of providing services and resources (Espina 2015). They have been discounted politically, left without internal political organization or formal institutional representation, and outside "civil society."

Another influence on the use of the term *civil society* in Cuba is its usage in the 1990s. At that time, civil society was primarily employed in liberal discourse that was critical of the Cuban state and often in opposition to it. Representatives of the Cuban state responded with such famous phrases that civil society was an example of "pasando gato por liebre" ("passing off a cat as a hare," i.e., a fraud) or a "Trojan horse of U.S. imperialism against the Cuban Revolution," among others. (For an early critical review of those positions, see Hernández 2002.)

Recent theoretical work also helps to explain official Cuban political reactions. For example, for institutionalists the state and the market are not distinct modes of organizing economic activity. Instead, they are mutually constituted spheres of activity (Block and Evans 2007). In this school of thought, the problem of development is critical for the theory of the state, and it is possible to construct synergies between the state, the economy, and civil society, without resorting to state "interference." From this perspective, the creation of independent small businesses in Cuba (the phenomenon of *cuentapropismo*) is an attempt to develop these synergies. These small businesses require independent organization and equal recognition by the state. It is a discourse of complementarity, not opposition, between civil society and the state (Fernández 2020).

In addition, new political vocabularies contradict the idea that civil society and the state must exist in opposition to one another. One example of this is the development of a new praxis of legal activism or legal mobilization, which has been used to address disputes after the approval of the constitution of 2019. The Law for the Protection of Constitutional Rights has been particularly significant, as it deals with the right to protest and to gather, along with the Law for Social Communication, dealing with film and communications (Pérez Martín 2021). This has been a new development in Cuban legal history, which had not emphasized these issues since the early 1960s. For decades, protections and guarantees flowed exclusively from the state, but it is now possible to challenge the state in domestic political disputes over rights. In this regard, there are the growing complaints to state institutions of illegitimate police behavior, for example, the complaints of the historian Alina B. López Hernández about harassing interviews by State Security officials and trans activist Mel Herrera's experience of threats and invasions of privacy.

This activism requires a degree of recognition by the state, which can also be understood as a subject of debate: it allows for possible areas of coordination/confrontation with the state that are different from those allowed in the 1990s, when this was especially viewed as an essentialist conflict between civil society and the state.

Another reason to question the use of the term *civil society* is the political intent for which it is used, according to which in Cuba there is a form of civil society without any agency, completely subordinated to the dictates of the state. Scholars have disagreed with the validity of this proposition. According to the art critic Iván de la Nuez (2021), "I do not know a better map of the landscape of Cuban diversity than contemporary art. It is a tradition that builds on four decades of incorporating all types of themes and problems of this place called Cuba." De la Nuez speaks of "a Cuba that becomes more Cuba-ist over time."

In this *increasingly Cuba-ist* Cuba, the depth of conflicts has increased. They have evolved to include women who take to the streets to display empty refrigerators, individuals who protest by squatting in unoccupied houses, transportation workers staging strikes, individuals painting protest slogans on the streets, and demonstrations in numerous locations around the country. Civil society has also been mobilized in ways that do not always come into conflict with the Cuban state, such as popular solidarity responses to the tornado that hit part of Havana in 2019, the organization of non-state workers to present demands to the Ministry of Labor and Social Security, and independent marches by the LGBTQIA+ community. Despite significant pressures, there have also been protests by students and teachers dissenting with Ministry of Higher Education policies, and many more actions of protest.

In 2019, three topics were taken up by the National Assembly of People's Power (Asamblea Nacional del Poder Popular [ANPP]) following a speech by the president: racism, cruelty against animals, and gender-based violence. These were "transcendent and extremely significant topics," according to the Cuban president, Miguel Díaz-Canel (2019). Legislative attention to these issues would not have been possible without the continuous, sustained efforts of feminist, antiracist, and animal welfare social militants. The Law against Gender-Based Violence presented in the National Assembly faced significant controversy in 2019 because it bore a resemblance to a proposal by the dissident Varela Project—despite conceptual differences.

El Pueblo and Social Movements

These domestic developments are evidence of a dynamic political sphere in Cuba, which is linked with global social movements. On a global scale, these social movements and identity-based demands on the state do not consistently align with the political axes of right and left. Rather they cross several interests and involve many different actors. The Cuban government appears unsure of how to address these heterogeneous influences or how to process these complex differences, declaring instead that all conflict can be reduced to "revolutionaries versus counterrevolutionaries."

To date, the Cuban state has responded to such conflict with a variety of approaches: stigmatization and exclusion, tokenism (making small concessions to minority groups to give the appearance that accusations of prejudice or discrimination are without merit), co-optation of certain topics, and the dismissal of their authors (denying the authors' origins and motivation). The Cuban state has also attempted to address social conflict by recognizing certain problems and making them the focus of specific state attention, as in the case of gender-based violence and racism. However, the practical efficacy of these efforts and the timelines for their execution are questionable.

Opponents of the Cuban state, in turn, also limit attention to social problems raised by civil society to a framework of "everything against the state." For example, in one 2017 colloquium of Afro-Cuban activists at Harvard University, certain dissident organizations whose work focuses on the issue of race were notably absent. The organizer of the colloquium, the historian Alejandro de la Fuente, explained that "their non-inclusion was a mutual decision, based on the groups' views that the struggle against racial discrimination was not their principal objective" (Gámez Torres 2017). Similar events unfolded in the debate over the Cuban Families Code in 2022. Certain opponents rejected the Families Code on the grounds that the "fundamental problem" was the recognition that the Cuban state was granting with the code rather than the rights and resources that would be made available to LGBTQIA+ Cubans under it.

New theoretical paradigms that are more reflective of the actual political context in Cuba can explain the complexity of relations between the Cuban state and civil society or el pueblo. For example, the sociologist Cecilia Bobes advocates using elements from classical and Latin American literature to describe and analyze recent social movements in their contentious negotiations with the state (Bobes 2021). Bobes observes that in a one-party political system where rights of association and assembly are limited, activists will have strong motivations to interact in non-conflictive ways with the state. Cooperation offers certain benefits: Activists obtain forums in which they can make their voices heard, promote their causes, and defend their positions in the public sphere. For its part, the state benefits from the collaboration on the international stage, where it can claim to collaborate with civil society and respond to international claims by offering participation in the political system (Bobes 2021).

However, this strategy can be tailored to co-opt and neutralize demands rather than to foster influence. This appears to be one reason for the rise of more independent activism, such as when Black feminists distance themselves from antiracist activism linked with the state. (This was also done by the collective of the journal *Afrocubanas* [2020].)

Everything Changes, Not Just Civil Society

It is not just civil society that has experienced and expressed changes. The Cuban government and state discourse have evolved as well. It is useful to identify some of these changes. In the days surrounding 11J, Miguel Díaz-Canel instructed Cubans to assume "battle formation"—a call for parastate groups to confront protestors in the streets. Following this order, for a brief time, the government then employed the language of conciliation and calls for solidarity, unity, and peace. Yet the following year, the official language changed again, celebrating the government's victory over an attempted "vandals' coup." This official discourse denied that there had been peaceful protests, as well as any legitimacy to the protesters' demands.

The debate over the 2019 constitution also employed new variations on older terms, particularly the word *republic*. It revived the term, which had last been widely used in 1960. The draft 2019 constitution reduced mentions of the term *communism*, which was more prominent in prior constitutions, but ultimately retained the term in the final text. However, around the 11J protests, Miguel Díaz-Canel issued a direct call to the "revolutionaries, and specifically the communists," to join in "combat." In this situation, we can observe that the Cuban state may be changing into "a Communist state, obligated to govern, represent, and satisfy the needs of a society that is already post-Communist" (De la Nuez 2021). That same Communist state has also been obliged to apply liberal reforms to its socialist system. As a result, the space given to market reforms nowadays is markedly different from what had been possible in Cuba in the 1960s.

Alongside the calls to combat, the Cuban state also promoted rhetoric that called revolutionaries to a sort of romantic love (the slogan "Give your heart to the struggle" is one example) and familial or domestic love (such as that between the president and his spouse that was frequently emphasized on social media, as a metaphor for the Cuban nation's love confronting anti-Cuban hate). This rhetoric played a more limited role in official statements, which indicates the efforts to experiment and innovate.

The Law, Civil Society, and Social Protest

Another aspect of the civil society question is the issue of how political performance is regulated in the Cuban constitution and legal code. The formal right to protest is moderated by a demand that the protestors respect the constitutional order. There are similar phrasings of this right and its limitations in other parts of the legal code as well. This is particularly restrictive because in Cuba the "constitutional order" is synonymous with the "socialist political order." As a result, one specific political ideology becomes the basis for limiting the exercise of constitutional rights. The question over the legitimate right to protest should be merged with criticism of the presence of political discrimination in practice based on the constitutional order and norms. Within the legal code, progressive language like that included in the constitution of 2019 is diluted further. For example, the new Penal Code includes provisions to discourage social protest. The minimum penalty for sedition was increased to three years and the maximum to thirty, and other penalties include life sentences and the death penalty.

The concept of civil society, or el pueblo, as I have referred to it in this chapter, does not specifically deal with what is sometimes called the "law of the excluded": the legal defense of persons who, through political exclusion and social disadvantage, have their condition reinforced by the violence of poverty and a lack of political representation *through the law itself.* As a result, these individuals' victimization is multiplied, and they face legal sanction for protesting the conditions of poverty.

The Crisis of Paternalism and Future Avenues for Change

The current crisis in Cuba is based on several previous and parallel crises: there is an economic crisis, a demographic crisis, a crisis of caregiving, the pandemic crisis, and several international crises (which come with increasingly shorter periods). Each compounds the other, and is then compounded by the ongoing, immoral, and illegal US policies of aggression against Cuba. There is also a crisis of future prospects—a clear driving force for migration. Confidence in the availability of political spaces and political institutions is likewise in crisis, and all of this in the midst of difficult socio-economic conditions. And this despite several institutional successes, such as Cuba's domestic production and distribution of COVID-19 vaccines.

A further crisis is that of hegemony, or a "crisis of paternalism" that has evolved in recent decades. In the 1980s, it was common to couch criticism of conditions in Cuba by claiming that the criticism in fact supported the Revolution, and expressions such as "the Revolution cannot permit this problem" or "I demand this change in the name of the Revolution, because I am loyal to Fidel [Castro] and a revolutionary" were used. In these statements, "the Revolution" has been a normative mechanism, used to express demands. This is a pattern observed in certain other countries. Alan Knight (2005, 116) observed that "when revolutions cease to fulfill their promises and procla-mations, their official platforms provide a canon from which one can make judgments and appeal for change, in the name of causes such as human rights, land and liberty, or socialist precepts."

This normative mechanism has broken down since the 1990s and now appears to be permanently ruptured. It is based on a crisis in the "paternal" authority of the state. The state can no longer claim that loyalty, a situation that makes the political scenario much more complex. Growing sectors of society no longer recognize that of-ficial discourse, nor do they recognize its authority—because all forms of paternalism are always based upon an authoritarian model. Moreover, many demands have been framed outside claims of "being inspired by the Revolution."

Seeking to recultivate legitimacy based on the performance of state institutions and efforts at political inclusion that it generates may be the most promising avenue for change and a resolution to the crisis of paternalism. However, it remains to be seen if the Cuban state understands, wants to take, and can successfully pursue this avenue for change. Another key question is whether future developments will push the balance between civil society and the state toward a path of cooperation or toward disruptive antagonism.

References

Afrocubanas Equipo de Redacción. 2020. *Afrocubanas: La Revista*, accessed at https://afrocubanas. com.

Block, Fred, and Peter Evans. 2007. "El Estado y la economía." In *Instituciones y desarrollo en la era de la globalización neoliberal.* Bogotá: Colección En Clave de Sur. 1st Edition: ILSA.

Bobes, Velia Cecilia. 2021. "De los discursos de identidad al activismo social: los movimien-tos sociales en la coyuntura de la nueva constitución cubana." *Revista Brasileira de Ciência Política*, no. 34, e240521: 1–48.

De la Nuez, Iván. 2021. "La gran innovación del socialismo solo puede estar en compaginar la justicia social con una democracia plena de respeto al distinto." Interview with Julio César Guanche and Harold Bertot. *OnCuba News*, September 10. Accessed at https://oncubanews

.com/voces-cubanas/voces-cubanas-la-gran-innovacion-del-socialismo-solo-puede-estar-en-compaginar-la-justicia-social-con-una-democracia-plena-de-respeto-al-distinto.

Díaz-Canel Bermúdez, Miguel. 2019. "Díaz-Canel en la Asamblea Nacional: ¡Unidos hemos vencido! ¡Unidos venceremos!" Cubadebate, December 21. Accessed at http://www.cubadebate.cu/opinion/2019/12/21/diaz-canel-en-la-asamblea-nacional-unidos-hemos-vencido-unidos-venceremos.

Dussel, Enrique. 2006. *20 Tesis de política*. Madrid: Siglo XXI de España Editores.

Espina, Mayra. 2015. "Desigualdades en la Cuba actual. Causas y remedios." In *Presencia negra en la cultura cubana*, ed. Denia Garcia Ronda. Havana: Ediciones Sensemayá.

Fernández, Oscar. 2020. "¿Neoliberalismo en la Conceptualización?" Rebelión, May 23. Accessed at https://rebelion.org/neoliberalismo-en-la-conceptualizacion/?fbclid=IwAR2nFciD6iLtnuoTnUwvvuelnUQvsWNoZ16IlU6cJcmXBl84uXVtbQ9-4yo.

Gámez Torres, Nora. 2017. "El Movimiento Afrocubano se discute en la Universidad de Harvard." *El Nuevo Herald* 17, no. 4. Accessed at https://www.elnuevoherald.com/noticias/america-latina/cuba-es/article144816059.html.

Hernández, Rafael. 2002. *Mirar a Cuba. Ensayos sobre cultura y sociedad civil*. México: Fondo de Cultura.

Knight, Alan. 2005. *Revolución, democracia y populismo en América latina*. Santiago: Centro de Estudios Bicentenario.

Pérez Martín, Amalia. 2021. "La Movilización Colectiva (del Derecho y los derechos) en Cuba." Sinpermiso, February 1. Accessed at https://www.sinpermiso.info/textos/la-movilizacion-colectiva-del-derecho-y-los-derechos-en-cuba.

Pérez Varona, Wilder. 2021. "Unas palabras sobre la Cuba de los humildes." CTXT: Contexto y acción, July 14. Accessed at https://ctxt.es/es/20210701/Firmas/36651/cuba-protestas-bloqueo-eeuu-castro-wilder-perez-varona-la-cosa.htm.

Santiago Muiño, Emilio. 2021. "El estallido social cubano. Motivaciones inmediatas (I)." CTXT: Contexto y acción, July 21. Accessed at https://ctxt.es/es/20210701/Politica/36701/cuba-protestas-dualidad-monetaria-covid.htm.

Zurbano Torres, Roberto. 2015. "Racismo vs. socialismo en Cuba: un conflicto fuera de lugar (apuntes sobre/contra el colonialismo interno)." In *MERIDIONAL: Revista Chilena de Estudios Latinoamericanos*, no. 4 (April): 11–40. Accessed at https://meridional.uchile.cl/index.php/MRD/article/view/36529.

CHAPTER 4

July 11 Is Still Present in Cuba

Ailynn Torres Santana

Translated by Erin Goodman

In many ways, it continued to be July 2021 in Cuba long after the protests ended. The causes of the social protests that took place on July 11, 2021, remained relevant, as economic and social reproduction crises persisted and worsened. The political scene continued to transform swiftly.

Analyzing the economic and sociopolitical arenas, as well as their interrelation, allows for an assessment of the Cuban situation not limited to the current moment. This is essential for a more comprehensive perspective on contemporary Cuba and to understand how the shorter-term political situation, which is usually invoked to explain the protests, has been conflated with a longer cycle, which encompasses the cleavages of today's myriad concurrent crises.

What follows are some essential elements for understanding the economic adjustment process of recent years and its social consequences, which serves as a partial explanation for the protests that took place in July 2021 (11J) and what unfolded thereafter. Then, I suggest keys for analyzing the 11J political ecosystem, which continues to evolve.

Between Economic Adjustment and the US Blockade: The Cuban People and Their Social Reproduction Crises

Cuba's persistent and dire structural economic crisis has had suffocating reproductive consequences. The beginning of that crisis dates to the 1990s, although its root causes can be traced back further.[1] The last major mitigating program began in 2011, with the approval—under the administration of Raúl Castro—of the official reforms roadmap, the "Guidelines for the Economic and Social Policies of the Party and the Revolution." In terms of social justice, the Guidelines began to institutionalize an ongoing process: reducing the state's participation in ensuring the well-being of the citizenry, consequently putting greater responsibility on families to get by and increasing market dependence (Torres 2020).

The 11J protests were a reaction against these changes and the evident failure of the economic reforms over the previous decade; the escalation of scarcity, inequality, and impoverishment; the tension between the successive official declarations that no one would be left unprotected; and the reality of an increasingly precarious situation. The protesting voices called for an effective state response to the lack of food, medicine, and electricity.

The acute social consequences of the global COVID-19 pandemic and its impact in Cuba, together with a new phase of the government's currency reunification process (*Tarea Ordenamiento* [TO])—the implementation of which began in January 2021— helped catalyze 11J. The TO included, among other measures, the partial dollarization of domestic economies through the expansion of the sale of consumer goods in foreign currencies, which was initially limited to luxury goods but soon became the primary or only means of obtaining necessities. Especially for families that depend exclusively on state salaries or pensions, this made it even more difficult to cover the basic basket.

The situation was also aggravated by the narrowing of remittance channels from the United States to Cuba (Delgado 2021). This was part of the US policy to asphyxiate the country, which resulted, on the one hand, in the economic, commercial, and financial blockade against the island and, on the other, in a systematic policy of regime change. The reduction in remittances was also influenced by the decrease in travelers in the context of the global pandemic, which limited the hand-to-hand channel for sending remittances.

In December 2021, the then-minister of economy said at the National Assembly session that the TO had not turned out as planned (*OnCuba News* 2021). This was not news—the July protests had already confirmed it months before.

Economic analyses (Catalejo 2022a, 2022b; Carmona and Izquierdo 2022) have highlighted at least four main problems of the Cuban economy: external debt, a distorted investment structure, serious problems in agricultural policy, and very high inflation—in 2021 the Economist Intelligence Unit registered inflation of 740 percent, and Vidal and Everleny (2022a) calculated it at 500 percent for that same year.

The investment structure is the most-cited problem. For years, investment in hotel infrastructure has been disproportionately high vis-à-vis the real demand for tourism. Since 2016, the hotel occupancy rate has only gone down. Even at its peak in recent years, only about 60 percent of available rooms were occupied. However, public investment in the sector has continued to be high, and the construction of five-star hotels has increased. In 2022, the national economic plan projected the completion of 4,607 new hotel rooms, and 24 percent of the country's total investment was dedicated to tourism (Triana 2022).

A 2020 ranking of Latin American hotel chains placed the Gaviota Tourism Group in second place in hotel capacity in the region. Cuba also took the fifth-place spot, held by Cubanacán (*Reportur* 2020). Gaviota is part of Grupo de Administración Empresarial S.A. (GAESA), a military consortium that includes important and growing business actors related to the tourism and real estate sectors and to imports and exports, among others. The lack of transparency and data on GAESA's operations further obscures real estate and tourism investments, which is not justified by the actual dynamics nor by economic sector projections for the country.

Meanwhile, agriculture has not been a priority for state investment and its performance is precarious. In December 2020, shortly before 11J, new measures were announced with the objective of increasing national food production (Alonso et al. 2020), but they have not been successful (Vidal and Everleny 2022b). On the contrary, incompetent public management of agricultural policy has continued with disastrous social consequences, alongside the trade restrictions imposed by the United States on the Cuban government.

Therefore, to take advantage of the universal social policies that do still exist, people must increasingly depend on family income, which has also been affected by a reduction in subsidies and increases in the costs of public services such as electricity and water and the general cost of living. For more than a decade, Cuba has experienced a deterioration in social policies, decreased social spending in proportion to the state budget and GDP, fewer social assistance beneficiaries, a decrease in real wages, and the heterogeneity of labor markets, presumably with an increase in informal work (and non-salary income) and real unemployment (Zavala and Echevarría 2020; Torres 2021).

These inequalities were not reflected in the COVID-19 vaccination rates, which were very high and were achieved with a proprietary vaccine created by Cuban scientists. However, inequalities were amplified across different groups by the social consequences of the pandemic and the preexisting crises in Cuban society.[2] The socio-territorial composition of the protests revealed a clear class marker: the notable presence of popular, racialized, precarious neighborhoods and social sectors.

11J influenced some of the narrative about inequalities and impoverishment, without transcending the official jargon that speaks of vulnerabilities rather than poverty. Shortly after the protests, the government announced that it would resume a social plan to improve living conditions in popular neighborhoods. Along the same lines, the official press reported that social plans initiated by Fidel Castro in the early 2000s would be resumed. At the end of 2022, it was announced that "inequality and social vulnerability" would be "Cuba's priorities in 2023" (Cubadebate 2022a). The scope of these programs seemed to be limited, however.

The vast negative consequences of the US blockade against Cuba can be further specified. Vidal (2022) evaluated the sensitivity of the historical series of Cuban GDP growth and other indicators with respect to changes (flexibility/tightening) in US sanctions over the last three decades. His analysis concluded that tightening sanctions does not seem to have significant impacts on the state economy,[3] but rather on household consumption and the dynamics of sales and employment in the private sector. It could be that faced with the intensification of the blockade, the Cuban state has put more of the public budget into play as a cushioning effect for its economy and Cuban society. Yet recently, and for various domestic and international reasons, the buffer capacity is highly limited. In conclusion, the US government blockade against Cuba affects families and the private sector in increasingly cruel and direct ways—precisely the people who, in the US political rhetoric, it wishes to "save."

The crises, with their myriad causes, have continued to take shape and become more complex from July 2021 to the present.

The Political Uprising

11J cannot be explained only by the economic and social reproduction crises. The protests also were a reaction against the political situation. Demonstrators demanded political and civil rights. They shouted "*libertad*" (freedom) and showed a loss of confidence in the so-called established channels and party/government/state discourses, policies, and actors. Given these demands and the way in which they were expressed, important changes are visible in the protest repertoires of the citizenry. A few examples follow.

BODIES IN THE STREET

Occupying the streets as a form of protest is much more frequent in Cuba's recent history. However, 11J did not forge that path. Previously, there was news of women in the streets displaying their empty refrigerators and of young people, intellectuals, and artists doing a sit-in outside the Ministry of Culture to demand freedom of creation and expression and democratic solutions to the events in San Isidro (especially the arrest of members of the San Isidro Movement who were on a hunger strike protesting police harassment). Other young people who were more supportive of the government called for a sit-in in response to the previous one, which received government support. There was a march and a sit-in outside the Ministry of Agriculture to demand regulations that would ensure animal welfare, a self-convened LGBTIQ+ march, and public acts by religious neoconservative sectors against the preliminary draft of the constitution that included a provision legalizing same-sex marriage.

That repertoire, then, was already established. But 11J expanded the number of participants and territories where it was used simultaneously. After July 2021, the occupation of public space became a permanent, latent possibility and those in power constantly sound the alarm and have increased surveillance. Subsequent episodes included collective protests in various locations around the country unleashed by a complete power outage after Hurricane Ian in 2022, and periodic outages through most of the year. Meanwhile, sectors that are more aligned with the government also may occupy public spaces, and official channels advertise this as evidence of its possibility.

More than before, today the streets are a disputed terrain in which diverse actors aspire to display their dissent.

POLITICS AND THE LAW

Another recent change is related to regulations. In 1987, a survey carried out in twelve provinces reported that two-thirds of those surveyed were unaware that the constitution of the republic was the most important legal document and reference point in the country. Thirty years later, Guanche and Fernández (2016) stated that, although no public information was available to substantiate their claim, the situation likely remained at least the same as back then.

The constitutional changes of 2018–2019 transformed that landscape. There was extensive citizen involvement in the popular consultation of the preliminary draft of the constitution. The appeal to the constitution and the laws has become common in the political behavior of individuals and groups, who now show a clear interest in written regulations as a source of law, whether they use it to show dissent or support for the government or regarding particular events.

The government has increasingly used criminal law to manage social conflicts, and regulations have been created or modified to that end. For example, Decree Law 349 was approved in 2018, formalizing censorship in the artistic and cultural sector; and in 2019, Decree Law 370 was created, extending the possibilities of censorship to the rest of the citizenry (an unknown number of people have been fined on that basis).

The 11J protests appear to have increased possibilities of censorship. After 11J, Decree Law 35 was approved, which sanctions the possibility of fines and imprisonment for sharing content considered to be against state security on social networks, without defining what that entails. It thus allows for discretionary interpretations to potentially penalize, on a legal basis, dissent against the government (García 2021b).

All of this is part of a process of major regulatory change: the new constitution led to the approval of a timetable for the creation or modification of 107 laws and decree laws that has not yet been fully complied with. In terms of rights, this process has been uneven. For example, a Families Code was approved in a referendum that is strong on rights (Torres and Guanche 2022), while the National Assembly of People's Power approved a punitive criminal code that maintains problematic criminal legal charges such as sedition and contempt, increases the penalty ranges of "deprivation of liberty" for the crime of sedition, and classifies as crimes "other acts against State Security" without a clear framework of what that implies.

Cuban politics are played out in the very important realm of regulations, including as pertains to the 11J protests.

POLITICAL CRIMES: FROM 11J ONWARD

The government initially described the 11J protests as riots and/or US-backed counterrevolutionary destabilization. Later, the president recognized some legitimacy in the uprising, attributing it to the crises the country was undergoing. That stance was short-lived. The language used to describe the events as vandalism intensified, and the president celebrated the anniversary of 11J as a "dismantling of a vandal coup" (Prensa Latina 2022). Hundreds of people remain incarcerated and/or under judicial process.

For more than six months no specific official information was disseminated regarding those arrested. In January 2022, the attorney general's office published a report on the trials, describing the protests as "serious events . . . that undermined the constitutional order and stability of our socialist State." It was reported that "790 people were charged with acts of vandalism, which attacked authorities, people, and property, as well as serious disturbances of order"; 69 percent of them were provisionally detained as precautionary measures (Cubadebate 2022b).

The official press reported about forty violent acts, which did indeed occur. The overwhelming majority targeted the aforementioned foreign currency stores, as well as police stations and patrol cars. Analyses at the time drew attention to the sociological and class markers of these acts: How much did the political rage and violence during the protests target the objects, spaces, and actors identified as responsible for the hardships of daily survival of the working class (García 2021a)? What does it mean that the attacks against those businesses spread after the president's first political address issuing a "combat order" to revolutionaries (Hernández 2021)?

The imprisonment and/or trial of minors younger than eighteen years of age and the status as political prisoners of those who were being tried are two key issues. The president and the minister of foreign affairs had stated that there were no political prisoners nor incarcerated minors in the country. In its report, the prosecutor's office reported fifty-five accused persons between sixteen and eighteen years of age. According to the penal code then in force, they were not considered minors, although international standards to which Cuba is a signatory establish that the age of majority is reached at eighteen years.

The prosecutor's office did not refer to the political nature of the imprisonments, but the report recognized sedition among the charges. Until then, official communications had only mentioned common offenses—public disorder, attacks, resistance, contempt, and disobedience—whereas sedition can be considered a political crime (Guanche 2022). Sentences given for sedition reached their legal limit for imprisonment, twenty years.

All in all, the nature and scope of what authorities define as political crimes was activated and amplified by 11J.

Outside the Law and the Externalization of the Conflict

The processing of the conflicts that were both causes and consequences of 11J was not limited to criminal proceedings. There were also extensive interrogations by State Security, de facto temporary arrests or house arrests without criminal proceedings to justify them, videos broadcast on national television that were filmed without consent, and illegal access to the personal information and networks of those being denounced. None of this was new, but 11J made it even more visible, extending to disparate actors and sectors in terms of ideologies and political projections.

Another issue has been the clear strategy to externalize the conflict via the migration of actors considered politically inconvenient. There is a record of people who were detained under judicial processes and who were officially taken to the airport to leave the country, and others who have been prohibited from reentering the island for strictly political reasons. This is taking place within a general migratory crisis, though it does not correspond to it specifically.

So What Defines the Political Field?

The narrative of polarization has been used to explain the Cuban political arena, now more than before. Some speak of a continuous closure of spaces for dialogue and affirm that the country is more divided today. Others affirm that the possibilities for dialogue have been revitalized, citing meetings the president had with different social sectors after 11J, the creation of officially coordinated working groups, and so on. Both lines of discourse assume that political polarization exists.

That is not the only framework to explain what is happening in Cuba. An alternative is that the thought trends and political options in the country have diversified and become more complex since 11J. The protests did not have a predominant or clear ideological imprint. Rather they revealed Cuban society in its contemporary complexity.

Today, the anticommunist and anti-leftist narrative in Cuba is clearly gaining ground, in very similar ways as it is in the rest of the region and the world. There are also political voices that present themselves as de-ideologized, unmarked by any left-right or other distinction. There is the traditional opposition, proudly on the right in their statements and practices. At the same time, there is an evident diversification of the left, and myriad actors dispute that the government has exclusive legitimacy over that classifier and of socialism itself. Not all of these sectors participated in the protests. In fact, later there was a systematic effort to capture the protests' spirit and acts and attribute them to different agendas and programs. However, there certainly was a clear alignment of popular demands for rights and guarantees, which translated into an amorphous, headless collective performative act, which achieved little—albeit not zero—institutional capacity afterward.

11J did not emerge from a prior organized political plot nor did it generate one, at least not to an important extent, but it was a watershed in Cuban politics and society—not because it was a social explosion, but because it exposed a society that had already exploded in different ways before. 11J also repositioned Cuba in the Latin American conversation about social protests.

Despite all that, the framework of a polarized society explains little of the political situation that 11J brought to the fore nor its consequences. It may be more fruitful to think of a hyperpoliticization of social practices and responses, which do not fit into the oft-invoked dichotomous classification and reclassification of "revolutionaries" versus "counterrevolutionaries," or "communists" versus "dissidents," according to the interests at stake. The Cuban society of 11J brought forth much more complex challenges about what constitutes a good and fair life.

Notes

1. For a systematic analysis of interpretive frameworks and crisis periodization beginning in the 1990s, which may also be important for understanding crises in their current cleavages, see González (2022).

2. For a gender analysis that assesses consequences for women, see Maqueira and Torres (2021).

3. Understood as government consumption within total aggregate demand (GDP on the spending side), the real value of total fiscal spending in the state budget and gross fixed capital formation (dominated by investments by state companies and mixed capital companies with foreign investors).

References

Alonso, R., et al. 2020. "¿Cómo marcha la implementación de la Estrategia Económica y Social de Cuba?" Cubadebate, December 3. Accessed at http://www.cubadebate.cu/noticias/2020 /12/03/como-marcha-la-implementacion-de-la-estrategia-economica-y-social-de-cuba.

Carmona, E., and L. Izquierdo. 2022. "Las propuestas de tres economistas para controlar la inflación en Cuba." *Tribuna de la Habana*, February 4. Accessed at http://tribuna.cu/cuba /2022-02-04/las-propuestas-de-tres-economistas-para-controlar-la-inflacion-en-cuba?plat- form=hootsuite.

Catalejo. 2022a. "¿Cuáles son los principales nudos que Cuba tiene que enfrentar en 2022? (1 parte)." *Temas*, January 7. Accessed at http://temas.cult.cu/la-letra-de-temas-2022-cuales-son -los-principales-nudos-que-cuba-tiene-que-enfrentar-en-2022/?fbclid=IwAR2KMh4uGxfPK H7fVxwzUudT3Bp_fpZKIkwqt1epkTICfZLEkBxkjl33lJw.

———. 2022b. "¿Cuáles son los principales nudos que Cuba tiene que enfrentar en 2022? (2 parte)." *Temas*, January 7. Accessed at http://temas.cult.cu/cuales-son-los-principales-nudos -que-cuba-tiene-que-enfrentar-en-2022-segunda-ronda/?fbclid=IwAR0oEmchQzh081qy -rIONivMiC2217iIUZ3Hix-wpe8GIKcItKp8uulpq3k.

Cubadebate. 2022a. "Desigualdad y vulnerabilidad social, prioridades de Cuba en 2023." December 25. Accessed at http://www.cubadebate.cu/noticias/2022/12/25/desigualdad -y-vulnerabilidad-social-prioridades-de-cuba-en-2023/#:~:text=Desigualdad%20y%20 vulnerabilidad%20social%2C%20prioridades%20de%20Cuba%20en%202023,-En%20 este%20art%C3%ADculo&text=Foto%3A%20Archivo.,de%20acuerdo%20con%20las %20autoridades.

———. 2022b. "Fiscalía General de la República informa sobre estado de los procesos penales derivados de los disturbios provocados el 11 de julio de 2021." January 25. Accessed at http://www.cubadebate.cu/noticias/2022/01/25/fiscalia-general-de- la-republica-informa-sobre-estado-de-los-procesos-penales-derivados-de-los-disturbios- provocados-el-11-de-julio-de-2021/?fbclid=IwAR2-HSIcnB9KiLbqcnUT9So0aH4 QN4Ekny6eh8S3_7W0pRmbXL005d1_Uik.

Delgado, D. 2021. "Políticas restrictivas de Estados Unidos sobre las remesas cubanas: efectos sobre las familias y el emergente sector privado." *OnCuba News*, January 25. Accessed at https://oncubanews.com/cuba-ee-uu/politicas-restrictivas-de-estados-unidos-sobre-las -remesas-cubanas-efectos-sobre-las-familias-y-el-emergente-sector-privado.

García, C. 2021a. "¿Cómo le explico a mi abuela que no son delincuentes?" *OnCuba News*, July 15. Accessed at https://oncubanews.com/cuba/como-le-explico-a-mi-abuela-que-no-son -delincuentes.

———. 2021b. "Información, Internet, Derechos. Para leer el Decreto Ley 35." *OnCuba News*, September 14. Accessed at https://oncubanews.com/opinion/informacion-internet -derechos-para-leer-el-decreto-ley-35.

González, A. 2022. *Período Especial en Cuba. Estudios entrecruzados de la crisis.* México DF: UNAM.

Guanche, J. C. 2022. "El problema de la sedición." *OnCuba News*, February 1. Accessed at https://oncubanews.com/opinion/columnas/la-vida-de-nosotros/el-problema-de-la-sedicion/?fbclid=IwAR2DRGUrUPugIdAhqEGvKsDlmarn338YCgw2eZ0qPAW16q4tQ7exSX87Srg.

Guanche, J. C., and J. A. Fernández. 2016. "Se acta pero . . . se cumple. Constitución, República y socialismo en Cuba." In J. C. Guanche, *La verdad no se ensaya*, 2nd ed. Havana: Editorial Caminos.

Hernández, R. 2021. "Conflicto, consenso, crisis. Tres notas mínimas sobre las protestas." *OnCuba News*, July 21. Accessed at https://oncubanews.com/opinion/columnas/con-todas-sus-letras/conflicto-consenso-crisis-tres-notas-minimas-sobre-las-protestas.

Maqueira, A., and A. Torres. 2021. "Cuba in the Time of COVID-19: Untangling Gendered Consequences." *Agenda* 35, no. 4: 117–28.

OnCuba News. 2021. "Cuba: primer ministro reconoce 'problemas' del ordenamiento monetario y anuncia próximas medidas." December 14. Accessed at https://oncubanews.com/cuba/cuba-primer-ministro-reconoce-problemas-del-ordenamiento-monetario-y-anuncia-proximas-medidas.

Prensa Latina. 2022. "Díaz-Canel calificó a la cultura como espada y escudo de la nación." July 8. Accessed at https://www.prensa-latina.cu/2022/07/08/diaz-canel-califico-a-la-cultura-como-espada-y-escudo-de-la-nacion.

Reportur. 2020. "'Top 15' REPORTUR: Ranking de cadenas hoteleras latinoamericanas." July 29. Accessed at https://www.reportur.com/mexico/2020/07/29/top-15-reportur-ranking-cadenas-hoteleras-latinoamericanas.

Torres, A. 2020. "Regímenes de bienestar en Cuba: Mujeres y desigualdades." *Cuban Studies* 49: 6–31.

———. 2021. "Poverty and (un)Protection in the Cuban 'Conjuncture.'" *Cuban Studies Group* (blog), August 10. Accessed at http://cubastudygroup.org/blog_posts/poverty-and-unprotection-in-the-cuban-conjuncture.

Torres, A., and J. C. Guanche. 2022. "Cuba's New Family Code Is a Window into the Political Ecosystem." NACLA, November 11. Accessed at https://nacla.org/cubas-new-family-code-window-political-ecosystem.

Triana, J. 2022. "Más hoteles ¿más turistas?" *OnCuba News*, February 21. Accessed at https://oncubanews.com/opinion/columnas/contrapesos/mas-hoteles-mas-turistas/?fbclid=IwAR2plzvaJDO0K7_O4oO4Xv6Py3nEaZXhkAKn-jV0dhkQNrZABuyDHjRtYzk.

Vidal, P. 2022. "El impacto económico de las sanciones estadounidense a Cuba, 1994–2020." Real Instituto El Cano, February 7. Accessed at https://www.realinstitutoelcano.org/documento-de-trabajo/el-impacto-economico-de-las-sanciones-estadounidense-a-cuba-1994-2020/?fbclid=IwAR04omVLK8KxukA3wsIyQLG2naaFYc-OAqFfh5926jU7_TiercofJh9ribk.

Vidal, P., and O. Everleny. 2022a. "De qué depende la inflación y la recuperación de la economía (parte 1)." Cuba Capacity Building Project, Columbia Law School, February 3. Accessed at https://horizontecubano.law.columbia.edu/news/de-que-depende-la-inflacion-y-la-recuperacion-de-la-economia-cubana-parte-i.

———. 2022b. "De qué depende la inflación y la recuperación de la economía (parte 2)." Cuba Capacity Building Project, Columbia Law School, February 3. Accessed at https://horizontecubano.law.columbia.edu/news/de-que-depende-la-inflacion-y-la-recuperacion-de-la-economia-cubana-parte-ii.

Zabala, M. C., and D. Echevarría. 2020. "Las políticas sociales para la Cuba del 2030: elementos para su diseño e implementación." *Economía y Desarrollo* 164, no. 2.

CHAPTER 5

11J, "Patria y Vida," and the (Not So) New Cuban Culture Wars

Michael J. Bustamante

I can't be certain, but it was likely one of the first Cuban "viral" videos. The year was 2009, and huddled in the lobby of Havana's Hotel Nacional, Colombian pop star Juanes can be seen conferring with other headliners of his "Paz Sin Fronteras" concert, set to begin that morning at the Plaza de la Revolución. Fuming over Cuban authorities' attempt to reserve front-row seats for politically loyal students, the artists threaten to cancel the event. Yotuel Romero, member of the Cuban hip-hop super-group Orishas, then urges his fellow performers to not let "them" win and press on with the show (ABC 2009).

Revisited in the aftermath of mass protests in Cuba in July 2021, this moment of tension more than a decade ago appears quaint, but it also carries the weight of fore-shadowing. More recently, Romero has played much more than a side part in a secretly filmed argument. As cowriter of the viral anti-Cuban-government anthem "Patria y Vida," his voice provided the soundtrack and slogan for the largest outburst of popular discontent in Cuba in decades (Romero et al. 2021).

But looking back from a Miami still awash in "Patria y Vida" banners, it is impossible to ignore several ironies. For one, Romero and other participants in the 2009 concert were panned widely at the time for performing in Cuba at all (Miller 2009). South Florida critics deemed "Paz Sin Fronteras" an act of legitimation for the political system that Romero now opposes and that even then he hinted needed to change (RTVE 2009).

Another irony relates to the United States. Because Juanes's Miami-based production team required US government permission to pull off a concert on the island, "Paz Sin Fronteras" represented an opening salvo in a move toward US engagement with Cuba under the Obama administration. Yotuel Romero publicly, if gingerly, encouraged that move when Obama took office (ANDINA 2009). Seven years later, Romero even attended events organized by the president's historic delegation to Havana in 2016 (Herrero 2021). But by 2021, "Patria y Vida" was not only an anthem of protest in Cuba, it also became the clarion call of a diaspora (or much of it) that appeared to have moved on—momentarily? permanently?—from increasing support for bilateral rapprochement over the previous decade (Grenier and Lai 2020).

As the community went, so went other Cuban performers featured on the song. Just a few years ago, Gente de Zona and Descemer Bueno were churning out the reguetón-lite that became the soundtrack to US-Cuba normalization. Their transnational careers provided financially lucrative evidence of a breaking down of previous borders and the Cuban *gozadera* (or "enjoyment," the title of a 2015 smash hit) newly accessible to American visitors after the two governments announced a diplomatic breakthrough late in 2014. At the time, of course, these artists periodically took heat outside the island. In 2017, for example, Miami's then-mayor rescinded Gente de Zona's previously awarded keys to the city because they appeared on stage in Cuba with the grandson of Raúl Castro. For this reason, to see the group go from being censored from a Miami stage in 2019 (curiously in the name of democracy) to performing at a "Free Cuba Fest" under a year later—complete with a Trumpian "Make Cuba Great Again" banner—was enough to produce whiplash (Pentón and Moreno 2019; *Diario de Cuba* 2020).

What explains these dramatic shifts? And how did popular culture become such a prominent vector of the intensifying conflict between the Cuban state and portions of Cuban society after 2019, contributing to and culminating in the mass protests of July 11, 2021? Was commercial/political opportunism and a US-backed disinformation campaign to blame, as Cuban state media alleged (Falcón 2021)? Or did the Cuban authorities' own missteps lead them to lose the pulse of the island's crisis—and (at the time) pandemic-stressed streets?

To begin answering these questions, this essay reflects critically on the message of "Patria y Vida," why it caught on, and some of the contradictions surrounding its reception and circulation. It argues that the recent Cuban "culture wars" in which the song played a starring role are hardly new or mere distractions without consequences. Not only did "Patria y Vida" spawn imitations in Miami, but also in the wake of July 11, Cuban musicians once considered luminaries of socialist culture (e.g., Carlos Varela, Pablo Milanés, even Los Van Van) joined a wider cast of artists strongly criticizing the state's repressive response (Chirino 2021; *Rialta* 2021). This ferment reflects a powerful albeit decentralized political awakening on and off the island since Miguel Díaz-Canel became Cuba's head of state, especially among a generation to come of age after the 1990s. All told, Cuban authorities have not faced such a challenge to their political and discursive authority in decades. And they still have not recovered, even as the memory of the protests risks fading.

Culture Wars Have Always Mattered

The year 2021 was certainly not the first time that culture provided a flashpoint in Cuban life. Culture is not just "superstructure," after all; it is serious business. For that reason, I use the phrase *culture wars* warily, as in US usage it tends to be uttered with scorn, as if to describe superficial matters diverting attention from "real" issues.

That has never been true, not in the United States and not in Cuba. Look no further than March 1959, when the early revolutionary government founded the Cuban Institute for Cinematic Art and Industry (ICAIC), not even three months after the *barbudos* took power. This act presaged the eventual nationalization of all movie production, radio stations, television stations, and, most importantly, outlets of the printed press by the end of 1960. Insurgent leaders quickly recognized the power of art, song, film, or the printed word to shape narratives and identities—in this case, a conception of the Revolution as long-awaited deliverance from a history of national ills.

For that reason, the history of the Cuban Revolution is full of cultural battles. And as the effects of the Revolution spurred outmigration, these battles quickly assumed transnational dimensions. Island-based artists often rejected, or ignored, the content and politics of exile cultural production, while Cuban expatriate culture workers offered counternarratives to those amplified by, and through, the culture industries of the Cuban socialist state. For this reason, as a largely diaspora-created text, it was not a surprise to see "Patria y Vida" generate a rejoinder from Havana—Raúl Torres's decidedly less catchy "Patria o Muerte por la Vida"—thus joining a long tradition of politicized call and response (Torres et al. 2021). Thirty years before, for example, Miami artist Willy Chirino had hopefully predicted that "our day is coming" against the backdrop of Cuba's Special Period, while Silvio Rodríguez promised listeners he would "die as [he] lived"—that is, as a loyal socialist (Chirino 1991; Rodríguez 1992).

"Patria y Vida," *Ahora*

So if Cuba's song wars are not so new, what made "Patria y Vida" different? Past examples from the Special Period are relevant because Cuba's economic crisis since 2019—its worst since the 1990s—has generated intense popular frustration that Cuban fans channeled into their listening of the lyrics in early 2021 and then took to the streets on July 11. That crisis was aggravated, even partially precipitated, by Trump-era sanctions, which the incoming Biden administration in 2021 did not immediately change. But it was not reducible to them either. Indeed, for all that one can make a convincing argument that the United States bears significant responsibility for Cubans' current economic hardships (not even providing sanctions relief at the height of a global pandemic), more and more young Cuban citizens in recent years appeared no longer convinced or no longer seemed to care. Their *own* government's questionable decisions—a calamitous currency unification process, the expanding redollarization of the economy through *moneda libremente convertible* (MLC) stores, ongoing investments in hotel construction as Cuba's healthcare infrastructure suffered under stresses related to COVID-19—were the targets of most popular ire and indignation leading up to and during 2021, and they have remained so since (Morales 2021). Hence, the potency of the inversion of the revolutionary dyad "Fatherland or Death" to "Fatherland *and* Life."

But as many have pointed out, we would be mistaken to see the success of the song, or events of July 11, 2021, as simply the product of economic or pandemic grievances. Economic problems are themselves always political, and they can easily lead to questions about the political model that governs economic decision-making. Moreover, the months preceding July 11, and indeed preceding the release of "Patria y Vida" that February, saw sharp conflict between newer voices of Cuban civil society and the Cuban state—from the disrupted hunger strike of the members of the San Isidro Movement in November and a historic sit-in in front of the Ministry of Culture the next day, to various skirmishes, small demonstrations, and arbitrary arrests subsequently (Fusco 2020). It is significant, therefore, that the song "Patria y Vida"—though mostly the creation of Cuban artists now abroad—featured two Havana-based protagonists of these events: Maykel Osorbo and Eliecer Márquez Duany (alias El Funky). The video, in turn, included a cameo from the San Isidro Movement's leader, Luis Manuel Otero Alcántara. Otero Alcántara was later arrested on July 11, and he remains in jail at present writing. Osorbo is still incarcerated, too, having been detained the previous May.

Here, then, we confront a crucial difference between the Cuba of 2021 and the Cuba of the 1990s: the internet. For while the protests on July 11 were not the brainchild of recognized actors in Cuban civil society, access to social media on personal cellphones since 2019 made political activists' confrontations with Cuban authorities over freedom of expression and the freedom to organize increasingly visible in society (Marsh 2021). Social media, of course, is a contentious battleground, with state-backed Cuban information warriors angling for clicks as much as opposition news sites funded by USAID. But in this now more complicated informational playing field, the dissemination of "Patria y Vida," the profusion of memes ridiculing Cuban authorities, and the viral events of July 11 themselves all showed that the Cuban state had lost something of its communications monopoly. These dynamics, combined with almost two years of pandemic hardships at the time, meant that more and more young people previously content to not *meterse en política* (get involved in politics) were throwing previous cautiousness to the wind. The violation of citizens' rights, as much as any group's cause or message, began to attract steady criticism, including among Cubans who were not retweeting #patriayvida per se.

The identities of the artists behind "Patria y Vida" also help explain the song's resonance. Yotuel Romero, Descemer Bueno, and Gente de Zona are now wealthy stars, but it mattered that they, along with Osorbo and El Funky, were persons of color hailing from what remains a racially fractured society—despite the Cuban Revolution's claims to having "solved" the problem of racial inequality by 1962 (Spence Benson 2016). It also mattered that they were exponents of originally Black music genres, hip-hop and reguetón, at which Cuban cultural authorities and the guardians of socialist good taste have thumbed their noses repeatedly (Luci Pereira and Soares 2019). But especially reguetón (or Cubatón, in its insular appropriation) is the undeniable soundtrack of Cuban neighborhoods that, because of rising racial inequalities (in terms of access to remittances and MLC stores or previous ability to benefit from pro-market reforms), have felt the effects of the current economic crisis most acutely. No wonder many taking the streets and cheering "Patria y Vida" on July 11 were Cubans of color.

Contradictions around Race between *Adentro y Afuera*

And yet, it was impossible to avoid the sensation of cognitive dissonance around the issue of race when considering aspects of the song's message and circulation, particularly outside of the island. For if the image of Black men criticizing the Cuban state was part of the music video's potency, in more phenotypically white Cuban

Miami, that impetus was set against a history and contemporary reality of denying, or minimizing, a past and present of racism on the island and in Cuban diaspora communities (Bakeman 2020). One could not help cringe, then, when the song's creators made the rounds in spring 2021 on pro-Trump Miami influencer channels, where the mere mention of structural racism in the US context, or internationally, still prompts charges of a communist conspiracy (*Cubanos por el Mundo* 2021; Lanard 2020). Similarly awkward was when Romero himself, in an interview with *Esquire*, called the expression "Black lives matter" "racist," at best a gross misread of its meaning (Cordero 2021). Granted, neither did the Black Lives Matter Global Network Foundation's one-sided statement about Cuba after the July 11 protests help build bridges of understanding (Adams 2021).

Even more infuriating were the racist undertones and overtones of responses to the song from loyalist and official sectors on the Cuban side. It may be true that the description in "Patria y Vida" of the past sixty years as "stuck" was a better political slogan than history lesson. Regarding race, for example, while the Revolution's silencing of further debate after 1962 cut short a deeper reckoning, Black Cubans did experience important educational gains and upward mobility for three decades (De la Fuente 2001). But from there to imply, as some "Patria y Vida" critics did, that Black artists like Romero "had become what they are" because of the Revolution—suggestions that abounded in the comment boards on state media—was to demand eternal Black docility and gratitude as the price for any past advances toward equality (Rodríguez López 2021). This is one of the oldest tropes in racist thinking. Such claims also willfully ignored evidence of the erosion in those gains in more recent decades, let alone concomitant demands for greater *political* liberties (Hansing and Hoffmann 2020).

On the other hand, protesters on July 11, or their supporters in Miami, did not necessarily have convincing answers to the intractable problem of racial inequality on the island either, particularly as concerns the ways economic reforms have aggravated disparities in Cuba over the last thirty years. Cries for *libertad* in Cuba on July 11, and certainly in Miami, were not limited to, but presumably encompassed, the desire to see Cuba transition to a more free-market system. Yet to return to a point above, we know that the modest market openings that Cuba has tried so far have benefited white Cubans disproportionately, while receding state subsidies have had the heaviest impact on Black communities (Hansing and Hoffmann 2020). Here, then, we run into another potential tension within the protest imaginary fueled by "Patria y Vida" on and off the island—between those who saw the slogan as compatible with an economic vision wherein the state plays a highly limited role versus those arguably reacting as much to *declining* state social provision and capacity.

"Patria y Vida" through a Different Lens

To conclude, it is worth briefly addressing US policy under the Biden administration, as in the aftermath of the protests, another notable disjuncture emerged between the way that "Patria y Vida" was being invoked on the island and some of the agendas it was made to serve in Washington, DC. One of the recurring refrains in the wake of

July 2021 was that US policy had become irrelevant. The protesters, many insisted, were not demanding an end to the US embargo; they wanted freedom from a political system in which they did not have a voice. That may have been true, but that does not mean protesters on July 11 were demonstrating in *favor* of US sanctions either. It also does not mean most protesters supported a US military intervention, as some highly irresponsible politicians from South Florida advocated publicly (Kilander 2021).

The point is that there is no reason that forms of sanctions relief designed to mitigate the impact of the humanitarian crisis on Cuban citizens in the summer of 2021 were automatically incompatible with showing support for the protesters or their demands for political change. From a self-interested point of view, such actions might have shown the United States as magnanimous, precisely at a moment when the Cuban government was arguing that what had occurred was nothing more than the result of a US-backed plot. But unfortunately, the Biden administration responded reactively, calling Cuba a "failed state" (stretching the social scientific meaning of the term) and issuing largely symbolic targeted sanctions against Cuban government entities and individuals that did nothing to deter a highly repressive Cuban government response—namely, the arrests of hundreds of the protesters in subsequent months (Londoño and Robles 2021; Kurmanaev and Lopez 2022). It would take months of stalemate and an unprecedented Cuban migration crisis—more than 200,000 arriving at the US-Mexico border through fiscal year 2022, smashing previous records—to partially break the logjam and get both governments talking (Vicent 2022; DeYoung 2022; Sherwood 2022).

But Cuba's leaders also missed clear opportunities to do right by their citizens in ways that would have limited the bilateral fallout. In response to July 11, island authorities did fast-track the legalization of small- and medium-size enterprises—a potentially transformative economic reform (Frank 2021). An acceleration of immunization with Cuba's homegrown vaccines also eased the toll of the pandemic—one of the drivers of the protests—thus clearing the way for the government to reopen its borders to international travel on November 15 (Frank and Acosta 2021). However, the decision to throw and keep in jail hundreds of protesters on inflammatory charges also created a political obstacle to the more durable normalization of relations that Havana in theory seeks. By late 2022, moreover, European vacationers had not flooded back, inflation remained dire, and discontent—as demonstrated by sporadic street protests with renewed cries of *libertad* in response to severe electricity outages over the summer—remained palpable, all demonstrating the need for deeper economic reform.

What the Cuban government has succeeded in doing, as alluded to already, is using the border opening to export a startling amount of that discontent through migration (quite deliberately, as suggested by close ally Nicaragua's conveniently timed offer to allow Cubans entry visa free), as well as pressuring into exile those members of Cuban civil society that had tried in various ways to keep the spirit of the July 11, 2021, protests going (Reuters 2021; Bustamante 2021). This instrumental use of migration may have coaxed the United States back to the table to a degree, but only cynics can call it a victory.

Today, Cubans critical of their government continue to invoke "Patria y Vida," though the hope initially inspired by the protest anthem has dimmed in the dark intervening months. For all the song's contradictions, it took on a life of its own, revealing the weakness of the Díaz-Canel government's rhetorical insistence on "continuity" since taking office, as well as its attempt to peg a pop-culture phenomenon as nothing more than imperial "fourth generation warfare" (Fazio 2021). Time will tell whether the scale of protests from July 11, 2021, will ever be repeated or whether the US and Cuban governments will continue moving back to a modicum of more constructive ties. Regardless, it is long time for Cuban authorities to also listen to diverse Cuban voices simultaneously demanding the normalization of their political rights.

References

ABC. 2009. "Juanes y Miguel Bosé en Cuba, «¿Por qué nos castigan así? ¿Por qué nos maltratan así?»." September 25. Accessed at https://www.abc.es/internacional/abci-juanes -y-miguel-bose-cuba-castigan-maltratan-200909250300-103123060707_noticia.html?vca =compartirrrss.

Adams, Char. 2021. "Black Lives Matter Faces Backlash for Statement on Cuba Protest." *NBC News*, July 16, 2021. Accessed at https://www.nbcnews.com/news/nbcblk/black-lives-matter -faces-backlash-statement-cuba-protest-rcna1438.

ANDINA. 2009. "Trío de hip hop Orishas hace votos para que Obama propicie acercamiento con Cuba." January 20. Accessed at https://andina.pe/agencia/noticia-trio-hip-hop-orishas -hace-votos-para-obama-propicie-acercamiento-cuba-214445.aspx.

Bakeman, Jessica. 2020. "'There's a Lot of Denialism': How an Anti-racism Proposal Exposed Miami's Racial/Ethnic Fractures." WLRN, June 24. Accessed at https://www.wlrn.org /education/2020-06-24/theres-a-lot-of-denialism-how-an-anti-racism-proposal-exposed -miamis-racial-ethnic-fractures.

Bustamante, Michael J. 2021. "The Cuban Government Hasn't Won Yet." *Slate*, December 2. Accessed at https://slate.com/news-and-politics/2021/12/cuban-protests-achipielago-15n -government-suppression.html.

Chirino, Willy. 1991. "Nuestro día (Ya viene llegando)." *Oxígeno*. LP. Columbia Records.

———. 2021. "Que Se Vayan Ya." Accesssed at https://www.youtube.com/watch?v=46hSA3v- VPMM.

Cordero, Gonzálo. 2021. "Y ahora serio: Yotuel Romero, Cuba y el racism." *Esquire*, March 5. Accessed at https://www.esquire.com/es/actualidad/musica/a35690714/yotuel-romero -racismo-cuba-beatriz-luengo-hijos.

Cubanos por el Mundo. 2021. "Yotuel habla con Alex Otaola en exclusiva del tema musical 'Patria y Vida.'" February 18. Accessed at https://www.youtube.com/watch?v=iVaxPFOw8wc.

De la Fuente, Alejandro. 2001. *A Nation for All: Race, Inequality, and Politics in Twentieth-Century Cuba*. Chapel Hill: University of North Carolina Press.

DeYoung, Karen. 2022. "Biden to Lift Some Trump-Era Restrictions on Cuba." *Washington Post*, May 16. Accessed at https://www.washingtonpost.com/national-security/2022/05/16/ biden-cuba-travel-remittances-visas.

Diario de Cuba. 2020. "Gente de Zona en el Free Cuba Fest de Miami." October 11. Accessed at https://diariodecuba.com/cultura/1602406677_25593.html.

Falcón, Randy. 2021. "¿Patria? y Business." Cubadebate, May 7. Accessed at http://www .cubadebate.cu/opinion/2021/05/07/patria-y-bussines.

Fazio, Carlos. 2021. "Cuba vs. Terrorismo Mediático." Cubadebate, July 29. Accessed at http:// www.cubadebate.cu/opinion/2021/07/29/cuba-vs-terrorismo-mediatico.

Frank, Mark. 2021. "Cuba Dips Toe in Market Economy with Legalization of Small Businesses." Reuters, August 13. Accessed at https://www.reuters.com/world/americas/cuba-dips-toe-market-economy-with-legalization-small-businesses-2021-08-13.

Frank, Mark, and Nelson Acosta. 2021. "Cuba Aims to Fully Inoculate 90% of Residents against COVID-19 by December." Reuters, October 1. Accessed at https://www.reuters.com/world/americas/cuba-aims-fully-inoculate-90-residents-against-covid-19-by-december-2021-10-01.

Fusco, Coco. 2020. "The Right to Have Rights: A New 'Artivist' Movement Demands Freedom of Expression in Cuba." *MoMA*, December 23 Accessed at https://www.moma.org/magazine/articles/479.

Grenier, Guillermo, and Qing Lai. 2020. *2020 FIU Cuba Poll: How Cuban Americans in Miami View U.S. Policies Toward Cuba*. Miami: Florida International University.

Hansing, Katrin, and Bert Hoffmann. 2020. "When Racial Inequalities Return: Assessing the Restratification of Cuban Society 60 Years After Revolution." *Latin American Politics and Society* 62, no. 2: 29–52. Accessed at https://doi.org/10.1017/lap.2019.59.

Herrero, Ricardo. 2021. Personal communication to author, October 12.

Kilander, Gustav. 2021. "Miami Mayor Calls on Biden to Consider Airstrikes against Cuba." *The Independent*, July 14. Accessed at https://www.independent.co.uk/news/world/americas/us-politics/cuba-protests-airstrikes-miami-mayor-b1884238.html.

Kurmanaev, Anatoly, and Oscar Lopez. 2022. "Mass Trials in Cuba Deepen Its Harshest Crackdown in Decades." *New York Times*, January 14. Accessed at https://www.nytimes.com/2022/01/14/world/americas/cuba-mass-trials-crackdown.html.

Lanard, Noah. 2020. "Meet the YouTube Star Who's Pushing a Generation of Florida's Cuban Voters to Trump." *Mother Jones*, October 7. Accessed at https://www.motherjones.com/politics/2020/10/meet-the-youtube-star-whos-pushing-a-generation-of-floridas-cuban-voters-to-trump.

Londoño, Ernesto, and Frances Robles. 2021. "Biden Ramps Up Pressure on Cuba, Abandoning Obama's Approach." *New York Times*, August 9. Accessed at https://www.nytimes.com/2021/08/09/world/americas/cuba-government-biden-pressure.html.

Luci Pereira, Simone, and Thiago Soares. 2019. "Reguetón en Cuba: censura, ostentación y grietas en las políticas mediáticas." *Palabra Clave* 22, no. 1: 1–28. Accessed at https://doi.org/10.5294/pacla.2019.22.1.7.

Marsh, Sarah. 2021. "The Facebook Group That Staged First in Cuba's Wave of Protests." Reuters, August 9. Accessed at https://www.reuters.com/world/americas/facebook-group-that-staged-first-cubas-wave-protests-2021-08-09.

Miller, Carlos. 2009. "Juanes Stirs Up Tired Old Cold War Debates." NBC Miami, August 22. Accessed at https://www.nbcmiami.com/news/local/juanes-stirs-up-tired-old-cold-war-debates-in-miami/1843931.

Morales, Emilio. 2021. "Menos turistas y más inversions hoteleras en Cuba: ¿qué hay detrás de todo esto?" *Diario de Cuba*, May 28. Accessed at https://diariodecuba.com/economia/1622217681_31502.html.

Pentón, Mario, and Sarah Moreno. 2019. "Cuban Reggaeton Group Gente de Zona Pulled from New Year's Eve Miami Concert." *Miami Herald*, December 24. Accessed at https://www.miamiherald.com/news/local/article238696643.html.

Reuters. 2021. "Nicaragua Eliminates Visa Requirement for Cubans." November 23. Accessed at https://www.reuters.com/world/americas/nicaragua-eliminates-visa-requirement-cubans-2021-11-23.

Rialta. 2021. "Artistas reivindican el orígen popular de las protestas y condenan la repression del gobierno Cubano." July 13. Accessed at https://rialta.org/artistas-reivindican-el-origen-popular-de-las-protestas-y-condenan-la-represion-del-gobierno-cubano.

Rodríguez, Silvio. 1992. "El Necio." *Silvio*. LP. EGREM.

Rodríguez López, Yusimí. 2021. "Negros malaradecidos y sospechosos: el ataque del oficialismo cubano a los intérpretes de 'Patria y Vida.'" *Diario de Cuba*, March 5. Accessed at https://diariodecuba.com/cuba/1614947877_29269.html.

Romero, Yotuel, Gente de Zona, Descemer Bueno, Maykel Osorbo, and El Funky. 2021. "Patria y Vida." Accessed at https://www.youtube.com/watch?v=pP9Bto5lOEQ.

RTVE. 2009. "El concierto 'Paz Sin Fronteras,' una 'gran oportunidad' para 'olvidar el odio' en Cuba." September 17. Accessed at https://www.rtve.es/noticias/20090917/concierto-paz-sin-fronteras-gran-oportunidad-para-olvidar-odio-cuba/292728.shtml.

Sherwood, David. 2022. "Cuba, U.S. to Hold Second Round of Migration Talks in Havana." Reuters, November 14. Accessed at https://www.reuters.com/world/americas/cuba-us-hold-second-round-migration-talks-havana-2022-11-14.

Spence Benson, Devyn. 2016. *Antiracism in Cuba: The Unfinished Revolution*. Chapel Hill: University of North Carolina Press.

Torres, Raúl, Annie Garcés, Dayana Divo, Karla Monier, and Yisi Calibre. 2021. "Patria o muerte por la vida." Accessed at https://www.youtube.com/watch?v=Xu4Huw3i-lE.

Vicent, Mauricio. 2022. "Cuba y un éxodo al que no se ve fin." *El País*, November 13. Accessed at https://elpais.com/internacional/2022-11-13/cuba-y-un-exodo-al-que-no-se-ve-fin.html.

CHAPTER 6

Cuba Today through the Eyes of a Novelist

Leonardo Padura Fuentes

Editors: Cuba today is in the midst of the worst economic conditions since the Special Period—although the levels of frustration and disaffection seem greater than in the 1990s. Do you agree? Why is this the case? How will this end?

Leonardo Padura (LP): I don't think that anybody knows how or when this horizontal crisis will end—and that's one of the problems. What might at first appear to be a temporary, or contextual, situation is in fact turning into a systemic challenge, and the solutions provided by the authorities are often merely administrative ones, and little else. An example can be seen in the distribution of essential goods. They are badly lacking—all of them! The solution is to either use slogans ("it's all due to inflation") or reduce their supply (food imports). . . . In addition to these many shortages we can also mention the "historical fatigue" faced by Cuban society—since there have been far too many years living in the midst of difficulties, shortages, attempts to solve the problems. However, these strategies don't solve the problems, but in fact increase them (as seen in the currency reforms). People are so very tired, and indeed angry—but have no means of expressing that discontent, since the Cuban system does not allow any space for them to do so. As a result, people are left with a variety of solutions—migration, cynicism, resignation. . . . And all of these make our society even poorer.

Editors: Many people believe that the government doesn't have any practical plan to emerge from the current crisis—or at least hasn't been able to communicate effectively a program that the people can accept. How do you think the government is doing in its efforts to resolve the current economic crisis?

LP: I think that the government is doing a poor job, because apart from slogans ("We have resisted, and will continue to resist," "This year will be better," etc.), we have not seen the results of the many measures that the government says that it is taking—and which have definitely not resolved the major problems of people.

Editors: The lack of equity, of fairness, seems to be growing in Cuban society and is more visible than in previous years. Does this inequity represent a threat to the basic principle of social justice on which the revolutionary struggle was based? What impact is this challenge having on popular opinion?

LP: The lack of equity—even though it may be terrible to admit it—is in fact necessary. The concept of egalitarianism worked well while there was Soviet financing to sustain it. It was not based upon an efficient, capable economic base, and as a result the only thing it managed to do when the Soviet financing disappeared was to impoverish us all. It made us equal, but by driving down our financial well-being.

In order to increase the economic well-being of society it is necessary to have an efficient economic model—and we have seen that the economy, trade, state services just don't have the necessary efficiency to resolve the many problems that have accumulated and are now affecting us. There is practically not a single sector of the Cuban economy that is really efficient. . . .

For years we have been afraid of individuals becoming rich. But if people aren't allowed to become wealthy, there is no generation of wealth for society—and that is worse, because what is being generated is more misery. Social justice is indeed necessary, but it should be created on a realistic base, with an equitable distribution of income, but without fear of wealth being created—for the country and for those individuals who are capable of creating it. And, of course, all of this with the mechanisms to regulate personal income through a system of taxation. By contrast, what we have seen so far is a combination of suspicion, a lack of commercial space, changes in economic policy—all to maintain the same economic and social policies which have been in crisis for more than thirty years.

Editors: Independent civil society appears to have grown a great deal in recent years. How do you see the efforts of the government to either control or combat the sociopolitical model of these new groups? And how do you see the impact of these new groups?

LP: I don't know if in Cuba we can talk about the emergence of independent civil society as a phenomenon or an established reality—or even if that is possible. How many delegates to our political legislatures are representatives of such groups? What is the space for any political action of any independent civil society groups? Cuban society functions with a model of one sole political party, the Communist Party—and within that model there is no consideration given for the existence of independent space, with any real possibility of discourse and action. Yes, there are groups that vaccinate and sterilize stray dogs, and little else. . . . But is that independent civil society?

Editors: In comparison with the 1990s, is there a greater level of official corruption in Cuba nowadays? If that is the case, what types of corruption are the most prevalent?

LP: I can't give an opinion on government corruption nowadays because there are no data available on the topic. There are, of course, many rumors about individuals who have businesses and privileges, access to certain commercial possibilities—but little else in terms of hard evidence. What is indeed true, though, is that people with high levels of political responsibility do indeed have clear possibilities that the rest of the population does not. To put this in clear, simple terms—they don't have to line up for five hours to buy a package of poor-quality hot dogs (which nowadays is the basic food source for thousands of families in Cuba). The fact that they have a certain political responsibility should not exempt them from living under the same rules as the rest of the population. Indeed, by doing so they would have a more realistic understanding of what it is like to live in Cuba nowadays. I have no idea how much the president earns, the prime minister, or the governor of one of the provinces—but I am sure that if they were to live just off their salary, they wouldn't be able to dress in the way that they do—since a pair of stockings for a school student costs the third of a minimum salary. Just a pair of stockings! . . . Meanwhile government officials are seen wearing fancy linen guayaberas.

PART II

ECONOMY

Ricardo Torres Pérez

The process of updating the Cuban economic model—which continues today—formally began when the Communist Party of Cuba (Partido Comunista de Cuba [PCC]), in its Sixth Congress of April 2011, adopted a resolution approving the *Lineamientos*, a set of socioeconomic policy "guidelines" for the country's development.[1] Yet important modifications to Cuba's economic model were already under way. In 2008, Cuban nationals were authorized to purchase mobile phone lines and stay at hotels previously restricted to foreign tourists. In 2009, public access to the internet, albeit limited, was approved. In the economic realm, the government had taken several steps to activate idle arable land and increase food production to reduce imports. In 2010, the sale of building materials was deregulated. That same year, authorities expanded the possibilities to engage in private businesses, then known as *cuentapropistas*.

Shortly after the Sixth Party Congress, additional reforms were enacted. In 2011, Cuban nationals were authorized to trade their homes and vehicles. In 2013, overseas travel was liberalized. The same year, the creation of cooperatives outside of agriculture was authorized. That momentum, for a while, heralded the beginning of a more structured and consistent approach to economic reform compared to the back and forth of the previous decades.

In April of 2016, the Seventh Party Congress approved three documents that would guide the reform over the next five years: the updated *Lineamientos*, a Conceptualization of Cuba's economic and social model, and the National Development Plan to 2030.[2] The Eighth Congress of the Cuban Communist Party, in 2021, took place amid the worst economic crisis since the collapse of the Soviet Union. As expected, there were no novel initiatives related to the reform process beyond embracing, in general terms, the changes that were formally launched in 2011.

In assessing the progress of Cuba's reforms, branded as *actualización* (updating), since 2014, this chapter reviews policy initiatives, discusses overall economic performance, analyzes governmental responses to economic difficulties, and highlights the main points and economic implications of the new Cuban constitution.

Reforms 2014–2019: No Haste and Much Pause

Cuba went from adopting major policy initiatives to nearly a full stop in economic reforms by early 2016, as recognized by the government in a Council of Ministers meeting in March 2018. Cuban authorities argued that this was to be expected given the fact that initial steps were the easiest and some changes had not proceeded as anticipated. The trajectory of reform was also affected by transformational external events such as renewed US sanctions, economic setbacks in Venezuela, and in late 2018 the end of the Cuban doctors program in Brazil. At the same time, the political scene was affected by the Seventh Party Congress in April 2016; the passing of Fidel Castro, Cuba's top political figure for over fifty years; the rise of a new generation of leaders to the country's top positions in 2018; and the discussion of a new constitution in the last few months of the same year.

In terms of the pace of change and the nature of policy initiatives, the period since 2014 can be divided into two main phases. During the first, from 2014 to 2015, most changes were in line with the idea of reforming fundamental elements of the economic model. But in the second phase, which began in early 2016 and has continued up to the writing of this chapter in 2023, reforms almost stopped and policies became more restrictive, with the possible exception of foreign investment.

By 2014, attention increasingly focused on foreign investment, for which the old framework was at odds with the change in language put forward by the *Lineamientos*. The new language designated foreign direct investment (FDI) as a key component of the nation's economic strategy. Cuba first enacted a foreign investment law as early as 1995; however, the role played by FDI in the economy had been small. Compared to other countries, Cuba attracted only modest amounts of foreign capital.[3] In a centrally planned economy, with predominantly state ownership, the development of market relationships is still limited. Investment is effectively controlled by the government, which restricts foreign participation to specified sectors or forms of investment deemed by the government to serve that national interest. But despite these constraints, Cuba's current medium- and long-term economic and social development strategy now includes foreign investment to be an integral element of national investment, rather than merely a complement to it.

Two new laws were especially significant. At the end of 2013, Decree Law 313 created a unique Special Development Zone (ZDEM) at Mariel Harbor, west of Havana. It was followed in 2014 by a new foreign investment law (Law 118). Taken together, these laws offered increased tax incentives, infrastructure built for investors in the Mariel Zone, and greater flexibility in the state employment agency's operation than the previous FDI structure provided. The government now appears willing to compensate investors in some areas, such as taxation and infrastructure, for its unwillingness to compromise on more sensitive issues like hiring practices, approval delays, and lack of transparency.

The year 2014 ended with the unprecedented announcements on December 17 by the US and Cuban presidents that diplomatic relations would be restored. In January and September 2015, the United States introduced modifications to the policy of sanctions aimed at expanding the possibilities of trade, investment, financial links, and travel. In May 2015, Cuba was removed from the US State Department's list of states that sponsor terrorism, which lifted some financial restrictions. That summer, both countries reopened embassies, and agreements were signed to restore direct mail and commercial flights.

While direct economic relations remained limited, this dynamic positively affected the number of Americans visiting Cuba and, predictably, the flow of capital in the form of remittances. In addition, the indirect effect on third countries was remarkable; the US-Cuba rapprochement stimulated tourism, finance, and investments from elsewhere. One of the areas of benefit for Cuba was the restructuring of the external debt with the member countries of the Paris Club.

In the wake of the 2009–2010 world financial crisis, the Cuban government decided to start restructuring the country's foreign debt and improving its credit worthiness.[4] Since then, Cuba has significantly reduced its foreign indebtedness through bilateral negotiations of its long-term debt with major creditors, such as Japan, Russia, Mexico, and China. In all these cases, at least 70 percent of the total debt claims was written off and the repayment of the remaining debt was rescheduled on acceptable terms. In December 2015, an agreement was made with the Paris Club to settle Cuba's debt of $11.1 billion. Seventy-six percent of this debt was written off and an eighteen-year repayment schedule was established for the remaining claims. It can be argued that the agreement was possible because US-Cuban relations had improved significantly.

Improving ties with the United States, and the great attention the process received from the Cuban government, may have partially concealed the internal contradictions suffered as a result of Cuba's economic reforms. Complaints in the December 2015 session of the National Assembly about rising food prices led to a partial reversal of agricultural reforms, especially the ability of producers and intermediaries to set prices freely according to market conditions. In April, new regulations went into effect introducing price caps and granting a greater role to Acopio, the state agency with a monopoly on marketing agricultural products, whose inefficiency had been regarded as an obstacle to progress not so long before. In addition, to curb social criticism, some prices for goods sold in convertible pesos were cut just before the start of the 2016 Party Congress. This was contradictory given that the country had begun to confront serious problems in its balance of payments, which would necessarily result in restrictions on imports, the main source of the products sold in these stores. The price cuts could have been justified if an increase in foreign exchange earnings had occurred, but in practice, the opposite was happening.

April 2016 was a turning point in the process of economic reform. The apparent logic observed until then, based on the need for changes to improve economic performance, was set aside. The market and the participation of the non-state sector were considered responsible for the spike in prices and the consequent increase in inequality. In spite of the economic benefits, improved relations with the United States also generated reservations in influential circles in the government.

The combination of the two resulted in stalled reforms. However, at least on the formal political level, the 2016 Party Congress left some positive elements for the future of the reform. It recognized that only 22 percent of the 2011 Guidelines had been completely fulfilled, and it approved two new documents to replace the first generation of Guidelines. The first was the Conceptualization, a theoretical and political document that described the general outline of Cuba's future model. Second was the 2030 National Development Plan, which provided a concrete roadmap for the following fifteen years.

One key feature that stands out is the formal recognition that the Cuban model's sustainability depended directly on achieving greater development, which in turn is tightly linked to economic growth. The model leaves ample room for forms of property other than those owned by the state, including the recognition of private ownership over the means of production, a first since 1959. A clear distinction is also made between property and management. In addition, the model legitimizes a shift toward more indirect means of state intervention in the economy. One section goes so far as to declare that "the state will concentrate on the functions appropriate to it, such as planning, regulating, conducting, and controlling the process of economic and social development."[5]

The 2030 National Development Plan is an ambitious proposal of great reach. According to the plan, development is examined through the so-called strategic axes, understood as the critical areas of transformation. It was an incomplete proposal, though, because indicators, gaps, and goals were unelaborated, as were the corresponding financing needs and their possible sources.

By the time the final versions of those documents were released in 2017, it was apparent that priorities had shifted and reforms had been put on hold. A deteriorating environment domestically and internationally introduced hesitation into the government's plans, which undoubtedly arose from the planners' doubts.

In July 2016, the government recognized that the country was facing growing stress in its external finances and austerity measures were necessary, including but not limited to forced energy savings in the public sector and stricter control over imports. In November the results of the US presidential election came as a shock, as most experts were expecting a different result. In both capitals, supporters of US-Cuban engagement had hoped to have at least four more years to cement the new relationship.

Starting in 2017, external circumstances and the Cuban economy went from bad to worse. In June of that year, President Donald Trump announced a policy change aimed at partially dismantling President Barack Obama's Cuba policy legacy. On August 1, a Cuban Ministry of Labor and Social Security resolution published in the *Official Gazette* established that temporarily no new licenses for private-sector businesses would be issued for a variety of activities and that changes would be introduced in the *cuentapropistas* (self-employed) business environment. To justify that decision, a wide range of reasons were given, among them tax evasion, the use of illegally obtained raw materials, the imprecision and insufficiency of controls, and deficiencies in the contracting for the supply of services or products by individual entrepreneurs, cooperatives, and private companies.

More than eleven months later, on July 10, 2018, Cuba's *Official Gazette* published numerous new rules that included five decree laws, one decree, and fourteen resolutions, covering a grand total of 129 pages of changes in the relevant regulatory framework for the country's self-employed. This new episode in the endless zigzag around the private sector was announced under the euphemistic title of "Policy for the Perfection of Self-Employment." The overwhelming majority of the changes constituted new restrictions on the exercise of non-state economic activities.

The new course taken had negative repercussions at the socioeconomic level. In an economy facing a precarious fiscal scenario, millions of pesos were lost in taxes not collected when the state stopped issuing new licenses. Cuentapropistas pay an array of taxes which include a sales tax and taxes for the labor force, personal income, and social security. Although data is not available showing the amount that cuentapropistas contribute, it can be assumed that they pay an overwhelming part of total personal income taxes the government collects, based on the explosive growth of private-sector taxpayers until 2019, numbers that had tripled after 2009. Meanwhile, budget revenues (personal income tax) grew more than 4.8 times. On this basis, it can be estimated lost revenues (not considering other taxes and indirect effects) were on the order of 900 million pesos.[6] To put the loss in perspective, this amount is almost equal to what was spent on community projects and personal services in a typical year prior to the monetary reform in 2021.

From the start, when some of the new policies were announced, there was widespread discontent, including in academic sectors. It awakened activism that prompted the attention of the authorities. In an unusual decision, especially because of the sensitivity of the issue, Cuban officials reversed some of the regulations related to self-employment work just before they went into effect in December 2018. For example, the rules that denied Cubans the possibility of engaging in more than one kind of approved work activity and that limited coffee shops, restaurants, and bars to fifty chairs were scrapped. Since then, the chair limit has been determined by the capacity of the premises in question. Regarding another highly sensitive issue, business bank accounts were allowed greater flexibility with regard to their size. The decision-making process that led to the adoption of these regulations was opaque from the very beginning: the policy of "perfecting" self-employment was not and has not been shared with the public.

It is worth noting, however, that complaints of tax evasion and the purchase of stolen or "shady" goods are common concerns anywhere in the world. Self-employment in Cuba is part of a larger system whose failures cannot be attributed only to this sector.

Unfortunately, an experiment with transportation in Havana proceeded as initially announced. New regulations on private taxis, or *almendrones*, were met with a kind of passive resistance. As a result, the number of private cars serving the city dropped, as many failed to meet the new technical standards or their owners decided to wait until the business climate improved. The reduced supply quickly translated into higher prices and fewer alternatives for people to move around in a city whose public transportation system had long been inadequate.

A Brief Assessment of Economic Results: Disappointment as a Norm

Even a cursory review of the speeches and public interventions of Raúl Castro and his cabinet leaves few doubts that actualización of the economy was their dominant concern. The government devoted energy and time to the political process associated with actualización, creating new structures such as the Implementation and Development Commission charged with overseeing the execution of the reforms. But the economic results lagged well behind the ideological and political exhortations. As an indication of the popular dissatisfaction with the reforms, the commission was disbanded after the Eighth Party Congress in 2021.

When measured against the economic performance and structural problems that should characterize the development of the nation, the transformation has been superficial. The most telling example of this is that much of 2019 was marked by an acute balance-of-payments crisis that harshly affected links with Cuba's main external partners, resulting in a recurring shortage of products of all kinds, including essential goods like eggs and bread flour. The COVID-19 pandemic exacerbated those problems, effectively plunging Cuba into its worst economic crisis in at least three decades.

Table II.1 summarizes the main economic indicators for the 2014–2018 period.

The data show very low average economic growth, well below the needs of a country of Cuba's size and level of development. This performance is not compatible with a sustained improvement in the living conditions of a majority of Cubans. In the Cuban model, inflation and the unemployment rate as reported do not transmit the information they carry in other contexts, so they must be interpreted with great cau-

Table II.1.   Selected percentage annual growth rates* (2014–2018)

Indicator	2014	2015	2016	2017	2018
GDP (in constant 1997 prices)	1.0	4.3	0.5	1.8	2.2
Inflation**	2.1	2.8	-2.9	0.6	2.4
Unemployment rate (%)	2.7	2.4	2.0	1.7	1.7
Investment (% at current prices)	-8.9	24.9	10.2	23.8	15.4
Gross capital formation (% of GDP)	7.6	9.4	9.6	10.3	12.0
Exports of goods and services (current prices)	-4.2	-16.1	-8.4	2.9	3.0
Imports of goods and services (current prices)	-11.1	-9.2	-10.9	0.7	11.1
Trade balance (USD millions)	3,947	2,350	2,463	2,774	1,936
Budget balance (% of GDP)	-2.2	-5.8	-6.6	-8.6	-8.1

Source: author's calculations based on data from the Office of National Statistics (ONEI)
Note: Percentage annual growth rates
*except otherwise indicated
**inclusive only of prices in Cuban pesos (CUP)

tion. The consumer price index does not include price changes in convertible pesos, so its recent evolution would not adequately reflect the price dynamics in markets of great importance to the daily life of large segments of the population. Food and transport are two sectors in which there has been a clear upward trend, which is not sufficiently weighted in this index.

In relation to the unemployment rate, the increase in the informal economy and the current demographic characteristics of an aging population suggest that the rate of economic activity (i.e., the proportion of the working population with a formal job) would be a more useful measure of certain trends in the labor market. This indicator has been showing a systematic decline since 2011, when it went from 76.1 percent to 63.8 percent in 2018. Another cause of decreasing employment in the formal economy is the emerging phenomenon of Cubans who have emigrated but retain their residency status. Reflecting the challenges facing the nation since 2016, the total working-age population has begun to shrink in absolute terms. Currently, fewer formal employees contribute directly to the central budget, from which social services are financed for the population.

In this period, the country managed to maintain a surplus trade balance, mainly due to falling imports matching the drop in exports. This is, in perspective, an unsustainable trajectory with a high cost to growth.

In 2015, the growth in the gross domestic product (GDP) stood at 4.3 percent. That year there was more-balanced performance at the industry level: all branches showed increases in their activity, although some did not grow at the expected pace. International tourism benefited particularly from the new relationship with the United States, which had a positive impact on other markets as well.

Already in 2016, the economy began to slow down, and the outlook became even more adverse in the second half of the year. This period was marked by the impact of the austerity measures announced by the government in July and the weakness of general economic activity, except for international tourism. Energy rationing (due to the shortfall in oil shipments from Venezuela), although discretionally managed to avoid blackouts and impacts on strategic activities, had recessive effects. The planned restrictions in imports and investments accelerated the downward spiral.

International tourism was the only large industry that gave the economy a boost in 2016. However, the number of tourists from Canada (the main source of tourists) decreased by 6.7 percent, a trend that continued into 2018. The cause of the decline is still unclear, but the Ministry of Tourism in Cuba pointed to the depreciation of the Canadian dollar against the US dollar. The Cuban convertible peso (CUC) was pegged to the US dollar, and prices were set in CUCs. As a result, when the American currency appreciated, travel to Cuba became more expensive. In addition, the government was very conservative in taking on new international loans in order to avoid debt levels beyond its actual ability to repay them.

Amid growing external financial constraints, international tourism continued to be one of the pillars of the country's economic performance in 2017 but suffered setbacks in the last two quarters. That was the year of the takeoff in the number of cruise passengers, with estimated arrivals of almost 400,000 visitors. However, the sector faced enormous challenges, both at home and abroad. At least four shocks of varying intensity affected the upward trend that started in late 2014: Hurricane Irma (September 2017); travel alerts issued by the US Department of State (mid and late September 2017); the temporary moratorium on granting licenses in several categories of private business directly connected with tourism (July 2018); and the 2017 and 2019 restrictive measures of the Trump administration.

The year 2018 marked another complex situation for the economy. Cuban authorities estimated economic growth of around 2.2 percent, supported by sectors such as communications, retail, manufacturing, public health, and construction. Decreases were reported in tourism and the sugar industry. While the government invested only 85 percent of its budgeted goal, these expenditures still represented an almost 15 percent increase over 2017. However, the growing scarcity of foreign exchange affected imports, and the country experienced an increased scarcity of basic products toward the end of the year.

2019: A New Constitution

The most important political process in Cuba in 2019 was the public discussion surrounding the new constitution. Cuba's new Magna Carta proposes transformations in a group of key areas of the country's economic, political, and social life. However, the final form these changes take, and their true scope, are still being defined in the legislative process that is generating the corresponding laws and in their practical application.

The new Cuban constitution establishes the general lines already agreed upon in the documents approved in the 2016 Seventh Party Congress. Likewise, the popular debate led to the modification of certain aspects of the original version (60 percent of the articles were modified), although most of the adaptations can be considered formal, with a few potentially important ones. Cuba defines itself as a socialist state, with an economy based on social ownership over the main means of production and with "socialist" planning as the main coordination mechanism.

Sovereignty resides in the people, who exercise it through the National Assembly of People's Power as the supreme organ. Likewise, the Communist Party retains its role as the leading political entity, and the only party recognized in the constitution. The direct and secret vote of the people is reserved for the deputies to the Cuban National Assembly and for the delegates to the Municipal Assemblies of People's Power. The fundamental executive positions of the state and the government are chosen by these two bodies.

The constitution recognizes a wider variety of individual rights, including the possibility of suing the state and the government for bias, and incorporates the right of habeas corpus. However, as of the end of 2022, few of those rights had been incorporated into law. The text opened the door to the recognition of same-sex unions, which was included in the new Family Code that the populace approved in 2022.

One of the areas that incorporate significant changes is the organization of Cuba's economic model. Title II includes the so-called Economic Fundamentals, while other rights of this type are included in Title V's "Rights, Duties and Guarantees." In general, Title II follows three basic guidelines. First, it adheres to the provisions of the so-called Conceptualization of the Cuban economic and social model. Second, although the text emphasizes that in Cuba the typical market economy system does not apply, it does introduce appreciable transformations that bring the effective model closer to what are known as mixed economies in which different forms of property coexist and there is space for market relations. Third, the constitution explicitly recognizes private ownership over means of production.

This third element is one of the changes that has the greatest potential to generate future transformation, if properly used. In this regard, the document recognizes and extends the possibility of mixed ownership (i.e., property formed by the combination of two or more forms of ownership, such as a private restaurant and a cooperative farm), which can generate unpredictable dynamics. Likewise, for the first time, the market is mentioned as part of the economic and social model. The state also promotes and guarantees foreign investment. However, given the recognition of various forms of property in Article 22 and the protections provided for foreign investment in Article 28, it is notable that the constitution provides few guarantees to private property owned by Cuban nationals, which is a disincentive for investment.

In addition, the text includes the right of workers to participate in the planning, regulation, management, and control of the economy. The language that refers to the concentration of property in non-state subjects was modified with a more neutral tone, and this provision was also extended to entities of this type. Nonetheless, a bias against the private and cooperative sectors, especially the former, is maintained.

In many areas, the constitution is more modern and flexible than the one dating from 1976. Progress was made in shaping the economic model and individual rights. However, the essence of the old Cuban system remains intact through the economic and political model that it enshrines. Still, a constitution merely establishes the general framework; it is up to the Cuban government and people to develop the new elements contained in the text.

2020–2022: Crisis Is Back, Again

The Cuban economy experienced a severe downturn after 2019. Recovery in 2021 and 2022 was weak, and in some areas such as energy, transport, and inflation there were notable setbacks. During 2020, the island faced the negative external shock associated with COVID-19, with productive activity weakened by the accumulation of domestic problems, the hardening of external constraints, and natural disasters. As a result, both the fiscal deficit and inflation rose sharply in 2020. In the midst of these circumstances, the government decided to go ahead with the Monetary Ordering program, intended to unify the currency. Although currency unification previously was considered a key step in any meaningful reform, its implementation starting in January 2021 has contributed to accelerating price growth and the depreciation of the Cuban peso (CUP).

While the economy began to recover in 2021 and 2022 with modest increases in GDP, the levels were too small to have a favorable impact on people's standard of living. This slow recovery had two fundamental characteristics. On the one hand, macroeconomic imbalances remained and economic policy was not able to control the rise in prices. On the other hand, progress was asymmetrical at the level of economic activities. International tourism lagged behind other Caribbean countries and became more dependent on visits from Cubans living in other countries than on foreign visitors. The energy crisis resulted in widespread power outages and energy rationing in the public sector. All this, together with acute shortages of food and medicine, were major factors that would explain the social protests in 2021 and 2022, together with the emigration of more than 300,000 Cubans, mainly to the United States.

The reasons for the ongoing crisis include external and domestic aspects. The external economic context changed negatively for Cuba. First, there was the economic crisis in Venezuela, whose effects were felt strongly in foreign trade. That country had been Cuba's first market for medical services and pharmaceuticals, and it was the main supplier of Cuba's oil and derivatives. Between 2014 and 2020, the Venezuelan economy contracted by more than 50 percent according to the International Monetary Fund.[7] Oil production went from 2.5 million barrels per day in 2014 to only 555,000 in 2021, a contraction of 78 percent.[8]

The resulting drop in oil shipments to Cuba was substantial. Trade figures show that exchanges between the two countries declined by as much as 57 percent in the period 2014–2020, reflecting both a drop in the oil price and a reduction in supplies. In August 2017, the joint venture ended between the Venezuelan state oil firm PDVSA and Cuba's Oil Union CUPET at the Cienfuegos refinery. That association had enabled Cuba to export oil byproducts that had become a significant source of foreign exchange.

In addition, relations with Brazil, which had been Cuba's second-largest trading partner in the region, began to deteriorate in late 2018. In response to president-elect Jair Bolsonaro's November 2018 demand that Cuba renegotiate the terms of the agreement by which Cuban doctors served mostly poor and remote areas in Brazil, the Cuban government ended its involvement with the Mais Médicos program. The participation of Cuban doctors was made possible through a technical cooperation project between the Pan American Health Organization (PAHO), the World Health Organization (WHO), and the Ministries of Health of Brazil and Cuba. In the end Cubans represented almost two-thirds of the total professionals hired. The annual Brazilian transfers to Cuba were estimated to be between $250 and $300 million. In addition, export guarantees available to Brazilian food producers were suspended, almost halting sales to Cuba. Brazil had enjoyed a significant market share of the island's food purchases since 2004.

The third external problem related to the erratic performance of two of Cuba's main export industries, nickel and sugar, which were adversely affected by setbacks in production and a decline in world market prices. Nickel production stagnated in the 2014–2020 period after the closing of one of three production plants and operational setbacks in a second one. Sugar exports earned $105 million in 2021, a third of the amount earned in 2014. In addition, income from foreign visitors was flat from 2017 to 2021, owing in large part to restrictions in the US market, as well as drops in the Canadian and European markets. These latter years' losses were mainly due to the COVID-19 pandemic, during which the Cuban government closed the island to tourists for many months. Overall, Cuba lost more than half of its export revenues in the period.

A fourth problem was the policies of the Trump administration, which were then maintained by the Biden administration. These had a particularly adverse impact on travel, investment, trade, finance, and remittances. Following restrictions aimed at curbing travel to Cuba in November 2017, the US administration introduced further measures in April 2019, including a cap on remittances, sanctions on vessels and companies involved in fuel transportation from Venezuela to Cuba, the elimination of the "people-to-people" educational category for authorized travel, the banning of cruise ships from docking in Cuban ports, and stricter enforcement of financial sanctions leading to fines of European banks. The US government also activated the implementation of Title III and IV of the Helms-Burton Act, which had been waived by every administration since the law was enacted in 1996. Under Title III, lawsuits are allowed in US courts against American and foreign companies doing business in Cuba by using property nationalized by the Cuban government following the 1959 Revolution. This more hostile bilateral climate may well have dissuaded both potential investors from third countries and US companies that had an interest in commercial relations with Cuba. The Biden administration did not substantially modify this policy until mid-2022, when it eased some restrictions on remittances and travel.

Cuban authorities responded to this challenging scenario with a mix of traditional tools and unconventional approaches. Since July 2016, strong measures have been adopted to save resources in the public sector, particularly in relation to energy, by reducing physical allocations to state entities. Likewise, import controls have been used to maintain a positive trade balance. By way of illustration, between 2013 and 2021 imports fell by 30 percent, a reduction that could not be attributed solely to price moderation in international markets.

Taking into account the high proportion of intermediate goods in Cuban foreign purchases, which has reached 61 percent, the reduction in imports had a negative effect on domestic production, particularly in the manufacturing sector. Other effects could be seen in retail, which has suffered from recurrent shortages of high-demand products and medicines. Until October 2018, Cuba made the required payments corresponding to the agreement with the Paris Club but was forced to reschedule several commitments with suppliers and foreign investors after 2019. High borrowing costs are linked to domestic issues and the US sanctions. However, it is difficult to imagine how Cuba could restart its productive system without fresh resources to finance investments.

The government also implemented some countercyclical measures. First, the public budget has been used to stimulate the economy. Public spending has grown faster than GDP since 2015. In this context, the fiscal deficit widened from 2.2 percent (of nominal GDP) in 2014 to 11.7 percent in 2021 (it was 17.7 percent in 2020). The pressure on prices has grown steadily since 2019, and inflation has skyrocketed since 2020.

There was also a major change in the structure of investments, which has maintained an upward trajectory, although still far from the necessary amounts. In the period considered, total investment more than doubled, a pace that is faster than nominal GDP. Investment in tourism-related facilities, especially high-end hotels, has been the most dynamic component, despite the paucity of tourists. In 2020, it represented around 48 percent of overall investment in the country, whereas the amount spent on energy, gas, and water was only 9 percent.

Foreign investment has received growing attention in recent years, but results are far from what the country needs. A minimal review of the government's economic policy shows that the attraction of foreign investment is practically the only relevant area where there have been no backward steps since the reforms were launched. Foreign investment's role is a relatively new phenomenon in the Cuban context. Although it took off during the 1990s, at that time there was a high degree of discretion and gradualism in attracting new companies, which led to the consolidation of a relatively restrictive and selective process. Between March 2014 (when the current Foreign Investment Law was adopted) and the end of 2021, Cuba registered some 285 new businesses with foreign capital (49 in the Mariel Zone) and 29 reinvestments, with committed capital of more than $7 billion, or a rate of $1 billion per year. Yet these sums are less than half of what had been recognized as necessary.

A much smaller amount has actually been invested, so the impact on economic activity is still modest. The existence of unconventional mechanisms for the allocation of production factors and for the formation of key prices (exchange rates, wages) generates significant distortions in these areas, which are critically important for decisions to penetrate any foreign market. Once in the field, the foreign investor must deal with a decision-making process whose transparency could be significantly improved, which would help build trust. Decision-making is, in addition, generally dilatory with numerous administrative hurdles, which increases the opportunity cost of time and the resources invested.

Taken together, these actions were insufficient to avoid the crisis altogether or secure a fast recovery since 2021.

2022: Did the Economic Crisis Prompt Meaningful Reform?

On the domestic front, as discussed earlier, between mid-2015 and mid-2020, hardly any new measures were adopted as part of the actualización process, even though the country's economic troubles were alarming. The economic crisis triggered by the COVID-19 pandemic clearly exposed the great vulnerability of the Cuban production system. For decades, the Cuban economy had been stuck on a path of very low growth. For example, GDP growth fell from 2.7 percent in 2010–2015 to 0.9 percent between 2016 and 2019. Then in 2020, output contracted by around 11 percent, one of the biggest slumps in Latin America.

Not only was economic performance poor, but it also led to greater macroeconomic instability. The budget deficit increased in recent years. At the same time that the mountain of state debt was growing, there was considerable price pressure, and the national currency, the peso, lost value in the informal market, reflecting both internal and external disequilibria. While inflation officially clocked in at 77 percent in 2021, the GDP price index—a broader measure of price dynamics—suggests an actual increase of 500 percent, which is more consistent with partial data from informal retail vendors and anecdotal evidence. Skyrocketing prices coincided with shortages of practically all goods and services, long lines to buy basic goods, and blackouts.

Small but growing numbers of public protests and sustained, strident criticism on social media indicated a notable drop in popular confidence that the authorities could deal with this crisis. As it expanded electricity rationing, the government also warned that it did not have either a short- or long-term solution to the problem of power generation, as the chapter by Jorge Piñon in this book explains. The devastation at the Matanzas Supertanker Base in August 2022 was another setback to energy supply shortages and the broader economy. The health system lacks essential medications and supplies.

To respond to some of the more important economic problems, the government announced a series of measures during the National Assembly sessions in late July 2021. Most of the steps were aspirational rather than concrete changes in economic policy and were aimed at the short-term crisis. The government reopened a formal market where people could sell hard currency (although they cannot yet buy it); moved to adopt new regulations to open up foreign investment in private companies; and hoped to implement a program to reduce the fiscal deficit.

Notably, some of the measures could worsen the crisis. The announcement that the exchange market will start with only the state as a purchaser of hard currency, offering a rate similar to that in the informal markets, entails significant risks. To stabilize a market, transactions must go both ways, or else people will continue to buy currency at higher prices on the street—fueling its depreciation. The use of the hard currency market to finance the economy reflects the decline in productive capacity on the island, and the purchase of dollars without increasing the supply in pesos is inflationary. Moreover, the most impoverished Cubans do not receive relief from this step, which furthers the growing inequality in the country.

With regard to foreign investment, the dominant tendency has been to try to reproduce for private companies an operating framework similar to that of state enterprises. If the Cuban state hopes to give potential investors confidence by using, for example, investment mechanisms like its own, with unclear policies for approving projects or with extended delays for approval of investments, it will be repeating the same errors as in the past.

Even if robustly implemented, the measures at best focus on the symptoms of the economic crisis, while the short- and long-term real causes remain unaddressed. The ongoing recessive cycle is taking place in the middle of an international situation that is adverse for small countries dependent on imported energy and food, such as Cuba. The island is particularly vulnerable to a context featuring the dramatic effects of the pandemic, the Venezuelan crisis, the war in Ukraine, and continued US sanctions. But the government is not showing any resolve to fix the systemic problems rooted in the Cuban economic model itself.

Recycling measures implemented in the 1990s, such as reliance on the hard-currency market, will have limited effectiveness. Cuba's economy operates against a backdrop of structural problems that Cuban leaders have dodged for decades in an effort to avoid the social and political costs of a serious adjustment, because of ideological dogmatism in economic policy, and as a result of many years of having external allies that could "pay the bill" for inefficiencies of the system.

Some of these effects are unavoidable, but the poor results of the current strategy suggest an urgent need to adjust the course. Economic reforms have stalled due to ideological shortcomings, political maneuvering, and a lack of skilled professionals in the public sector. At the turn of the century, reluctance to implement the necessary changes meant that much of foreign trade was once again tied to political agreements. Therefore, the economic problems of Venezuela, a close partner, now present a burden for Cuba.

On countless occasions, well-intentioned directives have been twisted around and disconnected from their original content. There is a clear resistance to change, but not everyone is rejecting it for the same reasons. The bureaucracy has already been portrayed in public discourse as an obstacle to "modernization." Those affected are convinced that they have a lot to lose if administrative processes become less important and jobs are eliminated.

Furthermore, as a result of the limited, unfinished, and even chaotic corporate reforms since the 1990s, public institutions have broken down in various ways. They seem to be governed by inconsistently applied rules that inevitably favor some to the detriment of others. Even within the state apparatus itself, the same rules do not apply to all, and some are clinging to their privileges.

As a consequence, certain conservative circles have cleverly taken advantage of the spaces and legitimacy of public institutions to be critical of economic reform, sometimes in underhanded ways. However, the only alternative they offer is the current model, which is becoming less and less popular among large sections of the Cuban population, especially the younger generation.

Lacking direct external support, such as from the international financial institutions, Cuba has few options for reviving its moribund economy without radical changes. It is well established that partial reforms in centrally planned economies only lead to stagnation, external imbalances, and deterioration of macroeconomic indicators. Cuba suffers from all of these at this moment.

As seen in the experiences of China and Vietnam, the Soviet-style central planning model can only be successfully reformed if radical changes in the ownership structure and resource allocation mechanism are undertaken. Even in contexts where few changes in the political model have taken place, sustained economic growth depends on the expansion of the private sector and on ownership and management models that dramatically reduce the interference of public officials in the decisions of enterprises. Under those circumstances, the state's role becomes essentially financial (tax payments, dividends).

As a consequence of (or complement to) this, the market becomes the dominant mechanism for resource allocation. Cuba suffers, like China and Vietnam before it, from a model in which state enterprises are dominant and public officials who have multiple simultaneous objectives interfere in their management. Many of these objectives are arbitrary and extra-economic in nature. The allocation of resources and productive factors takes place through a centralized mechanism, where government agencies establish annual plans and set prices and production volumes.

Officials seek to simplify the management of this model, so a few large companies are preferred. To function, the model requires a huge bureaucracy to provide the discipline that markets deliver through bankruptcy and variable profits. But Cuban companies operate under soft budget constraints, which creates perverse incentives for efficiency in their management. This means that, as a rule, state-owned enterprises have significant influence over the determination of the final sales price, because of their privileged relationship with officials and their monopolistic position in a market dominated by supply (in the face of chronic shortages).

The tax system is established endogenously to the company: it lacks measurable and objective application criteria, and many companies receive exceptional individual exemptions. They also receive transfers from the state free of charge, to cover current operations and investments. Access to credit is very low and the criteria for access often is not under the control of the enterprise. The private and cooperative sector, which has only grown appreciably since 2010, is still small and subject to the deformations of the general model and suffers from discretionary decisions that limit its possibilities to decisively transform the economic model. Neither workers nor company managers face an incentive structure that links performance with rewards. The consequence of the model inevitably leads to low growth, inefficiency, low external competitiveness, and weak incentives for innovation. If the survival of the political system depends on a model designed for control, then its survival precludes economic progress.

Some Cuban officials believe that the United States and some groups in the country will take advantage of any change that transforms the distribution of power. They remember well the lessons of uncontrolled perestroika in the last days of the Soviet Union. Nevertheless, they must find a middle ground between micro-measures of little strategic value and potentially destabilizing change. They can tone down their ideological statements and media wars, and surround themselves with a competent economic policy team to draw up a roadmap for long-term reform. Instead of the Cuban government clinging to empty promises of reform, such an approach would potentially help it find some allies and recover the confidence of Cuba's citizens and, no less importantly, recover social peace. Without a strategic plan, as various Communist Party resolutions have warned over the years, the problems will multiply over time, as they have since 1990.

Economic Reform Remains a Work in Progress

Fulfilling the initial goal of the economic reforms remains a work in progress, at best. For years, the Cuban government has shown very little imagination when it comes to the role of foreign powers in the island's transformation process. The main focus has been on expanding alliances that provide preferential agreements to reduce the cost of US sanctions and, most importantly, postpone the need for major changes to address the dysfunctional economic model.

However, it is difficult to say whether China or Russia, Cuba's most important allies, are interested in offering unconditional aid at the level that would enable the crisis to be overcome. Cuba has great potential, but successful implementation depends on a radical reform of the national model. This would explain the marginal participation of Chinese companies and the abrupt decline in trade between the two countries since 2016. There is also the risk that reliance on China and Russia could once again catch Cuba in the net of a new cold war in which it is pitted against its closest neighbor. This is a course that Cuba's leaders should definitely avoid at all costs.

Notes

1. "Lineamientos de la Política Económica y Social del Partido y la Revolución," Sixth Congress of Cuba's Communist Party (Havana: Partido Comunista de Cuba, 2011).

2. "Actualización de los Lineamientos de la Política Económica y Social del Partido y la Revolución para el periodo 2016–2021," document of Seventh Congress of Cuba's Communist Party; "Conceptualización del Modelo Económico y Social Cubano de Desarrollo Socialista," document of Seventh Congress of Cuba's Communist Party; "Plan Nacional de Desarrollo Económico y Social hasta 2030: Propuesta de Visión de la Nación, Ejes y Sectores Estratégicos," document of Seventh Congress of Cuba's Communist Party" (Havana: Partido Comunista de Cuba, 2016).

3. O. E. Pérez, "La inversión extranjera directa en Cuba: necesidad de su relanzamiento," *Economía y Desarrollo* 152, no. 2 (2012): 37–52.

4. C. Mesa-Lago and P. Vidal, "The Impact of the Global Crisis on Cuba's Economy and Social Welfare," *Journal of Latin American Studies*, no. 42 (2009): 689–717.

5. "Conceptualización del Modelo Económico y Social Cubano de Desarrollo Socialista," document of Seventh Congress of Cuba's Communist Party.

6. Calculations are based on budget revenue data from the Office of National Statistics (ONEI). The assumption is that cuentapropistas accounted for most of personal income tax revenues during those years.

7. International Monetary Fund, *Data Mapper: Venezuela*, April 2019, accessed August 6, 2019, at https://www.imf.org/external/datamapper/NGDPD@WEO/OEMDC/ADVEC/WEOWORLD/VEN.

8. US Energy Information Administration, "Venezuelan Crude Oil Production Falls to Lowest Level since January 2003," *Today in Energy*, May 20, 2019, accessed at https://www.eia.gov/todayinenergy/detail.php?id=39532.

CHAPTER 7

State Enterprise in a New Economic Context

C. Juan Triana Cordoví

Translated by Rebecca Bodenheimer

Today the "Cuban enterprise system" is structured into at least several groups: the socialist state-owned company; companies that have various contractual terms related to foreign capital, including joint ventures with non-state management firms as well as micro, small, and medium-size enterprises (MPYMES); self-employed people (TCP); and even projects developed by local governments. In addition, there are agricultural, credit, service, and industrial cooperatives. Compared to just a decade ago, today we can say that the enterprise system has been diversified, not only because new members have emerged, like MPYMES, but also because others that aren't so new have spaces that they didn't have access to ten years ago. But it wasn't always like this.

To understand what is taking place with state enterprises, we need to take a brief look at the history of the process of nationalization of the economy that began in the early 1960s, and become familiar with elements that currently survive and elements of the national macroeconomic behavior in which it should function.

This chapter addresses in a concise manner issues related to Cuban socialist state-owned companies, beginning with a historical perspective in order to then delve into the current context in which state enterprise must operate, with an emphasis on two relatively new phenomena: the so-called unified monetary system and the emergence of a sector of small and medium-size private businesses.

Enterprises and the Nationalization of the Economy

The nationalization of the Cuban economy was the result of a long process of interventions undertaken by the government, almost from the first months after the triumph of the Revolution. The catalyst for this was the nationalization of US companies, which later continued with the nationalization of large properties of the Cuban bourgeoisie. Thus, as early as 1963, the presence of the state sector within the economy was overwhelming and dominant, as is shown in table 7.1. In 1968, after the "Revolutionary

Table 7.1.   Extent of state sector control

	20%	40%	60%	80%	100%	
Banking						100%
Foreign trade						100%
Wholesale trade						100%
Retail trade						75%
Transportation						95%
Construction						98%
Manufacturing						95%
Agriculture						70%

Source: García 2005.

Offensive," this process was completed, with only one small segment of agriculture—no more than 30 percent—in the hands of private owners.

It is also important to note that nationalization began even before the country explicitly took on the form of a socialist system, although undoubtedly it was the adoption of the socialist economic model that consolidated the role of state enterprise within the dynamic of the national economy and decisively supplemented the political power of the revolutionary government. Nationalization also universalized the existence of large monopolies as the preferred organizing principle of the entrepreneurial system, which the political leadership of the country found useful.

Various moments within the evolution of the state enterprise system after the 1960s can be pinpointed: beginning in 1975, the adoption of the System for Economic Planning and Management (SDPE); the phase corresponding to the so-called rectification of errors and negative tendencies that began in the mid-1980s; the period of the 1990s, during which two business types were formed that are distinct in terms of their functioning, degree of decentralization, and use of one of the two currencies; and the counter-reforms that President Fidel Castro initiated in 2003.[1] These reforms re-elevated the degree of centralization and concentrated the utilization of currencies at the highest levels of the government. Between 2003 and 2004, the bank accounts for state-owned companies that had been in dollars were converted to convertible pesos. There was a notable reduction in the number of companies that could operate in foreign currencies and a return to centralization in the use of the freely convertible currency (MLC) by way of Resolution 92 from the Central Cuban Bank (BCC), which established the only foreign currency account in 2004. As a result, we saw the emergence of the Committee for the Approval of Foreign Currency of the Cuban Central Bank, an entity charged with allocating resources in MLC to the entire state enterprise sector (Blanco 2020). Finally, the current phase is known as the "updating of the economic model," and it has been defined by a renewed attempt to increase the power of state companies and expand their areas of action and decision.

Humberto Blanco (2020) has described the transformations of the 1990s aimed at a greater autonomy for state-owned companies in the following manner:

1. The elimination of the monopoly of the foreign trade sector and the creation of an import market of goods and services in MLC.
2. An emerging business sector, headed by the tourist sector and business entities with structure and forms of operation similar to Western corporations: head offices, territorial divisions, etc.
3. Self-financing schemes in foreign currency and the replacement of planning based on material balances with income and expense balances in MLC.
4. The emergence of non-banking financial entities that mobilize resources temporarily free from the business networks to which they were tied, by offering financing possibilities for development and the promotion of production chains with other companies.
5. A process of reorganization of productive capacities in order to counter the prevailing trend toward mega-companies in the European Economic Community (EEC).

It is worth noting, however, that the state enterprise system has been identified since the beginning as the decisive element in the whole process of economic reform, not only due to its weight within the national economy, which is indisputable, but also for political and ideological reasons

In sum, Cuban state enterprises are now in the phase of what has been called the updating of the Cuban economic model (beginning in 2012), bringing with it all the weaknesses of previous decades, particularly a very marked subordination to the ministerial structures and the absence of an appropriate institutional framework. In 2019 and 2020, state enterprises again were the subject of new reforms. To this, we should note an international context that is inauspicious for any attempt at modernization and restructuring (Romero 2021).

It has been posited that the long process of reforms that spans the period from 2008 to 2020 and that had as one of its core ideas the reform of state enterprise "did not succeed in discarding the utilization of mechanisms of direct control over the economy in general" (Hidalgo and Triana 2022, 15). The other matter to consider is the performance/situation of the Cuban economy, especially since 2019, because a group of factors have impacted the dynamics of the national economy and logically also state enterprises.

On the one hand, the ramping up of the US economic blockade, beginning with the policies of the Trump administration toward Cuba, has made trade and financing more expensive, and has made commercial operations more difficult and raised the cost of inputs and financing. On the other hand, government expenses were increased to fight the COVID-19 pandemic. The pandemic also required companies to reduce their level of activity.

But a group of internal factors has also had a crucial impact in the post-2018 period. The slow or negative growth of the gross domestic product (GDP), a low rate of investment in relation to investment needs, the uneven sectoral structure of investments, scarce foreign investment flows, and foreign debt and debt service (Sánchez and Borras 2021) all created an unfavorable macroeconomic picture with respect to the health of the socialist state enterprise. At the same time, a burdensome inflation was generated by the increase in the average nominal salary (in 2020) coinciding with the abrupt decline of the supply of goods and services in the retail market engendered by the reduction of the national supply and of imports. To all of this, we should add fiscal instability and foreign exchange and monetary distortions.[2] It is in this context that the state enterprise has been forced to survive (Hidalgo and Triana 2022).

Monetary Restructuring

The process "monetary restructuring" was expressed in more than 9,000 rules. Currency and exchange unification had long been identified as a priority of economic reform, and in general terms it can be considered to be a program of structural adjustment that intended to have goals beyond the unification associated with macro- and microeconomic functioning, with a decisive effect on the state enterprise sector.

Among its goals were: the correction of relative prices in order to better allocate resources; generating incentives for the export sector and attempting to eliminate/reduce implicit subsidies on exports; salary adjustments that cushion the loss of purchasing power that devaluation would produce; the generation of greater transparency with positive impacts on macroeconomic management; and adapting/improving income distribution mechanisms (Hidalgo and Triana 2022). Nonetheless, all of this was implemented several years after its announcement, and at the worst time to introduce changes.

After almost two years of having been put into practice, the so-called monetary regulation has not achieved any of its goals. On the contrary, the currency and exchange environment has become more complex, which negatively impacts state enterprises, which in practice has to operate in four different currencies: the Cuban peso, freely convertible currency (MLC), liquidity certificates (CL), and transactions that are made directly in dollars, buying and paying from abroad.

Monetary regulation directly impacted the cost structure of the state enterprise that for years had operated with an overvalued official exchange rate, so that its results in terms of efficiency and productivity were always skewed. There has been a devaluation of almost 2,300 percent produced by monetary regulation and the necessary transfer onto costs and enterprises, and from there to the price of products and services they offer, even though the state designed a program that attempted to reduce the impact.

At the moment, there are more than 400 state-owned companies (21 percent of all companies) in debt, and a portion of these are technically bankrupt.

State Enterprises in a Changing Environment

States enterprises are recognized in official documents as the most important economic agent in Cuba. In this regard, it is stated that among the main transformation is "to consolidate the fundamental role of the socialist ownership of the people over the fundamental means of production, distinguish between the exercise of the powers of the owners and those corresponding to possession or management (administration)" (PCC 2021, 21). In 2017, state enterprises were defined in the following way: "Business entities are owned by the people. The State acts for the benefit of the owner, which is the people; legal persons with duties and rights; responsible for the production of goods and services of a commercial nature and obtains profits and fulfills social responsibilities; covers their expenses with income; plays an active role in the preparation, execution and control of plans and budgets; and endowed with autonomy for business administration or management" (PCC 2017).

"Conserving" state-owned enterprise and improving performance has been one of the central purposes of the economic reform as a whole. To this point, it is possible to identify a group of economic policy actions aimed at this goal, as Humberto Blanco and Juan Triana explain:

> Managed with extreme caution, the reform of state enterprise has recently experienced a new dynamic, after the establishment of 43 measures—28 at the end of 2019 and 15 in July 2020—all aimed at providing greater autonomy to the companies in decisive matters such as price configurations, salary determinations, utilization of profits, export incentives, access to currencies for reproduction, reduction of the leading indicators of the plan to only two, facilitation and promotion of relations with the non-state sector as well as joint ventures, and the reconversion of the Base Business Units (UEB) to subsidiary companies when appropriate. (Blanco and Triana 2021, 32)

In a diagnosis of state enterprise conducted in 2018 (Díaz 2019), it was pointed out that companies have been converted into intermediate entities between the Higher Organizations of Business Management (OSDE) and the Base Business Units (UEB). The number of companies has shrunk by 50 percent since 2000. In the period between 2011 and 2017, there was a decrease of 400 entities and many were eliminated or merged because they took losses. In addition, there was an explicit budget subsidy from the state toward state-owned companies that substitute imports or that export goods. State enterprises contribute 50 percent of their profits to the state budget, but the budget showed a decreasing trend until 2018, with the exception of 2017.

The weight of state enterprises within the national economy continues to be decisive if one considers its contribution/participation in GDP (PIB). Although national statistics don't allow us to quantify its participation, it is plausible to suppose it is roughly 80 percent of GDP. From the perspective of job generation, however, the role of the state enterprise has ceded territory, and today the participation of the different economic actors in employment is as shown in table 7.2.

As table 7.2 indicates, the participation of the non-state sector in employment follows that of the state sector in importance (the non-state sector is composed of self-employed workers, cooperatives of many types, and artisans and artists). This data does not yet include employment in the MPYMES (micro, small, and medium-size enterprises), as they were just authorized in October 2021. If we consider the data

Table 7.2.   Enterprises in the national economy by province (January–September 2022)

Province	Total	State Enterprises	Corporations	MPYMES*	Cooperatives
Pinar del Río	260	92	1	121	46
Artemisa	322	80	10	167	65
La Habana	2,218	631	239	1,322	26
Mayabeque	206	70	3	86	47
Matanzas	407	101	3	231	72
Villa Clara	476	119	2	241	114
Cienfuegos	231	84	2	76	69
Sancti Spíritus	299	76	1	159	63
Ciego de Ávila	227	80	1	80	66
Camagüey	387	110	2	130	145
Las Tunas	277	65	1	102	109
Holguín	484	120	5	233	126
Granma	635	93	1	365	176
Santiago de Cuba	527	118	6	228	175
Guantánamo	293	78	1	127	87
Isla de la Juventud	76	34	0	34	8
Cuba	7,325	1,951	278	3,702	1,394

Source: ONEI 2022b.
*The Cuban National Statistical Office (ONEI) reported only the number of MPYMES actually in operation. As of September 2022, the Ministry of the Economy and Planning had approved more than 5,000 registrations.

from the Statistical Yearbook of Cuba in 2021, participation of the non-state sector in employment had barely changed from the percentage of the 4.5 million Cubans employed: 31 percent in 2020 versus 32 percent in 2021 (ONEI 2022a, table 7.2).

The creation of MPYMES likely introduced changes to the employment structure. According to data supplied by the Ministry of the Economy and Planning, they have generated direct employment for 91,692 people (Alonso, Figueredo, and Fonseca 2022). If we take into account that the number of state-run MPYMES is minimal, it is very probable that in 2022 there was growth of employment in the non-state sector, which is consolidating its role as a more dynamic job generator in Cuba.

We do not have statistics on the participation of MPYMES in the sectoral structure of GDP. For 2022, we do not have the data that would allow us to know the number of MPYMES by sector and compare them with the number of state-owned companies. At the close of 2021, with barely two months of authorization for MPYMES, the situation was as can be seen in table 7.2.

The large trend of creating MPYMES (more than one hundred per week) has enriched the Cuban business fabric, so much so that by the end of October 2022 the participation of MPYMES in different activities had shifted dramatically, as the data on the number of them in various spheres of activity demonstrates in table 7.3.

If we compare the number of businesses by sector/activity, we can see how the MPYMES surpass the state-owned enterprises in various sectors. However, it would be a mistake to derive from this data that state enterprise has lost relevance in these or other sectors. State enterprises are still dominant in virtually all sectors of the Cuban economy, even though the number of companies is fewer. Its size, as well as its volume of sales and contribution to GDP, is far greater than that of the MPYMES.

Another aspect to consider is that this hegemony is also associated with the support state enterprises have received from the state, and consequently with its role that is recognized politically in the configuration of the Cuban economic and social model, and that has been expressed in the paternalistic treatment by the state. This includes subsidies received to cover losses, the government's lax enforcement of credit obligations, and the priority state enterprises are given when it comes to investment.

Thus, although it is possible to note the systematic growth in the number of small and medium-size businesses in Cuba, including the fact that they have overtaken the number of state enterprises, we cannot necessarily assume that the state sector has been displaced by the nascent private sector of small and medium-size businesses.

It is still true today that the portion of the economy constituted by the state enterprise system is the most powerful, at least in terms of physical infrastructure and installed production capacity, even though a part of this production capacity is more theoretical than real. Among other things due to the years of accumulated obsolescence, there is the technology gap, high energy consumption, the inability to access supplies, and the limited scale of production.

It is also true that in the last three years, more measures have been adopted to "stimulate" the good performance of state enterprises than ever before. Nonetheless, to exercise the necessary leadership and engage the rest of the system, to push it and pull it, requires much more. It requires responding to questions that remain in the wind like the dust of the song.

The first question to answer is the same that has occupied Cuba for the past fifty years: What should continue to be state-owned within the Cuban entrepreneurial system? The way in which Cuban socialism is still understood today has led to conserving, maintaining, and nourishing a state entrepreneurial system that is very large in terms of the number of companies, and very dispersed if we consider the definition of the fundamental means of production, which also disperses effort and scarce resources and is inefficient. In effect the question is, should a small state, highly dependent on external conditions outside of its control, with very high social commitments, continue wearing itself out and throwing resources at failing companies?

In addition to economic questions, there are others that may be even more decisive: Do we have any certainty that the reduction of the state enterprise system will guarantee greater levels of efficiency? Could the MPYMES be the alternative? Is it possible that the reduction of a substantial part of the state enterprise system will have an unwanted impact in terms of instability and political control? What are the opportunity costs of doing it and those of not doing it? These are the fundamental questions that Cuba faces in its attempt to update the economy.

Table 7.3. Enterprises in the national economy by sector (January–September 2022)

Economic Activity	Total	State Enterprises	Corporations	MIPYMES	CNA*	Agricultural Cooperatives
Fishing	44	22	2	20	–	–
Mining and quarrying	29	19	5	5	–	–
Sugar industry	57	57	–	–	–	–
Manufacturing industries (except sugar)	1,944	378	22	1,486	58	–
Electricity, gas, and water supply	72	65	–	4	3	–
Construction	1,181	165	9	931	76	–
Commerce: repair of personal and household goods	818	401	53	236	128	–
Hotels and restaurants	752	129	11	455	157	–
Transportation, storage, and communication	288	93	41	148	6	–
Financial intermediation	37	8	28	1	–	–
Business services, real estate, and rental activities	600	231	86	266	17	–
Public administration, defense, and social welfare	10	5	4	1	–	–
Science and technological innovation	40	34	5	–	1	–
Education	2	2	–	–	–	–
Public health and social work	4	1	3	–	–	–
Culture and sports	49	34	8	7	–	–
Other community service activities	138	31	1	81	25	–
Total	11,067	1,951	278	3,702	473	4,663

Source: ONEI 2022b.
*CNA: nonagricultural cooperatives.

Notes

1. "One of the major corrections the Party and Government undertook was to put an end to the privilege that 3,000 citizens had administering the country's currency. If they took on debt on behalf of the state, it was done without a guarantee that it could be paid back. When it came time to repay—regardless of the necessity if the investment—the State had to pay it" (Castro 2005).

2. The dual currency system lasted for more than twenty-five years, generating many skews in costs and pricing (anchored to the huge lag in the official exchange rate) in the corporate and financial balance sheets and public accounts (Hidalgo and Triana 2022, 35).

References

Alonso, R., O. Figueredo, and C. Fonseca. 2022. "Nuevos actores económicos: El reto está en fortalecer el entramado empresarial cubano." Cubadebate, October 12. Accessed at http://www.cubadebate.cu/noticias/2022/10/12/nuevos-actores-economicos-el-reto-esta-en-fortalecer-el-entramado-empresarial-cubano-video.

Blanco, H. 2020. "Treinta años de la empresa estatal en Cuba: recuento y reflexiones sobre su transformación." *Economía y Desarrollo* 64, no. 2: 91–109.

Blanco, H., and J. Triana. 2021. "Reflexiones sobre la nueva estrategia económica cubana." In *Miradas a la Economía Cubaba. Elementos: Claves para la Sostenibilidad*, ed. Ricardo Torres Pérez and Dayma Echevarría León, 21–36. Havana: Ruth Casa Editorial and CEEC. Accessed at https://library.fes.de/pdf-files/bueros/fescaribe/18406.pdf.

Castro, F. 2005. "Speech Delivered by Commander in Chief Fidel Castro Ruz at the Ceremony for the 60th Anniversary of His Admission to the University, Held in the Aula Magna of the University of Havana, on November 17, 2005." Accessed at http://www.fidelcastro.cu/es/discursos/discurso-pronunciado-en-el-acto-por-el-aniversario-60-de-su-ingreso-la-universidad-en-el.

Díaz, I. 2019. "Prosperidad y sostenibilidad: necesidad de encontrar (descubrir) la empresa estatal." In *Miradas a la Economía Cubana. Un plan de desarrollo hasta 2030*, 97–106. Havana: Ruth Casa Editorial.

García, A. 2005. *Sobre la estrategia de desarrollo de Cuba*. Havana: Centro de Estudios de la Economía Cubana.

Hidalgo, V., and J. Triana. 2022. "Macroeconomía y crecimiento en la agenda de transformaciones del modelo económico cubano en el período pospandemis de COVID-19." In *La economía cubana pospandemia de Covid-19*, 9–61. Havana: Universidad de la Habana.

ONEI (Oficina Nacional de Estadísticas e Información). 2022a. *Anuario Estadístico de Cuba 2021*. Havana: MEP.

———. 2022b. *Organización Institucional. Principales Entidades Enero-Septiembre 2022*. Accessed January 12, 2023, at http://www.onei.gob.cu/node/18786.

PCC (Communist Party of Cuba). 2017. *Conceptualización del modelo económico y social cubano y plan de desarrollo*. Havana: Comité Central.

———. 2021. *Conceptualización del Modelo Económico y Social Cubano de Desarrollo Socialista: Lineamientos de la Política Económica y Social del Partido y la Revolución para el Período 2021–2026*. Havana: Comité Central. Accessed at http://www.cubadebate.cu/especiales/2021/06/17/descargue-en-pdf-la-conceptualizacion-del-modelo-y-los-lineamientos-para-el-periodo-2021-2026.

Romero, A. 2021. "Cuba 2020. El escenario económico externo y sus perspectivas." In Torres and Echevarría, *Miradas a la Economía Cubana. Elementos*, 5–17.

Sánchez, M., and F. Borras. 2021. "La gestión de la deuda pública en Cuba. Los desafíos del endeudamiento externo." In *Miradas a la Economía Cubana. elementos claves para la sostenibilidad*, 69–82.

CHAPTER 8

The Economic Stakeholders in Cuba

INTERACTIONS AND ALLIANCES ON THE ECONOMIC STAGE

C. Maelia Esther Pérez Silveira

The private sector increasingly plays a significant role in the Cuban economy. Its advances are reflected not only in its growing numbers, but also in the types and scope of activity.

In Cuba, business activity consists of two fundamental sectors: the state sector, which is the prioritized sector of the economy, and the non-state sector (the "private sector"), which is assigned a complementary role. Nonetheless, it is experiencing a gradual evolution despite its characterization and position as complementary.[1]

According to Mildrey Granadillo, First Vice-Minister of the Ministry of Economy and Planning, both sectors share a space that is becoming increasingly harmonious.[2] A unique part of this change is the ability to interact and generate alliances, although this process also generates disagreements among actors and conflicts with existing regulations.

In the state business sector, there is a process of convergence of state enterprises, their subsidiary entities, and top-level business management organizations that focus on the management of strategic sectors, the provision of public services, and the management and execution of their assigned economic activities. In their commercial activities, state enterprises enjoy autonomy in administration and management. This is evident by their operations in the areas of production or services, labor, finances, credit, investment, and setting prices, among others.

For its part, the private sector consists of businesses and business owners with a variety of forms of organization, ownership, and principles of internal organization. Despite the advances and setbacks in the development of the private sector during the last few years, its diversity and growth have been supported since the adoption of the legal reforms regulating it. The different forms of organization range from cooperatives, including agricultural and nonagricultural cooperatives (CNAs) and micro-, small, and medium-size businesses (MPYMES), which are usually organized in the form of limited liability companies. Some include local development projects in the category of "private sector," although there is disagreement about whether they constitute businesses that have economic stakeholders other than the state.

Title II of the Constitution of the Republic of 2019 establishes the economic fundamentals of the Cuban socialist economic system as based on the people's ownership

147

of the fundamental means of production. This constitutes the main form of property ownership, with the state regulating and controlling it for the benefit of society. Without a doubt, this assigned priority places public ownership in a superior place in relation to other forms of property ownership also recognized in the constitution, and establishes guidelines for the interaction among them. Article 22 of the constitution defines the forms of property:

- Socialist property of all the people, for which the state acts as a representative and for the benefit of the people as the owner. In this order, the socialist state company is defined as the main actor of the national economy, to which a vital role in the production of goods and provision of services is attributed.
- The property of the cooperatives
- The property of political, mass, and social organizations
- Private property
- Mixed property
- The property of institutions and associative forms
- Personal property[3]

Article 22 itself, in its last paragraph, establishes that "all forms of ownerships of the means of production *interact in similar ways.* The state regulates and controls the way in which they contribute to the economic and social development." The clause defines the basic principle that governs the interaction between the different forms of property ownership and places them in a status of being similar but implicitly not equal to the state enterprises. It also informs the relationship between the different actors that are property owners.

In this way, the different forms of property ownership are positioned—and with them the actors or stakeholders that own and develop them—*in similar statuses and not as equals,* although they may appear to enjoy equal power over their property. This standing generates an uncertainty subject to multiple interpretations that could put them somewhat out of balance, resulting in irregularities not originally intended by the lawmakers.

The Socialist State Enterprise

As part of the process of updating the Cuban economic model, as well as due to the importance and need to advance in the perfection of the state enterprise system, Decree Law 34 of 2021 was approved. It regulates the organization and the operation of state enterprises, subsidiary entities, and top-level enterprise management organizations, which it identifies with the generic term *entities.* They are the business activities of the Cuban state enterprise system.

Among the General Provisions defined in the constitution, in its Article 9.1, the autonomy of these entities with respect to their administration and management is recognized. In its Article 10, Decree Law 34 authorizes these entities to form contractual associations for the purposes of creating strategic alliances, production chains, and

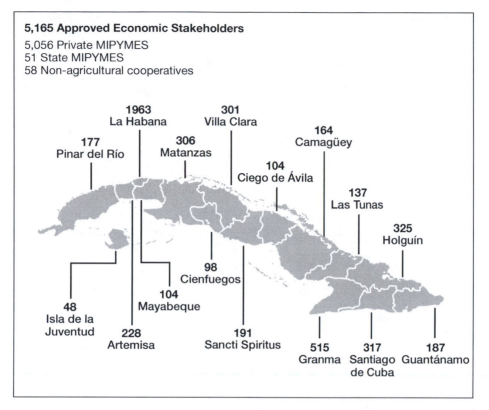

5,165 Approved Economic Stakeholders

5,056 Private MIPYMES
51 State MIPYMES
58 Non-agricultural cooperatives

1963
La Habana

301
Villa Clara

177
Pinar del Río

306
Matanzas

164
Camagüey

104
Ciego de Ávila

137
Las Tunas

325
Holguín

98
Cienfuegos

104
Mayabeque

48
Isla de la
Juventud

228
Artemisa

191
Sancti Spiritus

515
Granma

317
Santiago
de Cuba

187
Guantánamo

Figure 8.1.   Approved Economic Stakeholders. *Source*: Ministerio de Economía y Planificación; https://www.mep.gob.cu/sites/default/files/Documentos/Archivos/Listado%20de%20MIPYMES%20y%20CNA%20aprobadas%206505.pdf

access to technologies, among others. At the same time, it approves of their association with other state or non-state actors for the purposes of creating new legal entities.

The Self-Employed Worker (*Trajabador por Cuenta Propia* [TCP] or *Cuentapropista*)

TCP is the status that is granted to a natural person who is authorized to perform one or several economic production or service activities.[4] Business activities can be organized as one or more TCPs. As a result, self-employment work is understood to be the activity or activities autonomously performed by natural persons who may or may not own the means and objects of work they use to provide services and engage in the production of goods.

Decree Law 44 of 2021[5] updates the general provisions regarding the performance of self-employment work, the procedure for processing authorizations, and the organization and regulatory oversight of TCPs. In its Article 29, the regulation establishes that a TCP can market its products and services to Cuban and foreign natural persons and legal entities. It then authorizes TCPs to engage in the export of goods and services generated within the framework of their activities and the importation of raw materials or goods that are necessary for their products. This must be done through authorized exporter and importer entities. This appears to place the TCP in the status of any other economic stakeholder. With respect to legal entities, they can be formed in both the state sector and private sector.

Despite the broad authorization of Decree Law 44, TCPs are currently unattractive for a variety of reasons, including:

- The nature and lack of status as an entity offering limited personal liability. A TCP must accept the risks along with the rewards and incur personal liability and potentially loss of his or her individual assets.
- The expansion of the list of economic actors, including the CNAs and the MPYMES which organize themselves as limited liability companies. In both cases, they enjoy a status of independent legal entities, and the separation between the assets of the individual members and those of the entity, with the resulting limitation on the liability of the owners.
- Sustained resistance by state enterprises and governmental institutions to establishing commercial links with the private sector.

The Nonagricultural Cooperative (CNA)

Along with the constitutional recognition of cooperatives as property-owning associations, the legislation established the distinction between the agricultural cooperative companies and CNAs. Both are regulated through distinctive sets of regulations, each of which defines the scope and characteristics of the permitted relationships.[6]

Article 1 of Decree Law No. 47 of August 19, 2021, establishes the general rules applicable to nonagricultural cooperatives and the rules for their formation, operation, and expiration.[7] The regulation defines the CNA as an economic entity that is formed based on the voluntary association of people who contribute money, property, and other rights for the satisfaction of the economic, social, and cultural needs of its partners, as well as the public interest.

The second part of Article 2 establishes the status of the CNA as a legal entity, its equity interests, its rights of use and enjoyment regarding its assets, as well as its liability with respect to the obligations contracted with its creditors. It regulates the participation of CNAs in the contracting of the provision of goods and services with other actors, recognized in the current law, and *acknowledges their equal status with those*. In contrast, Article 22 of the constitution states that the various recognized actors have *similar status*.

Micro-, Small, and Medium-Size Companies

Decree Law 46/2021, regarding MPYMES, regulates the creation and operation of this new economic stakeholder.[8] MPYMES are defined as economic units with separate legal existence and size characteristics that have as their objective the development of the production of goods and the provision of services. They can be organized by the state or the private sector or be owned in partnership by both. They have business autonomy within the framework of the current law. They are generally organized as limited liability companies, thereby separating the ownership of the assets and commercial and other obligations imposed by the legal system from those of the individual members of the MPYMES.

Their enabling regulation produces an analogous framework as that for the CNAs. In Article 5.4 of Decree Law 46/2021, MPYMES, like CNAs, are given the right to engage in transactions for goods and services with other recognized economic actors and operate *with the same status*.

Future Composition of Economic Actors

The diversity of the economic actors, their presence in the Cuban economic space, and the recognition of their interaction by the constitution means they are not boxed into watertight compartments. Although a leading role is assigned to the socialist state company as the main form of property owner, that prerogative is not necessarily a detriment to the rest of the economic actors, including the private sector, which is today visible throughout the country and is becoming increasingly important.

The private sector's advances are demonstrated not only in the growth numbers, but also by the level of activity it is developing, the increase in its contribution to the country's economy, its use of modeling to adapt to a complex economic environment, its search for alternative solutions, and its interactions with other actors. This could well lead it to transcend its designated role as complementary or secondary in the country's economic development. However, as of this writing, only a few months after the approval of the laws that enable this new framework, it is too soon to make definitive forecasts.

Both the private sector alone and its relationship with the state sector have had to navigate difficulties, limitations, and conditions that impact their normal development, including:

- While the doors were opened to a new scenario, many of those working in the existing institutions are resisting the changes and hindering the way toward a range of broader and transparent exchanges and relationships.
- There is a general ignorance of the mechanisms, tools, and legal solutions that legitimate and empower these new actors and their alliances.
- Private entrepreneurs have had difficulty in adapting existing regulations for foreign commercial relations, banking, financing, and specific markets, which were designed for state economic activity, to the non-state sector.
- Those assigned to apply the regulations and supervise the activity are themselves ignorant of the purpose and appropriate application.
- Due to negative preconceptions about the private sector among state enterprise sector actors, and their resistance to change, many have been reluctant to establish relationships and interact with the different forms of private economic actors.

Notes

This chapter was originally published by the Cuba Capacity Building Project at Columbia University Law School (https://horizontecubano.law.columbia.edu) and is reprinted by permission.

1. David Pajón Espina, "The Expansion of the Private Sector in Cuba," *Horizonte Cubano*, April 2, 2021, accessed at https://horizontecubano.law.columbia.edu/news/expansion-private-sector-cuba.

2. Teyuné Díaz Díaz, "Empresas estatales y privadas en Cuba por impulsar la economía," Prensa Latina, November 14, 2022, accessed at https://www.prensa-latina.cu/2022/11/14/empresas-estatales-y-privadas-en-cuba-por-impulsar-la-economia.

3. Each of these forms is defined within the following scope: (a) socialist of the entire nation: in which the state acts in representation and for the benefit of it as owner; (b) cooperative: the property supported in the collective work of its owner partners and in the effective exercise of the principles of the cooperative movement; (c) regarding political, mass, and social organizations: the one that is exercised by these subjects on property intended for the achievement of its purposes; (d) private: the one that is exercised on specific means of production by natural persons or Cuban or foreign legal entities, with a complementary role in the economy; (e) mixed: the one formed by the combination of two or more forms of property; (f) regarding institutions and associative forms: the one that these subjects exercise on their property for the achievement of purposes of nonprofit nature; and (g) personal: the one that is exercised on the property which, without creating means of production, contributes to satisfying the material and spiritual needs of its owner.

4. Natalia Delgado and Saira Pons Pérez, "Legal Structures for the Non-state Sector Based on the Type and Scale of the Activity," *Horizonte Cubano*, July 7, 2019, accessed at https://horizontecubano.law.columbia.edu/news/legal-structures-non-state-sector-according-type-and-scale-activity.

5. Published in the Ordinary *Official Gazette of the Republic of Cuba* No. 94 of August 19, 2021.

6. Decree Law No. 365 on the agricultural cooperatives establishes the general principles regarding their formation, operation, splitting, and expiration; Decree No. 354 of December 18, 2018, establishes the regulation of the aforementioned Decree Law 365 of 2018. Both published in the Ordinary *Official Gazette* No. 37 of May 24, 2019.

7. Published in the Ordinary *Official Gazette* No. 37 of May 24, 2019. Decree No. 354 of the same date, which approves the regulations of the referenced decree law, is included.

8. Published in the Ordinary *Official Gazette* No. 94 of August 19, 2021.

CHAPTER 9

Economic Crisis, Foreign Investment, and the Challenges of Structural Transformation

Antonio F. Romero Gómez

Translated by Rozzmery Palenzuela Vicente

This chapter summarizes Cuban policy and performance in terms of attracting foreign direct investment (FDI) flows in recent years, linking this process with the general evolution and structural problems that the island's economy has faced.

The first section synthesizes the main factors and manifestations of the most recent crisis of Cuba's economy and society and concludes that these are an expression of an evident crisis of accumulation. The second section examines the dynamics of FDI inflows between 2011 and 2020, and the main changes in the policies and regulations related to foreign investment are presented. In the final section, the main challenges faced by the Cuban economy and authorities are synthesized according to their objective of attracting increasing FDI to overcome an important part of the structural obstacles that hinder the growth and socioeconomic development of the nation.

The Recent Economic Crisis and Its Determinants

The worsening of the economic and social dynamics of Cuba between 2019 and 2022 have multiple causal factors. These include:

- the sharp decline in bilateral relations with the United States since the Trump administration, and the increase in the sanctions applied—with extraterritorial implications—that harmed the nation's external economic transactions;
- the deep global economic recession that occurred since COVID-19 and its effects on external demand for goods, income from tourism and remittances, and the increase in the price of imports;
- the serious problems shown since 2014 by the economy of Venezuela, which was Cuba's main trade and external economic cooperation partner;
- the negative economic impacts generated from the Russia-Ukraine war in a context of slowdown-recession of the global economy with very high inflationary records;

- the high economic-financial costs assumed by the Cuban state to face the pandemic and its impacts.

However, at the core of the conflicting trends in Cuba in recent years are the contradictions and imbalances associated with a fragmented and partial implementation of the transformations in its economic model, which has not improved the levels of competitiveness and growth of the economy on an aggregate scale. This problem is transcendent if one considers that in 2011 a social consensus had been reached that modifications to gradually replace the economic structure of the country could no longer be postponed, because symptoms of a "crisis of accumulation" were becoming evident as resources to develop the industries and structures necessary for further growth needed to be acquired. By not proceeding as expected, the effects of the problems since 2019 were amplified and macro- and microeconomic distortions in the country have worsened.

Two key indicators are an expression of this: the average growth of economic activity in the medium term, and the level of fixed capital investment. Between 2011 and 2021, the Cuban economy registered an average annual economic growth—in real terms—of 0.51 percent, while the coefficient of gross fixed capital formation in that period barely averaged 12 percent of the generated gross domestic product (GDP). (Author's calculations are based on data from the National Office of Statistics and Information of Cuba [ONEI 2016 and ONEI 2022]). The inability to invest in the amounts required, not only to replace the capital consumed in the production process but—above all—to increase the potential production frontier of the country, acts as a perverse circle in the maintenance of a state of practical stagnation in the medium and long term. This is reflected in a drop in productivity and efficiency, the decapitalization of the country's physical and productive infrastructure, a drop in real income, and the deterioration of various indicators associated with social development.

External savings—particularly through FDI—under certain conditions, constitute a basic mechanism that can help to close the resource gap, and at the same time can contribute to technological modernization, productivity growth, and employment. To achieve these objectives, it is necessary for FDI to be directed in a way that has a multiplier effect on income and that generates efficient production chains in coordination with the national business fabric, promotes an increase in exports, and allows for efficient import substitution. The management of public policies and the institutional quality of the host country are essential to maximize these "desired positive effects" of FDI.

The Behavior of FDI in Cuba

Cuba has an extremely vulnerable external insertion profile, which is confirmed by the maintenance of a recurring deficit in the foreign trade of goods. In the absence of a surplus in the balance of international services transactions to compensate for said deficit, Cuba is obliged to adjust imports, which reduces the growth of its GDP and has a negative impact on the possibilities of increasing exports. Thus, attracting

FDI becomes a key element in any development strategy for the Cuban economy and has been recognized as a priority in the National Medium- and Long-Term Development Plan until 2030 and in the Social Economic Strategy, both of which were approved by the highest institutions of the country.

Since the early 1990s, the government has reiterated that FDI in Cuba is oriented toward the search for new foreign markets, competitive technologies, and capital. Additionally, it is recognized that it should serve as a source of employment generation, import substitution, improvement of chains of production, and the insertion of Cuba into the international economy. The approval in 2014 of the Foreign Investment Law No. 118, which modified the preceding legal text, provided a greater number of tax and foreign trade incentives for foreign capital, established the negotiation and approval mechanisms of entities with foreign capital, and exhaustively recognized the possibility and guarantee for the establishment of businesses owned 100 percent by foreigners in the country. In 2013, with the approval of Decree Law 313 of the Mariel Special Development Zone (ZEDM), the first Special Development Zone was opened in Cuba. It was designed to bring benefits to the country through investment projects that generate linkages within the national industry, innovation processes that increase competition, increased exports with high added value and a source of employment, and clean technologies.

Until a few years ago, it was common in the official discourse to point out that Cuba guaranteed important incentives to foreign investors based on what was stipulated in the "new regulations" and also because of the prevailing security climate in the country, political stability, availability of labor with high levels of education (and qualification), and the geographical position of the island. However, the results obtained are far from what was expected, and from the huge investment and technological reconversion needs that continue to be essential for the recovery and restructuring of the national economy today. In December 2016, the National Assembly of People's Power officially recognized that in order to grow at an average annual rate of 5 percent, the Cuban economy required at least FDI flows equivalent to US$2.5 billion per year. In addition, at the Seventh Party Congress (April 2016) foreign investment came to be considered not as a "complement" but as a "fundamental element" for the development of the country (Elizalde et al. 2016).

Between 2011 and 2020, channeled FDI flows averaged just $424 million (all figures USD) a year, which barely represents 17 percent of the annual amount required and expected from the official announcements of 2016 (ONEI 2022, Chapter 08, External Sector). In the first four years of the period, FDI decreased from around $400 to $241.2 million. FDI then began to have a growing trend, which could have been the result of incentives and regulatory changes that provide greater benefits to investors. In 2019, $715.8 million was raised, the maximum annual figure reached in Cuba, and then it dropped to just over $450 million in 2020.

According to official information, after the approval in 2014 of Law 118 on Foreign Investment, 272 new businesses with foreign capital have been completed outside of the Mariel Special Development Zone, and 51 within that area. Of this number, 104 are in the modality of mixed companies, 161 are contracts of the International Economic Association (IEA), and 56 are with wholly foreign capital. In total, the companies participating represent more than forty countries. As of November 2022, fifteen of these deals were in the process of winding down (Malmierca 2022a).

Consider that other countries in the region with an economic structure similar to Cuba received annual average flows of FDI higher than Cuban records in the same period (2011–2020): Panama, $3.684 billion; Dominican Republic, $2.626 billion; Costa Rica, $2.346 billion; Guatemala, $1.032 billion; and Ecuador, $926 million (ECLAC 2022).

Of course, the economic sanctions imposed by the United States on Cuba for six decades—with their extraterritorial nature in many cases—is a fundamental factor that serves as a disadvantage and conspires against national efforts to attract increasing amounts of FDI. For this reason, issues like flexibility, creativity, the elimination of bureaucratic obstacles, and strict compliance with the commitments assumed with foreign investors constitute central elements that determine the effectiveness of Cuban policy to attract foreign investment.

Between 2019 and 2022, Cuba implemented several measures to expedite the procedures and permits necessary for the establishment of businesses with foreign capital, among them: (1) the creation of the Single Window for Foreign Investment (VUINEX) in 2020; (2) the possibility of associating foreign capital with non-state legal persons; (3) the authorization of foreign majority participation in all sectors, except the extraction of natural resources and the provision of public services; (4) a new, more flexible methodology for preparing and presenting the technical-economic studies of the proposed investment; (5) the elimination of the restrictive policy regarding the establishment of bank accounts abroad; (6) the announcement of establishing measures to stimulate FDI in the biotechnology sector; and (7) the participation of FDI in domestic trade (wholesale and retail).

This last measure aroused perceptible interest in 2022. Its objective is to develop foreign investment businesses in domestic trade with a view to expanding access to supply markets and obtaining advanced management methods, technology, and marketing techniques in order to achieve a stable supply of merchandise, in the midst of a national context characterized by a high shortage and a growing inflationary spiral since the beginning of 2021. Among the provisions authorized in domestic trade is the approval of a differentiated financial scheme that would allow companies to operate in foreign currency and carry out all their collections and payments with full liquidity support in addition to registering their accounting in foreign currency, and the possibility of having accounts in convertible currency to freely order payments abroad.

It should be taken into account that the Portfolio of Opportunities for Foreign Investment 2022, presented at the International Havana Fair in November 2022, included 104 projects presented by local governments to promote production and services from the territories; this is a reflection of the "new government efforts" to make things more flexible, modify certain principles, and eliminate restrictions that still weigh on Cuban politics. In addition, four projects are incorporated in the financial banking sector, eight in wholesale and retail trade, and eleven business opportunities with new non-state actors presented through local governments (Malmierca 2022b). In total, the 2022 Opportunity Portfolio has 708 projects—30 more than in 2021.

Pending Challenges

While still insufficient, recent adjustments to policies to attract FDI reflect a consensus that in order to face the decapitalization of the country's productive fabric and physical infrastructure it is necessary to increase the role of FDI. However, it must be insisted that the measures adopted and those announced should not be seen independently or in isolation, but should be embedded as an important part of a coherent strategy for structural transformation, which is what will lead Cuba to recover from the very complex economic and social situation that it is currently facing.

The integral program of structural transformation must necessarily include substantive modifications in the flow of production, in the resource allocation mechanism, in the dialectical interrelationship of the various forms of property, in the income distribution profile, and in the terms of external economic relations of the nation.

Given the current conditions in which the economy operates, the state, through its economic policy, has to facilitate, promote, and foster the economic activity of all the actors, first, by providing macroeconomic stability. The current inflationary crisis, in the midst of growing distortions, makes it essential that the design and implementation of a macroeconomic stabilization program in Cuba be prioritized. This is a necessary, although insufficient, condition to recover activity levels, reduce distortions, and, therefore, generate a more propitious macroeconomic environment that would simultaneously favor the attraction of FDI flows.

However, some aspects of Cuba's political and economic reality that constitute areas for improvement in order for the country to advance further in terms of attracting FDI need to be highlighted for discussion and analysis:

1. The existence of state "employer companies or entities" that must be used by foreign investors for the hiring of their labor force is an element that is continually questioned by foreign counterparts; they do not constitute an internationally accepted practice and, apparently, only function for collection.
2. The severe limitations caused by the country's inefficient infrastructure (transportation, communications, modern storage facilities, availability of the container and packaging industry, and specialized business services, among others) have adverse implications for the attraction of FDI that are not always compensated by the existence of a labor force with high levels of education.
3. The increase of a segment of micro, small, and medium-size enterprises in Cuba (MPYMES)—the vast majority of them private—is one of the most important transformations that have taken place in the economic structure of the country. They have great potential to help overcome various limitations and contradictions in the economic functioning of the nation. Although it is already recognized that these entities must be authorized to enter into agreements with foreign capital, the same regulatory conditions that are in effect for state companies should not be applied to them.
4. Cuba has high levels of external debt with public and private creditors, foreign suppliers, and companies that have invested in the country. The latter have accumulated significant amounts of profits that, due to the chronic lack of liquidity

in the country's foreign currency, they have not been able to transfer abroad. This is perhaps the most sensitive issue that concerns foreign partners and requires a comprehensive solution—albeit negotiated—in a short period of time. Notably, in November 2022, the prime minister of Cuba reiterated the will to comply with international commitments and solve the delays that exist in the repatriation of profits abroad, and he thanked the trust and commitment of foreign businesspeople who have maintained their firms on the island (Fuentes and Padilla 2022).

Consolidating Elements of Cuba's International Economic Policy

The Cuban economy is currently facing one of the most complex critical periods of the last six decades which is determined by factors of an external nature but also—importantly—by internal elements. The attraction of FDI flows has been recognized for some time as an essential factor in overcoming the structural bottlenecks that impede national economic development.

In recent years, there have been changes in policies, regulations, and certain practices applied to attract resources for this concept—seeking to stimulate this flow and make it the main source of external financing. The changes made to FDI policies are positive, but insufficient, and should form part of a comprehensive project of structural transformations. Given the current conditions, simultaneously with this project, the design and implementation of a macroeconomic stabilization program must have the highest priority, as a necessary, but not sufficient, condition to overcome the crisis and create more favorable conditions for foreign investment in the country.

Three elements of the country's "international economic policy" are central to the consolidation and diversification of the channeling of FDI: (1) the design and implementation of a strategy for the renegotiation and/or rescheduling of the debt crisis; (2) the modification of certain practices and principles still in force in the foreign investment attraction policy; and (3) greater flexibility for the active participation of the emerging non-state sector of the Cuban economy in foreign transactions and business.

References

ECLAC (Economic Commission for Latin America and the Caribbean). 2022. *Anuario Estadístico de América Latina y el Caribe 2021 / Statistical Yearbook for Latin America and the Caribbean 2021 / United Nations*. Santiago: Comisión Económica para América Latina y el Caribe.

Elizalde, Rosa Miriam, José Raúl Concepción, Ismael Francisco, and Irene Pérez. 2016. "Marino Murillo: Vienen ajustes en la economía, sin afectar servicios fundamentales a la población." Cubadebate, July 8. Accessed at http://www.cubadebate.cu/noticias/2016/07/08/marino-murillo-vienen-ajustes-en-la-economia-sin-afectar-servicios-fundamentales-a-la-poblacion.

Fuentes Puebla, Thalía, and Abel Padrón Padilla. 2022. "Sesiona V Foro de Inversiones en Fihav 2022: ¿Cómo marcha la inversión extranjera en Cuba?" Cubadebate, November 15, 2022. Accessed at http://www.cubadebate.cu/noticias/2022/11/15/sesiona-v-foro-de-inversiones-y-presentacion-sobre-inversion-extranjera-en-fihav-2022.

Malmierca, Rodrigo. 2022a. "Discurso del Ministro del Comercio Exterior y la Inversión Extranjera de Cuba en el V Foro de Inversiones." 38th edition of the Havana International Fair (FIHAV), November 15, 2022.

———. 2022b. "Cartera de Oportunidades para la Inversión Extranjera." 38th edition of the Havana International Fair (FIHAV), November 15, 2022.

ONEI (National Office of Statistics and Information). 2016. *Economic Yearbook of Cuba 2015.* Havana: ONEI.

———. 2022. *Economic Yearbook of Cuba 2021.* Havana: ONEI.

CHAPTER 10

Social Inequality and Challenges for Attention in Cuba Today

María del Carmen Zabala Arguelles

Translated by Ann Halbert Brooks

Over the past six decades, Cuba has been the scene of profound economic, political, and social transformations which comprise an alternative experience of development, oriented toward achieving equity and social justice. Since 2008, further changes to the socioeconomic and legal environment, as well as changes to the central figures of the government, have altered the trajectory of Cuban development.

The purpose of this chapter is to discuss the changes around one of the key axes for Cuban society: social inequality and the policies that seek to address it and achieve greater equity. The discussion begins with a brief summary of the context in Cuba, followed by commentary on the impact of the crisis and economic reforms of the 1990s, and then an intersectional survey of key changes and continuities of social policies, as well as their impact in different settings. Finally, this chapter presents a series of challenges that must be addressed related to the problem of inequality in Cuba today.

The Cuban Context

Social policies directed by the Cuban state are central to development in Cuba. The fundamental principles guiding these efforts over the past six decades have been inclusion, equity, and social justice. These principles have been implemented with policies and programs characterized by universal and free access to basic social services, social protections, complementary social and economic programs, and the central role of the Cuban state in design, financing, and management thereof (Ferriol, Therborn, and Castiñeras 2004).

In Cuban social policy, equity is a multidimensional concept, including equality in the formal rights of all, equality of opportunity for all social groups in the areas of human capital and social protections, and guarantees of greater support to disadvantaged citizens who might otherwise have reduced access (Álvarez and Mattar 2004). In addition, Cuban social policies have emphasized the role of *spaces of equality* as a distributive mechanism, with guarantees of access, universality, integration, rights, participation, and homogeneity for all the social sectors (Espina 2008).

Metrics such as the social indicators of health, education, and social security, among others, demonstrate that there has been progress toward meeting these equity goals, but the Cuban government has identified economic performance as the greatest challenge to further progress. In addition, in recent years some progress has been rolled back. While United Nations development statistics rank Cuba as a country with high levels of human development, between 2015 and 2021 its ranking dropped seven places—to its current ranking in eighty-third place (UNDP 2022). Furthermore, the Cuban population has also been decreasing, due to a combination of declining fertility rates, negative net migration rates, and the continued aging and urbanization of the population.

Impact of the Crisis and Reforms of the 1990s on Equity

Though the Cuban government's management of the crisis of the 1990s was undertaken in accordance with the principles of preserving social gains in the areas of health, education, social security, etc.—in short, the protection of equity and all of Cuban society—one of the most prominent effects of the crisis was the increase in socioeconomic differentiation. The crisis of the 1990s led to the (re)production of gaps in equity and an increase in levels of poverty and vulnerability. These gaps have continued to the present.

One can quantify this socioeconomic differentiation and decrease in equity with the Gini coefficient. In Cuba's urban areas, the Gini coefficient between 1996 and 1998 was 0.38. However, in 1978 and 1987 the Gini coefficient for urban areas was 0.25 and 0.22, respectively (Ferriol, Therborn, and Castiñeiras 2004). Despite this increase in inequality, the multidimensional Human Development Index still ranks Cuba second in Latin America and the Caribbean (CIEM/PNUD 2000)—evidence that despite the crisis of the 1990s, the Cuban state continued to substantially guarantee basic rights and social protections and offer specific attention to disadvantaged groups.

Inequality particularly increased around the axes of gender, age, skin color, geography, and personal socioeconomic situation—comprised of income, consumption, employment, and living conditions, among other attributes. For example, as income and poverty levels diverged in the 1990s, 20 percent of the urban population met the criteria for classification as "at risk" by 1999 (Ferriol et al. 1998; Ferriol, Ramos, and Añé 2004). Among this at-risk population, women, the elderly, Cubans of color, persons with chronic illnesses or disabilities, the unemployed, and those with lower levels of education were overrepresented (Ferriol, Ramos, and Añé 2004). In addition, scholars have noted varying levels of inequality based on geography (Íñiguez and Ravenet 1999) and among households headed by women (Zabala 2009). These patterns have persisted, according to more recent studies. Recent studies also expand on related challenges including environmental problems, the impact of natural disasters, the failings of local government entities, migration, and cultural consumption (Zabala 2014).

Attention to Inequalities: Continuities and Changes in Social Policies

The crisis of the 1990s and resulting inequality was driven by a combination of external and internal factors, including the structural, systemic crisis associated with the end of the Soviet Union, the intensification of the economic blockade by the government of the United States, and Cuba's internal demographics. In 2007 the Cuban government took a new step to address the situation, seeking to update its model for economic and social development. Specific reforms included efforts to avoid the concentration of property in the hands of non-state entities, efforts to better redistribute wealth through the tax code, price controls on basic necessities provided by non-state businesses, and improvements to social services.

The National Plan for Social and Economic Development to 2030 (*Plan Nacional de Desarrollo Económico y Social hasta 2030*, or PNDES), which is oriented around the principles of human development, equity, and social justice, includes the objectives of progressively reducing economic and social inequality, preserving universal social programs, guaranteeing a universal system of social security and social assistance, and meeting the needs of diverse and potentially vulnerable communities. These vulnerable communities include those suffering food insecurity, the elderly, and persons with disability, among others. Specific programs undertaken as part of the PNDES focus on access to and quality of social services, improving living conditions, increasing access to dignified work, and the prevention of vulnerabilities and mitigation of existing vulnerabilities. The National Program for the Advancement of Women and the National Program against Racism and Racial Discrimination are also carried out in coordination with the PNDES.

One can observe significant continuities with prior Cuban social policies, particularly in the areas of equality of rights and opportunity, guaranteed access to basic social services, equity-focused development strategies, and universal social programs. However, there are important changes focused on ensuring the economic sustainability of social programs, reductions to social spending and the number of beneficiaries of social programs, ensuring the efficient use of resources, the gradual reduction of excessive subsidies, and refinements to the tax code. The role of the family and the market are also enhanced. In short, there is a process of moving from state-centric solutions toward market-based and family-centered solutions (Peña 2017).

While changes have been necessary, certain policies' implementation has reinforced preexisting inequality. For example, reductions to Cubans' food ration entitlements increase the net cost of procuring food for households (Anaya and García 2018). In the educational sector, reorganization has coincided with significant gaps in achievement on the basis of gender. The reorganization and consolidation of health care in Cuba has also reduced the real accessibility of certain services (Íñiguez 2012) and the accessibility of treatment options (Fuentes 2016).

Survey of Social Inequalities and Intersectional Analysis

Analyses of Cuban society today have identified patterns in inequality and inequity around characteristics including gender, skin color, age, class, degrees of ability, and geography, and in various spheres including economic well-being, living conditions, and social and cultural participation. Poverty, vulnerability, and marginalization also intersect with these factors (Zabala 2020a). Inequality among social classes has been identified in areas including resource access, use, and control; work and income; social capital, politics, and culture; consumption and access to services; and prestige and social recognition. Current levels of inequality and processes of impoverishment are associated, among other factors, with membership in the working class and employment by the Cuban state (Fundora 2020a).

Economic inequality in particular is associated with occupation and income, with salary differences observed between locations and economic sectors. Families whose primary income is from state salaries and pensions, or with limited access to foreign currency, also face particular challenges. Housewives, children, adolescents, elderly adults, and unemployed persons are among the individuals most affected (Echeverría 2020a). A survey of these factors related to inequality illustrates that an intersectional analysis is necessary to fully understand each and the full range of challenges to Cuba today.

For example, despite equity gains for Cuban women, gender-based gaps have remained. These include divisions of work within and outside the home: work in the home is disproportionately performed by women and disproportionately restricts women's time, and women are underrepresented in many higher-paid occupations outside the home. Early motherhood and gender-based violence also negatively impact Cuban women (Echeverría 2020b).

Gaps have also continued in outcomes for Cubans of color, who are underrepresented at the highest levels of leadership and academic attainment, overrepresented among those with lower incomes and worse living situations, and underrepresented in highly remunerative areas of non-state employment. Higher fertility rates early in life and higher mortality rates also contribute to inequality (Zabala 2020c).

Disparities correlated with geography also play a role. Population loss due to out-migration has been highest in Cuba's eastern provinces, for example (Hidalgo 2020a). Less-urbanized provinces have less-robust infrastructure, reduced access to services, less access to transportation, fewer cultural options, and, on average, lower-quality housing stock. School attendance rates, access to higher education, and overall educational attainment levels also lag in these provinces (Hidalgo 2020b).

Inequality can also be observed at all ages. For infants, inequality on the basis of gender and family of origin are significant factors. Sociopolitical participation, cultural consumption, and living conditions are all elements of the inequality experienced. Young people are also affected by differences in access to family remittances, labor market factors, cultural consumption, and other factors. For older adults, issues such as interpersonal violence and varying quality of life—including the effects of factors such as gender and geography discussed above—become particularly acute for single elderly adults (Díaz 2020a).

Persons with disabilities also experience socioeconomic inequality in access to employment, with the greatest challenges observed for those with intellectual disabilities. Environmental inequality such as housing inequality is also observed. Furthermore, access to technology, information, and internet access limit participation in community projects and social programs. Women with disabilities and women caregivers for persons with disabilities are particularly affected by these challenges (Díaz 2020b).

With regard to poverty rates in Cuba, there are no updated statistics on purely financial poverty; the multidimensional poverty rate across the Cuban population in 2021 was 0.44 percent, and there was no recorded incidence of severe, multidimensional poverty. The three highest indicators of poverty as of 2021 were in the areas of assets held, types of fuel available for cooking, and access to adequate health care (Grupo Nacional 2021). Women, Cubans of color, older adults, and the residents of less-developed regions were overrepresented in the population living in poverty. Poverty was also found to correlate with levels of civic participation, living conditions, access to public services and assistance, and cultural consumption (Zabala 2020d).

The varying quality of construction for existing housing is also a significant factor. Poor-quality construction is associated with residents living with greater precarity, reduced hygienic/sanitary conditions, lack of access to domestic appliances, and overcrowding, among other factors. Illegal construction of dwellings in rural areas, in Cuba's eastern provinces, or in areas not included in national development plans is also associated with challenges (Jiménez 2020). For young adults in particular, sociocultural participation is correlated with family poverty and living situations (Jiménez and Álvarez 2020).

An intersectional analysis of these factors highlights the relevance of considering all of the following in the study of inequality: gender, skin color, class, age, and geography. In addition, factors such as disability, migration, sexual orientation, family cultural capital, and family and marital situation also affect the advantages and disadvantages available to individuals and communities (Zabala 2020b). With regard to Cuban public policy, the most influential factors around creating, (re)producing, and reducing inequality are in the areas of work, education, health, social assistance, and living situation (Fundora 2020b). Effects have been mixed, with equity gaps remaining despite recent efforts.

The Persistence of Inequality

The crisis brought about by the COVID-19 pandemic has had the greatest impact on the most vulnerable groups, despite special measures taken in the areas of health, employment, social security, social assistance, education, economic activity, and nutrition (Zabala 2021). The elimination of the dual-currency system in Cuba—which also coincided with the COVID-19 pandemic—effected a notable increase in the price of goods and services and reinforced inequalities in income and consumption.

Reducing equity gaps is one of the most important measures of Cuban society, but inequality has persisted and morphed in response to changing policies and programs. Greater attention to the economic sustainability of social programs, a balance between social equity and economic efficiency, attention to the value of universal programs for impoverished or vulnerable groups, and the intersectional impacts of policies and programs is needed. In addition, further work is needed to develop and refine methodologies to evaluate social programs from the perspective of equity.

Despite these challenges, opportunities exist: there is a shared understanding that equity and social justice must be pursued, and that universal social services are a key tool for improving equity and social justice. In addition, efforts targeted at vulnerable or at-risk populations and specific regions with greater need—likely through decentralized local initiatives—show promise.

References

Álvarez, Elena, and J. Mattar, eds. 2004. *Política social y reformas estructurales: Cuba a principios del siglo XXI*. Mexico City: CEPAL/INIE/PNUD.

Anaya, Betsy, and Anicia García. 2018. "Dinámica de gastos básicos en Cuba (1ra parte)." Inter Press Service of Cuba, September 28. Accessed at https://www.ipscuba.net/economia/dinamica-de-gastos-basicos-en-cuba-primera-parte.

CIEM/PNUD. 2000. *Investigación sobre desarrollo humano y equidad en Cuba 1999*. Havana: Caguayo S.A.

Díaz Pérez, Danay. 2020a. "Desigualdades etarias e interseccionalidad: Análisis del contexto cubano 2008-2018." Facultad Latinoamericana de Ciencias Sociales (Programa-Cuba). Havana: Publicaciones Acuario, Centro Félix Varela. Accessed at https://biblioteca-repositorio.clacso.edu.ar/bitstream/CLACSO/5788/1/6-Desigualdades-etarias.pdf.

———. 2020b. "Desigualdades, discapacidad e interseccionalidad: Análisis del contexto cubano 2008-2018." Accessed at https://biblioteca-repositorio.clacso.edu.ar/bitstream/CLACSO/5787/1/8-Desigualdades-discapacidad.pdf.

Echevarría, Dayma. 2020a. "Desigualdades económicas e interseccionalidad: Análisis del contexto cubano 2008–2018." In *Colección Tensión y complicidad entre desigualdades y políticas sociales*.

———. 2020b. "Desigualdades de género e interseccionalidad: Análisis del contexto cubano 2008–2018." In *Colección Tensión y complicidad entre desigualdades y políticas sociales*.

Espina, Mayra. 2008. *Políticas de atención a la pobreza y la desigualdad: Examinando el rol del Estado en la experiencia cubana*. Buenos Aires: CLACSO-CROP.

Ferriol, Angela, G. Carriazo, O. U-Echavarría, and D. Quintana. 1998. "Efectos de políticas macroeconómicas y sociales sobre los niveles de pobreza: El caso de Cuba en los años noventa." In *Politica Macroeconomica y Pobreza en Americalatina y el Caribe*, edited by Enrique Ganuza, Lance Taylor, and Samuel Morley, 355–99. Madrid: Ediciones Mundi-Prensa. Accessed at https://repositorio.cepal.org/bitstream/handle/11362/31171/S301441G211_es.pdf.

Ferriol, Angela, M. Ramos, and L. Añé. 2004. *Reforma económica y población en riesgo en Ciudad de La Habana, Informe de investigación*. Havana: INIE-CEPDE-ONE (unpublished).

Ferriol, Angela, G. Therborn, and R. Castiñeiras. 2004. *Política social: el mundo contemporáneo y las experiencias de Cuba y Suecia*. Havana: INIE.

Fuentes, Susset. 2016. *El acceso a los servicios de salud y la capacidad de enfrentamiento familiar ante situaciones de quebrantamiento de la salud. ¿Un lugar desde el cual pensar la reproducción de desigualdades en la Cuba actual.* Havana: Tesis de Maestría en Desarrollo Social, FLACSO-Cuba.

Fundora, Geydis. 2020a. "Desigualdades clasistas e interseccionalidad: Análisis del contexto cubano 2008–2018." In *Colección Tensión y complicidad entre desigualdades y políticas sociales.*

———. 2020b. "Políticas sociales y sus efectos en las desigualdades." In *Colección Tensión y complicidad entre desigualdades y políticas sociales.*

Fundora, Geydis, María del C. Zabala, Vilma Hidalgo, Jagger Álvarez, Danay Díaz, and Reynaldo Jiménez Fundora. 2021. "¿Eliminación, disminución o ampliación de brechas de equidad? Propuesta metodológica para el análisis prospectivo de desigualdades en diferentes escenarios de políticas." *Revista Estudios del Desarrollo Social: Cuba y América Latina* 9, no. 3 (September–December 2021): 54–73. Accessed at https://biblioteca-repositorio.clacso.edu .ar/bitstream/CLACSO/11554/1/Metodologia-escenarios.pdf.

Grupo Nacional para la Implementación de la Agenda 2030. 2021. *Informe Nacional Voluntario Cuba 2021*. Havana: Ministerio de Economía y Planificación de Cuba. Accessed at https://www.mep.gob.cu/es/documento/informe-nacional-voluntario-cuba-2021-sobre-la-agenda-2030.

Hidalgo, Vilma. 2020a. "Desigualdades territoriales e interseccionalidad: Análisis del contexto cubano 2008–2018." In *Colección Tensión y complicidad entre desigualdades y políticas sociales.*

———. 2020b. "Desigualdades, ruralidad e interseccionalidad Análisis del contexto Cubano 2008–2018." In *Colección Tensión y complicidad entre desigualdades y políticas sociales.*

Íñiguez, Luisa. 2012. "Aproximación a la evolución de los cambios en los servicios de salud en Cuba." *Revista Cubana de Salud Pública* 38, no. 1: 109–25.

Íñiguez, Luisa, and Mariana Ravenet. 1999. *Desigualdades espaciales del bienestar en Cuba: Aproximación a los efectos de los nuevos procesos en las realidades sociales Informe de investigación*. Havana: CESBH (unpublished).

Jiménez, Reynaldo. 2020. "Vivienda, hábitat y desigualdades: Análisis interseccional del contexto cubano 2008–2018." In *Colección Tensión y complicidad entre desigualdades y políticas sociales.*

Jiménez, Reynaldo, and Jagger Álvarez. 2020. "Desigualdades, participación y consumo cultural." In *Colección Tensión y complicidad entre desigualdades y políticas sociales.*

ONEI (Oficina Nacional de Estadísticas e Información). 2012. *Censo de Población y Viviendas 2012*. Havana: ONEI.

Peña, Ángela. 2017. *Regímenes de bienestar y pobreza familiar en Cuba*. Havana: Editorial Ciencias Sociales.

UNDP (United Nations Development Programme). 2022. *Human Development Report 2021/2022: Uncertain Times, Unsettled Lives: Shaping our Future in a Transforming World*. New York: United Nations Development Programme.

Zabala, María del Carmen. 2009. *Jefatura femenina de hogar, pobreza urbana y exclusión social: Una perspectiva desde la subjetividad en el contexto cubano*. Buenos Aires: CLACSO.

———, ed. 2014. *Algunas claves para pensar la pobreza en Cuba desde la mirada de jóvenes investigadores*. Havana: FLACSO / Publicaciones Acuario.

———. 2020a. *Análisis interseccional del contexto cubano 2008–2018*. Facultad Latinoamericana de Ciencias Sociales (Programa-Cuba). Havana: Publicaciones Acuario, Centro Félix Varela. Accessed at https://biblioteca-repositorio.clacso.edu.ar/handle/CLACSO/5799.

————. 2020b. "Análisis interseccional de las desigualdades en Cuba." In *Colección Tensión y complicidad entre desigualdades y políticas sociales.*

————. 2020c. "Desigualdades por color de la piel e interseccionalidad." In *Colección Tensión y complicidad entre desigualdades y políticas sociales.*

————. 2020d. "Pobreza, vulnerabilidad y marginación." In *Colección Tensión y complicidad entre desigualdades y políticas sociales.*

————. 2021. "Grupos vulnerables y COVID 19 en Cuba: alcances y retos para la protección social." In *Enfrentando la COVID-19 en el Caribe: Experiencias en República Dominicana y Cuba.* Friedrich-Ebert-Stiftung (FES) and FLACSO-Cuba. Available at http://library.fes.de/pdf-files/bueros/fescaribe/17971-20210701.pdf.

CHAPTER 11

The Food System and Food Production in Cuba

Armando Nova González

For any economy, the food agro-industrial system is extremely complex. For the Cuban economy and agricultural system, there are similar complexities. What makes the situation more challenging in the Cuban context is that for several years there have been restrictions and obstacles that have prevented the proper development of the productive forces.

Structure and Operation

Cuba's agro-industrial system is made up of several variables, all contributing to a framework of networks. The starting point, and the most important, is the role of the agricultural workers who produce the food throughout the country. To date, this network of networks has not produced sufficient amounts of food on a national scale—and has not met the demands of the country. This has resulted in a steady increase in the importation of food and thus greater dependency on food from abroad, thereby compromising national sovereignty.

In terms of the domestic structure of the food industry, there is a series of channels, for both products and services, through which farmers are linked to suppliers, consumers, industries, distributors, marketers, and financiers. In other words, through the agents or variables that make up the food system, all linked to the various regions of the country.

As is well known, the first obstacle facing the food system in Cuba lies in the economic blockade or embargo of the United States, which has been maintained and strengthened by the various administrations. The second major obstacle is seen in the domestic situation, and specifically the resistance to change.

In search of a solution to this second obstacle, we urgently need to implement a new model of productive economic management in agriculture, one that starts at the local, grassroots level and then continues, promoting changes at the higher levels of management. The macro components of the system consist of sources of financing, science-technology and innovation, the workforce, a supply of inputs (both domestic and imported), agricultural and livestock production, internal marketing (for population and industry) and external marketing, and logistics, among other factors.

The solution to the food problem begins with the municipality and local development and, given the current complex situation regarding food, requires speed, simplification of administrative procedures, decentralization, and empowerment of decision-makers at the levels of municipal government management. It is necessary to achieve the real and effective separation of management between the government and the enterprise itself. There are various enterprises such as Cooperatives of Credits and Services (CCS) and Cooperatives of Agricultural Production (CPA), as well as private landholders and others who have been loaned the land by the government on fixed leases (*usufructuarios*). These are responsible for 81 percent of national vegetable production, more than 40 percent of meat production, and 70 percent of milk. In addition, there are Basic Units of Cooperative Production (UBPC), state enterprises, urban and suburban agriculture, and people's own yards and plots of land, as well as new economic forms—the small and medium-size enterprises (MPYMES), industrial cooperatives, and self-employed persons (TPCs).

Local agriculture—urban, suburban, and family-run—is an important component in the production of food. Food produced at these locations is easily accessible and beneficial to local consumers from the economic point of view, since the production costs are lower—resulting in cheaper prices for the produce. It is necessary to employ all these business forms in order to obtain cooperation with other groups, as well as develop collaborative relations and the autonomy required in productive economic management.

National Food and Nutrition System

In July 2022 the Council of Ministers approved the Law on the National and Nutritional Food System (SANN), which has as its fundamental objective to enforce the provisions of Article 77 of the Constitution of the Republic: "Everyone has the right to a healthy and adequate food supply. The state creates the conditions to strengthen the food security of the entire population . . ." The concept of food security is a key component of the SANN plan and includes the availability of food, physical and economic access, sustainability, and management in terms of production/supply.

The proposal establishes a completely new model of economic-productive management that is controlled at the municipality and is fully participatory, inclusive, and transparent. It guarantees and consolidates efficiency in key areas (economic, energy, nutritional), in harmony with the environment. This implies the practice of agroecological agriculture, as set out in the conceptual framework, action plan, and strategic themes contained in the SANN. Achieving the highest possible level of food sovereignty is also presented as a basic objective to be achieved. At present, there is an external food dependence of close to 70 percent.

Agroecological Agriculture

To confront the circumstances in which Cuba finds itself, the application of science-technology and innovation is required, together with the use and conservation of our own sources of wealth in harmony with the environment and nature. As a result of this approach, agroecological agriculture offers a way of producing food in order to achieve economic and social development in a systemic way. It combines biophysical and socioeconomic elements that make up three pillars of sustainable development: social, economic, and environmental. Agroecology as a scientific discipline analyzes the interaction between the various components of the system. As a social movement, it generates economic benefits for rural communities and strengthens their cultural identity, while also applying a set of actions to optimize production. It relates the lessons of science and traditional knowledge to generate food in a sustainable way.

As a recognized science, agroecology is based on how people, animals, plants, and the environment interact. Its solutions, usually local and/or regional, aim at the use and maintenance of biodiversity, generally resorting to natural and renewable energy sources and recycling animal biomass and excreta. It offers a distinctive agricultural model, a viable alternative to conventional practices and the more recent introduction of genetically modified organisms (GMOs), which generally use technologies supported by intensive use of chemicals, monoculture practices, and nonrational use of natural resources such as soil and water. By contrast, agroecological agriculture adapts to different contexts and to different productive economic scales—the very small for self-consumption and the small and medium scale. It considers that the soil and its surroundings constitute an ecosystem. It takes into consideration all the components of the ecosystem and identifies them as a unit, favoring the sustainable practices.

The economic-social-ecological processes, which agroecological agriculture promotes with its production, show that it is a strategy for transformative change in the production of sustainable food. This approach becomes more evident in periods of economic crises and pandemics. It should be noted that during the decade known as the Special Period (1990–2000), a new form of food production resulted, which was seen as a transitory phase toward agroecological agriculture (see table 11.1).

One can see that while the production of plants increased, it was strongly impacted by circumstances in the 1991–2000 period. The exception was rice, which registered a reduction in the nineties (it is a crop highly dependent on agrochemical input and agro-industrial technology). The adaptation process for rice was delayed until 2001. In the following decades it recorded a small level of recovery compared to the period 1986–1990.

In the rest of the crops there was an increase, during the 1990s and higher in the years 2001–2010 and 2011–2018, highlighting the root crops and vegetables that registered greater increases. An analysis of the yields of other crops shows similar results.

This performance in terms of production and harvests cannot be questioned even from the logic of linear analysis of conventional agriculture (volume of production and

Table 11.1. Production of vegetables, 1986–2018

Crops	Average Production (Mt)				Average Yield (t/ha)		
	1986–1990	1991–2000	2001–2010	2010–2018	1991–2000	2001–2010	2010–2018
Root crops	989	1,291	2,442	2,558	5.3	7.6	8.5
Vegetables	577	788	2,965	2,371	6.3	11.6	11.9
Rice	510	395	519	533	2.5	3.1	3.4
Corn	43	131	336	382	1.2	2.3	2.4
Bean	13	32	103	134	0.4	1	1/1
Total	2,132	2,637	6,365	5,978			

Imported Inputs	1986–1990	1991–2000	2001–2010	2010–2018	% Reduction Compared to 1986–1990		
					1991–2000	2001–2010	2010–2018
Fuel (MMtm)	12,461.7	8,847.8	3489.2	3,240.0	29	72	74
Fertilizers (Mtm)	946.4	356.2	179.0	187.5	62	81	80
Pesticides (Mtm)	23.9	12.4	10.0	9.9	48	58	58.6

Source: Prepared by R. Caballero and A. Nova, based on the Anuario Estadístico de Cuba (Annual Statistical Data Report) from 1986 to 2018, published by ONEI, and official sources of the Ministry of Agriculture.

crop yield). Agroecological-based agriculture is systemic and therefore its assessment must consider various criteria. It should be noted that there are important additional contributions from agroecological agriculture from 1990 to the present day, such as reducing natural imbalances, promoting healthier foods, greater diversity of products, and decreases in the importation of inputs. One can also see that the transition to agroecological agriculture during the economic crisis of the Special Period resulted in higher yields than were obtained during the 1986–1990 period, when high industrial inputs were used.

Several factors specific to agroecological agriculture contributed to these results, including

- reduction in the scale of production units (from large companies to cooperatives, and then to smaller units and farms);
- decentralization of administration, accompanied by an increase in the number of people directly administering the land;
- use of practices appropriate to the characteristics of the production units;
- adoption of methods that reduce the demand for traditional inputs used in conventional agricultural management;
- integration of various renewable energy sources;
- greater use of the cultivated area (polycultures, rotations of crops);
- adoption of favorable official policies and programs;
- intense training and technological innovation activity in the centers of research, universities, and Cuban NGOs, and with international collaboration.

The availability of fertilizers and pesticides was much higher during the 1980s and has been reduced since the 1990s. Although traditionally there has been a high correlation between the use of fertilizers and food production, in terms of agricultural production in Cuba the results have been quite different. This is precisely because the factors listed above were used in Cuba and were not considered in traditional experiments. Of course, the increase in the capacity to obtain bioinputs in a decentralized manner and to integrate them into the management of the systems contributed to a high level of substitution of agrochemical imports.

These results show that agriculture that today occupies about 80 percent of the land found in different types of cooperatives and private landholdings, despite having a low level of physical and financial capital, in fact shows greater productive, economic, and energy efficiency, in addition to guaranteeing more than 70 percent of the food consumed. It is in these landholdings where you can currently see different degrees of adoption of agroecology. Public policies that lead to progress and sustainability must be directed toward this approach if we are to achieve true food sovereignty. In the same way, the distribution of land in usufruct (loaned at no cost to landholders over fixed periods of time, provided that the land is farmed) has been a positive factor, despite the limitations, restrictions, and bureaucratic conduct, reflected initially in Decree Law 259 (2008) and subsequent ones, which have continued to the present.

Profound Transformations from the Local to Higher Levels

The progress of countries on the road to development has been preceded by transformations previously initiated by agriculture—such as land distribution, agrarian reforms, technological innovations, new management methods, decentralization, and autonomy—which have been seen as essential conditions for economic and social development. More recent examples are found in Vietnam and China, with economic, social, and political systems similar to Cuba's. Agriculture provides food, raw materials, and sources of employment, while it also generates surpluses for trade. It promotes the sovereignty and food security of a nation, virtues that this primary sector provides.

To address and seek appropriate and timely solutions, at least sixty-three measures have been proposed, and several working groups have been created. The first task is to propose the new model of agricultural management from the grassroots to the highest government level. This model implies the necessary replacement of the current model of economic management of food production with a totally new one, starting with the local bases of food production. The need to consider agroecological agriculture an indispensable pillar is a part of the SANN.

The New Management Model: What Is It? What Does It Mean?

Between 2013 and 2022, academics raised the urgent need for the implementation of a totally new agricultural management model that fully replaces the current management model (Nova 2014). The proposed model considers the diversity of actors or productive forms existing at the base, and facilitates collaborative and horizontal relations between producers—all in search of autonomy and the solution of problems at the local level.

Among the fundamental purposes and objectives to be achieved are autonomy, as well as the following:

- Eliminate monopolistic centralization and vertical decision-making practices. Bring about the effective separation of business management of the state within the municipality.
- Achieve the independence of producers in terms of use of the land. This means recognizing the right of the producers to decide what they must produce, to combine necessary productive factors, to decide to whom they can market their products, to set the price for their produce, and to purchase the required inputs and means of production at the appropriate time—all in order to ensure the successful productive cycle (production-distribution-exchange-consumption).
- Recognize the real and objective existence of the market, taking into account necessary planning, and always bearing in mind the needs of the population.

- Strengthen the municipal government with the necessary authority and autonomy, bearing in mind the diversity and particular factors of each municipality.
- Recognize that each productive base would possess equal rights as all the others.
- Establish a new organization, the Municipal Food Agro-industrial Directorate, which will support and facilitate producers and receive the required information on the various productive forms, which will develop thorough business management structures. With this, the new organization will achieve the separation of state management from business management at the local level.

The proposed new management model would break the umbilical cord, the vertical top-down management approach, that exists between the National Institutional Directorate of Agriculture (Ministry and Provincial and Municipal Administration of Agriculture) and the various productive bases existing in the municipality. At present state management is mixed in with the local businesses, with limited input of the actual food producers.

The current Municipal Delegation of Agriculture would be eliminated and the Municipal Agri-food Directorate would be created, subordinate to the municipal government, which would carry out exclusively the functions of government, supporting producers, and be independent from the Ministry of Agriculture. A Producers' Council would be created, made up of the various cooperatives in the area, state enterprises, MPYMES, and vertical companies existing locally. The council would contribute to collaboration among local members and the development of horizontal, equal relations. Within its capabilities the Producers' Council would seek to provide solutions among its members to the problems that each productive base faces. While acting as an independent organization it would maintain links with the Food Agro-industrial Directorate of the Municipality and would identify problems and solutions. National, provincial, and vertical companies that exist in the municipality would be invited to the sessions of the council. With the participation of local universities, research institutions, the National Association of Small Farmers (ANAP), and the National Association of Economists and Accountants of Cuba (ANEC), the municipalities could convene and organize market observatories in order to assess the behavior of supply, demand, prices, income, and consumer price index.

The establishment of this new model would help to achieve three basic objectives: (1) marketing would be carried out directly by the producers; (2) producers would gain direct access to inputs, without interference from intermediaries; and (3) demographic stability for farm workers and their families would be assured.

References

Alburquerque, F. 1997. "Globalización y competitividad y desarrollo económico local." Boletín ILPES/CEPAL, Santiago de Chile.

Bú, A., Á. García, and A. Nova. 2022. "Análisis de la seguridad alimentaria y nutricional en Cuba." In *Agricultura en Cuba, entre Retos y Transformaciones*, edited by Armando Nova González. Havana: Editorial Caminos.

García, A. 2022. "El mercado agropecuario y su contexto." In *Agricultura en Cuba, entre Retos y Transformaciones*.

Echevarría León, D., Y. Bombino, B. Anaya Cruz, and M. García. 2022. "Políticas para mejorar la condición y posición de las mujeres rurales. Reflexiones críticas." In *Agricultura en Cuba, entre Retos y Transformaciones*.

Funes, F. 2022. "Proyecto agroecológico territorial Finca Marta beneficio económico-social y ambiental." In *Agricultura en Cuba, entre Retos y Transformaciones*.

Molina, E., and E. Victorero. 2022. "Sugerencias de mecanismos no tradicionales para el Financiamiento de la agricultura en Cuba." In *Agricultura en Cuba, entre Retos y Transformaciones*.

Nova, A. 2006. *La agricultura en Cuba. Evolución y trayectoria (1959–2005)*. Havana: Editorial Ciencias Sociales.

———. 2013. *El Nuevo modelo agrícola y los lineamientos de la política económica y social en Cuba*. Havana: Editorial Ciencia Sociales.

———. 2014. "Un nuevo modelo cubano de gestión agrícola." *Revista Temas*, no. 77.

———. 2020a. "Nueva política agrocoercializadora en Cuba." IPS, November 26. Accessed at https://www.ipscuba.net/espacios/por-su-propio-peso/camino-al-andar/nueva-politica-comercializadora-agropecuaria-en-cuba.

———. 2020b. *Caminando el cooperativismo en Cuba*. Havana: Editorial Temas.

Prego, J. C., A. Nova, and L. Robaina. 2022. "Formas de integración cooperativa y sus principales técnicas de realización." In *Agricultura en Cuba, entre Retos y Transformaciones*.

CHAPTER 12

How the Cuban Military Became an Economic Powerhouse

William M. LeoGrande

The civil-military boundary in Cuba has always been permeable. With the collapse of the old regime in 1959, state administration fell largely on the shoulders of the Rebel Army. Local commanders implemented the Revolution's policies, and much of the new government's bureaucracy grew out of the National Institute of Agrarian Reform, staffed by the army. During the 1960s, senior leaders of the Revolution circulated freely, moving among top posts in the armed forces, party, and government as circumstances required.[1]

During the 1970s, civilian and military roles were gradually differentiated as the army became more professional, developing a reputation as the country's best-organized and most efficient institution. Raúl Castro's success in creating a well-trained, effective leadership team meant that senior military officers were frequently called upon to run civilian ministries when the civilians made a mess of things—a phenomenon dating back to the late 1960s when the civilian bureaucracy proved unable to manage the epic struggle to produce ten million tons of sugar in 1970.[2]

The role of the armed forces in the economy began modestly in the late 1960s when troops were deployed to help bring in the ten-million-ton harvest. In 1973, the armed forces created the Army of Working Youth to separate its agricultural labor force from regular combat units. In the 1980s, when Soviet assistance began to decline, Cuba built its own military industries to provide basic supplies. Known collectively as the Defense Industry Group, these enterprises were run by the Ministry of the Revolutionary Armed Forces (MINFAR) itself. A lack of experienced managers led Raúl Castro to start a training program for military cadres, sending hundreds abroad to study management in Western Europe and Asia. This corps of military managers made possible the subsequent growth of the military's economic might.

When the Soviet Union collapsed, throwing the Cuban economy into deep recession, the armed forces took on greater economic responsibility, first by focusing on food production to feed its own troops and to augment civilian supplies. The military also became a major player in Cuba's expanding tourism industry, converting the military's infrastructure of rest and recreation installations into modern tourist facilities. With foreign investors and partners providing the capital, the military's Grupo de Turismo Gaviota became one of the largest tourist enterprises on the island.[3] Gaviota's success led MINFAR to take on a larger role managing other enterprises in telecommunications, import-export, and retail operations, all of which are gathered under the umbrella of a holding company, the Grupo de Administración Empresarial S.A. (GAESA).[4]

The military's expanding role in the economy created new career opportunities for an officers corps that otherwise would have been significantly downsized when the number of men and women under arms was cut by half due to the economic exigencies of the Special Period. Senior officers, still on active service, were moved into the expanding military business sector as senior managers.[5]

Surprisingly, the regular military services did not receive much, if any, of the rapidly growing revenue generated by their fellow officers running GAESA's businesses. World Bank estimates of Cuba's military expenditures have been flat at $1.3 billion annually since 2012.[6] This has reportedly caused some friction between regular officers and the officers turned business leaders.[7]

The Military's Role in Tourism, the "Locomotive" of the Economy

The shift from sugar to tourism as the "locomotive" of the Cuban economy, as President Díaz-Canel called it, happened gradually.[8] The US embargo imposed in 1962 demolished the prerevolutionary tourist industry, but as Cuba's relations with Western Europe warmed in the late 1970s and 1980s, Cuban officials came to see Europe as a potential market. The turn to tourism accelerated during the Special Period—the decade-long depression caused by the loss of Soviet assistance when the Soviet Union collapsed. As Cuba sought foreign capital to fuel economic recovery, tourism proved to be the sector most attractive to investors.

The military's role in tourism began modestly in 1988 with the creation of Gaviota, operating a single hotel, the Kurhotel, formerly a rest and recreation center for military officers. In just two years, Gaviota was managing twenty-seven properties with 3,600 rooms, about 10 percent of the tourist market.[9] As the corporation grew, it diversified into a variety of tourism-related businesses including travel agencies, package tours, tour buses, car rentals, marinas, and a domestic airline.

In 2016, Gaviota acquired Habaguanex S.A., the tourism company founded in 1994 by Eusebio Leal, the Historian of the City of Havana. Historic preservation was Leal's passion. He convinced Fidel Castro to give him a million dollars seed money and a free hand to rehabilitate the city's colonial section. Habaguanex was allowed to keep all the tourism revenue from the hotels, restaurants, and shops in Old Havana to reinvest in expanding renovations.[10] Within a decade, Habaguanex was generating over $100 million in revenue. However, as Leal's health declined, subordinates became involved in a corruption scandal, leading to the decision to bring Habaguanex under the Gaviota umbrella.[11]

By 2016, Gaviota had become the dominant corporation in Cuban tourism, with over one hundred hotels controlling 40 percent of available rooms—almost as many as the two civilian-run companies, Cubanacan (24 percent) and Gran Caribe (19 percent), combined. Gaviota held an even greater advantage in the most lucrative part of the market, holding 59 percent of the rooms in four- and five-star properties and 83 percent of the five-star rooms.[12] With an annual growth rate of 12.8 percent and revenue of $700 million, Gaviota was the clear leader.[13]

The government's ambitious plans envisioned rapid expansion of the luxury segment of the market in partnership with international hotel brands. Gaviota's model has been to build hotels with its own resources, retaining 100 percent of the equity, and then contract with foreign hotel chains to manage the hotels and handle marketing and reservations.[14] Investment in the construction of hotels and tourism facilities has consumed, on average, 40.1 percent of total annual investment since 2017, dwarfing all other categories of investment, including agriculture (4.9 percent) and industrial manufacturing (11 percent).[15]

The COVID-19 pandemic did not slow Gaviota's torrid pace of investment and expansion, despite the fact that the number of foreign visitors fell by 86.6 percent from 2019 to 2021. The desperate shortage of foreign exchange currency that afflicted Cuba as a result of losing tourism revenue and the Trump administration's restrictions on remittances sparked a debate about whether some of the money spent on building luxury hotels ought to be reallocated to import food, fuel, and medicine or to invest in agriculture and manufacturing. Economist Pedro Monreal pointed out that the occupancy rate for Cuban hotels had been declining even before the pandemic, dropping from 61.5 percent in 2016 to 41.8 percent in 2019, suggesting that the room supply was already outstripping demand.[16]

President Díaz-Canel addressed these concerns directly, arguing that tourism was Cuba's best source of badly needed foreign exchange revenue, that the sector's "corporate culture" (presumably referring to its efficiency) was a model for state enterprises, and that with better linkages to domestic production, tourism could serve as the locomotive of national development.[17] Moreover, Díaz-Canel noted, the tourism sector was subject to the government's new policy of letting enterprises make investment decisions based on economic criteria rather than the state dictating priorities by "administrative methods." Perhaps he was hinting at an unspoken reason for staying the course on tourism development—the fact that the investment capital was coming from Gaviota's retained profits, not the central budget.

The Military's Role in Finance and Commerce

CIMEX S.A. (short for Comercio Interior, Mercado External), one of GAESA's largest holdings, began in 1978 as the Ministry of the Interior's trade and finance hub for evading the US economic embargo and managing the financial side of the government's relationship with the Cuban American diaspora. CIMEX set up front companies in several countries, Panama being the most important, through which it purchased goods that US companies could not legally sell directly to Cuba. CIMEX also handled travel arrangements for Cuban American visitors through its Havanatur subsidiary and processed remittances through Financiera Cimex S.A. (FINCIMEX). CIMEX was spun off from the Ministry of the Interior in 1989, after revelations that senior officers responsible for conducting clandestine trade had used their positions to enable the Colombian Medellín cartel to smuggle drugs into the United States through Cuba. Although an independent company, CIMEX remained under the direction of senior military officers who had Fidel Castro's trust.

In the early 1990s, Cuba's capacity to import fell 75 percent as a result of losing Soviet economic aid and favorable terms of trade with Communist Eastern Europe. The government was in desperate need of foreign exchange currency at a moment when the flow of remittances from Cuban Americans was growing in response to the humanitarian crisis on the island. To capture this new source of revenue, CIMEX created a chain of several hundred retail stores—TRD Caribe, short for Tiendas de Recuperación de Divisas (literally, stores to recover convertible currency)—selling imported consumer goods for US dollars (later, convertible pesos) at markups of 200 percent or more.

When Raúl Castro became president in 2008, he initiated a drive to consolidate and centralize competing state corporations operating in the same markets. In 2009, the government abolished Cubalse, a conglomerate of twenty-one companies with annual revenue of more than $400 million, distributing its component parts to CIMEX and Gaviota.[18] Just a year later, CIMEX was acquired by GAESA.

In 2019–2020, the government began replacing TRD-Caribe stores with MLC (short for *moneda libremente convertible*, or freely convertible currency) stores that only accepted US dollar-denominated debit cards. Cubans abroad could wire any convertible currency to their relatives' MLC debit card accounts via FINCIMEX, enabling the government to capture the convertible currency immediately. The recipient could then shop in the MLC stores for scarce consumer goods unavailable for sale in Cuban pesos. CIMEX used revenue from the MLC sales to import goods to restock the stores, and the government used its share of the profits to import necessities like food, fuel, and medicine to sell for Cuban pesos. In effect, this reproduced the mechanism invented to capture remittances through TRD stores during the Special Period. Before the COVID-19 pandemic, CIMEX generated an estimated $2.6 billion in revenue annually.[19]

One element of Raúl Castro's economic reform program was the acknowledgement that foreign direct investment (FDI) would have to play a significant role in financing Cuba's economic development. In 2014, Minister for Foreign Trade and Investment Rodrigo Malmierca declared that Cuba hoped to attract between $2 and $2.5 billion in FDI annually.[20] That same year, Cuba opened a new modern port at Mariel, surrounded by the Mariel Special Development Zone (Zona Especial de Desarrollo de Mariel [ZEDM]). Designed and built by the Brazilian engineering firm Odebrecht, the port at Mariel was Cuba's largest capital investment project in decades. Of the estimated $957 million cost, the Brazilian Development Bank provided $682 million in concessionary credits.[21] Modeled on the Special Economic Zones China opened early in its economic reform process, the Mariel ZED offered investors highly favorable terms to attract manufacturing both for re-export and for the Cuban domestic market. The port, the ZEDM, and their associated infrastructure represented the cutting edge of Cuba's strategy for attracting foreign investment. Opening the port in January 2014, Raúl Castro called it "a project of transcendental importance for the national economy."[22] As of 2022, sixty-two companies had signed investment contracts to build facilities in the zone, totaling over $3 billion.[23] The Cuban companies overseeing the port and ZEDM are subsidiaries of GAESA.

Washington Targets Cuba's Military Enterprises

In 2015, reacting to President Barack Obama's policy of normalizing relations with Cuba, Cuban American representative Maria Díaz-Balart and Senator Marco Rubio introduced legislation to prohibit US business transactions with firms managed by the Cuban armed forces. Given the wide scope of economic activities under the GAESA umbrella, this would have seriously inhibited commercial ties between Cuba and the United States, undercutting Obama's policy. The bill never became law, but when Donald Trump was elected president, Díaz-Balart and Rubio convinced him to use his regulatory authority to impose this restriction on a long list of Cuban enterprises managed by Gaviota, CIMEX, and GAESA.[24]

Initially, the regulations exempted remittance service providers, including FINCI-MEX, which handled remittances under a contract with Western Union. However, on October 26, 2020, in a bid to energize Cuban American supporters in Florida for the 2020 election, Trump prohibited US remittance service providers from doing business with FINCIMEX.[25] Western Union was forced to close its 407 offices that delivered remittances throughout the island.[26] The impact on the Cuban population was significant, since some 56 percent of families received remittances, more than 90 percent of which came from the United States.[27] When the COVID-19 pandemic cut off travel, Cuban Americans lost the alternative of hand-carrying remittances on family visits or hiring "mules" to deliver the funds for them. Remittances fell from an estimated $3.7 billion in 2019 to $2.4 billion in 2020 and $1.9 billion in 2021.[28]

The Biden campaign denounced Trump's remittances cutoff as a "cruel distraction . . . denying Cuban-Americans the right to help their families."[29] In office, however, Biden was reluctant to lift the sanction because, he said, "it's highly likely that the regime would confiscate those remittances or big chunks."[30] This mistaken view originated with Senator Robert Menendez, who claimed that the Cuban government was "taking 20 percent of remittances to Cuban families, then converting the balance of the remittance to Cuban pesos that are worth a fraction of what Americans send to their families," a claim that was both exaggerated and outdated.[31] Nevertheless, the Biden administration stuck by the position that remittances via wire service would not be restored if any of the money went to the military's commercial businesses.

In 2022, the Cuban government licensed a new civilian-managed remittance service provider, Orbit S.A., to take over from FINCIMEX, and in early 2023, Western Union was able to resume processing remittances. The economic impact on GAESA from the lost business was not great. The main profit that GAESA received from remittances came not from the small 1 percent processing fee charged by FINCIMEX, but from GAESA's control of the network of MLC retail stores where Cubans spent their remittances. In 2021, MLC stores generated an estimated $1.3 billion in revenue, enabling the government to import $300 million worth of basic goods sold for Cuban pesos at subsidized prices.[32]

The Military Business Sector's Example

Overall, the enterprises under GAESA's umbrella held strategic positions in almost all the sectors of the Cuban economy generating convertible currency—tourism, remittances, dollar-denominated retail sales, and foreign direct investment. Cuban economists estimated that GAESA generated between 40 and 60 percent of Cuba's foreign exchange earnings.[33] GAESA and its subsidiaries rarely report their gross or net revenue, how much of their net revenue is returned to the central bank, or how much is retained to finance new investments. Other state enterprises retain half their after-tax profits. The ability of Gaviota to invest hundreds of millions of dollars in new hotel construction illustrates its commercial success. In 2018, the Havana Consulting Group estimated GAESA's annual revenue at $4.2 billion, or about 4.3 percent of Cuba's 2018 GDP.[34]

The elevation, in 2021, of GAESA's president, Luis Alberto Rodríguez López-Calleja, to the Political Bureau of the Communist Party underscored how the political influence of the military's business sector had grown in tandem with its economic power. His sudden death from a heart attack in July 2022 meant the loss of a highly qualified and politically well-connected manager (he was Raúl Castro's former son-in-law). Notably, his successor at GAESA did not assume his seat on the Political Bureau.

The military has been a powerful and influential institution in Cuba ever since 1959, second only to the Communist Party. Prior to the creation of the party, Fidel Castro referred to the Revolutionary Armed Forces as the vanguard of the revolution. It has always had a major voice on policy through the substantial representation of senior military officers in the highest councils of both party and government. The strategic role it has developed in the Cuban economy strengthens its institutional influence, especially on questions of economic reform. The military's experience provided the blueprint for the reform (or "updating") of Cuba's economic model proposed by Raúl Castro in 2011. The process of *perfeccionamiento empresarial* (business improvement) aimed at forcing state enterprises to operate efficiently and generate profits rather than deficits originated in the Defense Industry Group in the 1980s.[35]

In the internal bureaucratic debates over the pace and depth of Cuba's economic reform program, or "updating" of the economy launched by Raúl Castro in 2011, the military business sector was a powerful voice for reform. GAESA's businesses already operated under the strict accounting procedures that many state enterprises had yet to fully adopt. Because so many of the military's enterprises dealt in external markets, they had to become efficient enough to compete globally. Their demonstrable success offered a powerful example to civilian enterprises of what was possible.

There was nothing inherently military about the management systems used to run the business enterprises managed by the armed forces, nothing to prevent the lessons learned from GAESA's expansion from being exported to the civilian sector. The slow pace of diffusion of those lessons to the wider economy was testament to the discipline and efficiency of the military institution Raúl Castro built during his tenure as minister of the Revolutionary Armed Forces, and to a deficit of those virtues in the civilian state bureaucracy.

Notes

1. William M. LeoGrande, "The Politics of Revolutionary Development: Cuban Civil-Military Relations," *Journal of Strategic Studies* 1, no. 3 (December 1978): 260–94.

2. LeoGrande, "Politics of Revolutionary Development."

3. Gaviota Tourism Group, "About Us," accessed September 19, 2022, at http://www.gaviota-grupo.com/en/inicio.

4. Hal Klepak, *Cuba's Military, 1990–2005* (New York: Palgrave Macmillan, 2005), 75–102; José de Cordoba, "Cuba's Military Puts Business on Front Lines," *Wall Street Journal*, November 15, 2006, accessed at https://www.wsj.com/articles/SB116356024065223514.

5. Hal Klepak, *Raúl Castro and Cuba: A Military Story* (New York: Palgrave Macmillan, 2012), 64–66.

6. World Bank, "Military Expenditure (Current USD)—Cuba, 2018," accessed October 1, 2022, at https://data.worldbank.org/indicator/MS.MIL.XPND.CD?locations=CU.

7. Frank Mora, Brian Fonseca, and Brian Latell, *Cuban Military Culture* (Miami: Florida International University, 2016), 5, accessed at https://digitalcommons.fiu.edu/jgi_research/16.

8. Oscar Figueredo Reinaldo et al., "Asamblea Nacional: Ministerios de Turismo e Industrias brindaron información a los diputados, asistió el Presidente Cubano," Cubadebate, July 11, 2019, accessed at http://www.cubadebate.cu/noticias/2019/07/11/asamblea-nacional-ministerios-brindan-informacion-a-los-diputados-asiste-el-presidente-cubano.

9. Julio Batista, "La apuesta hotelera en Cuba: El esquema gaesa para construir hotels," *El Toque*, October 24, 2019, accessed at https://hoteles.eltoque.com/El-esquema-GAESA-para-construir-hoteles.

10. David Montgomery, "Eusebio Leal, the Man Who Would Save Old Havana," *Washington Post*, May 20, 2012, accessed at https://www.washingtonpost.com/lifestyle/style/eusebio-leal-the-man-who-would-save-old-havana/2012/05/20/gIQAAW31dU_story.html.

11. Tony Perrottet, "The Man Who Saved Havana," *Smithsonian Magazine*, May 2018, accessed at https://www.smithsonianmag.com/travel/man-who-saved-havana-180968735.

12. Richard E. Feinberg and Richard S. Newfarmer, *Tourism in Cuba Riding the Wave Toward Sustainable Prosperity*, Brookings Institution, December 2016, accessed at https://www.brookings.edu/wp-content/uploads/2016/11/fp_20161202_tourism_cuba_feinberg_newfarmer.pdf; Jessica Dominguez Delgado, "La apuesta hotelera en cuba: el negocio hotelero," *El Toque*, October 24, 2019, accessed at https://hoteles.eltoque.com/El-negocio-hotelero-en-Cuba.

13. Feinberg and Newfarmer, *Tourism in Cuba*; Gaviota Hoteles, "Business," accessed September 19, 2022, at https://www.gaviotahoteles.com/en/negocios.

14. Miguel Alejandro Figueras, "Foreign Participation in the Development of Tourism in Cuba," Columbia University Law School Cuba Capacity Building Project, February 27, 2020, accessed at https://horizontecubano.law.columbia.edu/news/foreign-participation-development-tourism-cuba.

15. USD estimate based on official exchange rate of 24 pesos to the dollar. Oficina Nacional de Estadística e Información Cuba, *Anuario Estadístico de Cuba 2021*, "Construcción e Inver-

siones," Table 12.5 (Havana: ONEI, 2022), accessed at http://www.onei.gob.cu/sites/default/files/12_construccion_e_inversiones__0.pdf.

16. Pedro Monreal, "¿Debería moderarse la inversión en el turismo en Cuba?" El Estado Como Tal, July 12, 2019, accessed at https://elestadocomotal.com/2019/07/12/deberia-moderarse-la-inversion-en-el-turismo-en-cuba.

17. Figueredo Reinaldo et al., "Asamblea Nacional."

18. Julio Cerviño and Jaime Bonache, "Cuban Retailing: From a Centrally Planned to a Mixed Dual System," *International Journal of Retail & Distribution Management* 33, no. 1 (2005): 79–94; Andrea Rodríguez, "Gobierno cubano cierra la corporación estatal Cubalse," Associated Press, June 2, 2009.

19. "Grupo GAE, the Business Emporium of the Armed Forces," Havana Consulting Group, January 3, 2018, accessed at http://www.thehavanaconsultinggroup.com/en/Articles/Article/58.

20. Daniel Trotta, "Cuba Set to Approve Law Aimed at Attracting Foreign Investment," Reuters, March 29, 2014, accessed at https://www.reuters.com/article/cuba-investment/cuba-set-to-approve-law-aimed-at-attracting-foreign-investment-idUSL1N0MQ0B720140329.

21. Juan Pablo Spinetto and Sabrina Valle, "Odebrecht Set to Profit as Brazil's Cuban Bet Vindicated," Bloomberg, December 19, 2014, accessed at https://www.bloomberg.com/news/articles/2014-12-19/odebrecht-set-to-profit-as-brazils-cuban-bet-vindicated#xj4y7vzkg.

22. Raúl Castro, "Esta Terminal, muestra concreta del optimismo de los Cubanos," Cubadebate, January 27, 2014, accessed at http://www.cubadebate.cu/opinion/2014/01/27/discurso-de-raul-castro-esta-terminal-muestra-concreta-del-optimismo-de-los-cubano-por-el-futuro-so-cialista-y-prospero-de-la-patria.

23. EFE, "Cuba Has Approved 62 Businesses in Mariel Special Development Zone," *OnCuba News*, July 12, 2022, accessed at https://oncubanews.com/en/cuba/economy/cuban-economy/cuba-has-approved-62-businesses-in-mariel-special-development-zone.

24. US Department of the Treasury, "Treasury, Commerce, and State Implement Changes to the Cuba Sanctions Rules," November 9, 2021, accessed at https://home.treasury.gov/system/files/126/cuba_fact_sheet_11082017.pdf.

25. US Department of the Treasury, "Treasury Prohibits Cuban Military from Processing Remittance Related Transactions," October 26, 2020, accessed at https://home.treasury.gov/system/files/126/cuba_fact_sheet_20201026.pdf.

26. "In Blow to Struggling Cubans, Western Union Offices Close as Sanctions Bite," Reuters, November 23, 2020, accessed at https://www.reuters.com/article/us-cuba-remittances-idUSKBN2840CI.

27. Katrin Hansing and Bert Hoffmann, *Cuba's New Social Structure: Assessing the Re-stratification of Cuban Society 60 Years after Revolution*, German Institute of Global and Area Studies (GIGA) Working Paper No. 315, February 2019, accessed at https://www.giga-hamburg.de/en/publication/cubas-new-social-structure-assessing-the-re-stratification-of-cuban-society-60-years.

28. "COVID-19 puede hacer declinar las remesas a Cuba entre un 30 y 40% en el 2020," Havana Consulting Group, March 20, 2020, accessed at http://www.thehavanaconsultinggroup.com/en-us/Articles/Article/74.

29. EFE, "Biden's Campaign Criticizes Blocking of Remittances to Cubans," *OnCuba News*, October 29, 2020, accessed at https://oncubanews.com/en/cuba-usa/bidens-campaign-criticizes-blocking-of-remittances-to-cubans.

30. Nora Gámez Torres and Alex Roarty, "Amid Wave of Repression in Cuba, Biden Says He Won't Lift Restrictions on Remittances," *Miami Herald*, July 15, 2021, accessed at https://www.miamiherald.com/news/nation-world/world/americas/cuba/article252821163.html.

31. William M. LeoGrande, "Biden Stalls on Reinstating Cuban Remittances for No Good Reason," Responsible Statecraft, July 21, 2021, accessed at https://responsiblestatecraft.org/2021/07/21/biden-stalls-on-reinstating-cuban-remittances-for-no-good-reason.

32. Dave Sherwood, "Cuba's Dollar Shops Stoke Anger, Division amid Economic Crisis," Reuters, March 10, 2022, accessed at https://www.reuters.com/article/cuba-economy/cubas-dollar-shops-stoke-anger-division-amid-economic-crisis-idUKL1N2UY27G.

33. Marc Frank, "Cuban Military's Tentacles Reach Deep into Economy," Reuters, June 15, 2017, accessed at https://www.reuters.com/article/idUSKBN1962VK.

34. "Grupo GAE," Havana Consulting Group.

35. "Perfeccionamiento empresarial," Ecured, accessed September 19, 2022, at http://www.ecured.cu/index.php/Perfeccionamiento_Empresarial.

CHAPTER 13

Cuba's Energy Challenges

Jorge R. Piñón

Cuba faces far-reaching energy challenges that threaten its economic development. Energy is a central element of development that enables investments, technological innovations, and the emergence of new industries that are the engines of job creation. Access to energy and to efficient, clean, and renewable energy for that matter is needed in order to ensure a positive impact on people and their environment. Electricity is essential for the well-being of households and commercial activities, and the quality of most public services, such as health and education, depend on it (Kelsey 2022). Moreover, the global energy sector is undergoing a massive transformation, as a result of increasing pressure to reduce carbon emissions and rapid and profound technological developments.

But Cuba lacks a detailed strategic road map toward a comprehensive national energy policy that addresses these challenges. A consistent policy and regulatory framework are essential in order to facilitate an energy transition that neither disrupts Cuba's energy supply nor locks it into political supply relationships, short-term price subsidy programs, or inefficient technologies.

Oil, Petroleum Products, and Natural Gas Value Chain

Cuba lacks sufficient domestic hydrocarbon resources to meet its current or future energy needs. Its mature crude oil field production has declined by 22 percent from 50,000 barrels per day in 2010 to approximately 39,000 barrels per day in 2021. Without heavy conversion and desulfurization refinery capacity, Cuba's heavy and sour crude oil production is difficult to upgrade into high-value refined products. As a result, its sole use today is as a highly polluting industrial and electric power sectors fuel (ONEI 2022b).

Associated natural gas production has also declined from 2016 levels by 24 percent, from 20.4 thousand barrels of oil equivalent per day (boed) to 14.6 thousand boed in 2020. Natural gas production is used by ENERGAS, Cuba's largest independent power

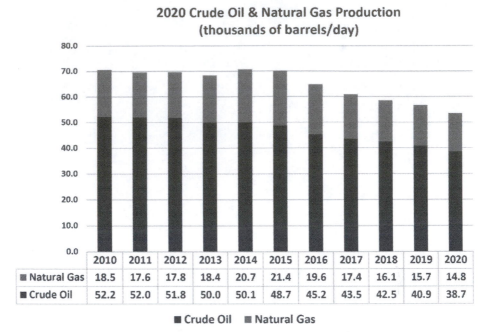

2020 Crude Oil & Natural Gas Production
(thousands of barrels/day)

	2010	2011	2012	2013	2014	2015	2016	2017	2018	2019	2020
■ Natural Gas	18.5	17.6	17.8	18.4	20.7	21.4	19.6	17.4	16.1	15.7	14.8
■ Crude Oil	52.2	52.0	51.8	50.0	50.1	48.7	45.2	43.5	42.5	40.9	38.7

■ Crude Oil   ■ Natural Gas

Figure 13.1.   Crude Oil and Natural Gas Production. *Source*: Oficina Nacional de Estadísticas e Información de Cuba; http://www.onei.gob.cu.

producer, a joint venture with Canada's Sherritt with over 500MW of combined cycle power units in situ in the Varadero, Puerto Escondido, and Boca de Jaruco oil fields (Sherritt 2022).

The *Oil & Gas Journal* estimates Cuba's proven oil reserves to be 124 million barrels, with primary recovery factors at less than 10 percent due to the viscosity of the oil and porosity of the reservoirs. The 2010 US Geological Survey report "Geologic Assessment of Undiscovered Oil and Gas Resources of the North Cuba Basin" estimated that the mean volumes of undiscovered resources of the North Cuba Basin are 4.6 billion barrels of oil and 8.6 trillion cubic feet of natural gas (Schenk 2010).

Based on this and other industry proprietary geological assessments, a number of international oil companies carried out exploratory drilling campaigns in 2012 of four deepwater prospects in Cuba's Gulf of Mexico and Florida Strait economic exclusive zone. All four were declared as noncommercial discoveries, and no further offshore exploratory activity has been reported, nor is any anticipated. Cuba faces strong headwinds in attracting deepwater oil and natural gas exploration investments when competing with other regions with proven reserves such as the US Gulf of Mexico, Guyana-Suriname Basin, Brazil, and West Africa.

Currently there is an onshore campaign of two exploratory wells in Matanzas Province by Australia's Melbana Energy in partnership with Angola's national oil company, Sonangol. As of this writing, results are inconclusive. In addition, if oil were found it would take twelve to eighteen months to drill the production wells and build the gathering and logistics infrastructure necessary to monetize any potential commercial discovery (Searancke 2022).

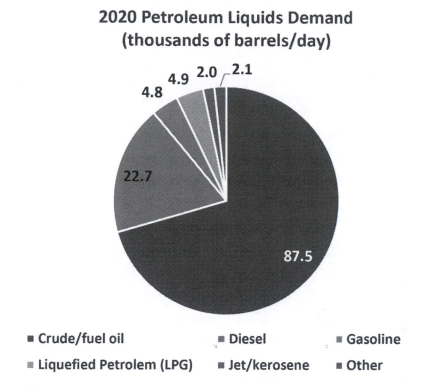

2020 Petroleum Liquids Demand (thousands of barrels/day)

4.8   4.9   2.0   2.1

22.7

87.5

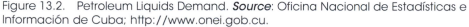

- ■ Crude/fuel oil
- ■ Diesel
- ■ Gasoline
- ■ Liquefied Petrolem (LPG)
- ■ Jet/kerosene
- ■ Other

Figure 13.2.   Petroleum Liquids Demand. *Source*: Oficina Nacional de Estadísticas e Información de Cuba; http://www.onei.gob.cu.

Cuba's Oficina Nacional de Estadísticas e Información (ONEI) reports 2020 petroleum liquids total demand at 124 thousand barrels per day, a drop of 15 percent from 2016 levels of 146 thousand barrels per day (ONEI 2022a). Cuba's oil demand is skewed toward a high-sulfur crude/fuel oil blend for the industrial and electric power sector, representing 70 percent of total demand.

Diesel represents 18 percent of total demand, 30 percent of which is destined for the electric power sector (distributed energy, or *grupos electrógenos*) and 18 percent for the transportations and agricultural sectors. Low gasoline consumption of less than 5,000 barrels per day of total demand reflects the size and age of the vehicular park, compared to countries such as the Dominican Republic and Guatemala which each consume over 20,000 barrels per day.

We have seen over the last ten years an increase of over 50 percent in the Cuban demand for liquefied petroleum gas—butane LPG—as it has become the cooking fuel of choice of a large percentage of the population (ONEI 2022a). Much of Cuba's petroleum liquids consumption today is not the result of actual end-user demand but losses as a result of energy-inefficient industrial transformation processes, road and rail transportation constraints, lack of weatherization of commercial and residential buildings, and losses in public utilities such as water management and electric power generation and distribution systems (Alonso et al. 2021).

Based on ONEI's supply/demand balance it is estimated that Cuba's current oil deficit is approximately 70 thousand barrels per day. This deficit is partially supplied by 55 thousand barrels per day of petroleum liquids imports from Venezuela on a noncommercial services-for-oil barter agreement, and approximately 15 thousand barrels per day from other international sources including Russia.

The rationalization of the island's oil refining sector is inevitable due to its low conversion factors, energy inefficiency, obsolete technology, and air, water, and surface environmental levels of contamination of its three refineries.

Electric Power Sector

Electric power has become the Achilles' heel of Cuba's energy sector and economy, as its oil baseload thermoelectric and distributed generation are collapsing due to age and lack of scheduled and capital maintenance. According to ONEI, Cuba's electric grid (Sistema Eléctrico Nacional, or SEN) has a total generation rated capacity of 6,767 MW, consisting of 2,608 MW of high-sulfur crude/fuel-oil-blend-fired baseload thermoelectric power plants and 2,671 MW of oil-fired distributed generation.

In 2022 less than 40 percent of the sector's total oil thermoelectric generation capacity was operational, which resulted in prolonged blackouts of eight to twelve hours throughout the country (Cubadebate 2022). Only twelve of twenty total generating units were operating within eight thermoelectric base-load power plants according to 2022 year-end reports by Unión Eléctrica (UNE), Cuba's electric power state monopoly. The distributed generation (*grupos electrógenos*) strategy introduced during the 2006 *Revolución Energética* resulted in a total failure. The 2022 year-end UNE reports document that 59 percent of Cuba's distributed generation installed rated capacity is out of service as a result of equipment failure and shortage of diesel fuel. Moreover,

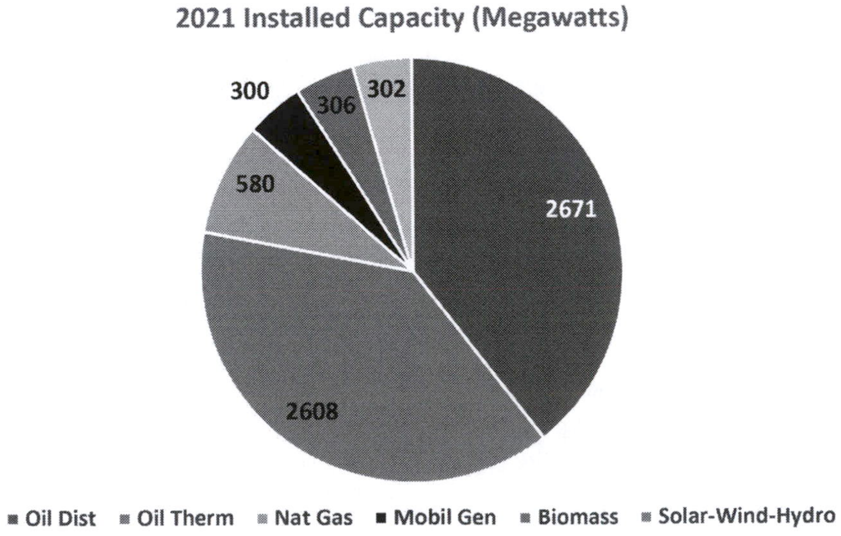

Figure 13.3.   Installed Electric Generating Capacity and Electric Generation. *Source*: Oficina Nacional de Estadísticas e Información de Cuba; http://www.onei.gob.cu.

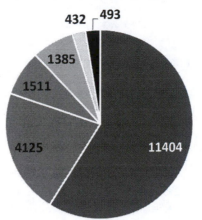

2021 Installed Generation (Gigawatt Hours)

- Oil Therm - Oil Dist - Nat Gas - Mobil Gen - Biomass - Solar-Wind-Hydro

Figure 13.4.   Installed Electric Generation. *Source*: Oficina Nacional de Estadísticas e Información de Cuba; http://www.onei.gob.cu.

electric power losses of 15 percent of generation in the transmission and distribution of electricity, particularly in the local distribution networks, continues above acceptable industry losses of 2 to 5 percent (ONEI 2022b).

There is no short-term solution to Cuba's electric power generation challenges. The total recapitalization of its baseload and distributed generation and renewable electric power matrix is the only solution, which regrettably would take time and as much as $5 to $7 billion of investments (EIA 2020).

Renewable Energy Sources

The Cuban National Economic and Social Development Plan 2030 (PNDES), presented in 2016 before the Seventh Party Congress, included an ambitious goal of 25 percent of renewables in the national electric power energy matrix, but failed in fully addressing how the balance of 75 percent would be fueled.

Wind and solar have not materialized to their fullest potential due to the lack of utility-scale battery storage systems needed to levelize excess renewable power for use when electricity demand exceeds supply as a way to resolve the intermittent nature of renewable energy. However, Cuba did see a 230 percent increase (2017–2021) in grid-connected and stand-alone solar photovoltaic installed capacity (ONEI 2022b).

Sugarcane has been a major disappointment when viewed for its long-term potential, not only as a source of biomass for electric power generation but also as a source of fuel ethanol for the transportation sector. According to *Granma*, Cuba's 2021–2022 sugarcane harvest fell to just 52 percent of the goal for the season, for approximately 474,000 tons, the worst since 1908 (Sherwood 2022).

Cuba's first major biomass foreign investment joint venture between Azcuba and British Havana Energy, a $185 million 60MW sugarcane biomass power-generation project, connected to the grid in December of 2021. But the generator sits idle, as there is no sugarcane biomass to supply it.

The sugarcane industry is a sustainable business model. Its products and byproducts of sugar, fuel ethanol, bioelectricity from bagasse, and biofertilizers offer the competitive advantage and flexibility to switch from one product to another as market forces dictate. The revamping of the sugarcane industry deserves high consideration and focus within Cuba's future national energy policy. This would bring considerable economic benefits with new investments and employment creation, support the national balance of payments by reducing the demand for imported oil, and create new sources of export revenue. With a land-reclamation development plan and the recapitalization of the island's sugarcane processing industry under a decentralized agricultural economic model, Cuba has the potential of again becoming a major producer of sugarcane and its derivatives.

However, in 2002, Cuba began a drastic downsizing of its sugarcane industry in what was a myopic strategic decision that did not consider long-term implications and possible market and technological changes. Moreover, the outlook for returning to past levels of sugarcane production is challenging unless the Cuban government undertakes substantial reforms of its agricultural economic model. The mills and the biomass plants can be built but they are worthless without sugarcane. That is why the recapitalization and ownership/production model of the agricultural sector is so important.

Decisions by Cuba's leadership on this subject are also constrained by Fidel Castro's disapproving views of the role of the sugarcane industry on the island's economic and social development. It has become political dogma within some political circles in Cuba to substantially and deliberately phase out the sugarcane industry, as Fidel Castro declared in 2005: "Sugar will never be the source of life in this country again. . . . [Sugar] belongs to the era of slavery and illiteracy" (as quoted in Arreola 2005).

Brazil's sugarcane industry best practices and mistakes are a good case study for Cuba. That country's experiences in creating a sugarcane economy have the potential to help Cuba in developing its strategy and select the best paths in how to successfully integrate sugarcane fuel ethanol and biomass into the island's energy matrix. Sugarcane bioelectricity, produced from bagasse and field debris, supplied Brazil's national power grid with more than 8 percent of the country's electricity consumption in 2020, enough to power more than ten million homes per year (UNICA 2021a).

The Brazilian automobile industry has developed flex fuel vehicles (FFVs) that operate with any proportion of gasoline (E20-E25 mix) or hydrous ethanol (E100). Available on the market since 2003, the existing fleet of FFVs grew from 10.8 percent in 2006 to 88.6 percent of licensed light commercial vehicles in 2018 (UNICA 2021b).

The US Environmental Protection Agency (EPA) reports that ethanol made from sugarcane is a low-carbon renewable fuel, which can contribute significantly to the reduction of greenhouse gas (GHG) emissions. It designated sugarcane fuel ethanol as an advanced biofuel that lowers GHG emissions by more than 50 percent (US Environmental Protection Agency 2022).

Liquefied Natural Gas

Cuba should consider a fuel-switching strategy from high-sulfur oil to cleaner-burning liquefied natural gas (LNG) as it rebuilds its baseload thermoelectric and distributed generation.

Natural gas is an energy source of fossil origin that offers many advantages: it is price competitive, ensures availability of supply, and is less polluting than oil and/or coal. Natural gas, like any other fossil fuel, produces CO_2; however, its emissions are 40 to 50 percent lower than those of coal and 25 to 30 percent lower than those of fuel oil, making it the cleanest of fossil fuels. Natural gas has a sulfur content of less than 10 ppm (parts per million), so the emissions of sulfur dioxide (SO_2), the main cause of acid rain, are 2,500 times less than that emitted by fuel oil (EIA 2020).

It is critical for Cuba to develop a baseload electric power system that offers the flexibility to operate on a number of diverse fuels such as liquefied natural gas and/or liquid fuels. This is a choice to be made based on available technology and on a fuel's Btu value/price, market availability, and associated environmental costs. Companies such as GE, Siemens, Wartsila, and others are developing technologies that can provide baseload flexible fuel engine power plants, providing an optimized transition to cleaner fuels.

LNG could play an important role in Cuba's future energy mix, as Cuba needs to decarbonize its electric power generation while still providing reliable and cost-competitive power by investing in technologies that will make this possible while avoiding stranded assets as technologies change.

Environmental Impact of Burning High-Sulfur Crude and Fuel Oil

Cuba's INSMET Centro de Contaminación y Química Atmosférica (CECONT) identified sulfur dioxide as the most important pollutant emitted into the atmosphere on the island, followed by nitrogen dioxide (NO_2) and carbon monoxide (CO), all associated with the burning of fossil fuels (Pelaez 2022).

CECONT carried out an analysis of the spatial distribution of air pollutants, with SO_2, NO_2, and PM10 (particulates) contaminants having the highest concentrations. The mean monthly concentrations of particulates pollutants were correlated with the number of cases treated monthly for acute respiratory infections and bronchial asthma. According to the study, the metropolitan areas with the worst level of air pollution were Mariel, La Habana, Matanzas, Nuevitas, Moa, Santiago de Cuba, and Cienfuegos. All are cities where Cuba's eight high-sulfur oil-fired baseload thermoelectric plants are located (Préndez, López, and Carillo 2014).

National Energy Policy Roadmap

Cuba's energy challenges begin with its future economic growth and rising standard of living within a decentralized economic system. This should be supported by the adoption of a public-private partnership (PPP) development model, which would attract much-needed foreign direct investment (FDI) and technology. There will be no sector of Cuba's economy and social well-being that will not be directly impacted and/or influenced by such a national comprehensive energy policy. Cuba's growth will depend largely on the development of a competitively priced, readily available, and environmentally sound long-term energy plan that considers three basic pillars: (1) energy security and reliability, (2) clean sustainable energy, and (3) energy efficiency.

ENERGY SECURITY AND RELIABILITY

Geopolitical uncertainties such as political instability, civil conflicts, economic downturns, economic sanctions, and natural disasters impact the supply/demand balance and global price of petroleum liquids and natural gas. These uncertainties affect all regions of the world and threaten both rich and poor nations alike. Cuba's domestic hydrocarbon resources deficit makes the country vulnerable to the market volatility described above, but fuel type and supply source diversification provides the ability to manage these risks. The uninterrupted performance of the infrastructure is critical for the delivery of energy to both consumers and industry, and this is a strategy that must be in place to facilitate recovery from disruptions to energy generation, transmission, and/or distribution.

CLEAN SUSTAINABLE ENERGY

Renewable energies are clean and increasingly competitive energy sources. They differ from fossil fuels mainly in their diversity, abundance, and potential for use as fuel for electric power generation. Above all, they do not produce greenhouse gases, hence minimizing climate change and polluting emissions. Their costs, too, are steadily declining. A balanced energy matrix of renewable sources such as wind, solar, and biomass, supported by low-carbon fossil fuel baseload generation such as liquefied natural gas, can play an important role in reducing fossil fuel greenhouse emissions in both the electric power and transportation sectors, Cuba's two largest sources of carbon dioxide emissions.

ENERGY EFFICIENCY

Energy efficiency simply means using less energy to perform the same task—that is, eliminating energy waste. Energy efficiency brings a variety of benefits: reducing greenhouse gas emissions, reducing demand for energy imports, and lowering costs. It is the most efficient way for Cuba to reduce its use of fossil fuels. Industrial transformation processes, upgraded road and rail transportation, weatherization of residential and commercial buildings, and improved efficiency of public utility sectors are the principal areas of focus (Panfil 2017).

Foreign Direct Investments through Public-Private Partnerships

Cuba can be categorized as a frontier market, a country that is more established than the least-developed countries but still less established than emerging markets because it is too small, carries too much inherent risk, or is too illiquid to be considered an emerging market (Khambata and Ajami 1992). Risks of frontier markets include political instability, poor liquidity, inadequate regulations, the lack of the rule of law, substandard financial reporting, large currency fluctuations, high inflation or deflation, unregulated markets, and unsound monetary policies.

An analysis of the southern Mediterranean by Emmanuel Bergasse and his colleagues is germane to the challenge faced by Cuba as a frontier market:

> The current energy situation in the region [southern Mediterranean countries] is characterized by a rapid increase in energy demand, low energy efficiency, and low domestic energy prices due to extensive universal consumption subsidy schemes. In short, the current energy policies do not appear to be sustainable and pose several risks to the prospects of socio-economic development of the region. (Bergasse et al. 2013, 10)

Thus, Cuba should consider, within a decentralized economic model, promoting the use of public-private partnerships (design-build-operate-maintain-finance) which would attract private capital financing to infrastructure projects, freeing the government to spend much-needed revenues for education and health care while still maintaining regulatory control over public infrastructure projects.

The Solution to Cuba's Energy Challenges

There is no short-term solution to Cuba's energy challenges. The country does not have the necessary domestic oil and natural gas resources to supply its own needs and will have to continue to depend on imports of petroleum liquids and liquefied natural gas to fuel its future economic growth.

Cuba's electric power infrastructure is old, tired, and broken beyond repair. Years and billions of dollars would be needed to reconstruct its thermoelectric baseload and distributed generating capacity and to achieve its goal of 25 percent of renewables within its electric power sector energy matrix. Two things that Cuba urgently needs and does not have are time and money. There are a number of issues that Cuba must first address if it desires to attract much-needed direct foreign investments and the support of multilateral international financial institutions.

- Cuba must reassess its centralized economic model and develop a socially open and decentralized market economy.
- Cuba and the United States must find a political solution that removes the restrictions of the codified Cuban Democracy Act of 1992 and the Helms-Burton Act of

1996, which constraints US trade, investments, and access to multilateral financial institutions with Cuba.
* Cuba's population must reach a standard of living necessary to afford the nonsubsidized cost of clean and sustainable energy commensurate with an acceptable rate of return to the investor.

Cuba faces a long and hazardous road ahead in order to achieve the goals of a comprehensive national energy policy road map: energy security and reliability, clean sustainable energy, and energy efficiency.

References

Alhajji, A. F. 2008. "What Is Energy Security? Definitions and Concepts." *Oil, Gas and Energy Law Journal* 3. Accessed at www.ogel.org/article.asp?key=2786.

Alonso Falcon, Randy, et al. 2021. "Ante la actual situación hidrometeorológica, ¿cómo enfrenta Cuba la sequía?" Cubadebate, May 13. Accessed at http://www.cubadebate.cu/noticias/2021/05/13/ante-la-actual-situacion-hidrometeorologica-como-enfrenta-cuba-la-sequia-video.

Alvarez, Jose. 2001. *Cuba's Sugar Industry.* Gainesville: University Press of Florida.

———. 2004. "The Current Restructuring of Cuba's Sugar Agroindustry." Institute of Food and Agricultural Sciences, University of Florida, Gainesville. Accessed March 19, 2020, at https://edis.ifas.ufl.edu/publication/FE472.

Arreola, Gerardo. 2005. "Cuba 'no volverá a vivir jamás' de la industria azucarera: Fidel Castro." *La Jornada*, March 20. Accessed at https://www.jornada.com.mx/2005/03/20/index.php?section=mundo&article=030n1mun.

Benjamin-Alvarado, Jonathan, ed. 2010. *Cuba's Energy Future: Strategic Approaches to Cooperation.* Washington, DC: Brookings Institution Press.

Bergasse, Emmanuel, et al. 2013. "The Relationship between Energy and Economic and Social Development in the Southern Mediterranean." Mediterranean Prospects Technical Report No. 27, February 7. Accessed at https://www.ceps.eu/ceps-publications/relationship-between-energy-and-economic-and-social-development-southern-mediterranean.

Brazilian Sugarcane Industry. 2010. "EPA Reaffirms Sugarcane Biofuel Is Advanced Renewable Fuel with 61% Less Emissions than Gasoline." Cision PR Newswire, February 3. Accessed at https://www.prnewswire.com/news-releases/epa-reaffirms-sugarcane-biofuel-is-advanced-renewable-fuel-with-61-less-emissions-than-gasoline-83483922.html.

Cubadebate. 2022. "Unión Eléctrica Pronostica Afectación de 800 MW En El Horario Diurno Y 1 266 MW en el Pico Nocturno." Cubadebate, November 7. Accessed at http://www.cubadebate.cu/noticias/2022/11/07/union-electrica-pronostica-afectacion-de-800-mw-en-el-horario-diurno-y-1-266-mw-en-el-pico-nocturno.

EIA (US Energy Information Administration). 2020. *Capital Cost and Performance Characteristic Estimates for Utility Scale Electric Power Generating Technologies.* February 2020. Washington, DC: US Department of Energy. Accessed at https://www.eia.gov/analysis/studies/powerplants/capitalcost/pdf/capital_cost_AEO2020.pdf.

———. 2021. "Country Analysis Executive Summary: Brazil." June 14. Accessed at https://www.eia.gov/international/analysis/country/BRA.

EPE (Empresa de Pesquisa Energética). 2020. *Balanço Energético Nacional 2020: Ano base 2019.* Rio de Janeiro: EPE. Accessed at https://www.epe.gov.br/sites-pt/publicacoes-dados-abertos/publicacoes/PublicacoesArquivos/publicacao-479/topico-528/BEN2020_sp.pdf.

González Martínez, Ortelio. 2022. "Bioeléctrica del Central Ciro Redondo: Sueños de Matrimonio Divorciado." Cubadebate, March 20. Accessed at http://www.cubadebate.cu/especiales/2022/03/20/bioelectrica-del-central-ciro-redondo-suenos-de-matrimonio-divorciado.

Harrison, M. R., T. M. Shires, J. K. Wessels, and R. M. Cowgill. 1996. "Methane Emissions from the Natural Gas Industry." United States Environmental Protection Agency, National Risk Management Research Laboratory. Accessed at https://www.epa.gov/sites/default/files/2016-08/documents/1_executiveummary.pdf.

International Energy Agency. 2019. "Country Profile: Cuba." Accessed January 4, 2023, https://www.iea.org/countries/cuba.

Katz, Cheryl. 2020. "In Boost for Renewables, Grid-Scale Battery Storage Is on the Rise." Yale Environment 360, December 15. Accessed at https://e360.yale.edu/features/in-boost-for-renewables-grid-scale-battery-storage-is-on-the-rise.

Kelsey, Jack. 2022. "How Much Do We Know about the Development Impacts of Energy Infrastructure?" World Bank Blogs, March 29. Accessed at https://blogs.worldbank.org/energy/how-much-do-we-know-about-development-impacts-energy-infrastructure.

Khambata, Dara, and Riad Ajami. 1992. International Business: Theory and Practice. New York: Pearson, 1992..

Melbana Energy. 2021. "Cuba Block 9 Production Sharing Contract." Accessed January 4, 2023, at https://www.melbana.com/site/cpfile/8c59ca95-7db5-49ea-971f-9a78d86f58e7/20211213CubaFlyerBlock9.pdf.

Ministerio de Economía y Planificación. 2021. "Plan Nacional De Desarrollo Económico y Social 2030." Accessed January 4, 2023, at https://www.mep.gob.cu/es/pndesods-2030/plan-nacional-de-desarrollo-economico-y-social-2030.

Musacchio, Aldo, and Eric Werker. 2016. "Mapping Frontier Economies." Harvard Business Review, December. Accessed at https://hbr.org/2016/12/mapping-frontier-economies.

Oil & Gas Journal. 2021. "World Crude Oil Reserves and Production." Accessed January 4, 2023, at https://www.ogj.com/general-interest/document/17299007/worldwide-crude-oil-and-natural-gas-production.

ONEI (Oficina Nacional de Estadística e Información). 2022a. Anuario Estadístico de Cuba 2021, capítulo 10, "Minería y Energía."Havana: ONEI. Accessed at http://www.onei.gob.cu/sites/default/files/10_mineria_y_energia_2021.pdf.

———. 2022b. Electricidad en Cuba: Indicadores Seleccionados. Enero-Diciembre 2021. Havana: ONEI. Accessed at http://www.onei.gob.cu/sites/default/files/publicacion_electricidad_en_cuba._2021_edic_2022.pdf.

Panfil, Michael, et al. 2017. The Cuban Electric Grid Lessons and Recommendations for Cuba's Electric Sector. Washington, DC: Environmental Defense Fund. Accessed at https://www.edf.org/sites/default/files/cuban-electric-grid.pdf.

Pelaez, Orfilio. 2022. "¿Cómo se comporta la calidad del aire en Cuba?" Granma, July 15. Accessed at https://www.granma.cu/ciencia/2022-07-15/como-se-comporta-la-calidad-del-aire-en-cuba-15-07-2022-20-07-44.

Pérez-López, Jorge F., and José Álvarez, eds. 2005. Reinventing the Cuban Sugar Agroindustry. Lanham, MD: Lexington Books.

Préndez, Margarita, Rosemary Lopez, and Ernesto Carrillo. 2014. "Physical and Chemical Components of Cuba's Rain: Effects on Air Quality." International Journal of Atmospheric Sciences, August 12. Accessed at https://www.hindawi.com/journals/ijas/2014/680735.

Schenk, Christopher J. 2010. "Geologic Assessment of Undiscovered Oil and Gas Resources of the North Cuba Basin." United States Geological Survey, February 13. Accessed at https://pubs.usgs.gov/of/2010/1029.

Schwarz, Peter M. 2017. Energy Economics. Milton Park, UK: Routledge.

Searancke, Russell. 2022. "Cuban Oil Exploration Well Suspended as Owners Return to Previous Discovery." *Upstream*, October 31. Accessed at https://www.upstreamonline.com/exploration/cuban-oil-exploration-well-suspended-as-owners-return-to-previous-discovery/2-1-1343698.

Sherwood, Dave. 2022. "Cuba's Sugar Harvest Worst in Over Century, Another Hit to Ailing Economy." Reuters, May 25. Accessed at https://www.reuters.com/markets/commodities/cubas-sugar-harvest-worst-over-century-another-hit-ailing-economy-2022-05-25.

Sherritt International Corp. 2022. *Annual Reports 2010–2021*. Accessed January 4, 2023, at https://www.sherritt.com/English/Investor-Relations/Annual-Meeting-Material/default.aspx.

UNICA 2021a, *UNICAdata*, União da Indústria de Cana-de-Açúcar e Bioenergia, Accessed June 30, 2023, at https://unicadata.com.br/listagem.php?idMn=145.

UNICA 2021b, *UNICAdata*, União da Indústria de Cana-de-Açúcar e Bioenergia, Accessed June 30, 2023, at https://unicadata.com.br/listagem.php?idMn=147.

United Nations. 2020. "Renewable Energy—Powering a Safer Future." Accessed January 4, 2023, at https://www.un.org/en/climatechange/raising-ambition/renewable-energy.

US Environmental Protection Agency. 2022. "Can Ethanol Produced from Sugarcane Molasses through a Fermentation Process in a Mixed Sugar/Ethanol Mill Generate D-Code 5 RINs under the Existing Pathway in Table 1 to §80.1426 for Ethanol Produced from Sugarcane through the Fermentation Process?" August 30. Accessed at https://www.epa.gov/fuels-registration-reporting-and-compliance-help/can-ethanol-produced-sugarcane-molasses-through.

Varela Pérez, Juan. 2003. "Restructuración Azucarera: El Compromiso de Dar Uso a las Tierras que Pasan a Otros Cultivos." *Granma*, October 26. Accessed at https://www.granma.cu/granmad/2003/10/26/nacional/articulo12.html.

World Bank. 2018. "Access to Energy Is at the Heart of Development." April 18. Accessed at https://www.worldbank.org/en/news/feature/2018/04/18/access-energy-sustainable-development-goal-7.

PART III

INTERNATIONAL RELATIONS

John M. Kirk

The situation facing Miguel Díaz-Canel as he assumed the presidency in April 2018 was radically different from just a few years earlier. In July 2015, for example, the United States had officially resumed diplomatic relations, and in March 2016 Barack Obama became the first sitting president in over eighty years to visit Cuba. Cuba's relationship with the European Union was also progressing well, with frequent exchanges resulting in substantial aid. Canadian-Cuban relations were also solid, and in 2015 1.36 million Canadian sun-seekers made up 36 percent of all tourists to the island.

Ongoing medical collaboration with the Global South was successful, with tens of thousands of Cuban medical personnel working in developing countries, both winning political support and generating Cuba's largest source of hard currency. Relations with traditional allies Russia and China continued strong. Very different, however, was the relationship with Latin America where, with the exception of a handful of left-wing governments referred to by the Trump administration as the "troika of tyranny," tensions were noticeable.

This complex kaleidoscope of international relations was soon to change dramatically, and few in Havana could have foreseen the extent of the reversal of policies undertaken by the Trump administration (2017–2021), much less the continuation of similar policies under President Biden. This in turn had a "knock on" effect of other key facets of Cuba's ties with other countries—both positive and negative. Nevertheless, Cuba still had many allies, many of whom remained opposed to US policy.

Recent years have constituted a diplomatic roller coaster for Cuba, in no small part due to the necessary survival struggle when faced with extremely rigorous punitive measures enacted by Washington, compounded with economic mismanagement by the Cuban government and the COVID-19 pandemic. Nevertheless, through pragmatic politics fostered by Havana, as well as the support of various ideological allies including China and Russia (largely the result of their own strained relationship with the United States), Cuba has managed to keep its increasingly tattered revolutionary process alive. This has been an extremely complex process, made all the more challenging because of differing interpretations of human rights and democratic process questions among some of Cuba's international commercial partners—particularly after the street protests in the summer of 2021.

Cuba-US Relations

The single largest influence on Cuba's international relations has traditionally been US policy toward the island. The Obama years represented a major shift in the long-standing US policy of enmity, as the president noted after arriving in Cuba: "I've come to Havana to extend the hand of friendship to the Cuban people. I'm here to bury the last vestige of the Cold War and to forge a new era of understanding to help improve the daily lives of the Cuban people" (Obama 2016).

Under Obama, American tourists flooded into Cuba (over 638,000 in 2018), US exports grew, Cuba became a popular stop for cruise ships, remittances to families on the island increased, flights from the United States reached a dozen Cuban cities, cultural ties grew rapidly (with American TV programs being filmed in Cuba), and US business interests in tourism started. Corporate executives from Airbnb, Google, General Electric, PayPal, Pfizer, and Xerox arrived to investigate possible business ventures. Even representatives from the Trump organization looked into tourism opportunities. As an illustration of the possibilities of a new stage in international relations, Beyonce, Rihanna, and the Rolling Stones all visited. The French fashion house Chanel staged a show—the first in Cuba since 1959. It did indeed look as if the Cold War in this troubled bilateral relationship was about to end.

Then along came Donald Trump, who presented a radically different perspective—as can be seen from his words in Miami on June 16, 2017: "It's hard to think of a policy that makes less sense than the prior administration's terrible and misguided deal with the Castro regime. . . . Therefore, effective immediately, I am canceling the last administration's completely one-sided deal with Cuba" (Office of the Press Secretary 2017). Given the enormous influence of this bilateral relationship, the many sweeping policy changes introduced by the Trump administration (some 240 according to the Cuban government) had an immense negative effect on events in Havana. In 2018 the United Nations estimated the cost of the embargo to Cuba at $130 billion (Adler 2022).

As noted by William LeoGrande in chapter 14, the Trump administration methodically dismantled all the Obama initiatives toward Cuba. Cruise ships were prohibited from traveling between US ports and Cuba, flights to Cuban cities were canceled (apart from to Havana), and private charter flights were forbidden. Trade and investment were banned for US companies seeking to do business in Cuba. Americans were no longer allowed to stay at hundreds of hotels owned by the government. Remittances to family members on the island were severely limited by Washington, and some 400 Western Union outlets were forced to close. Illustrative of this broad punitive sweep was the decision in the last days of the Trump administration to place Cuba on the list of countries allegedly supporting terrorist activities—once again overturning the Obama policy. (This had a particularly negative impact, since it made it extremely complex for Cuba to have any international commercial dealings, and Cuba was now seen—along with Syria, Iran, and North Korea—as an international pariah.)

A further irritant to the relationship was the emergence of the so-called Havana Syndrome, an unexplained malady that affected US diplomats, who complained of a variety of symptoms ranging from hearing and balance issues to vision and brain problems. These symptoms were first experienced in late 2016 but became publicly known in 2017. The Trump administration quickly accused Cuba of responsibility for these events, claiming that it was either involved in the "sonic attacks" against American diplomats or complicit in allowing these to occur. As a result, the US embassy was radically reduced, diplomats were sent home, and the consular section was shut down. (The latter was particularly problematic for Cubans seeking to visit family members or emigrate to the United States, and an established quota of 20,000 Cuban immigrants a year leaving for US destinations was immediately stopped.)

At the time of this writing, the cause of this mysterious "syndrome" has not been discovered, and the Biden administration is beginning to increase the size of embassy staff. In late 2022 officials in both the State Department and the CIA debunked the idea of any conspiracy to commit attacks against diplomats, replacing the term *sonic attacks* with the more general *anomalous health incidents* to illustrate that the health "threat" had been downgraded to an unknown medical condition.

Many Cubans hoped that with the election of Joe Biden in November 2020, the United States would return to a more liberal policy on Cuba. Speaking before the election in September 2020, Biden condemned the Trump approach and promised that, if elected, he would "try to reverse the failed Trump policies that inflicted harm on Cubans and their families," noting that Trump "had done nothing to advance democracy and human rights" (Sesin 2020). Expectations ran high following his election. He had been the vice president in the popular Obama administration, and his wife, Dr. Jill Biden, had visited Cuba in late 2016. Sadly, during the first two years of his administration, little changed on the Cuba file. As a result, and despite some minor changes in 2022 and 2023 to reduce irritants in the bilateral relationship, US policy toward Cuba remained frozen in Cold War rhetoric.

A resounding condemnation of the Biden policy on Cuba was given in September 2022 by Ben Rhodes, Obama's deputy national security adviser who was responsible for negotiating the renewal of US relations with Cuba. He accused Biden of maintaining and even strengthening Trump policies toward the island: "Why would any Cuban official ever negotiate anything with America ever again after this? We had Trump—in the most grotesque, callous way—politicizing this. But then to have a Democratic administration legitimize what Trump did by continuing it—it's a gaslighting to those people in Cuba" (Isikoff 2022).

The brusque transition from heightened expectations about the improvement of bilateral relations under the Obama administration to despondency under his successor, and then the dashed hopes for renewal under Biden, have resulted in a particularly strained relationship between Havana and Washington. That said, some minor improvements have occurred since the midterm elections in November 2022. Consular offices in the embassy were reopened and resumed issuing immigrant visas. Several government and business delegations visited Cuba. Flights from various US cities increased to cities across the island. It became somewhat easier to send financial remittances to the island. Talks on orderly migration processes started and were characterized as "constructive" by both sides. It remains to be seen, however, if any major changes will be implemented during the remainder of the Biden presidency. Significantly, any changes taken during his administration will be executive orders, not new legislation, and could be reversed by the next US president.

In the meantime, many Cubans—despondent at the possibilities of improving their conditions on the island and frustrated at the tardiness in improvements to bilateral relations—have taken advantage of the preferential treatment accorded Cubans seeking refugee status in the United States under the Cuban Adjustment Act. Between October 2021 and September 2022 some 224,000 Cubans reached the United States, while 6,100 were interdicted at sea by the US Coast Guard and returned to the island (significantly more than the number of migrants in 1980, when 125,000 left from the port of Mariel, and 1994, when 31,000 "rafters" left; it also represents a 400 percent increase over 2021 figures). By opening a new immigrant processing program (albeit one designed to reduce the number of Cuban immigrants, supported by regulations to deport Cubans not following the new quota system which relies heavily on US-based sponsorship of exiles), five years after this was stopped, the Biden administration finally provided a safe, legal way for Cubans to emigrate, avoiding the dangerous journey through Mexico or across the Florida Strait.

Diplomatic Representation and Medical Internationalism

One of the reasons Cuba has maintained international support when faced with massive opposition from the United States is its extensive role abroad, both through its diplomatic missions and its program of medical support, particularly in the Global South. Cuba, for example, has been elected to three bodies of the UN Economic and Social Council (ECOSOC) as well as the International Labor Organization's Governing Body (2021–2024), the Executive Board of the Pan American Health Organization (2020–2023), the United Nations Children's Fund (2020–2022), the World Food Program (2020–2022), the UN Human Rights Council (2020–2023), and the Commission for Social Development (2020–2024). In September 2022 Cuba was also elected to chair the Group of 77 for the year 2023. This is the largest intergovernmental organization in the world and was set up in 1964 with the support of 77 developing countries. There are now 134 countries that are members, and Cuba is highly respected by the membership.

Cuba has successfully pursued a policy of strengthening international ties, largely as a means of reducing the strategy of diplomatic isolation pursued by Washington. This extensive international role has understandably strengthened Cuba's profile abroad. In addition, Cuba has 125 embassies and 20 consulates abroad. In terms of the number of embassies and consulates based in Havana, there is again a large number—112 embassies and 8 consulates in the capital (EmbassyPages 2023). This is more than would be expected for a Latin American country of just 11.2 million (in Mexico City there are 86) and illustrates the significance of Cuba in international politics. While a Third World country, Cuba has in many ways assumed the profile, and foreign policy, of one from the First World. This successful policy has continued in recent years, as can be seen in the number of international bodies on which it is represented.

Support for Cuba has also resulted from its successful medical support abroad. Since 1960 Cuba has pursued a policy of medical internationalism, sending personnel around the globe to provide humanitarian assistance. Cuban prime minister Manuel Marrero noted in July 2022 that during this sixty-year period some 605,000 Cuban medical personnel had treated some two billion patients from 165 countries (Díaz Ballaga 2022). In recent years Cuba has provided medical support for countries dealing with several natural disasters and epidemics, most recently the COVID-19 pandemic. While critics of Cuban medical collaboration condemn this medical support, the dozens of nations that employ their services continue to accept them—and to praise Cuba's contribution, as is analyzed in the chapter by Erisman and Kirk. Cuba, which on a per capita basis has approximately three times as many physicians as the United States, will continue to send medical missions abroad, and in so doing gains international respect—while also generating badly needed hard currency.

In recent years opponents of the Cuban government have used the role of medical internationalism as evidence of slave labor: the doctors receive only a portion (usually between 20 and 25 percent of the amount paid by the country receiving medical assistance); they live in difficult (and at times dangerous) circumstances and are not allowed to bring their family members with them; they usually have to give their passports to the leader of their contingent; and they are expected to live a modest lifestyle and not to fraternize with locals. Supporters of their role indicate that since they do indeed live in areas where local medical personnel prefer not to work (because of either the primitive conditions or the reduced income), it would be unwise to be accompanied by family members. Moreover, while they receive only a portion of the funds paid by the host government, this nevertheless represents a significant increase in the income that they would have received in Cuba. (The Cuban government maintains that the bulk of the convertible currency received is plowed back into the public healthcare system on the island.)

In addition, given the radically different interpretation of the role of health care in socialist and capitalist approaches, and the nature of medical education in Cuba, opponents and supporters argue from radically different standpoints. In the Cuban case this role can be traced to the preamble of the national constitution, which stresses the responsibility of a socialist society to share its natural talents.

Whether the role of Cuban medical brigades abroad constitutes exploitation can be supported or attacked depending on one's approach to the human right to access medical care. It would appear, however, that the scores of governments that contract Cuban medical services are aware of such arguments but are still prepared to hire Cuban medical personnel. Their willingness to pay for such services illustrates that they do not believe that the Cuban doctors and nurses they hire (in essence to save lives) are slave labor. Support from the World Health Organization (WHO) and the Pan

American Health Organization (PAHO) would appear to agree with Havana—providing health care has traditionally trumped conservative ideology.

Erisman and Kirk analyze the extent of Cuba's medical role during the recent COVID-19 pandemic and suggest that this significant contribution (almost 5,000 medical personnel in some 40 nations) is another significant factor in explaining international support. Speaking at the June 2022 Summit of the Americas, the prime minister of Belize and chairman of the Caribbean Community (CARICOM) gave a pertinent perspective from the Global South: "Cuba has provided consistent, unmatched cooperation in health to almost two-thirds of the countries in this hemisphere including Belize. Cuban healthcare experts of the Henry Reeve Brigade were on the frontline in the very early and uncertain days of Belize's COVID-19 response. Many Belizean doctors and healthcare professionals are trained in Cuba" (Briceño 2022). One could argue that medical internationalism has been criticized by exile groups precisely because it has been so successful abroad, and is widely appreciated. It has also saved countless lives.

Support from Traditional Allies (and US Adversaries)

It is not surprising that two of Cuba's oldest allies, Russia and China, have been among the greatest supporters of Cuba in recent years—especially during the years when policies of the Trump administration most affected the island. Russia's support (particularly in economic matters) has been significant, while China has provided political and economic aid at crucial times.

China is Cuba's second-largest trading partner (after Venezuela), as well as a major ideological ally. In 1960 Cuba was the first Latin American country to establish diplomatic relations with the People's Republic. At a time when US-China relations are rapidly deteriorating, Beijing has been steadily increasing its influence in the Global South, particularly in trade and investment. As Fulton Armstrong indicates, in terms of its long-term goal of increasing relations with Latin America, Cuba has proved a useful base for China, given its geostrategic position and influence in the region. In December 2021 Cuba also signed an agreement to participate in China's long-term development strategy, the Belt and Road Initiative. This will involve cooperation in a variety of areas—technology, tourism, energy, biotechnology, public health, and culture (Devonshire-Ellis 2022).

In recent years Cuba's cooperation with (and commercial dependence upon) China has increased notably. The national telephone/internet company Etecsa, for example, uses only Chinese equipment (Huawei, TP-Link, and ZTE). Geely cars and Yutong buses are ubiquitous, while domestic appliances and electronics found in Cuba are mainly Chinese. There are also several biotechnology research centers in China where Cuban scientists participate in collaborative medical projects, most notably cancer research.

There are close ties between the armed forces of both countries, and a particularly strong political relationship. For example, high-level Chinese officials have visited

Cuba twenty-two times since 1993, while their Cuban counterparts have visited China twenty-five times since 1995. In Cuba in 2014 President Xi Jinping emphasized the close ties: "The two countries advance hand in hand . . . on the path of the construction of socialism with its own characteristics, offering reciprocal support on issues related to our respective vital interests" (Lazarus and Ellis 2021).

Bilateral trade has been relatively consistent in recent years, although heavily weighted in favor of Chinese exports to the island. Imports to Cuba from China from 2019 to 2021 were $1.2 billion (2019), $963.3 million (2020), and $972.1 million (2021). For these years exports from Cuba to China were $442.6 million (2019), $371.7 million (2020), and $417.7 million (2021) (ONEI 2022).

In recent years China has provided support for Cuba in several ways. A $120 million loan was used to modernize the port of Santiago. Beijing is also supportive of Havana's interests to develop alternative energy sources and has provided thousands of solar panels—some 5,000 in May 2022 alone. Given shortfalls of food in Cuba, China has traditionally donated rice—5,300 tons in February and March of 2022. Likewise, it was one of the major supporters of Cuba during the COVID-19 crisis, supplying planeloads of medical equipment, lung ventilators, oxygen concentrators, personal protection equipment, Sinopharm vaccines, and syringes.

Cuba is a traditional supporter of Beijing's foreign policy, particularly its "One China" policy, and condemned the 2022 visit to Taiwan of US House of Representatives Speaker Nancy Pelosi. The Cuban government declared the trip as "interference in internal Chinese affairs" while noting "the aggressive policy and increased military presence of the United States and its allies in the Strait of Taiwan." Significantly it ended by stressing "the key role of China as a factor of international stability and balance" and "the importance of its cooperation, without any political conditions, for developing countries" (MINREX 2022).

In November 2022 when Díaz-Canel visited Bejing, he was received by President Xi Jinping, Premier Li Keqiang, and Li Zhanshi, President of the National Assembly. A dozen agreements were signed—in trade, infrastructure, technology, and commercial cooperation. China agreed to restructure Cuban debt and to provide new trade credits, while also donating $100 million to meet the most pressing needs. Díaz-Canel spoke about Cuba's economic challenges and stated that he "counted on the support of friendly countries like China." For his part, Xi stated clearly: "No matter how the international situation changes, China's commitment to our longstanding friendship with Cuba will not change. China's determination to support Cuba in pursuing socialism will not change. China's determination to work alongside Cuba to safeguard international equity and justice, and to oppose the hegemony of the powerful will not change" (*OnCuba News* 2022b).

Russian support for Cuba has been somewhat different. There is a similar geostrategic interest as with the case of China, but during the Putin era there has also been a clear desire to maximize its influence over Cuba, one of its closest allies in the Global South. This is particularly important given the diplomatic shunning by the international community in the war against Ukraine and concern about Putin's objectives.

From the Russian perspective Cuba once again represented a major irritant to Washington—and thus was worthy of Moscow's support. As was the case sixty years ago at the time of the Missile Crisis, Cuba offered the opportunity to remind the United States of Russian influence in the region. While the historical ties with Havana are understandably important, the ideological connections are less so, since Russia abandoned socialism when the Soviet Union collapsed in 1991. In fact, the major element to explain Moscow's support is geostrategic pragmatism, as seen in the ability to remind Washington of Russia's potential (negative) influence just ninety miles away.

Relations between Cuba and Russia deepened in recent years. Significantly, the first stop by Díaz-Canel in his initial international tour after becoming president was to Moscow, and he returned there in October 2019 and again in November 2022. The 2019 visit came after a July mission to the island led by Russian foreign minister Sergey Lavrov and a later visit by Prime Minister Dmitry Medvedev and Russian Security Council secretary Nikolai Patrushev. Lavrov returned in February 2022 to show Moscow's continued support.

The tone of bilateral relations was set by Dimitry Medvdev, former Russian president and current deputy chair of Russia's Security Council: "In Russia, Cuba has partners and dependable friends. . . . With President Miguel Díaz-Canel we've decided to reinforce our strategic cooperation" (AFP 2019). A variety of initiatives resulted—in scientific cooperation, nuclear medicine, pharmaceuticals, oil, steel production, biotechnology, airline updating, and the railway sector. As the Trump administration brought in scores of measures designed ultimately to bring about regime change in Havana, the support of Moscow was enormously important in the survival of the Cuban Revolution.

Russian deputy prime minister Yuri Borisov and his Cuban counterpart Ricardo Cabrisas have also met several times to further support these development projects. Speaking in Havana in April 2021, Borisov emphasized the sweeping nature of bilateral connections, calling Cuba a "key partner and reliable ally," adding: "We intend to preserve and multiply the existing achievements on the entire range of Russian-Cuban relations: from political to military-technical" (teleSUR 2021). He returned in January 2022, noting Russian medical aid for Cuba in the midst of the COVID-19 pandemic and seeking support for Russia in countering NATO expansion in Eastern Europe.

In recent years bilateral trade has held steady, but was not spectacular—with Russian exports heavily outweighing imports from Cuba. Russian exports for the last three years were $528.4 million (2019), $320.1 million (2020), and $627.9 million (2021). By contrast, Cuban exports to Russia illustrate the difficult economic situation on the island: $26.3 million (2019), $7.4 million (2020), and $5.3 million (2021) (ONEI 2022).

Despite the poor export record of Cuba, Moscow has been a steady supporter of Cuba in recent years. It has provided loans of $43 million to update Cuba's aging military equipment and has plans to modernize Cuba's rail network, a $1 billion project. Particularly helpful from the Cuban perspective was Moscow's decision in 2014 to write off 90 percent of Cuba's debt (estimated at some $35.3 billion), while in 2022, given Cuba's ongoing difficult economic circumstances, Russia postponed repayment of credits provided the island—some $2.3 billion between 2006 and 2019—until 2027.

During the COVID-19 pandemic Russian aid was noteworthy, as Mervyn Bain notes in his chapter. In April 2022, for instance, 19,000 tons of wheat were donated to Cuba. In previous months several shipments had also arrived—83 tons of medical supplies and 170 tons of food supplies (*OnCuba News* 2022a). The disastrous fire in August 2022 at the country's largest oil terminal at Matanzas offered an opportunity for Russia to show solidarity with its ally. Moscow responded by sending a supertanker with 700,000 barrels of oil—extremely important given the shortage of fuel available on the island (resulting in several widespread protests at the resultant blackouts). Two further shipments of crude (300,000 and 700,000 barrels) occurred in the next four months to support Cuba's desperate energy needs. In all, by late October 2022 Russia had sent oil worth $352 million since the start of the Ukraine war (some 4.3 million barrels), with further shipments planned (Associated Press 2022). In December 2022 Moscow also agreed to donate 25,000 tons of wheat to Cuba, to be delivered in 2023.

Russian ties with Cuba have clearly grown substantially in recent years, and in many areas. Russian warships have visited Havana, Cuba has participated in joint war games, and there was even talk—since discarded—of reestablishing a Russian military base on the island. Generous trade credits have been provided to buy Russian cars and trucks and to upgrade steel mills. There is even an initiative to allow Russian credit cards (MIR) to be used in Cuba, due to the growing number of Russian tourists. In 2021, for example, Russians displaced Canadians as the largest group of tourists and represented 40 percent of the number of tourists on the island—a situation that stopped following the war with Ukraine (when Russian planes were forbidden from flying over European airspace) but has since been revived when several flights a week to tourist destinations Varadero and Cayo Coco started again in October 2022. A fitting symbol of this deeply rooted historical partnership was that Russian craftsmen restored the gilded dome of the Havana Capitol building to celebrate the 500th anniversary of the founding of Havana in 2019.

That said, the Russian invasion of Ukraine in 2022 obviously represented a major challenge for Cuban diplomacy—in many ways similar to the situation in 1968 when the Soviet Union invaded Czechoslovakia. On the one hand, Cuba supported the need for smaller countries to be politically independent and rejected the use of force by a larger neighboring country. At the same time, it understood (and shared) Russia's concerns at growing NATO influence close to the Russian border, and in particular the major role of the United States in criticism of Putin. Cuba also did not want to lose the political and commercial support of Moscow.

The result—surprising to many—was Cuba's decision to abstain on key UN General Assembly votes on the issue of Russia's invasion. At the same time, however, Cuban official media clearly followed a pro-Moscow line (Padrón Cueto 2022). In September 2022 Cuba also voted against allowing the request by Ukrainian president Volodymyr Zelenskyy to address the UN General Assembly virtually (as opposed to being present, required according to UN regulations). In all, 101 countries voted in favor of Ukraine's request, with 6 countries opposed. In sum, Cuba has pursued a delicate balance between supporting Ukraine's right to independence and Russia's fear of NATO expansion.

From Moscow's perspective the bilateral relationship is largely based upon the geostrategic value offered by the island's position. As tensions between Moscow and

Washington have grown in recent years, so too has the importance of Cuba. With ties going back to the 1962 Missile Crisis and its strategic location, Cuba offers the Putin government the opportunity to goad the United States and remind it that the decades-long ties with Havana offer Russia a unique opportunity to counter US dominance in the region.

The November 2022 visit to Moscow by President Díaz-Canel was extremely important on many fronts. In addition to talks about collaboration on steel, fuel, tourism, and trade, both presidents emphasized their similar interpretation of international politics, and the closeness of their ties. President Putin noted that both the Soviet Union and Russia "have always supported the Cuban people in their struggle for independence and sovereignty." For his part Díaz-Canel, while not supporting Russia's role in Ukraine, emphasized the "unjust and arbitrary sanctions that are based upon the same enemy: the Yankee empire." He went further, supporting Putin's claim that the root cause of the war in Ukraine was the expansion of NATO toward Russian territory, while criticizing the role of the EU in supporting these goals: "We reject the conduct of the European Union, which has given in to the interests of Washington" (Duch 2022). A week later Esteban Lazo, president of Cuba's National Assembly, visited Moscow and repeated Cuba's concerns about the offensive nature of NATO's growth.

Changing Positions: Pro and Con . . .

A significant change in recent years can be seen in the EU's relationship with the island, and its decision to adopt a strongly critical position concerning the human rights situation in Cuba. In this way it is similar to the "Common Position" of the EU—in place from 1996 until 2016. At that time its concern about the island was very clear: "The objective of the European Union in its relations with Cuba is to encourage a process of transition to pluralist democracy and respect for human rights and fundamental freedoms, as well as a sustainable recovery and improvement in the living standards of the Cuban people" (Hare 2008). In 2016 this position was dropped when it became clear that EU policies had exercised minimal influence on political developments on the island.

The 2016 decision to eliminate the Common Position was also carried out because the response of individual EU members was anything but "common." Despite the rhetoric about the official position, most continued to trade with Cuba, while its citizens flocked to Cuban beaches for vacations—a quarter of tourists to the island in 2019. As a result, a new agreement, the Political Dialogue and Cooperation Agreement, came into force in 2016. Its objective was to engage in a process of constructive engagement with Havana, with the expectation that this softer diplomatic approach would prove to be a confidence-building measure and would encourage the Cuban government to adopt more-liberal policies.

The next stage in EU-Cuba relations, from 2016 to 2021, saw the EU tone down criticism of the government and increase development assistance, while continuing to condemn the US embargo. In September 2019 Federica Mogherini, the High Representative for Foreign Affairs and Security for the twenty-eight-nation EU, noted in Havana that the EU remained the major trading partner and investor in Cuba, and that cooperation support had tripled in the previous two years to 140 million euros.

This changed in July 2021, following mass demonstrations in Cuba protesting the shortage of food and electricity services and the increase in COVID-19 cases. The government responded with repression, and some 1,400 people were arrested. There were claims of prisoners being abused and beaten, and long prison sentences were given to some protestors. The EU, which had deliberately avoided confrontation with the Cuban government since the abrogation of the Common Position five years earlier, condemned the reaction by Cuban security forces.

Josep Borell, the EU's leading diplomat, did not mince words: "We call on the Cuban government to respect the human rights and freedoms enshrined in the universal Human Rights convention. . . . We urge [the government] to release all arbitrarily detained protestors, to listen to the voices of its citizens, and to engage in an inclusive dialogue on their grievances" (Marsh 2021). In September 2021 a resolution of the European Parliament condemning Cuban government repression passed with 426 members supporting it and 146 opposing it. Clearly the diplomatic gloves were off, as the EU doubled down on criticism of Cuban government actions in repressing what Brussels saw as a basic human right to protest government policies.

Not surprisingly, Havana reacted strongly to these statements, rejecting the accusations made by Borrell about abuses of human rights and encouraging the EU to deal with the many human rights abuses within its own member states. The 2016 agreement, the Cuban government noted, had been based upon equality, noninterference, and respect for national sovereignty—and it was time for the EU to refrain from any interference in internal Cuban matters, particularly when (Havana argued) they were fueled by US interference. Regardless of the arguments bandied about by both sides, it was clear that relations between the EU and Cuba had suffered a serious setback.

A similar position concerning the July 11 demonstrations in 2021 was taken by Canada. In Cuba's Ministry of Foreign Affairs (MINREX) the Canada desk is housed in the same department as Europe, and there are similar diplomatic traditions and interests of both the EU and Canada with Havana. A long history of sound diplomatic ties exists between Canada and Cuba. Canada (along with Mexico) was the only country in the Americas not to break relations with Cuba in the early 1960s, and in 1976 Pierre Trudeau became the first leader of a NATO country to visit Cuba. When Canada extended its 12-mile marine limit to 200 miles in 1977, Cuba was the first country allowed to fish within the new boundaries. For most of the past two decades Canadians have been the largest group of tourists to the island, and between 1994 (when the Cuban Ministry of Tourism was established) and 2021, over 18.3 million Canadians visited the island (Perelló 2022). Cuba is Canada's principal market in the Caribbean–Central American region, and Canada is Cuba's second-largest source of direct investment there. The Toronto-based nickel producer Sherritt International is one of the largest investors in Cuba.

Despite Canada having a fairly solid relationship with Cuba, there remain significant differences—similar to those expressed by Borrell. The Global Affairs Canada (the foreign ministry) website, for instance, outlines Canadian policy:

> Canada is committed to strengthening democracy in Cuba and will continue to work with likeminded partners to ensure our respective and collective responses to the situation in Cuba [to] support the rights and legitimate democratic aspirations of the Cuban people. Canada supports a future for Cuba that fully embraces the fundamental values of freedom, democracy, human rights and the rule of law. Canada has consistently recognized Cuba's strong commitment to economic and social rights, with its particularly important achievements in the areas of education and social rights. At the same time, Canada has stressed the importance of basic civil and political rights, such as freedom of speech, association and the press. (Global Affairs Canada 2022)

Understandably, Ottawa was shocked by the Cuban government's response to the July 11, 2021, street protests and the sentences given the demonstrators, and reacted by condemning government conduct. The Canadian government continues to express its concern about the human rights situation, much like its European counterparts.

A further area of concern in recent years has arisen over the question of "sonic attacks," or the "Havana Syndrome," since several Canadian diplomats also complained of similar symptoms shortly after the first complaints by US diplomats. Ottawa reacted to the strange medical condition by withdrawing much of its embassy staff and providing medical care for those affected. Overshadowing bilateral relations was the $28 million lawsuit brought against Global Affairs Canada by diplomats claiming to be affected by the mysterious syndrome and criticizing Ottawa's conduct in failing to protect them. Several Royal Canadian Mounted Police investigators came to the island to seek the cause of the medical condition, and a certain amount of tension arose between Ottawa and Havana—largely because of uncertainty about the Havana Syndrome. For several years the Canadian embassy was badly neglected by Ottawa, and the number of staff dwindled. The consular section was closed, and any incoming diplomats were not allowed to bring family members. The Havana embassy became an unpopular post, as Ottawa struggled to find staff to maintain a skeleton diplomatic presence.

As was the case with the US embassy, these concerns began to dissipate in 2021, as the number of cases began to fall. Ottawa started to increase the number of staff members in the embassy, and the consular section was again opened. Indicative of the slow but noticeable strengthening of relations is that the Havana Syndrome—as is the case with US diplomats—is now referred to as an "anomalous health incident" by Ottawa. No cause has ever been found to explain this bizarre medical phenomenon, and it is clear that Ottawa does not blame Cuba for the condition. A diplomatic page has been turned.

While fundamental differences remain over the questions noted above by Global Affairs Canada, there appears to be a determination to move on in its relationship with Havana, or at least to seek to project a degree of normalcy. The decline in COVID-19 cases has also given a psychological boost, resulting in the return of Canadian vacationers, who once again represent the single largest group of tourists on the island. To put this in context, in 2021—and in the midst of COVID-19—some 68,944 Canadian tourists arrived in Cuba, 19.3 percent of the total number of tourists to the island. In 2022 the number of Canadian tourists, and their representation as a percentage, had risen significantly. By August of 2022 some 298,410 Canadians had arrived—30.7

percent of the number of tourists to the island (Perelló 2022). In sum, an attempt has been made to seek to return to a normal relationship—although fundamental differences, and concerns, remain.

The Evolution of the Latin American and Caribbean Position

Cuba's relations with Latin America and the Caribbean have strengthened considerably in recent years, in no small degree due to the election of left-of-center leaders in Mexico, Bolivia, Honduras, Argentina, Colombia, Chile, and Brazil. Cuba continues to have strong relations with leftist governments in Nicaragua and Venezuela, the latter being extremely important because of strong ideological ties and Venezuela being the source of approximately half of Cuba's oil.

There is, however, a great difference in ideology among the new cohort of elected leftist leaders. Gabriel Boric, Chile's president, for example, is a traditional democrat and has been critical of both human rights abuses and the Cuban political system. By contrast the newly elected president of Colombia, Gustavo Petro, was a leader of the M-19 guerrilla movement and is supportive of Cuba's government. What unites this new cohort of leftist leaders, however, is a shared platform of continentalism and the need for reform, nonintervention in political affairs, respect for each country's right to determine its own development model, the full practice of human rights (including social and economic rights), and concern over Washington's traditional role in Latin America—particularly during the Trump years. These principles produced a common alignment against Washington's policy toward Cuba of economic sanctions and regime change.

Speaking in Miami in April 2019, National Security Adviser John Bolton summarized the Trump perspective by recalling the 1823 policy that constituted a paternalistic claim to dominate the hemisphere, and defended the United States' right to intervene in any nation of the Americas: "Today we proudly proclaim for all to hear: the Monroe Doctrine is alive and well" (Newman 2019). The election of several left-of-center presidents in the region in recent years illustrates a firm rejection of such positions.

Cuba's greatest supporter in the region continues to be Venezuela, and it is difficult to imagine Cuba surviving without oil from Caracas. Julio Borges, an outspoken critic of the Maduro government, claims that the amount of assistance provided over the past twenty years is some $60 billion—consisting mainly of oil, but also reflected in infrastructure, food, power plants, and medical supplies (Translating Cuba 2022). In fact, there is a model of mutual dependence in the relationship, or "economic complementarity," as Richard Feinberg terms it. This is largely based upon a barter arrangement, in which Cuba provides a variety of services to Venezuela (mainly medical, but also in education, security, and sports) and in return receives highly subsidized oil. An estimated 219,000 Cuban professionals served in Venezuela between 2000 and 2018, while some 300,000 Venezuelans received free medical treatment in Cuba (Feinberg 2020). The numbers of Cuban medical personnel working in Venezuela has since dropped to approximately 20,000, while Venezuelan oil supplies have been erratic—from 44,000 barrels per day (bpd) in 2022 to 22,000 bpd in the first quarter of 2022 (Parraga 2022).

Despite these reductions, both countries need each other—oil in the case of Cuba, and a variety of services for Venezuela. The political ties remain strong, particularly as US policies have sought to bring about regime change in both countries.

A good measuring stick to assess the strength of Cuba's relationship with countries in the region can be seen in their response to the Summit of the Americas, held in Los Angeles in June 2022. One issue dominated pre-summit planning—whether or not to allow Cuba, Venezuela, and Nicaragua to participate in official meetings. During the Obama years Cuba was present at the summits in Panama City (2015) and Lima (2018), but the hardened Cuba policy of Trump and inherited by Biden made Cuba's presence risky for Biden, who seemed to believe that it could cost the Democrats votes in the 2022 midterm elections.

In the end Cuba, Venezuela, and Nicaragua were not invited, based on their ideological positions and "undemocratic" form of government. Leaders of Latin America and the Caribbean were divided as to whether to boycott the summit or to attend and voice their criticism. Mexican president Andrés Manuel López Obrador summed up the feelings of many: "If there is to be a Summit of the Americas, then all—yes all—the countries have to participate. All the countries of the Americas. . . . Nobody should be allowed to exclude anybody. Moreover, we have to change politics toward the region. In Latin America we cannot hang on to the policies of two hundred years ago" (López Obrador 2022a). In the end twenty-three (of the thirty-five) heads of government attended the Los Angeles summit.

Perhaps the most significant development in Cuba's relations with Latin America is the growing connection with Mexico, under the leadership of López Obrador (AMLO). This has continued to develop in 2022 and 2023, but it had been obvious since AMLO was elected in 2018 that he would follow a progressive continent-wide policy, and that Cuba would be a key element in that approach. During the COVID-19 crisis, Mexico imported Cuban vaccines and paid for medical services provided by several hundred Cuban medical personnel (some 300 from December 2020 to the following April, and 586 from April to July 2020).

Several key cultural exchanges have helped to cement the relationship—with ballet, modern dance, film, and literature activities figuring prominently. In October 2021 at the prestigious Festival Internacional Cervantino, Cuba was the invited guest of honor and key Cuban cultural personnel participated. In February 2022 Havana returned the honor at the International Book Fair, with Mexico as the "invited country," or guest of honor, at the massive celebration. A boatload of Mexican books was delivered to the book fair by the Mexican navy ship *Huasteco*—a follow-up to the visit of the Mexican navy training vessel *Cuauhtémoc* in September 2018.

Underlining the growth in this relationship, President Díaz-Canel was a special guest of AMLO's at celebrations to mark the independence of Mexico in 2021. AMLO used the opportunity to appeal to Joe Biden to condemn the embargo against Cuba, terming it a "perverse strategy." His praise for the Cuban Revolution was clear: "Miguel Díaz-Canel represents a people which has known, like few in the world, to defend its dignity, its right to live free and independent, rejecting interference in its internal matters from any foreign power. . . . To have resisted 62 years without surrendering is an undisputable historical feat" (Manetto 2021). No Mexican president in decades had been as outspoken in supporting Cuba as AMLO.

In May 2022 the Mexican president was feted in Havana, where he received the José Martí Order, the highest award granted to foreigners by the Cuban government. There he continued some of the themes from the meeting in Mexico, calling on Biden to drop the "blockade" (his term) against Cuba, and concluding by noting that Cuba's survival had shown that "reason is more powerful than force" (López Obrador 2022b). In view of Mexico's need for medical assistance in underserved communities, an agreement was reached for the services of some 600 Cuban doctors, and in midsummer of 2022 the first contingent arrived. Mindful of Cuban medical support during the worst of the COVID-19 pandemic, Mexico also agreed to purchase Cuban vaccines—and to have Mexican medical personnel further their education in Cuba.

In terms of the Caribbean, Havana maintains strong ties with all countries. Its program of medical collaboration has been particularly successful, with hundreds of Cuban medical personnel working around the region. Generous scholarship support for Caribbean students in Cuba, active participation in CARICOM meetings, lobbying to support Caribbean interests in international gatherings, cultural exchanges, and hurricane relief have all strengthened ties. Comments by Caribbean leaders in the chapter on medical internationalism illustrate this support.

Views similar to those expressed by the Mexican president were sounded by John Briceño, chairman of CARICOM and prime minister of Belize. Addressing the initial plenary session at the 2022 Summit of the Americas, he condemned Cuba's exclusion and criticized US policy in the region:

> It is therefore inexcusable that all countries of the Americas are not here, and the power of the Summit diminished by their absence. It is incomprehensible that we should isolate countries of the Americas which have provided strong leadership and contributed to the hemisphere on the critical issues of our times. . . . The illegal blockade against Cuba is an affront to humanity. It continues to cause untold suffering. It is inconsistent with our values. In fact, it is unamerican. (*Jamaica Observer* 2022)

President Petro of Colombia expressed his own opposition to US policy toward Cuba in a letter to US vice president Kamala Harris, in which he explained how Cuba had been unjustly accused of supporting terrorism, when in fact it had been one of the prime movers in the peace accords in Colombia. He urged Harris to remove Cuba from the list of countries that allegedly support terrorism: "This is an unfair ruling that goes not only against the human rights of the Cuban people, but also threatens the aspirations for peace in our own country" (*Semana* 2022).

Realpolitik and New Possibilities in Cuban Foreign Policy

The ancient aphorism "the enemy of my enemy is my friend" is certainly borne out in some key facets of Cuban foreign policy. In recent years Cuba has strengthened bilateral relations with several countries that have had a strained relationship with Washington. Most of these ties were based on older ideological connections (such as with China and Russia, and to a certain extent, Venezuela), but in recent years stronger political ties have emerged with other countries such as Syria, and in particular Iran.

In order to survive—just ninety miles from its self-declared enemy, and a major superpower—Cuba has managed to blend principles and pragmatism: "Realpolitik dictates that Cuba cultivate good relations with major powers like Russia and China so long as it lives in the shadow of a hostile United States" (LeoGrande 2022). While relying on these two major powers for financial and political support, Cuba has also pursued a significantly pragmatic approach in its relations with Europe and the Global South. In so doing, it has been remarkably successful.

A symbolic representation of the evolution of Cuba's foreign policy can be gleaned from the international response to two major disasters that Cuba confronted in 2022: the massive refinery fire in Matanzas in August and Hurricane Ian a month later. The fire was a major humanitarian and ecological disaster—the largest in the history of Cuba—and just ninety miles from Florida. The greatest level of aid came from traditional allies Russia and Venezuela. Russia's contribution was referenced earlier; Venezuela sent two tankers of replacement fuel to Santiago and Antilla. Spain sent twenty-seven tons of medical equipment and supplies. The Dominican Republic donated forty tons of medical supplies and food, while Nicaragua sent a shipload of food and Chile also provided material support. The Chinese Red Cross sent $150,000 to its counterpart organization, while Vietnam also donated financial support. Iran sent a team of specialists to provide advice on fighting oil tank fires and to train Cuban firefighters on risk assessment and safety measures. Iran also sent firefighting equipment, and Cuban firefighters were invited for further training programs in Iran. Canada donated $1.2 million in emergency assistance, while Italy provided 2.3 million tons of medical supplies. Bolivia sent sixty-two tons of food and medical supplies, and Colombia sent 3,000 square centimeters of skin for burn victims.

The most immediate support came from Mexico and Venezuela, which within days of the fire between them sent over twenty flights of supplies (including four planeloads of firefighting chemicals and foam) as well as some 120 specialists in controlling fuel blazes (85 from Mexico and 35 from Venezuela). Mexico also sent two navy ships to assist—the fireboat *Bourbon Artabaze* and the supply ship *Libertador*. On the latter there were supplies of firefighting equipment (including retardant foam, pumps, and hoses) and medical supplies. Officials from PEMEX (Petróleos Mexicanos, the state-owned company with a monopoly over the Mexican oil industry) also offered to help rebuild the burned-out facility. In addition to sending specialists in fighting fires, Venezuela also sent twenty tons of supplies. Perhaps most important, Venezuela committed to help rebuild the oil terminal (the largest in Cuba), which had lost approximately 40 percent of its storage capacity, while Mexico also offered its services in this reconstruction.

Despite an appeal for aid to the international community, and despite a request from almost twenty US organizations representing religious, environmental, and research groups, Washington expressed its condolences and provided technical advice—but little more. The bureaucratic (and unhelpful) position was summed up by a State Department spokesperson who noted: "We have had general discussions with the government of Cuba on this tragic disaster. However, the government of Cuba has not formally requested U.S. government assistance." The Cuban response from the deputy director of US affairs at the Cuban Foreign Ministry revealed Cuban frustration at this bureaucratic position: "So far, the US offered a phone number to an emergency local authority. We accepted, Cupet [Cuba's state-run oil company] made the phone call. . . . The rest is old same US abyss saying/acting." (Sesin and Murray 2022). In late August 2022, however, an exchange took place between the Cuban Ministry of Science and Technology and the Environmental Protection Agency in the United States, in which Cuba requested specific technical assistance in the environmental rehabilitation of the site. Washington responded by donating a hundred fire suits.

Hurricane Ian in September 2022 had a devastating effect on Cuba. Winds of over 120 miles per hour wreaked havoc over western Cuba. Sixty-three thousand homes were destroyed or severely damaged, and electricity was cut off for several days (and in some cases, weeks). Three people were killed, and 50,000 were evacuated. It was again Mexico and Venezuela that provided the greatest amount of aid. Mexico sent 113 tons of badly needed materials in 16 flights—including 13 tons of equipment for electrical repairs. In addition, seventeen specialists came to supervise repairs. For its part Venezuela sent two ships with a cargo of emergency food, electrical transformers, electrical cables, and zinc sheets (for housing). Once again Cuba requested assistance from Washington, and the United States responded by sending $2 million in hurricane relief—in symbolic terms a significant gesture, but in reality a paltry sum. Havana expressed appreciation for the aid, but Foreign Minister Bruno Rodríguez Parrilla noted that punishing US sanctions, in place for over six decades, represented "a constant hurricane" (Associated Press 2022).

The last few years in Cuba's international relations have revived and indeed strengthened traditional patterns of the last six decades, while also hinting at possible new directions. The major thrust of Cuban foreign policy has understandably been to bolster its poor economy through greater relations with allies China and Russia. Without that support Cuba would face a truly disastrous situation. Havana has been able to take advantage of the animosity between both countries and Washington, and has been rewarded in terms of trade, investment, and political support, particularly in the case of Russia. This has understandably irritated the Trump and Biden administrations—whose focus on electoral politics as a basis for their policy to the island has been counterproductive.

Significant changes have occurred in Cuba's international relations in recent years. The diplomatic cold shoulder offered by the EU during this time has been a blow to the island, although individual EU members have maintained bilateral trade ties with Cuba. Given the question of human rights and democracy, the differences seem difficult to resolve. Much, of course, hinges on US policy toward Cuba, with Havana consistently defending its actions as justified due to US measures designed to bring about regime change. This diplomatic ballet of hostility seems destined to continue, and US policy toward the island shows no interest in any significant change.

A key development has been the strengthening of ties with Latin America as several left-center governments have come to power across the region. Cuba can count on significant international support—mostly symbolic, some ideological, but with just enough material aid to keep the system ticking over. In November 2022 (for the thirtieth time) the UN General Assembly gave a resounding condemnation of the US embargo of Cuba, with two countries voting against (the United States and Israel) and two abstaining (Ukraine and Brazil), while 185 supported the motion.

In the wake of COVID-19, Cuba is facing an economic and social crisis of a magnitude that rivals the "Special Period" after the implosion of the Soviet Union. Yet despite the odds the Cuban Revolution continues to survive. In no small degree this is due to the complex, and skillful, development of foreign policy by Havana—which has been of crucial importance in keeping the revolutionary process afloat. It is also aided by significant international support and respect from the Global South, which understands and sympathizes with Cuba's desire for independence and will to survive.

References

Adler, David. 2022. "Cuba Has Been under US Embargo for 60 Years. It's Time for That to End." *The Guardian*, February 3, 2022. Accessed at www.theguardian.com/commentisfree /2022/feb/03/cuba-us-embargo-must-end.

AFP. 2019. "Russia's Medvedev Says Cuba Can 'Rely' on Moscow." *Daily Star*, October 2. Accessed at https://www.thedailystar.net/backpage/news/russias-medvedev-says-cuba-can -rely-moscow-1809490.

Associated Press. 2022. "Cuba Is in the Middle of an Escalating Tug-of-War between Russia and the U.S." October 27. Accessed at https://www.nbcnews.com/news/latino/cuba-middle -escalating-tug-war-russia-us-rcna54389.

Briceño, John. 2022. "Statement by Hon. John Briceño, Prime Minister of Belize and Chairman of CARICOM, to the Plenary Session of the IX Summit of the Americas, June 10, 2022." Accessed at https://caricom.org/statement-by-hon-john-briceno-prime-minister-of -belize-and-chairman-of-caricom-to-the-plenary-session-of-the-ix-summit-of-the-americas.

CBS News. 2009. "Text: Obama Press Conference after Summit." April 20. Accessed at www .cbsnews.com/news/text-obama-press-conference-after-summit.

Cuba Archive. 2022. "Cuba's Disproportionate International Influence." June 8. Accessed at https://mailchi.mp/cubaarchive.org/diplomaticpresence?e=82923a4953.

Devonshire-Ellis, Chris. 2022. "Unlocking US Sanctions: China Signs Construction & Energy Deals with Cuba." Silk Road Briefing, January 3. Accessed at https://www.silkroadbriefing.com /news/2022/01/03/unlocking-us-sanctions-china-signs-construction-energy-deals-with-cuba.

Díaz Ballaga, Wennys. 2022. "En 59 años, los médicos cubanos atendieron a 2000 millones de pacientes en otros países." *Granma*, July 9. Accessed at https://www.granma.cu/cuba/2022 -07-09/en-59-anos-los-medicos-cubanos-atendieron-a-2-000-millones-de-pacientes-en-otros -paises-09-07-2022-00-07-35.

Duch, Juan Pablo. 2022. "Rusia y Cuba refrendan su programa de cooperación." *La Jornada*, November 23. Accessed at https://www.jornada.com.mx/2022/11/23/mundo/032n1mun.

DW (Deutche Welle). 2022. "López Obrador defiende contratación de médicos cubanos en Nayarit." July 24. Accessed at https://www.dw.com/es/lópez-obrador-defiende-contratación de médicos-cubanos-en-nayarit/a-62575841.

EmbassyPages. 2023. "Cuba Embassies & Consulates." Accessed April 15, 2023, at https:// www.embassypages.com/cuba.

Feinberg, Richard E. 2020. "The Geopolitics of Cuba-Venezuela-U.S. Relations: An Informal Note." In *Venezuela and Cuba: The Ties That Bind*." Washington, DC: Wilson Center. Accessed at https://www.wilsoncenter.org/publication/venezuela-and-cuba-ties-bind.

Global Affairs Canada. 2022. "Canada-Cuba Relations." September 2. Accessed at https://www
.international.gc.ca/country-pays/Cuba/relations.aspx?lang=eng.

Hare, Paul. 2008. "The Odd Couple: The EU and Cuba, 1996–2008." Brookings Institution,
September 14. Accessed at https://www.brookings.edu/research/the-odd-couple-the-eu-and
-cuba-1996-2008/.

Isikoff, Michael. 2022. "Former Top Obama Aide Accuses Biden of 'Gaslighting' Cuba:
'Disappointed doesn't begin to scratch the surface.'" Yahoo News, September 14. Accessed
at https://news.yahoo.com/former-top-obama-aide-accuses-biden-of-gaslighting-cuba-disap-
pointed-doesnt-begin-to-scratch-the-surface-160058896.html.

Jamaica Observer. 2022. "Caricom Leader Slams 'Unforgivable' Decision by US to Exclude
Cuba, Venezuela from Summit," June 10. Accessed at https://www.jamaicaobserver.com
/latest-news/Caricom-leader-slams-unforgivable-decision-by-us-to-exclude-cuba-venezuela
-from-summit.

Lazarus, Leland, and Evan Ellis. 2021. "How China Helps the Cuban Regime Stay Afloat and
Shut Down Protests." *The Diplomat*, August 3. Accessed at https://thediplomat.com/2021
/08/how-china-helps-the-cuban-regime-stay-afloat-and-shut-down-protests.

LeoGrande, William. 2022. "Why Cuba Has Threaded the Russia Needle for 60 Years." Responsible Statecraft, March 9. Accessed at https://responsiblestatecraft.org/2022/03/09/why
-cuba-has-threaded-the-russia-needle-for-60-years.

López Obrador, Andrés Manuel. 2022a. Morning Press Conference of May 3, 2022. Accessed
at https://youtube.com/watch?v=M7_LMu5TLTI.

———. 2022b. "Discurso del presidente Andrés Manuel López Obrador en su visita a Cuba."
May 8. Accessed at https://lopezobrador.org.mx/temas/amlo-Cuba.

Manetto, Francesco. 2021. "López Obrador lanza el Día de la Independencia un alegato en
defensa de la soberanía de Cuba." *El País*, September 16. Accessed at https://elpais.com/
mexico/2021-09-16/lopez-obrador-hace-del-dia-de-la-independencia-un-alegato-en-defensa
-de-cuba.html.

Marsh, Sarah. 2021. "EU Urges Cuba to Free 'Arbitrarily Detained' Protestors." Reuters,
July 21. Accessed at https://www.reuters.com/world/americas/eu-urges-cuba-free-arbitrarily
-detained-protestors-2021-07-29.

MINREX (Ministerio de Relaciones Exteriores). 2022. "MINREX: Cuba reafirma apoyo a la
posición de una sola China." Cubadebate, August 2. Accessed at http://www.cubadebate.cu
/especiales/2022/08/02/minrex-cuba-reafi.

Newman, Lucia. 2019. "Trump Revives Monroe Doctrine as Warning to China and Russia."
Al Jazeera, June 19. Accessed at https://www.aljazeera.com/news/2019/6/19/trump-revives
-monroe-doctrine-as-warning-to-china-and-russia.

Obama, Barack. 2016. March 21 Facebook post, from the White House, "Charting a New
Era in Cuba." Accessed at https://obamawhitehouse.archives.gov/issues/foreign-policy/cuba.

Office of the Press Secretary, The White House. 2017. "Remarks by President Trump on the
Policy of the United States Towards Cuba." June 16. Accessed at https://uy.usembassy.gov/
remarks-president-trump-policy-united-states-towards-cuba.

OnCuba News. 2022a. "Cuba recibe más de 19 mil toneladas de trigo donadas por Rusia."
April 21. Accessed at https://oncubanews.com/cuba/cuba-recibe-mas-de-19-mil-toneladas
-de-trigo-donadas-por-rusia.

———. 2022b. "Cuba y China firman una docena de acuerdos en Pekín." November 25.
Accessed at https://oncubanews.com/cuba/cuba-y-china-firman-una-docena-de-acuerdos-en
-pekin.

ONEI (Oficina Nacional de Estadística e Información). 2022. "Intercambio comercial de mer-
cancías por países seleccionados y áreas geográficas." In *Anuario Estadístico De Cuba 2021*,

capítulo 8: "Sector Externo Havana." Havana: ONEI. Accessed at www.onei.gob.cu/sites/default/files/08_sector_externo_2021-_1.pdf.

Padrón Cueto, Claudia. 2022. "Cuban Gov. Media Promotes Russia's Narrative about Ukraine." *Havana Times*, March 31. Accessed at https://havanatimes.org/features/cuban-gov-media-promotes-russias.

Perelló, José L. 2022. "Canadá como principal emisor de turismo para Cuba. Una reseña obligada." *Correo*, September 15. Accessed at https://www.correo.ca/2022/09/canada-como-principal-emisor-de-turismo-para-cuba-una-resena-obligada.

Parraga, Marianna. 2022. "Cuba Struggles to Buy Fuel as Imports from Venezuela Dwindle—Data." Reuters, April 5. Accessed at https://www.reuters.com/business/energy/cuba-struggles-buy-fuel-imports-venezuela-dwindle-data-2022-04-05/?rpc=401&.

Semana. 2022. "'Es una injusticia': presidente Gustavo Petro apoya petición para que EE.UU. saque a Cuba de la lista de países promotores del terrorismo." September 22. Accessed at https://www.semana.com/politica/articulo/es-una-injusticia-presidente-gustavo-petro-apoya-peticion-para-que-eeuu-saque-a-cuba-de-la-lista-de-paises-promotores-del-terrorismo/202208.

Sesin, Carmen. 2020. "Biden Slams Trump on 'Abject Failure' on Venezuela, as Well as Cuba Policies." NBC News, September 6. Accessed at https://www.nbcnews.com/news/latino/biden-slams-trump-on-abject-failure-venezuela-well-cuba-policies-n12393561.

Sesin, Carmen, and Mary Murray. 2022. "U.S. Faces Mounting Pressure to Do More to Help Cuba Fight a Deadly Blaze at an Oil Facility." NBC News, August 9. Accessed at https://www.nbcnews.com/news/latino/us-faces-mounting-pressure-help-cuba-fight-deadly-blaze-oil-facility-rcna42118.

Tass. 2019. "Russia to Continue Supporting Cuba in Dealing with US Sanction Pressure—Foreign Ministry." November 7. Accessed at https://tass.com/politics/1087542.

teleSUR. 2021. "Russia's Deputy Prime Minister Borisov: Cuba Is a 'Key Partner.'" April 1. Accessed at www.telesurenglish.net/news/Russias-Deputy-Prime-Minister-Borisov-Cuba Is-a-Key-partner-20210401-0015.html.

Translating Cuba. 2022. "Venezuelan Oppositionist Julio Borges Estimates Venezuela's Aid to Cuba at 60 Billion Dollars." July 1. Accessed at https://translatingcuba.com/venezuelan-oppositionist-julio-borges-estimates-venezuelas-aid-to-cuba-at-60-billion-dollars.

CHAPTER 14

US-Cuban Relations

THE NEW COLD WAR IN THE CARIBBEAN

William M. LeoGrande

On December 17, 2014, President Barack Obama and President Raúl Castro announced the restoration of formal diplomatic relations, broken in 1961, and began a process to normalize US-Cuban relations overall. The announcement was hailed around the world as a historic breakthrough—the final end of the Cold War in the Caribbean. But the last two years of Obama's second term were not time enough for the new policy to establish roots deep enough to make it "irreversible."[1] President Donald Trump reinstated a policy of "regime change" in deference to the conservative Cuban American diaspora, and President Joe Biden, in his first two years in office, did little to change it.

Trump Strikes Back

Donald Trump energized the Republican Party's Cuban American base in Florida in 2016 by pledging to roll back Obama's Cuba policy. Trump won just over 50 percent of Florida's Cuban American vote, polling only slightly better than Mitt Romney in 2012.[2] Nevertheless, Trump felt he owed the exile community a political debt, an idea reinforced at every opportunity by Senator Marco Rubio (R-FL). The president himself was not especially invested in Cuba policy, outsourcing it to Republican Cuban American legislators on Capitol Hill. "Make Rubio happy," he instructed his staff.[3]

On June 16, 2017, Rubio tweeted a photo of himself and Representative Mario Díaz-Balart (R-FL) in Rubio's Senate office, captioned "the night @MarioDB and I hammered out the new Cuba policy." The next day, Trump, speaking to a cheering crowd of Cuban exiles in Miami, declared, "Effective immediately, I am canceling the last administration's completely one-sided deal with Cuba." Trump denounced the Cuban government as brutal, criminal, depraved, oppressive, and murderous. He imposed an initial round of sanctions limiting "people-to-people" educational travel and prohibiting transactions with a long list of Cuban enterprises managed by the armed forces, including major hotels where most US tour groups stayed.[4]

In September, Secretary of State Rex Tillerson downsized the US embassy in Havana after two dozen US personnel reported suffering unexplained neurological symptoms—the so-called Havana Syndrome.[5] The embassy's consular section stopped processing Cuban visa requests and suspended both the Family Reunification Program and the refugee program in violation of the 1994 and 2017 migration accords signed with Havana. Cubans seeking visas were forced to travel to a third country to apply. Immigrant visas issued to Cubans fell 90 percent. Pressured by Rubio, Tillerson also expelled an equivalent group of Cuban diplomats from Washington.

In 2019, the Trump administration launched a "maximum pressure" campaign to cut off Cuba's principal sources of foreign currency in hopes of collapsing the Cuban economy and the regime along with it. Trump activated Title III of the 1996 Cuban Liberty and Democratic Solidarity Act, enabling US nationals, including Cuban Americans, who lost property after the 1959 revolution to sue Cuban, US, or foreign companies in US federal court for "trafficking" in (i.e., making beneficial use of) their confiscated property.[6] The aim was to deter foreign investments in Cuba by raising the specter of extended litigation.

The administration targeted Cuba's energy supply by imposing sanctions on companies shipping Venezuelan oil to Cuba, aggravating fuel shortages.[7] The State Department pressured countries to end their medical assistance contracts with Cuba, and conservative governments in Brazil, Ecuador, Bolivia, and El Salvador quickly obliged. The Brazilian program alone involved over 11,000 medical personnel, generating $250 million in annual revenue for Cuba.[8]

Trump's most serious sanctions focused on travel and remittances. The administration eliminated the people-to-people travel category entirely, blocking most non–Cuban American travelers.[9] It severed commercial and charter air links to all Cuban cities except Havana, and prohibited US cruise ships, which carried some 800,000 people to Cuba in 2018, from docking there.[10] Remittances, unlimited under Obama, were capped by the Trump administration at $1,000 per quarter, and just weeks before the 2020 presidential election, Trump blocked Cuban Americans from wiring funds through Western Union.[11] Remittances fell from an estimated $3.7 billion in 2019 to $1.9 billion in 2021.[12] By the end of the Trump administration, US economic sanctions, aggravated by the COVID-19 pandemic, were wreaking havoc on the Cuban economy.

Biden's Unkept Promises

During the 2020 presidential campaign, Joe Biden criticized Trump's policy because it had "inflicted harm on the Cuban people and done nothing to advance democracy and human rights." He promised that he would resume Obama's policy of engagement "in large part," lifting sanctions that hurt Cuban families, restoring Americans' right to travel, and reengaging the Cuban government diplomatically. When Trump closed the main channel for wiring remittances to the island, the Biden camp called it a "cruel distraction . . . denying Cuban Americans the right to help their families."[13]

Biden and the Democrats took a beating among Cuban American voters in 2020. Trump won more than 60 percent of their vote in Miami-Dade, and Democrats lost two House seats in South Florida.[14] This electoral rout made the incoming administration hypersensitive about the domestic political risks of any opening to Cuba.

Biden also had to contend with Senator Robert Menendez (D-NJ), chair of the Senate Foreign Relations Committee and a bitter foe of engagement with Cuba. To assure Menendez's cooperation on Biden's foreign policy agenda, the president consulted him regularly on Cuba, while pro-engagement congressional Democrats found it hard to get an audience at the White House.[15]

Despite his campaign promises, Biden left Trump's sanctions in place during his first sixteen months in office. White House press secretary Jen Psaki claimed the policy was under review, but that it was "not among President Biden's top priorities."[16] Juan Gonzalez, Senior Director for Western Hemisphere Affairs on the National Security Council staff, repeatedly voiced skepticism about engagement. "The idea that . . . a president has to just go back to the way things were with Cuba does not understand our current context," he said.[17]

A variety of constituencies urged Biden to resume Obama's policy to no avail. The US Agricultural Coalition for Cuba (USACC), including most of the major farm associations in the United States, urged Biden to lift the embargo to encourage agricultural trade.[18] In February 2021, fifty-six progressive church and foreign policy groups wrote to the president urging him to resume normalization.[19] As Biden's first year in office drew to a close, 114 Democratic members of the House of Representatives—more than half the caucus—signed a letter calling on the president to "prioritize the well-being of the Cuban people" by lifting sanctions on travel and remittances.[20] None of these groups, however, could deliver any sizable bloc of voters in South Florida or counter Menendez's power in the Senate.

In the streets of Havana, Cubans honked their horns and applauded when Biden's election was confirmed.[21] President Miguel Díaz-Canel reiterated Cuba's willingness to reengage with Washington, tweeting, "We believe in the possibility of constructive bilateral relations respecting one another's differences."[22] In January 2021, Carlos Fernández de Cossio, director general of the US division of the Foreign Ministry, expressed guarded optimism that Biden would move fairly quickly to reengage.[23] But as time passed with no change in US policy, Havana's optimism turned to frustration and anger.

The Biden administration initially said that, as part of its policy review, it would reassess Trump's last-minute designation of Cuba as a state sponsor of terrorism. But in May 2021, the State Department reaffirmed Trump's determination that Cuba was not cooperating with US counterterrorism efforts. The Cuban Foreign Ministry angrily rejected the designation as "unfounded and mendacious . . . irresponsible and shameful," noting that it was the United States, not Cuba, that had abandoned the counterterrorism cooperation talks begun by President Obama.[24] In December 2021, the State Department reaffirmed the claim that Cuba was a state sponsor of terrorism.

July 11: Cuba Moves Up on the President's Agenda

The July 11, 2021, protests in Cuba forced the issue onto Biden's agenda. As videos of Cubans chanting antigovernment slogans and fighting with police went viral, Biden made a brief statement in support of the protestors.[25] On July 22, Biden imposed sanctions on senior officials of Cuba's security forces for their role in suppressing the demonstrations, and two more rounds of such sanctions followed on July 30 and August 13. The sanctions froze the assets of the targeted individuals and banned their entry to the United States—a largely symbolic exercise since none of the people sanctioned had assets in the United States (such assets would have been frozen already by the embargo) and none were likely to apply for visas.

Biden also promised to increase support for Cuban dissidents and explore ways to provide internet service independent of the Cuban government, which had suspended certain social media apps on July 11 to halt the viral spread of the protests. Ideas floated by Republicans ranged from satellites to powerful Wi-Fi hot spots at the US embassy or Guantánamo Naval Station to balloons in the stratosphere (reminiscent of the blimp known as "Fat Albert" that once broadcast Radio Martí to Cuba before it was destroyed by hurricanes).[26] Meanwhile, Washington continued to provide $20 million annually to opponents of the Cuban government under the guise of "democracy promotion."

To mollify pro-engagement Democrats, Biden created a Remittances Working Group to find a way to get remittances to Cuban families, circumventing the Cuban government. He also affirmed that the State Department was working on how to safely re-staff the US embassy in Havana and reopen the consular section. However, despite these pledges, policy did not change. "After July 11, we hit the pause button," explained Juan Gonzalez.[27] If the demonstrations presaged collapse of the regime, there was no reason for the administration to change policy in ways that might ease the acute economic crisis on the island and, in so doing, give the regime "oxygen."

Over the ensuing months, Cuban courts convicted hundreds of people arrested during and after the July 11 protests, imposing heavy sentences ranging from five to twenty years in prison for those charged with violence against police, government, or commercial establishments. The proceedings drew international criticism, making it even more difficult politically for Biden, who prided himself on his support for human rights, to take any positive steps to improve relations.

Summit of the Americas

Biden's Cuba policy might have remained paused indefinitely if the White House had not been pushed into action by the surge of Cuban migrants at the US southern border, and the prospect of embarrassment at the Summit of the Americas. From October 2021 through May 2022, the number of irregular Cuban migrants was more than three times as many as in the entire previous year. Meanwhile, several Latin American presidents, foremost among them Mexico's Andrés Manuel López Obrador, threatened to boycott the 2022 summit over Biden's decision to exclude Cuba, Venezuela, and Nicaragua.

On May 16, 2022, the administration announced policy changes on immigration, travel, and remittances in hopes of avoiding a Summit of the Americas boycott, although in the end Mexico and half a dozen other states still sent lower-level delegations rather than their heads of state.[28] The May measures included a pledge to resume compliance with the 1994 and 2017 migration agreements. The US embassy began to gradually re-staff, but the consular section did not resume full processing of immigrant visas until 2023.[29]

Meanwhile, the migration surge continued unabated. In 2022, US Customs and Border Protection encountered more than 300,000 irregular Cuban migrants—twice as many as arrived in the 1980 Mariel boatlift and the 1994 rafters crisis combined.[30] Up until January 2023, Cubans arriving at the southern US border received preferential entry into the United States, enabling them to adjust their status under the Cuban Adjustment Act after one year and remain as permanent residents—a practice that incentivized more Cubans to make the dangerous journey through Mexico.[31] In January, to reduce the flow of irregular migrants, the Biden administration announced it would provide humanitarian parole for up to 30,000 Cubans, Nicaraguans, and Haitians monthly. Others attempting to enter the United States without prior approval would be deported.[32]

Biden also restored people-to-people educational travel, which had accounted for more than 638,000 US visitors a year until Trump abolished it.[33] US air service to cities other than Havana was restored, making it easier for Cuban Americans to visit family members living in the interior. However, the State Department continued to prohibit US travelers from staying at hotels in which the Cuban government had an ownership interest, a ban that included almost all major hotels. Biden also retained the Trump-era prohibitions on individual people-to-people travel and cruise ship visits, so the new travel measures had limited practical effect. In 2022, non–Cuban American US visitors numbered fewer than 100,000.

In potentially the most important change, Biden lifted Trump's limits on remittances, which promised to put more money into the hands of Cuban families at a time when access to foreign exchange currency was decisive for a family's standard of living. However, the administration retained the prohibition on US remittance service providers like Western Union doing business with their Cuban counterpart, FINCI-MEX, because it was part of the military's business conglomerate. In November 2022, Washington licensed a small US firm to wire remittances to a Cuban financial institution unconnected to the armed forces, and in January 2023, Western Union launched a pilot program wiring remittances to Cubans' bank accounts.[34]

In short, Biden's May measures looked good on paper, but were limited in practice because the administration was slow to take the steps necessary to make them effective. This was a recurrent pattern in the first two years of Biden's presidency: promises of policy change never materialized into significant change on the ground.

Inching toward Engagement

On August 5, 2022, lightning touched off a fire at Cuba's Matanzas oil base, the island's largest oil storage facility and depot for receiving oil imports. The fire burned out of control for five days, consuming four of the base's eight large storage tanks.

The initial US response hinted that the tragedy might become a step toward US-Cuban reconciliation. The US embassy put out public statements offering condolences to the victims, reminding US organizations that they could legally provide Cuba humanitarian aid and offering US technical assistance. Vice Minister Fernández de Cossio responded with "profound gratitude."[35]

Behind the scenes, both governments were in conversation with a US company experienced in responding to oil spills and fires, but the Biden administration decided it was too politically sensitive to provide humanitarian assistance to fund the company's involvement. The United States ended up standing on the sidelines while Mexico and Venezuela helped Cuba extinguish the fire.[36]

Just two months later, Hurricane Ian gave the Biden administration a second chance to use humanitarian aid to improve relations. The storm devastated Cuba's western provinces and knocked out power to the entire island. On several occasions, previous US administrations had offered Cuba assistance after hurricanes, but Havana had always refused.[37] After Ian, Cuba took the unprecedented step of asking for help, and the Biden administration agreed to provide $2 million for "emergency relief" to those impacted by the storm. The Cuban Foreign Ministry immediately expressed its appreciation.[38] The offer was a small gesture financially, but an important one symbolically.

The elections of Gabriel Boric as president of Chile in March 2022, Gustavo Petro in Colombia in June 2022, and Luiz Inácio Lula da Silva in Brazil in October 2022 marked the return of the of the so-called pink tide in Latin America, with leftist or center-left governments in every major country in the region. Biden's appointment in November 2022 of former senator Chris Dodd as Special Presidential Advisor for the Americas signaled that Biden was aware his Latin America policy was in trouble and in need of sustained high-level attention after the partial boycott of the Summit of the Americas in May.

Dodd's appointment signaled a new look at Cuba policy. The level of diplomatic dialogue increased and the two governments resumed talks on a range of issues of mutual interest. In January 2023, the two governments resumed talks on law enforcement cooperation broken off by Trump in 2018. "The policy *has* changed," acknowledged Juan Gonzalez at the National Security Council. "It's taken some time, but our policy has changed." He was not clear, however, on what the new policy would be, other than that it would be different than either Obama's or Trump's.[39] Both publicly and privately, diplomats on both sides expressed the desire to improve relations, but both governments seemed reluctant to take the first step to initiate significant rather than just marginal improvement.

Politics and Ideology

Biden's Cuba policy was a product of both domestic politics and his approach to foreign policy. In the White House, political calculations remained unchanged from the 2020 campaign: do nothing on Cuba because anything positive entailed political costs, especially in Florida, with no off-setting political gains. Speaking at the U.S. Institute for Peace in September 2022, Juan Gonzalez observed that Latin America, more than most regions, involved "tremendous domestic equities. . . . It's hard to take politics out of consideration when you're making policy."[40]

A Florida International University poll conducted in mid-2022 showed Democrats at a deep disadvantage among Cuban American voters in South Florida, outnumbered by Republicans two-to-one in party registration. Support for the embargo, which had been falling prior to President Trump's election, rebounded to 63 percent, with recent immigrants almost as strongly in favor as early ones. Only pro-engagement policies involving family ties garnered majority support. Cuban Americans overwhelmingly opposed President Biden's Cuba policy, 72 percent to 28 percent—even though Biden's policy was not substantially different than Trump's. In fact, Cuban American antipathy toward Democrats went beyond Cuba policy, reaching across a wide range of policy issues, foreign and domestic.[41] According to exit polls, 67 percent of Cuban Americans in Florida voted for Rubio in the 2022 midterm elections, and 69 percent for Governor Ron DeSantis.[42]

Despite this clear alignment of most Cuban Americans with the Republican Party, Biden nevertheless gave the diaspora a privileged role crafting his Cuba policy, calling Cuban Americans "a vital partner" and "the best experts on the issue." After a number of consultations with Cuban Americans by White House officials, Biden met with nine prominent members of the community on July 19, 2021, at the suggestion of Senator Menendez. The president promised to "make sure that their voices are included and uplifted at every step of the way."[43] Just as President Trump outsourced his Cuba policy to Senator Rubio, Biden outsourced his to Senator Menendez and select members of the Cuban American diaspora.

The White House's deference to domestic politics was reinforced by the president's framing of his foreign policy around the conviction that the struggle between democracy and autocracy would determine "the future and direction of our world."[44] The Biden doctrine had strong echoes of the early cold war when the United States and its Western European allies were arrayed against the Soviet Union and Communist China—the same geostrategic adversaries Biden identified as contemporary authoritarian threats.[45]

The new cold war did not bode well for Cuba. As a "strategic partner" of Russia and a commercial partner of China, Cuba—despite efforts in recent years to diversify its international relations—appeared to Biden to be firmly in the adversaries' camp, a view underscored by President Díaz-Canel's November 2022 trip to Russia and China. Cuba's socialist ideology, one-party system, and intolerance of organized opposition reinforced the administration's framing of Cuba as an authoritarian adversary of Washington's global allies. That, in turn, revived the strategic concerns that were the foundation of US hostility toward Havana during the first cold war, before Cuban Americans became a potent political force. With both foreign policy and domestic politics reinforcing a hostile US stance toward Cuba, the likelihood of Biden restoring Obama's policy of engagement was remote.

Notes

1. Karen DeYoung, "Opening to Cuba Is 'Irreversible,' Senior Obama Aide Says," *Washington Post*, June 9, 2016, accessed at https://www.washingtonpost.com/world/national-security/opening-to-cuba-is-irreversible-senior-obama-aide-says/2016/06/09/9143435e-2e8c-11e6-9b37-42985f6a265c_story.html.

2. Patricia Mazzei and Nicholas Nehamas, "Florida's Hispanic Voter Surge Wasn't Enough for Clinton," *Miami Herald*, November 9, 2016, accessed at www.miamiherald.com/news/politics-government/election/article113778053.html#storylink=cpy.

3. Jonathan Blitzer, "The Fight for the Latino Vote in Florida," *The New Yorker*, September 16, 2019, accessed at https://www.newyorker.com/magazine/2019/09/23/the-fight-for-the-latino-vote-in-florida.

4. Julie Hirschfeld Davis, "Trump Reverses Pieces of Obama-Era Engagement with Cuba," *New York Times*, June 16, 2017, accessed at https://www.nytimes.com/2017/06/16/us/politics/cuba-trump-engagement-restrictions.html.

5. Julian E. Barnes, "Most 'Havana Syndrome' Cases Unlikely Caused by Foreign Power, C.I.A. Says," *New York Times*, January 20, 2022, accessed at https://www.nytimes.com/2022/01/20/us/politics/havana-syndrome-cia-report.html.

6. Niraj Chokshi and Frances Robles, "Trump Administration Announces New Restrictions on Dealing with Cuba," *New York Times*, April 17, 2019, accessed at https://www.nytimes.com/2019/04/17/world/americas/cuba-trump-travel-lawsuits.html.

7. Doina Chiacu and Marianna Parraga, "U.S. Slaps Sanctions on Firms Moving Venezuelan Oil to Cuba," Reuters, September 24, 2019, accessed at https://www.reuters.com/article/us-usa-venezuela-sanctions/us-slaps-sanctions-on-firms-moving-venezuelan-oil-to-cuba-idUSKBN1W91XV.

8. Mario J. Pentón, "Cuba Will Lose Millions in Revenue if It Pulls Its Doctors Out of Brazil, Experts Say," *Miami Herald*, November 16, 2018, accessed at https://www.miamiherald.com/news/nation-world/world/americas/cuba/article221727185.html#storylink=cpy.

9. Matthew Lee and Michael Weissenstein, "Trump Administration Halts Cruises to Cuba under New Rules," AP News, June 4, 2019, accessed at https://apnews.com/article/travel-leisure-travel-ap-top-news-barack-obama-cruises-67c721daee8143d4a2e6ee8c401bf215.

10. Tariro Mzezewa, "Cruises to Cuba Are Abruptly Canceled, after New Travel Ban," *New York Times*, June 5, 2019, accessed at https://apnews.com/article/travel-leisure-travel-ap-top-news-barack-obama-cruises-67c721daee8143d4a2e6ee8c401bf215.

11. Kirk Semple, "Cuba Says U.S. Restrictions Will Force Western Union Offices to Close," *New York Times*, October 28, 2020, accessed at https://www.nytimes.com/2020/10/28/world/americas/cuba-western-union-remittances.html.

12. The Cuban government does not report remittances separately, so estimates are rough. "COVID-19 puede hacer declinar las remesas a Cuba entre un 30 y 40% en el 2020," Havana Consulting Group, March 20, 2020, accessed at http://www.thehavanaconsultinggroup.com/en-us/Articles/Article/74; RevoluGROUP Canada Inc., "RevoluSEND Remittances Adds Cuba and Morocco Topping 116 Countries," news release, February 28, 2022, accessed at https://www.globenewswire.com/en/news-release/2022/02/28/2393095/36545/en/RevoluGROUP-Canada-Inc-RevoluSEND-Remittances-Adds-Cuba-and-Morocco-Topping-116-Countries.html.

13. "On Anniversary of Obama Visit, Cubans Fret over Whether Biden Will Resume Détente," Reuters, March 19, 2021, accessed at https://www.reuters.com/world/americas/anniversary-obama-visit-cubans-fret-over-whether-biden-will-resume-detente-2021-03-19;

EFE, "Biden's Campaign Criticizes Blocking of Remittances to Cubans," *OnCuba News*, October 29, 2020, accessed at https://oncubanews.com/en/cuba-usa/bidens-campaign-criticizes-blocking-of-remittances-to-cubans.

14. Mary Ellen Klas, "'Total Systemic Failure': Florida Democrats Suffer Devastating Election Losses," *Tampa Bay Times*, November 4, 2020, accessed at https://www.tampabay.com/news/florida-politics/elections/2020/11/04/total-systemic-failure-florida-democrats-suffer-devastating-election-losses.

15. Andrew Desiderio and Nahal Toosi, "The Road to Joe Biden's Foreign Policy Runs through Bob Menendez," *Politico*, March 2, 2021, accessed at https://www.politico.com/news/2021/03/01/biden-foreign-policy-bob-menendez-472097.

16. "Press Briefing by Press Secretary Jen Psaki," The White House, Office of the Press Secretary, March 9, 2021, accessed at https://www.whitehouse.gov/briefing-room/press-briefings/2021/03/09/press-briefing-by-press-secretary-jen-psaki-and-deputy-director-of-the-national-economic-council-bharat-ramamurti-march-9-2021.

17. Latin America Program, Woodrow Wilson Center for Scholars, "Transcript: Trump or Biden: What Would It Mean for Latin America and the Caribbean?" September 21, 2020, accessed at https://www.wilsoncenter.org/sites/default/files/media/uploads/documents/Transcript_Trump%20or%20Biden_%20What%20Would%20it%20Mean%20for%20Latin%20America%20and%20the%20Caribbean.pdf.

18. P. Scott Shearer, "Senate Ag Supports Vilsack Confirmation," *National Hog Farmer*, February 5, 2021, accessed at https://www.nationalhogfarmer.com/agenda/senate-ag-supports-vilsack-confirmation.

19. Latin America Working Group, "56 Groups Urge the Biden-Harris Administration to Take Immediate Action to Normalize U.S.-Cuba Relations," press release, February 10, 2021, accessed at https://www.lawg.org/wp-content/uploads/Cuba-letter-to-President-Biden-February-2021.pdf.

20. Karen DeYoung, "More than 100 House Democrats Urge Biden to Implement Changes in Cuba Policy," *Washington Post*, December 16, 2021, accessed at https://www.washingtonpost.com/national-security/cuba-biden-letter/2021/12/16/7d4d9152-5e8c-11ec-8665-aed48580f911_story.html.

21. Nelson Acosta, "Cubans Applaud Biden Win, Hope for Easing of Sanctions," Reuters, November 7, 2020, accessed at https://www.reuters.com/article/us-usa-election-cuba/cubans-applaud-biden-win-hope-for-easing-of-sanctions-idUSKBN27N0Z5.

22. "Cuba's President Acknowledges Biden's U.S. Election Win," Reuters, November 8, 2020, accessed at https://www.reuters.com/article/us-usa-election-cuba/cubas-president-acknowledges-bidens-u-s-election-win-idUSKBN27O0MC.

23. "La Habana espera que Biden revierta las sanciones de Trump 'en el corto plazo,'" *Diario de Cuba*, January 21, 2021, accessed at https://diariodecuba.com/cuba/1611259928_28214.html.

24. Ministry of Foreign Affairs, "Cuba Rejects US Slanders about Counterterrorism Cooperation," May 27, 2021, accessed at http://www.minrex.gob.cu/en/node/4640.

25. The White House, "Statement by President Joseph R. Biden, Jr. on Protests in Cuba," July 12, 2021, accessed at https://www.whitehouse.gov/briefing-room/statements-releases/2021/07/12/statement-by-president-joseph-r-biden-jr-on-protests-in-cuba.

26. David Shepardson, "U.S. Reviewing whether It Can Help Restore Internet Access in Cuba—Biden," Reuters, July 15, 2021, accessed at https://www.reuters.com/world/americas/us-reviewing-whether-it-can-help-restore-internet-access-cuba-2021-07-15.

27. Carmen Sesin, "After Historic Protests, Biden 'Hit the Pause Button' on Cuba Policy, Senior Official Says," NBC News, November 30, 2021, accessed at https://www.nbcnews.com/news/latino/historic-protests-biden-hit-pause-button-cuba-policy-senior-official-s-rcna7110.

28. US Department of State, "Biden Administration Measures to Support the Cuban People: Fact Sheet," May 16, 2022, accessed at https://www.state.gov/biden-administration -measures-to-support-the-cuban-people.

29. Dave Sherwood, "Cuba, U.S. to Hold Second Round of Migration Talks in Havana," Reuters, November 14, 2022, accessed at https://www.reuters.com/world/americas/cuba-us -hold-second-round-migration-talks-havana-2022-11-14.

30. US Customs and Border Protection, "Nationwide Encounters," accessed February 1, 2023, at https://www.cbp.gov/newsroom/stats/nationwide-encounters.

31. Christine Armario and Nick Miroff, "Cubans Arriving in Record Numbers along Mexico Border," *Washington Post*, accessed at April 7, 2022, https://www.washingtonpost.com /national-security/2022/04/07/cuba-migration-border-miami.

32. Nora Gámez Torres et al., "U.S. Will Step Up Expulsions of Cubans, Haitians and Nicaraguans at the Border, Expand Legal Pathway," *Miami Herald*, January 5, 2023, accessed at https://www.miamiherald.com/news/local/immigration/article270803257.html.

33. Oficina Nacional de Estadística e Información, *Cuba Anuario Estadístico de Cuba 2021*, "Turismo," Table 15.6 (Havana: ONEI, 2022), accessed at http://www.onei.gob.cu/sites/ default/files/15_turismo_.pdf.

34. Nora Gámez Torres, "Western Union Quietly Resumes the Business of Remittances to Cuba with a Pilot Program," *Miami Herald*, January 11, 2023, accessed at https://www.miami- herald.com/news/nation-world/world/americas/cuba/article271039062.html.

35. Carlos F. deCossio, Twitter, August 6, 2022, accessed at https://twitter.com/ CarlosFdeCossio/status/1555988313147842560.

36. Nora Gámez Torres, "Cuba Has Not Officially Requested U.S. Help to Put Out Oil Fire, State Department Says," *Miami Herald*, August 9, 2022, accessed at https://www.miami- herald.com/news/nation-world/world/americas/cuba/article264342816.html#storylink=cpy.

37. William M. LeoGrande and Marguerite Rose Jiménez, "Disease, Disaster, and En- vironmental Degradation: How Cuba and the United States Can Collaborate on Common Interests," in *Cuba in a Global Context: International Relations, Internationalism, and Transna- tionalism*, ed. Catherine Krull (Gainesville: University Press of Florida, 2014), 27–43.

38. Karen DeYoung, "U.S. Will Provide $2 million of Hurricane Aid in Cuba," *Washington Post*, October 18, 2022, accessed at https://www.washingtonpost.com/national-security/2022 /10/18/biden-cuba-hurricane-ian.

39. "AQ Podcast: The White House's Juan Gonzalez on Mexico Relationship, Venezuela and More," *Americas Quarterly*, January 9, 2023, accessed at https://www.americasquarterly .org/article/aq-podcast-the-white-houses-juan-gonzalez-on-mexico-relationship-venezuela-and -more.

40. A video of the event is available at https://www.usip.org/events/there-path-greater-unity -western-hemisphere.

41. Guillermo Grenier and Qing Lai, *2022 FIU Cuba Poll: How Cuban Americans in South Florida View U.S. Policies toward Cuba, Critical National Issues, and the Upcoming Elections* (Miami: Florida International University), accessed at https://issuu.com/fiupublications/docs/ sipa_cuba_poll_report_2022_2882279691_final_noblee.

42. "Florida Midterm Election 2022," NBC News, November 9, 2022, accessed at https:// www.nbcnews.com/politics/2022-elections/florida-results?icid=election_statenav.

43. "Remarks by President Biden at Meeting with Cuban American Leaders," The White House, July 30, 2021, accessed at https://www.whitehouse.gov/briefing-room/speeches -remarks/2021/07/30/remarks-by-president-biden-at-meeting-with-cuban-american-leaders; "Statement by President Joseph R. Biden, Jr. on Continuing Crackdown in Cuba," The White House, July 22, 2021, accessed at https://www.whitehouse.gov/briefing-room/statements

-releases/2021/07/22/statement-by-president-joseph-r-biden-jr-on-continuing-crackdown-in -cuba.

44. "Remarks by President Biden at the 2021 Virtual Munich Security Conference," The White House, February 19, 2021, accessed at https://www.whitehouse.gov/briefing -room/speeches-remarks/2021/02/19/remarks-by-president-biden-at-the-2021-virtual-munich -security-conference.

45. See Biden's introduction to *The National Security Strategy*, October 2022, https:// www.whitehouse.gov/wp-content/uploads/2022/10/Biden-Harris-Administrations-National -Security-Strategy-10.2022.pdf.

CHAPTER 15

Havana-Moscow Relations Following Fidel and Raúl Castro

Mervyn J. Bain

As detailed throughout this book, historic change occurred in Cuba between April 2018 and April 2021 with Miguel Díaz-Canel first becoming the president of Cuba and secondly the first secretary of Communist Party of Cuba (PCC). Díaz-Canel was not part of the historic generation of Cuban leaders who had governed the country since the Cuban Revolution in January 1959, and furthermore he was also born after the victory of the Revolution. This chapter's focus is Havana-Moscow relations, and the consequence of this historic change in Cuba was that for the first time since the reestablishment of diplomatic relations between Havana and Moscow after the Cuban Revolution (diplomatic relations were initiated on May 8, 1960), neither Fidel nor Raúl Castro were at the pinnacle of the Cuban ruling elite.

From the reestablishment of bilateral relations in May 1960 until December 1991 and the dissolution of the Soviet Union, Havana's relationship with Moscow had been of great importance for both countries. In this period a multifaceted relationship developed with Moscow providing political support for Havana, the Soviet Union was Cuba's chief trading partner, and numerous joint projects were completed on the island—crucial as Cuba faced continuous aggression from the United States, not least the ongoing economic embargo. For Moscow, the relationship was key for its attempts to rebalance the Cold War in its favor.

Although this was the case, and global politics in the 2020s is very different from the Cold War era, under Díaz-Canel's presidency the relationship continues to be highly significant for both the Cuban and Russian governments. The importance of the relationship to Havana and Moscow is demonstrated by it being classed as a "strategic partnership" by both governments (Ferrer Fonte 2022a). Moreover, the relationship's significance is further highlighted by Russia being part of Díaz-Canel's extensive overseas trip in October 2018, with Díaz-Canel returning to Moscow in October 2019. Moreover, Dmitry Medvedev, Russian prime minister, visited Cuba in October/November 2019. This chapter will chart and analyze the pressures and issues at play within Cuban-Russian relations under Díaz-Canel's presidency to detail its continuing significance. It will focus on key areas within the bilateral relationship and will examine the following topics: politics, geopolitical significance, trade, bilateral agreements, tourism, culture, and a reconceptualization of the relationship's past.

Politics

Politically the bilateral relationship continues to be mutually beneficial for Havana and Moscow, particularly concerning both countries' relationships with the United States. Tension remains in Havana-Washington relations, and Russia's relationship with the United States and the West in general has deteriorated, exacerbated by Russia's February 2022 invasion of Ukraine.

Russian ongoing support for Havana concerning its relationship with Washington is evident in various international fora; that is, in November 2022 Russia once again supported the UN resolution calling for the end of the US embargo against the island (United Nations 2022). Furthermore, the Russian Foreign Ministry statement made in the aftermath of the spontaneous protests that surfaced in Cuba on July 11, 2021: (1) criticized US policy toward Cuba over the last sixty years; (2) criticized Washington's policy toward the island since the onset of the COVID-19 global pandemic; and (3) compared the United States' Cuba policy to its policy concerning the "coloured revolutions" of the twenty-first century in post-Soviet Eurasia (Russian Foreign Ministry 2021). Moreover, this Russian government statement correlated with the humanitarian aid that it provided Cuba in April 2021, necessary due to the island's economic difficulties resulting from both the ongoing US embargo and the impact of the COVID-19 pandemic on the Cuban economy (Translating Cuba 2021). Russia providing support for Cuba concerning its relationship with the United States was further evident in May 2021 when Washington placed Cuba on a list of nations that are perceived as not collaborating in the fight against terrorism. The Russian government described Washington's decision as "absurd and unjustified" (MINREX 2020b).

Support in international fora is reciprocated by Cuba, apparent at the UN with issues over Russian involvement in the war in Georgia in 2008, Syria, and in 2014 the annexation of Crimea. In February 2022 while calling for peace, acknowledging Russia's security concerns but nonobservance of international norms in its invasion of Ukraine, the Cuban government attached blame to US and North Atlantic Treaty Organization (NATO) provocations, including NATO expansion to the east, for a situation which could have been avoided (Cuban Government 2022). Havana also abstained in subsequent UN General Assembly votes condemning this Russian invasion (Duffy 2022a). Moreover, in October 2022 Cuba again abstained in the UN General Assembly vote that condemned Russia's annexation of the Ukrainian regions of Donetsk, Luhansk, Zaporizhzhia, and Kherson (Duffy 2022b). In short, the bilateral relationship permits both Havana and Moscow to counter US policies toward Cuba and Russia.

In sum, Havana and Moscow have a common perception of the international system and Washington's role within it. Both Havana and Moscow perceive Washington as hostile, but each other as friendly. Collective memory of the relationship's past and the economic sanctions that both Cuba and Russia face (both detailed below) exacerbates this shared perception. The shared perception of the international system was evident in October 2022 when during a meeting between Ricardo Cabrisas and Dmitry Chernyshenko, deputy prime ministers of Cuba and Russia, Chernyshenko stated, "We will continue working together to shape a polycentric international order based on respect for generally-accepted principles and rules of international law" (Russian Government 2022). Moreover, a January 2021 telephone conversation between Bruno Rodríguez Parrilla and Sergey Lavrov, the Cuban and Russian foreign ministers, further highlighted the significance of the political aspect of the relationship and shared international outlook. The press release on the conversation focused on the close political ties, shared outlook on many international issues, mutual support for each other in various international fora, and increasing cooperation in various economic collaborations (Prensa Latina 2021).

Geopolitical Significance

The result of the above political aspect of the relationship is that Cuba once again has geostrategic significance for Moscow. This is not to suggest that this geostrategic significance has returned to the level of the Cold War era (a key determinant in Moscow's attention in the Cuban Revolution in the late 1950s/early 1960s), but it has returned. In early 2022 Russian deputy foreign minister Sergei Ryabkov spoke of the possibility of a Russian military deployment to Cuba and Venezuela to counter the buildup of Western forces in Ukraine as tension between the West and Russia increased (Rankin, Harding, and Borger 2022). This military buildup did not materialize, but the return of geostrategic significance also evidences the importance of legacies from previous eras of the relationship's history, outlined below.

Trade

In 2021 bilateral trade between Havana and Moscow was US$633,358 million (ONEI 2021, 8.4). This level of trade is a mere fraction of the level of Cuban-Soviet trade in the 1960 to 1991 era when in 1985 it reached almost US$10 billion (*Vneshiaia Torgovliia Sssr 1989–1990*, 5). Moreover, bilateral Cuban-Russian trade has never been of a high level during Díaz-Canel's presidency, illustrated by table 15.1.

However, Cuban-Russian trade had been at low levels for several years prior to 2018, and in 2021 Russia remains Cuba's fourth-most-important trading partner. Moreover, the 2021 level of Havana-Moscow trade is the highest level of bilateral trade conducted between Cuba and Russia in the twenty-first century. Simply, trade with Russia remains key for Cuba, especially as the island's economic situation is adversely affected by the impact of the COVID-19 pandemic on the global economy, fall in trade with Caracas due to the deteriorating internal Venezuelan situation, and the

Table 15.1.   Cuban-Russian trade 2018 to 2020/21 (millions of US dollars)

2018	2019	2020	2021
451,155	554,784	327,613	633,358

Source: Anuario Estadístico de Cuba 2021 (ONEI 2021, 8.4).

continuing US embargo. The significance of trade was demonstrated in November 2022 when Russian once again participated in the Havana International Fair, FIHAV 2022, Cuba's major trade and exhibition event (Ferrer Fonte 2022b).

In the 2020s both Cuba and Russia face economic sanctions, increasing the possibility that bilateral trade will increase as both countries endeavor to circumvent these sanctions. In March 2022 Cabrisas and Chernyshenko discussed the potential for bilateral transactions to be conducted in Russian roubles, which would help facilitate trade due to the difficulties of conducting trade in US dollars as a result of the economic sanctions that Russia faces (Russian Government 2022). Moreover, the political will exists in both Havana and Moscow for trade to increase, further illustrating its significance.

Bilateral Agreements

For similar reasons to those detailed above concerning bilateral trade (the impact of the COVID-19 pandemic on the global economy, fall in trade with Venezuela, and the ongoing US embargo), bilateral agreements with Russia focusing on other areas of the relationship remain significant for Cuba. Since April 2018 a number of such agreements have been signed. This includes eight during Medvedev's October/November 2019 trip to Cuba, which focused on several areas of the relationship including infrastructure and oil (Russian Government 2019a and 2019b). Energy security has been a persistent issue for Cuba throughout the revolutionary period.

Additionally, since Díaz-Canel became president of Cuba several other bilateral agreements have been signed, illustrating the multifaceted nature of the relationship. In July 2019 Cabrisas signed an agreement with Russian defense minister Sergei Shoigu for bilateral cooperation between their countries, helping to provide continued security within the Caribbean (Cubadebate 2019a). In September 2018 collaborations in geophysics and astronomy, technologies, palaeontology, and metallurgy were signed, and in November an 2018 agreement was reached for increased collaboration between Cuban and Russian universities (Prensa Latina 2018). Moreover, in February 2020 an agreement of intent between Cuban and Russian universities was signed for the creation of a Russian language training school in Havana to provide Cuban students with the necessary language skills to study at Russian universities (Prensa Latina 2020). In May 2022 it was reported that an agreement between the Russian Federal Service for Veterinary and Phytosanitary Control and the Cuban Ministry of Agriculture was reached for the veterinary certificates required for Russia to supply Cuba with meat, dairy, and fish products; canned food; and processed meat products (Ramos Martin 2022).

It is also apparent that both Havana and Moscow intend to broaden the relationship, as several other topics have been discussed for possible future bilateral agreements. This was evident in October 2020 while Cabrisas was in Russia. During this visit Cabrisas met Ksenia Yudaeva, first vice governor of the Central Bank of Russia; Alexander Novak, Russian energy minister; and Mikhail Murashko, Russian health minister (MINREX 2020c). Furthermore, in the spring of 2022 a pilot scheme permitting the use of Russian MIR cash cards in automated teller machines (ATMs) in Cuba commenced. This pilot scheme is to benefit the number of Russian tourists who now visit Cuba (Russian Government 2022).

Tourism

The importance of the Russian MIR cash cards working in Cuban ATMs results from the increase throughout the 2010s of Russians vacationing in Cuba. The outcome is that the most Russians are now traveling to Cuba since the dissolution of the Soviet Union in 1991. Until the onset of the COVID-19 pandemic, which curtailed international travel, this trend continued under Díaz-Canel's presidency. In 2018 189,813 Russians vacationed in Cuba, an increase of over 250 percent compared to 2013 (ONEI 2018, 15.6). In 2019 the figure was 177,977 (ONEI 2021, 15.6). The 2019 figure is the last before international travel was interrupted by the COVID-19 pandemic, but it made Russia Cuba's third-most-important source of tourists. The number of Canadian tourists visiting Cuba has historically far exceeded the number of Russians (traditionally over one million Canadians visit Cuba each year), but Russia is still an important source of tourists for the island. Moreover, diversifying the source of tourists also helps mitigate negative consequences if a decrease occurs in one of Cuba's other chief tourist markets.

The significance of Russian tourists to Cuba was further evident in August 2019 when an air route from Moscow to Varadero was announced (Cubadebate 2019b). Moreover, once travel returned after the COVID-19 pandemic the significance of Russian tourists for Cuba became even more apparent. In 2021 146,151 Russians visited Cuba. This number of Russians tourists had both almost returned to pre-pandemic levels and accounted for 41 percent of the number of tourists visiting the island. In 2021 Russia was the most important source of tourists for Cuba (ONEI 2021, 15.6).

In the future as the global tourist industry reverts to more pre-COVID-19 practices the number of Canadian tourists vacationing in Cuba is likely to exceed the number of Russian tourists, as has traditionally been the case. However, it is likely that Russia will remain one of Cuba's chief tourist markets, particularly if travel remains restricted for Russians due to sanctions imposed after the Russian invasion of Ukraine in February 2022.

Culture

As with increasing numbers of Russians visiting Cuba throughout the 2010s, a similar process has taken place with bilateral cultural links. This process has continued since April 2018 until again these cultural links were adversely affected by the restrictions on travel due to the COVID-19 pandemic. November 14, 2019, marked the beginning of a Cuban film week in Russia (Prensa Latina 2019), and also in November 2019 the St. Petersburg ballet performed *Alicia Alonso* in Havana's Gran Teatro de la Habana

(Acosta and Pérez 2019). Additionally, at the end of November 2019 the Academy of Arts in Moscow hosted an exhibition of Cuban art to celebrate the 500th anniversary of Havana (Cubadebate 2019c).

Reconceptualization

The bilateral cultural links not only evidence the multifaceted nature of Havana-Moscow relations in the 2020s, but are also illustrative of legacies of previous eras of the relationship. Simply, similar cultural exchanges are not taking place between Russia and other Latin American countries with which Moscow does not have such longstanding links. Moreover, both the Cuban and Russian governments are also highlighting the relationship's heritage. In November 2022 it was announced that a statue of Fidel Castro would be unveiled in Moscow's Sokol District (TASS 2022). Additionally, both governments are also emphasizing the pre-1959 relationship that existed between the two countries. This relationship was at a much-reduced level compared to the 1960 to 1991 era, but both governments are emphasizing the links between the two countries from the earlier period.

These links include the first diplomatic contact between the two countries being made in 1902, and diplomatic relations between Havana and Moscow existing for ten years beginning in 1942 (severed by Fulgencio Batista when he returned to the Cuban presidency in March 1952). In 1927 Alexander Alekhin and José Raúl Capablanca competed against each other for the title of world chess champion, the Russian ballerinas Anna Pavlova and Maya Plisetskaya performed in Cuba, and the Cuban ballerina Alicia Alonso performed at the Bolshoi Theatre in Moscow. Moreover, in 1896 three Russians—Pyotr Streltsov, Yevstafy Konstantonovich, and Nikolai Melentyev—joined General Antonio Maceo's army in the Cuban War of Independence. Medvedev paid respects to them in October 2019 when he visited the Tomb of the Unknown Mambi (Cuban Independence fighter). Three Cubans—Aldo and Jorge Vivó and Enrique Vilar—also fought for the Red Army during World War II (MINREX 2020a).

This reconceptualization process illustrates the longevity of the bilateral relationship, the interlinked nature of the two countries, and importantly its continuation. Significantly, a generation of Cuban and Russian citizens have been born in both countries after the dissolution of the Soviet Union in 1991 who could question the relationship's continuation due to the geographical distance between Cuba and Russia. This reconceptualization process answers this question with it further evidencing the importance of the relationship to both countries.

A Mutually Beneficial Relationship

Under the presidency of Miguel Díaz-Canel, Havana-Moscow relations remain key for both countries, which is illustrated by the multifaceted relationship being classed as a "strategic partnership." Various reasons and pressures underpin the relationship, with many of these reasons and pressures remaining the same as in earlier eras of the relationship, specifically the 1960 to 1991 era. At the forefront of these reasons and pressures is the mutual support that the two countries can provide for each other in various international fora—crucial because in the early 2020s both Havana's and Moscow's relationship with Washington remain strained.

Moreover, the relationship now possesses a long heritage (highlighted by both governments), with it being evident that going forward Havana and Moscow wish to expand the relationship. Endeavoring to circumvent economic sanctions that both countries face is likely to further increase the importance of bilateral trade, which has been at a persistently low level for several years.

Although this is the case, at the time of this writing the governments in both Havana and Moscow face a number of challenges that in the long term could begin to challenge the bilateral relationship. However, since the 1960s the relationship has faced several challenges, not least the end of the Cold War and Fidel and Raúl Castro no longer being at the forefront of Cuban politics. As this chapter has illustrated, not only has the bilateral relationship survived these challenges, but it continues to be mutually beneficial and highly important for both Cuba and Russia. Consequently, it is highly likely that the relationship will in the short to mid term continue in its present form.

References

Acosta, Dinella García, and Irene Pérez. 2019. "Asiste Díaz-Canel a la gala del ballet de San Petersburgo en La Habana." Cubadebate, November 15. Accessed at http://www .cubadebate.cu/noticias/2019/11/15/asiste-diaz-canel-a-la-gala-del-ballet-de-san-petersburgo -en-la-habana.

Cubadebate. 2019a. "Vicepresidente cubano Ricardo Cabrisas se reúne en Moscú con Ministro de Defensa Ruso." July 23. Accessed at http://www.cubadebate.cu/noticias/2019/07/23/ vicepresidente-cubano-ricardo-cabrisas-se-reune-en-moscu-con-ministro-de-defensa-ruso.

———. 2019b. "Inaugurada nueva ruta Moscú-Varadero que afianzará mercado en Cuba." August 10. Accessed at http://www.cubadebate.cu/noticias/2019/08/10/inaugurada-nueva -ruta-moscu-varadero-que-afianzara-mercado-ruso-en-cuba.

———. 2019c. "Dedican mega exposición de arte en Rusia al aniversario 500 de La Habana." November 28. Accessed at http://www.cubadebate.cu/noticias/2019/11/28/dedican-mega -exposicion-de-arte-en-rusia-al-aniversario-500-de-la-habana.

Cuban Government. 2022. "Statement by the Revolutionary Government." Official Website of the Cuban Government, February 26. Accessed at http://www.minrex.gob.cu/en/cuba -champions-solution-guarantees-security-and-sovereignty-all-statement-revolutionary-gov- ernment.

Duffy, Nick. 2022a. "UN Russia Vote: Full Voting Breakdown as North Korea and Syria Back Putin over Ukraine Invasion." *i*, March 2. Accessed at https://inews.co.uk/news/un-russia -vote-full-voting-breakdown-north-korea-syria-back-putin-ukraine-invasion-1494907.

———. 2022b. "UN General Assembly Russia Vote List in Full as World Condemns An- nexations in Ukraine but China, India Abstain." *i*, October 12. Accessed at https://inews.co .uk/news/world/un-general-assembly-russia-vote-list-in-full-world-condemns-russias-illegal -annexations-ukraine-1908831.

Ferrer Fonte, Ileana. 2022a. "Putin and Diaz-Canel Discuss Strategic Cooperation." Prensa Latina, January 24. Accessed at https://www.plenglish.com/news/2022/01/24/putin-and -diaz-canel-discuss-strategic-cooperation.

———. 2022b. "Havana Trade Fair FIHAV 2022 Opens in Cuba." Prensa Latina, November 14. Accessed at https://www.plenglish.com/news/2022/11/14/havana-trade-fair-fihav-2022 -opens-in-cuba.

MINREX (Ministry of Foreign Affairs of Cuba). 2020a. "Joint Article by Foreign Minister Sergey Lavrov and Foreign Minister of Cuba Bruno Rodriguez Parrilla on the 60th Anniversary of Restoring Russian-Cuban Diplomatic Relations." May 8. Accessed at https://cubaminrex .cu/en/node/1952.

———. 2020b. "Russia Rejects Cuba's Inclusion in US Terrorist List." May 21. Accessed at https://cubaminrex.cu/en/node/2097.

———. 2020c. "Russia and Cuba Boost Energy, Banking and Health Cooperation." October 1. Accessed at https://cubaminrex.cu/en/node/3456.

———. 2021. "Cuba, Russia Are Strategic Partners, Top Russian Leader Says." October 13. Accessed at https://cubaminrex.cu/en/cuba-russia-are-strategic-partners-top-russian-leader -says.

ONEI (National Office of Statistics and Information). 2018. *Anuario Estadístico de Cuba 2018*. Accessed at http://www.onei.gob.cu/sites/default/files/aec_2019_0.pdf.

———. 2021. *Anuario Estadístico de Cuba 2021*. Accessed at http://www.onei.gob.cu/sites/ default/files/08_sector_externo_2021-_1.pdf.

Prensa Latina. 2018. "Higher Education Projects Strengthen Ties between Russia and Cuba." November 14. Accessed at http://www.plenglish.com/index.php?o=rn&id=35769&SEO =higher-education-projects-strengthen-ties-between-russia-and-cuba.

———. 2019. "Cuban Film Week to Be Held in Russia." November 5. Accessed at https:// www.plenglish.com/index.php?o=rn&id=48631&SEO=cuban-film-week-to-be-held-in -russia.

———. 2020. "Russian Language Training School Opens in Cuba." February 12. Accessed at http://www.plenglish.com/index.php?o=rn&id=52105&SEO=russian-language-training -school-opens-in-cuba.

———. 2021. "Cuba, Russia FMs Hold Talks on Bilateral Relations." January 21. Accessed at https://www.plenglish.com/index.php?o=rn&id=63710&SEO=cuba-russia-fms-hold-talks -on-bilateral-relations.

Ramos Martin, Alina. 2022. "Russia and Cuba Agree on Food Products Export." Prensa Latina, May 13. Accessed at https://www.plenglish.com/news/2022/05/13/russia-and-cuba-agree-on -food-products-export.

Rankin, Jennifer, Luke Harding, and Julian Borger. 2022. "Russia Threatens Military Deployment to Cuba and Venezuela as Diplomacy Stalls." *The Guardian*, January 13. Accessed at https://www.theguardian.com/world/2022/jan/13/russia-says-talks-with-nato-over-ukraine -are-hitting-a-dead-end.

Russian Foreign Ministry. 2021. "Comment by the Official Representative of the Russian Foreign Ministry, Maria Zakharova, on the Situation in Cuba." Official Website of the Russian Foreign Ministry. July 15.

Russian Government. 2019a. "Dmitry Medvedev Holds Talks with Miguel Mario Díaz-Canel Bermudez, President of the Council of State and the Council of Ministers of Cuba." Official Website of the Government of the Russian Federation, October 3. Accessed at http:// government.ru/en/news/38007.

————. 2019b. "Dmitry Medvedev Visits Boca de Jaruco Oil Drilling Site." Official Website of the Government of the Russian Federation, October 4. Accessed at http://government.ru/en/news/38013.

————. 2022. "Dmitry Chernyshenko Meets with Deputy Prime Minister of Cuba Ricardo Cabrisas." Official Website of the Government of the Russian Federation, October 6. Accessed at http://government.ru/en/news/46734.

TASS. 2022. "Preparations Underway for Communication between Russian, Cuban Leaders, Says Kremlin." November 11. Accessed at https://tass.com/politics/1535233.

Translating Cuba. 2021. "Russia Sends Cuba 253 Tons of Oil and 430 of Tons of Wheat Flour." April 27. Accessed at https://translatingcuba.com/russia-sends-cuba-253-tons-of-oil-and-430-of-tons-of-wheat-flour.

United Nations. 2022. "General Assembly: 28th Plenary Meeting, 77th Session." November 3. Accessed at https://media.un.org/en/asset/k16/k16o4lsqf3.

Vneshiaia Torgovlia Sssr 1989–1990. 1992. Moscow: mezhdunarodnye otnosheniia.

CHAPTER 16

Cuba-China Relations

SOLIDARITY AND PRAGMATISM

Fulton T. Armstrong

The rhetoric of solidarity between Cuba and the People's Republic of China is clear and sincere, but it glosses over a web of transactional relations that ebb and flow as circumstances change. Both countries emphasize their commitment to building Communism "with national characteristics" and proclaim the "mutual benefit" they get from the relationship. Chinese officials call Cuba "a good brother, good comrade, good friend." But the practical pillars of the relationship have not always been as solid as the slogans suggest.

Relations between the two peoples have deep, if not at first egalitarian, roots. Along a major avenue in Havana, in a plaza on Línea and L, is a unique tribute to the longstanding ties between the Cuban and Chinese people—and the latter's loyalty to Cuba. It is a monument that proclaims, "There was no Chinese Cuban deserter; there was no Chinese Cuban traitor." No other immigrant community has received such praise.

In the mid-nineteenth century, amid the chaos of the Opium Wars, tens of thousands of Chinese were dragooned to go to Cuba as indentured slaves. About 5,000 more came from the United States to escape anti-Chinese laws and discrimination. Some 170,000 "Coolies"—almost all men—were eventually working in Cuban agriculture, particularly sugar. Outcry over their treatment led China to investigate and negotiate an agreement committing Spain to end recruitment by force or trickery and China to establish a consulate in Havana—its first diplomatic mission in Latin America (Ng 2014).

Many Chinese stayed and went on to fight in the Cuban wars of independence, earning the epithet on the monument. Their grandchildren's loyalty showed again during the Cuban Revolution in the 1950s, when military commanders Armando Choy, Gustavo Chui, and Moisés Sío Wong figured prominently among the ranks of Fidel Castro's forces, later becoming generals in Cuba's Fuerzas Armadas Revolucionarias.

Young Revolutions Feel Their Way

Cuba is proud to be the first country in Latin America to recognize the People's Republic of China. Chairman Mao Zedong and the Chinese Communist Party (CCP) defeated the US-favored General Chiang Kai-shek in October 1949, almost ten years before Fidel Castro marched victorious into Havana. Early on, the young Cuban revolutionary government emphasized solidarity with Chinese socialism and sovereignty, making Cuba the first country in the Western Hemisphere to embrace a "One China" policy—that Taiwan is an inalienable part of China with Beijing as its capital.

Relations had a strong start. In 1960, the two countries held talks and Che Guevara headed the first high-level delegation to China, resulting in trade agreements by which China agreed to buy Cuban sugar in return for Chinese rice and consumer goods (Zuo 2010). China extended $60 million in interest-free loans and offered to train Cuban technicians. In the early 1960s, according to Chinese Foreign Ministry officials, relations were so cozy that Fidel and Raúl Castro and Che Guevara would make unannounced visits to the Chinese embassy hoping to enjoy a good Chinese dinner, particularly Beijing duck. This occurred frequently enough that the foreign ministry in Beijing sent additional cooks to the embassy (Cheng 2007).

Such happy times were not to last, however. Cuba's relationship with the Soviet Union, China's strategic competitor, became an obstacle to the full blossoming of ties with Beijing and, at times, caused great acrimony. In a speech in January 1966, for example, Fidel Castro announced that China was cutting a planned $250 million exchange of goods to $170 million and implied that Beijing was punishing Cuba for its cooperation with the USSR. According to press reports at the time, China was demanding that trade be balanced and would extend no more credit, returning trade to its 1961 level. Several weeks later, Cuba's press agency, Prensa Latina, quoted Castro as saying that China's reaction to his speech was "extremely deceptive" and reflected "hypocritical, contemptuous procedures." Castro said the Chinese government was committing "a criminal act of economic aggression against our country." He referred to Chinese "perfidy, hypocrisy, malevolent insinuations, and disdain for our small country." Castro went so far as to refer to Mao as a "senile idiot" (Castro 1966).

Relations remained off-balance for years as Cuba continued to align with the Soviets' proletarian internationalism, with activities in Latin America and Africa (although not always with Moscow's approval or even knowledge). As China was engineering its rapprochement with the United States in the 1970s—from the first Nixon administration feelers in 1971 to full normalization in 1979—Cuba was deepening its role as a Soviet partner in "anti-imperialist" enterprises. Castro was furious when China in 1979 sparked a border dispute with Vietnam, which he considered heroic in its victory against the United States just years before. At a rally, Castro referred to China's leaders as a "mad, neo-fascist faction" and called then-chairman Deng Xiaoping a "sort of caricature of Hitler," "an idiot" (*mentecato*), and "a puppet" (*títere*) (Castro 1970).

The Soviet Patron Exits

Relations changed drastically as the Soviets' desire and ability to continue their special trade relationship with Cuba diminished, culminating in the collapse of the Berlin Wall in 1989 and the USSR itself in 1991. Without Soviet markets and subsidies, the Cuban economy contracted an estimated 35 percent in 1990–1991—thrusting the island into the "Special Period in Peacetime" and giving Havana a huge incentive to rebuild relations with China and other potential partners around the world.

The outreach coincided with important shifts in China, reflected in the crackdown on protests in Tiananmen in the summer of 1989. Fidel Castro privately endorsed the suppression as necessary to defend Communism and social order. Chinese foreign minister Qian Qichen was in Havana during the Tiananmen incident and, according to an oral history by Chinese officials, Castro told him that he completely supported the Chinese government and would offer "whatever occasions and facilities" China needed (Cheng 2007). Castro may also have assessed that the crackdown meant that Chinese officials were going to slow the economic reforms that had diluted socialist purity and, in his view, contributed to such disorder.

High-level exchanges resumed. Cuban foreign minister Isidoro Malmierca reciprocated Qian's visit in 1989, and heads of state followed several years later. CCP chairman Jiang Zemin was the first Chinese head of state to visit Cuba, in November 1993, and Fidel Castro reciprocated with a nine-day visit two years later. Raúl Castro made his first trip to Beijing in 1997, spending twenty days and visiting six provinces. Chinese leaders have visited every several years since then, often as part of larger trips. Chairman Xi Jinping made his first (and so far only) visit in 2014, when Raúl Castro gave him the Order of José Martí—Cuba's highest honor for a foreigner. According to Xu Yicong, the Chinese ambassador to Havana in 1993–1995, Fidel Castro resumed his 1960s-era practice of dropping in at the embassy unannounced—eight times in one year (Cheng 2007). (Cuba's first president in the post-Castro era, Miguel Díaz-Canel Bermúdez, made his first official visit to China in November 2018.)

Good Friends but with Conditions

Many observers believed—and perhaps Cuba hoped—that the revamped ties were going to lead to China filling the Soviets' old shoes as generous benefactor. Beijing undoubtedly helped its comrade in need, but it also imposed conditions on that help as it nudged Cuba to a more realistic definition of "mutual benefit." China offered credits in the hundreds of millions of dollars and let Cuba run up significant debt, but it slowed exports when Cuba didn't pay and gently urged Fidel and Raúl to implement the sort of reforms that enabled Chinese Communism to transition from a backward, bureaucratic variety to a productive, vibrant one. Chinese officials at the highest levels praised Fidel's resolve to preserve socialism—particularly in the face of the US embargo and other measures meant to weaken the Cuban government—but they were perplexed and, at times, displeased by his skepticism of China's reforms.

Solidarity rhetoric remained robust, but trade became the major driver of the relationship. Venezuela, by virtue of its oil dealings with Cuba, was the island's biggest trading partner, but China has for many years been its second—albeit still only 13.3 percent of Cuba's total trade, according to the government's *Anuario Estadístico* (ONEI 2021). In 1990, two-way trade grew rapidly—doubling to about $500 million a year. It was at first largely on a barter basis; China extended little credit and almost no aid. Over time, however, Beijing loosened the purse strings for particular purchases that Cuba needed. In the early 2000s, for example, it provided about $500 million in credits for Cuba to buy buses, communications equipment, and electronic gear. Havana also needed chemicals, food (particularly dried legumes), textiles, and other light manufacturing goods. China imported Cuban sugar and nickel and other metals such as zinc ore and scrap metal (Foreign Ministry of China 2022). In 2020, a Cuban news website, Cubadebate, reported that China was paying for the services of Cuban doctors in "various Chinese regions" and that joint enterprises in the biotechnology sector were expanding production of new products in advanced clinical trials (Blanco Silva 2020).

Data on debt and assistance are piecemeal and difficult to corroborate, but they fall within similar oscillating patterns as trade. AidData, a research lab at the College of William & Mary, estimates that Cuba owes China $4.643 billion in sovereign and "hidden" debt (Malik et al. 2021). Information on Chinese direct assistance is largely anecdotal. In 2008–2009, for example, China provided humanitarian assistance and credits in the wake of three major hurricanes that hit the island in a three-week period in August and September 2008. The interest-free credit line was reportedly for purchase of maritime and communications equipment (Sánchez Ramírez 2012).

Is Cuba Becoming Less Special to China?

Havana still has a special niche in Beijing's heart, but China's recent massive effort to build ties in Latin America has created relationships in the region that dwarf Cuba's. As a "good brother, good comrade, good friend," Cuba still edges out others in "comprehensive strategic partnerships" (such as Mexico, Brazil, Argentina, Chile, Peru, and Ecuador) or lesser "cooperative partnerships," and solidarity rhetoric remains a constant in the relationship (Myers and Barrios 2021). In September 2020, on the sixtieth anniversary of bilateral diplomatic relations, Chairman Xi and former president Raúl Castro issued glowing statements. Xi spoke of "the unique friendly relations . . . the deep friendship through mutual understanding, mutual trust, and mutual support . . . the all-round and in-depth development," and Castro praised the "friendship [that] will be passed down from generation to generation and last forever" (*Asia News Monitor* 2020). More recently, President Díaz-Canel has reiterated that the Cuban government and Communist Party had the "will [to continue] deepening the close [*entrañable*] friendship" (*Noticias Cubanas* 2022).

But, interestingly, neither of two official policy papers that China has published on its relations with Latin America, in 2008 and 2016, mentioned Cuba (nor other individual countries for that matter). They state that the Chinese government views its relations with the region "from a strategic plane and seeks to build and develop a comprehensive and cooperative partnership featuring equality, mutual benefit and common development with Latin American and Caribbean countries" (USC Annenberg 2009).

The numbers show the importance of China's efforts. In the first two decades of this century, trade between China and Latin America grew from $21 to $330 billion—1,300 percent. Chinese foreign direct investment (FDI) in the region was negligible in the early 2000s, but grew to approximately $160 billion between 2005 and 2020. The contrast between Cuba, with its relatively small debt, and countries like Ecuador—a country of eighteen million receiving billions in Chinese investment for hydroelectric and other projects—is stark. Even in the Caribbean, Cuba is not China's biggest partner. At $4 billion in 2019, the value of Chinese trade with the Dominican Republic—which also has about eleven million inhabitants—was three times greater than with Cuba (Ellis 2021).

Beijing continues to provide Cuba politically significant assistance in crisis situations, such as during the dark days of the COVID-19 pandemic. It sent hundreds of tons of medical supplies, including pulmonary ventilators, oxygen concentrators, antigen tests, and various kinds of protective gear. When a huge Cuban fuel storage facility in Matanzas was devastated by fire in August 2022, President Xi sent a condolence message and pledged $150,000 in support to the Red Cross of Cuba to help deal with injuries. After Hurricane Ian slammed into western Cuba two months later, destroying homes and infrastructure, China's International Development Cooperation Agency (CIDCA) made an "important cash donation" of an unspecified amount, according to officials in both countries.

But trade—more important to Cuba than handouts—has declined steeply in recent years. Two-way trade totaled more than $2.5 billion in 2016 but dropped to almost $1.4 billion in 2021—a decrease of 46 percent, according to Cuban government figures, which generally coincide with Chinese government and World Bank data. Cuba ran up a trade deficit with China of $555 million in 2021. The COVID-19 pandemic caused a roughly 11 percent contraction of the Cuban economy in 2020 and forced Havana to make emergency reductions of about 20 percent in imports. Revamped US economic sanctions explain another significant part of the drop, targeting Cuban revenues from tourism and remittances as well as its third-country trade. While the foundation of China-Cuba trade—Cuban minerals and sugar for equipment, technology, and food—remains largely the same, the old long-term agreements have been replaced by more ad hoc, shorter-term deals with clear parameters on credit terms.

Public statements by both countries' leaders continue the same, however. After phone calls between Chairman Xi and President Díaz-Canel in 2021, the Chinese government released statements emphasizing that it, "as always, supports Cuba's adoption of a development path that's in line with its national conditions" (Foreign Ministry of China 2021). But a longtime foreign correspondent in Havana and others reported in the same time frame that foreign diplomats and businessmen active in Cuba cited their Chinese peers as being frustrated with Cuban business practices and payment problems. The elephant in the room is that, as a European businessman said, "the Cubans have no money" (Frank 2021).

Speculation that Cuba would adopt reforms similar to China's—to increase growth and productivity—has proliferated for years. Since the 1990s, according to a number of sources, Chinese officials privately have urged Fidel and Raúl Castro to shift toward China's sort of "market socialism." Fidel resisted, but Raúl is widely credited with steering the debates that led to modest reforms approved during Cuba's Sixth Party Congress in 2011—the *Lineamientos de la Política Económica y Social del Partido y la Revolución*—that did inch Cuba toward opening to private enterprise, foreign investment, and deeper property rights. But implementation of even these modest measures, slowed by distrustful hardliners and bureaucrats in Havana, has been painfully halting and partial.

The two countries' military and intelligence relations—cause of concern among some US politicians—are, understandably, shrouded in secrecy. Their defense ministers exchange visits every couple years, typically reiterating public pledges of friendship and cooperation. During a visit by Cuban minister of the Revolutionary Armed Forces Leopoldo Cintra Frías in 2018, his Chinese counterpart, State Councilor Wei Fenghe, said China was "ready to work with the Cuban side to continue building up military-to-military strategic mutual trust and practical cooperation" in pursuit of peace and development (State Council 2018). Neither provided any details, and observers in Havana have identified no significant shifts in training or hardware. A US senator in 2016 alleged that China had a "listening station" in Bejucal, where the Soviets had one in the past, but publicly available evidence of such facilities is lacking.

Might Relations Change?

Some of the unifying factors of the Cuba-China relationship, such as the desire to limit US influence in their regions, are almost certain to carry into the future. Both countries will condemn US "imperialism," "hegemony," and "intervention." For sixty years, China has supported Cuba's efforts to resist the comprehensive US economic embargo—the *bloqueo*—and US efforts to attack the government's legitimacy through diplomacy, radio broadcasts, and "democracy promotion" regime-change programs. For its part, Cuba will continue to speak out for China. When US presidents Donald Trump and Joe Biden took positions suggesting a shift away from the US "One China" policy, Havana joined Beijing's complaints. Both countries like to poke Washington in the eye on other issues when doing so does not compromise other diplomatic objectives.

China's Belt and Road Initiative (BRI) appears likely to sustain, and maybe increase incrementally, trade and investment. Cuba was one of the first countries in Latin America to join it, formalized when President Díaz-Canel signed a Memorandum of Understanding in 2018. Data on the impact of BRI is incomplete, but public information suggests some potential for expanding cooperation. Several communications projects appear to have taken off, including expansion of mobile phone networks and public Wi-Fi hotspots. When Cuba joined the BRI Energy Partnership (BREP) in October 2021, Chinese vice-premier Han Zheng emphasized the group would undertake international "joint efforts . . . to promote green and low-carbon energy transformation and deepen cooperation on nuclear electricity, new-energy generation, and smart energy" (Xinhua 2021). A few projects in Cuba reported since then, including several biomass power plants funded by China Eximbank, suggest more will come as cost-efficient ways of addressing Cuba's energy problem on a local level.

Several factors can alter the broader relationship, however. Although both countries have exercised great caution in their public statements, the gap between their two systems could grow to a point that trade stumbles even more. The Chinese—like watching a Cuban mechanic fixing a 1950s Chevy sedan—admire Cuban ingenuity, audacity, and discipline in resisting US policies, but they surely wish Cuba would reform its economy and pay its bills on time. As others in Latin America advance their relations with Beijing, this impatience will probably increase.

Nevertheless, other policies in Beijing and Havana could steer them toward closer relations. The Chinese Communist Party's selection of Chairman Xi to serve a third five-year term in October 2022 as he strengthens the party, clamps down on dissent, and increases efforts to exert China's influence vis-à-vis the United States suggests at least some openness to greater Chinese generosity. This could take the form of increased credits, assistance, and joint diplomatic efforts to resist US efforts to hem in China and to effect regime change in Cuba. Havana, on the other hand, could undertake internal reforms, starting with the *Lineamientos* the party approved in 2011, to improve the economy and its ability to trade.

Shifts in US policy toward Cuba could affect Cuba-China relations dramatically. If Washington resumes the normalization process that President Obama started in 2014, Trump suspended in 2017, and Biden has been reluctant to restore (so far), the influx of travelers and other revenues would fuel the private sector as a motor for Cuba to open up, as it began to do during the late Obama period, and enable it to trade more with everyone, including China—especially if Chairman Xi loosens the terms of trade.

China's global role, tensions among the great powers, and vexing problems such as climate change all represent potentially powerful drivers of change in Cuba-China relations. Barring such game-changers, the pattern established since the collapse of the Soviet Union seems likely to persist: heavy doses of political solidarity, many promises of collaboration (some of which are fulfilled), waiting for the United States to accept the failure of its embargo, and pragmatism in trade.

References

Asia News Monitor. 2020. "China: Xi Jinping Exchanges Messages with First Secretary of the Central Committee of the Communist Party of Cuba Raul Castro Ruz and President Miguel Diaz-Canel of Cuba [. . .]." October 7. Accessed at https://www.proquest.com/docview/2448644794.

Blanco Silva, Alberto. 2020. "Cuba-China: La amistad borra la distancia." Cubadebate, September 27. Accessed at http://www.cubadebate.cu/temas/politica-temas/2020/09/27/cuba-china-la-amistad-borra-la-distancia.

Castro, Fidel. 1966. "Castro Statement on Cuban-CPR Relations, February 6, 1966." Accessed at http://lanicutexas.edu/project/Castro/db/1966/19660206.html.

———. 1970. Speech to the Councils of State and Ministers at the "National Act of Solidarity with Vietnam and Condemnation of Chinese Aggression." Council of State records, February 21. Accessed at http://www.cuba.cu/gobierno/discursos/1979/esp/f210279e.html.

Cheng, Yinghong. 2007. "Fidel Castro and 'China's Lesson for Cuba': A Chinese Perspective." *The China Quarterly* 189 (March 2007): 24–42. Published online by Cambridge University Press at https://doi.org/10.1017/S0305741006000786.

Ellis, Evan. 2021. "Chinese Engagement in the Dominican Republic: An Update." Global Americans, May 7. Accessed at https://theglobalamericans.org/2021/05/chinese-engagement-in-the-dominican-republic-an-update.

Foreign Ministry of China. 2021. "Xi Jinping Speaks with First Secretary of the Communist Party of Cuba Central Committee and President Miguel Diaz-Canel on the Phone." May 7. Accessed at https://www.fmprc.gov.cn/ce/cgla/eng/topnews/t1874080.htm.

———. 2022. "China-Cuba Relations." Accessed May 7, 2023, at https://www.fmprc.gov.cn/web/gjhdq_676201/gj_676203/bmz_679954/1206_680302/sbgx_680306.

Frank, Marc. 2021. "Cuba's Imports from China Slump 40 Percent in 2020, Extending Long Decline." Reuters, February 5. Accessed at https://www.reuters.com/article/cuba-china-trade/cubas-imports-from-china-slump-40-in-2020-extending-long-decline-idUSL1N2K919P.

Malik, A., B. Parks, B. Russell, J. Lin, K. Walsh, K. Solomon, S. Zhang, T. Elston, and S. Goodman. 2021. *Banking on the Belt and Road: Insights from a New Global Dataset of 13,427 Chinese Development Projects*. Williamsburg, VA: AidData at William & Mary. Accessed at https://www.aiddata.org/publications/banking-on-the-belt-and-road.

Myers, Margaret, and Ricardo Barrios. 2021. "How China Ranks Its Partners in LAC." Inter-American Dialogue, February 3. Accessed at https://www.thedialogue.org/blogs/2021/02/how-china-ranks-its-partners-in-lac.

Ng, Rudolph. 2014. "The Chinese Commission to Cuba (1874): Reexamining International Relations in the Nineteenth Century from a Transcultural Perspective." *Transcultural Studies* 5, no. 2: 39–62. Accessed at https://doi.org/10.11588/ts.2014.2.13009.

Noticias Cubanas. 2022. "Cuba define su relación con China como de 'largo plazo' y 'alta prioridad.'" March 23. Accessed at https://noticiascubanas.com/2022/03/23/cuba-define-su-relacion-con-china-como-de-largo-plazo-y-alta-prioridad.

ONEI (National Office of Statistics and Information). 2021. *Anuario Estadístico de Cuba 2021*. Accessed at http://www.onei.gob.cu/node/18491.

Sánchez Ramírez, Pablo Telman. 2012. "Recent Developments in Sino-Cuban Relations: Particularities and Advances." *Latin America Policy* 3, no 2: 259–71. Accessed at https://onlinelibrary.wiley.com/doi/abs/10.1111/j.2041-7373.2012.00073.x.

Small, Andrew. 2008. "Fidel's Choice." *New York Times*, November 27. Accessed at https://www.nytimes.com/2008/11/27/opinion/27iht-edsmall.3.18204430.html.

State Council of the People's Republic of China. 2018. "China, Cuba Pledge to Deepen Military Ties." November 24. Accessed at http://english.www.gov.cn/state_council/state_councilors/2018/11/24/content_281476403871348.htm.

USC Annenberg. 2009. "China's Policy Paper on Latin America and the Caribbean." April 20. Accessed at https://china.usc.edu/chinas-policy-paper-latin-america-and-caribbean.

Xinhua. 2021. "Vice-premier Stresses Belt and Road Energy Cooperation." October 19. Accessed at https://english.www.gov.cn/statecouncil/hanzheng/202110/19/content_WS616dfbe9c6d0df57f98e3734.html.

Zuo, Pin. 2010. "A Survey of the Relationship between Cuba and China: A Chinese Perspective." The Association for the Study of the Cuban Economy. November 30. https://www.ascecuba.org/asce_proceedings/survey-relationship-cuba-china-chinese-perspective.

CHAPTER 17

Cuba and a Changing Western Hemisphere

Philip Brenner

At the start of the twenty-first century, Latin America was the region that offered Cuba the greatest promise of mutually beneficial relations. Nearly every country in the region experienced meaningful economic growth between 1990 and 2010. By 2009, all of the countries in the Western Hemisphere except the United States had established diplomatic relations with Cuba. After pressure from Latin American and Caribbean countries in 2012 influenced President Barack Obama to break with prior US policy, even the United States began to engage with Cuba constructively. Those negotiations led to the restoration of diplomatic relations between the two countries.[1] Yet within the next decade, Cuba's relations with many of the region's countries took a roller-coaster ride. This chapter examines the ups and downs of Cuba's foreign relations with Latin America and the Caribbean, which appeared once again to be on an upswing at the end of 2022.

Latin America Turns Left

A leftward turn in Latin American politics at the turn of the twenty-first century dramatically benefited Cuba. Hugo Chávez's election in 1998 as Venezuela's president was followed by the victories of Brazil's Luiz Inácio Lula da Silva in 2002 and Argentina's Néstor Kirchner in 2003. The change in governments was one reason that Latin American countries elected Cuba to hold one of the region's six seats on the United Nations Human Rights Commission in March 2003, despite Cuba's harsh sentencing of seventy-five people the prior month. (At the time, the General Assembly voted by region in choosing the fifty-three members of the commission, which was replaced by the UN Human Rights Council in 2006.) The vote was a clear rebuke to the United States, which had lobbied against Cuba's selection.[2] Subsequently, Uruguay's Tabaré Ramón Vázquez was elected in 2004, Ecuador's Rafael Correa in 2005, and Chile's Michelle Bachelet and Bolivia's Evo Morales in 2006.

The Cuban-Venezuelan association was held together by three interconnected ties: the personal relationship between Fidel Castro and Chávez, the mutually beneficial exchange of goods and services between the two countries, and the shared political goals for the hemisphere of the Cuban and Venezuelan leaders.[3] Chávez looked to Castro as his spiritual mentor and once in office turned to the Cuba leader for advice. He told Larry King in 2009 that Castro is "like a father to me, like a father, a political father."[4]

In October 2000, Venezuela began to sell oil to some South American countries and Cuba at a price that was one-third lower than the world market price. The purchases could be made with credit; the interest rate was 2 percent and the loan would be due in fifteen years. By 2001 Cuba was importing more oil from Venezuela than it had imported from the Soviet Union in 1990. Under a 2005 agreement, Venezuela sold 53,000 barrels of oil daily to Cuba at a subsidized rate of $27 per barrel. Cuba paid for oil, in part, by sending sports trainers, teachers, and doctors and nurses to Venezuela. As a result, Venezuela became Cuba's largest trading partner until 2016.

More than three million Venezuelans benefited from the Barrio Adentro Deportivo (Sports in the Neighborhood) program, and Cuban coaches trained 68 of the 109 Venezuelan athletes who participated in the 2008 Beijing Olympics.[5] Teachers in Cuba's Misión Robinson program contributed to the reduction of illiteracy in Venezuela, and the doctors helped Venezuela establish a medical program for the poor, Barrio Adentro (Inside the Neighborhood). Cuba sent 30,000 medical personnel to Venezuela, began training a planned 40,000 doctors, and provided eye operations to more than 100,000 Venezuelans though Operación Milagro (Operation Miracle).[6]

Operación Milagro later expanded to other countries in Latin America and had "restored sight to two million people" by 2014.[7] The medical services Cubans provided in Brazil, Bolivia, Haiti, Jamaica, Venezuela, and Ecuador brought care to rural communities and urban pockets of poverty that had never seen a doctor. In turn, it strengthened the popularity of leaders in those countries, which reinforced their inclination to support Cuba.

Cuba also engaged Brazil in several ways. It established a joint venture with Odebrecht, the Brazilian engineering conglomerate, to modernize the Port of Mariel at a cost of $1 billion. Cuban officials envisioned that the port would be a hub for commerce with both North and South America. In addition, following Lula da Silva's assumption of the presidency in 2003, Brazil began to rely on Cuban doctors to provide medical care in the country's poorest areas. Brazil's political support also was critical in Cuba gaining full membership in 2008 in the Rio Group, an association of twenty-three Western Hemispheric countries that served as a semiformal forum to discuss regional issues.

Three years later, the Rio group institutionalized itself as the Community of Latin American and Caribbean States (CELAC in the Spanish acronym). Its membership included every country in the Western Hemisphere except Canada and the United States. CELAC presented a potential challenge to the Organization of American States (OAS) as the main forum for handling hemispheric issues. Just prior to the group's 2013 summit, the EU announced that CELAC, not the OAS, would be its counterpart organization for bi-regional negotiations, significantly increasing CELAC's importance. The organization's 2014 summit meeting was held in Havana, because the members had chosen Cuba to cochair CELAC. Their choice was meant as a not-too-subtle message to Washington, which had prevented Cuba from participating in a 2012 OAS-led hemispheric summit.

Also meeting in Havana at the same time were peace negotiators from the Colombian government and the Revolutionary Armed Forces of Colombia (FARC), the main insurgent group in the country. Their negotiations began in mid-November 2012 in Norway and quickly moved to Havana where Cuban diplomats played an essential role in helping to bring about an agreement four years later to end the civil war. Cuba also contributed to the settlement by offering 1,000 medical school scholarships to Colombians.[8]

At the start of the millennium, Cuba and Venezuela also began to implement an ambitious project, as Fidel Castro described it in October 2000, "to unite the Latin American and Caribbean nations and to struggle for a world economic order that brings more justice to all peoples."[9] What started with the sale of oil and free medical care emerged in 2004 as ALBA, the Spanish acronym for Bolivarian Alternative for the Peoples of Our America. (The name was changed in 2009 to the Bolivarian Alliance for the Peoples of Our America.) Aimed at competing with the US-proposed Free Trade Area of the Americas, ALBA sought to economically integrate Latin American and Caribbean countries. It also created a development bank and served as a coordinating mechanism for development projects. While only eleven countries in the Western Hemisphere were members of ALBA at its height, its projects extended to many other nations in the region.

The various ways that Cuba interacted positively with other countries in the region—through its medical assistance, education, and athletic programs and engagement in CELAC and the Caribbean Community (CARICOM), as well as via popular culture—contributed to a key underpinning of Cuba's foreign policy, its so-called soft power. Soft power is a term that connotes the ability of a country to influence others by example rather than by coercion. Cuba's soft power contributed to a positive image that enabled Cuba "to be seen as a trusted and valued partner in many international arenas and institutions," despite its lack of Western liberal democracy, as historians Julia Sweig and Michael Bustamante observed.[10]

Small states historically have sought to use international organizations as a means of enhancing their power vis-à-vis a large powerful neighbor.[11] Certainly Cuba's most notable recent success in relation to the United States was gaining participation in the 2015 Summit of the Americas. In effect, the political support that Latin American countries gave to Cuba was enough to counter the hard power—military strength and financial levers—the United States traditionally used to dominate the hemisphere. It was an instance of what political scientist Tom Long terms "collective foreign policy," where a small country can influence a larger one as a result of its "ability to win international allies and to work with other small and medium states."[12]

A Changed Context

By 2020 circumstances in Latin America had changed in ways that were less favorable to Cuba. Between 2013 and 2020, Venezuela's economy declined significantly due to a drop in world oil prices, corruption, the government's failure to maintain the petroleum industry's infrastructure, the out-migration of technical experts, and international sanctions. It was no longer able to provide the same level of subsidies to Cuba or to support ALBA, and its shipments of oil to the island declined by 50 percent. By 2017 Cuba already had turned to Algeria to replace some of the oil it could no longer obtain from Venezuela.[13]

Corruption also led to the downfall of Brazilian governments that had good relations with Cuba. In 2018, Brazilian president-elect Jair Bolsonaro effectively ended the program of Cuban medical assistance by demanding doctors meet untenable conditions. In turn, Cuba removed 8,000 doctors from underserved Brazilian areas. Elections in Chile, Ecuador, Peru, Argentina, and Colombia, as well as a coup in Bolivia, also brought conservatives to power who sought to gain favor with the administration of President Donald Trump by distancing their countries from Cuba. As a result Cuban medical missions departed from Bolivia and Ecuador.

Cuba's decreased engagement with the region is evident from the decline in its trade with Latin America. In 2018, 13.4 percent of Cuba's imports came from Latin America and the Caribbean; in 2019 it had dropped to 2.8 percent.[14] Venezuela had been Cuba's top trading partner until 2016, when China replaced it.

ALBA's success depended on Venezuela's financial support, which it derived from the sale of oil. In 2016 Venezuela's oil production declined by 60 percent. Consider that Venezuela's oil exports to Latin America totaled $2.38 billion in 2013 and only $154 million in 2019.[15] By 2019, Ecuador and Bolivia had withdrawn their memberships in ALBA, and ALBA's influence in the region—and by extension, Cuba's influence—declined.

Cuba's decreased engagement along with the region's turn to the right naturally undermined its famed "soft power." This is evident from the change in Latin American public opinion about Cuba between 2015 and 2020. Surveys done by Latinobarómetro showed that favorable attitudes toward Cuba declined in nine of the seventeen countries surveyed, while favorable attitudes toward Cuba increased in only four countries.

The one bright spot in Cuba's relations with the region was the Caribbean. Cuba began sending doctors to Haiti at no cost in 1998. By 2022, they had performed 660,000 surgeries and carried out 192,414 deliveries, and were on the front lines in Haiti during the COVID-19 pandemic.[16] In all, Cuba sent 500 medical personnel to countries in the Caribbean in 2020 in response to the pandemic. This was one of the reasons Caribbean leaders repeatedly cited in recent years as they called for an end to US sanctions against Cuba.[17] In 2020, the prime ministers of CARICOM issued a declaration that asserted "their deep appreciation for the medical assistance provided by Cuba to the Member States of the Community over the years that helped build their health sectors to the benefit and wellbeing of their people. . . . They repudiated the statement that this medical assistance given by the Cubans was a form of human trafficking."[18]

In addition, Cuba was able to locate a few new sources of capital in the region, from the Development Bank of Latin America and the Central American Bank for Economic Integration, in 2017.[19]

A Pink-ish Tide Reemerges

Some notable changes in the region seemed to offer auspicious conditions for improved Cuban relations with Latin America. Elections in Chile, Colombia, and Brazil in 2022 brought progressives to power, and this followed the removal in 2021 of right-wing governments in Bolivia, Ecuador, and Peru.

In mid-2021, Mexican president Andrés Manuel López Obrador signaled a renewed Mexican interest in pressuring the United States to reduce or abolish sanctions against Cuba. In belittling President Joe Biden's claim that the United States "stands with the Cuban people," the Mexican leader said, "The truth is that if one wanted to help Cuba, the first thing that should be done is to suspend the blockade of Cuba as the majority of countries in the world are asking."[20] Even though López Obrador sought to work with the United States on trade and migration issues, he again denounced US policy toward Cuba as "genocidal" in May 2022 and then pointedly absented himself from the US-hosted Summit of the Americas because the United States refused to invite Cuba, Venezuela, and Nicaragua.[21]

Most of the countries in the Western Hemisphere also registered their opposition to US policy by refusing to endorse the Biden administration's denunciation of Cuban government arrests in response to demonstrations on July 11, 2021.[22] In October 2022, the CELAC foreign ministers demanded that the United States remove Cuba from its list of state sponsors of terrorism.[23] The designation significantly increased the cost of Cuba's international financial transactions and made it difficult for citizens from hemispheric countries to enter the United States if they had also visited Cuba. The next month, eighteen former Latin American and Caribbean leaders sent "a letter to U.S. President Joe Biden asking the United States to remove its six-decade embargo on Cuba."[24]

It was unclear whether the Biden administration perceived these various demands as "pressure," especially as it gave little attention to the region except for problems related to migration and drug trafficking. However, Cuban–Latin American relations gained greater importance for the United States toward the end of 2022, as President Biden's November appointment of former senator Christopher Dodd as Special Presidential Advisor for the Americas indicated. Three factors stand out as possible explanations for the renewed US attention to both Cuba and Latin America.

First, the new Colombian and Brazilian presidents seemed to have judged that good relations with Cuba were in their countries' national interests. Consider that Cuba's ambassador to Colombia was the first emissary with whom President Gustavo Petro met. During a joint press conference with US Secretary of State Antony Blinken, the Colombian leader praised Cuba for serving as an interlocutor in the Colombian government's negotiations with the National Liberation Army (ELN) and called Cuba's inclusion on the US list of state sponsors of terrorism "an injustice."[25] In the case of Brazil, it appeared that President Lula da Silva hoped to restore a leadership role in the Western Hemisphere for his country, particularly through institutions such as CELAC. US sanctions against Cuba served as impediments to the cohesive hemispheric relations the Brazilian leader sought in his second term of office. In addition, it seemed likely that he would be requesting the return of some Cuban doctors, though not as many as had served in Brazil until 2018, to provide medical care in areas where Brazilian doctors had been reluctant to work.

Second, Cuban and Venezuelan migrants, not Central Americans, had become the largest group trying to enter the United States through Mexico in 2022. This new wave led the Biden administration to resume migration talks with Cuba that President Trump had discontinued.[26] In addition, it may have led the Biden administration to push the Venezuelan opposition to resume talks in Mexico with the Venezuelan government.

The third element was China. Whether or not China's investments in and trade with Latin America were a serious threat to US national security, the conventional wisdom in Washington had become that China's engagement with Latin America posed a danger.[27] In part, this is because President Biden saw the world from a Cold War, bi-polar framework. (As British historian G. M. Young remarked in 1943, in a statement often attributed to Napoleon Bonaparte, that to understand the character of a public person, one needs to look at what was happening in the world when the person was twenty years old.[28]) The president tended to conflate Russian and Chinese positions as a singular threat to the United States. The perceived Chinese threat thus increased the region's importance and made paying attention to Latin Americans more important.

Future Challenges Await

Cuba's return to better relations with Latin America in the early 2020s was unlikely to follow the pattern of the earlier period in the century, because the earlier context was not neatly reproduced in the latter period.

First, economic conditions in the region were less favorable in 2023 than they were just ten years earlier. The COVID-19 pandemic had negatively impacted every country, resulting in negative or minimal growth. For Latin America and the Caribbean as a whole, gross domestic product declined from US$5.83 billion in 2017 to US$4.74 billion in 2020. While it grew in 2021, it was still below the 2017 mark.[29] Notably, the UN Economic Commission for Latin America and the Caribbean estimated that regional exports for 2023 were likely to decline because "the outlook for world trade in 2023 is not favorable."[30] As a consequence, countries that could afford medical and educational services from Cuba earlier were less able to purchase them in 2023, even if they wanted them. Consider, as an example, the difficulties President Lula da Silva had during his first weeks in office as the Brazilian legislature resisted budgeting funds for his progressive social agenda.[31]

Second, the personal ties and respect Fidel and Raúl Castro had with regional leaders did not carry over to President Miguel Díaz-Canel. The kind of adoration that Hugo Chávez expressed was no longer evident, even from avowedly sympathetic leaders. Chilean president Gabriel Boric, for example, did not hesitate to criticize human rights violations committed by Cuban authorities in the wake of the July 2021 demonstrations.[32]

Third, Cuba's outreach to China, Russia, and Iran—which Cuban leaders judge is necessary for the Revolution's survival—could create difficulties for some countries in Latin America and the Caribbean as they seek to engage with the United States in pursuit of their own national interests. To the extent that US foreign policy fully embraces a cold war, zero-sum framework, under which it would perceive any country as either fully "with or against" the United States, it may pressure countries in the region to distance themselves from Cuba.

In short, as Cuba's roller-coaster relationship with Latin America returned to its previous heights, the track on which it traveled was clouded in a fog of new circumstances that make the journey less congenial than it had been before.

Notes

1. William M. LeoGrande and Peter Kornbluh, epilogue to *Back Channel to Cuba: The Hidden History of Negotiations between Washington and Havana* (Chapel Hill: University of North Carolina Press, 2015). Also see Ben Rhodes, *The World as It Is: A Memoir of the Obama White House* (New York: Random House, 2018), 209–16.

2. Ari Fleischer, "Press Briefing," Office of the Press Secretary, The White House, April 29, 2003, accessed at https://georgewbush-whitehouse.archives.gov/news/releases/2003/04/20030429-3.html#2.

3. Max Azicri, "The Castro-Chávez Alliance," *Latin American Perspectives* 36, no. 1 (January 2009): 108. Also see Carlos Romero, "Venezuela and Cuba," in *Cuban Foreign Policy Transformation under Raúl Castro*, ed. H. Michael Erisman and John M. Kirk (Lanham, MD: Rowman & Littlefield, 2018).

4. Hugo Chávez, "Interview," *Larry King Live*, CNN, September 24, 2009, accessed January at https://transcripts.cnn.com/show/lkl/date/2009-09-24/segment/01.

5. Carlos A. Romero, "South-South Cooperation between Venezuela and Cuba," in *Special Report on South-South Cooperation, South-South Cooperation: A Challenge to the Aid System?* (Quezon City, Philippines: Reality of Aid Network, 2010), 108, 110, accessed at http://www.realityofaid.org/wp-content/uploads/2013/02/ROA-SSDC-Special-ReportEnglish.pdf.

6. Philip Brenner and Peter Eisner, *Cuba Libre: A 500-Year Quest for Independence* (Lanham, MD: Rowman & Littlefield, 2018), 286.

7. John M. Kirk, "Cuban Medical Internationalism Under Raúl Castro," in *A Contemporary Cuba Reader: The Revolution Under Raúl Castro*, ed. Philip Brenner, Marguerite Rose Jiménez, John M. Kirk, and William M. LeoGrande (Lanham, MD: Rowman & Littlefield, 2014), 258. Also see H. Michael Erisman and John M. Kirk, "Cuban Medical Internationalism and 'Soft Power,'" in the current volume.

8. "Cuba Offers Colombia 1,000 Medical School Scholarships," Associated Press, March 16, 2017, accessed at https://apnews.com/827ae08af1144c8688bcc3732f5e5a1f/cuba-offers-colombia-1000-medical-school-scholarships.

9. Fidel Castro Ruz, "Key Address to a Solemn Session of the National Assembly," Caracas, Venezuela, October 27, 2000, accessed at http://www.cuba.cu/gobierno/discursos/2000/ing/f271000i.htm.

10. Michael J. Bustamante and Julia E. Sweig, "Cuban Public Diplomacy," in *A Contemporary Cuba Reader*, 269.

11. Tom Long, *Latin America Confronts the United States: Asymmetry and Influence* (New York: Cambridge University Press, 2015), 12–18; Tom Long, *A Small State's Guide to Influence in World Politics* (New York: Oxford University Press, 2022), chap. 3.

12. Long, *Latin America Confronts the United States*, 224.

13. "Algeria Sends More Oil to Cuba as Venezuelan Supplies Fall," Reuters, January 10, 2018, accessed at https://www.reuters.com/article/us-algeria-oil-cuba/algeria-sends-more-oil-to -cuba-as-venezuelan-supplies-fall-idUSKBN1EZ28O.

14. Economic Commission for Latin America and the Caribbean, *International Trade Outlook for Latin America and the Caribbean, 2019*, LC/PUB.2019/20-P (Santiago: ECLAC, 2019), accessed at https://repositorio.cepal.org/bitstream/handle/11362/44919/6/S1900747 _en.pdf.

15. Organization of Export Oil Countries, "Where Does Venezuela Export To?" 2013 and 2019, accessed January 15, 2023, at https://oec.world/en/visualize/tree_map/hs92/export/ven /show/all/2013 (2013) and https://oec.world/en/visualize/tree_map/hs92/export/ven/show/all /2019 (2019).

16. Emily J. Kirk and John M. Kirk, "Cuban Medical Cooperation in Haiti: One of the World's Best-Kept Secrets," *Cuban Studies* 46 (2010): 166; "The Cuban Brigade Celebrates 23 Years of Care in Haiti, *Haiti Libre*, December 12, 2021, accessed at https://www.haitilibre .com/en/news-35493-haiti-health-the-cuban-brigade-celebrates-23-years-of-care-in-haiti.html.

17. Wazim Mowla, "A Cuban Lifeline to CARICOM," *Global Americans*, May 7, 2020, accessed at https://theglobalamericans.org/2020/05/a-cuban-lifeline-to-caricom; "Caribbean Community Countries Call for an Immediate End to US Financial Blockade against Cuba, Vowing to Enhance Cooperation," *Global Times*, December 8, 2022, accessed at https://www .globaltimes.cn/page/202212/1281419.shtml.

18. CARICOM, "Communiqué Issued at Conclusion of 31st CARICOM Intersessional Meeting," February 20, 2020, accessed at https://caricom.org/communique-issued-at-conclusion -of-31st-caricom-intersessional-meeting.

19. "Firman primer acuerdo de colaboración Cuba y Banco de Desarrollo de América Latina," Radio Rebelde, September 2, 2016, accessed at http://www.cuba.cu/economia/2016 -09-02/firman-primer-acuerdo-de-colaboracion-cuba-y-banco-de-desarrollo-de-america-latina /33110; "Cuba Joins the Central American Bank for Economic Integration," *Granma*, August 29, 2017, accessed at https://en.granma.cu/cuba/2017-08-29/cuba-joins-the-central-american -bank-for-economic-integration.

20. Dave Graham, "Mexico President Calls for End to Cuba Trade Embargo after Protests," Reuters, July 12, 2021, accessed at www.reuters.com/world/americas/mexico-president-calls -end-cuba-trade-embargo-after-protests-2021-07-12.

21. Kylie Madry, "Mexican President Slams U.S. Embargo on Cuba as 'genocidal policy,'" Reuters, May 17, 2022, accessed at https://www.reuters.com/world/americas/mexican-president -calls-us-embargo-cuba-genocidal-policy-2022-05-17. Also see Oscar Lopez, "Mexico President Will Not Attend Americas Summit in Blow to Biden," *New York Times*, June 6, 2022, accessed at https://www.nytimes.com/2022/06/06/world/americas/mexico-obrador-americas-summit .html.

22. Sarah Marsh, "Latin America's Resurgent Left and Caribbean Spurn U.S. Policy on Cuba," Reuters, August 2, 2021, accessed at https://www.reuters.com/world/americas/latin -americas-resurgent-left-caribbean-spurn-us-policy-cuba-2021-08-02.

23. Telesur, "CELAC Demands US to Remove Cuba from Terrorist Sponsors List," October 27, 2022, accessed at https://www.telesurenglish.net/news/CELAC-Demands-US-to -Remove-Cuba-From-Terrorist-Sponsors-List-20221027-0004.html.

24. Megan Janetsky, "Former Latin American Leaders Urge U.S. Change on Cuba," AP News, November 1, 2022, accessed at https://apnews.com/article/hurricanes-biden-colombia -caribbean-united-states-222dbeb17eb63388b394ef835427d8cb.

25. Office of the Spokesperson, US Department of State, "Secretary Antony J. Blinken and Colombian President Gustavo Petro at a Joint Press Availability," October 3, 2022, accessed at

https://www.state.gov/secretary-antony-j-blinken-and-colombian-president-gustavo-petro-at-a
-joint-press-availability.

26. Karen DeYoung and Nick Miroff, "U.S., Cuba Hold Talks over Migration for the First
Time in Four Years," *Washington Post*, April 21, 2022, accessed at https://www.washingtonpost
.com/national-security/2022/04/21/us-cuba-migration-border.

27. Mark Sullivan and Thomas Lum, "China's Engagement with Latin America and the
Caribbean," in *In Focus*, Congressional Research Service, Report No. IF10982, December 28,
2022, accessed at https://crsreports.congress.gov/product/pdf/IF/IF10982.

28. George Malcolm Young, "Burke," Annual Lecture on a Master Mind, Henriette Hertz
Trust of the British Academy, February 17, 1943, accessed at https://gutenberg.ca/ebooks/
younggm-burke/younggm-burke-00-h.html.

29. The World Bank, "GDP (Current US$)—Latin America & Caribbean," accessed January 14, 2023, at https://data.worldbank.org/indicator/NY.GDP.MKTP.CD?locations=ZJ.

30. Economic Commission for Latin America and the Caribbean, introduction to *International Trade Outlook for Latin America and the Caribbean, 2022*, LC/PUB.2022/23-P (Santiago: ECLAC, 2023), accessed at www.cepal.org/en/publications/48651-international-trade
-outlook-latin-america-and-caribbean-2022-challenge-boosting.

31. "Big Plans, Not Much Money: Brazil's New President Faces a Fiscal Crunch and a
Fickle Congress," *The Economist*, December 31, 2022, accessed at https://www.economist.com
/the-americas/2022/12/31/brazils-new-president-faces-a-fiscal-crunch-and-a-fickle-congress.

32. Jon Lee Anderson, "Letter from Santiago: Can Chile's Young President Reimagine
the Latin American Left?" *The New Yorker*, June 13, 2022, accessed at www.newyorker.com
/magazine/2022/06/13/can-chiles-young-president-reimagine-the-latin-american-left.

CHAPTER 18

Cuban Medical Internationalism and "Soft Power"

H. Michael Erisman and John M. Kirk

> Of all the so-called developing nations, Cuba has by far the best health system. And their outreach program to other nations is unequaled anywhere.
>
> —President Jimmy Carter

This chapter focuses on Cuban medical internationalism in recent years and asks to what extent it can be seen to have influenced diplomatic relations with recipient countries. There is of course no way to determine precisely the extent of such influence—but at the same time influence can be inferred, or at least understood. And certainly, there is a great deal of appreciation expressed for Cuban medical collaboration by world leaders—as well as clear examples of support for Havana.

There are two sections to this chapter. The first analyzes the nature of Cuban medical internationalism, providing some background information, and then focuses on the post-Castro years (and specifically Cuba's international role in the COVID-19 campaign). The second section analyzes the essence of soft power and reflects on the extent to which Cuban medical cooperation impacts its foreign relations.

Some Examples of Cuban Medical Internationalism

Cuban medical internationalism has a long tradition, starting in 1960 when the first mission headed to Chile following an earthquake. In 1963 a larger delegation went to newly independent Algeria, to help establish a national medical service. Since then, Cuba has been involved in hundreds of related initiatives. In recent years readers might remember Cuba's leadership in dealing with the earthquake in Haiti (2010) or the Ebola outbreak in West Africa (2014). In 2005, when Hurricane Katrina took place in New Orleans, Cuba offered to send 1,200 specialists in emergency medicine and thirty-two tons of medicines to help the local population. From dealing with tsunamis in Asia to flooding in Mexico, earthquakes in Pakistan and Guatemala to cholera epidemics in Africa, and most recently in sending medical missions to dozens of countries to fight COVID-19, Cuban response to such emergencies has been widely lauded in the developing world. It has also been largely ignored by media in the industrialized world.

There are well-established Cuban programs in medical internationalism that deserve to be noted. Among these are the establishment of the Latin American Medical School (ELAM) in Havana in 1998, where by 2020 free medical training had been provided to over 30,000 students from 118 developing countries (Reed 2020). Some 200 US students had also graduated as physicians from ELAM. Also significant is the ophthalmological program, Operación Milagro, which has provided free eye care to over 3.2 million patients, mainly in Latin America and the Caribbean (Noda Alonso 2021). Following the nuclear implosion in 1986 at the Chernobyl nuclear reactor in Ukraine, Havana provided free medical treatment in Cuba to 26,000 people (mainly Ukrainian children) from the affected region. And finally, one can mention the Henry Reeve Brigade, established in 2005, which has provided medical assistance to five continents affected by natural emergencies and epidemics. (Henry Reeve was a US citizen who was killed fighting for Cuba's independence from Spain in 1878.) In all, 13,467 specialists have participated in these missions, according to the minister of public health (Portal Miranda 2022).

This is an extraordinary record, especially for a small (pop. 11.2 million) developing country like Cuba. In all, since the inception of Cuba's medical internationalism program, some 605,000 personnel have served approximately two billion patients in 165 countries (Díaz Ballaga 2022). At the time of the COVID-19 outbreak there were already approximately 24,000 Cuban medical personnel working abroad, and in May of 2022 there were over 26,000 medical personnel working in fifty-eight nations, mainly in the Global South (Prensa Latina 2022a).

Cuba can do this because it has a surplus of doctors and nurses. In 2020, for example, it had 103,835 doctors (or 108 patients per physician) and 85,000 nurses—roughly three times more per capita than the United States (MINSAP 2021). There are ideological, historical, political, and commercial reasons for Cuba's medical internationalism program, and Havana is able to mobilize such large numbers of personnel because it has the staff to do so.

During the years under study, there have been many examples of diverse medical collaboration from Cuba. Cuba has set up vaccine and pharmaceutical production facilities in several countries, especially China and Iran. In September 2022 Cuba agreed to a technology transfer program with Nigeria to produce vaccines and has sent specialists to Ghana, Angola, Zambia, Equatorial Guinea, Benin, and Gabon to deal with malaria and dengue. In Qatar it maintains a hospital, with 475 Cubans working as doctors, nurses, and technicians. At the time of COVID-19, Cuba sent 346 members of the Henry Reeve Brigade to combat the pandemic there.

It has also established medical schools in several African nations, and has sent vaccines against COVID-19 to various countries, including Mexico, Venezuela, Iran, Nicaragua, Syria, and Vietnam. Following the August 2021 earthquake in Haiti, over 250 Cuban members of the Henry Reeve Brigade flew in to provide assistance. In July

2022 some 594 new medical graduates who had studied in Cuba returned to South Africa. (This Nelson Mandela/Fidel Castro Program has trained 2,556 doctors since its inception in 1997.) That same month the government of Jamaica issued a special recognition of the 500 Cuban medical personnel who had worked on the island during the COVID-19 pandemic. In May 2022 an agreement was signed between Barbados and Cuba to establish a permanent medical presence there—following the successful Cuban role in dealing with the pandemic in Bridgetown.

In terms of providing medical support to countries affected by the COVID-19 pandemic, some 4,700 members of the Henry Reeve Brigade participated, working in forty-two countries. In all there were fifty-eight missions, since some countries, such as Italy, received more than one Cuban delegation (Prensa Latina 2022a). The case of Cuban medical support in both Crema and Turin in Italy illustrates well Cuba's role. Italy asked for assistance, first in the Lombardy region of Italy and later in Turin. As the Cubans were leaving Turin following three months of working there, the mayor thanked them for their support: "It is the victory of the values represented by those who came from the other side of the ocean, of solidarity and generosity" (Frank et al. 2020).

Two of the largest post-COVID programs were announced in late 2022—in the Calabria region of Italy, where 497 medical personnel would be posted for three years, and Mexico, 610 doctors for three years. Cuba's earlier role in the COVID-19 campaigns in Italy was highly regarded, while for Havana it also represented recognition from a major European country. The shortage of medical personnel in the Calabria area, and the difficulty in recruiting them, as well as the successful Cuban record in the COVID-19 campaign in Italy, made this an understandable arrangement. Roberto Occhiuto, president of the Calabria region, summed up the situation clearly: "There are not enough doctors in Italy. . . . All the regions are doing everything to recruit doctors, and they are failing. . . . So what do we do? Do we close the hospitals? Shall we close the emergency rooms? Do we not guarantee the right to care of Calabrian citizens?" (Dyer 2022).

The Mexican program was more controversial, with criticism on several levels. First, it was claimed (incorrectly) that the Cubans were taking posts from Mexican doctors. Critics of the government also referred to the fact that the Cuban medics would only receive a small portion of their salaries, with the bulk going to the Cuban state. On a related note, some saw the Cubans as exploited. Medical associations claimed that the Cubans were in fact not "real" doctors and lacked the skills to be dealing with patients. Some opposition politicians used this issue as a means of attacking Mexican president Andrés Manuel López Obrador, stating that the doctors were in fact spies, members of state security, and officials in the Cuban military.

The human rights critique became amplified in recent years. Human Rights Watch condemned the "draconian rules on doctors deployed in medical missions globally that violate their human rights," and their director criticized the "Orwellian system that dictates with whom doctors can live, fall in love, or talk" (Human Rights Watch 2020). It is a position assumed by Washington which, in its 2022 report on human trafficking, singled out Cuba, along with a handful of other countries, as having a "documented 'policy or pattern' of human trafficking, trafficking in government-funded programs, forced labor in government-affiliated medical services or other sectors" (US Department of State 2022).

The response to these criticisms is that Cuba possesses a different approach to public health, grounded on different principles of the prevailing socialist system. In the case of Mexico, as in Calabria, the government initially sought qualified local medical personnel to fill the positions in the healthcare system. Out of 10,495 positions advertised, only 521 Mexicans applied—4.96 percent of the total number of vacancies (Prensa Latina 2022b). Simply put, most of Mexico's doctors—principally from privileged socioeconomic backgrounds—prefer to stay in the cities (where remuneration is better) rather than work in underserved, and often dangerous, locations. For his part the Mexican president expressed clearly his views: "I took the decision to hire foreign medical specialists, and Cuban doctors will be coming. I did so because health has nothing to do with ideology. Instead, this is a matter of human rights. And if we have to bring them from the United States, from Russia, from Cuba, from Japan or France—then so be it" (Olivares 2022).

The Cuban motivation for providing medical support is a combination of altruism and commercial interest. Some of the countries that received Cuban medical support did so without being asked for payment (such as countries in sub-Saharan Africa), while others (such as Mexico, Italy, and Andorra) pay for Cuban medical services in internationally convertible (hard) currency. This sliding scale is based upon a combination of ability to pay, basic needs, and geopolitical influence. Cuban doctors receive 25 to 30 percent of the payment, which would be a typical percentage earned by any individual professional whose company is hired to perform a service.

The Question of Soft Power

The recipients of Cuban medical assistance are not, however, its only beneficiaries, for there is evidence that also flowing from this humanitarianism is a crucial diplomatic/political resource for Havana—soft power. This concept, coined by Joseph Nye, has been defined by him as follows:

> Power is the ability to alter the behavior of another to get what you want. There are basically three ways to do that: coercion (sticks), payments (carrots), and attraction (soft power). . . . A country's soft power can come from three sources: its culture (in places where it is attractive to others), its political values (when it lives up to them at home and abroad), and its foreign policies (when they are seen as being legitimate and having moral authority). (Nye 2006)

The soft power characteristics that Nye lists may result in one country influencing the behavior of another. However, it can be difficult to determine precisely the impact of soft power on a country's behavior in specific circumstances, since we often rely on "circumstantial evidence." In the case of Cuba's medical internationalism, this can be seen in the Global South's support for Cuba in various international organizations.

For example, 1992 marked the first year that a resolution condemning US sanctions on Cuba was passed at the UN General Assembly, with fifty-one members voting for it and seventy-one abstaining. Many of the abstentions were cast by least developed countries (LDC), cautiously adjusting to the post–Cold War world and Washington's evolving attitude toward them. Such resolutions have been passed every following year. An analysis of the "abstentions" versus "for" votes in subsequent years shows how the Global South shifted solidly behind Havana. In November 2022, for instance, there were 185 votes supporting the resolution, 2 opposing it (the United States and Israel), and 2 abstentions (Brazil and Ukraine). This support is indicative of Havana's soft power, with its ongoing medical internationalism representing a significant contributing factor to the last of Nye's key criteria listed above.

A similar soft power pattern can be seen in support for Cuba from the Global South in other national organizations. The Non-Aligned Movement (NAM), founded in 1961 and composed overwhelmingly of developing nations, chose Cuba as its leader in 1979 and 2006. The only other country elected to lead the NAM on two occasions was Yugoslavia.

This soft power momentum, with Havana's medical collaboration programs representing a major "fueling factor," has carried over into the post–Raúl Castro period as Cuba was elected (with strong Global South support) to the following organizations: three bodies of the UN Economic and Social Council (ECOSOC); the Governing Body of the International Labor Organization (2021–2024); the Executive Board of the Pan American Health Organization (2020–2023); the United Nations Children's Fund (2020–2022); the World Food Program (2020–2023); the Commission for Social Development (2020–2024); and a fifth term on the UN Human Rights Council (2020–2023).

There are, of course, instances where key participants in international affairs perceive clearly the potential of soft power. One illustration of this with respect to Cuba's medical internationalism occurred at the 2009 Summit of the Americas in Trinidad, where during a press conference President Barack Obama observed:

> One thing that I thought was interesting—and I knew this in a more abstract way but it was interesting in very specific terms—was hearing from these leaders who when they spoke about Cuba talked very specifically about the thousands of doctors from Cuba that are dispersed all throughout the region, and upon which many of these countries heavily depend. (Obama 2009)

Basically, then, this represented an acknowledgment on Washington's part that Havana's medical internationalism constitutes a major source of competition for the United States in the realm of Latin American soft power politics.

There are dozens of comments from world leaders thanking Cuba for its medical collaboration, which support this hypothesis. Typical was the comment of Prime Minister Ralph Gonsalves of Saint Vincent and the Grenadines: "They [Cuban medical staff] are lifesavers. . . . In some Caribbean countries, they constitute the backbone of the response to the pandemic" (Reuters 2020).

A similar sentiment was expressed by the prime minister of Dominica, Roosevelt Skerrit, in 2022. He commented on the role of Cuba's medical support, both in providing opportunities to study medicine in Cuba and in sending doctors to the island: "Without them the health care system would not have been able to sustain itself, especially during the challenging times . . . of the COVID epidemic." He then went on to explain the nature of the bilateral relationship: "It is a mutually beneficial relationship, we respect the sovereignty of Cuba, we respect their right to self-determination and we will always continue as a matter of principle to call on the United States to remove the economic blockade of Cuba" (Kendy 2022).

An African perspective is also pertinent. In July 2022 President Uhuru Kenyatta of Kenya thanked the Cuban foreign minister, Bruno Rodríguez Parrilla, for the training Kenyan doctors had received, and he directly linked medical collaboration and support for Cuban foreign policy: "I just want to say that we value your support and reiterate that Cuba has a true friend in Kenya. We will always stand in solidarity with you in whatever fora at the multilateral level" (Mwende 2022).

In November 2022 at the Sixth International Conference on Cooperation of the Association of Caribbean States, further evidence of appreciation can be found. Granada's Foreign Minister Joseph Andall thanked Cuba for its support: "Almost half of doctors found in Caricom nations have been trained in Cuba. Indeed, in many countries here those former students, now graduated, occupy government positions" (Padrón 2022). His counterpart from Saint Vincent and the Grenadines, Keisal Melissa Peters, added that her father had received cataract surgery from a Cuban-run program "and has never stopped praising the Cuban doctors who gave him back his sight." She also mentioned the modern diagnostic center, with chemotherapy, dialysis, and other treatments, there which had resulted from Cuban cooperation. They concluded that "Cuba can always count upon the support of its brothers and sisters" (Padrón 2022).

Soft Power *a la Cubana*

This chapter has provided data on the nature of Cuban medical collaboration (Cuba prefers to use this term instead of the paternalistic concept of "aid"). It has also examined the concept of "soft power" and has suggested that Cuba's medical internationalism may well have influenced recipient countries' support for Cuba's sovereignty. Indeed, it seems logical that if a country comes to your assistance and provides a badly needed service (in this case, public health) that you otherwise could not afford, then you would naturally respect the donor nation.

In the final analysis, then, there appears to be a viable—although admittedly somewhat circumstantial—case for a dynamic interplay between Havana's South-South relations in general, its medical internationalism programs in particular, and soft power as a significant component of Havana's foreign affairs toolbox. In short, the evidence suggests that Cuba's foreign policies, especially their South-South dimension with its heavy emphasis on medical internationalism, possess the legitimacy and moral authority that Nye claims are critical in generating soft power.

That said, and regardless of the relationship between soft power and Cuba's medical collaboration, what is perhaps more important is to recognize the potential afforded by this large medical cohort. A recent article in the *British Medical Journal* summarized the post-COVID-19 pandemic threat, and the potential role of Cuba in dealing with future medical challenges of a global nature: "Pandemics are a common challenge faced by human beings in an age of globalisation. This has highlighted an important principle: we are all in this together and cooperation is a necessity, not a choice. Hence, in relation to the provision of healthcare and solidarity, one can learn a lot from Cuba, a country that time after time globalises solidarity" (Escobedo et al. 2021).

References

Díaz Ballaga, Wennys. 2022. "En 59 años los médicos cubanos atendieron a 2000 millones de pacientes en otros países." *Granma*, July 9. Accessed at https://www.granma.cu/cuba/2022-07-09/en-59-anos-los-medicos-cubanos-atendieron-a-2-000-millones-de-pacientes-en-otros-paises-09-07-2022-00-07-35.

Dyer, Owen. 2022. "Italy and Mexico Turn to Cuban Doctors to Fill Gaps in Underserved Regions." *BMJ*, August 31. Accessed at https://www.bmj.com/content/378/bmj.o2130.

Escobedo, Ángel A., et al. 2021. "Cuba: Solidarity, Ebola and COVID-19." *BMJ Paediatrics Open* 5, no. 1 (May 19): e001089. Accessed at https://www.ncbi.nlm.nih.gov/pmc/articles/PMC8136810.

Frank, Marc, et al. 2020. "Pandemic Deepens Divide over Cuba's International Medical Squads." *Financial Times*, July 24. Accessed at https://www.ft.com/content/06069a-7066-4cc0-bbe3-285a1dcaa465.

Human Rights Watch. 2020. "Cuba: Repressive Rules for Doctors Working Abroad." July 23. Accessed at https://www.hrw.org/news/2020/07/23/cuba-repressive-rules-doctors-working-abroad.

Kendy. 2022. "Dominica's PM Skerrit on Official Visit to Cuba." *Nation News*, April 25. Accessed at https://www.nationnews.com/2022/04/25/dominicas-pm-skerrit-official-visit-cuba.

MINSAP (Ministerio de Salud Pública). 2021. *Anuario estadístico de salud 2020.* Havana: Ministerio de Salud Pública, 2021. Accessed at https://salud.msp.gob.cu/wp-content/Anuario-2020.pdf.

Mwende, Sharon. 2022. "Uhuru Meets Cuban Foreign Affairs Minister." *The Star*, July 2. Accessed at https://www.thestar.co.ke/news/2022-07-02-uhuru-meets-cuban-foreign-affairs-minister.

Noda Alonso, Sheila. 2021. "Misión Milagro: luz de esperanza para millones en el mundo." MINSAP, July 9. Accessed at https://salud: msp.gob.cu/mision-milagro-luz-de-esperanza-para-millones-en-el-mundo.

Nye, Joseph S. 2006. "Think Again: Soft Power." *Foreign Policy*, February 23. Accessed at https://foreignpolicy.com/2006/02/23/think-again-soft-policy.

Obama, Barack. 2009. "Text: Obama Press Conference after Summit." CBS News, April 20. Accessed at https://www.cbsnews.com/news/text-obama-press-conference-after-summit.

Olivares Alonso, Emir. 2022. "Anuncian la llegada de los primeros 60 médicos cubanos." *La Jornada*, July 24. Accessed at https://www.jornada.com.mx/2022/07/24/politica/004n1pol.

Padrón Padilla, Abel. 2022. "Cancilleres de Granada y San Vicente y las Granadinas: Cuba siempre podrá contar con sus hermanos del Caribe." CubaDebate, November 16. Accessed at http://www.cubadebate.cu/especiales/2022/11/16/cancilleres-de-granada-y-san-vicente-y-las-granadinas-cuba-siempre-podra-contar-con-sus-hermanos-del-caribe.

Portal Miranda, José Angel. 2022. "Diecisiete años de profesionalidad y altruismo." MINSAP, September 19. Accessed at https://salud.msp.gob.cu/diecisiete-anos-de-profesionalidad-y-altruismo.

Portland. 2019. *The Soft Power30: A Global Ranking of Soft Power 2019.* Accessed at https://softpower30.com/wp-content/uploads/2019/10/The-Soft-Power-30-Report-2019-1.pdf.

Prensa Latina. 2022a. "Colaboración médica de Cuba, una historia de altruismo y solidaridad." May 23. Accessed at https://prensa-latina.cu/2022/05/23/colaboracion-medica-de-cuba-una-historia-de-altruismo-y-solidaridad.

———. 2022b. "Cuba se une a esfuerzo de México para cubrir carencias médicas." August 9. Accessed at https://www.prensa-latina.cu/2022/08/09/cuba-se-une-a-esfuerzo-de-mexico-para-cubrir-carencias-medicas.

Reed, Gail A. 2020. "Fallen in the Face of COVID-19: Graduates of Cuba's Latin American School of Medicine (ELAM)." *MEDICC Review* 20, no. 4 (October 4). Accessed at https://mediccreview.org/fallen-in-the-face-of-covid-19.

Reuters. 2020. "Cuba Sends 'White Coat Army' of Doctors to Fight Coronavirus in Different Countries." NBC News, September 14. Accessed at https://www.nbcnews.com/news/latino/cuba-sends-white-coat-army-doctors-fight-coronavirus-different-countries-n1240028.

US Department of State. 2022. *2022 Trafficking in Persons Report.* Washington, DC: US Department of State. Accessed at https://www.state.gov/reports/2022-trafficking-in-persons-report.

CHAPTER 19

The Battle over Cuban Transnational Ties

EXILES VERSUS THE NEW CUBANS

Susan Eckstein

The United States welcomed Cubans after Castro came to power to demonstrate their preference for capitalist democracy over an anti-American, increasingly Soviet-aligned regime in the throes of the Cold War. It offered them unique entitlements, and in so doing contributed to the creation of a powerful diaspora that went on to press for continued entitlements for Cuban immigrants after the Cold War's end. At the same time, Cuba changed, in ways that transformed both the lived experiences, values, and yearnings of incoming Cubans and relations among the Cubans who immigrated with the different homeland experiences.

The Donald Trump and Joe Biden administrations have had to deal with the long-term impact of Cuban immigration policies previous administrations implemented and with tensions the policies set in motion, including between the different waves of arrivals. Below, I briefly summarize unique entitlements the United States offered Cubans since 1959 and why. I then describe how and explain why Barack Obama, followed by Trump, revoked Cuban entitlements, how Cubans resisted the entitlement cutbacks, and how President Biden has had to address consequences earlier entitlements unleashed.

Unique Cuban Immigration Entitlements

Unique entitlements granted Cubans since Castro assumed power in 1959 include special entry privileges, special rights to become lawful permanent residents (LPRs) and citizens when they entered the United States without authorization, and rights to special benefits once settled in the US.[1] Successive presidential administrations piled new entitlements onto entitlements earlier administrations granted, and on several occasions Congress passed legislation to provide Cubans with unique privileges.

Cubans received multiple entry privileges. Presidents arranged, in total, for nearly one-third of a million Cubans to be flown to America at US taxpayers' expense. So too did they extend various types of temporary entry rights to Cubans that became the basis for permanent residency rights and then citizenship, such as admitting them as tourists and as refugees when known to be neither. Presidents also permitted unauthorized Cubans to be paroled into the United States, that is, awarded temporary entry rights regardless of where they entered the country when other immigrants could only be admitted at official ports of entry with visas. In addition, presidents created unique immigration statuses to admit Cubans that circumvented congressional restrictions on entry;[2] they allowed Cubans to operate one of the only privately run immigration programs in US history; and they agreed to admit a minimum of 20,000 Cubans yearly, a guarantee offered nationals of no other country.

The United States, in turn, offered Cuban entrants unique entitlements to help them adapt. They were beneficiaries of the most generous refugee program in US history, even when they did not meet the near-universally agreed-upon criteria for refugee status. In addition, they have been the only immigrants eligible for federally funded welfare benefits upon arrival, whether or not they entered the US with authorization. Authorized immigrants from other countries are ineligible for welfare benefits their first five years in the US, and unauthorized immigrants from other countries never are eligible.

For over half a century Democrat and Republican administrations alike granted Cubans new entitlements as well as honored entitlements earlier administrations initiated. Obama was the first president to break the precedent. He granted Cubans no new entitlements and in his last full week in office he ended Cuban exceptionalism "as we knew it," in revoking Cuban rights to parole entry, the basis on which most Cubans had been admitted to the United States. However, legislated entitlements that only Congress can retract have remained in effect, most notably the Cuban Adjustment Act (CAA) which, since 1966, has entitled most Cubans who arrived without authorization the right to LPR status after one year in the US. No other unauthorized immigrants have had the lawful means to routinely upgrade their residency status.

Why the Privileging of Cubans between 1959 and 2017?

The Cuban experience reveals that neither presidents with their discretionary power nor Congress with its legislative power treat all immigrants and all aspiring immigrants equally and equitably. Fortunately for Cubans, for over half a century both presidents and Congress singled Cubans out for special entitlements.

Initially presidents and Congress leveraged immigration for foreign policy gain. President Eisenhower and his immediate successors privileged Cubans with hopes thereby to cause the Castro-led government to collapse: by draining Cuba of its "best and brightest," by demonstrating Cubans' preference for a capitalist democracy, and by recruiting Cubans for covert activity to destabilize the revolutionary regime. Arguably, Washington may have unwittingly strengthened Castro's hold on power in welcoming its opponents.

Cuban immigrants quickly became agents of the continued privileging of people from their homeland. They pressed for honoring entitlements previously granted, for new entitlements, and for entitlements for more Cubans. They came to lobby, make campaign contributions, bloc-vote, and mobilize in the streets of Miami and Washington to defend and promote Cuban immigrant interests. Settling mainly in Florida, which came to have the third-largest number of electoral college votes as more of the US population settled in the state and has become the largest swing state, they attained outsized political influence, despite comprising less than 1 percent of the total population. In the process, domestic politics became the driving force behind continued Cuban immigrant privileging, already during the Cold War but especially afterward when Washington's foreign policy priorities no longer justified singling Cubans out for unique entitlements.

Working further to Cubans' advantage, they were light-skinned. US immigration policy had notoriously favored light- over dark-skinned foreign-born when Washington, between the 1920s and mid-1960s, enforced a national origins admission quota system (favoring northern Europeans). The 1965 immigration reform, which remains in effect, introduced a so-called preference system that ostensibly put the racist admissions policy to rest. It prioritized admission of family of US residents and persons with economically useful skills. Despite the reform, though, most Cubans have been admitted based on their nationality, owing to entitlements that enabled them to circumvent the preference system. Their skin color worked to their advantage. According to the US census, the vast majority of Cuban immigrants are white.

Why the Obama Administration Ended the Privileging of Cubans "As We Knew It"

President Obama retracted Cubans' unique right to parole entry against the backdrop of a surge in visa-less Cubans making their way to the US border—at great risk to their lives. Nearly 57,000 unauthorized Cubans came in FY2016. Human smugglers guided them thousands of miles under dangerous conditions through Central American countries and Mexico. Since the mid-1990s Coast Guard policing of the Florida Straits made the most direct route to the United States near-impossible. President Obama hoped that in revoking Cubans' parole rights the US would regain control over its borders. With prospects of parole entry Cubans had presumed that if they touched American soil they could secure legal rights to stay.

President Obama revoked the parole rights when unconstrained by Cuban American political pressure, including from Cuban American members of Congress who influenced US Cuba policy. He made the policy change in his parting days in office, in January 2017, when unconcerned about courting Cuban American voters and against the backdrop of changes in the Cuban American community that spared him political pushback. Cuban American politicians, from families who immigrated in the early years of the Revolution (who viewed themselves as Exiles),[3] during Obama's presidency criticized Cuban entitlements they until then had defended and promoted.

Committed to a "wall" across the Florida Straits to isolate and strangulate "Castro's Cuba" economically (under the leadership of Fidel, then of his brother Raúl, and, since 2019, Miguel Díaz-Canel), Cuban American politicians, with the support of the broader Exile community, opposed the mounting homeland travel and remittance-sending of post–Soviet era arrivals (I refer to them as the New Cubans). The New Cubans, who experienced the crisis the abrupt ending of Soviet aid and trade unleashed, viewed themselves more as economic migrants than as political refugees and, accordingly, wanted to bond with and help family they left behind. Their transnational family morality conflicted with the Exiles' political morality.[4]

Resentful of the New Cuban cross-border ties, beginning in 2015 Cuban American politicians—among them Representatives Mario Díaz-Balart and Carlos Curbelo and Senators Marco Rubio and Bob Menendez—argued for restricting Cuban immigration and for restricting entitlements to Cuban arrivals who made no homeland trips. In making their arguments they cited a series of articles published in the South Florida newspaper *Sun Sentinel* in October 2015 that reported Cuban Americans breaking the law, including in ways embedded in cross-border ties: committing crimes to pay debts to smugglers who brought them to the United States and partaking in highly organized Miami-based criminal networks claimed to be rooted in the ease with which visa-less Cubans gained US entry, with the ringleaders traveling frequently back and forth to Cuba smuggling millions of dollars and bringing Cubans to the US to work as foot soldiers in their criminal organizations. In essence, the Cuban American politicians argued that Cuban immigrant transnational ties were not merely morally reprehensible, in defying the personal embargo to which they were committed, but also grounded in illicit activity.

At the same time, the Cuban American legislators who critiqued continued Cuban immigrant entitlements did not support legislation Republican Paul Gosar, along with nine other members of Congress, proposed in 2015 to sunset the CAA (Kestin and O'Matz 2016). In not supporting Gosar's proposed legislation the Cuban Americans revealed that they were not really interested in repealing the CAA that provided unauthorized Cuban entrants a path to lawful permanent residence and citizenship. Rather, they wished to threaten its repeal to pressure Cuban immigrants to comply with the people-to-people embargo. Instead, Representative Curbelo and Senator Rubio proposed legislation (also in 2015) to terminate Cubans' automatic rights to welfare. The legislation called for restricting welfare rights to Cubans who made no homeland trips (O'Matz and Kestin 2016). Mustering insufficient support from other legislators, Congress continued to fund welfare for all incoming Cubans.

The divergent views toward cross-border ties among the earlier and more recent Cuba immigrants derived from their different experiences in Cuba before uprooting. Exiles, who immigrated in the early years of the Revolution, typically wanted nothing to do with the country transformed under Castro's rule and sought to bring the regime to heel. In contrast, the New Cubans, who "lived the Revolution" but became disillusioned with it when experiencing the crisis caused by the Soviet Union's collapse and the consequent abrupt ending of Soviet aid and trade, perceived themselves as immigrants. Like immigrants from other countries, after moving to America they wanted to visit and financially help family they left behind (see Eckstein 2009, especially chapter 4). However, with no political organizations or political leadership of their own, and without financial resources to make political contributions that might convince politicians to promote their interests, they did not publicly challenge the Cuban American politicians' critique of their entitlements.

Trump Administration Further Retraction of Cuban Immigrant Entitlements

Although unintended, President Obama's parting reforms appealed to President Trump's anti-immigrant base. Trump fervently attacked immigrants and made no exception for Cubans. He further restricted Cuban immigrant entitlements, but de facto more than de jure. Cubans who tried to circumvent new restrictions became victims of his general "war on immigrants." He had little interest in reinstating entitlements that would serve as an "escape valve" for aggrieved Cubans; he would rather they not uproot and spur regime change at home. Furthermore, Senator Rubio, to whom President Trump turned for Cuba policy advice, opposed resumption of entitlements of old, as noted above.

What entitlements did Trump retract? For one, he refused to honor the 1994 bilateral migration agreement that committed the United States to grant a minimum of 20,000 Cubans immigration visas yearly. Between FY2016 and FY2018 his administration admitted no more than half the US' commitment (see DHS 2016, 2017, and 2018 table 10 and CRS 2020), and in 2018 the US embassy in Havana suspended visa-processing. Instead, Cubans needed to apply for visas in third countries, with no guarantee that they would be awarded visas, or awarded visas in a timely manner. The Trump administration also introduced new bureaucratic hurdles to the implementation of the Cuban Family Reunification Parole Program (CFRPP), a program initiated by George W. Bush which President Obama had continued. Then, in 2019 his administration officially suspended the program. New Cubans had been the main beneficiaries of the CFRPP in that, as more recent arrivals, they had more family in Cuba seeking to immigrate (FIU 2020).

Faced with new barriers to lawful immigration and no recourse to parole entry, Cubans creatively turned to a new immigration strategy: request asylum. Cubans became the third-largest group of asylum claimants (Bier 2019). As a result, President Obama's retraction of parole rights did not stop Cubans from coming. If Cubans won their asylum cases they gained lawful entry. Although, as of 2020, immigration judges rejected more than half of the claims Cubans filed (Center for Democracy 2020; for slightly different figures see TRAC 2020a), the Trump administration suspended immigration court hearings when faced with the COVID-19 pandemic. Fortunately for Cuban asylum-seekers, if in the United States for one year they could draw on the Cuban Adjustment Act to become lawful residents. No other asylum-seekers had such a path to legal entry.

While unsuccessful on its own in blocking Cubans from immigrating, the Trump administration rallied the Mexican and Central American governments to its cause. It required asylum-seekers (from all countries, not just from Cuba) to wait in Mexico, often for months, until their asylum hearings. While waiting in Mexican border cities

Cubans were at the mercy of criminal gangs, armed robbers, and kidnappers (Atta-nasio 2019). The Trump administration also pressured the Mexican government to detain and deport Cubans so that they would not reach the US border to make asylum claims. As a result, Cubans found themselves subjected to far worse conditions than those they fled.

With the outsourcing of immigration control to Mexico insufficiently effective in blocking asylum-seekers, in 2019 the Trump administration also offshored US immigration control to the governments of Guatemala, El Salvador, and Honduras. It convinced the Central American governments to sign Asylum Cooperation Agree-ments that required migrants to seek asylum in the first country through which they passed. If migrants passed through a country before reaching the United States, the Trump administration deemed them ineligible for asylum in the US, a ruling that went on to be challenged in the courts (Liptak 2019). The countries through which asylum-seekers trekked to reach the US border had some of the highest homicide rates in the world (Rappaport 2019).

The Trump administration, in turn, sought to deny lawful rights to the Cubans who successfully evaded entry barriers. Detention of Cubans soared, 700 percent between President Obama's last year in office and the end of FY2018 (Rivero 2019), and in 2019 US Immigration and Customs Enforcement (ICE) detained more Cubans than other nationals (TRAC 2020b). Cubans were detained under such deplorable conditions that they rebelled (Lanard 2020). Once detained, they needed to fight for asylum in the courts. If their claims were rejected, they were deported. Cuban deporta-tions increased more than eighteen-fold during Trump's presidency.

The Trump administration even constricted Cuban visits to family in the United States. It stopped issuing multiple-entry visas instituted by President Obama that had made get-togethers among family living on the two sides of the Florida Straits easier and less costly. Instead, it reinstituted single-entry visas, the policy under the Bush administration. More significant, it required Cubans to go to embassies outside Cuba to attain visas for visits as well as for immigration, and absorb the costs on their meager earnings. It thereby made US cross-border family get-togethers near-impossible. As unpopular as the barriers to visits were among New Cubans with family still on the island (FIU 2020), the Cuban American politicians, from Exile families, made no ef-fort to facilitate ties that defied the personal embargo to which they were committed.

In sum, the Trump administration made authorized as well as unauthorized Cu-ban immigration more difficult. Yet, with Congress maintaining the CAA as the law of the land, Cuban asylum-seekers had a path to lawful entry independently of winning asylum claims.

The Biden Administration Confronted with a Cri-sis in Cuba and a New Cuban Immigration Crisis

The retraction of immigrant rights did not keep Cubans from coming when Cuba fell on hard times. The pandemic led the government to shutter tourism, which had been a pillar of the economy; Venezuela slashed subsidized oil deliveries on which Cuba had depended (which caused unpopular electricity blackouts); scarcities fueled extraordinary inflation; and officials introduced a single currency that drove more Cubans into dire economic straits. The Trump administration added to Cubans' woes when it imposed new restrictions on remittance-sending to Cuba. Cubans had relied on remittances from family in the United States to supplement their meager domestic earnings.

By July 2021 the crisis in Cuba reached a boiling point. Angry Cubans took to the streets in protest (and did so again in 2022, in smaller numbers). Met with government repression, not reforms that would improve living conditions, more Cubans envisioned emigration as their best hope. In FY2022 Customs and Border Patrol (CBP) reported (as of August) some 197,000 "encounters" with Cubans at the US-Mexico border;[5] this exceeded the number who fled to the United States in 1980 and 1994 combined, during the so-called Mariel and rafter crises, the largest exoduses until then of visa-less Cubans. President Obama's retraction of parole rights proved not to keep visa-less Cubans from coming.

Confronted with the mounting immigration crisis, in May 2022 the Biden administration announced changes in US policy (see Sneed and Alvarez 2022). It announced that it would reinstate the CFRPP, which the Trump administration had suspended, to admit relatives of US citizens. With the CAA still the law of the land, the Cubans paroled into the country through the CFRPP could apply for permanent residency status.

The Biden administration also announced plans to fully restore immigrant visa processing at the embassy in Havana, which could allow resumption of Washington's commitment to the bilateral agreement to grant a minimum of 20,000 Cubans immigrant visas annually. Plans were also announced to lift the Trump administration's $1,000 quarterly cap on remittance-sending. With greater income, remittance-recipients might be disinclined to immigrate. At the same time, transnational ties among donors and recipients of remittances are likely to be strengthened, especially among the New Cubans most committed to relatives in Cuba—undermining the Exiles' commitment to the people-to-people embargo.

The Impact of the New Cuban Exiles

Ever since Castro assumed power in 1959 the United States has granted Cuban immigrants a range of unique entitlements that have enabled many of them to live the American Dream and become a political force contributing to their continued receipt of special entitlements. Obama was the first president to extend no new entitlements to Cuban immigrants, as well as rein in entitlements previously granted. Yet, despite the retraction of entitlements Cubans have continued to find ways to take advantage of remaining entitlements, and to leverage unauthorized for authorized entry.

The large-scale arrival of Cubans in the post-Soviet era proved, however, to transform the Cuban community in the United States and to create tensions among the immigrant waves. The more recent arrivals remain committed to family on the island, whereas the more politically influential earlier émigrés have promoted a "wall" across the Florida Straits designed to isolate and strangulate the Cuban economy in hopes thereby to bring the Cuban government to heel.

In resisting Exile pressures the New Cubans are quietly deepening ties that know no country borders. In the process, they are changing the Cuban community in the United States and changing Cuba.

Notes

1. I discuss the gambit of entitlements in greater detail in *Cuban Privilege: The Making of Immigrant Inequality in America* (Eckstein 2022).

2. For example, President Carter created the category of "Entrant: Status Pending" to grant temporary entry rights to some 125,000 unauthorized arrivals from the Cuban port of Mariel. President Reagan proceeded to grant the entrants refugee status in the absence of evidence that they had fled persecution, the internationally agreed-upon criteria for refugee status, and thereby enabled them to become lawful permanent residents.

3. Marco Rubio and Bob Menendez came from families who immigrated shortly before the Revolution. However, they identified with the Exiles, from whom they received substantial political contributions.

4. See my book *The Immigrant Divide: How Cuban Americans Changed the US and Their Homeland* for more detail on differences between the immigrant waves (Eckstein 2009).

5. "Encounters" include expulsions/deportations, and "apprehensions" involve detentions by CBP. The number of encounters can differ from the number of individuals attempting US entry, in that some individuals make repeat attempts to enter and therefore have multiple encounters with CBP. However, Cubans are less likely than other nationalities to make repeat attempts because they rarely have been subject to expulsion, for example, under Title 42. As a result, Cuban encounters are likely to approximate the actual number of Cuban arrivals. See Center for Democracy in the Americas, "U.S.-Cuba News Brief," September 27, 2022.

References

Attanasio, Cedar. 2019. "Migrants Face Violence as US Makes Them Wait in Mexico," AP News, June 27. Accessed at https://apnews.com/0d4a28d1153547a7a777e29489e7fb85.

Bier, David. 2019. "Cuban Credible Fear Asylum Claims Surge after Ending Wet Foot, Dry Foot." *Cato at Liberty*, March 20. Accessed at https://www.cato.org/blog/cuban-credible-fear-asylum-claims-surge-after-ending-wet-foot-dry-foot.

Center for Democracy in the Americas. 2020. "U.S.-Cuba News Brief." January 17. Accessed at https://cubacentral.wordpress.com/2020/01/17/u-s-cuba-news-brief-01-17-2020.

———. 2022. "U.S.-Cuba News Brief." September 27. Accessed at https://cubacentral.wordpress.com/2022/09/27/u-s-cuba-news-brief-09-27-22/#more-3773.

CRS (Congressional Research Service). 2020. *Cuba: US Policy in the 116th Congress.* May 14, 2020. Accessed at https://fas.org/sgp/crs/row/R45657.pdf.

DHS (Department of Homeland Security). 2016, 2017, and 2018. Yearbooks of Immigration Statistics. Accessed at https://www.dhs.gov/immigration-statistics/yearbook.

Eckstein, Susan. 2009. *The Immigrant Divide: How Cuban Americans Changed the US and Their Homeland*. New York: Routledge.

———. 2022. *Cuban Privilege: The Making of Immigrant Inequality in America*. Cambridge: Cambridge University Press.

FIU (Florida International University). 2020. *2020 FIU Cuba Poll: How Cuban Americans in Miami View U.S. Policies toward Cuba*. Miami: FIU, Steven J. Green School of International and Public Affairs.

Kestin, Sally, and Megan O'Matz. 2016. "Rubio Bill Would Curb Welfare Abuses by Cuban Immigrants." *Sun Sentinel*, January 12. Accessed at www.sun-sentinel.com/news/nation-world/fl-rubio-cuba-welfare-bill-filed-20160112-story.html.

Lanard, Noah. 2020. "Trump Panders to Cubans, Nicaraguans, and Venezuelans While He Deports and Detains Them." *Mother Jones*, February 5.

Liptak, Adam. 2019. "Justices Permit U.S. to Exclude More Asylum Seekers." *New York Times* September 12.

O'Matz, Megan, and Sally Kestin. 2016. "Rubio to Propose Bill to Cut Aid to Cuban Migrants." *Sun Sentinel*, January 7. Accessed at www.sun-sentinel.com/local/broward/fl-rubio-bill-cuba-aid.

Rappaport, Nolan. 2019. "Trump's Latest Gambit: Send Asylum Seekers to 'Safe Third Countries' That Are Less than Safe." *The Hill*, November 24.

Rivero, Daniel. 2019. "Number of Cuban Nationals Detained by ICE Has Skyrocketed, New Data Shows." WLRN-Miami, June 18. Accesssed at https://www.wlrn.org/post/number-cuban-nationals-detained-ice-has-skyrocketed-new-dta-shows#stream/0.

Sneed, Tierney, and Priscilla Alvarez. 2022. "Biden Reverses Some Trump Policies Related to Cuba, Making It Easier for Families to Visit Relatives in Country." CNN, June 30. Accessed at https://www.cnn.com/2022/06/30/politics/supreme-court-immigration-remain-in-mexico/index.html.

Sullivan, Mark. 2022. "Biden Administration's Cuba Policy Changes." Congressional Resource Service, May 25.

TRAC. 2020a. "Asylum Decisions." Accessed at https://trac.syr.edu/phptools/immigration/asylum.

———. 2020b. "Immigration and Customs Enforcement Detention." Accessed at https://trac.syr.edu/phptools/immigration/detention.

PART IV

SOCIETY

Hope Bastian

In Cuba, the period between 2018 and 2022 was one of rapid social changes that significantly altered Cubans' everyday lives and reconfigured the complex relationships between the people and the state. Five significant changes are worth noting: (1) the impacts of the expansion of the internet and new technologies on everyday life; (2) declining standards of living and widespread economic insecurity; (3) the orientation of leaders toward continuity and control and away from change and openness to economic and social entrepreneurship; (4) the state's inattention to inequalities and social vulnerability; (5) the increased visibility of diverse perspectives and new spaces in which problems are debated openly, no longer mediated or controlled by the state. These changes, and the state's responses, are likely to have distinct repercussions for the future of the Revolution, Cubans living on the island, and the rapidly increasing numbers of Cubans in the diaspora who maintain active connections with the island in ways that were not possible in previous generations.

Internet and New Technologies Transform Everyday Life in Cuban Society

Increased access to the internet, social media, and other new technologies changed everyday social practices and relationships among Cubans and strengthened relations between Cubans abroad and in the homeland. It also altered the relationship between the state and the citizenry. In December 2018, data services became available to prepaid customers of Cuba's sole telecommunications company (ETECSA), expanding internet access and the roles of internet and phones in Cuban social life. In just the first two weeks, users bought more than 700,000 data packages.[1] Two months later, 40 percent of cellphone users were using data and 5,000 additional new users were joining each day.[2]

Since 2015, those without access through work or school connections have connected to Wi-Fi routers in select public parks. While Wi-Fi connectivity was expensive, it was a breakthrough, and much cheaper than international calls. Many people began to use the public Wi-Fi areas to communicate with friends, family, and clients around the world through messaging and VoIP services. When cellular data became available in 2018, it began to change not only the way Cubans connected with the world, but also the way they communicated with friends just across town via WhatsApp, Messenger, Facebook, and Telegram.[3] In a country where many dwellings still do not have landlines, WhatsApp provided a more affordable way to stay connected.

The COVID-19 pandemic accelerated the transition toward making online social networks a significant part of Cubans' daily lives. During the first months of the pandemic, most stores were closed and the state promoted online commerce. However, demand quickly overwhelmed online platforms.[4] TuEnvío, a state online commerce platform developed in November 2019, saw average daily visitors jump from 100 to 6,000–8,000. In February 2020 the site took 1,356 orders, and in March 6,000.[5] By April, it was receiving more than 73,300 orders, and in the first two weeks of May, another 78,800 orders were made.[6] In late June, ETECSA lowered the price of 4G data, facilitating the turn to digital spaces.

Internet connectivity also created opportunities for alternative employment when workplaces shut down or turned to remote modalities. New businesses opened during the pandemic often focused on just one product, such as *croquetas*, frozen mangos, or cloth diapers.[7] More-established businesses also used groups to keep in touch with their clientele and build brand loyalty, despite required closures during lockdowns. Groups of friends and families also used WhatsApp and Facebook groups to notify each other when products appeared in stores around the city.

New online provisioning strategies came with many barriers, stratifying access to basic consumption.[8] A data-ready cellphone and funds in a bank account configured for online payments were needed to take advantage of online commerce. Payments were processed instantly, while deliveries took weeks or even months to arrive. Low-income people, stressed to put food on the table today, could not spend their limited funds in this way. To relieve logistical bottlenecks, stores began to create combinations (called *combos*) of products—chicken, detergent, sodas, cleaning supplies, tomato paste, cooking oil—at set prices. This increased consumers' expenses and forced them to dedicate extra time to reselling or trading unwanted goods from *combos* to recoup their costs.

Employees of state institutions, on their own initiative and expense, also used WhatsApp and Telegram groups to reach the people they served. Parents chipped in to pay for data for classroom teachers so that they could deliver lessons and support student learning informally to supplement televised lessons during school closures that lasted in Havana from March 2020 to November 2021. Psychologists provided mental health services, from group to individual therapies, via WhatsApp. In late 2022, many neighborhood People's Power Municipal Assembly delegates created groups to communicate with their constituents about the arrival of products in assigned stores. Their constituents also used the groups to provide feedback on how the process was working and to complain about corruption and favoritism by store employees, demanding delegates take action.

The internet also changed leisure practices in Cuba. While once Cubans had to invent *El Paquete* and Snet to stay connected and share media, as the price per giga-byte fell and with reduced rates after 1:00 a.m., what people did with data changed. Internet usage began to expand to streaming or downloading videos and podcasts, and services that consumed more data. Access to social media also gave Cubans without professional training the opportunity to become content creators in spaces like Face-book, Telegram, Twitter, Instagram, iVoox, and YouTube. During the pandemic, the number of podcasts made in Cuba distributed on Anchor to international distribution sites Spotify, Google Podcasts, and Apple Music boomed.[9]

Limited mobility during lockdowns, the migration of people who were the foot soldiers of media copiers, and cheaper internet access (largely because of inflation) changed the market and made media-streaming more attractive and convenient than *El Paquete*.[10] Cubans' use of these new technologies also changed the way they migrate, allowing them to keep in contact with friends and family and coordinate with coyotes along the way. Upon arrival, they posted videos montages of the *travesía* (the journey to the United States).[11]

As Cubans connected online, the state moved to populate the new digital com-mons. Cuban leaders set up Twitter accounts and began to use Facebook Live to stream everything from the daily morning COVID-19 updates to presidential ad-dresses. Important policy decisions were communicated through official social media accounts. In December 2018, Cubans learned via a tweet from the People's Power National Assembly that Article 68, which would have allowed same-sex marriage, had been excised from the proposed constitution. In September 2021, the Ministry of Education decided to postpone the implementation of a new inclusion-focused sexual education program it had already approved in response to pressure from evangelical sects. The announcement was made on Facebook.

Internet use expanded access to information and the diversification of media sources.[12] During the presidency of Raúl Castro in the 2010s, the number of inde-pendent comprehensive news reporting platforms began to expand. Before Wi-Fi and data became accessible, outlets like *Progreso Semanal, OnCuba News, Periodismo del Barrio,* and *el Toque* largely had reached their audiences on the island via email. New digital magazines—such as *Vistar* and *Garbos,* which focus on fashion and lifestyle, and *Play-off,* which covers Cuban sports—previously had reached readers only through *El Paquete*.[13] As internet access expanded in late 2018, publications like *AM/PM* (an inde-pendent Cuban magazine about music, founded in 2018) and *Q de Cuir* (a magazine "for LGBTIQ+ people's empowerment," founded in 2019) were designed to reach a Cuban audience directly online rather than exclusively through email bulletins and PDFs in *El Paquete*. Many of these alternative media spaces were founded by gradu-ates of Cuban university programs in journalism, design, and the arts and employed Cuban-trained creative professionals. Some journalists working for state media also did freelance digital reporting to supplement their low salaries. In response to state pres-sure, many left state media, leading to its apparent decline in professionalism.

The internet also changed the way state media outlets reached their audiences. Although state digital media articles are often direct copies from print, TV, and radio platforms, Cubans find it is a more convenient way to access information than having to tune in at set times. The information is also more accessible than printed newspapers, which have a limited circulation. Online, smaller weekly provincial newspapers have been able to reach larger national audiences. Their reporting can be less formulaic than national platforms, and tends to respond more closely to local readers' concerns and incorporate information from local officials.

Online state media platforms also created more of a two-way exchange between readers and state media. The shift to online publishing created opportunities for people to express opinions on state discourses, decisions, and priorities. Rather than a couple of letters to the editor a week in *Juventud Rebelde*'s "Acuse de Recibo" section and *Granma*'s "Cartas a la Dirección," the comments sections of articles in state online media allow unlimited anonymous responses from people anywhere in the world.[14] While these responses were sometimes censored, these sections often seemed to be open, even to critical opinions.

For a short period, state media appeared to be making an effort to compete with alternative media by renovating *Somos Jóvenes* (for teens) and *Alma Mater* (for university students) by appointing talented young directors. *Alma Mater* content reached readers via Medium and profiles in Facebook, Telegram, Twitter, Instagram, iVoox, and YouTube as well as twenty-five WhatsApp groups. However, these efforts were short-lived. In 2018, the director of *Somos Jovenes*, Darío Alejandro Escobar, was reassigned, and in 2019, Armando Franco Senén, director of *Alma Mater*, was "liberated of his responsibilities" by the Union of Young Communists (UJC).[15] The teams of talented journalists they had brought together left en masse.

Declining Standards of Living and Household Economic Insecurity

A third social change during the period was the expansion of economic instability, insecurity, and downward mobility, as crisis after crisis overwhelmed Cuban households. The number of people who could be considered middle and upper class had grown as a result of economic reforms after 2011, and so inequality increased during the period. Those at the top of the economic pyramid had been unaffected by the disparities the dual currency system caused and by everyday struggles for food security in the 2010s. Food security, reliable access to three meals a day, separated Havana's middle class from its lower class.[16] During the pandemic, however, those at the top found themselves no longer immune to these daily difficulties. After a decade of upward mobility and freedom from want, Cuba's relatively privileged found themselves slapped back into an economic reality frequently compared to the 1990s Special Period.

From March 31 to November 15, 2020, international travel was interrupted to Havana by the pandemic. Immediately, the country lost international tourism and remittances—two of its top three sources of income. According to Reuters, "Money transfers from the United States via Western Union were estimated at more than $1 billion [in 2019], the majority of which was sent from Florida."[17] Another $1 to $2 billion was estimated to have been delivered through informal channels by "mules" (individuals who traveled back and forth carrying cash and goods). This channel was interrupted by the closure of airports due to the pandemic. With borders closed, Western Union became the only way to send money directly to Cuba. In November 2020, President Trump interrupted this lifeline, leaving people in Cuba no legal channel for receiving money from abroad.

In a few short months, the pandemic changed Havana's food system.[18] At the beginning, upper-class and middle-class households with savings and private transportation moved freely throughout the city, or to the countryside, to fill their pantries, refrigerators, and chest freezers, despite the suspension of public transit. Those with smartphones, internet access, and hard currency could take advantage of new online commerce systems set up by state stores, or could afford to buy from intermediaries at markup. This allowed them to guarantee their food security without exposing themselves to risk of infection in long lines for basic goods.[19]

Havana's transit system is a complex combination of state-owned, collectively operated, private, and individual solutions. With the availability of cellphone data, many new apps and WhatsApp groups emerged to make getting around simpler. However, in the summer of 2019, fuel shortages began to impact Havana's transit system. In September 2019, President Miguel Díaz-Canel promised that these problems were merely a temporary situation, or *coyuntura*.[20]

In 2020, pandemic control measures frequently interrupted public transit in Havana and between provinces and collective taxis became harder and harder to find. Because of the difficulty of obtaining fuel, most drivers preferred high-paying direct taxi trips rather than the collective routes that many middle-class Cubans used to get around the city with a modicum of comfort. When you could get them, standard collective taxi prices for a short ride soared from $10 to 50 and 100 Cuban pesos. Bicycles shot up in price, as people sought options to avoid coronavirus exposure. Electric motor scooters became an increasingly popular mobility option for those who had parked their cars for lack of fuel or were left stranded by the deterioration of the collective taxi system. These barriers to mobility affected Cubans' lives in myriad ways, from limiting job opportunities and the ability to maintain social networks to providing for the needs of vulnerable people in their care (children, elderly, people with disabilities, etc.).

The impacts of domestic economic policies on household economies were especially severe after the currency reunification began on January 1, 2021. New salaries and pensions were no match for rampant inflation and an unraveling safety net. Hard currency became central to basic survival, and poorly stocked stores failed to meet basic needs. Many private businesses that previously charged in CUC (the Cuban "hard currency" equivalent until 2021) began to charge exclusively in internationally convertible currencies: US dollars, euros, or MLCs (*moneda libremente convertible*), which are funds denominated in dollars or euros and accessible from a Cuban bank with an MLC card.

As the COVID-19 pandemic lockdowns dragged on, the struggle to meet basic consumption needs began to affect even Cubans of relative privilege. The interruption of informal commodity chains (suitcase imports) affected the availability of all manner of household goods and inputs for small businesses.[21] Days-long lines for gasoline made personal cars useless, and having a freezer full of food became a source of stress, rather than security, as twelve-, twenty-four-, and forty-eight-hour power outages in 2021–2022 meant losing hundreds of dollars worth of food. This could only be avoided with a personal generator (which would also require days-long lines to buy fuel). These changes made sacrifice an everyday experience for upper-echelon households that had emerged during the reform period.

As described in the chapter on COVID-19 and health in this volume, the coronavirus pandemic and economic crises in Cuba severely impacted the state's ability to maintain the public health system and guaranteed access to quality healthcare services, leaving many Cubans afraid of getting sick and believing that their legendary public health system had failed them. Limited access to pharmaceuticals to manage chronic conditions and the lack of reagents for diagnostic testing, along with shortages of materials needed for surgeries and the loss of health professionals, further stressed the system. Beyond the impacts of the crises on health infrastructure and access to care for chronic and acute illness, the deterioration of the living conditions of Cuban families made it increasingly difficult for them to live healthy lives.

Because of pandemic border closures, US consular shutdowns, and the limited flights authorized by Cuban aviation authorities, leaving the country became an extremely difficult option, even for those with the resources to do so. The lack of an escape valve led to increased pressures on the state, and protests became more frequent. (In September 2022 protests occurred for the first time in middle-class municipalities of Havana such as Plaza of the Revolution and Playa.[22]) In late 2021, borders reopened and immigration began to flow immediately.[23] The most common migrant route from Cuba to the United States before the pandemic was through Guyana in South America, which did not require visas for Cuban travelers but did require a dangerous trip through Panama's Darién Gap.[24] On November 21, 2021, Nicaragua announced that Cuban citizens could enter without a visa. For those looking to make the *travesía* to the United States, starting in Nicaragua represented a significant shortcut. By the next month, 6,178 Cubans had already entered Nicaragua.[25]

Leadership Vision and Relationship with *el Pueblo*: From Change and Collaboration to Continuity and Control

Changes in state leadership and the government's messaging accompanied the transition from the administration of Raúl Castro to that of Miguel Díaz-Canel. Raúl was of the generation of revolutionary leaders who in the 1950s and 1960s toppled a bloody dictatorship, made radical changes in the social structure, and created opportunities for improving the lives of those most marginalized under the previous US-dominated governments. As Raúl's pick, Díaz-Canel enjoyed conditional support from the population. However, it was common to hear Cubans express a cautious "wait and see" attitude: "I didn't choose you, *they* gave you the position, let's see what you are going to do with it." The distancing in the relationship between state leadership and people is also seen in the change from the intimacy of referring to the leader on a first-name basis, as was the case with Fidel and Raúl.

The new leadership discourse focused on ensuring the *continuity* of power, which represented a significant change from his predecessor's focus on "changing what needed to be changed." As Raúl knew that he was not Fidel, he dedicated his presidency to building political capital by holding listening sessions, publishing people's letters to the editor in *Granma*, and encouraging popular participation to bring new generations on board with the collective (but still state-led) project of building a new "Prosperous Socialism." In response to the expectations expressed by the population, he proposed wide-ranging changes to the nation's political-economic system, overseeing the emergence of new economic actors.[26] He also encouraged new forms of popular participation and debate. However, as described in the introduction to the politics section in this volume, Raúl's recalibration of state discourse contributed to a shift in Cuban political culture. It changed the grammar of state-*pueblo* relations to incorporate protests from diverse sectors of civil society.

From the beginning, Díaz-Canel's administration was plagued by disasters. Some were inherited and some, like the COVID-19 pandemic, were unexpected. Before he took office, the economy was already suffering, and the Trump administration's escalating aggressive policies toward Cuba added to the problems. International tourism, the motor of the Cuban economy, declined in 2018, and after Hurricane Irma, sugar brought in its smallest harvest in over a century. In the first years of his administration, Díaz-Canel had to respond to the deadliest crash in the history of Cuban aviation, major hurricane damage in the capital and the province of Pinar del Rio, a freak tornado, a deadly explosion at a luxury hotel within view of the iconic *Capitolo*, and a massive deadly fire at Cuba's largest oil tank field with the attendant loss of 40 percent of fuel for power generation. With each disaster people compared his response as a leader to "what Fidel would have done." These were very big shoes to fill and, by most accounts, Cubans perceived that the new president was not up to the task.

In addition to the coronavirus crisis and the unfolding economic crisis, a crisis of poor communication earned President Díaz-Canel offensive nicknames. He began his term promising to be a force for continuity at a time when people were already demanding significant changes to "socialism as usual." His seeming failure to understand the accumulated exhaustion of a population that had been repeatedly chided to sacrifice was read as a sign of a disconnect between the lives of the country's leaders and its population, which has eroded the leadership's legitimacy.

A contributing factor to the loss of legitimacy has been the behavior of the Cuban president's wife, Lis Cuesta, on social media. She opened her Twitter account (@liscuestacuba) in March 2022. By June 2022 her 142 tweets had gained her 30,000 followers, and six months later she had generated 512 tweets and her number of followers had grown to almost 80,000. Her frequent tweets included: messages commemorating historical events, birthday wishes to her "friends" (important figures in the Cuban political and cultural sphere) with the hashtag #TeMolestaMiAmor, messages and pictures with her husband on official state visits, and family snapshots of the president with messages like "He is so beautiful! Inside and outside: the dictator of my heart!" (April 10), which she tagged with the hashtag #ElDictadorDeMiCorazon. It led to an explosion of satirical memes. On April 20 she tweeted a love letter to the president, "My LOVER yesterday, my LOVER tomorrow and my LOVER FOREVER. I will whisper it in your ear and I will scream it on twter. Because together we are much more than two people." It was followed by #TeMolestaMiAmor and #ElDictador-DeMiCorazon.

As crisis after crisis dealt blows to all areas of daily life in Cuba, government officials tended to blame the population for not being willing to sacrifice even more, admonishing them during the 2019 *coyuntura* to *pensar como país* (think as a country), instead of building consensus and bringing people (back) on board by presenting coherent plans to improve social conditions on the island.[27] In the summer of 2020, in the face of a serious episode of food shortages, traditional state media engendered popular outrage by blaming shortages on women from urban peripheries waiting in lines (*coleros*). The state responded by unleashing a force of 20,000 deputized agents to fight against these women in what was declared the *Lucha Contra Coleros* (Fight against *Coleros* [LCC]). Despite frequent complaints about corruption by LCC agents, the ineffective program and the discourse continued for more than two years.[28]

On May 22, 2022, in the midst of frequent, long-lasting power blackouts, Lis Cuesta tweeted: "My heart is wrung out like a scouring pad by the suffocating power outages that left me unable to sleep, I went to Meteoro and then to the Closing Ceremony of #25Cubadisco. I am thankful for my work: Cubans and North Americans embraced by music. Truly delightful!" Few believed that the president's household was suffering the same daily power outages they experienced, and many felt offended by her disrespectful false populism. Immediately the memes and stickers began.

These tweets have affected the image of the president and the state by positioning them as disconnected from the everyday realities of the country. Although other official accounts rarely retweet Lis Cuesta's messages, they cause incalculable damage to the president's popular support.

On July 11, 2021, Díaz-Canel responded to the widespread demonstrations with a televised national address in which he called on Cubans to take arms against protestors to defend the Revolution.[29] Many Cubans were shocked to hear their president openly encouraging Cubans to take up arms against other Cubans. More than 1,400 protestors were arrested, including teens and young adults. Hundreds were convicted of serious crimes, from violence to sedition, and sentenced to long prison terms.[30]

For many Cubans who had long been faithful to the government, despite decades of difficulties and personal sacrifices, Díaz-Canel's response in promoting street violence against protesters provoked a personal existential crisis that deepened with the news of the harsh treatment and sentencing of protesters. They began to doubt how such actions could come from a leader of the Revolution who claimed to stand for the continuity of Fidel's struggles for social justice.

After the protests, Díaz-Canel began a tour of marginalized neighborhoods that was heavily reported across state media platforms, including Twitter.[31] Though he promised to direct assistance to these communities, the visits resulted in little change and had perhaps even less impact in improving the state's image. To do that would have required results in improving the declining standard of living on the island.[32] It was clear that the type of continuity Cubans were most desperate for was continuity of a social contract in which the state guaranteed citizens a better life and the rights to high-quality health and education services, as Louis A. Pérez observes in his conversation at the beginning of this volume.

State Management of Inequalities and Social Vulnerability

The inequalities that became more visible during the first decade of the twenty-first century have impacted the position from which Cuban households have been able to confront the multiple crises of Díaz-Canel's term. In justifying the need for structural transformations in the early 2010s, Raúl described the country's economic situation in simple terms, comparing the controversial decisions ahead with the decisions faced by all households: "Nobody, no individual nor country, can indefinitely spend more than she or he earns."[33] His approach to balancing the budget depended on eliminating "unnecessary subsidies," laying off workers from "bloated payrolls," and stimulating the development of small businesses to absorb them.

Katrin Hansing and Bert Hoffmann's chapter on racial inequalities in this volume describes the uneven playing field Cubans found themselves on with the transformations of structures of opportunity with the 2011 "Guidelines for the Economic and Social Policies of the Party and the Revolution." As the results of Hansing and Hoffmann's research show, there were winners and losers coming out of these structural adjustments, despite the frequent promises that "no one would be left behind." The changes reinforced patterns of racialized exclusions established during the Special Period.[34]

While the vast majority of social science research on and in Cuba focuses on understanding social phenomena in Havana and other urban centers, Vilma Hidalgo López-Chávez's contribution in this volume helps us to understand the challenges rural families have faced from the decapitalization of rural areas since the 1990s economic crisis and especially since 2011. In the 2010s, the Cuban economy reoriented toward encouraging growth in spheres that excluded rural communities far from urban areas. Agrarian policies, such as the distribution of land in usufruct in 2008, were unsuccessful at stemming the decades-long migration from rural to urban areas. The closure of most of Cuba's remaining sugar mills in 2012 dealt a deafening blow to rural communities, leaving families increasingly dependent on the state at a time in which severe cuts were made in education, health care, and basic infrastructure—all of which threatened to reverse the achievements of the Revolution.[35]

During the reform era of the 2010s, poor people's struggles for basic survival were normalized by pundits who acknowledged the existence of acceptable levels of inequality in a socialist society. Gradually, the marginalized became non-subjects in Cuban political life. People living in precarious situations at the margins of Cuban society

were only occasionally visible in student thesis films, and through the documenta-
tion of Silvio Rodríguez's tour through the barrios.[36] Their needs were addressed by
international charitable organizations, evangelical missionaries, international NGOs'
development projects, and grassroots community organizations operating under the
radar, rather than as a result of government programs aimed at achieving social justice.

Kirenia Criado Pérez and Dachelys Valdés Moreno's chapter describes the emergence of fundamentalist evangelical sects as political actors in Cuba, rooting their
emergence in the crises of household social reproduction in Cuba in the 1990s–2010s
which paralleled processes of neoliberal dispossession of working-class people in Latin
America. As elsewhere in the region, poverty in Cuba has contributed to the growth of
fundamentalist evangelical sects with ideological and political agendas that are contrary
to the social and political platform of the Cuban Revolution. As the authors describe,
the absence of state efforts to adequately address the inequalities that emerged during the Special Period and provide for the basic needs of vulnerable populations now
diminishes the state's ability to mobilize support for its agenda.

During the debates in 2018–2019 around the Cuban Constitution, evangelical
churches erupted onto the scene as new political actors, making demands on the state
by virtue of their ability to organize and mobilize large numbers of members to reject
state projects inconsistent with their beliefs.[37] This is a new challenge to the capacity
of the government to implement progressive social reforms if it chose to do so. From
LGBTQ+ rights to inclusive sexual education, these legislative proposals are consistent
with obligations under international treaties signed by Cuba, and are needed to address
social problems in the communities most affected by current crises. For example, high
rates of teenage pregnancy in rural areas contribute to increased infant and maternal
mortality, and threaten the ability of the state to guarantee protection of health and
well-being.

New Spaces for Public Debates and Increased Visibility of Diverse Perspectives Escape State Control

Increased access to the internet was also a factor in politicizing Cubans who had not
previously participated in political activities. In early 2019, as the number of cellphone
data users grew, digital infrastructures were key in facilitating the coordination of
grassroots actions in Havana around issues as diverse as disaster recovery, LGBTQ+
rights, urban planning, and medical aid.

On January 27, 2019, a kilometer-wide E4 tornado hit Havana, leaving 4 dead,
195 injured, and 1,225 homes partially collapsed. It was social media, not the state,
that was decisive in connecting young volunteers to people in need in the disaster
area. "Right after the tornado social networks made it possible for us to come together to find ways we could help people who had been affected by the tornado in a
way that had never been possible before. We didn't wait for the state to help, we just
went in and did whatever needed to be done," explained one University of Havana

student who spent her break working with initiatives she learned about on Facebook. Cubans abroad raised funds that enabled displaced residents to buy food, water, and construction materials. Locally, donation collection sites and pick-up spots where volunteers could get rides to help with cleanup efforts were announced online. Volunteers detailed the needs of affected households on a Facebook group called Alternativas.[38] They also used Google Maps and Docs to create collaborative lists. Social media users shared information on road closings and ways to engage with local authorities. Posts with pictures and testimonies kept donations flowing from Cubans abroad who were eager to see their aid go directly to those affected.

In 2018, LGBTQ+ Facebook users and their allies used social media to fight back against the evangelical churches. When churches began to campaign heavily against the proposed Cuban Constitution and Article 68 that would have legalized same-sex marriage, many LGBTQ+ people became social media activists. The 68 Va! Facebook campaign gained close to 2,000 followers by asking Cubans to upload selfies to show their support of Article 68. Abriendo Brechas de Colores released short videos telling stories of LGBTQ+ Cubans and calling for "all rights for all people."[39]

After the removal of Article 68 and the constitution's approval, these groups remained active and members marched together for the first time with rainbow flags in Havana's May First workers' parade. When the Ministry of Public Health canceled the yearly Conga against Homophobia and Transphobia in 2019, a spontaneous Pride march was organized online for May 11.[40] Many active in the campaigns for an inclusive constitution joined together to found the 11M (May 11) Telegram group commemorating this date, and on the 11th of each month they have organized online activities to keep the movement alive. In 2023, the march resumed for the first time since 2018.

As the debates around the Cuban Families Code began in 2021, an all-female group reacting to sexism within the LGBTQ+ activist community launched the campaign Ahora Sí.[41] In a month they had 2,000 Facebook followers and organized local teams with captains on the ground in Santa Clara, Trinidad, Ciego de Ávila, Cienfuegos, Bayamo, Las Tunas, Manzanillo, Guantánamo, Holguín, Santiago, and Havana to pass out their flyers and stickers in the street. Their daily updates with colorful photos of their teams' work were shared by 11M activists and others on Facebook and other platforms.[42] However, the growing movement was quickly interrupted by a worsening epidemiological situation in Matanzas, and the energy of many of the core activists was consumed by this new crisis.

By the end of the decade, the new independent Cuban media that grew in the early 2010s under Raúl's watch found itself attacked and criminalized. One month after the July 2021 protests, the government began to air *Con Filo*, a television program intended to frame the debate about protests, describing critical Cuban voices online as part of "the bombarding of a media war against Cuba." Each fifteen-minute capsule scours social media for "enemies" of the Revolution and accuses critics of being funded by the United States. In late 2022, state media unleashed a campaign against *el Toque*, an independent publication.[43] State security agents have also used intimidation tactics to encourage journalists and people active in social media groups to emigrate.

In addition to its use of traditional media platforms, the government has attempted to use diverse methods in an attempt to control spaces of public debate and action. In 2017 and 2018, events for university students were organized with free food and Wi-Fi to post "my selfie against the blockade" with the hashtags #NoMasBloqueo, #HacemosCuba, and #UnblockCuba on Twitter.[44] As data use has expanded, the state has attempted to make sure that "its side" is represented in online conversations, growing the ranks of *cibercombatientes* (cyber combatants) by providing students and state workers with mobile data to participate in online debates on Facebook, Twitter, and other social networks.

In 2019 and 2020, internet outages became common occurrences whenever protests took place. These unscheduled outages, sometimes lasting for hours, created frustrations and real problems for people who used the internet for work. It led many Cubans to assume that anytime the ETECSA connection was slow, it was because of a protest somewhere. During the November 2020 artists' protests and July 11 street protests, internet blocking was most extensive. These experiences led Cuban internet users to become familiar with the use of VPNs to circumvent restrictions. ETECSA also collaborated by blocking the delivery of SMS messages with keywords like VPN, dictatorship, and protest; names of VPN services; and statements and hashtags like Patria y Vida, SOSMatanzas, and words related to specific protests and groups like Archipiélago, 11J, 15N, 20N, and the catchall DPEPDPE (*de pinga el país de pinga este*, which roughly translates to "fuck this fucking country").[45]

President Díaz-Canel has pointedly attacked critics, and the government has promulgated a series of laws to criminalize dissent, rather than recognizing legitimate grievances. Cuba's 2022 Penal Code is one example of legislation that has the potential to control online threats to state power.[46] During the consultations and state-facilitated debates around the 2019 Constitution and the 2022 Families Code, the state released cellphone apps and special websites to make the proposed texts and analysis about possible changes widely available and accessible to the public. In contrast, the new Penal Code was approved in May 2022 by the National Assembly without extensive popular consultation. Instead of being published immediately, as is the regular process, it was not made public until September 2022. The law went into effect three months later. It increased the number of offenses punishable by death and life imprisonment, making it a crime to attempt to change any aspect of the Cuban Constitution or the form of government established by it. Notably, this prohibition includes commentary on internet and social media channels, which held out the potential of suppressing online activism. The Penal Code also places any person or entity receiving vaguely defined "external funding" at considerable risk of being accused of treason.

Conclusion

As 2022 ended, daily life for more Cubans was harder than ever. It had been a year of "sustained economic crisis, accentuated shortages, skyrocketing inflation, scheduled and also unforeseen blackouts, migratory stampede, accidents, explosions, and a major hurricane," as an article in *OnCuba News* succinctly summarized the problems.

It listed "Five Questions for 2023" that hinted at the greatest worries on the mind of the average Cuban: (1) How far will prices go up? (2) Will the endless days of blackouts return? (3) Will tourism in Cuba be able to take off in 2023? (4) Will there be more hurdles or more freedoms for the private sector? (5) Will the migratory tsunami stop?[47]

Perhaps the biggest change between Cuba in 2018 and Cuba in 2022, visible in all of these questions, was the lack of hope and confidence in the future. Everyday life in Cuba has changed significantly, and so has the way that people and state relate to each other. There has been a shift in their vision of the Revolution as one of change and prosperity to one that is characterized by continued control and sacrifice. Technological advances played a key role in creating spaces in which conversations between diverse sectors of the population, about the problems affecting the country, were no longer mediated by the state. Technology also allowed the rapidly growing numbers of Cubans in the diaspora to continue to participate in social and political life on the island in ways that were not possible in the past.

The desperation felt by Cubans pushed to the limit by food insecurity, failing electrical infrastructure, and shortages of basic goods that threaten the ability of the public health and education systems to function as they had in the past made these conversations feel more urgent than ever. This pressure also made people more willing to take risks to have their voices heard, whether by critiquing state policies or state leaders on social media or alternative press or stepping out into the streets to bang on pots or by throwing rocks at MLC stores while yelling "Patria y Vida," "Díaz-Canel Singao," and "Libertad." The government has been significantly challenged in adjusting to this new social environment and making effective use of new technologies to engage in productive relationships with the population that provides Cubans with hope.

Notes

1. Xenia Reloba de la Cruz, "How to Stay Connected in an 'Offline' Country? Stories of Cubans' Internet Experience," MA thesis, Queen's University, Kingston, Ontario, Canada, April 2019, 1, accessed at https://qspace.library.queensu.ca/bitstream/handle/1974/26131/RelobadelaCruz_Xenia_201904_MA.pdf?sequence=3&isAllowed=y.

2. Susana Antón, "Conexión por datos 3G, ¿qué se hace para mejorarla?" *Granma*, February 28, 2019, accessed at http://www.granma.cu/cuba/2019-02-28/conexion-por-datos-3g-que-se-hace-para-mejorarla-28-02-2019-23-02-15.

3. Hope Bastian, "From Facebook to the Streets: Digital Infrastructures and Citizen Activism in Connected Cuba," in *The Road Ahead: Cuba after the July 11 Protests* (virtual symposium, Center for Latino and Latin American Studies, American University, 2021), ed. William M. LeoGrande, John M. Kirk, and Philip Brenner, accessed at https://www.american.edu/centers/latin-american-latino-studies/cuba-after-the-july-11-protests-bastian.cfm.

4. Oscar Figueredo Reinaldo, "Paso a paso: ¿Cómo comprar a través de la plataforma Tuenvio.cu?" Cubadebate, April 15, 2020, accessed at http://www.cubadebate.cu/especiales/2020/04/15/paso-a-paso-como-comprar-a-traves-de-la-plataforma-tuenvio-cu-listado-de-tiendas.

5. Oscar Figueredo Reinaldo, Lisandra Romeo Matos, Edilberto Carmona Tamayo, and Abel Padrón Padilla, "Tiendas virtuales en Cuba: ¿Dónde está 'mi envío'?," Cubadebate, June 9,

2020, accessed at http://www.cubadebate.cu/especiales/2020/06/09/tiendas-virtuales-en-cuba
-donde-esta-mi-envio/amp.

6. Reinaldo et al., "Tiendas virtuales en Cuba."

7. Hope Bastian, "You Can Buy This Croqueta on WhatsApp in Havana," *Startup Cuba TV*, March 23, 2012, accessed at https://startupcuba.tv/2021/03/23/havana-whatsapp-users-fill
-gaps-by-selling-on-the-app.

8. Hope Bastian, "COVID-19 and Inequalities in Havana: Segmented Consumption Opportunities in Cuba's Changing Food System," *ReVista: Harvard Review of Latin America*, August 5, 2020, accessed at https://revista.drclas.harvard.edu/book/covid-19-and-inequalities
-havana.

9. Yohan Amed Rodríguez Torres, "Un recorrido por el podcasting con sabor a Cuba," Podcasteros, accessed January 31, 2023, at https://podcasteros.com/un-recorrido-por-el-pod-casting-con-sabor-a-cuba.

10. *El Paquete* is a black market service that provides access to international television pro-grams and films. See Steffen Köhn and Nestor Siré, "Swap It on WhatsApp: The Moral Econ-omy of Informal Online Exchange Networks in Contemporary Cuba," *The Journal of Latin American and Caribbean Anthropology* 27 (2022): 80–100. Also see https://elpaquetesemanal
.org.

11. As seen in the 2020 film *La Opción Cero* by Cuban filmmaker Marcel Beltrán, who used more than one hundred hours of migrants' personal cellphone footage as they made the journey through the jungle of the Darién Gap.

12. For a description of changes in the media ecosystem and the role that emerging online civic media play in the professional exodus from state press and contribution to the construction of space for transnational debates about the future of the country, see Carlos Manuel Rodríguez Arechavaleta, "Prensa y Estado en Cuba. Aproximaciones a un escenario en transición," *Dixit* 34 (June 1, 2021): 30–47, accessed at https://revistas.ucu.edu.uy/index.php/revistadixit/article
/view/2299.

13. Steffen Köhn and Nestor Siré, "Fragile Connections: Community Computer Networks, Human Infrastructures, and the Consequences of Their Breakdown in Havana," *American Anthropologist* 124, no. 2 (June 2022): 383–98, accessed at https://anthrosource.onlinelibrary
.wiley.com/doi/10.1111/aman.13727.

14. Martin K. Dimitrov, "The Functions of Letters to the Editor in Reform-Era Cuba," *Latin American Research Review* 54, no. 1 (2019): 1–15, accessed at https://www.cambridge.org/
core/services/aop-cambridge-core/content/view/F46BFAEDCCF8A730A46E041C3F2ED615
/S0023879100005069a.pdf/functions_of_letters_to_the_editor_in_reformera_cuba.pdf. All the letters published in "Cartas a la Dirección" from 2008–2014 are available at https://www
.granma.cu/granmad/secciones/cartas-direccion/index.html.

15. Darío Alejandro Escobar directed *Somos Jovenes* from 2017 to 2019. See "Reacciones ante 'liberación' de director de la revista Alma Mater," Inter Press Service in Cuba, May 4, 2022, accessed at https://www.ipscuba.net/sociedad/reacciones-ante-liberacion-de-director-de
-la-revista-alma-mater. Also see "La burocracia cubana destituye a joven director de medio de prensa gubernamental," *COMUNISTAS*, April 25, 2022, https://www.comunistascuba.org
/2022/04/la-burocracia-cubana-destituye-joven.html.

16. Bastian, "COVID-19 and Inequalities in Havana."

17. "In Blow to Struggling Cubans, Western Union Offices Close as Sanctions Bite," Re-uters, November 23, 2020, accessed at https://www.reuters.com/article/us-cuba-remittances/in
-blow-to-struggling-cubans-western-union-offices-close-as-sanctions-bite-idUSKBN2840CI.

18. Hope Bastian and Hanna Garth, "Cuban Food Security in a Time of COVID-19," *An-thropology News*, September 25, 2020, accessed at https://www.anthropology-news.org/articles

/cuban-food-security-in-a-time-of-covid-19. Also see Bastian, "COVID-19 and Inequalities in Havana."

19. Köhn and Siré, "Swap It on WhatsApp."

20. "En vivo: Presidente de Cuba anuncia medidas para la coyuntura energética del país," *Granma*, September 11, 2019, accessed at https://www.granma.cu/cuba/2019-09-11/en-vivo -presidente-de-cuba-anuncia-medidas-para-la-coyuntura-energetica-del-pais-video-11-09-2019 -15-09-41.

21. Jennifer Cearns, "'The Mula Ring': Networks of Material Circulation and Exchange through the Cuban World," *Journal of Latin American and Caribbean Anthropology* 24, no. 4: 864–90. Repatriation flights began again in October, 2021, but with severely limited luggage policies.

22. Proyecto Inventario compiled a map of protests in 2022 at https://maphub.net /proyectoinventario/protestas-verano-2022-en-cuba. Also see "Havana Protests Flare for Second Night as Cuba Scrambles to Turn on Lights," Reuters, October 1, 2022, accessed at https://www. reuters.com/world/americas/protests-havana-flare-up-second-night-blackouts-persist-2022-10 -01.

23. "Nicaragua Eliminates Visa Requirement for Cubans," Reuters, November 23, 2021, accessed at https://www.reuters.com/world/americas/nicaragua-eliminates-visa-requirement -cubans-2021-11-23.

24. Karl Vick, "Cuba: The Long Way to America," *Time*, October 12, 2016, accessed at https://time.com/cuba-the-long-way-to-america.

25. Elmer Rivas, "Nicaragua Is the Key to Escape from the Prison That Is Cuba," *Havana Times*, July 14, 2022, accessed at https://havanatimes.org/interviews/nicaragua-is-the-key-to -escape-from-the-prison-that-is-cuba.

26. Communist Party of Cuba, *Resolution on the Guidelines for the Economic and Social Policies of the Party and the Revolution*, April 18, 2011, accessed at http://www.cuba.cu/gobierno/ documentos/2011/ing/l160711i.html.

27. Miguel Díaz-Canel Bermúdez, "Gracias por 'Pensar como País,'" Cubadebate, October 2, 2019, accessed at http://www.cubadebate.cu/opinion/2019/10/02/gracias-por-pensar-como -pais. During the difficult *coyuntura* in August 2019, the presidency opened a space online for people to leave 280-word comments of what it meant to them: "¿Qué significa para usted pensar como país?" at https://www.presidencia.gob.cu/es/pensar-como-pais/que-significa-para -usted-pensar-como-pais. A critique of the effort is available at Julio Antonio Fernández Estrada, "¿Pensar cómo, país?" *el Toque*, October 25, 2019, https://eltoque.com/pensar-como -pais.

28. Hope Bastian and Maya J. Berry, "Moral Panics, Viral Subjects: Black Women's Bodies on the Line during Cuba's 2020 Pandemic Lockdowns," *The Journal of Latin American and Caribbean Anthropology* 27 (2022): 16–36. Also see "Nuevas medidas en La Habana para la venta de productos," *Granma*, December 1, 2022, https://www.granma.cu/cuba/2022-12 -01/nuevas-medidas-para-la-venta-de-productos-liberados-controlados-de-alta-demanda-en-las -cadenas-de-tiendas-cimex-y-caribe.

29. A map created by Proyecto Inventario reported protests on July 11, 2021. Each listing includes a link to photographs or video in the public domain taken at the location (https://www .google.com/maps/d/u/0/viewer?mid=1AQAArlWutvq3eqA2nK_WObSujttknlxZ&hl=en_US &ll=22.33383601546799%2C-81.82677047123681&z=60). "Díaz-Canel al pueblo de Cuba: "La orden de combate está dada, a la calle los revolucionarios," Cubadebate, July 11, 2021, accessed at http://www.cubadebate.cu/noticias/2021/07/11/miguel-diaz-canel-comparecera -en-cadena-de-radio-television-a-las-400-pm/?fbclid=IwAR2KlQ3t-8SM1w_uMHvZO7yrfA cqKYwSeRqHS9t2ThONjxuPyi7uxoho_-o.

30. "Fiscalía cubana confirma sanciones contra 381 personas por protestas de julio de 2021," *OnCuba News*, June 13, 2022, accessed at https://oncubanews.com/cuba/fiscalia-cubana-confirma-sanciones-contra-381-personas-por-protestas-de-julio-de-2021; "Emiten condenas de hasta 15 años de cárcel a manifestantes del 11J," *OnCuba News*, January 28, 2023, accessed at https://oncubanews.com/cuba/emiten-condenas-de-hasta-15-anos-de-carcel-a-manifestantes-del-11j.

31. Alina Perera Robbio, "En los barrios: cambios que van más allá de las paredes," *Granma*, September 28, 2021, accessed at https://www.granma.cu/cuba/2021-09-28/en-los-barrios-cambios-que-van-mas-alla-de-las-paredes-28-09-2021-20-09-36. Also see "Hasta Pocito-Palmar, en Marianao, llegó Díaz-Canel este viernes," Cubadebate, November 12, 2021, http://www.cubadebate.cu/noticias/2021/11/12/hasta-pocito-palmar-en-mariano-llego-diaz-canel-este-viernes.

32. Zuleica Romay Guerra, "Grietas en la pared: una mirada al contexto social del 11J," in *The Road Ahead*, accessed at https://www.american.edu/centers/latin-american-latino-studies/cuba-after-the-july-11-protests-romay-guerra.cfm.

33. Marc Frank, "Raúl Castro Pushes Cubans to Rethink Socialism," Reuters, September 22, 2009, accessed at https://www.reuters.com/article/us-cuba-debate/raul-castro-pushes-cubans-to-rethink-socialism-idUSTRE58L3QF20090922.

34. An expanded version of these results were published in Katrin Hansing and Bert Hoffmann, "Cuba's New Social Structure: Assessing the Re-stratification of Cuban Society 60 Years after Revolution," *GIGA Working Papers*, Series 315 (Hamburg: German Institute for Global and Area Studies, 2019), https://www.giga-hamburg.de/en/publications/giga-working-papers/cuba-s-social-structure-assessing-re-stratification-cuban-society-60-revolution.

35. A. Vera, *Guajiros del siglo XXI* (Havana: Instituto Cubano de Investigación Cultural Juan Marinello, 2012).

36. *Buscándote Habana* (2006) is a film about internal migrants in an irregular neighborhood in Havana, directed as a student thesis film by Alina Rodríguez at the Universidad de las Artes–FAMCA. The documentary *Canción de barrio* (2014), directed by Alejandro Ramírez Anderson, tells the story of Cuba troubadour Silvio Rodriguez's concerts in Cuba's most vulnerable neighborhoods that began in 2010. The documentary had close to three million views on YouTube (https://www.youtube.com/watch?v=2FczuWyxfMM) after Ramírez posted it in 2015. It became accessible to general Cuban audiences in 2021 when it was shown on Cuban television.

37. Rubén Padrón Garriga, "Apaga el termostato y abre la ventana," *Alma Mater*, April 3, 2022, accesssed at https://medium.com/revista-alma-mater/apaga-el-termostato-y-abre-la-ventana-fa4313b497cd.

38. Alternativas, Facebook, February 27, 2019, accessed at https://www.facebook.com/groups/1708025335966356/permalink/1749023281866561 and https://www.facebook.com/groups/1708025335966356/permalink/1748882851880604.

39. Proyecto Abriendo Brechas de Colores–LGBTI, Facebook, September 25, 2018, accessed at https://www.facebook.com/watch/?ref=search&v=329201631170782&external_log_id=5039790e-3e5e-400b-8176-f141337187d9&q=abriendo%20breachas%20de%20colores%20cuba, and November 1, 2018, accessed at https://www.facebook.com/watch/?ref=search&v=2033824253346827&external_log_id=5039790e-3e5e-400b-8176-f141337187d9&q=abriendo%20breachas%20de%20colores%20cuba.

40. After the 2019 cancellation, Congas did not take place in 2020 and 2021 due to the COVID-19 pandemic. In 2022, it was canceled due to the explosion of the Saratoga Hotel. Cenesex, "Ajuste al programa de las Jornadas Cubanas contra la Homofobia y la Transfobia en su duodécima edición," Facebook, May 5, 2021, accessed at https://www.facebook.com/notes

/3686886767996215; Cubadebate, "Suspenden actividades festivas de las XV Jornadas Cubanas Contra la Homofobia y la Transfobia," May 9, 2022, accessed at http://www.cubadebate.cu/noticias/2022/05/09/suspenden-actividades-festivas-de-las-xv-jornadas-cubanas-contra-la-homofobia-y-la-transfobia.

41. Ahora Sí, "¿Quiénes están detrás de #AhoraSí? Conoce al equipo," Facebook, June 3, 2021, accessed at https://www.facebook.com/AhoraSiCuba/posts/pfbid0VVwAuHzeVBn9Hap1tZBarqnYt9eJhVDZXLK1vVSHuprq5hLWhwMn2RA5d3CTBuA3l.

42. Ahora Sí, "Ha pasado un mes . . . Ahora Sí," Facebook, June 27, 2021, accessed at https://www.facebook.com/AhoraSiCuba/posts/pfbid02fF6W1eD5XUBaA3KSCiMcHE5VWMfJBVwXWGHPtFzFuEXvFnHJrpDJGMFxGDm6BXNQl.

43. Antonio Rodríguez Salvador, "El Toque exchange y un apocalipsis de dos centavos," Cubadebate, August 28, 2022, accessed at http://www.cubadebate.cu/noticias/2022/10/28/el-toque-exchange-y-un-apocalipsis-de-dos-centavos-video. Also see "Editorial: 'La noche no será eterna,'" el Toque, August 31, 2022, https://eltoque.com/editorial-la-noche-no-sera-eterna.

44. "Hoy: avispero contra el bloqueo en universidades cubanas," Granma, October 31, 2018, accessed at https://www.granma.cu/cuba/2018-10-31/hoy-avispero-contra-el-bloqueo-en-universidades-cubanas-31-10-2018-09-10-47.

45. "Palabras censuradas en los mensajes de texto SMS en Cuba," Proyecto Inventario, June 15, 2022, accessed at https://proyectoinventario.org/palabras-censuradas-en-mensajes-de-texto-sms-cuba-etecsa. Also see Michael Bustamante's chapter in this volume for a discussion of the song "Patria y Vida."

46. Hope Bastian, "Cuba's Pandemic Crisis," Current History 122, no. 841 (February 1, 2023): 56–62, accessed at https://doi.org/10.1525/curh.2023.122.841.56.

47. Eric Caraballoso, "Cuba: Five Questions for the Year That Begins," OnCuba News, January 9, 2023, accessed at https://oncubanews.com/en/cuba/cuba-five-questions-for-the-year-that-begins.

CHAPTER 20

The Comeback of Racial Inequalities

ASSESSING THE RE-STRATIFICATION OF CUBAN SOCIETY

Katrin Hansing and Bert Hoffmann

Social and racial inequalities are rapidly increasing in Cuba. The "erosion of racial equality" (Blue 2007) has taken on a new quality, in which not only living standards become less equal, but a comprehensive structural reconfiguration of Cuban society is taking place. From a comparative perspective, the socioeconomic cleavages on the island are not as profound and the racial imbalances are not yet as deeply ingrained as in numerous other Latin American countries. Nevertheless, given that overcoming social inequalities and racial discrimination has been at the very core of the revolutionary project, the re-stratification is dramatic and has a number of immediate political implications.

The debate on social inequalities has become an issue of public discourse in Cuba; however, the racial connotations of these inequalities are largely dismissed. Scholars and activists on the island have called for the National Office of Statistics to publish data on the relationship between race and social inequality in more meaningful ways. In the words of the Afro-Cuban scholar Esteban Morales (2018): "The Cuban population is treated as a homogenous mass. This is an error of incalculable dimension. . . . 'black skin color' has always been a category of social differentiation—a category that is not taken into consideration by our national statistics apparatus."

The 1959 Cuban Revolution radically broke with a past in which "class" overlapped with most aspects of social life, including "race," gender, income, education, and territory. The centralized, state-sponsored economy was the great social elevator of the lower strata of society. As a result, by the 1980s Cuba had become one of the most egalitarian societies in the world. However, ever since the economic crisis of the 1990s new social inequalities have emerged, and they have become more and more visible in everyday life.

Whereas Cuba's National Office of Statistics (ONEI) publishes little data on Cuban society's re-stratification, between January 2017 and April 2018, Hansing and a four-member Cuban research team conducted a unique nationwide survey with 1,049 respondents across the island. By selecting a cross section of Cuban society based on age, gender, race, educational background, profession, and territorial location, a semi-representative survey and reliable results were achieved. This chapter draws on

Hansing and Hoffmann (2020), in which method and findings are described in more detail.

Our data show patterns of growing socioeconomic disparity in which, most disturbingly, Afro-Cubans have significantly less income through remittances or private business activities, less savings, and less access to the internet, goods, and mobility. In other words, it reveals how strongly racialized Cuba's emerging social structure is.

A note is due on the terms and method used in our survey defining the respondents' racial identity. The official Cuban census rejects the term *race* and instead uses the term *skin color* (ONEI 2016, 7–9). International studies on Latin America and the Caribbean use the terms *race* or *ethnicity/ethnic group*. In this chapter these terms are used interchangeably.

The Cuban census allows for three different categories of skin color: white, black, and mulatto (ONEI 2016, 4). In our survey we only used two categories—namely, white and Afro-Cuban, based on self-identification. We are well aware that neither two nor three categories will do justice to the complexity and diversity of racial identities in Cuba. But given the societal relevance "race" has historically had and continues to have today, coping with the deficiencies of such categories is in our view better than not using them at all and, by doing so, being blind to the current social realities.

Social Inequalities along Racial Lines

The National Office of Statistics does not report on key income inequalities, as its publications only provide data on salaries in the highly devalued Cuban peso (CUP), thereby explicitly excluding hard-currency earnings (e.g., ONEI 2017, 4). As the average monthly CUP salary translates into a mere US$30 on the black market,[1] with this type of accounting, official income differences are low. In contrast, our survey asked for income as measured in the US-dollar-pegged convertible peso (CUC). While the data show that a sector of well-off Cubans is emerging with far higher incomes than the majority, the contrasts are much stronger when we break this data down by race (see table 20.1).

Among Afro-Cubans, 95 percent report a yearly income below CUC 3,000. In contrast, only 58 percent of white Cubans fall into this lowest income category. In turn, income levels above CUC 5,000 are limited almost exclusively to white Cubans.

There are some counterweights. Monetary income is not the only factor defining material status, particularly in a socialist country like Cuba, where state subsidies are prevalent. Cuba's welfare provisions have largely been nonmonetary, and although their quality and scope have eroded over time, they still need to be taken into account. Despite harsh cutbacks the food-rationing system still distributes basic food supplies at almost symbolic CUP prices. Education and health care are free, and public transportation as well as arts/cultural and sports events are heavily subsidized. Also, given that most Cubans own their own home and rents are subsidized, housing costs are not as central a concern as elsewhere. Still, most state-run and private businesses as well as the black market are based on hard-currency prices, and it has become impossible for ordinary Cubans to satisfy their daily needs with their state salaries.

Table 20.1. Income and savings by race (percentage)

Annual income in US dollars		<3.000	3.001–5.000	5.001–10.000	10.001–20.000	20.001–40.000	40.001–60.000	>60.000
Total		74.2	11.9	3.3	2.0	2.8	2.4	0.8
White		58.5	18.3	8.6	4.4	4.2	4.7	1.3
Afro-Cuban		94.9	3.5	0.9	0.7	0	0	0
White	Without remittances	24.4	13.0	13.3	8.9	17.0	18.5	5.9
	With remittances	68.5	20.2	7.2	3.0	0	0	0
Afro-Cuban	Without remittances	97.2	1.5	0.3	0.9	0	0	0
	With remittances	89.1	6.6	2.3	0	0	0	0

Personal savings (in CUC)	0	1–100	101–250	251–500	501–3.000	>3.000
Total	6.8	26.8	17.9	19.2	17.4	11.9
White	1.3	11.0	19.1	23.6	25.1	19.9
Afro-Cuban	14.1	47.8	16.4	13.2	7.2	1.3

Source: Authors' survey data.

The increased monetization of socioeconomic affairs is a key ingredient of Cuba's ongoing economic reform process. Access to a bank account is a good indicator of how prepared people are for this. Here, too, our survey provides strong evidence of the increasing race-based inequalities. Among white Cubans, 50 percent of respondents reported having a bank account; among Afro-Cubans, this was a mere 11 percent (see table 20.2).

Savings show a similarly stark divide. The level of savings shows not only how prepared people are to face adverse material circumstances, but also how able they are to take advantage of possibilities in the market sector of the Cuban economy. More than 62 percent of Afro-Cubans but only 12 percent of whites in our survey report savings of less than CUC 100 (see table 20.1). On the other end of the spectrum, while 45 percent of white Cubans have savings above CUC 500, this is only the case for 8 percent of Afro-Cubans.

Finally, travel: A key step undertaken under Raúl Castro's leadership was the migration law reform in 2013, which eliminated the domestic administrative obstacles for Cubans when leaving the island. Since then travel has increased greatly. In a context in which the petty import business into Cuba is booming, travel possibilities constitute an important material asset. In our survey, 31 percent—almost one-third—of white

Table 20.2.   Bank account, internet access, travel abroad, and remittances (percentages by race)

		White	Afro-Cuban
Bank account holders			
	Yes	50.4	11.5
	No	49.6	88.5
Internet access			
	Does not have	25.2	70.0
	In public areas	62.1	27.8
	At home	12.7	2.2
Travel abroad			
	Yes	30.9	3.3
	No	69.1	96.7
Remittance receivers			
	Total	78.1	21.9
	Yes	77.3	28.5
	No	22.7	71.5
Reasons for not receiving remittances			
	I'm fine	62.2	0.3
	Family abroad does not send	9.6	14.8
	I do not have family abroad	28.1	84.9

Source: Authors' survey data

Cubans reported having traveled since the migration law reform; among Afro-Cubans this figure was a mere 3 percent (see table 20.2).

Whether we look at income, access to a bank account, savings, or travel abroad, our survey results show that the inequalities that have opened up in Cuban society are profoundly marked by race. We now turn to the driving forces behind this process.

Past Migration Patterns and the Impact of Family Remittances

If after the 1959 Revolution the state-run economy became the powerful social elevator for the upward mobility of Afro-Cubans, it was precisely the decline of Cuba's socialist state economy after 1989 that reversed this process. At the depth of the crisis in 1993, the government saw itself forced to legalize the US dollar—essentially to secure the minimum of foreign exchange revenues deemed necessary for survival by tapping into remittances from emigrated relatives.

Migrant remittances have become an important source of external finance in much of the developing world. Although a latecomer to the group of remittance-receiving countries, Cuba received an estimated US$3.5 billion in money transfers a year before the pandemic. This is a huge portion of the island's yearly hard currency intake. However, the distribution of remittances in Cuban society is untypical. In Mexico, Central America, and other countries in the region it has mostly been the lower strata of society that have emigrated, mainly to the United States. In contrast, in Cuba the 1959 Revolution sparked the exodus of hundreds of thousands of mostly white upper- and middle-class Cubans, who had lost their power, property, privileges, and businesses. Between 1959 and 1973 more than half a million Cubans immigrated to the United States, most of whom settled in South Florida.

In the following decades, other migrant cohorts enlarged the Cuban émigré community. In many ways the Cuban diaspora has come to reflect Cuba's own diversity, with the exception of one key aspect—namely, the island's racial composition. Respondents of Cuban origin were much more likely than the total Hispanic population to report as white alone (85 percent) (Ennis, Ríos-Vargas, and Albert 2011). Also, the much smaller Cuban diaspora in Europe is predominantly white, not least due to the large inflow on the basis of the 2007 Spanish "grandchildren's law" which awarded citizenship to Cubans with Spanish ancestry.

This strongly racialized migration pattern has immediate consequences for remittances. Our survey confirms that remittances mainly flow along family lines. In fact, for 98 percent of respondents the sender of their remittances was a family member. The cleavage is clear: Among white respondents, 93 percent had a family member abroad; among Afro-Cubans, only 34 percent did. This translates into unequal access to remittances. In our survey, a total of 56 percent of respondents received remittances. Of these, 78 percent were white and only 22 percent were Afro-Cuban (see table 20.2).

However, the most striking racial divide comes from the 44 percent of respondents who did not receive remittances. Among Afro-Cubans, 85 percent did not have family abroad, while among whites this was the case for only 28 percent (see table 20.2). Among Afro-Cubans, the remaining 15 percent said that their relatives abroad don't send money; for whites, this was 10 percent. However, there was a third category: of the whites without remittances, a full 62 percent said they don't receive remittances because they "are fine" (*estoy bien*). In other words, they don't need monetary support from their family abroad but are what we could call "living above the remittance line." Among Afro-Cubans, not a single respondent answered in this manner.

There may, however, also be a semantic issue at work. The concept of remittances (*remesas*) usually refers to a relatively small amount of money that is sent to help cover basic monthly costs. The Cubans who "are fine" may, in fact, be seeing the money from relatives abroad not as remittances; instead, they may view it as start-up capital or as a joint "family investment" to purchase a house or car, renovate a home, or start a business. The new economics of labor migration conceive of "remittances as an intra-family loan arrangement" (Poirine 1997), and this is the prototypical Cuban version of it.

Self-Employment and Small Enterprises

When the US dollar was legalized in Cuba in the 1990s and remittances started to pour in, they mainly served as a private "social safety net." This is still the case for many, but with the economic opening for private businesses, even if limited, remittances now have become a key source of capital for investment.

There is enormous diversity in terms of what falls under so-called private sector activities, ranging from street vendors, who sell peanuts for a few pesos, to people who own and rent out entire apartments to foreigners in hard currency. Our survey reflects this. Of the 286 respondents undertaking private sector activities, more than 60 percent reported sales of less than CUC 500 per month. However, the racialized stratification within this sector becomes evident when this data is disaggregated along racial lines (see table 20.3). Of the Afro-Cubans engaged in private sector activities, 77 percent have sales below CUC 250 per month; among whites this is a mere 30 percent. Among high-revenue businesses we find the opposite. Almost half of the self-employed whites have monthly sales above CUC 500, compared to a mere 7 percent among self-employed Afro-Cubans. Almost a third of white Cubans in this sector reported monthly sales above CUC 1,000; not a single Afro-Cuban did.

There are two types of businesses that can be considered high-revenue activities: room rentals for foreign tourists and private restaurants (*paladares*), which cater to tourists and to the small number of relatively high-income Cubans. As the laws do not allow the leasing or acquisition of state property for these activities, both depend crucially on the availability of large private homes.

Here, the issue of prerevolutionary property kicks in. After 1959 the revolutionary government confiscated all rental housing properties; however, an individual was allowed to keep one private home (house or apartment) and one vacation home, at the beach or in the countryside. With the legalization of private room rentals and restaurants in the 1990s, the grand mansions and spacious apartments from the pre-

Table 20.3. Business sales and type of business (by race percentages)

Monthly sales (in CUC)	1–250	251–500	501–1,000	1,001–3,000	>3,000
White	29.8	22.2	17.3	17.8	12.9
Afro-Cuban	77.0	16.4	6.6	0	0

Type of business	Room rental/ B&B	Restaurant	Simple gastronomy	Beauty services	Production	Services (crafts)	Vendor	Other services
White	30.0	4.4	13.7	13.7	8.0	10.2	5.8	14.2
Afro-Cuban	1.6	0	14.8	11.5	6.6	19.7	27.9	18.0

Source: Authors' survey data.

revolutionary era became the crucial base for entering the most lucrative segments of the new market economy. Given the racialized stratification of Cuba's pre-1959 society, the access to such real estate—and hence the possibility of opening a restaurant or a bed-and-breakfast—has starkly disfavored Afro-Cubans.

This "property bias" was given further fuel by Law 288, which as part of Raúl Castro's economic reform agenda legalized the buying and selling of private property. This re-commodification evidently favors prerevolutionary elites who kept their property, as well as revolutionary cadres who were allotted confiscated property. In this context Bastian (2018, 125) speaks of the beneficiaries as "Cuba's two historical ruling classes: the children and grandchildren of pre-revolutionary elites who remained in Cuba after the Revolution, and the descendants of revolutionary leaders." It also favors a third, often overlapping, sector—namely, those with family members abroad willing and able to finance real estate acquisitions on the island. In racial terms, this circumstance again tilts strongly in favor of white Cubans.

Our survey data on occupations in the emergent private sector provide evidence of the resulting imbalances. Among self-employed Afro-Cubans the largest share is that of petty vendors (28 percent), followed by craftsmen (20 percent) and small-scale gastronomic services (15 percent) (see table 20.3). In our survey, no Afro-Cuban owns a private restaurant, and only one respondent (2 percent) reported renting out accommodation. In contrast, among whites, renting private accommodation is the single biggest category (30 percent); restaurants are relatively few, at only 4 percent, but this is a category in which Afro-Cubans are entirely absent. Petty vendors, the number one category among Afro-Cubans, only accounts for 6 percent of white respondents. Private taxi and transport services are another sector in which prerevolutionary property—and hence pre-1959 ethnic hierarchies—weigh heavily.

The Privilege of Additional Foreign Citizenship

As we have seen, transnational links based on past racialized migration patterns have an enormous impact on the restructuring of Cuban society currently taking place. As part of this, another factor comes into play—namely, the ability, or inability, to obtain a second, foreign citizenship. This issue gained prominence in Cuba when in 2007 a Spanish law—of historical memory (*memoria histórica*)—gave the right to acquire Spanish citizenship to whoever could claim to have a Spanish parent or grandparent who had fled fascist Spain under Franco. In Cuba the impact was enormous. As of 2018, more than 110,000 Cubans had become Spanish citizens under this law and another 70,000 applications were being processed.

In our survey, 68 of 1,049 respondents reported holding second citizenship. Of these, 85 percent held Spanish citizenship; the remainder were split up among different nationalities, acquired mostly through marriage. This underscores the crucial impact of Spain's "grandchildren's law." As it is based on Spanish ancestry it is of little surprise that access to Spanish citizenship is, exceptions apart, a privilege of white Cubans.

In Cuba, the privileges of an EU passport are immediately tangible, as it is the key to international mobility. The survey data shows how much higher international mobility is among dual citizens: 98 percent had traveled abroad since the 2013 migration law, compared to a mere 14 percent of those with only Cuban citizenship.

Travel possibilities are the key resource for the flourishing petty import business that brings everything from clothes to cellphones and from makeup to air conditioners into the country. In addition, an EU passport paves the way to opening a bank account abroad, which is of much value for transnational business, renting apartments, or getting a credit card.

The impact is particularly striking because the coveted EU passport is accessible almost exclusively to a social group that is already better off—namely, white Cubans with family abroad. It is a privilege that comes "on top" of and reinforces an already favorable social status.

Cuba's Socio-racial Re-stratification: Conclusions

The increasing social inequalities lend urgency to the reform of Cuba's social welfare system. At present, the system is based on the principle of universal, equal coverage. As such, all Cubans, for example, receive the highly subsidized food provisions via a ration system, regardless of whether they need them or not. The issue of moving from a universal ration-card system to a targeted social safety program based on need has been on Cuba's reform agenda for many years without being implemented. Postponing its implementation has not helped to curb social inequalities.

There is much at stake. For the socialist government, rising inequalities touch upon a key pillar of political legitimacy. While Raúl Castro's economic reform agenda bid farewell to the excessive egalitarianism of the past, the state and party leadership still claim to be the guardians of social justice and societal cohesion. A central instrument in this regard has been putting the brakes on the growth of the private sector. However, not only is this at odds with the hopes of economic growth through reform, it also overlooks that the root cause of the widening social gap is not the opening of small businesses, but rather the collapse of the purchasing power of wages in Cuba's state sector.

This is what our research has addressed. Its analysis shows how strongly the pre-revolutionary, racialized social structure is shaping the current reproduction of social inequalities, leaving Afro-Cubans clearly disadvantaged. In the current re-stratification of Cuban society, this racial bias is turning back one of the proudest historic achievements of the Cuban Revolution.

Impact of the Post-COVID Crisis

The research for this chapter was completed before the COVID-19 pandemic. As elsewhere, this profoundly challenged the country's health system and brought severe lockdown measures. Moreover, with the collapse of international tourism, the island also lost its main industry overnight. Together with the preexisting deficiencies of the island's economy and stepped-up US sanctions from the Trump government, which the Biden administration has to date not undone, the fallout from the pandemic led to a desperate economic crisis on the island. Shortages of all kinds severely impact daily life.

The slump in foreign tourists hit hard the bed-and-breakfasts and small restaurants which had been at the heart of the emerging private business sector—and which have been overwhelmingly "white." But this has not reversed the socio-racial hierarchies: as supplies in the peso economy dried up, access to hard-currency shops and the black market became all the more important. The monetary reform of January 2021 eliminated the CUC but did not result in making the CUP the single currency used in Cuba. Instead, a new, digital-only currency called *moneda libremente convertible* (MLC) has taken the CUC's place; it was also pegged officially at 1:1 to the US dollar and is the currency needed to obtain goods in the hard-currency shops. In the streets, US dollars and euros have gained ground as tangible hard currency, whereas the CUP has continued its devaluation. The deeper the crisis cut, the more access to remittances from abroad became essential for getting by.

However, as a result of the worsening crisis and the waning hopes of improvement, emigration has soared. Here, too, the new social inequalities weigh heavily. Those with a second passport or well-established transnational ties may just take a flight out and settle in Madrid, Mexico, or the United States. The majority of emigrants—no less than 225,000 to the US alone over the past twelve months—have taken the perilous route via Nicaragua or South America to then make their way north to cross the US border by foot.

With a cost of approximately US$10,000 for overpriced tickets and the indispensable "guides" on the migration route, this is quite an investment. Some have sold their house or car for it. For many others, relatives in the United States shouldered the cost. In a way this is another type of "remittance in kind": not to provide financial help in the struggle with the daily hardships nor to invest in a business, but to provide an intra-family loan to get out. Those with neither property to sell nor family abroad—and this disproportionately applies to Afro-Cubans—don't have this exit option. Hence, to some extent even the current wave of out-migration shows the same socio-racial bias that is reshaping Cuban society on the island.

Note

1. The latest data available on average salary is 3,830 CUP for 2021 (ONEI 2022, 5). The black market rate reached 175 CUP for 1 USD in December 2022.

References

Bastian, Hope. 2018. *Everyday Adjustments in Havana: Economic Reforms, Mobility, and Emerging Inequalities*. Lanham, MD: Lexington Books.

Blue, S. A. 2007. "The Erosion of Racial Equality in the Context of Cuba's Dual Economy." *Latin American Politics and Society* 49, no. 3: 35–68. Accessed at https://doi.org/10.1111/j.1548-2456.2007.tb00382.x.

Ennis, Sharon R., Merarys Ríos-Vargas, and Nora G. Albert. 2011. *The Hispanic Population: 2010.* Accessed December 5, 2018, at https://www.census.gov/content/dam/Census/library/publications/2011/dec/c2010br-04.pdf.

Hansing, Katrin, and Bert Hoffmann. 2020. "When Racial Inequalities Return: Assessing the Restratification of Cuban Society 60 Years after Revolution." *Latin American Politics and Society* 62, no. 2: 29–52. Accessed at https://doi.org/10.1017/lap.2019.59.

Morales, Esteban. 2018. "El tema racial en Cuba y el informe a Naciones Unidas del 2018. Un balance crítico." *Esteban Morales Domínguez* (blog), August 14. Accessed at http://esteban moralesdominguez.blogspot.com/2018/08/el-tema-racial-en-cuba-y-el-informe.html.

ONEI (Oficina Nacional de Estadísticas e Información). 2016. *El Color de la Piel según el Censo de Población y Viviendas 2012.* Havana: ONEI.

———. 2017. *Panorama Territorial Cuba 2016.* Havana: ONEI.

———. 2022. *Salario Medio en Cifras. Cuba Enero-Diciembre 2021.* Havana: ONEI. Accessed at http://www.onei.gob.cu/sites/default/files/publicacion_salario_medio_en_cifras._2021.pdf.

Poirine, Bernard. 1997. "A Theory of Remittances as an Implicit Family Loan Arrangement." *World Development* 25, no. 4: 589–611.

CHAPTER 21

Infrastructures and Inequalities in Rural Cuba

CHALLENGES FOR FAMILIES

Vilma Hidalgo López-Chávez

Cuba's rural population has faced growing inequalities and the weakening of the welfare system as a result of reforms that prioritize economic goals. This chapter examines failures in infrastructure to deliver services, transportation, markets, public education, and care in rural areas, and describes how these characteristics of rural communities structure gender relations within households that subject rural women and girls to extreme levels of gender violence.

Rurality and Social Policy from 1959 to the Present

The 1959 Revolution radically changed the conditions of precarity and poverty in which rural Cubans lived; however, the dominant development model in the first decades of the Revolution often prioritized urban areas (García et al. 2019). The creation of state cooperatives and urbanization of rural communities to improve living conditions left an imprint on the rural population and gave rise to a process of depopulation that began in the 1970s (Íñiguez, Figueroa, and Frómeta 2019). This rural exodus has been difficult to reverse and is extremely critical in dispersed and mountain settlements in eastern Cuba.

Measures implemented in response to the Special Period crisis of the 1990s also had uneven effects on rural communities. While some rural areas maintained a stable population and experienced economic growth through efficient land use, diversification, and opportunities for articulation with local productive chains, territories with little entrepreneurial capital and opportunities for economic diversification connected to emerging sectors of the economy experienced a stark decline (Leyva and Arias 2015). Strong decapitalization has led to insufficient infrastructure and services and low standards of living, which further encourage migration and demographic aging, leaving community well-being increasingly dependent on decision-makers (Leyva and Arias 2015).

The contrast between thriving and struggling rural communities is clearly seen in the upward mobility of producers in eastern Cuba dedicated to various crops and livestock in comparison with the stagnation and downward mobility of members of Cooperatives of Agricultural Production (CPAs) and Basic Units of Cooperative Production (UBPCs), state workers, and peasants linked to crops like coffee (Espina Prieto et al. 2010). Between 2002 and 2012, the agricultural sector experienced a loss of 135,196 workers, creating significant labor shortages which continue to impact agricultural production (Íñiguez and Figueroa 2018, 60).

Because of the urgent need to increase agricultural productivity, the 2011 "Guidelines for the Economic and Social Policies of the Party and the Revolution" emphasized decentralization and local development, the expansion of the private and cooperative sector, and the distribution of idle land in usufruct to increase production, promote employment, and encourage the repopulation of rural areas (Bombino 2014). In addition to measures aimed at increasing production, the Guidelines also reorganized social spending, attempting to "reinforce the sustainability of social policy" through budget cuts for social assistance, education, and health services (PCC 2017). To cut costs, the number of family doctor-nurse offices, polyclinics, rural hospitals, and primary and secondary schools decreased significantly (Hidalgo 2020).

Outside of a small number of prosperous rural communities, the well-being of Cuba's rural population was particularly affected by the weakening of the welfare system and the reduction of educational, healthcare, and other basic services. Limited mobility due to a lack of transportation and deterioration of roads contributed to widening the urban and rural gap in access to income, education, and conditions for well-being (Hidalgo 2020). For example, the concentration of educational centers has meant that children and adolescents must travel longer distances for education, resulting in lower school attendance rates in rural areas: 30.89 percent of rural adolescents are not studying (compared to 12.24 percent of urban youth) (Íñiguez, Figueroa, and Rojas 2017). While they may have saved money, these new agrarian policies and programs failed to reverse the complex migratory dynamics affecting rural communities and instead increased social stratification (Leyva 2018).

Rural Families Today

In Cuba, around 150,000 rural families are dedicated to agricultural production; however, little research is available to show how rural families are affected by and respond to processes of social change (FAO 1995). Rural and urban Cuban households share similar demographic trends: they tend to form stable partnerships early, between 15 and 20 years of age, and live in consensual partnerships rather than formal legalized marriages. Fertility rates are low, and female migration rates are high. Rural households tend to be organized in small nuclear families, with an average of 2.87 people. The majority (63 percent) of rural households do not have children, and the number of single-person households made up of people over 60 years of age has increased (García et al. 2019, 12).

Increased access to technologies, communication products, and transnational and urban exchanges promote an ideal of progress typical of urban and transnational life in rural communities. Cultural globalization penetrates audiovisual tastes, clothing preferences, and consumer expectations that cannot be fulfilled in the rural environment. In this sense, feelings of frustration appear, which stimulate migratory projects and the detachment of young people from agricultural activity.

> This is a life of suffering, even if you have money you can't stop working. We are tired of this. I don't want this life for my child. I want him to study, to become a professional, to become somebody in life and that is why we keep fighting, this is his father's dream and mine. (41-year-old female)

Infrastructure and Gendered Vulnerability

While rural housing stock quantities are sufficient, structural conditions are much worse than in urban areas and the insufficiency of water, sanitation, and electricity services directly impacts the living conditions of rural families (MINCONS 2018). Although 96.2 percent of rural households are connected to electrical infrastructure, water aqueducts only connect 42.6 percent of households: 12.9 percent do not have access to drinking water, while 89.1 percent use pits and latrines (ONEI 2017). The lack of basic goods in rural households, especially in eastern Cuba, is evidence of high levels of poverty and precarity (Pupo 2017; Nodal 2011; Chávez et al. 2008). Compared to urban homes, rural households own fewer key household appliances: only 74 percent have a television, of which slightly more than a third are black-and-white; 54 percent have a refrigerator; 42 percent a washing machine; and 75 percent have a rice cooker and multipurpose cooker (García et al. 2019).

The growing insufficiency of social support services for the care of vulnerable people such as children, the elderly, and people with disabilities has displaced care to the family environment and increased the dependency burden of households (Hidalgo 2020). Deficiencies in infrastructure demand an extra effort from families that falls mainly on female figures responsible for caring for and carrying out domestic chores, which on many occasions extend to unpaid agricultural labor (ONEI 2016).

Gender asymmetries in relation to occupation and property structure show that rural women have few opportunities for paid employment and a greater presence in the state sector and in lower-paid administrative and service positions (Muster and Fleitas 2014). In her study, Echevarría found that less than 15 percent of rural women of working age were engaged in paid work (2013). In the communities I studied, only 23 percent of women are employed, compared to 75 percent of men. New post-reform opportunity structures continue to privilege men in access to assets and means of production as well as employment in better-remunerated sectors of the economy. Women's employment was concentrated in the state sector and in UBPCs in food processing, security, education, and office administration, positions with low salaries and social prestige (Hidalgo 2020). Men are concentrated in sectors that respond to the logic of change and emerging opportunities in the country's agrarian and economic structure, such as Cooperatives of Credits and Services (CCSs) and self-employment, with a greater diversification of the activities. All the community members employed outside the state sector were men. A wide disproportion in access to land between men and women is evident. Women represent only 9.5 percent of small farmers with usufruct rights (Echevarría 2013). In my sample, there was only one female small farmer.

The unequal structure of opportunities for employment is one way that the patriarchal culture affects the internal and relational dynamics of rural families, generating strong asymmetries of power which mediate the distribution of roles, the use of public and private spaces, relational dynamics that reinforce the culture of obedience and respect for the father, and climates charged with violence, as well as parenting patterns entrenched in sexist stereotypes. Rural households headed by women represent only 16 percent of the total, compared to 44.9 percent nationally (ONEI 2012). Empirical evidence confirms the prevalence of strong power imbalances in male-female partners, which place the man as an authority figure and are linked to the high incidence of domestic violence toward women and girls naturalized, legitimized, and invisibilized in the communities in which they occur (Hernández, Ramírez, and Graham 2017). This situation is made more complex by the high consumption of alcoholic beverages by rural men (García et al. 2019).

> The boss is the first God and then me as the head of the household. I am the only man. I live with my three girls and my wife. They have to follow my orders. I am the one looking out for them and the one who speaks for them, you see? (31-year-old male)

The proportion of separations or divorces is significantly lower in rural areas. Only 9 percent of all rural mothers are single and less than 3 percent are divorced (compared to urban rates of 13.98 percent single and 7.2 percent divorced). Two-parent households represent 58.8 percent of the total rural households, while female single parents are only 27.97 percent. Rural nuclear households are frequently integrated into networks of nearby kin that lead to a type of economic and functional exchange more typical of the extended family. Sexist parenting models combined with structural limitations for education contribute to the frequency of adolescent marriage.

> I finished middle school and didn't want to continue, the school was very far away and I didn't have a way to get there. Now I am with a guy who is doing his military service. We live together right here, but we sleep in my grandmother's house next door. What I do is help my mother with things around the house, whatever needs to be done. I get up at 8:00 a.m. and I get started helping with the pigs' food, or cleaning, washing, straightening up the house. I've been cooking since I was 9 years old! (15-year-old female)

Cuba's total fertility rate (TFR) of 1.57 children per woman (ONEI 2020) is below the replacement line, and the rural TFR of 1.53 is actually lower than the urban rate of 1.74 (Rodríguez, Molina, and Quintana 2015). However, when this indicator is crossed with the age dimension, a significant increase in adolescent fertility is observed in rural areas. In 2014, fertility among rural 10- to 14-year-olds was 44 percent higher than their urban agemates (Molina 2019, 85). Fertility rates of rural 15- to 19-year-olds were 20 percent higher than their urban peers (Molina 2019, 85). Recent studies show that this troubling pattern has continued through 2020 (Molina 2021).

How People Feel about Their Lives in Rural Areas

Cuban researchers have long called for more attention to rural communities whose daily realities and family lives have been largely invisible (Vera 2012). Participants expressed the greatest dissatisfaction with relationships between the family and schools and the state and work, as well as with public transportation and the care provided by the health system. The quality of life of rural families is negatively affected by the lack of basic services (commerce, care institutions, education and health, transportation, recreation options) as well as weak connectivity and accessibility that restrict connections with other rural and urban settings. In terms of employment, emerging opportunities since the 2011 economic reforms can only be taken advantage of in rural settlements close to urban spaces. These characteristics are the cause of deep dissatisfaction and devalue individuals' sense of the place where they live and, in addition, have fractured the relationships of families with social institutions, whose support and protection functions they perceived as deficient.

> Transportation is bad, the bus now comes by on Tuesdays and Saturdays and today it didn't actually come. This is difficult to accept, people say that if the road was in good condition and there was good transportation they wouldn't leave. If instead of this bad dirt road there was a good path you could even go to Aguada by bike. The people with money have their electric scooter and trucks and they don't have to leave. With a good road the doctor could come every day on an electric scooter, but with the road the way it is they can't come. (31-year-old female)

> The shortages are extreme because even with money you can't find the things you need. You could have thousands of pesos, but if you can't get to Covadonga or Aguada . . . we don't have anything here. Things to eat for example, seasonings, vegetables, a little piece of meat, you have to go buy it there and sometimes when you get there there is nothing left because you didn't make it in time. (30-year-old female)

Families describe impoverished formal support networks, centered on workplaces and for those with religious beliefs, the church. To compensate for the deficient relationships between the family and state support systems, informal networks have become extremely important. Relatives, neighbors, and religious relationships make up solid networks of reciprocal exchange of goods, services, and support for child and elderly care. Even commercial relations privilege the informal/submerged market in the purchase of basic products (food, hygiene, clothing, footwear, medicines, instruments, and work supplies), for compensation in the face of shortages and the long distances that families must travel to access them.

> My husband needs a special diet, he has to have chicken, vegetables, and medicines. If I can't find it in the pharmacy I have to buy them wherever they show up. Some people sell them for 10 CUC for 100 pills. Sometimes you can find them for 5 CUC. (54-year-old female)

> My grandmother or my mother take care of the kid. There is no state child
> care here, just first grade, that's it. If a woman wants to work she has to have
> family nearby, if not she is out of luck. (37-year-old woman)

Reforms aimed at reducing rural schools, polyclinics, and hospitals and subsidies have exacerbated the dissatisfaction accumulated by families and strained their relationship with the state, translating into feelings of isolation and exclusion. The perception of a conflict between the policies implemented and their own needs and interests has impacted community participation, and ties to political organizations have declined.

> This stopped working here many years ago. The Federation of Cuban
> Women representative lives nearby, she is a good person and all, but the
> poor thing is old. The Committee for the Defense of the Revolution guy
> lives downstairs and they say that they do a caldosa on the 28th, but I never
> hear anything about it, nor do I care. (41-year-old female)

The sustained invisibility of rural families in the framework of the reforms that are being carried out is an area of great concern, as is the gap between current social policies and the needs, interests, and problems faced by families. The cost of implementing reforms that do not correspond to the subjectivities of the rural protagonists is still evidenced in lingering effects of the resizing of the sugar industry in the early 2000s, and the migratory trends and loss of agricultural labor force that resulted from the urbanization and concentration of rural communities with a strong peasant tradition. Studying the experiences of families in rural contexts contributes to understanding how gendered vulnerabilities rooted in infrastructural failures to deliver services, transportation, markets, public education, and care in rural areas reinforce unequal gender relations that subject women and girls to gender violence.

References

Bombino, Y. 2014. "La juventud rural en el contexto de reordenamiento del modelo económico cubano." *Revista Estudio* (Centro de Estudios Sobre la Juventud) 18: 54–63.

Chávez, E., et al. 2008. "Las familias cubanas en el Parteaguas de dos siglos." Informe de investigación. Grupo de Estudios sobre Familia. Havana: Centro de Investigaciones Psicológicas y Sociológicas.

Echevarría, D. 2013. "Procesos de reajuste en Cuba y su impacto en el empleo femenino: dos siglos y repetidas desigualdades." In *Miradas a la economía cubana: Entre la eficiencia económica y la equidad social*, ed. O. E. Pérez and R. Torres, 54–67. Havana: Editorial Caminos.

Espina Prieto, M., et al. 2010. "Sistematización de estudios sobre heterogeneidad social y desigualdades en Cuba. 2000–2008." Informe de investigación. Havana: Centro de Investigaciones Psicológicas y Sociológicas.

FAO (Food and Agriculture Organization of the United Nations). 1995. "Las familias rurales." Chap. 4 in *Mirando hacia Beijing 95—Mujeres rurales en América Latina y el Caribe: Situación, perspectivas, propuestas*. Accessed at http://www.fao.org/3/x0248s/x0248s05.htm.

García, M., et al. 2019. "Condición y posición de las mujeres rurales en Cuba." Informe de Investigación. Centro de Estudios de la Economía Cubana (CEEC). Havana: Universidad de La Habana.

Hernández, Y., A. Ramírez, and M. Graham. 2017. "Bajo el silencio: violencia contra mujeres y relaciones incestuosas en el medio rural. Lecturas culturales de un estudio de caso en Moa." In *Políticas públicas y procesos rurales en Cuba: Aproximaciones desde las Ciencias Sociales*, ed. A. Leyva and D. Echevarría, 250–71. Havana: Ruth Casa Editorial

Hidalgo López-Chávez, V. 2020. *Desigualdades, ruralidad e interseccionalidad: Análisis del contexto cubano 2008–2018*. FLACSO-Cuba. Havana: Publicaciones Acuario. Accessed at http://biblioteca.clacso.edu.ar/Cuba/flacso-cu/20201103114047/9-Desigualdades-ruralidad.pdf.

Íñiguez, L., E. Figueroa, and J. Rojas. 2017. "Atlas de la Infancia y la Adolescencia en Cuba." Análisis a partir del Censo de Población y Vivienda del 2012. Havana: Editorial UH.

Íñiguez Rojas, Luisa, and Edgar Figueroa Fernández. 2018. "Los territorios rurales de Cuba: Las disyuntivas de su determinación." In *Cuba rural: transformaciones agrarias, dinámicas sociales e innovación local*, ed. A. Leyva, D. Echevarría, and R. Villegas, 105–34. Havana: Editorial de Ciencias Sociales.

Íñiguez Rojas, Luisa, Edgar Figueroa Fernández, and Enrique Frómeta Sánchez. 2019. "La heterogeneidad territorial en las actuales estrategias de desarrollo rural en Cuba." *Temas* 98 (April–June 2019): 56–64.

Leyva, A. 2018. "Cooperativas agropecuarias en Cuba: Dinámicas socioestructurales entre dos siglos." In *Cuba rural*, 135–88.

Leyva Remón, A., and M. Arias Guevara. 2015. "Reforma, ruralidades y nuevos campesinos/as en Cuba. Desafíos y propuestas para las políticas públicas." In *Cuba: los correlatos socioculturales del cambio económico*, ed. M. Espina Prieto and D. Echevarría León, 153–78. Havana: Editorial Casa Ruth.

Molina Cintra, M. C. 2019. "La fecundidad adolescente en Cuba." Havana: Editorial CEDEM.

———. 2021. "Tendencias de la fecundidad adolescente en Cuba hasta el 2020." *Novedades en Población* 17, no. 34. Accessed at http://www.novpob.uh.cu.

MINCONS (Ministerio de la Construcción de la República de Cuba). 2018. "Política de Vivienda en Cuba." Accessed at http://www.micons.gob.cu.

Muster, B., and R. Fleitas. 2014. *Equidad vs. Inequidad de género en el sector agropecuario en Cuba*. Centro de Investigaciones de la Economía Mundial. Universidad de La Habana.

Nodal, T. 2011. "Feminización de la pobreza en áreas rurales y periferias de San Antonio de los Baños." Tesis de diploma. Facultad de Filosofía, Historia y Sociología. Universidad de La Habana.

ONEI (Oficina Nacional de Estadística e Información). 2012. *Informe Nacional del Censo de Población y Vivienda*. Havana: ONEI.

———. 2016. *Encuesta Nacional sobre Igualdad de Género, ENIG-2016*. Havana: ONEI.

———. 2017. *Anuario Estadístico de Cuba, 2016*. Havana: ONEI.

———. 2020. *Anuario Estadístico de Cuba, 2019*. Havana: ONEI.

PCC (Partido Comunista de Cuba). 2017. "Conceptualización del Modelo Económico y Social Cubano de Desarrollo Socialista." Documentos del 7mo. Congreso del Partido aprobados por el III Pleno del Comité Central del PCC el 18 de mayo de 2017. Accessed at https://www.granma.cu/file/pdf/gaceta/tabloide%202%20%C3%BAltimo.pdf.

Pupo, A. 2017. "Pobreza rural en el oriente cubano: lecturas desde las perspectivas de género y espacio." In *Políticas públicas y procesos rurales en Cuba*, 226–49.

Rodríguez, G., M. C. Molina, and L. Quintana. 2015. "Fecundidad. Estudio y comportamiento. América Latina y Cuba." *Novedades en Población* 17, no. 21: 65–77.

Vera, A. 2012. *Guajiros del siglo XXI*. Havana: Instituto Cubano de Investigación Cultural Juan Marinello.

CHAPTER 22

Evangelical Christianity, the State, and New Political Alliances

Kirenia Criado Pérez and Dachelys Valdés Moreno

Translated by Ann Halbert Brooks

Between 2018 and 2022, Cuban Neo-Pentecostal Evangelical churches spearheaded campaigns to oppose two of President Miguel Díaz-Canel's most important legislative priorities: the new Cuban Constitution (2018–2019) and the new Families Code (2021–2022).[1] In each case, as it attempted to update legislation to reflect the Revolution's historical commitments to gender equality and to guarantee the rights of Cuba's LGBTQ+ citizens, the state faced fierce opposition from emerging religious leaders, acting outside of traditional spaces for ecumenical dialogue.

It is impossible to understand contemporary Cuban political life and recent grassroots mobilizations against social equality without analyzing the phenomenon of Christian fundamentalism. Written by a Cuban pastor and popular educator and a Cuban LGBTQ+ activist, this chapter describes how a small group of Neo-Pentecostal Evangelical churches in Cuba have successfully capitalized on larger processes of social and economic change to emerge as powerful political actors, and reflects on how these changes might impact future activist movements for inclusion and social justice.

Fundamentalism: Its Definition and Roots

Perhaps it was only a matter of time before Christian fundamentalism, a phenomenon born and developed so close to the Caribbean island, would forcefully insert itself into Cuban society. Despite Cuba's unique social system, and the Revolution's atheist and Communist past, successive economic crises in Cuba have created social vulnerabilities remarkably similar to elsewhere in Latin America.

Understanding the origins of fundamentalism is essential to understanding its role in popular movements and the control of "empty" spaces in the periphery. The advance of neoliberalism in Latin America in the 1990s had devastating consequences for the working classes and strongly influenced the rise of religious fundamentalism. The lack of state attention to the working classes precluded the development of solutions to their pain and suffering. By growing close to marginalized and disfavored communities that had suffered natural disasters or been left behind by state aid efforts, Evangelicals emerged as a uniquely powerful new political force in the region.[2] A number of Evangelical churches in Latin America received support from successive US administrations to bring popular classes in conflict with efforts to demand social justice and progressive economics. The same strategy has allowed these groups to build power in Cuba, where the end of the Soviet Union and many other Soviet-aligned socialist governments also led to a profound precarity.

Many Cubans found acceptance, a sense of community, and the promise of material prosperity in new Evangelical churches. These congregations' Neo-Pentecostal focus on material prosperity was accompanied by new liturgy and new organizational forms, known as the Prosperity Gospel, which "teaches that Christians have the right to well-being, the right to good health, and the right to a good financial outlook . . . to enjoy the Earth and the privileges associated with being children of God."[3] Prosperity is posited as an outcome of, and reward for, believers' adherence to the divine project. A new faith capable of bringing about material prosperity especially appealed to Cubans facing difficult material circumstances, people who could not otherwise expect to regain the dignity or abundance they had lost.

Contrary to popular impressions, the Prosperity Gospel was not the first to imagine the possibility of change in the lives of believers in the here and now. In the 1970s, Latin American Liberation Theology held that communities of faith could work together for material well-being and happiness in this life. Based on a critical rereading of history and the Bible, it emphasized Jesus's opposition to oppression and the temporal authorities that supported it. To be a Christian was to fight against injustice and work for the liberation of the poor and oppressed; the Christian's mission was to collectively create a new, better society on Earth, free of suffering. This, of course, is incompatible with capitalism, the source of workers' oppression.

Latin American Neo-Pentecostals in the 1990s also focused on tangible improvements to the lives of believers, however with a key modification. In Neo-Pentecostalism, prosperity was the result of *individual* effort, rather than collective action. These efforts were not understood to be impacted by systems of oppression, and capitalist markets were seen as a God-given arena of personal enrichment. Believers could expect material benefits through conversion and adherence to rigid rules and teachings grounded in fundamentalist readings of the Bible. The goal of Neo-Pentecostalism was not the construction of a society free of systemic oppression, nor to escape the evils of current power structures and their reproduction in the future. Individual enrichment did not depend on mutual uplift or increasing the prosperity of the society as a whole.

The Political Project of Christian Fundamentalism in Cuba

The crisis of meaning that the Cuban social project has endured in the face of symbolic and practical shortages created a fertile ground for a fundamentalist communications strategy that challenges the political authority of secular leaders and ecumenical institutions worldwide. Fundamentalism seeks to win influence in the public sphere, legitimating itself and mobilizing believers to support fundamentalist priorities.

In Cuba, the ultimate goal is to force a dialogue with the state and ensure that fundamentalist priorities are heard, and heeded. Fundamentalist discourse in Cuba has focused on discrediting the Cuban state, denouncing its alleged inattention to religious affairs, lack of support for churches, and violations of the right to freedom of religion, insisting that the state provide equal space for the public expression of Christian viewpoints. After four decades of movement building, Christian fundamentalism in Cuba today is an organized reactionary movement particularly strong in rural and marginalized communities, capable of mobilizing large numbers of believers and other citizens to support its political projects.

In order to understand this movement, one must understand both the dogma taught in the churches and the political ambitions that accompany it. Neo-Pentecostal fundamentalism seeks to foreclose opportunities for dialogue, and de-contextualized Bible verses are used to justify an agenda centered around "moral" issues that primarily affect the bodies of women and LGBTQ+ people. Those who challenge the absolute truth of the Bible become an enemy to destroy, active threats to the full and prosperous life to which converts are entitled. This "spiritual war" of good against evil is in dialogue with a theological tradition called Dominion Theology that seeks to rebuild a theocratic state in contemporary society, "fulfilling Christian theories of predestination that those in positions of power (presidents, ministers, parliamentarians, governors of provinces and states, municipal leaders, and jurists) must be believers. Once in power, these authorities can work to bring about Christian religious rule and influence public life."[4]

Theologically speaking, fundamentalism as practiced in Cuba today includes calls for believers to build their lives around religious identity and conservative norms of sexuality, family, and marriage. For example, the biblical interpretation considered most valid in fundamentalist discourse is one that recognizes marriage as a union between a man and a woman only, indissoluble until death or adultery (Matthew 19:4–6). Biblical figures, such as Joshua (Joshua 24:15b), who chose to obey God in times of crisis, are also invoked. They preach about the fate of those who seek to practice evil, recalling what occurred in biblical accounts of the fall of Sodom and Gomorrah and the exhortation "Woe unto them that call evil good and good evil" (Isaiah 5:20). Believers are called to a life that renounces all of these evils (Titus 2:11–12).

Fundamentalist teachings also reinforce patriarchal family structures by citing the biblical creation story that portrays women as reproductive figures. Fundamentalists in Cuba seek to promote a literalist reading of the Bible that precludes critical analysis and interpretation based on contemporary context. Jesus, the historic context in which he lived, and the works he and his followers performed are not discussed. Fundamentalist churches in Cuba today proselytize with messages that the nation and the family are fundamental institutions, while also proclaiming that there are abundant signs of the coming End of Days and the Second Coming of Christ.

Cuban fundamentalism has sought to build power through action in three spheres:

1. On social media, where the goal is to (mis)inform about certain topics, promote fundamentalist priorities, amplify messaging that is compatible with a fundamentalist worldview, and forge alliances with ideologically aligned communities.

2. In communities of faith, neighborhoods, families, and communities through fundamentalist religious services, meetings, lectures, and pamphlets that utilize moralistic messaging to instill fear that the family is in danger and actions must be taken to "protect the family." In these spaces, believers' hope and newfound religious paradigm for their lives is manipulated in service of a political agenda.
3. In relations with other institutions, where fundamentalists use alliances and make demands that break with norms of ecumenicalism.

Cuban Evangelical political campaigns have honed their flocks into a de facto army, making successive claims against the state, pushing the Cuban state to adopt policies that reinforce the fundamentalist worldview around family, sexuality, and morality. Using legislative processes as a focus for their energies, fundamentalist churches claim that new legislation should reflect their worldview. Rhetoric against the LGBTQ+ community is especially virulent and the term *gender ideology* has been copied from Latin American campaigns as a tool to prevent believers from developing a critical conscience, and to oppose efforts to combat racism, machismo, sexism, homophobia, and gender-based violence.

Evangelical Mobilization to Oppose Expanding Human Rights

The first large-scale mobilization of Christian fundamentalist churches in the Cuban political arena was in the debate about the new constitution, which began in the summer of 2018. A particular flashpoint in the debates was Article 68, which proposed a change in the definition of marriage from a union between a man and a woman to one between two persons, without specifying their gender. The draft constitution was discussed in neighborhoods, workplaces, and schools, and members of fundamentalist churches attended public comment sessions to oppose the inclusion of Article 68. They publicly prayed for the "traditional Cuban family," displaying large signs outside their churches, on flyers in the streets, and even in government offices where they worked.[5]

As access to the internet grew after December 2018, social media became a site of conflict between the faithful, who sought to defend "the family," and the LGBTQ+ community, motivated by hopes that for the first time they might be acknowledged in the national constitution and have a path to reparative justice. Public opinion was split between churches that sought to recodify the "Original Design" of the heterosexual family and LGBTQ+ Cubans and their allies. The Cuban state did not respond directly to this fractured social environment, instead focusing on campaigning for popular support for the constitution's approval. Church leaders threatened that their congregants would vote against the entire constitution if Article 68 was not removed. And so, Article 68, which defined marriage equality, was separated from the constitutional project. It was decided that Cubans would be asked to decide how marriage would be defined in the upcoming Family Code two years later. With these changes, the Cuban constitution went on to be approved via referendum in February 2019 and the churches celebrated their victory.

It was inevitable that, two years later, when the new Families Code came under consideration, marriage equality and recognition of family diversity would be a point of conflict along the same battle lines drawn during the constitutional debate. In 2021–2022, the fundamentalist mobilization against same-sex marriage kicked into high gear, mobilizing in opposition from the very beginning until the day it was approved by referendum.[6] Around the same time, they also mobilized to collect signatures against a Comprehensive Sexual Education program, approved by the Ministry of Education.[7] They encouraged parents to take the radical action of removing their children from public schools so that they would not be "indoctrinated" in the "ideology of gender."[8] Fundamentalist opposition to the Resolution was presented in terms of rights—to freedom of expression and religious freedom—albeit freedoms they aimed to exercise in order to restrict the rights of others.

The LGBTQ+ side of the Families Code conflict garnered significant support from civil society. Stuck at home by curfews and limitations on mobility during the coronavirus pandemic, confrontations moved from public spaces to the internet. Social media offered a safe space to share ideas and educational material and graphics to educate about the importance of the new Families Code. Other efforts included a widely shared digital audiobook with community members reading the draft Families Code, making the dense law more engaging and accessible.[9] COVID-19 transmission rates permitting, campaigners also spread their message in the streets, distributing stickers and fliers with messages of inclusion. Cuban citizens used to the omnipresent repetitiveness of official state messaging were surprised by the variety of communications that surged from the independent community-led Families Code campaigns. This creativity was effective in building support for long-neglected rights for LGBTQ+ citizens.

Because of the lack of knowledge about religious diversity in Cuba, one unfortunate result of these conflicts has been the growing apprehension among progressive Cubans toward people of faith. The lack of understanding of religious diversity creates a risk that all Cuban Christians are unfairly perceived as a threat to human rights and just policies despite wide differences in theology.[10] Given the history of discrimination and exclusion experienced by members of ecumenical movements in the early decades of the Revolution, such a development would be a sad regression in the acceptance of diversity in Cuba.

While fundamentalists were victorious in imposing their views in the drafting of the constitution, the LGBTQ+ community and allies won the debate over the Families Code. The high-profile pressure campaigns waged on the state by Christian fundamentalists have made it clear that they are now a part of the Cuban social landscape that can no longer be ignored. The power of their numbers and ability to organize give them the ability to make demands on the state. Christian fundamentalism and political fundamentalism in Cuba will complicate future struggles to recognize and empower historically marginalized communities and challenge patriarchal norms. We can expect to see campaigns in the future that will continue to complicate upcoming legislative struggles for inclusive sex education, to protect trans Cubans, curb gender-based violence, advance the status of women, and combat racism.

Notes

1. While the 1976 family law was called the Family Code, the bill proposed in 2021 was deliberately called the Famil*ies* Code, in the plural, in recognition of the many diverse forms Cuban families take, implying the law would provide legal recognition and protection for all families. See Caridad Rosa Jiménez Morales, "De la familia a las familias: Un ejercicio de interpretación colectiva," Cubadebate, September 12, 2022, accessed at http://www.cubadebate.cu/especiales/2022/09/12/de-la-familia-a-las-familias-un-ejercicio-de-interpretacion-colectiva.

2. The implementation of this strategy in Cuba during the 1990s economic crisis is described by one of its major proponents, Teo Babún Jr., in the article "Faith-Based NGOs: Their Role in Distributing Humanitarian Aid and Delivering Social Services in the Special Period," *ASCE Blog*, November 30, 2001, accessed at https://www.ascecuba.org/asce_proceedings/faith-based-ngos-their-role-in-distributing-humanitarian-aid-and-delivering-social-services-in-the-special-period.

3. Andrea Dip, *Em nome de quem: A bancada evangélica e seu projeto de poder* (Rio de Janeiro: Civilização Brasileira, 2018), 81.

4. Magali Cunha, *Fundamentalismos, crise da democracia e ameaça aos direitos humanos na América do Sul: Tendências e desafios para a ação* (Salvador: Koinonia, 2020), 18, accessed at https://kn.org.br/wp-content/uploads/2020/10/FundamentalismosPT-1.pdf.

5. Sarah Marsh and Nelson Acosta, "Iglesias abogan contra el matrimonio gay en una inusual campaña en Cuba," Reuters, October 16, 2018, accessed at https://www.reuters.com/article/cuba-constitucion-idESKCN1MQ2NN-OESEN.

6. Rubén Padrón Garriga, "Apaga el termostato y abre la ventana," *Revista Alma Mater*, April 3, 2022, accessed at https://medium.com/revista-alma-mater/apaga-el-termostato-y-abre-la-ventana-fa4313b497cd.

7. Ministerio de Educación de la República de Cuba, "El Ministerio de Educación aplaza la aplicación de la Resolución 16," February 26, 2021, accessed at https://www.mined.gob.cu/el-ministerio-de-educacion-aplaza-la-aplicacion-de-la-resolucion-16-del-26-de-febrero-de-2021.

8. Asociación Convención Bautista de Cuba Occidental, "Declaración de la Asociación Convención Bautista de Cuba Occidental: Con relación a la Resolución No. 16/2021 del Ministerio de Educación," May 22, 2021, accessed at https://acbcocc.org/2021/05/22/declaracion-de-la-asociacion-convencion-bautista-de-cuba-occidental.

9. "Lectura colectiva del proyecto de ley del código de las familias," accessed January 23, 2023, at https://drive.google.com/file/d/1vwJqu3NiwDG1qH7BFEVowCcjxgAQBuql/view?usp=drivesdk and https://mega.nz/file/BOoSzTSS#ott6lAGv01J06hbZuQ9ZyPRgTrsBN7FX4lQenNw-g20.

10. Susana Hernández Martin, "What Cuba's Religious Fundamentalists Want to Sweep under the Carpet," *el Toque*, November 30, 2018, accessed at https://en.eltoque.com/what-cubas-religious-fundamentalists-want-to-sweep-under-the-carpet.

CHAPTER 23

Aging and Care in Cuba
MAGELA ROMERO ALMODÓVAR INTERVIEW

Translated by Elise Arnold-Levene

Dr. Magela Romero Almodóvar has coordinated the Cuban Care Studies Network since its founding in 2020 and is an internationally recognized expert on care and gender.

Editors: Thanks so much for taking the time to talk with us about aging in Cuba. Can you begin by talking us through some of the statistics and demographic indicators that are central to understanding the dynamics of aging in Cuba? Are there regional differences in these dynamics between Havana and other provinces or between rural and urban areas?

Magela Romero Almodóvar (MRA): The stages of life can never be seen as disconnected. From the time we are born until we die, we are part of the unique process that is life, both individual and collective life—which must be framed within a greater context to understand its development and possible future evolution. From the demographic perspective the definition of aging has to do with the increase in the proportion of people of an advanced age in relation to the rest of the population. Nevertheless, it is important to also define it as the inversion of the age pyramid, since the phenomenon does not only indicate an increase in the proportion of the elderly, but also a reduction in the proportion of children and youth between zero and fourteen years of age.

The aging of the demographic structure is the focus of research internationally, even in countries with a relatively small aging population. Currently, some societies are unable to look at themselves without observing the beauty of their gray hair. I say beauty because living in a country with a considerable increase in elderly people not only makes you more sensitive to the human element with respect to their experiences, but it necessarily focuses your attention time and time again to the concept of the stages of life.

In Latin America and the Caribbean, Cuba was one of the countries that began its demographic transition the earliest, given the sharp decline in fertility, the gradual increase in life expectancy, and the persistent negative migratory balance. The interaction between these components, along with multiple other determinations, led to the accelerated aging of its population. According to the United Nations Economic Commission for Latin America and the Caribbean, since 2010 the island has been the most aged economy in the region. Analyzing the aging process of the demographic structure of a population almost always leads to reflecting on the behavior of fertility and mortality. But in some cases, as in the case of Cuba, this exercise inevitably leads us to examine migration, particularly given the migratory wave the country experienced from 2021 to 2022.

According to statistics, Cuba has had a fertility rate below replacement level since 1978, leading to a reduction in the percentage of the population under fifteen years of age. At the same time, the sustained decrease in mortality contributed significantly to the increase in life expectancy—factors that have led to an increase in the proportion of people over the age of sixty at a faster rate than any other age group. In 2021, 21.6 percent of the population was sixty-plus and it is expected that by the year 2050 they will represent 34.9 percent, making Cuba the country with the oldest population in the Latin American region (ONEI 2021; ONEI 2022).

Looking at aging across Cuba, the distribution of elderly residents is similar to the distribution of the population overall: more than 70 percent of the population above age sixty lives in urban areas. At the close of 2021, the municipality of Plaza de la Revolución in Havana became the most aged with 29.3 percent, while Yateras in Guantánamo was the least aged municipality with 15 percent (ONEI 2022). Villa Clara continues in first place as the most aged province with 24.5 percent (ONEI 2021). On countless occasions the changes we have highlighted here have been mistakenly assessed as a "social problem"; however, I believe it is better to take it for what it is: a significant challenge. Cuba's aging population is a challenge that involves cultural obstacles and must be addressed in the country's economic, social, and political planning.

Editors: What are some of the challenges that the dynamics of aging in Cuba present for the state, the Ministry of Public Health, health systems, the economy, and the workforce?

MRA: The challenges are significant, and the first is changing the frame to understanding that the problem is not aging in itself, but our own readiness for facing this process and doing so without alarm or false triumphalism. It is important to note that in terms of public policies, the process of aging of the socio-demographic structure of the country warrants first a transformation in the way that old age is understood, and subsequently the redesign of many policies.

We need to transform the traditional conception of the policies that frame the older adult population as inactive, dependent, and passive into a conception that also understands this population as energetic in its contributions and social, political, cultural, and economic involvement and engagement. This entails understanding that in Cuba, given the state's intention to take maximum advantage of the potential of this age group, we do not think of older people as inactive entities.

Editors: What are some of the challenges that the dynamics of aging in Cuba present for families and for women? How are Cuban women differentially impacted by the aging population in relation to their participation in the workforce, their other care commitments, and their physical and emotional well-being?

MRA: Discussing the changes that transformations to the socio-demographic structure of the country entail for the social organization of care means taking several points into consideration. We must consider not only the aging of the socio-demographic structure, but also the impact of other processes—like low birthrates and emigration—on the demand for care and the difficulties of satisfying these demands. It is important to link this complex panorama with a context of socioeconomic crisis in which across the board it is difficult to satisfy the needs associated with dependence and access the supplies necessary to provide care.

This complex panorama directly impacts Cuban families and particularly women who continue to be the primary caregivers within households. Statistics in Cuba show that women continue to bear the excess burden of domestic functions and caregiving. Weekly, women dedicate approximately fourteen hours more than men to care work. Another significant statistic that the National Survey on Gender Equality shows is that women continue to be the ones to abandon their studies and paid positions in the public sphere earlier and with greater frequency to provide care. According to this survey of approximately 1,000 people, 964 respondents reported having been in this situation and, of these, 832 were women. This data point is illustrative of the way in which women continue to be the primary caregivers, often to the detriment of their own health and well-being.

The uneven distribution of and participation in caregiving work negatively impacts not only women's time and employability, but also their ability to retain employment, participate socially and economically, develop their professional skills, and advance in their careers. When we think about the costs of this uneven distribution for women, we generally locate the affected areas on an economic plain, in terms of women's sociopolitical labor participation. Similarly, we can see the way in which, because of these excessive burdens, women lose opportunities to generate their own income and to establish autonomy. But if we begin to analyze further we see that, at the psychological level, this uneven distribution of and participation in care work implies excessive burdens and loads that are often invisible, which can lead to stress, depression, and health effects associated not only with the care dynamics themselves, but with deferment of medical attention, where women are not able to take care of their own health needs because of the immediacy of caring for someone else. These are core aspects because they may not be visible at first glance and yet they affect women directly. We must continue working to change the way in which the sexual division of labor "naturally" occurs and this excess burden is unevenly distributed.

We know that many women, when faced with a caregiving situation, depend on their families and on a social and familial order that establishes them as the primary caregivers. They find themselves in the dilemma of being good workers or good daughters, wives, mothers, and nieces, and this situation leads to many contradictions that affect their well-being and their ability to fulfill their dreams. Studies have revealed the existence of a never-ending care cycle among Cuban women, whereby as soon as they leave the workforce to care for their children, they are tied down by other demands that arise over time. From caring for their children, they move on to caring for the fathers, mothers, mothers-in-law, fathers-in-law, uncles, other family members—moving from short-term to long-term care dependencies—to finally focusing on caring for grandchildren or partners. While they are happy to have fulfilled their obligations within the patriarchal model, they also express frustration at not having been able to work in their chosen professions and at having developed professionally only to fulfill other dreams and goals. It is a very sad and invisible reality—one that is also dangerous in a country like Cuba in which women represent more than 65 percent of the technical and professional workforce.

Editors: Can you describe the cultural norms surrounding aging in Cuban society? For example, what are older people's expectations of what their old age will be like? What are the most common choices for how, where, and with whom they will live? What role do they hope to have within the family and society? What type of care do they feel they want, need, and deserve? And who do they feel should provide this care—the family or the state? Are there any barriers to living out old age as they envision it?

MRA: The cultural norms associated with elderly people in Cuba are diverse, but if you had to group them and describe them, you would find that norms of respect, admiration, protection, and care predominate. For this age group, policies and programs have been designed to meet their needs, taking into account their rights and well-being. I can't cite a specific study about the way in which elderly people in Cuba perceive themselves, but I would say that at the forefront of these perceptions is engagement, the desire to contribute to society and to their families, the aspiration to live well and in good health to an advanced age, and to remain socially, economically, culturally, and politically active.

Regarding care, we can say that elderly people in general feel secure that they will be cared for, be it by their families in a country where family has played a central role in the provision of care, or by state institutions given the express political will evident in specific programs and services. Nonetheless, it would be unfair to say that the elderly think of themselves or should think of themselves as dependent groups since at this age, grandparents play a very important role in the family setting: in the care they provide for the youngest in the household, for people with disabilities, and for elderly people in need of care. Older adults and elderly people should be thought of as a diverse population that make considerable contributions, and they can't be disregarded in the construction of a new social order of care.

Editors: Can you tell us a little about the work being done in Cuba now around issues of care?

MRA: For a long time now, Cuba has been working to create national programs to care for elderly people and to generate projects and initiatives that contribute to their well-being—programs that understand their participation as social actors as integral to their care. Since 2019, we have been advocating for the creation of a National System for Comprehensive Care throughout the Lifecourse and, to make this dream a reality, building capacity for research and transformation at all levels. The role of academia and Cuban feminism in this undertaking has been fundamental. The Cuban Care Studies Network, created in 2020, has played a fundamental role in bringing together specialists from the three regions of the country who, with their contributions, help to improve national care policies and priorities.

On December 1, 2021, a government project focusing on unpaid labor was approved in Cuba. Beyond the obvious goal of improving existing policies and programs, the project's innovative approach aims to better understand the social organization of care in Cuba and the gendered gaps in access to quality care services which affect women, but also other vulnerable groups who face barriers in accessing quality care services appropriate to their needs and the characteristics of their families. In this project, we examine the protection, the well-being, and the improvement of conditions not only for dependents, those receiving care, but also for the people that provide care.

Among the most important actions envisioned for this project are those related to training decision-makers and caregivers. Important advances have been made in this first phase: we created a training program for the country's decision-makers, the first of which took place from November 28 to December 2, 2022. Starting from the principle that a National System for Comprehensive Care throughout the Lifecourse can only function well if it has the workforce and skill sets in place that allow it to move forward with changes, we have worked to improve the existing educational program for caregivers coordinated by the Ministry of Public Health. The program has undergone important transformations to achieve a shift in the underlying approach and a greater scope and relevance. It is worth noting that among the goals of the next phase is to begin issuing graduates certifications to allow them to work as professional paid caregivers. We also aim to strengthen care support services and initiatives that improve the ability of each territory to increase its offerings.

The project includes annual communications campaigns to accompany this process. A transcendental aspect of the initiative relates to the intention of establishing national studies on care work that will allow for a better understanding of this work, and the calculation of the contribution that it represents for the national GDP. Finally, and most importantly, is the construction of a National System for Comprehensive Care throughout the Lifecourse within the framework of this initiative. This is an initiative for which Cuba has important precedents and that the current context favors.

The construction of comprehensive care systems in the region is a challenge for many countries, and Cuba is no exception given the existence of a context with a marked crisis of care that demands it. The stakes are high, but the alliance between diverse social actors and the political will of the state is the key to achieving our goals. You might say that this aspiration will require radical changes and you would be right. This commitment to social and gender equity and transforming life in Cuba through a model of social justice stems from an understanding of care as a right and a social duty.

References

ONEI (Oficina Nacional de Estadística e Información). 2021. *El envejecimiento de la población: Cuba y sus territorios 2020*. Havana: ONEI.
———. 2022. *El envejecimiento de la población: Cuba y sus territorios 2020*. Havana: ONEI.

CHAPTER 24

Tarea Vida

CUBA'S STATE PLAN TO CONFRONT CLIMATE CHANGE

Helen Yaffe

In April 2017, the Cuban government approved the State Plan to Confront Climate Change, known as *Tarea Vida* (Life Task). With a projection up to 2100, *Tarea Vida* is currently the world's only truly long-term state plan to address climate change.[1] Despite being responsible for only 0.08 percent of global CO2 emissions, like other Small Island Developing States (SIDS), the Caribbean nation is already disproportionately hard-hit by the effects of climate change. Cuba's state plan builds on decades of environmental protection regulation, the promotion of sustainable development, and scientific investigations into climate change that date back to the 1990s. In this chapter, I will explain how Cuba's *Tarea Vida* has been driven by necessity and facilitated by capacity.

The Threat of Climate Change in Cuba

Climate change currently impacts Cuba in multiple, diverse, and reinforcing ways: increasingly frequent and intense extreme weather events (hurricanes, drought, and torrential rain), coastal flooding and erosion, and rising sea levels. Cuba is already undergoing a transition from a tropical humid to a tropical sub-humid climate, which will extend the dry season, raise average annual temperatures and minimum and maximum temperatures, increase evaporation processes, reduce soil and air humidity and water availability, decrease cloud cover, increase solar radiation, change the precipitation regime (falling average rainfall but increased extreme events), and further raise sea levels leading to greater penetration of the saline wedge, with hurricanes temporarily flooding larger territories, significantly impacting coastal settlements (CITMA 2021a, 7–8).

By 2017, many of these impacts were already evident. For example, between 2001 and 2017, Cuba was struck by an unprecedented nine intense hurricanes (Pérez Montoya 2017). In their evaluation of the 499 coasts Cuban investigators found that 82 percent showed signs of accumulated erosion and the deterioration of coastal protections (sandy beaches, wetlands, and the ridges of coral reefs) (Pell del Río and

Herrera Cruz 2017, 81). The coastline on sandy beaches is already receding 1.2 meters per year; this is particularly serious for Cuba which, like other Caribbean countries, depends on tourism revenues. While sea level rose by an average of 6.77 centimeters between 1966 and 2017, the rise has happened at an accelerated rate in the last five years of that period (Pérez Montoya 2017)

The situation is projected to deteriorate dramatically in the mid to long term, with sea levels rising 29.3 centimeters by 2050 and 95 centimeters by 2100 (CITMA 2021a, 9). This scenario will see 2.3 percent of Cuba submerged by 2050 and 122 coastal towns wiped out by the end of the century, forcing one million people (about 9 percent of the population) to relocate. Freshwater shortages can be expected to be compounded by the salinization of aquifers due to seawater flooding, and agricultural lands will be destroyed.

In the very long term, by 2100 the air temperature could have risen by 4.5°C, leading to desertification, water deficits, falling agricultural yields, the disappearance of certain crops (rice, tobacco, and pork), and increasing disease vectors and plagues. Rainfall will decrease by between 20 and 60 percent (CITMA 2021a, 8).

Features of *Tarea Vida*

While Cuba shares this harrowing climate scenario with its neighbors, the Cuban state's response is unique. There are five distinctive features of *Tarea Vida*. First, multiple state institutions coordinate and contribute, with the country's leadership (including the president) regularly evaluating progress. The state plan does not rely on private interests. Second, the policy is led by science; environmental scientists are central to policy-making. Third, *Tarea Vida* focuses on "natural" solutions (such as restoring mangroves to protect beaches) and draws on national resources, avoiding dependence on external finance, management, or technologies. Fourth, community mobilization and participation are integral to the state plan. Fifth, *Tarea Vida* is part of a broader process of transition to more decentralized sustainable development, with responsibilities, powers, and budgets increasingly devolved to local communities. Flexibility is built in, enabling each sector and territory to adapt the approach to their specific needs.

Tarea Vida starts by identifying at-risk populations and regions and formulating a hierarchy of "strategies" and "tasks" through which climate scientists, ecologists, and social scientists work alongside local communities, specialists, and authorities to respond to specific threats in short- (2017 to 2020), medium- (up to the year 2030), long- (to 2050), and very long-term (to 2100) stages. It involves a process of research, design of interventions, participation, experimentation, review, and revision. *Tarea Vida* is a key element of Cuba's National Environmental Strategy (NES), which was first approved in 1997 and frequently updated in 2007, 2011, and 2016. The function of the NES is to "identify the principal environmental problems and establish the priorities and lines of action" (CITMA 2021b, 5). Environmental considerations are integral, not marginal, to Cuba's national development strategy. This builds on a long history of addressing environmental degradation.

Centuries of colonial and then imperialist exploitation and the imposition of the agro-export model led to chronic deforestation and soil erosion in Cuba. The expansion of the sugar industry reduced the island's forest cover from 95 percent pre-colonization to 14 percent in 1959, turning Cuba "from rainforest to cane field" (Funes Monzote 2009). Redressing this historical legacy became part of the project for revolutionary transformation post-1959, which sought to break the chains of underdevelopment.

Despite the revolutionaries' early aspirations for economic diversification, post-1959 Cuba continued to be dominated by the sugar industry, and increasingly mechanized agricultural production, through trade with the Soviet bloc. The government adopted the so-called Green Revolution on its predominant state farms, relying on imported natural gas–based fertilizers, oil-based pesticides, and diesel-powered machinery—the island used 90,000 tractors. Other productive activities that contributed to pollution and erosion continued. However, the detrimental effects were gradually recognized and incrementally redressed, particularly from the 1990s. More generally, there has been increasing concern with protecting the natural endowments of the Cuban archipelago (1,600 islands and islets), which include extraordinary biodiversity and coastal resources of global importance.

How Cuba Built Capacity to Address Climate Change

The threat of climate change establishes the necessity for the state plan. However, without the capacity fostered by Cuba's socialist development, such a comprehensive, welfare-based approach would not be possible. Several factors explain Cuba's capacity in relation to *Tarea Vida*: first, the legal and institutional framework; second, the state-dominated centrally planned economy, that is, the political economy context; third, the Civil Defense System which coordinates its world-leading response to risk and natural disasters; fourth, the capacity to collect and analyze data (and associated scientific expertise); fifth, the influence of geographers and environmentalists; and sixth, political will. These factors are discussed below.

THE LEGAL AND INSTITUTIONAL FRAMEWORK AND THE POLITICAL ECONOMY CONTEXT

The first and second factors cited above overlap. The socialist system is established in the Cuban constitution and national laws. Key Cuban legislation states that the system prioritizes people, "and the social character of property facilitates the adoption of measures that guarantee comprehensive environmental protection and the rational use of natural resources" (República de Cuba 1981). The state-dominated, centrally planned economy facilitates the government to mobilize national resources and direct national strategy without negotiating with, or seeking to incentivize, private profit-seeking interests—unlike countries that rely on "market solutions." Law scholar Oliver A. Houck notes that "post-revolutionary Cuban law promoted public and collective values from the start. Environmental laws fit easily into this framework" (Houck 2000, 17).

As early as May 1959, the Agrarian Reform Law gave the state responsibility for protecting natural areas, initiated reforestation programs, and excluded forest reserves from distribution to agricultural collectives. In 1975, the First Congress of the Cuban Communist Party (CCP) agreed on the need to pay greater attention to the protection and improvement of the environment and the exploitation of natural resources (Funes Monzote 2019, 411). Scientific-technical investigations were launched to enable this.

The following year, 1976, a new constitution was approved. Article 27 made "the state and the society" responsible for protecting nature (flora and fauna) and preventing contamination (water, air, and soil). The National Commission for the Protection of the Environment and the Rational Use of Natural Resources (COMARNA) was also set up in 1976 to "establish a system based on the most advanced scientific-technical knowledge to allow the harmonious development of human activity with the least possible degree of environmental and natural resource damage" (cited by Funes Monzote 2019, 412). Thus, Cuba was among the first countries in the world to include environmental issues in its constitution and to issue environmental laws (FAO 2013). Over the following decades, further studies and projects followed, and environmental regulations were introduced.

In 1981, Law 33 on the Protection of the Environment and the Rational Use of Natural Resources was enacted. It was accompanied by complementary laws, addressing specific issues, while reforestation efforts were stepped up. In the late 1980s, Plan Turquino and Plan Manatí programs were introduced to protect and improve Cuba's mountainous regions. In 1995 they were combined in the Programme for Comprehensive Development of Cuban Mountains, covering the mountain population and managed by the central government, with decentralization to the provincial or municipal levels for local projects. In 1990, a new Law 118 allocated responsibility for environmental protection to state agencies, to provide better enforcement mechanisms.

In August 1990, the Special Period in a Time of Peace was announced, propelling the Cuban state and people into survival mode. In 1991, first the Council of Mutual Economic Assistance, the socialist countries' trading bloc, and then the USSR itself collapsed. By 1993, Cuba's GDP had plummeted 35 percent as the island lost 86 to 87 percent of its trade and investment. Russian oil imports fell from thirteen million tons in 1989 to zero in 1993. State farms were converted into cooperatives, and organic and urban farming and agroecology were introduced nationwide. It was a question of survival. Rationed electricity cuts, mass cycling, and collective hitch-hiking were other solutions to the acute fuel scarcity (Yaffe 2020, 37–68). The need for a shift to sustainable development was now imperative.

During this process, in 1992, Fidel Castro went to the UN Earth Summit in Brazil where he warned of the threat of extinction due to environmental damage and a commitment to sustainable development was added to the Cuban constitution. In 1994, the new Ministry of Science, Technology and Environment (CITMA) was created. In 1997, CITMA's National Environment Strategy was adopted, and the new

Environmental Law 81 gave CITMA broad powers to control, direct, and execute environmental policy while putting boundaries and limits on the activities of foreign companies operating in Cuba. In 2017, *Tarea Vida* was approved by the Council of Ministers. In 2019, the new Cuban constitution established "the right to enjoy a natural environment that is healthy and stable," adding that "the State protects the environment and the country's natural resources" (Constitution, Article 75, 2019). That year, Jason Hickel's new Sustainable Development Index (SDI), which measures the ecological efficiency of human development, ranked Cuba best in the world between 1990 and 2015 (Hickel 2020, 1).

CIVIL DEFENSE AND DATA ANALYSIS

The third and fourth factors listed above are results of Cuba's welfare-based development strategy and scientific, technical, and institutional capacity. The island is recognized globally for its record of anticipating and responding to risk and natural disasters. This is organized through the Civil Defense System, which was established in 1963 after the deadly Hurricane Flora.

The national system provides early detection and monitoring of threats, and coordination of the necessary response. The process is reproduced at provincial, municipal, and neighborhood levels throughout the country. Meteorologist Eduardo Planos Gutiérrez explains: "At the local level, risk-study centers focus on the specific phenomenon, and the neighborhood is organized. The social organizations in each area take preventative measures. Local governments set up local Defense Councils, which organize how the system works, distribute basic foodstuff so people don't go without, and check electrical installations and the evacuation plan" (DaniFilms 2021). Cuba's Civil Defense also contributed to the containment of COVID-19, alongside the public health system and medical science sectors. Even factoring in the COVID-19 surge of summer 2021, the island had relatively low contagion and fatality statistics and was the first country in the world to fully vaccinate its complete population over two years of age. And it did so with domestically produced vaccines.

Linked to that is Cuba's competence in the collection and analysis of local data, a precondition for evaluating specific territorial threats. Cuba's scientific capacity, the result of investments in science and technology education since the early 1960s, is crucial in facilitating this. For example, the Cubans have adapted data from the Intergovernmental Panel on Climate Change (IPCC) on global sea level rises to sixty-five specific points of the national territory to determine differences depending on local conditions, and to use that information as the basis for planning actions. As advisor to CITMA, Orlando Rey Santos points out, "That can only be done if you are backed up by strong science" (DaniFilms 2021).

EARLY "ENVIRONMENTALISTS" AND POLITICAL WILL

The fifth and sixth factors cited above are also linked. Political commitment has been fostered by geographers and environmentalists who put concern for the natural environment on the agenda of the revolutionary government post-1959. Outstanding among them is Antonio Núñez Jiménez, a socialist and professor of geography in the 1950s who served as a Rebel Army captain and headed the National Institute of Agrarian Reform from 1959 to 1962, among other roles. Fidel Castro also propelled Cuba's environmental program. According to Tirso Sáenz, who presided over COMARNA, Cuba's first environmental commission, in 1976, "Fidel was the main driving force for the incorporation of environmental concerns into Cuban policy" (Sáenz 2020). More generally, as Houck underscores, the Cuban Communist Party's "open endorsement of environmental protection and sustainable growth provides significant legitimacy to environmental programs" (Houck 2000, 11). Given this political will, the CCP and the government can mobilize state institutions to get behind environmental policy and channel public and sectoral participation.

The Study of Climate Change and Policy Formation

The first domestic study to assess the impact of climate change on Cuba was carried out in 1991. Following two devastating hurricanes in 2004, national investigations into "dangers, vulnerabilities and risks" were stepped up. In 2007 the Council of Ministers approved the first program to confront climate change. CITMA was charged with carrying out a major investigation into coastal hazards and vulnerabilities, projecting forward to 2050–2100. Known as the "macro-project," this incorporates ongoing annual investigations carried out by multidisciplinary groups of scientists. Annually, in February and March, results are presented to the country's leadership to inform policy.

In 2015, CITMA was tasked with developing a state plan, to convert scientific research into state policy. Two years later, *Tarea Vida* was approved. By then, 103 studies had been concluded throughout the country. Early studies focused on hydrometeorological dangers (strong winds, flooding due to sea penetration, and heavy rain) before expanding to include drought, rural fires, and dangers of a geological, technological, or sanitary nature. The results of these investigations informed *Tarea Vida*, and measures of prevention, preparation, response, and recuperation to prevent and reduce risks and vulnerabilities. As Minister Pérez Montoya says, "Cuba is completely vulnerable"; however, resource restraints prevent Cuba from taking action in every region simultaneously, so an incremental process is established on the basis of priorities. This is why *Tarea Vida* is divided into stages, and the actions and tasks are listed in the accompanying boxes (CITMA 2017). The strategic actions indicate the long-term approach, which implies a cultural change among the government and population, and the tasks concern the roles and responsibilities of the social and economic stakeholders.

Strategic Actions

1) Prohibit construction of new homes in threatened coastal settlements predicted to disappear as a result of permanent flooding. Reduce population density in low-lying coastal areas.

2) Develop constructive concepts in infrastructure, adapted to coastal flooding in low-lying areas.

3) Adapt agricultural activities, particularly those with the greatest impact on the country's food security, to changes in land use due to rising sea levels and drought.

4) Reduce cultivation in areas near the coasts or affected by saline intrusion. Diversify crops, improve soil conditions, and introduce and develop varieties resistant to the new temperature scenario.

5) Plan, within specified timescales, the urban reorganization processes of the threatened settlements and infrastructures, in correspondence with the economic conditions of the country. Start with lower cost measures, such as induced natural solutions (beach recovery, coastal reforestation, and so on).

Tasks

1) Identify and undertake actions and projects of adaptation (coastal protection of cities; relocation of human settlements; integral recovery of beaches, mangroves, and other protective natural ecosystems; and hydraulic works and coastal engineering, among others) to climate change, of a comprehensive and progressive character, necessary to reduce the existing vulnerability in fifteen zones identified as priorities. These are assessed in the order of threats to the population, food security, and the development of tourism.

2) Establish the legal norms necessary to support the implementation of the state plan, as well as ensure strict compliance, with particular attention to measures aimed at reducing vulnerability of the built heritage, prioritizing threatened coastal settlements.

3) Conserve, maintain, and fully recover sandy beaches, prioritizing urbanized beaches for tourist use and reducing the structural vulnerability of the built heritage.

4) Ensure the availability and efficient use of water to combat drought, based on water-saving technologies and to satisfy local demands. Improve the hydraulic infrastructure and its maintenance, as well as introduce actions to measure efficiency and water productivity.

5) Direct reforestation toward maximum protection of the soils and waters in quantity and quality, as well as the recovery of the most affected mangroves. Prioritize reservoirs, canals, and hydro regulatory strips of the tributary basins of the main bays and coasts of the insular platform.

6) Stop the deterioration and rehabilitate and conserve coral reefs throughout the archipelago, with priority given to the ridges that line the insular platform and protect urbanized beaches for tourist use. Avoid overfishing fish that favor coral reefs.

7) Maintain and introduce the scientific results of the macro-project on hazards and vulnerability in the coastal zones (2050–2100) within the land and urban plans. In addition, include the studies regarding disaster vulnerability and risk reduction. Use this information for future decision-making.

8) Implement and control measures of adaptation and mitigation of climate change derived from sectoral policies in the programs, plans, and projects linked to food security, renewable energies, energy efficiency, land and urban planning, fishing, agricultural activity, health, tourism, construction, transport, industry, and forest management.

9) Strengthen monitoring, surveillance, and early warning systems to systematically assess the status of the coastal zone, water, drought, forest, and human, animal, and plant health.
10) Prioritize measures and actions to increase the perception of risk, improve the knowledge and participation of the entire population in tackling climate change, and promote a culture of water conservation.
11) Manage and use the international financial resources available, from global and regional climate funds as well as from bilateral sources, to execute the investments, projects, and actions that derive from each of the state plan's tasks.

Short- and Medium-Term Phases

The 2017–2020 "short-term" phase of *Tarea Vida* coincided with Donald Trump's presidency in the United States and the onset of the COVID-19 pandemic. The Trump administration severely tightened US sanctions against Cuba, further obstructing its access to resources and finances. The pandemic further battered the economy through the loss of tourism revenues as borders were closed. In 2020, Cuba's GDP shrank by 11 percent. Nonetheless, there were tangible achievements: 11 percent of the most vulnerable coastal homes were relocated; coral farms were set up and coral reefs recovered; 380 km² of mangroves were recovered, serving as a natural coastal defense; and a significant investment was made in the country's hydraulic program to improve the quality, availability, and management of water, particularly in remote areas. Reforestation programs since 1959 had raised forest cover to 31.8 percent by 2018 (CITMA 2021a, 10). Reforestation contributes to removing CO_2 from the atmosphere and reduces Cuba's relatively very low net emissions (70.5 percent of which are from the energy sector). Cuba plans to shift 24 percent of electricity generation to renewable sources by 2030, which will also contribute to lowering that figure.

The "medium-term" (2021–2030) phase of *Tarea Vida* is under way. In its projections for the new "cycle" (2021–2025), CITMA commits to more rigorous planning and clearer identification of the efficacy of their measures, incorporating social and economic issues in their evaluation (CITMA 2021a, 12). The impact of COVID-19 has reinforced the need for a more inclusive and strategic approach, it states, to achieve a greener recovery "so that the crisis generated by the pandemic becomes an opportunity to advance in environmentally sustainable development" (CITMA 2021a, 12). Despite the current hardships, including severe financial restrictions, CITMA is optimistic that "actions can be deployed that simultaneously benefit health, economic recovery, local development, and adaptation and mitigation of climate change" (CITMA 2021a, 13).

While the strategic actions and tasks of *Tarea Vida* have not changed, there are specific objectives for the next cycle. These include greater efficiency in implementation and evaluation at the sectoral and territorial levels; ensuring the state plan contributes to the broader national development strategy; increasing awareness and participation of the population; using public policy to reduce territorial and social inequalities; and capturing disaggregated data and implementing a geo-referenced information system. CITMA lists the priority action, results expected, and indicators to be used for evaluation. In this new phase, the contribution of social, economic, and political scientists will be more integrated into science programs related to climate change. Toward the end of this 2021–2025 cycle, new mechanisms will be in place for monitoring, registering, and verifying emissions, to facilitate the goal of achieving "carbon neutrality" in Cuba in a way that is consistent with the country's economic and social development priorities and programs.

Obstacles and Challenges

The greatest obstacle to *Tarea Vida* is Cuba's lack of access to financial resources and technologies for climate change adaptation and mitigation. This is largely a result of US sanctions, which stop Cuba from joining multilateral development banks and oblige international financial institutions to categorize Cuba as "high risk" and avoid transactions related to Cuba. The island depends on bilateral cooperation and financing through the UN system. Even there, third countries are often subject to US pressure to end projects with Cuba, or blocked by US sanctions regulations. For example, the United States prohibits the sale to Cuba of equipment in which 10 percent or more of the components are made by US companies. Cubans are unable to acquire the latest equipment, such as advanced early warning systems for their Civil Defense. The goals of *Tarea Vida* would be easier and quicker to reach without these externally imposed restrictions.

The Cuban approach offers an alternative to globally dominant paradigms based on the private sector or public-private partnerships. At the annual UN Climate Change Conferences (Conference of Parties, or COP) Cuba participates in negotiations as part of the Alliance of Small Island Developing States (SIDS-AOSIS), with ALBA (Bolivarian Alliance for the Peoples of Our Americas) countries and the Like-Minded Developing Countries (LMDC) group, which represents over 50 percent of the world's population and vociferously demands reparations ("loss and damage") from the developing countries which historically caused climate change. These groups in turn participate in the Group 77 and China coalition, integrating all developing countries.

Through these forums, those countries are learning about *Tarea Vida*. "There is definitely a lot of interest," Rey Santos says. "It draws recognition and even some amazement" that a state plan of such scope could be implemented despite the hardships Cuba endures (Rey Santos 2021). The Cubans are sharing their analyses, experiences, and results, while expanding cooperation with these developing countries, particularly those most vulnerable, like Cuba, to climate change.

Note

1. Other countries' plans mostly focus on reducing carbon emissions, while those addressing "climate resilience" are shorter-term than Cuba's and the state is not the key actor.

References

CITMA (Ministerio de Ciencia, Tecnología y Medio Ambiente). 2017. "La Tarea Vida—Plan de Estado para el enfrentamiento al Cambio Climatico en Cuba." Approved April 25, 2017. Accessed at http://misiones.cubaminrex.cu/sites/default/files/archivos/editorucrania/articulos/esp_tarea_vida.pdf.

———. 2021a. *Proyecciones Tarea Vida 2021–2025*. Havana: CITMA.

———. 2021b. *Estrategia Ambiental Nacional 2021–2025*. Havana: CITMA.

Constitution, Republic of Cuba. 2019. Approved February 24, 2019. Accessed at https://www.constituteproject.org/constitution/Cuba_2019?lang=en.

DaniFilms. 2021. *Cuba's Life Task: Combating Climate Change*, coproduced by Helen Yaffe. Accessed at https://youtu.be/APN6N45Q6iU.

FAO (Food and Agricultural Organization of the United Nations). 2013. "Strengthening the Programme for Comprehensive Development of Cuban Mountains." Last updated July 9, 2013. Accessed at http://www.fao.org/forestry/watershedmanagementandmountains/74916/en.

Funes Monzote, Reinaldo. 2009. *From Rainforest to Cane Field in Cuba: An Environmental History since 1492*. Chapel Hill: University of North Carolina Press.

———. 2019. *Nuestro Viaje a la Luna: la idea de la transformación de la naturaleza en Cuba durante la Guerra Fría*. Havana: Fondo Editorial Casa de Las Américas.

Hickel, Jason. 2020. "The Sustainable Development Index: Measuring the Ecological Efficiency of Human Development in the Anthropocene." *Ecological Economics* 167: 106331. https://doi.org/10.1016/j.ecolecon.2019.05.011.

Houck, Oliver A. 2000. "Environmental Law in Cuba." *Journal of Land Use & Environmental Law* 16, no. 1: 1–81.

Pell del Río, C. Silvia Miriam, and Juan N. Herrera Cruz. 2017. "Tarea Vida: plan del estado para el enfrentamiento al cambio climático." *Revista Bimestre Cubana* (July–December), 3:47.

Pérez Montoya, Elba Rosa. 2017. "Tarea de Vida." Entrevista con René Tamayo León. *Juventud Rebelde*, June 10. Accessed at http://www.juventudrebelde.cu/ciencia-tecnica/2017-06-10/tarea-de-vida.

República de Cuba. 1981. Ley Nº 33, "Ley de protección del medio ambiente y del uso racional de los recursos naturales." Accessed at http://extwprlegs1.fao.org/docs/html/cub6802.htm.

Rey Santos, Orlando. 2021. Interview with the author, November.

Sáenz, Tirso W. 2020. Email interview with the author, June 12.

Yaffe, Helen. 2020. *We Are Cuba: How a Revolutionary People Have Survived in a Post-Soviet World*. New Haven, CT: Yale University Press.

CHAPTER 25

COVID-19 and Health in Cuba

Hope Bastian

Cuba's public health system is well known for its focus on comprehensive primary care and the practice of community-based medicine with a strong focus on prevention through the use of doctor-nurse teams who live and work in the neighborhoods they serve. This strong base is supported by a network of polyclinics staffed by specialists and tertiary-level hospitals and research institutes internationally recognized for their ability to perform advanced medical procedures and engage in pharmaceutical research and production.

However, more than three years into the COVID-19 pandemic, both high-touch and high-tech medicine commonly practiced in Cuba have been severely impacted. In this chapter, I provide a brief description of the multisectoral response to coronavirus in early 2020, which was initially extremely successful in controlling the spread of the virus during the first two waves of infections. Next, I describe the measures that contributed to the gradually increasing rates of infection in 2021, leading into the third wave of infections. While the first two waves peaked at 847 and 676 daily active cases respectively, during the summer of 2021, Cuba's daily per capita contagion rates were the highest in Latin America. On July 31, 2021, at the peak of the third wave, there were 9,747 *new* cases and 50 deaths each day (Beldarraín Chaple et al. 2022, 4).

While during earlier periods, COVID-19 protocols called for preventative hospitalization and treatment of all suspected/confirmed cases, during the third wave the public health infrastructure was insufficient to continue providing the same level of care. Especially impacted were the provinces of Matanzas, Ciego de Ávila, Cienfuegos, and Guantánamo. These difficulties led to strong internal critiques of the state's incapacity to fulfill popular expectations of the public health system.

At that moment of extreme health crisis, it was Cuban scientists and the pharmaceutical development and production infrastructure that saved the day. While the deployment of experimental vaccination campaigns with vaccines developed by Cuba's pharmaceutical industry was affected by delays and lack of communication, they were ultimately successful in bringing case rates back under control in the last quarter of 2021. Thanks to domestic vaccines, Cuba was able to vaccinate its population over the age of two significantly earlier than mRNA vaccines for these age groups were available in the United States. At the end of 2022, Cuba led the region with 90 percent of the population and 97.5 percent of the pediatric population fully vaccinated against COVID-19 (MEDICC 2022b, 3).

In the final part of the chapter, I discuss challenges for health in a "new normal" as the pandemic exposed vulnerabilities in infrastructures of care. Even with the pandemic "under control," the island's health system faced extreme shortages of pharmaceuticals and inputs to diagnose and treat acute and chronic conditions, and a significant outmigration of health personnel with impacts on health education. To understand the severity of the current health crisis, I examine the deterioration of Cuba's maternal-infant health indicators, a top priority of the Ministry of Public Health (MINSAP) since its inception. The case highlights the changing social determinants of health in Cuba and the mark that the pandemic and economic crisis left on the population's health and the health system's capacity to address urgent health concerns.

2020: Multisectoral Action in Cuba Controls the Pandemic

In Cuba, health is considered "a right of the people and the responsibility of the state, achieved through laws and regulations in all sectors of the economy" (Vela Valdés 2020, 2). Cuba's first Plan for the Prevention and Control of the Coronavirus was approved by the Council of Ministers on January 29, 2020. When Cuba's first coronavirus cases were identified on March 11, 2020, the country's Civil Defense infrastructure was activated.

The Temporary Government Working Group, headed by President Miguel Díaz-Canel, began to meet daily to analyze the epidemiological situation via videoconference with leaders from each province (Vela Valdés 2020). Every morning, Dr. Francisco Durán, Cuba's National Epidemiologist, gave a televised update of the number of new cases and the health status of active cases. To control the spread of the virus, efforts centered on the strict control of people with respiratory symptoms from abroad and contacts of confirmed cases. Neighborhood doctor-nurse teams and medical students went door to door to ask if anyone was experiencing symptoms (Pérez Riverol 2020). Suspected cases were transported to isolation centers for observation until they tested negative. Confirmed cases were hospitalized for treatment and all of their contacts for the last fourteen days were traced and examined.

On March 20, the president announced a package of pandemic control measures: international arrivals were quarantined, and Cubans were instructed to stay at home, avoid large groups, cancel social events, wear masks, and practice social distancing. Shortly after, international flights were suspended, schools closed, and many workers transitioned to remote work. Cuban doctors fighting the virus in neighborhood clinics, quarantine centers, and international missions were a source of nationalist pride, reinforcing the prestige of the public health system as the embodiment of the Revolution's moral commitments. Every evening, across Havana, Cubans stepped onto their balconies to applaud the heroic efforts of healthcare workers.

The island with its well-developed universal health system and strong political will to protect health seemed a safe place to be as Cubans contemplated the collapse of powerful health systems around the globe. In the first months, 20 hospitals were dedicated to COVID cases in addition to 61 centers to isolate suspected cases, 286 for contact quarantine, and 73 for travelers (Beldarraín Chaple et al. 2022, 6). Early in the pandemic, 2,579 Cuban healthcare providers were sent to 24 countries to fight the pandemic, joining some 28,000 Cuban health workers on international missions in 59 countries (Lamrani 2021).

In 2020, the initial success in controlling the pandemic was achieved through primary prevention strategies that reached beyond the health sector and required the collaboration of all sectors of society. As expected, the focus on prevention, contact tracing, testing, and quarantine kept national case counts in the single and double digits. In mid-June 2020, the Cuban government declared victory in the fight against the coronavirus and restrictions were gradually lifted.[1] In Havana this new freedom was short-lived: on August 8 a new lockdown was imposed. On September 1 new measures included a 7:00 p.m. curfew, the closing of beaches and parks, and banning exercise in public places. Children were not allowed outside their homes, and provincial travel required special permission.

In October, limited flights repatriated Cubans stranded abroad. When Havana's airport opened in November, passengers were not required to present a negative pre-arrival PCR (polymerase chain reaction test); instead they were given PCRs upon arrival. After a long separation, Cubans abroad were eager to visit their families. Although expected to isolate during their first five days, many did not observe the isolation periods. It wasn't until after the busy New Year's travel season that travelers were required to show a negative PCR test before flying. Predictably, COVID cases began to climb as a result of cases introduced by foreign visitors and Havana returned to the most restrictive phase of health regulations (Beldarraín Chaple et al. 2022, 7).

2021: Coronavirus Becomes a Crisis

In early 2021, new coronavirus cases quickly shot to over 800 per day and a 9:00 p.m. curfew was implemented. Flights from major hubs were suspended. US airlines were later limited to one flight per week. Visitors were quarantined at designated hotels (at their own expense) until receiving a second negative PCR. Throughout the spring, curfews continued and localized quarantines closed off buildings, blocks, or neighborhoods with high case rates. Extended power outages became more regular, disrupting access to water for basic hygiene. As shortages became severe, every day was consumed by finding food. At times you could only shop in stores in your municipality, and social distancing measures were difficult to enforce in high-stakes lines. Reminiscent of the Special Period, many households began to eat just once a day, prioritizing food for children and the elderly members.

The drive to produce COVID-19 vaccines meant a significant reduction in the production of other medications, exacerbating previous shortages. In 2021, Cuba's pharmaceutical industry received only half its normal budget and provided only 33.7

percent of the products normally manufactured (Efe 2022). Of the 627 products on MINSAP's Basic National Formulary, 369 were produced by BioCubaFarma. Throughout 2021, an average of 121 BioCubaFarma medications were unavailable each month (Efe 2022).

In July, the highly contagious Delta variant appeared in Cuba and many more children and young adults without preexisting conditions were infected than in previous waves (Beldarraín Chaple et al. 2022). Both official statistics and social media showed a health crisis in Matanzas Province that overwhelmed the public health system. For more than a year, from the safety of the island Cubans had watched health systems collapsing under the strain of COVID-19 cases from New York to Milan. Now, despite months of strict measures, nightly curfews, limitations on mobility, and closed borders, sick Cubans were languishing in the hallways of health centers and in blocks-long queues for testing and treatment. Especially impacted were the provinces of Matanzas, Ciego de Ávila, Cienfuegos, and Guantánamo. Through private chats on WhatsApp, friends and relatives called for help. Matanzas was the epicenter of COVID-19 in Cuba, a country that itself had become the epicenter in Latin America.

Cuba's Pharmaceutical Industry and COVID-19 Vaccination Campaigns

Early in the pandemic, the Cuban pharmaceutical industry began developing vaccine candidates based on well-known vaccine technologies. The Abdala vaccine is similar to the hepatitis B vaccine produced in Cuba since 1992 (MEDICC 2022b, 12). Cuba's second vaccine, Soberana, is based on conjugate technology available since the 1980s. Both vaccines use a protein sub-unit technology requiring only household refrigeration, important for low-resource settings (MEDICC 2022a, 11).

With growing coronavirus case numbers throughout the spring of 2021, the state gambled on immunizing the population with Cuban vaccine candidates although they had not yet completed phase 3 clinical trials or been granted emergency use authorization (EUA). In March 2021, the Cuban Center for the Control of Medicines and Medical Devices (CECMED) approved the experimental use of Soberana and Abdala vaccines in high-risk groups and territories, including 164,000 essential public health workers (MEDICC 2022b, 14). Abdala's phase 3 clinical trials showed a 92.28 percent efficacy against symptomatic infection and 100 percent against severe disease and death (MEDICC 2022b, 11). With this information, a public health intervention began to vaccinate people in high-risk communities in Havana, Matanzas, Ciego de Ávila, and Santiago provinces. Shortly thereafter, Abdala (July 9) and Soberana 02 (August 20) received EUA. By the end of August, 88.4 percent of the population was vaccinated.

In September and October, juvenile vaccine regimens for children aged two and older received EUA (MEDICC 2022b,15). As observed by an international fact-finding delegation of scientists, "Cuba's COVID-19 vaccination rate in children and adolescents 2–18 years old (97.5 percent) is far greater and was achieved far earlier than any country in the world" (MEDICC 2022a, 12). This massive effort allowed in-person classes to resume in Havana for the first time since March 2020. Three months after the initial series, booster campaigns began. On May 31, 2022, Cuba's mask mandate, in place since March 2020, was lifted.

Cuban vaccines are beginning to gain international recognition. In November 2022, the Mexican federal health regulatory agency, recognized by the Pan American Health Organization, issued an EUA for Soberana (*OnCuba News* 2022). Iran, Vietnam, Saint Vincent and the Grenadines, Belarus, and Venezuela have also granted EUAs and signed commercial import contracts (MEDICC 2022b, 3). In 2022, the Central American Bank for Economic Integration provided a 46.7 million euro credit to strengthen Cuba's pharmaceutical production infrastructure (MEDICC 2022b, 19).

Challenges for Health in Cuba in "the New Normal"

When vaccination rates reached 63 percent, infections began to fall. In late September 2021, restaurants, bars, and beaches reopened. In November, curfews and interprovincial travel restrictions were lifted, signaling a return to "normality" after Cuba's third and most deadly coronavirus wave. Despite the successes of Cuba's vaccination campaigns in resolving the epidemiological crisis, the economic and political damage has been more difficult to address.

The current economic crisis in Cuba has impacted state provision of resources needed to maintain the public health system and guarantee access to quality healthcare services. Limited access to pharmaceuticals to manage chronic conditions and the lack of reagents for basic diagnostic testing became common barriers to timely diagnosis and treatment. Shortages of inputs for surgeries and the loss of health professionals across all levels of the public health system impact individual health outcomes and medical education. Shortages have also affected public health efforts to control dengue (Boza Ibarra 2022; Carmona Tamayo and Fariñas Acosta 2022).

In late 2022, it was often up to patients to find their own medications, resorting to the black market or support from abroad. Monthly reports by CubaBioFarma showed that severe shortages continued: in October 2022, 160 of the 369 medications produced by BioCubaFarma were unavailable (BioCubaFarma 2022). Due to difficulties in accessing raw materials and equipment, BioCubaFarma established three categories for prioritizing production. Priority level 1 includes pharmaceuticals for cancer treatments, maternal infant health, dialysis, patients in intensive care, and chronic conditions managed through Pharmaceutical Control Cards (Alonso Falcón et al. 2022). Severe shortages meant that people with epilepsy, heart conditions, and mental illness and those receiving gender-affirming care had to do without. Pregnant people also struggled to find prenatal vitamins, folic acid, and iron supplements. Due to the lack of antibiotics, simple infections could cause life-threatening complications. In October 2022, pharmaceutical shortages included twenty-eight products for management of chronic conditions and seventy-eight additional priority level 1 pharmaceuticals

(BioCubaFarma 2022). In an aging population of eleven million, six million Cubans depend on medications on the priority level 1 list to manage chronic illnesses.[2]

Condoms and birth control were unavailable, leading to higher rates of STIs and unplanned pregnancies (Caraballoso 2022). Reagents were unavailable for HIV testing and many other diagnostic tests in local polyclinics and hospitals. Without the basic materials needed for surgeries, doctors regularly asked patients if they had family abroad in order to give them detailed lists of the materials needed to operate. Access to abortion was similarly complicated by lack of reagents for necessary tests and materials for surgeries.

The migration of experienced healthcare providers, laboratory technicians, and allied health professionals also has been significant. At the end of October 2022, Dr. Tania Margarita Cruz, deputy minister of MINSAP, reported "incomplete payrolls" in nine of Cuba's fifteen provinces (Rojas 2022).

In addition to impacting patient care and health outcomes, the pandemic has also impacted medical education. Cuban medical students do practical rotations early in their education and have had few opportunities to gain experience in managing chronic conditions, as this type of care was frequently suspended. Education and training opportunities for residents were interrupted, especially in surgical specialties where elective procedures were discontinued or postponed indefinitely (Céspedes-Tamayo and Ulloa-Cedeño 2021). Even in 2022, when coronavirus rates were lower, the lack of resources and professionals to perform surgeries provided students with fewer learning opportunities.

The growth of dengue cases in 2022 was closely linked to infrastructure deficiencies and social conditions in which people live. In September, active dengue transmission was taking place in fourteen provinces (González 2023). Dr. Dennys Pérez, of Cuba's prestigious Pedro Kourí Tropical Medicine Institute, described social determinants of health as key in controlling dengue cases, which cluster in low socioeconomic areas with high population density and limited access to potable water (Fariñas Acosta and Héctor Rodríguez 2022). The number of foci identified set a 15-year record in Cuba, leading to a surge in cases—3,036 confirmed and another 14,256 potential cases (Carmona Tamayo and Fariñas Acosta 2022).

In the comments section of a 2022 Cubadebate article, the population highlighted factors such as infrequent municipal trash removal, leaky aqueducts, and large potholes where water accumulates, creating breeding grounds for mosquitoes (Fariñas Acosta and Héctor Rodríguez 2022). At the individual level, mosquito repellant was only available with cards denominated in freely convertible currency (*moneda libremente convertible*, or MLC), and both lidded tanks and mosquito nets for sleeping were expensive or simply unavailable. Without mosquito nets, people used electric fans to keep mosquitoes away, which left them vulnerable during frequent blackouts in 2021 and 2022 (Fariñas Acosta and Héctor Rodríguez 2022). Shortages of abate larvicide, insecticides, and diesel for fumigation made it impossible for MINSAP to implement vector-control strategies that had proven successful in the past (Carmona Tamayo and Fariñas Acosta 2022).

As a result of these difficulties, many Cubans came to feel that their legendary public health system had failed them. Insufficient state budgets to improve conditions in hospitals made it difficult to follow protocols and led to the appearance of infections acquired in health facilities (Rojas 2022). In the coming years, health statistics can be expected to show increased death and disability from preventable causes across the population, the result of scarce treatments for chronic conditions, the loss of healthcare professionals to migration, and increasingly difficult social conditions.

Social Determinants of Health: Maternal and Infant Mortality

Public health is not only about access to health care, but also about creating the conditions in which communities can have the best chance at health. Social determinants of health are "the conditions in which people are born, grow, work, live, and age, and the wider set of forces and systems shaping the conditions of daily life" that affect individual and population health (WHO, n.d.). Beyond the impacts of the crises on health infrastructure and access to care for chronic and acute illness, upstream, the deterioration of the living conditions of Cuban families made it increasingly difficult for them to live healthy lives.

On January 1, 2021, currency reunification came to Cuba. Minimum wage increased from $400 pesos to $2,100 pesos (US$17 to US$87) but so did prices on almost everything else. Notably, the cost of rationed goods increased 780 percent and soup kitchens for Cuba's most vulnerable families stopped subsidizing meals. Rampant inflation, food insecurity, income insecurity, and infrastructure that fails to provide Cuban homes with reliable access to clean water, sewage, and electricity "undermine Cuba's efforts to maintain the public's health" (Burke 2021, 6).

Both the pandemic and the current economic crisis left a mark on the population's health profile and weakened the public health system's capacity to take action to address urgent health concerns. The severity of the health crisis is reflected in the health of Cuba's most vulnerable. Maternal-infant health was severely impacted by the coronavirus crisis and deteriorating economic and social conditions in Cuba. Maternal mortality is extensively recognized as not only a key indicator of health systems, but also a proxy for socioeconomic development. Between 2020 and 2021, maternal mortality increased from 40 to 176.6 deaths per 100,000 births (Noda Alonso 2022).

Cuba's infant mortality rate, long among the region's lowest, increased 55 percent in one year. In 2021, infant mortality rates in the province of Ciego de Ávila, 13.6 per 1,000 live births, were almost double the national rates (Noda Alonso 2022). In an article in the provincial newspaper, Dr. Luis Carmenate Martínez, head of the Provincial Group of Gynecology and Obstetrics, explained that "prenatal care, the evaluation of risks in pregnant women and the application of protocols has failed" as he described a health system lacking key personnel responsible for the community-based preventive care (Castilla Padrón 2021).

Other researchers have highlighted the ways in which poor nutrition and stress affect the health of low-income black and mestiza women in rural communities and people experiencing housing precarity (Edith 2022). Low birth weight and prematurity are key risk factors for infant mortality. Both are associated with adolescent pregnancy, a complex phenomenon which has increased on the island (Edith 2022). Early and unplanned pregnancies become more common when insufficient sexual education is combined with contraceptive scarcity (Edith 2022).

Looking ahead, Cuba's health system faces many challenges to make the constitutional right to health a reality in the face of extreme economic hardship. From the beginning of the pandemic until December 2022, more than a million Cubans were diagnosed with COVID-19. Thanks to a coordinated nationwide effort, 42.6 million Cuban COVID-19 vaccine doses were administered, allowing 90.3 percent of the population to be completely vaccinated (González 2023). Just as it took a multisectoral approach to keep the novel coronavirus under control in the early days of the pandemic, in the years ahead it will take all hands on deck for Cuba's public health system, and Cubans' health, to recover.

Notes

1. Dates in this section from author's fieldwork in Havana and reports from A3M's COVID-19 event page for Cuba (2022).

2. These twelve most-prescribed medications include five antihypertensives, two diuretics, one anticoagulant, metformin for diabetes, isosorbide dinitrate for heart failure, and salbutamol and fluticasone inhalers for asthma.

References

A3M. 2022. "Event Page: COVID-19 Pandemic—Cuba." Accessed January 31, 2023, at https://global-monitoring.com/gm/page/events/epidemic-0002030.IIuBQc37EVO0.html?lang=en.

Alonso Falcón, Randy, Oscar Figueredo Reinaldo, Thalía Fuentes Puebla, Andy Jorge Blanco, Lisandra Fariñas Acosta, Claudia Fonseca Sosa, and Rogelio Carmenate. 2022. "¿Cuál es la situación actual y las perspectivas de la producción de medicamentos en Cuba?" Cubadebate, September 14. Accessed at http://www.cubadebate.cu/noticias/2022/09/14/cual-es-la-situacion-actual-y-las-perspectivas-de-la-produccion-de-medicamentos-en-cuba.

Beldarraín Chaple, Enrique, Pedro Más Bermejo, Ileana Regla Alfonso Sánchez, María Vidal Ledo, and Ileana Morales Suárez. 2022. "Dieciséis meses de pandemia de COVID-19 en Cuba." *Infodir*, no. 38 e1197 (August 1). Accessed at http://scielo.sld.cu/scielo.php?script=sci_arttext&pid=S1996-35212022000200005&lng=es&tlng=.

BioCubaFarma. 2022. "Reporte Medicamentos en Falta." October 2022. Accessed at https://www.biocubafarma.cu/doc/medicamentos_falta_2022_10.pdf.

Boza Ibarra, Glenda. 2022. "Dengue en Cuba: qué hay detrás de las cifras oficiales." *el Toque*, July 25. Accessed at https://eltoque.com/dengue-en-cuba-que-hay-detras-de-las-cifras-oficiales.

Burke, N. J. 2021. "Precarity in the Time of COVID-19: Aging Housing and Aging Population in Cuba." *Global Perspectives* 2, no. 1: 29703.

Caraballoso, Eric. 2022. "Aborto en Cuba: un derecho a blindar (I)." *OnCuba News*, August 3. Accessed at https://oncubanews.com/cuba/aborto-en-cuba-un-derecho-a-blindar-i.

Carmona Tamayo, Edilberto, and Lisandra Fariñas Acosta. 2022. "Dengue en Cuba: Cómo se comporta hasta la fecha y claves para su control." Cubadebate, July 20. Accessed at http://www.cubadebate.cu/especiales/2022/07/20/dengue-en-cuba-como-se-comporta-hasta-la-fecha-y-claves-para-su-control/?fbclid=IwAR1CmdTC8IttYdAOkqjZ1TgGPz1uDpAwHtmchooZIbJP_1w7Z-VmJSaNdE8.

Castilla Padrón, Ailén. 2021. "Mortalidad infantil en Ciego de Ávila, seguimos sin ver la luz." *Invasor*, December 14. Accesssed at http://www.invasor.cu/es/secciones/sociedad/mortalidad-infantil-en-ciego-de-avila-seguimos-sin-ver-la-luz.

Céspedes-Tamayo, Leonel Gustavo, and Héctor Alejandro Ulloa-Cedeño. 2021. "Carta al Director: Médicos residentes cubanos durante la COVID-19." *Educación Médica* 22, supp. 2. Accessed at https://doi.org/10.1016/j.edumed.2020.10.001.

Edith, Dixie. 2022. "Maternidad en la adolescencia: Un dato no es suficiente." Cubadebate, April 12. Accessed at http://www.cubadebate.cu/especiales/2022/04/12/maternidad-en-la-adolescencia-un-dato-no-es-suficiente.

Efe. 2022. "Cuba produjo en 2021 solo el 34 % de su cartera de medicamentos." *OnCuba News*, January 31. Accessed at https://oncubanews.com/cuba/cuba-produjo-en-2021-solo-el-34-de-su-cartera-de-medica mentos.

Fariñas Acosta, Lisandra, and Yilena Héctor Rodríguez. 2022. "¿Por qué el dengue sigue siendo un problema creciente a pesar de ser una enfermedad conocida hace siglos?" Cubadebate, November 13. Accessed at http://www.cubadebate.cu/noticias/2022/11/13/por-que-el-dengue-sigue-siendo-un-proble ma-creciente-a-pesar-de-ser-una-enfermedad-conocida-hace-siglos.

González, Carlos Alberto. 2023. "Salud pública cubana en 2022: epidemias, retrocesos y crisis." *OnCuba News*, January 4. Accessed at https://oncubanews.com/cuba/ciencia/salud-en-cuba/la-salud-publica-cubana-en-2022.

Lamrani, Salim. 2021. "The Health System in Cuba: Origin, Doctrine and Results." *Études caribéennes*, no. 7 (September 13). Accessed from https://journals.openedition.org/etudescaribeennes/24110.

MEDICC. 2022a. "Insights from Cuba's COVID-19 Vaccine Enterprise: Report from a High-Level Fact-Finding Delegation to Cuba Executive Summary." *MEDICC Review* 24, no. 3–4. Accessed at http://mediccreview.org/wp-content/uploads/2022/10/MEDICC-Cuba-COVID-19-Vaccin e-Executive-Summary_2022.pdf.

———. 2022b. "Insights from Cuba's COVID-19 Vaccine Enterprise: Report from a High-Level Fact-Finding Delegation to Cuba Technical Report." *MEDICC Review* 24, no. 3–4. Accessed at http://mediccreview.org/wp-content/uploads/2022/10/MEDICC-Cuba-COVID-19-Vaccin e-Full-Report_2022.pdf.

Noda Alonso, Sheila. 2022. "Cuba registra una tasa de mortalidad infantil de 7,6 por mil nacidos vivos, en un año complejo debido a la pandemia." Cubadebate, January 2. Accessed at http://www.cubadebate.cu/noticias/2022/01/02/cuba-registra-una-tasa-de-mortalidad-infantil-de-76-por-mil-nacidos-vivos-en-un-ano-complejo-debido-a-la-pandemia.

OnCuba News. 2022. "Autoridades mexicanas autorizan uso de emergencia de dos vacunas cubanas contra la COVID-19." November 20. Accessed at https://oncubanews.com/cuba/ciencia/salud-en-cuba/autoridades-mexicanas-autorizan-uso-de-emergencia-de-dos-vacunas-cubanas-contra-la-covid-19.

Pérez Riverol, Amilcar. 2020. "The Cuban Strategy for Combating the COVID-19 Pandemic." *MEDICC Review* 22, no. 3: 64–68. Accessed at https://www.redalyc.org/journal/4375/437567141015/html.

Rojas, Lucia. 2022. "Cuba Returns to an Infant Mortality of the Last Century." *OnCuba News*, November 11. Accessed at https://oncubanews.com/en/cuba/cuba-returns-to-an-infant-mortality-of-the-last-century.

Vela Valdés, J. 2020. "Los principios de la salud pública socialista cubana ante la pandemia de COVID-19." *Revista Cubana de Salud Pública* 46. Accessed at https://revsaludpublica.sld.cu /index.php/spu/article/view/2791/1629.

WHO (World Health Organization). n.d. "Social Determinants of Health." Accessed January 31, 2022, at https://www.who.int/health-topics/social-determinants-of-health#tab=tab_1.

Chronology of Key Events: 2014–2022

2014

January 28–29: The Second Summit of the Community of Latin American and Caribbean States (CELAC) takes place in Havana with President Raúl Castro chairing the conclave as the organization's copresident. CELAC's members include every state in the Western Hemisphere except the United States and Canada.

March 29: Cuba's National Assembly approves a new foreign investment law as part as the economic reforms to attract hard currency to the country.

May: The Council of Ministers approves the general bases for writing a 2016–2030 Social and Economic Development Program.

October: Cuba sends a medical brigade of 165 people—the largest foreign medical team from a single country—to Sierra Leone to fight the Ebola epidemic.

December 17: Presidents Raúl Castro and Barack Obama announce that their two countries will reestablish diplomatic relations. At the same time, Cuba releases Alan P. Gross on humanitarian grounds. Gross had been a USAID subcontractor charged with committing "acts against the integrity or territorial independence of the state" for installing sophisticated satellite communications transmitters, which may have included the capability of being undetectable for a radius of 250 miles. Gross and the US State Department claimed that his goal was to provide Cuba's Jewish community with equipment that would enable its members to access the internet without Cuban government interference. The United States releases the three remaining members of the Cuban Five still in US prisons in exchange for Cuba's release of a jailed US spy. The Five were Cuban intelligence officers who received long prison terms in 2001 after being convicted of conspiracy to commit espionage and murder. The Cuban government asserted that their mission was to monitor exile groups that had engaged in acts of terrorism against Cuba.

2015

January: The Cuban government commutes the sentences of fifty-three people whom the United States had identified as political prisoners.

April 9–11: Cuba participates for the first time in the Summit of the Americas, which is being held in Panama. Castro and Obama engage in the first private bilateral meeting between a Cuban and US president.

May 29: The US State Department removes Cuba from its list of state sponsors of terrorism.

July 20: The Cuban and US embassies officially reopen in Washington, DC, and Havana, respectively.

July: The Cuban government begins the expansion of broadband Wi-Fi access throughout the country by creating "hot spots" at which users can connect to the internet.

September 11: Cuba and the United States hold the inaugural session of a bilateral commission created to organize and provide continuity to the process of normalizing relations.

September 20–22: Pope Francis visits Cuba, during which time he officiates at three public masses.

September 29: Presidents Castro and Obama hold another bilateral meeting at the UN General Assembly.

2016

March 20–22: Obama visits Cuba along with his family and a bipartisan congressional delegation. Castro and Obama hold official meetings, give a joint press conference, and attend a baseball game between the Tampa Bay Rays and the Cuban national team. Obama gives a televised speech to the Cuban people from Cuba's National Theater, the Gran Teatro de La Habana Alicia Alonso.

March 25: The Rolling Stones perform at a free outdoor concert in Havana.

April 16–19: At the Cuban Communist Party's Seventh Congress, delegates approve resolutions affirming Cuba's socialist economic model and the proposed vision for the 2030 National Economic Development Plan, and elect Raúl Castro as first secretary for a five-year term.

July 4–8: Castro reports to the National Assembly that Cuba's gross domestic product grew by only 1 percent in the previous year, half of what was planned.

August 24: The Colombian government and the Revolutionary Armed Forces of Colombia (a group engaged in armed struggle against the government since the 1960s) sign a peace agreement in Cuba. After Colombian voters reject the accord in a referendum, the parties renegotiate its terms in Havana. The Colombian Congress approves the final agreement on November 30.

October 14: Obama issues a Presidential Policy Directive (PPD-43), which consolidates changed policy with regard to Cuba, and the Treasury Department issues new regulations authorizing transactions related to Cuban-origin products, the sale of Cuban pharmaceuticals, joint medical research, and civil aviation safety-related services. This is the fifth package of regulatory reforms easing the embargo on Cuba issued by the Obama administration since December 17, 2014.

October 26: For the first time since 1992, when the UN General Assembly began annual votes on a resolution to end the US embargo, the United States and Israel abstain instead of voting against the resolution. The final vote is 191–0–2 in favor.

November 25: Fidel Castro Ruz dies at the age of ninety in Havana. Cuba declares nine days of mourning, a period that culminates in his burial on December 4 at Santa Ifigenia Cemetery in Santiago de Cuba.

December 12: Cuba and the EU sign a Political Dialogue and Cooperation Agreement, which provides a framework for a relationship based on equality, reciprocity, and mutual respect. The signing comes in the wake of the EU's revocation of its 1996 Common Position conditioning economic cooperation on Cuba's human rights performance.

December: Cuban bilateral trade with China totals $1.8 billion in 2016, making China the island's largest trading partner.

2017

January 12: US officials meet in Havana for the third technical exchange on certified property claims by US nationals.

January 12: President Obama ends the 1995 policy known as the "wet foot, dry foot" via executive order. Cubans arriving on US soil can no longer have an unrestricted path to permanent residency and are instead processed in the same fashion as migrants from other nations. The US Department of Homeland Security also ends the Cuban Medical Professional Parole Program, which allowed Cuban doctors serving on humanitarian missions abroad to enter the United States legally if they defected.

January 17: Cuba and the United States sign agreements to cooperate on air and maritime search-and-rescue in the Florida Straits.

March 8: The Association of Caribbean States holds its first Cooperation Conference in Havana. The parties discussed new opportunities for cooperation, especially in development efforts.

April 10: Cuba invites UN Special Rapporteur Maria Grazia Giammarinaro to the island, the first time in a decade that a UN human rights Special Rapporteur has been allowed to visit Cuba.

May 3: Cuba and Russia sign an agreement allowing Cuba to purchase 1.9 million barrels of oil and diesel fuel from Russia, which eases pressure felt by the decline in Venezuelan imports.

May 22: Cuba opens five new *merca hostales* (wholesale markets) selling food items to *cuentapropistas*, bringing the total to eight *merca hostales*.

June 16: Speaking in Miami, President Donald Trump announces that he is "canceling" President Obama's policy of engagement with Cuba and returning to a policy of hostility and regime change. On stage at a theater named for the leader of the Cuban exile brigade that was defeated at the Bay of Pigs, he signs a National Security Presidential Memorandum (NSPM–5) that limits educational travel to Cuba by US citizens to trips only with a licensed tour provider, and that imposes sanctions for engaging in commerce with entities controlled or operated by the Cuban military.

June 23: Since the beginning of 2017, Cuban authorities have confiscated 1.8 tons of drugs, triple the amount taken in the same period in 2016. Cuba and the United States had signed a Counter Narcotics Agreement one year earlier that made increased cooperation and information sharing possible to prevent the illegal trafficking of narcotics.

July 5: The EU Members of Parliament approve a Political Dialogue and Cooperation Agreement with Cuba, which replaces the EU Common Position on Cuba. The Common Position had imposed sanctions on the island.

July 13: Reports from state-run oil companies show that Cuba's oil imports from Venezuela slid almost 13 percent in the first half of 2017. Since 2016, Cuba has reduced fuel allocations 28 percent to the majority of public companies.

September 9: Hurricane Irma reaches Cuba as a Category 5 storm, leaving ten dead and severely impacting the economy. The storm damages 300,000 hectares of sugarcane crops and 40 percent of Cuba's sugar refineries. The cost totals $13 billion, including over 150,000 homes damaged.

September 18: US and Cuban officials meet in Washington for the sixth session of the bilateral commission, the first to occur since the Trump administration took office.

September 29: The US State Department recalls 60 percent of its staff at the US embassy in Havana following allegations of "sonic attacks" on officials there, and issues a travel advisory warning US residents against traveling to Cuba. The United States also demands that Cuba reduce its embassy staff in Washington and designates the entire commercial section of the embassy to be withdrawn. Earlier in the week, Cuba reiterated its desire to cooperate with the United States in uncovering the source of the incidents.

November 1: The UN approves a resolution condemning the US embargo against Cuba. Israel and the United States are alone in opposing the resolution, which passes with a vote of 191–2.

November 26: Armando Hart Dávalos dies at age eighty-seven. A founding member of the July 26th Movement, he served as director of Cuba's 1961 literacy campaign, as minister of education, and as the first minister of culture.

December: Cuba ends the year with a record of 4.7 million international visitors, including 620,000 from the United States. But the number of US travelers declined in December from the previous year as US State Department travel warnings began to have a negative impact.

December 21: Raúl Castro announces he will step down from the presidency in April 2018, rather than February as previously planned, due to delays caused by Hurricane Irma.

2018

January 1: Policy changes take effect that the *Gaceta Oficial* announced in October. The estimated 800,000 Cubans living abroad no longer need an *habilitación* stamp on their passports in order to travel to the island. Children born abroad to Cuban citizens may also apply for citizenship.

January 3: Federica Mogherini, the EU's top diplomat, visits Havana to follow up with the implementation of the Political Dialogue and Cooperation Agreement, ratified in November. Shortly after the visit, Cuba announces that the EU will invest $22.4 million over the subsequent five years in renewable energy projects on the island.

January 10: Cuba announces the intention to import an additional 2.1 million barrels of crude oil from Algeria in an attempt to make up for the loss of imports from Venezuela.

February 26: Cigar manufacturer Havanos S.A. reports that Cuba's cigar sales reached a record of $500 million in 2017, due largely to rapidly rising demand from China.

March 29: The US State Department announces processing and interviews for immigrant visas for Cuban nationals are to be conducted in Georgetown, Guyana, rather than in Colombia, as they had been since January.

April 16: The United States and Cuba reestablish direct postal service.

April 19: The National Assembly elects Miguel Díaz-Canel Bermúdez as the new president, replacing Raúl Castro (Salvador Antonio Valdés Mesa is elected first vice president, replacing Díaz-Canel). This follows March elections in which 83 percent of the electorate turn out to elect 605 deputies to the National Assembly and 1,265 delegates to Cuba's provincial assemblies.

May 8–20: The Kennedy Center in Washington, DC, hosts the Festival of Cuban Arts, the largest-ever exhibition and celebration of Cuban art and culture in the United States, with more than one hundred Cuban artists, singers, dancers, and musicians participating.

May 29: Díaz-Canel calls corruption in state enterprises the "number one enemy of the Revolution."

June 6: President Trump appoints former Miami mayor Tomás Regalado, a self-described "hardliner" regarding Cuba policy, to head Radio and TV Martí, the US-based propaganda outlets.

June 2: The Cuban National Assembly chooses Raúl Castro to lead the commission tasked with rewriting the Cuban constitution.

July 10: The Cuban government announces private sector reforms that include requirements for labor contracts, sanctions for workplace discrimination, and limits on the number of licenses individuals and households can hold. All transactions will have to be carried out through state-run banks.

July 16: Cuba's state-run communications company begins providing data-based internet access to select mobile phones.

September 4: As part of its ongoing effort to support the peace process in Colombia, Cuba receives the first of 200 scholarship recipients participating in a Cuban program to assist veterans of the Colombian civil war in finding new career paths.

September 26: The first-ever biotech venture between the United States and Cuba, named Innovative Immunotherapy Alliance S.A., is announced. The venture is intended to research new cancer treatments and promote new, potentially life-saving medications.

November 1: With a vote of 188–2–0, the UN General Assembly votes again for a resolution to end the US embargo of Cuba. Israel and the United States vote in opposition.

November 1: In a Miami speech during the week before the midterm elections, US national security adviser John Bolton calls Cuba, Venezuela, and Nicaragua a "troika of tyranny" and announces there will be new sanctions against the three countries.

November 1: Díaz-Canel arrives in Moscow, marking the beginning of an international tour that takes him also to North Korea, China, Vietnam, Laos, and the United Kingdom.

November 14: Cuba announces it will withdraw most of the 8,600 doctors working in rural Brazilian towns under a Pan American Health Organization program in response to president-elect Jair Bolsonaro's demand that the doctors obtain new licenses and that they receive 100 percent of the salaries paid by the Brazilian government.

November 14: The Trump administration adds twenty-six popular tourist attractions in Cuba, including sixteen hotels, to the State Department's list of places Americans are prohibited to visit.

December 6: The day before new restrictive regulations on the private sector go into effect, the government responds to complaints by private entrepreneurs by eliminating two of the most criticized provisions limiting licenses and the size of restaurants. The government also promises to consult with Cuban artists before implementing a new restrictive law on the arts.

December 6: Cubans gain internet access via cellphones as Etecsa, the state-owned telecommunications company, begins 3G service for everyone.

December 19: US Major League Baseball announces an agreement with the Cuban Baseball Federation intended to facilitate the hiring of Cuban baseball players by US professional teams.

December: The number of international visitors to Cuba increased slightly in 2018 to 4.75 million. But the number of US tourists declined by 6.8 percent.

2019

January 7: Florida International University's 2018 poll of Cuban Americans finds respondents were evenly split between those favoring and opposing continuation of the US embargo against Cuba, with 68 percent favoring US companies expanding or maintaining business relations with the island.

January 28: The worst tornado ever to hit Havana leaves 7 dead, close to 200 injured, and some 10,000 people displaced as about 8,000 homes are severely damaged. Cubans use newly acquired cellphone access to mobilize support for the victims via social media apps.

February 6: Russia announces that it has approved a $43 million loan to Cuba for the purpose of purchasing military equipment such as armored vehicles.

February 24: Cuban voters approve the new constitution in a referendum with 87 percent voting in favor. Turnout was 84.4 percent of the 8.7 million eligible voters. Opponents of the constitution—mainly evangelical Protestant churches and the Roman Catholic Church—were permitted to freely campaign publicly against it.

April 8: The Trump administration cancels the agreement between Major League Baseball and the Cuban Baseball Federation that would have established a system to allow Cuban players to join US professional teams without giving up their Cuban citizenship.

April 11: A march for animal welfare takes place in Havana with local government approval.

May 3: Despite opposition from US allies, President Trump activates Title III of the 1996 Cuban Liberty and Democratic Solidarity [Libertad] Act, also known as the Helms-Burton Act. Since its passage, both Republican and Democratic presidents had waived Title III, which permits US citizens to sue in a US court corporations and individuals allegedly using the property previously owned by the claimants and expropriated by the Cuban government, even if the claimant had not been a US citizen at the time of the expropriation.

May 11: MINSAP cancels the annual Conga against Homophobia and Transphobia, claiming "certain circumstances make it difficult for the march to take place successfully." Still smarting from the removal of a proposed Article 68 from the new constitution, which would have provided rights for LGBTQ+ Cubans, a group of people spontaneously organize an LGBTQ+ March from the Parque Centrale to the Malecon.

June 5: The US Treasury and Commerce Departments issue regulations canceling licenses for organizations engaged in "people-to-people" educational travel for Americans and prohibiting US-based cruise ships from docking at Cuban ports. The seventeen companies and twenty-seven ships affected by the prohibition had contributed between $63 and $107 million dollars to the Cuban economy annually. The new regulations also cap at $1,000 every three months the previously unlimited amount of remittances Americans could send to their families in Cuba.

June 27: President Díaz-Canel announces a gradual increase in state salaries and pensions that will affect 2.7 million people. The minimum wage will increase to 400 pesos, and the average income of public sector workers from 767 Cuban pesos (about US$31) to 1,067 pesos (US$44).

July 20: Roberto Fernández Retamar, director of the Casa de las Américas and renowned poet and essayist, dies.

July 24: Panama stops issuing $20 tourist cards to Cuban visitors, requiring them to apply for visas through the consulate in Cuba in a more complicated and expensive process. The new barrier reduces the number of Cubans traveling to Panama to make purchases and those using the country as a path to arrive to the US southern border. The tourist card for Cubans was created in 2018 and allowed Cubans to enter Panama to make purchases for up to thirty days.

July 25: Cardinal Jaime Ortega dies. He had served as archbishop of Havana for more than three decades, helping to create new public spaces for Catholic voices and facilitating a dialogue between Cuba and the United States.

July 29: New communications regulations take effect that allow Cubans to create privately owned and managed local wireless and wired networks for personal and commercial uses. The rules, which will enable the expansion of internet use to homes, also permit the importation of routers and other networking equipment.

September 6: The US Treasury Department imposes additional sanctions on Cuba, including a limit of family remittances to $1,000 dollars per quarter, a prohibition on remittances to relatives of Cuban officials and members of the Communist Party, and denying the transfer of funds through US banks.

September 11: President Díaz-Canel asserts that recent energy shortages—which forced the state to cut by half fuel allocations for state companies and limit public transportation—are the result of US government measures to prevent the arrival of oil to the island. He promises the problem is a "temporary situation" (*coyuntura*) and not the beginning of a new Special Period like the one that affected the island during the 1990s.

October 17: Legendary ballet dancer and choreographer Alicia Alonso dies at age ninety-eight. In 1959, she founded the famed National Ballet of Cuba and helped to make the country an international center for classical ballet.

October 18: US secretary of state Mike Pompeo issues a regulation that bans funding in Cuba by any US organization for cultural exchange programs.

October 22: Betsy Díaz, minister of domestic trade, reports that Cuban industries would be able to meet only 50 percent of the country's demand for basic toiletries and cleaning materials due to the intensification of US sanctions.

October 29: President Díaz-Canel meets in Moscow with Russian president Vladmir Putin to discuss increasing trade between the two countries.

November 15: Havana residents begin celebrations of the capital's 500th anniversary.

November 27: Cuba launches a National Program against Racism and Racial Discrimination. The campaign, which is intended to expand education about Cubans' African roots and spur a public debate about racial issues, will include the creation of a commission headed by President Díaz-Canel to organize the effort.

December 10: A US ban on commercial airline flights to all Cuban airports except Havana goes into effect, making it difficult for Americans to visit family members outside the capital.

December 12: The Cuban government reports that four million visitors will have arrived in Cuba by the end of the year, one million fewer than had been projected,

2020

January 10: The Trump administration suspends US charter flights to Cuban cities other than Havana and limits the number of flights to the capital. This follows a similar December 2019 limitation of scheduled airline service to Cuba.

February 3: The Inter-American Commission on Human Rights criticizes Decree Law 370, issued in 2019, because it "could establish a censorship regime in the country and serve as a legal instrument to punish the independent press."

February 26: The Ministry of Communications reports that 63 percent of the Cuban population had internet access at the end of 2019, and of these, about half accessed the internet by using cellphones.

March 10: More than 3,000 people sign a petition calling for the release from detention of Luis Manuel Otero Alcántara, a performance artist–activist. The list of signatories includes famed folksinger Silvio Rodríguez and painter-sculptor Alexis Leiva ("Kcho").

March 24: Cuba suspends entry to the country by non-Cubans, essentially shutting down its tourism industry, as a preventive measure against the spread of COVID-19. (The first case on the island was reported on March 11, with an Italian tourist who subsequently died from the virus.) The suspension comes one day after the government announced cancellation of public activities such as sporting events and the closure of schools and public facilities such as pools and disco clubs.

April 1: The Ministry of Public Health reports that it has dispatched 593 medical workers to fourteen countries to help them fight the outbreak of COVID-19. The first contingent was sent to Italy on March 21.

April 27: Former vice president Joseph Biden asserts in an interview with CBS's Miami affiliate that he intends to restore most of the Obama administration's Cuba policies if he is elected president.

May 12: The US State Department places Cuba on a list of countries that did not "fully cooperate" with US counterterrorism efforts in 2019, in large part because it permitted members of Colombia's National Liberation Army (ELN) to live in Cuba. Cuba had served as the interlocutor for negotiations between the Colombian government and the ELN.

June 18: The Cuban Ministry of Justice (MINJUS) issues a birth certificate for Paulo César Bastian Valdes, the first time the law recognizes that a child legally can have two mothers.

June 19: The nineteen-member Paris Club, a group of wealthy, mainly European nations, grants Cuba a one-year moratorium on its debt repayment.

July 16: The Council of Ministers announces a series of economic reforms, including the right of private businesses to import and export goods through thirty-seven designated state enterprises.

July 31: Eusebio Leal Spengler dies at the age of seventy-seven. He was widely respected for his work as the official historian of Havana in leading the restoration of Old Havana and the effort to name the neighborhood a UNESCO World Heritage Site.

August 30: Marriott International ends its management of Havana's Four Points Sheraton Hotel as a result of the US Treasury Department's refusal to renew the company's license for conducting business in Cuba.

September 24: The US Treasury Department issues regulations that further restrict travel to Cuba by US citizens, including limitations on attendance at professional meetings and participation in or organizing "certain public performances, clinics, workshops, other athletic or non-athletic competitions, and exhibitions."

October 13: The UN General Assembly elects Cuba to the UN Human Rights Council, with 170 of the 192 members voting in favor.

October 22: Foreign Minister Bruno Rodríguez Parrilla asserts that US sanctions had cost Cuba $5.57 billion between April 2019 and March 2020, an increase of $1.23 billion over the prior twelve months.

November 23: Western Union closes its 407 offices in Cuba, effectively cutting off most remittances from the United States to Cuba. This comes as a result of the Trump administration's decision in June to place Financiera Cimex S.A. (FINCIMEX) on a list of "restricted" entities with which US citizens and companies cannot trade. Registered in Panama, and owned by the Cuban military's Grupo de Administración Empresarial S.A. (GAESA), FINCIMEX had been the principal correspondent financial institution that Western Union used to transmit remittances.

November 27: More than 300 demonstrators protest outside of the Ministry of Culture against alleged increases in government control over artists' freedom of expression, and in support of Luis Manuel Otero Alcántara, a founder of the San Isidro Movement (MSI), who had been arrested the previous day. A group of artists and writers formed MSI in 2018 to protest the government's codification of extended control over artistic expression, which appeared to be codified in Decree Law 349. The demonstration led to a rare dialogue between representatives of the protestors and Vice Minister of Culture Fernando Rojas and an agreement to hold further meetings. The subsequent unwillingness of the government to engage in further dialogue with MSI in part contributed to a wellspring of discontent that erupted on July 11, 2021.

December 10: In an effort to attract foreign investment, the government announces that it will permit foreign investors to own more than 50 percent of a company.

2021

January 1: The government initiates the long-awaited task of unifying the currency and exchange rates (Tarea Ordenamiento), eliminating the convertible peso (CUC) and pegging the exchange rate of the Cuban peso (CUP) to the US dollar at 24:1. Over the coming year, the black market exchange rate will top 100:1.

January 11: With just days remaining in the Trump administration, Secretary of State Mike Pompeo designates Cuba as a state sponsor of international terrorism, damaging Cuba's ability engage in international financial transactions and complicating the incoming Biden administration's relations with Havana.

January 15: The outgoing Trump administration imposes Magnitsky sanctions on the Cuban Ministry of the Interior and its minister for alleged human rights violations. Magnitsky sanctions prohibit US persons from engaging in transactions with listed entities and bar listed persons from entering the United States.

January 27: A planned meeting between the minister of culture and artists who demonstrated against censorship and police harassment at the ministry on November 27, 2020, turns into a shoving match between demonstrators and ministry officials, ending any chance for dialogue.

February 16: The music video "Patria y Vida" (Homeland and Life) is released. Produced by Cuban American filmmaker Asiel Babastro with a group of dissident Cuban hip-hop artists, it mocks Fidel Castro's signature slogan, "Patria o Muerte" (Homeland or Death), declares the Cuban Revolution "over," and is viewed by millions on the internet.

March 10: The Cuban government announces it will accept foreign direct investment from Cubans living abroad, although the US embargo prohibits investing in Cuba except in private businesses.

April 10: Almost two years to the day after a protest march demanding an end to animal cruelty, the government approves an animal protection law.

April 16–19: The Communist Party of Cuba holds its Eighth Congress, reaffirming its commitment to the economic reform program launched at the Sixth Congress in 2011. Miguel Díaz-Canel is elected first secretary of the party, replacing Raúl Castro, who retires from the leadership along with several other leaders from the "historic" generation that took power in 1959.

May 12: Cuba begins a mass vaccination campaign against COVID-19 with vaccines developed by its own bio-pharmacological industry.

June 23: For the twenty-ninth consecutive year, the UN General Assembly approves—by a vote of 184 in favor, 2 against (the United States and Israel), and 3 abstentions—a resolution calling on the United States to lift the embargo against Cuba.

June: The Delta variant of COVID-19 causes a surge in infections in Havana and Matanzas provinces, overwhelming Cuba's healthcare system, already short on supplies.

July 1: The annual US report on human trafficking designates Cuba as a "Tier 3" country responsible for trafficking because Cuba's medical assistance missions abroad allegedly do not meet International Labor Organization standards. Cuba denounces the report as false and an effort to prevent it from earning income from the export of medical services.

July 11–12: Thousands of Cubans in dozens of towns and cities take to the streets to protest the surge in COVID-19 cases; electricity blackouts; shortages of food, fuel, and medicine; and the government's inability to remedy these problems. Most marches are peaceful, but in some places demonstrators loot stores and clash with police, who are accused of using excessive force. Over the next several weeks, an estimated 1,400 people are arrested for participating in the protest.

July 22 and 30 and August 13: The United States imposes Magnitsky sanctions on senior officials and special units of the Cuban police and armed forces for human rights violations against July 11 protestors.

July 26: The Cuban government announces a program to prioritize improving infrastructure and services in 302 vulnerable communities, 65 of them in Havana, including a number in which large protests occurred on July 11–12.

July 29: The EU calls on Cuba to respect internationally recognized human rights and free protestors arbitrarily detained.

August 7: After expanding the number of occupations open to private businesses in February, the Cuban government approves a new law giving micro, small, and medium-size private businesses (MPYMES) status as legal entities, spurring a major increase in the number of such businesses over the next two years.

August 16: The US Department of State allows family members to resume accompanying diplomats stationed at the embassy in Havana for the first time since 2017, when the Trump administration downsized the staff and ordered dependents to depart in response to the so-called Havana Syndrome.

August 17: Decree 35, a new law on cybersecurity, imposes criminal penalties for hacking, the dissemination of disinformation, "inciting mobilizations" that disrupt public order, "subverting the constitutional order," and defaming the country's prestige.

September 20: Young artists in the Facebook group Archipiélago, in coalition with traditional dissidents, petition the government for permission to hold a Civic March for Change in various cities, making political demands of the government. Permission is denied and the organizers declare they will march anyway.

September 25: The first shipment of Cuba's Abdala COVID-19 vaccine arrives in Vietnam, which authorized the purchase of ten million doses.

November 15: On the date scheduled for the Civic March for Change, police confine most of the organizers to house arrest and no other marchers show up. Over the next few months, most of Archipiélago's leaders go into exile.

November 22: Nicaragua eliminates the visa requirement for Cubans, facilitating emigration by Cubans planning to travel the US southern border to seek asylum.

December 19: Minister of Economy and Planning Alejandro Gil Fernández reports to the National Assembly that Cuba will end 2021 with a 2 percent increase in GDP and 60 percent inflation for the year.

December 24: Cuba and China agree to a construction plan that begins implementation of a 2018 Memorandum of Agreement that Cuba signed when it joined China's Belt and Road Initiative.

2022

January 20: A CIA investigation reveals that no evidence has been found that any country is responsible for the mysterious ailment known as the Havana Syndrome.

February 7: Cuba's Central Bank authorizes Orbit S.A., a private corporation, to process remittances from the United States as a way to circumvent US restrictions on state-owned financial institutions.

February 22: Russia postpones Cuba's repayment of $2.3 billion in loans until 2027. The next day, Cuba criticizes "the progressive expansion of NATO towards the borders of the Russian Federation" and called for a diplomatic solution to the conflict in Ukraine.

April 21: Cuban and US officials meet in Washington to resume semiannual migration talks that the Trump administration suspended in 2017.

April 30: Ricardo Alarcón de Quesada dies. A longtime government leader, he served as foreign minister, Cuba's ambassador to the UN, and president of the National Assembly from 1993 to 2013.

May 6: An explosion from a gas leak at Havana's famed Hotel Saratoga kills twenty-six people.

May 15: The National Assembly approves a new penal code, which then goes into force in August 2022. While it creates penalties for domestic and gender-based violence, the new code also includes provisions so broad they could be invoked to charge people for nonviolent criticism or protest.

May 16: The Biden administration announces it will relax some sanctions against Cuba. These include removing the cap of $1,000 on family remittances every three months, the resumption of the Family Reunification Parole Program, and increased flights to the island.

June 5: President Biden withholds invitations to Cuba, Nicaragua, and Venezuela to participate in the Summit of the Americas. In response, Mexican president Andrés Miguel López Obrador and Honduran president Xiomara Castro refuse to attend the meeting in Los Angeles.

June 24: Prominent members of the San Isidro Movement, Luis Manuel Otero Alcántara and Maykel Castillo, receive jail sentences of five and nine years, respectively, for assault and defaming the Cuban flag.

August 3: Cuba's Central Bank announces that the government will begin to buy dollars and other convertible currencies at roughly five times the official rate of 24 pesos to the dollar.

August 6: Lightning strikes cause explosions and fires at the Matanzas Supertanker Base oil storage facility, injuring 125. Controlled after five days, the fire destroys 40 percent of Cuba's main fuel storage facility, causing massive blackouts. The gasoline shortages and subsequent blackouts aggravate earlier summer tensions and lead to scattered local protests.

September 1: The US embassy announces that, for the first time since 2017, it will begin processing applications for the Cuban Family Reunification Parole Program.

September 26: President Díaz-Canel and Esteban Lazo, president of the National Assembly, sign into law the Families Code, which Cubans had ratified the previous day in a nationwide referendum, with 67 percent in favor (74 percent of eligible voters participate). The legislation legalizes marriage between and adoption by same-sex couples and includes an extension of children's rights.

September 27: Hurricane Ian, a Category 4 storm, hits Cuba with winds up to 125 mph. It destroys 10,000 houses and damages an additional 79,000 homes in Pinar del Río Province, kills three people, and forces the national power grid to shut down. In all, 21,000 acres of crops are affected, including the main portion of Cuba's tobacco crop.

September 30: The fiscal year ends with a record 224,607 Cubans attempting to cross the southern US border. The US Coast Guard reports that for the same period it had intercepted 6,182 Cubans at sea (a 600 percent increase over 2021).

October 2: President Díaz-Canel condemns "vulgar" street protests against fuel and food shortages, calling them "illegitimate."

October 5: Colombian president Gustavo Petro tells visiting US secretary of state Antony Blinken that US inclusion of Cuba on the list of states supporting terrorism was "an injustice."

October 17: The United States offers to donate $2 million in emergency relief to Cuba after Hurricane Ian. Cuba accepts the offer of US aid—the first time it does so.

October 25: A Florida International University poll of Cuban Americans in South Florida finds that 63 percent favor continuation of the embargo; 64 percent and 72 percent, respectively, support selling food and medicine to Cuba; and 71 percent favor the resumption of air travel to all regions of Cuba.

November 2: The UN General Assembly votes (for the thirtieth year) in favor of a motion condemning the US embargo of Cuba, by a vote of 185–2–2. The United States and Israel vote against; Ukraine and Colombia abstain.

November 5: The Cuban government announces that only 41 percent of the planned sugarcane had been planted. It estimates that the resulting harvest will produce 14,000 fewer tons than in the previous year, and that very little sugar would be exported.

November 14: The annual International Havana Fair opens after a two-year lapse due to COVID-19. Intended to attract trade and foreign investment, 400 business representatives from sixty countries attend. President Díaz-Canel announces that Cuba is open to investment from US companies and Cuban Americans.

November 15: Cuban and US officials meet in Havana. They discuss a full resumption of immigrant visa processing at the US embassy in Havana, and Cuba agrees to accept US deportation flights of Cubans apprehended at the Mexican border.

November 16–27: President Díaz-Canel visits Algeria, Russia, Turkey, and China, seeking to restructure Cuba's debt, obtain new investment financing and aid, and obtain help with Cuba's energy problems. China agrees to give $100 million in financial aid.

November 22: Pablo Milanés dies. The beloved poet and folksinger was a founding member in the 1960s of the *nueva trova* movement, which blended folk music with political themes.

November 29: Cuban municipal elections take place—with the lowest turnout in forty years. Approximately 69 percent of registered voters participate (compared to 89 percent in 2017).

November 30: A US Department of Justice agency recommends denial of Cuba's application to link up to a US undersea telecommunications cable. Nine days later Cuba signs an agreement linking the island to a similar cable via Martinique.

December 2: The United States adds Cuba and Nicaragua to its list of "countries of particular concern" for allegedly abusing religious freedom.

December 12: Alejandro Gil Fernández, Minister of Economy and Planning, reports that between January and October 2022 the price of basic goods and services had increased 29 percent. GDP had grown 2 percent, half of what had been forecast. Only 1.7 million tourists arrive in 2022, 800,000 fewer than the government had predicted.

December 31: The government announces that 6,273 micro, small, and medium-size enterprises (MPYMES) had been registered. Of these, 6,138 are private businesses, 75 are state-run, and 60 are industrial cooperatives, with an estimated 106,400 new jobs having been created as a result.

Note

The editors appreciate the assistance of Teresa García Castro, Elisabeth Hutcheson, and Rafael Miller in compiling the chronology.

Index

About the Contributors

Fulton T. Armstrong has worked on Cuba in various senior positions in the US government and, since 2012, at American University's Center for Latin American and Latino Studies. He served two terms as a director for Inter-American Affairs at the White House National Security Council during the Clinton administration, and later as US National Intelligence Officer for Latin America. He also worked at the State Department, at the US Interests Section in Havana, and on the Senior Professional Staff at the Senate Foreign Relations Committee. For a number of years he also specialized in China affairs.

Mervyn J. Bain is a professor in the Department of Politics and International Relations at the University of Aberdeen (United Kingdom). He has published on Havana-Moscow relations in a variety of journals and is the author of four books on the bilateral relationship: *Moscow and Havana: 1917 to the Present*; *From Lenin to Castro, 1917–1959*; *Soviet-Cuban Relations, 1985 to 1991*; and *Russian-Cuban Relations since 1992*.

Hope Bastian is assistant professor of anthropology at Wheaton College, Massachusetts. She is the author of *Everyday Adjustments in Havana: Economic Reforms, Mobility and Emerging Inequalities* (2018), which examines the impacts of economic reforms on everyday life and inequalities in Socialist Cuba. From 2015 to 2021 she taught at the University of Havana. Her current research explores social movements in Cuba's emerging virtual public sphere around birth, breastfeeding, LBGTQ+ rights, and gender violence.

Philip Brenner is emeritus professor of international relations and history at American University in Washington, DC. Among his books and articles are several about Cuban history, US-Cuban relations, and Cuban foreign policy. His most recent books are *Cuba Libre: A 500-Year Quest for Independence* (2018) and *Cuba at the Crossroads* (2020).

Michael J. Bustamante is associate professor of history and the Emilio Bacardí Moreau Chair in Cuban and Cuban-American Studies at the University of Miami. He is the author of *Cuban Memory Wars: Retrospective Politics in Revolution and Exile* (2021) and coeditor of *The Revolution from Within: Cuba, 1959–1980* (2019).

Kirenia Pérez Criado is the pastor of Havana Friends Church (Quakers) and coordinates education programs at the Martin Luther King, Jr. Memorial Center in Marianao, Havana, where she has worked in multiple roles since 2004. She is professor of New Testament and Greek at the Matanzas Evangelical Theological Seminary and director of the Centro de Estudios of the Cuban Council of Churches.

Susan Eckstein is professor of international relations and sociology at the Pardee School of Global Studies, Boston University. Her research focuses on Latin America and Latin American immigration. She has written extensively on Mexico, Cuba, and Bolivia and, in recent years, on immigration and its impact across borders, as well as immigration policy. Her most recent book is *Cuban Privilege: The Making of Immigrant Inequality in America* (2021).

H. Michael Erisman is emeritus professor of politics at Indiana State University. He is the author of *Cuba's International Relations: The Anatomy of a Nationalistic Foreign Policy*, *South-South Relations in the Caribbean*, and *Cuba's Foreign Relations in a Post-Soviet World* and the coauthor (with John M. Kirk) of *Cuban Medical Internationalism: Origins, Evolution and Goals*. He is also the coeditor (with Kirk) of *Cuban Foreign Policy Confronts a New International Order* and *Redefining Cuban Foreign Policy: The Impact of the "Special Period."*

Julio Antonio Fernández Estrada is a professor of Roman law at the Universidad Iberoamericana de México and a fellow in Harvard's Scholars at Risk program. He holds a 1998 law degree, a 2003 degree in history, and a 2005 doctorate in law from the University of Havana. He was a professor at the University of Havana Law School and the Center for Public Administration Studies from 1999 to 2016.

Julio César Guanche holds a law degree from the University of Havana (1997), a master's degree in public law from the University of Valencia (2005), and a PhD in social sciences from FLACSO-Ecuador (2017). He is the author, among others books, of *En el borde de todo. El hoy y el mañana de la Revolución en Cuba* (2007), *La verdad no se ensaya. Cuba: el socialismo y la democracia* (2012), and *La libertad como destino. Valores, proyectos y tradición en el siglo XX cubano* (2013).

Katrin Hansing is associate professor of sociology and anthropology at Baruch College, City University of New York. Previously she was the associate director of the Cuban Research Institute at Florida International University. She has spent the last thirteen years conducting research in the Caribbean (especially Cuba) and southern Africa and its diasporas. Currently she is working on a book about Cubans' memories of the Angolan Civil War. Dr. Hansing is the author of numerous publications including *Rasta, Race, and Revolution: The Emergence and Development of the Rastafari Movement in Socialist Cuba* (2006).

John M. Kirk is emeritus professor of Latin American studies at Dalhousie University in Canada. He is the author/coeditor of several books on Cuba, dealing with José Martí, religion and politics, culture, and international relations. His most recent works are *Healthcare without Borders: Understanding Cuban Medical Internationalism* (2015), *Cuban Foreign Policy: Transformation under Raúl Castro* (2018), and *Cuba at the Crossroads* (2020).

William M. LeoGrande is professor of government in the School of Public Affairs at American University in Washington, DC. He specializes in Latin American politics and US relations with Latin America, with a particular focus on Cuba. He has written for a wide range of scholarly and popular publications and is coauthor of *Back Channel to Cuba: The Hidden History of Negotiations between Washington and Havana* (2015) and coeditor of *Cuba at the Crossroads* (2020).

Vilma Hidalgo López-Chávez is a professor and researcher at the Facultad Latinoamericana de Ciencias Sociales (FLACSO) in Havana. As an expert on gender, family, social inequalities, and public policies she has served as a consultant and evaluator of development projects on gender, employment, rurality, and disability. She has an MS in clinical psychology and health psychology and a PhD in psychology from the University of Havana.

Bert Hoffmann is lead research fellow at the German Institute for Global and Area Studies (GIGA), head of the GIGA Berlin Office, and professor of political science at Freie Universität Berlin. He also serves as a principal investigator in the German-Latin American Centre of Infection & Epidemiology Research & Training (GLACIER). He has published widely on political and economic issues in Latin America, and in particular Cuba, for more than thirty years.

Arturo López-Levy is assistant professor of politics and international relations at Holy Names University and director of the podcast *Conversaciones Americanas*. He is the coauthor of *Raúl Castro and the New Cuba: A Close-Up View of Change* (2012) and author of numerous articles in scholarly and popular journals on contemporary Cuban politics. He received his PhD in international studies from the University of Denver.

Armando Nova González is professor of economics at the University of Havana and senior researcher at the Center of International Economic Research. A specialist on issues related to agricultural economics, he is the author or coauthor of more than seventy articles and seven books, the most recent of which is *Agricultura en Cuba, entre Retos y Transformaciones* (2022). He has also served as an international advisor to the United Nations Food and Agriculture Organization and the Economic Commission for Latin America and the Caribbean.

Leonardo Padura Fuentes is a Cuban novelist and journalist, and one of Cuba's best-known writers internationally. He has written screenplays, two books of short stories, and a series of detective novels translated into ten languages. In 2012 Padura was awarded the National Prize for Literature, Cuba's national literary award, and in 2015 he was awarded the Premio Principe de Asturias de las Letras of Spain, one of the most important literary prizes in the Spanish-speaking world.

Louis A. Pérez Jr. is the J. Carlyle Sitterson Professor of History at the University of North Carolina, Chapel Hill. The author or editor of more than twenty books on Cuban history, including *Cuba: Between Reform and Revolution* (five editions), *The Structure of Cuban History: Meanings and Purpose of the Past* (2013), and *Cuba and the United States: Ties of Singular Intimacy* (1997), his most recent book is *Rice in the Time of Sugar: The Political Economy of Food in Cuba* (2019). He is a member of the American Academy of Arts and Sciences and Cuba's Academy of History.

C. Maelia Esther Pérez Silveira is professor of law at the University of Havana, where she specializes in commercial law and private international law. The author of several articles and book chapters, she was also a professor at the Center for the Study of Public Administration (2018–2022) and coordinator of the Ibero-American Network on Law, Family, International Migrations and Conflict Resolution, sponsored by the Iberoamerican College Association Graduate Program (AUIP).

Jorge R. Piñón is a senior research fellow at the University of Texas at Austin's Energy Institute. He previously served as director of the Latin American and Caribbean Program at the university's Center for International Energy and Environmental Policy. He has been a visiting energy fellow at the University of Miami's Center for Hemispheric Policy and served as president of Amoco Oil de México, president of Amoco Oil Latin America, and manager of BP Oil Europe's western Mediterranean petroleum supply and logistics operations.

Magela Romero Almodóvar is professor of sociology at the University of Havana and coordinator of the Cuban Care Studies Network (Red Cubana de Estudios sobre Cuidados). She is also a member of the advisory team for the Prevention of and Attention to Gender Violence (Equipo Asesor para la Prevención y Atención de la Violencia de Género) of the Federation of Cuban Women and working groups of the Latin American Council of Social Sciences on "Feminism, Resistance and Emancipation" and "Gender and Care." Dr. Romero is the author of more than seventy scientific articles and the author or editor of ten books.

Antonio F. Romero Gómez is professor of economics at the University of Havana, where he holds the "Norman Girvan" Caribbean Studies Chair. The author of more than sixty journal articles on economics, development, and international relations, he served for a decade as director of the International Economics Research Center (CIEI) at the University of Havana, and on the staff of Permanent Secretariat of the Latin American and Caribbean Economic System (SELA).

Ricardo Torres Pérez is adjunct professor of economics at American University, Washington, DC, and a research fellow at the university's Center for Latin American and Latino Studies. Previously he was a professor and deputy director of the Centro de Estudios de la Economía Cubana at the University of Havana. He is the editor-in-chief of the series Miradas a la Economía Cubana and a columnist for *Progreso Semanal / Progreso Weekly*. He is the coeditor of *No More Free Lunch: Reflections on the Cuban Economic Reform Process and Challenges for Transformation* (2014).

Ailynn Torres Santana is a visiting professor at the Latin American Faculty of Social Sciences (FLACSO), Ecuador. She recently finished her postdoctoral research at the International Research Group on Authoritarianism and Counter-Strategies (IRGAC) at the Rosa Luxemburg Foundation. She has been an associate professor at Universidad de la Habana (2006–2012); a visiting professor at Freie Universität Berlin, Universidad de Barcelona, and the University of Massachusetts Amherst; and a visiting scholar at Harvard University.

C. Juan Triana Cordoví is professor of economics and president of the Scientific Council of the Center for the Study of the Cuban Economy at the University of Havana. The author of numerous journal articles on the Cuban economy and economic reforms, he is a regular contributor to *OnCuba News*.

Dachelys Valdés Moreno is a clinical psychologist, educator, and LGBTQ+ activist. She has taught psychology at the Calixto Garcia Medical School in Havana, provided counseling for LGBTQ+ families at the University of Havana's Center for Psychological Well-being (Centro de Bienestar Psicológico-CEBPSI), and managed social media and produced a podcast for the grassroots Afro-Cuban community group Lo llevamos rizos.

Helen Yaffe is a senior lecturer in economic and social history at the University of Glasgow, specializing in Cuban and Latin American development. She is the author of *We Are Cuba! How a Revolutionary People Have Survived in a Post-Soviet World* (2020) and *Che Guevara: The Economics of Revolution* (2009) and coauthor of *Youth Activism and Solidarity: The Non-stop Picket against Apartheid* (2017).

María del Carmen Zabala Arguelles is professor of economics at the University of Havana and a member of the Facultad Latinoamericana de Ciencias Sociales (FLACSO) and Cuba's Academy of Sciences. She is the author of *Jefatura Femenina de Hogar, Pobreza Urbana y Exclusión Social: Una perspectiva desde la subjetividad en el contexto cubano* (2010) and editor of *Pobreza, exclusión social y discriminación étnico-racial en América Latina y el Caribe* (2008).

Made in the USA
Middletown, DE
27 January 2024

48536475R00216